Thunder Bay Press

An imprint of the Advantage Publishers Group

5880 Oberlin Drive, San Diego, CA 92121-4794

www.thunderbaybooks.com

ISBN 1-59223-372-4

Library of Congress Cataloging in Publication Data available upon request

DESIGN Paul Cooper
EDITOR Tony Bacon

Printed by Colorprint Offset Ltd. (Hong Kong)

1 2 3 4 5 09 08 07 06 05

The Monkees play live at the Pittsburgh Civic Arena, December 30th 1966, on their first tour.

THE
monkees

The day-by-day story of the '60s TV pop sensation

THUNDER BAY
P · R · E · S · S
San Diego, California

Andrew Sandoval

Contents

1942–64

Micky Dolenz appears in his first TV series, *Circus Boy* … Davy Jones lands acting roles in BBC-TV play, in TV soap *Coronation Street*, and as the Artful Dodger in *Oliver!* stage musical … Peter Tork plays folk clubs in New York … Michael Nesmith performs solo, as half of Mike & John duo, and as part of a folk troupe, and releases his first single … Micky sings and plays in a few groups … Peter tours with Phoenix Singers folk group … Davy signs as solo artist to Colpix Records and records his first single.
pages 10 – 17

1965

Davy has first singles released, tours in stage musical *Pickwick*, signs to Columbia Pictures … Raybert Productions sells idea for what becomes *Monkees* TV series to Screen

Gems … Davy's debut LP recorded and released … Michael records for Colpix Records as Michael Blessing, releases two singles, plays with Survivors folk group … Raybert places ads for musicians, singers, and actors to audition for parts in *Monkees* TV series; screen tests held for best candidates … Davy, Michael, Micky, and Peter chosen as The Monkees and pilot show made.
pages 18 – 31

1966

Monkees TV series sold to NBC … filming begins for TV series and continues through year … music producer is appointed to direct recordings … instrumental recordings by session players begin at RCA Hollywood for first single and LP; Monkees supply vocals … producers include Boyce & Hart, Michael Nesmith … music coordinator Don Kirshner and RCA Records set up special Colgems label for Monkees product

… 'Last Train To Clarksville' first single, makes #1 … personal appearance tour to promote single and TV show … weekly *Monkees* show debuts on NBC TV … first LP *The Monkees*, makes #1 … some instrumental recording shifts to New York, including 'I'm A Believer' with producer Jeff Barry … recording for second album starts … 'I'm A Believer' second single, makes #1 … first live concerts.
pages 32 – 77

1967

More Of The Monkees second LP, makes #1 … more concerts … TV series continues on NBC … more TV series filming … first recording sessions with Monkees as self-contained band, Chip Douglas producing … Jeff Barry continues New York sessions … London visit, meeting various Beatles, Kinks, Stones … TV show achieves biggest audience, 12 million plus … tussle over inclusion of 'group' side on new single leads to dismissal of Don Kirshner … third single 'A Little Bit Me, A Little Bit You' with group-recorded B-side 'The Girl I Knew Somewhere,' makes #2 … concerts in Canada … shooting starts of second TV series as first nears end … *Headquarters* third LP, makes #1 … first TV series reruns with some new music … more U.S. concerts … 'Randy Scouse Git' released as 'Alternate Title' single in U.K., makes #2 … TV episode shot in Paris, France … concerts in London, England … fourth single 'Pleasant Valley Sunday,' makes #3 … long U.S. summer concert tour; Jimi Hendrix quits after seven shows … last rerun of first TV season; second season debuts … fourth LP *Pisces, Aquarius, Capricorn & Jones Ltd.* and fifth single, 'Daydream Believer,' both make #1 … Michael records *The Wichita Train Whistle Sings* … group members record separately … Boyce & Hart remake 'Valleri.'

pages **78 – 153**

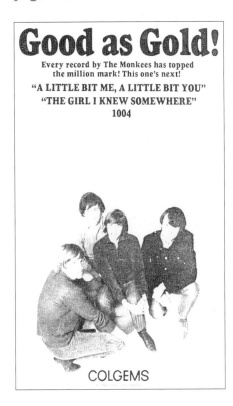

Good as Gold!
Every record by The Monkees has topped the million mark! This one's next!
"A LITTLE BIT ME, A LITTLE BIT YOU"
"THE GIRL I KNEW SOMEWHERE"
1004

COLGEMS

1968
Davy, Michael, Micky, and Peter recording self-produced sessions separately … second season TV series continues on NBC … script developed for forthcoming Monkees movie *Changes* … 'Valleri' sixth single, makes #3 … filming starts on *Changes* movie … NBC says no to third TV season … movie name changed to *Untitled* … TV reruns start as second season ends

… *The Birds, The Bees & The Monkees* fifth LP, makes #3 … Michael's instrumental *Wichita Train Whistle Sings* LP released … Michael records in Nashville … 'D.W. Washburn' seventh single, makes #19, the first 'flop' … rare meeting of four Monkees in studio, for spoken-word piece … movie name changed to *Head* … final primetime TV episode of *The Monkees* shown … concerts in Australia, Japan … 'Porpoise Song' eighth single, makes #62 … Bones Howe is new Monkees record producer … *Head* sixth LP, makes #45 … *Head* movie is (briefly) released … recording and filming for TV special … Peter leaves The Monkees.

pages **154 – 221**

1969
Monkees now a trio: Davy, Michael, and Micky … Davy makes solo TV appearances … producer Bones Howe continues Monkees recording sessions … *Instant Replay* seventh LP, makes #32 … 'Tear Drop City' ninth single, makes #56 … concerts as trio, backed by Sam & The Goodtimers … TV ads for Kool Aid soft drink mix … TV special *33 ⅓ Revolutions Per Monkee* shown on NBC … 'Someday Man' tenth single, makes #81 … Davy, Michael, and Micky resume separate recording sessions … concerts continue … *Greatest Hits* compilation LP, makes #89 … Boyce & Hart return to Monkees production … 'Good Clean Fun' 11th single, makes #82 … Saturday TV reruns of *The Monkees* on CBS, some with new music … *The Monkees Present* eighth LP, makes #100 … more concerts … Michael begins a gradual departure from the group.

pages **222 – 257**

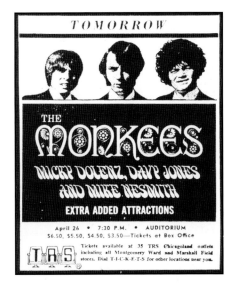

1970
Michael effectively leaves The Monkees, except to make more ads … Michael secures deal for his new group … Davy tells press he plans solo career … reruns of *The Monkees* continue on CBS TV … Michael's First National Band start recordings … Micky and Davy record as Monkees with producer Jeff Barry … 'Oh My My' 12th and last single, makes #98 … Michael's group release first single, 'Little Red Rider,' and LP, *Magnetic South* … *Changes* ninth and last Monkees LP, fails to chart … Micky makes stage-acting debut … Davy opens his shopping mall in Los Angeles … Michael's First National Band release second single, 'Joanne,' and play European dates … Davy and Micky make final Monkees recording session … second album and third single by First National Band, *Loose Salute* and 'Silver Moon.'

pages **258 – 278**

Afterword 279
Musicians index 280
Songography 286
Acknowledgements 304

Introduction

They say everything happens for a reason. On July 10th 1989 I received from the State of California a license to drive a motor vehicle. I had failed my driving test twice before and was glad to be finally on the road as a part of the Golden State's car culture. I mention this because it was not only a momentous day in my life, but also an important date for The Monkees. (Get ready: this book is filled with important dates for The Monkees.)

Only minutes after my picture was snapped and I was bequeathed a temporary license, The Monkees were acknowledged by their fans with the great honor of a star on Hollywood's *Walk Of Fame*. All four Monkees assembled on Hollywood Boulevard in front of the Vogue Theater – where their movie *Head* had premiered in November 1968 – and they were awarded a commemorative plaque. Afterwards the group headed over the hill to Universal City to give their first press conference as a foursome since '68.

Miraculously, I drove to both events. Without incident, I might add. Somehow I asked the very first question put to the reunited group. "Now that you've settled a few differences, do you plan to have an official biography?" The Monkees laughed at the thought of having settled any differences, and Micky quietly asked his former bandmates to "wake me when it's over." Ever the diplomat, Davy offered a more thoughtful response: "There are a few [books] out there on the market that tell most of the information," he explained. "Obviously you'd have to be a fly on the wall to know the rest."

Well, this is not The Monkees' official biography, nor am I the fly on the wall that Davy described. Yet, through the magic of magnetic tape and microfilm, I was able to transport myself

back to the 1960s and compile the book you now hold. It didn't take much. Just a little patience and 15 years of studiously listening through hundreds of hours of original session recordings made for and by The Monkees. There was also the review of dozens of original documents relating to their television series and talking with many of the original participants in the project. I was nearly there. The real challenge came in tracking down the thousands of contemporary press clippings that I knew existed. I told myself that it was just something that had to be done.

"So who wants to know all this stuff anyway?"

No, this was not the question my publishers asked me, but rather the words of a surprised Michael Nesmith upon seeing some early pages of this book. His skepticism was not misplaced. As in the 1960s, The Monkees are either loved or loathed. Anyone giving The Monkees serious coverage must be looked upon with at least some suspicion.

"The Monkees was like a circus," Micky Dolenz once told me. "Most people just went and looked at the tent; nobody went inside. Years later, the very fact that there is still this interest … well, it's nice to have that kind of justification."

It is my sincere belief that this book not only provides further justification for that interest but also is an accurate glimpse at the circus that was The Monkees' life during the 1960s. Perhaps it will change a few opinions, or at least put to rest a couple of urban myths.

The Monkees deserve some respect. After all, they have made millions of people happy with their music and their humor. If I can make just a fraction of those people happy with this book, I will have done my job. So let mine be the post-hypnotic voice that wakes Micky from his self-induced slumber: "Wake up, it's finally over!" The complete Monkees story is now at your fingertips.

Andrew Sandoval
Hollywood, February 2005

P.S. This book is dedicated to my parents, who made me a music lover, and to The Monkees, who have been a very big part of my life.

Core recordings

The following CDs and vinyl records are the core collection of recorded works that will be referred to throughout this book.

ORIGINAL ALBUMS

1966
The Monkees CD Rhino #71790 (1994)

1967
More Of The Monkees CD Rhino #71791 (1994)
Headquarters CD Rhino #71792 (1995)
Pisces, Aquarius, Capricorn & Jones Ltd. CD Rhino #71793 (1995)

1968
The Birds, The Bees & The Monkees CD Rhino #71794 (1994)
Head CD Rhino #71795 (1994)

1969
Instant Replay CD Rhino #71796 (1995)
The Monkees Present CD Rhino #71797 (1994)

1970
Changes CD Rhino #71798 (1994)

COMPILATIONS
featuring unique or previously unissued material

Missing Links ('Missing Links 1') CD Rhino #70150 (1988)
Live 1967 CD Rhino #70139 (1988)
Missing Links Volume Two ('Missing Links 2') CD Rhino #70939 (1990)
Listen To The Band CD boxed set Rhino #70566 (1991)
Greatest Hits CD Rhino #72190 (1995)
Missing Links Volume Three ('Missing Links 3') CD Rhino #72153 (1996)
The Monkees Best!! CD (Japan only) East West #AMCY-978 (1996)

Hey Hey We're The Monkees (CD-ROM) nu.millennia #CD0131 (1996)
I'm A Believer & Other Hits CD Flashback #72883 (1997)
Daydream Believer & Other Hits CD Flashback #75242 (1998)
The Monkees Anthology CD Rhino #75269 (1998)
Headquarters Sessions CD Rhino Handmade #RHM 7715 (2000)
The Monkees Summer 1967: The Complete U.S. Concert CD Rhino Handmade #RHM2 7755 (2001)
Music Box CD boxed set Rhino #76706 (2001)
The Best Of The Monkees CD Rhino #73875 (2003)

SOLO RECORDINGS
1960s through 1970

Davy Jones
David Jones vinyl album Colpix #493 (1965)
'Dream Girl' / 'Take Me To Paradise' vinyl single Colpix #764 (1965)
'The Girl From Chelsea' vinyl single Colpix #789 (1965)
Just For The Record Volume One CD Hercules #Y6120E (1995)

Michael Nesmith
'Well Well'/ 'Wanderin'' vinyl single Highness #HN-13 (1963)
'How Can You Kiss Me' / 'Just A Little Love' vinyl single Omnibus #239 (1965)
'The New Recruit' / 'A Journey With Michael Blessing' vinyl single Colpix #787 (1965)
'Until It's Time For You To Go' / 'What Seems To Be The Trouble Officer' vinyl single Colpix #792 (1965)
The Wichita Train Whistle Sings vinyl album Dot #25861 (1968)
Magnetic South/Loose Salute CD Camden #660442 (1999)
Nevada Fighter (w/ *Tantamount To Treason*) CD Camden #822352 (2001)

Micky Dolenz
'Don't Do It' vinyl single Challenge #59353 (1967)
'Huff Puff' vinyl single Challenge #59372 (1967)

Glossary of recording terms

assembly Compilation of recorded elements (usually taped) for the purpose of future reproduction and release on disc etc.

bounce, bounced, bouncing Bouncing is a process of combining recorded elements that were originally taped separately, in order to create space on the tape so that more instruments and/or vocals can be added. *See also* reduction.

compressed, compression, compressor Compression is an electronic effect that smoothes dynamic range, minimizing sudden leaps in volume and increasing perceived overall loudness.

cue Incidental musical piece used in the score or soundtrack of a film or television program.

date Slang for recording session.

demo Abbreviation of demonstration recording. Usually a rough sketch of a song or proposed production.

double-tracked, double-tracking, doubling Double-tracking is a technique in which a second performance of similar content is added to an already existing recording to create a fuller, louder, or 'wider' sound. The process is most often used on vocals to create a natural echo or phasing type effect.

dub, dubbing, dubdown Alternative terms for mix, mixing, mixdown. *See also* mix.

equalization, equalize, equalizer An equalizer is a sophisticated tone control that can raise or lower the levels of selected frequencies.

master, mastering Mastering is a process involving the transfer of the final mixed-down mono or stereo master tapes or masters to another recorded medium for the purpose of mass-producing recorded discs, tapes, or compact discs (CDs).

This usually includes the enhancement of a master recording through such electronic processes as equalization, compression, vari-speed oscillating, and reverb.

mix, mixing, mixdown Mixing is a process similar to reduction in which all of the content recorded for a particular piece of music is reduced down to a 2-track (stereo) or full-track (1-track or mono) tape for the purpose of disc-cutting or manufacturing into recorded discs, tapes, or compact discs (CDs). *See also* mastering.

mono A single channel of recorded sound. For most of the period discussed in this book, mono was the most common format for radio and television broadcasts. Mono was also an option (alongside stereo) for consumers purchasing vinyl records.

multi-track Recording format in which the tape machine's recording head records multiple tracks or 'bands' of individual recorded sound along the tape.

Regular analog tape formats for the period discussed in this book were half-inch 3- or 4–track, one-inch 8- or 10–track, and two-inch 16–track. The 'inch' measurement indicates the width of the tape; the 'track' number indicates the maximum number of tracks that the machine records on the tape.

Multi-track recording enables a producer to have more control of various recorded elements by separating them on the individual tracks. Furthermore, the performer can embellish an existing performance by adding to it on an adjacent track of the same tape.

Multi-track recording is also used in live recordings to make it possible to achieve greater separation between instrumentation and in some cases to delete a vocal, instrument, or effect that the producer or performer may find undesirable.

overdub, overdubbing Overdubbing is a recording process in which new instrumentation or vocals are added to an existing recording. An overdub is usually added on a separate track of a multi-track tape.

pick-up piece A recording made for use in editing to enhance or correct an existing performance.

punch-in Short new recorded piece inserted within an existing take.

reduction Process in which elements of a recording are combined and copied onto another tape in order to make room for further instrumentation or overdubs. *See also* bounce and mixing.

reverb Abbreviation of reverberation. Mechanical or electronic effect that uses delay to recreate room ambience.

During the period that this book covers, reverb was most often generated by using an echo chamber. These chambers, or rooms of varying size, were usually tiled or painted with reflective material and housed a single loudspeaker in a cabinet and a microphone.

The length of reverberation could be controlled by the size of the chamber and the situation of the microphone and/or loudspeaker within the chamber.

stereo Two channels of recorded sound played in tandem to create a natural soundstage. Alongside mono, stereo was also a format option for consumers purchasing vinyl records.

sweetening Another term for overdubbing. Basically the same process, but the term is usually used in reference to adding the 'final touch' or embellishment in a production, for example strings or a solo instrument.

take Individual attempt at a recording.

track Non-technically, an individual recording of a piece of music, as in 'backing track.' Technically, a 'band' of recording on a multi-track tape. *See also* tracking.

tracking Recording of basic instrumentation, usually including guitars, bass, and drums.

Other instrumentation such as brass and strings are in most cases recorded as overdubs after tracking is completed.

Vocals and backing vocals are also usually added later in the recording process.

transfer Process of making a recorded copy to another machine or tape.

treat, treated To treat is to process or distort a previously recorded item electronically. A sound is said to be 'treated' if it is processed in this way.

vari-speed oscillator (VSO) Electronic device, external or internal, that controls the speed of a tape machine's 'capstan' or drive motor.

It can be used to speed up or slow down recordings at any stage of the production process, sometimes for special effect.

1942-64

Micky Dolenz appears in his first TV series, *Circus Boy* ... Davy Jones lands acting roles in BBC-TV play, in TV soap *Coronation Street*, and as the Artful Dodger in *Oliver!* stage musical ... Peter Tork plays folk clubs in New York ... Michael Nesmith performs solo, as half of Mike & John duo, and as part of a folk troupe, and releases his first single ... Micky sings and plays in a few groups ... Peter tours with Phoenix Singers folk group ... Davy signs as solo artist to Colpix Records and records his first single.

Premonition? Micky Dolenz in his first TV role, as Corky in *Circus Boy*, with a significant animal.

1942

PETER TORK is born Peter Halsten Thorkelson to Virginia and John Thorkelson at Washington D.C.'s Doctor's Hospital on February 13th 1942. The Thorkelsons move to Detroit, Michigan, in 1945, and the following year to Berlin, Germany, where Peter's father is stationed in the Army. In 1948 they return to the United States, settling in Badger, Wisconsin, and later shift to Madison, Wisconsin. Peter attends Wyndham High School there in 1954.

MICHAEL NESMITH is born Robert Michael Nesmith in Houston, Texas, to Bette and Warren Nesmith on December 30th 1942. Warren and Bette are divorced in 1945. In 1949 Michael and his mother move from Houston to Dallas, Texas, where Bette supports the family by working as a secretary at Texas Bank & Trust (during which time she develops the formula for a product later known as Liquid Paper).

MICKY DOLENZ is born George Michael Dolenz at Cedars Of Lebanon Hospital in Los Angeles, California, to Janelle and George Dolenz on March 8th 1945. The Dolenz family reside in Tarzana, California, and then in 1948 move to a new house on Camarillo Street in North Hollywood, California. In 1951 'Mickey' attends Eunice Knight Saunders private school in the San Fernando Valley. (He will drop the 'e' from his name some time around 1964; we will call him Micky throughout the book.)

DAVY JONES is born David Jones to Doris and Harry Jones in Manchester, England, on December 30th 1945. The youngest of four children, he lives with his family in a two-up two-down terraced house in Leamington Street, Openshaw. He attends school at Varna Street Infants and throughout the 1950s acts in various school and church play productions.

1956

● Peter receives a ukulele from folk singer Tom Glazer, starting his career as a musician. He will soon move on to guitar among other instruments.
● Micky's father George stars in television's *The Count Of Monte Cristo* as Edmund Dantes. Through his parents' industry connections and natural ability Micky lands commercials for products including Kellogg's cereal and Oscar Mayer wieners. Last year he landed the lead in a TV series of his own, *Circus Boy*, that debuts this September.

SEPTEMBER

● Monday 17th
● Eleven-year-old Micky makes one of his earliest television appearances on the NBC network morning show, *Today*. He is plugging *Circus Boy*'s debut this Sunday. Today – and for the next several years – he is billed under the stage name Mickey Braddock.

● Sunday 23rd
● *Circus Boy* debuts on NBC television at 7:30pm. The adventure series revolves around Micky's character, Corky, an orphan boy who grows up among the crew of a turn-of-the-century traveling circus. *Circus Boy* will switch from NBC to the ABC television network in September 1957.

Mickey Braddock, star of Screen Gems' new family adventure series, CIRCUS BOY, which premieres on NBC-TV on Sunday, September 23, at 7:30 pm EDT, waves a greeting from aboard Sinbad, a racing camel. Mickey proves that camels run faster than horses in "The Amazing Mr. Sinbad," the October 14 adventure in the CIRCUS BOY series.

1957

JANUARY

● Friday 4th
● *The Los Angeles Times* writes: "Eleven-year-old Mickey Braddock of the *Circus Boy* series was the envy of every youngster in his neighborhood the other day. A sequence called for him to take a balloon ride. He did it in a specially constructed 14,000-cubic-foot balloon which soared 140 feet in the air. Mickey tells everyone it's even more fun than baseball."

FEBRUARY

● Saturday 9th
● Mickey Braddock performs for a combined audience of more than 14,000 youngsters during two shows at the annual May Co. Jamboree held at the Shrine Auditorium in Los Angeles. This program is part of Boy Scout week; the crowd includes Scouts, Cubs, and Explorers.

1958

● Michael Nesmith attends Thomas Jefferson High School in Dallas, Texas.
● With his *Circus Boy* TV series about to end, Micky attends Walter Reed Junior High School in North Hollywood, California.

SEPTEMBER

● Thursday 11th
● The final primetime episode of *Circus Boy* airs on the ABC network, at 7:30pm. The show will reappear in syndicated re-runs on Saturday mornings from October 1958 through September 1960. Micky recalls: "I don't remember being disappointed when the series

Micky stars (RIGHT) in the Screen Gems TV series *Circus Boy*, starting September 1956. The promo shot has a caption (ABOVE) that includes his stage name, Mickey Braddock.

stopped after three years. I think I was so young I didn't understand much of what was going on. All I knew was that we weren't going to film any more. Then I went right into school. Because I had had a private tutor, I skipped ahead two grades, so I started into high school at 13."

OCTOBER

● Michael's mother Bette Nesmith markets her own invention called Liquid Paper through The Mistake Out Company. The product is a small bottle of thin white paint that can be applied to paper to correct minor mistakes in handwriting or typing. (Later, in the 1970s, Michael will inherit his mother's substantial royalties from her sale of the Liquid Paper formula.)

NOVEMBER

● Thursday 27th
● Micky makes a guest appearance on the television program *Zane Grey Theatre*. In tonight's episode of the series that presents a different play each week, Micky (credited as Mickey Braddock) plays Ted Matson in *The Vaunted*.

1959

● Michael appears in Thomas Jefferson High School's production of *Oklahoma* as Andrew Carnes.
● Micky attends North Hollywood Junior High. On January 22nd, still using his stage surname of Braddock, he appears in an episode of the *Playhouse 90* series written by Rod Serling. This will be his last major television role for several years.
● Davy's mother dies. With no further interest in school he pursues his dual interests in acting and becoming a jockey.
● Bert Schneider is named assistant treasurer at Screen Gems, the television production arm of Columbia Pictures. He is the son of the head of Columbia, Abe Schneider, and started working for Screen Gems in 1954. Bert will later play an important part in the development of The Monkees.

1960

● Michael attends Thomas Jefferson High School in Dallas, Texas, where he participates in the Concert Choir.
● By mid-year Davy lands a role and performs in the BBC television play *June Evening*. He spends his summer holidays at Basil Foster's Holland House stables in Newmarket, Suffolk in southern England. By year's end Foster invites Davy to live and work there as a stable boy.
● Micky switches schools to Van Nuys Junior High, in the San Fernando Valley suburb of Los Angeles.
● Peter attends Carleton College in Northfield, Minnesota.

1961

● From January 5th to 8th Davy is in Leeds, England taping the BBC radio play *There Is A Happy Land*. His part is the longest ever written for a teenager in the show. He also appears this year in a Granada television program, *A Man And A Dog*. Davy meanwhile continues to work as a stable boy at Holland House through May, but after his appearance as Colin in television soap-opera *Coronation Street* his stable boss Basil Foster encourages him to pursue acting full-time.
● Sixteen-year-old Micky is also showing a shift in focus. In the first year he is eligible to drive he wins an award at the Rod & Custom Motorama for the overall best custom car.
● Michael attends his senior year at Thomas Jefferson High School in Dallas, Texas.
● Peter has flunked out of college and finds work at the American Thread Company's thread mill in Willimantic, Connecticut.

1962

● Davy makes theatrical contacts with agents and managers involved in various West End stage productions in London as the result of efforts by his boss Basil Foster. He is initially turned down for a part in *Oliver!*, the musical based on Dickens's tale of Oliver Twist, due to

LEFT Micky's first TV series, *Circus Boy*, draws to a close in September 1958. RIGHT The Tork & Farwell duo – Bruce Farwell on guitar and Peter Tork on banjo – performing in Greenwich Village, New York City, in 1963.

his inability to forge a cockney accent. Luckily, he quickly lands the part of Michael in a touring company of *Peter Pan*. During the show's six-week run, co-star Jane Asher (later the companion of Paul McCartney) will coach Davy on his tone of voice. This effort will prove successful, and Davy will win the part of the Artful Dodger on his second audition for *Oliver!*.

● Michael enlists in the Air Force after a brief runaway trip to California. He is stationed at Sheppard Air Force Base in Wichita Falls, Texas. On weekend leave he visits Oklahoma and attends a gig by Hoyt Axton. Michael: "[Axton] sat up there with a guitar and all of those people were nourished by it, and he was too. It was a very high experience. I remember coming away absolutely convinced I was going to get a guitar." By Christmas he will indeed have his own instrument.

● Peter returns to Carleton College in Northfield, Minnesota, and works as the school's DJ as well as taking part in some folk ensembles. Once again he will flunk out. He soon sets his sights on performing folk music in New York's Greenwich Village.

● Micky appears briefly on television this year, but only as a member of a studio audience. During the October 10th edition of *The Steve Allen Show* he can be spotted sporting a shirt (and apparently a sign too) that reads "Little Black Things Club." Host Steve Allen is intrigued by the display and briefly talks on camera to Micky about this unusual slogan.

● Bob Rafelson, a fledgling writer, producer, director, and frustrated musician, develops the initial idea for the *Monkees* television series and tries unsuccessfully to sell it to Revue, the TV division of Universal Pictures. Rafelson: "I got the idea for the series in 1962, before Dick Lester's *Hard Day's Night*. I have great respect for his work, and I don't want to be drawn into controversy, but I worked in advertising for some time and a lot of the technique I use I picked up there.

"I tried to sell it as a folk-rock group, something about which I knew because I had traveled with a group of unruly and somewhat chaotic musicians in Mexico in 1953. We were itinerant musicians and I [later] used many incidents that happened to me in Mexico in *The Monkees* episodes."

JANUARY

● **Wednesday 3rd**
● Davy makes a guest appearance in the British television series *Z Cars*.

MARCH

● **Friday 23rd**
● Davy auditions for the part of the Artful Dodger in the London stage version of *Oliver!*.

MAY

● Bert Schneider is named treasurer of Screen Gems, the television production arm of Columbia Pictures. He will go on to play an important part in the development of the *Monkees* TV series.

● **Monday 7th**
PERFORMANCE Davy has won the part on his second try and opens as the Artful Dodger in the London stage version of *Oliver!* at the New Theatre (later renamed the Albery).

NOVEMBER

● Producer David Merrick decides to integrate Davy into his North American production of *Oliver!*, replacing the current Artful Dodger, Michael Goodman, before the show hits Broadway. In December, Davy will journey to Toronto, Canada, prior to his opening night.

DECEMBER

● Monday 17th
PERFORMANCE Davy opens as the Artful Dodger in the Broadway production of *Oliver!* at the Imperial Theatre on 45th Street in New York City.

● Tuesday 25th
● Michael receives his first guitar. His career as a singer-songwriter is underway.

1963

● Peter Thorkelson is now using the stage surname of Tork. He moves to New York's Greenwich Village and plays at various folk music 'basket' houses, where musicians collect donations from the audience after each performance. He can be found gigging at clubs such as The Pad, Abdo's, and The Playhouse Cafe. His early repertoire includes comedic songs penned by his brother Nick, including 'Alvin' and 'Under The Undertaker.' He takes part briefly in a group called Casey Anderson & The Realists. He also teams with Bruce Farwell during this period as Tork & Farwell and they perform at The Why Not?, The Basement, The Cyclops, The Third Side, The Four Winds, The Samurai, The Dragon's Den, The Raven, and The Id. The duo are sometimes joined by Carol Hunter to become Tork & Farwell Plus One.

● Micky attends Valley Junior College in the San Fernando Valley suburb of Los Angeles and forms his first group, The Spartans. The group features Micky on vocals and guitar, and his friends Bob Nigg and brothers Gary and Eddie Graham. The unit will last approximately six months.

● Davy continues to perform in the musical *Oliver!* at the Imperial Theatre in New York City. Around this time he enters a studio to record some basic demonstration tapes of his singing. Material includes 'A Lot Of Livin' To Do' (from the musical *Bye Bye Birdie*), the standards 'More' and 'Misty,' the Kay Starr-popularized 'If You Love Me (Really Love Me),' and Eddie Hodges's early-'62 hit 'Bandit Of My Dreams.' All of these will surface in 1995 as a part of Davy's self-released archival disc *Just For The Record – Volume One*.

● Michael attends San Antonio College in San Antonio, Texas, as a drama major. There he meets his wife-to-be Phyllis Barbour. In addition to performing solo, Michael has formed a folk troupe for events such as shopping-center openings and private parties. This aggregation features Phyllis, her boyfriend Mark Weakley, brothers David and Bob Price, Bill Collins, Tommy Piper, Bill Holloway, and various others.

  As an aspiring singer-songwriter, Michael also releases his first recording during this period, as Mike Nesmith, on Highness Records. One SAC student will recall later that this may have been a label available for small 'vanity' pressings. Both sides of the release, 'Wanderin'' and 'Well Well,' are self-penned compositions. Also at this time Michael composes the song 'Go Somewhere And Cry,'

which is recorded by Denny Ezba & The Goldens; Michael features as whistler and additional guitarist on the disc.

● Bob Rafelson now works as director of program development for the ABC network. He will become heavily involved in one of the projects that comes across his desk during the fall season.

● Bert Schneider moves from his post as treasurer of TV company Screen Gems to vice president.

JANUARY

● Tuesday 8th
● Davy has his first mention in the U.S. press in today's *New York Times*. In a generally favorable review of *Oliver!*, theatre critic Howard Taubman calls Davy's turn as the Artful Dodger "impudent and genial."

● Monday 14th
● The musical in which Davy is appearing, *Oliver!*, is the featured cover story in today's issue of *Playbill*, the weekly magazine for theatergoers.

● Friday 18th
● *Life* magazine publishes a three-page spread on *Oliver!* featuring the first nationally published photos of Davy Jones.

FEBRUARY

● Friday 8th
● Micky's father, George Dolenz, dies of a heart attack.

APRIL

● Sunday 28th
● Davy attends the 17th Annual Tony Awards ceremony at the Hotel Americana Imperial Ballroom in New York City. *Oliver!* has received ten theatre-industry Tony Award nominations this year. Davy is among those nominated for best supporting actor in a musical, but the prize goes to David Burns of *A Funny Thing Happened On The Way To The Forum*. The event is aired on WWOR-TV Channel 9 in New York City in a telecast produced by David Yarnell. Next year, Yarnell will pitch a television concept called *Liverpool U.S.A.* to Screen Gems.

JUNE

● Saturday 23rd
PERFORMANCE Michael heads a folk hootenanny at Wonderland Shopping City in San Antonio, Texas. Alongside fellow students

from San Antonio College he reportedly performs to as many as 3,000 spectators. Two hours of this event are televised on San Antonio's Channel 12. Michael tells the *San Antonio Light* newspaper that he will be traveling to New York in July to record for Warner Bros, though it is doubtful that the trip really happens.

JULY

● Tuesday 16th
TV Davy makes his American network television debut on the CBS show *Talent Scouts*. He is introduced by host Merv Griffin and *Oliver!* cast member Georgia Brown, who discuss how Davy has adapted his Mancunian accent to suit his role as the Artful Dodger. Davy sings a medley of two songs from *Oliver!* – 'Consider Yourself' and 'Where Is Love.'

SUMMER

PERFORMANCE Michael performs solo at the Grey Gables Inn, Cape Cod, Massachusetts, and upon his return to San Antonio makes a club appearance, which is privately taped. His live set at this point includes Woody Guthrie's 'Pastures Of Plenty,' folk standards 'Winken Blinken And Nod' and 'Pick A Bale Of Cotton,' and 'Don't Let Your Deal Go Down,' as well as his original songs 'Looks Like Rain' and 'One And Twenty.'

SEPTEMBER

● Michael meets bassist John London (formally Kuehne) during fall semester at San Antonio College. London is impressed by his original material and the two form an almost instant musical bond. Over the next few months they work on material together, and the two soon appear publicly as a duo.

● Tuesday 17th
● Bob Rafelson's latest venture, *The Greatest Show On Earth*, debuts on the ABC network at 9:00pm. Rafelson works on this program about the circus for Desilu Productions, but his involvement in the project, like the series itself, won't last long. Rafelson: "I never seemed to be able to keep a job. When I got to Hollywood I was fired from every studio because they wouldn't let me do my job the way I saw it. When I was an associate producer on a TV series, the head of the studio recut one of the episodes. I went a little crazy and turned his desk upside down. They physically threw me off the lot."

DECEMBER

PERFORMANCE Michael and John London make their performing debut together at a San Antonio pizza parlor called Mama's. Their repertoire includes Nesmith originals 'Pretty Little Princess' and 'Different Drum.'

● Friday 31st
● Phyllis Barbour breaks up with her boyfriend and folk-bandmate Mark Weakley. She will marry Michael Nesmith in 1964.

1964

● Micky transfers from Valley Junior college to Los Angeles Trade Tech, while musically he fronts a five-piece group known as The Missing Links. They make some recordings for the Rosco and Deville labels, though none including Micky. In addition to Micky, the group consists of Danny Delacy (later a member of Australia's The Loved Ones), Jim Stanley, Larry Duncan, and Mike Swain. For at least one gig the band is billed as Micky & The One Nighters. Micky reportedly performs for several weeks with singer Eddie Hodges at The Sugar Shack Club in Denver, Colorado. and it is also reported that The Missing Links play at Denver's La Pitcher. "Micky Dolenz [at this time] was strictly San Fernando Valley rock'n'roll," Michael will tell *The Saturday Evening Post* later, describing the style as "comb your hair back into a pompadour and sing everybody else's music."
● Also this year, Micky returns to acting with two guest appearances on the NBC network series *Mr. Novak*.
● Davy meets Columbia Pictures employee Ward Sylvester in New York. Sylvester is interested in bringing Davy to Hollywood for various performance opportunities. Davy continues in his role as the Artful Dodger, eventually joining the touring production of *Oliver!*, which travels to several U.S. cities including Cleveland, Detroit, Milwaukee, and Chicago. By year's end, Davy will sign a recording contract with Colpix Records, a subsidiary of Columbia Pictures.
● Michael Nesmith and John London win San Antonio College's Headliner Of The Year talent contest award, and after play a regular gig at The Rebel. They will soon set their sights on greater things.

LEFT Michael's first record release, as Mike Nesmith on the small Highness label, combines two of his songs, 'Wanderin'' and 'Well Well.' **ABOVE** An early snap of Michael the singer-songwriter in 1963 at an audition for Texas television station WFAA.

● At the beginning of the year, 23-year-old Peter travels to Venezuela to visit his family who have migrated there in one of their regular relocations. On his return he lands in New York for some further gigs, and by mid-year is married – though only for a matter of days. Peter also forms a brief musical union with Steve Stills and another player, John Hopkins.

● Bob Rafelson is now seasoned in the world of television, co-producing the pilot for a show called *The Wackiest Ship In The Army*. It is easily sold and will debut next year on NBC. Yet the ever restless Rafelson still longs to produce his pet musical TV project. He recalls later: "If I couldn't be a rock'n'roll singer, I wanted as a filmmaker to create a rock'n'roll group. I was fulfilling my ambition and not thinking of [it as] any kind of perpetration at all. At the time, I didn't have any idea if The Monkees would be a hit or anything."

FEBRUARY

PERFORMANCE Peter plays at Carnegie Hall during the New York City Folk Festival with Peter LaFarge, composer of the folk classic 'The Ballad of Ira Hayes,' made famous by Johnny Cash. Other acts on the bill include Cash himself, Phil Ochs, and Mississippi John Hurt.

● Sunday 9th

TV Davy sings 'I'd Do Anything' with the Broadway cast of *Oliver!* on the CBS network's *The Ed Sullivan Show* at 8:00pm. Also appearing on this telecast are The Beatles, making their live stateside debut, Tessie O'Shea, and Frank Gorshin. Although the show is videotaped

at New York City's Studio 50 before a live audience of just 728, an estimated 73 million people view this historic telecast. (Decades later it will be made available in its entirety on DVD.)

APRIL

● Peter joins folk group The Phoenix Singers as an accompanist on banjo and guitar. The Belafonte Singers-like group recorded without Peter during 1963 for the Warner Bros. label and will take him on tour for the next seven months.

MAY

● Tuesday 19th

● *The Hollywood Reporter* writes that Bob Rafelson has been hired by Screen Gems to work on television projects for the company. Rafelson: "Bert [Schneider] and I had this conversation about how we wanted to make films and then nothing happened. I was working at Screen Gems in New York and one day he called and said, 'Do you remember our conversation?' And I said, 'What conversation?' And he said, 'Jesus Christ, you don't remember our conversation?' You see, we had had these meetings which were more or less secret because we were both employed at the time. We took long walks and talked about things we wanted to do and about the bullshit that you couldn't do them in Hollywood. We decided to make a company that would do things our way. I realized the only reason it hadn't been done before was that it lacked someone like Bert. He's an incredible guy, a brilliant guy, a positive person, a very moral person. We didn't have any burning ambition or slogan to change Hollywood; it wasn't that animated. We just knew there was a way to do something groovier than the way it was being done. I knew that, and he knew that; but I didn't know it was going to work, and he didn't know it was going to work. We just believed in each other."

JUNE

PERFORMANCE Twenty-one-year-old Michael travels to Dallas after school lets out for the summer at San Antonio College. John London and his pal/manager Charlie Rockett will soon join him for gigs at The PM Club and Rubyait. After this, Michael will return to San Antonio to marry Phyllis Barbour.

● Friday 5th

● Peter marries his 16-year-old girlfriend Jody Rabb at her parents' home in Nyack, New York. The union is shortlived; the couple will separate in three months and later divorce.

● Saturday 27th

● Michael marries Phyllis Barbour at the Ft. Sam Houston Chapel in San Antonio, Texas. After the ceremony the newlyweds take off for the West Coast where they hope to meet up with their friends John London and Charlie Rockett, who have both already moved to Los Angeles.

JULY

● The Beatles' first Richard Lester-directed feature film, *A Hard Day's Night*, is released to critical and commercial acclaim. This movie's undeniable success will reignite and legitimize Bob Rafelson's concept for the *Monkees* television series. Rafelson soon teams with his friend Bert Schneider to bring his idea to fruition.

Rafelson: "I had a hard time selling it until The Beatles came along and lent credence to the popularity not only of the music but of using film in the fashion it was being used by them. After all, Lester was a director of commercials at the time and was really borrowing heavily from nouvelle French techniques."

Schneider: "The Beatles made it all happen, that's the reality. Richard Lester is where the credit begins for The Monkees and for Bob and me. Our ambitions were to make movies. We began with a TV series because that was a foot in the door. It was easier to get a pilot of a TV series made than it was to get a movie made."

● Wednesday 1st

● Newly married Michael and Phyllis Nesmith arrive in Los Angeles and find an apartment through the *Valley News & Green Sheet*. The manager of their new abode has a daughter, Jackie Sherman, who is a business associate of crooner Frankie Laine. She takes the Mike & John duo under her wing and arranges for some performances and demo recordings.

AUGUST

● Friday 14th

● *The Los Angeles Times* reports that Bob Rafelson will produce a pilot called *Possessed* for Screen Gems. This hour-long costume drama, which Rafelson has written and developed with William Wood, is set around the turn of the century and stars actor Steven Hill. It is not picked up as a series.

SEPTEMBER

● Davy appears in the teen bible, *16* magazine. The end of the article says: "You'll soon be hearing Davy on the Colpix label."

● Wednesday 30th

The Hollywood Reporter says that Davy "has been signed to a long-term contract by Screen Gems. In addition to appearing in future TV series for Screen Gems, Jones will also record for the firm's Colpix Records and make features for Columbia Pictures."

OCTOBER

PERFORMANCE Michael Nesmith and John London head out on an ill-advised tour of Texas school assemblies set up by Jackie Sherman. Leaving a now-pregnant Phyllis in Los Angeles, Michael and London will earn little for their travels.
● Davy has his appendix removed at St. John's Hospital in New York.

● Saturday 10th

TV Peter makes his television debut today as a sideman with The Phoenix Singers folk group who perform three songs – 'Run Come See,' 'Song Of The Land,' and 'Glory Glory' – on the Canadian folk program *Let's Sing Out*.

Not long after this broadcast the group will perform a fundraising show in Denver for the Lyndon B. Johnson presidential campaign. Following the gig, Peter falls out with the group and is subsequently asked to leave.

DECEMBER

RECORDING In the week before Christmas, Davy cuts his first session for Colpix Records. Produced by Jack Lewis in New York City, the date yields at least two recordings, 'Dream Girl' and 'Take Me To Paradise.' The musical arrangements are by Charlie Calello and the results will be issued on Colpix early next year.

● Friday 25th

● Michael and John London have completed their grueling tour of Texas schools, and Michael and Phyllis spend Christmas together in Dallas, Texas.

LEFT **Davy Jones in a New York studio in December 1964 working on two songs for the Colpix label, issued next year as his debut single.** RIGHT **The Mike &** **John duo – Michael Nesmith (right) on guitar and John London on bass – performing in 1964. London will have a long musical relationship with Michael.**

1965

Davy has first singles released, tours in stage musical *Pickwick*, signs to Columbia Pictures … Raybert Productions sells idea for what becomes *Monkees* TV series to Screen Gems … Davy's debut LP recorded and released … Michael records for Colpix Records as Michael Blessing, releases two singles, plays with Survivors folk group … Raybert places ads for musicians, singers, and actors to audition for parts in *Monkees* TV series; screen tests held for best candidates … Davy, Michael, Micky, and Peter chosen as The Monkees and pilot show made.

The Monkees are formed late this year; they are pictured in November filming the pilot show for the proposed TV series *The Monkees*.

● Davy is contracted to Screen Gems as a television actor and Columbia Pictures for potential movie roles. During this year he begins a tour with the stage musical *Pickwick*. It is hoped that the show will make it to Broadway in the fall.

● Michael straddles two musical scenes this year as he leads his own electric combo, Mike & John & Bill, and assumes the solo acoustic folk persona of Michael Blessing. Shifting management from Frankie Laine's organization to Bob Krasnow, he will find a home alongside Davy Jones at Colpix Records.

He also begins hanging out at a West Hollywood nightclub called The Troubadour. At the Troub he will cross paths with songwriter-musician Bill Chadwick who recruits Michael (and bandmate John London) to join The Survivors, a large folk ensemble in the tradition of The New Christy Minstrels. Other members of this unit include Owens Castleman and Michael Murphey (both of whom will later contribute songs to The Monkees), and Nyles Brown, who will become an extra on the *Monkees* TV series. Michael's stint in The Survivors will also bring about an association with folk impresario Randy Sparks, who will publish several original Nesmith compositions this year.

● Peter performs in Greenwich Village at clubs such as The Café Id, Café Wha', Café Why Not, Flamenco Café, The Gaslight, The Basement, The Pad, The Four Winds, The Cyclops, and The Night Owl. By mid-year he feels the pull of the West Coast and decides to hitch a ride towards Los Angeles.

● Micky performs sporadically this year at The Red Velvet Club, mainly on Mondays when the club hosts an all-comers 'open microphone' night. Nevertheless, his main focus will be his architectural studies at Los Angeles Trade Technical College. He has long-term plans to join his family, now relocated to Northern California, in the fall, but spends the summer attending auditions to see if there are any roles left for a one-time child star.

● Bert Schneider leaves New York City and moves to Los Angeles, saying goodbye to the security of his executive post at the Screen Gems television company. He is hoping to start a new venture with fellow TV exec Bob Rafelson, who is now also based in Hollywood. Rafelson recalls: "Bert straightened me out; we started a company of our own, and he protected me from all the ugly phantoms of Hollywood."

JANUARY

● Michael and Phyllis Nesmith return to Los Angeles from Texas, moving back to the apartment they were renting at the end of '64. During the first half of this year, Michael and John London will audition their folk-rock band unsuccessfully at a number of Los Angeles-area clubs, after which they reportedly take their act to Las Vegas, Nevada. Following that engagement they move on to the Safari Hut in San Jose, California. Some time before the summer, producer Chance Halladay will record the group in Hollywood. With musician Bill Sleeper on drums, they will issue a single on Omnibus as Mike & John & Bill. In addition to these two issued recordings, 'How Can You Kiss Me' and 'Just A Little Love,' the combo likely demos more Nesmith material with Halladay including 'All The King's Horses' and 'I've Been Searchin'.'

Michael: "Chance was a typical Hollywood type of the time – hair, clothes, car, attitude, etc. Stereotypical, as I think back. Nice enough. He worked for Frankie Laine's management company, which was my first management outfit. Awful. The lady there stole money from me, tiny amounts, which speaks volumes. I don't think

Chance was involved with that, at least as far as I know. About the only thing I remember was him coming into the studio when we were making that record and yelling at me to relax! It had the effect you might imagine.

"Can't remember the studio though, somewhere on Sunset maybe. I often wondered what his real name was. Could it actually have been Chance Halladay?"

● Davy performs as the Artful Dodger in a Chicago production of *Oliver!*. One of the performances is taped and possibly broadcast locally on radio.

● Tuesday 12th

The Los Angeles Times reports that "Mickey Braddock" (Micky's old stage name) has been signed for a feature role in an upcoming episode of the television show *Peyton Place*. It will be Micky's only television appearance this year.

FEBRUARY

'Dream Girl' / 'Take Me To Paradise' single by David Jones is released in the U.S.A. This Colpix 45 is Davy's debut single.

● Saturday 6th

● *Billboard*, the music-business journal, runs the first in a series of teaser advertisements for Davy's debut release, this one featuring a picture of the singer with his eyes covered in text, reading: "who is david jones?".

● Saturday 13th

● *Billboard* runs a second teaser ad for Davy's Colpix release, with the same picture as last week but the singer's eyes now uncovered. Again the ad copy reads: "who is david jones?".

● Saturday 20th

● Davy, having been facially revealed to the public, now appears in a full-page ad in *Billboard* for the new single. The copy reads: "David Jones is the British teen-age sensation – the 'Artful Dodger' of the Broadway and London productions of *Oliver!*. David Jones is already a teen-age favorite – his fan club membership is in the thousands and he has been featured in teen magazines reaching hundreds and thousands! David Jones' first record is on Colpix – an exciting new single now breaking nationally!" Though this single will never reach the charts, it will be the first of several releases from Davy on Colpix.

● Sunday 31st

● Michael's first son, Christian DuVal Nesmith, is born at the Griffith Park maternity home.

MARCH

● Friday 5th

● Songwriting team Tommy Boyce and Bobby Hart have their composition 'I Can't Get Him Out Of My Mind' copyrighted by Picturetone Music today. With a gender change it will be transformed into 'I Can't Get Her Off My Mind,' a song The Monkees will record and perform during 1966 and 1967.

● **Saturday 13th**
● Davy does his final turn as the Artful Dodger in *Oliver!* during a stage show in Chicago.

APRIL

● Davy begins two weeks of 14-hour-a-day rehearsals for his new role as Sam Weller in the musical *Pickwick*.
● Colpix Records appoints Hank Levine as its new West Coast A&R director. Davy will soon record under Levine's guidance.

● **Friday 16th**
● Raybert Productions, the new company that unites Bob Rafelson and Bert Schneider, sells the concept of what is to become the *Monkees* TV series to Schneider's former employers, Screen Gems. Reportedly, the company's Jackie Cooper allocates a $225,000 budget for Raybert to set up offices, audition actors, and film a pilot. Rafelson says: "We considered only one existing group for the show before we picked The Monkees one by one – The Lovin' Spoonful. They were unknown at the time, but eventually it just wasn't practical." (The Lovin' Spoonful will reach the national charts for the first time in August with their single 'Do You Believe In Magic.')

● **Tuesday 20th**
● Davy opens as Sam Weller in the musical *Pickwick*. The production runs for the next seven weeks in San Francisco, California, before moving to Los Angeles.

MAY

● **Friday 7th**
● The first-ever copyright is filed today for a Michael Nesmith composition, by a publisher known as Melo-Art Music. The song, 'Pretty Little Princess,' has been a staple of Michael's repertoire since 1963. It is reportedly sold to Frankie Laine's talent agency for a mere $50.

● **Saturday 29th**
● *Cash Box*, the music-business journal, reports that Colpix's Hank Levine has now completed his orientation as the company's A&R director and is planning a "heavy schedule" that includes some recording dates with David Jones.

JUNE

● **Monday 7th**
● *Daily Variety*, the showbiz paper, reports that David Jones has been signed to an exclusive contract by Columbia Pictures. The deal is set to begin August 1st. Davy recalls later: "One of the pilots they offered me was great – and who knows, I might yet do it. It's about a policeman and a leprechaun. Only the policeman can see the leprechaun. He gets into situations and I get him out of them – sort of like *Bewitched*. Then they shelved that for a while and decided that the thing to do was to write a brand new series idea."

● **Tuesday 8th**
● The musical *Pickwick*, featuring Davy in the role of Sam Weller, opens at the Pavilion of the Music Center in Los Angeles. The show, starring Harry Secombe, reunites Davy with Peter Coe and David Merrick, with whom he worked on *Oliver!*. During this period Davy's manager Ward Sylvester begins to look seriously for a starring vehicle that will showcase his client's musical and theatrical talents.

● **Thursday 10th**
● *The Hollywood Reporter* reviews *Pickwick* in today's issue, saying: "David Jones, a bouncy, comical youth with a fine musical comedy voice, is a standout here."
● *The Los Angeles Times* announces that Bert Schneider and Bob Rafelson's Raybert Productions will film an adaptation of *Midnight Plus One*, a suspense novel recently acquired by Columbia Pictures. It is unlikely that the project ever gets past the planning stages.

● **Friday 11th**
● *The Los Angeles Times* publishes an interview with Davy. He tells the paper's Nadine M. Edwards that "hanging up my stirrups was probably the best thing that ever happened to me. I've been under a lucky star ever since. I love the stage, but I would like to break into films. I feel this is the biggest method of exploitation and surest way to success for any performer. I've been living in New York, but after *Pickwick* closes I'm going to live in Los Angeles. My dad is joining me here, which pleases me very much. I hope some day to buy a house for him." Edwards notes that Davy has another Colpix single due at the end of the month, and indeed his next recording session is only a few days away.

● **Tuesday 15th**
RECORDING United Recorders *6050 Sunset Blvd, Hollywood, CA* 2:00-5:00pm. Hank Levine *prod*; Eddie Brackett Jr. *eng*; tracking.
1. **'This Bouquet'**
   David Jones
2. **'Baby It's Me'**
   David Jones
3. **'A Little You'**
   unissued
4. **'What Are We Going To Do'**
   David Jones
Personnel Red Callender (bass), Al Casey (guitar), Gene Garf (organ), Bobby Gibbons (guitar), Gene Page (piano), Earl Palmer (drums), Don Peake (guitar), Emil Richards (percussion, including bells), Tommy Tedesco (guitar), unknown (backing vocals), unknown (strings 1).
● The original union contract refers to the artist as "Dick Jones" but this is the first of three recording sessions for the self-titled *David Jones* debut album on Colpix Records. Four songs are taped during this three-hour date; 'This Bouquet' and 'Baby It's Me' will both be featured on the next single. Davy, who is in Los Angeles as a member of the *Pickwick* cast, probably overdubs his vocals at a separate session. Additional elements such as backing vocals and the strings on 'This Bouquet' are also likely added at a later session.
  The tapes for this and all of Davy's Colpix sessions will later go missing, and subsequently all reissues will be made from copies of the vinyl album and singles.

● **Late June**
● Peter travels towards Los Angeles in a '37 Chevy. The car blows a rod outside of Las Vegas, forcing him to hitchhike the rest of the way. When he arrives in L.A. Peter stays with friend Susan Haffey, a

waitress at The Golden Bear club in the Los Angeles suburb of Huntington Beach. After Peter tries once too often to enter the venue without paying he is asked to wash dishes and draw beers. He will also perform sporadically at The Golden Bear and Sid's Bluebeat club throughout the second half of this year.

JULY

● Michael comes to the attention of music-industry impresario Bob Krasnow. Krasnow suggests that he adopt the name Michael Blessing because "Nesmith stinks," and so Michael records 'The New Recruit' and 'What Seems To Be The Trouble Officer' for Colpix Records under the new name. During this period, Nesmith/Blessing also becomes involved with folk ensemble The Survivors, assembled by Randy Sparks. Michael's membership in this group will not only provide opportunities to have his songs published but also comes with a handy $50 a week salary to help his young family survive.

● Wednesday 7th
● *Daily Variety* reports that *Pickwick* in the fourth week of its Los Angeles run has earned $126,000, making it the city's top grossing stage play this week.

● Tuesday 13th
● *Pickwick* scores another $125,000 at the box office this week.

● Wednesday 14th
● Today's *Hollywood Reporter* reveals that Davy is due to appear in the Columbia feature film of *Oliver!* and is scheduled to leave *Pickwick* on August 1st to return to England. He is expected back in the States "in September to prepare for [a] TV pilot for Bert Schneider and Bob Rafelson." This is the first indication that Davy is linked to the *Monkees* project. The *Reporter* also notes that a movie "with Peter Sellers is slated to roll next February in London, with John Bryan directing. [Davy] is also up for an MGM film here." These projects, including Davy's appearance in the film of *Oliver!*, will never materialize.

● Friday 16th
● A number of Michael's songs are copyrighted by Randy Sparks's Country Music Inc. publishing company. They include: 'Bound Away,' 'Different Drum,' 'Don't Call On Me,' 'East O' Texas,' 'Ebenezer,' 'Hollywood,' 'How Can You Kiss Me,' 'I've Found A Girl,' 'Just A Little Love,' 'Sparrow On A Wing,' and 'This All Happened Once Before.'

A rumored album featuring these songs performed by Michael with John London, Michael Martin Murphey, and John Raines under the band name of The Trinity River Boys and released by Phil Spector's Prospector label does not exist, according to Michael, who also says he was never part of such a band.

● Saturday 17th
● *Cash Box* reports that Colpix "hosted a cocktail clambake at the Beverly Hills Hotel for David Jones who's currently appearing in *Pickwick* (singing and acting 'like the Dickens'). Local stations are

playing his single 'What Are We Going To Do.'" The single, recorded only a month ago, is indeed now on sale to the public.

● Saturday 24th
● *Pickwick* ends its run in Los Angeles. It will move on to Cleveland, Ohio, though Davy will only stay for another week's worth of performances before returning to Los Angeles. His recording career is on the upswing, evidenced by today's *Cash Box* that features a full-page ad for his latest disc, 'What Are We Going To Do.'

● Tuesday 26th
RECORDING United Recorders *Hollywood, CA* 1:00-4:00pm, 5:00-8:00pm. Hank Levine *prod*; tracking.
1. **'Theme For A New Love (I Saw You Only Once)'**
   David Jones
2. **'My Dad'**
   David Jones
3. **'Face Up To It'**
   David Jones
4. **'Maybe It's Because I'm A Londoner'**
   David Jones
5. **'Put Me Amongst The Girls'**
   David Jones
6. **'Any Old Iron'**
   David Jones
7. **'It Ain't Me Babe'**
   David Jones
Personnel Victor Arno (violin), Arnold Belnick (violin), Red Callender (bass), Al Casey (guitar), Jim Decker (French horn), Elliott Fisher (violin), Gene Garf (piano), Jimmy Getzoff (violin), Carol Kaye (guitar), Earl Palmer (drums), Bill Pitman (guitar), George Price (French horn), Lou Raderman (violin), Kurt Reher (cello), Emil Richards (percussion, including bells, marimba), Henry L. Roth (violin), Harold Schneier (cello), Paul Shure (violin), Tommy Tedesco (guitar), unknown (backing vocals).

● At this double session work is completed on the David Jones album for Colpix. Musically, 'Theme For A New Love' is a kind of precursor for Davy: he will later recite love lyrics to an orchestral backing in a similar way on 'The Day We Fall In Love' on *More Of The Monkees*. Bob Dylan's 'It Ain't Me Babe' has just been covered in folk-rock style by Los Angeles band The Turtles (their recording will reach *Billboard's* Hot 100 Bound national charts tomorrow), and while Davy's version is musically similar, his recording features verses left out of The Turtles' pop arrangement. The rest of today's material finds Davy aping the British 'music hall' repertoire currently being revived by Herman's Hermits.

● Thursday 29th
● *The Los Angeles Times* announces that Bert Schneider and Bob Rafelson's Raybert Productions have signed novelist and poet William Wood to write his first original screenplay, *The Crucified*. Like Raybert's proposed *Midnight Plus One* last month, *The Crucified* will be sidelined when their attentions drift towards filming a pilot of *The Monkees*.

● Saturday 31st
● 'What Are We Going To Do' single by David Jones breaks into

Billboard's Hot 100 Bound chart at #135. It will flounder its way into the Hot 100 next month.

AUGUST

● A newsletter from the David Jones National Fan Club reports that Davy will travel to England for a three-week holiday this month, after which he is due back in Hollywood. During the overseas visit he treats his family to a jaunt in Spain.

Sunday 8th
● The *San Antonio Express* reports that Michael Nesmith (along with John London) has a contract with Columbia Records – probably meaning Colpix – and that their new recordings of 'All The King's Horses' and Tom Paxton's 'The Last Thing On My Mind' are scheduled for release in September. In fact, no release of these Mike & John recordings is known.

Tuesday 10th
PERFORMANCE Michael plays at Frost's department store's second floor Young Shop in downtown San Antonio, Texas, at 11:00am, alongside John London on bass, Bill Chadwick on a unique nine-string guitar, and drummer Jimmy Messinger. Michael also autographs every purchase of his recently released 'How Can You Kiss Me' single. According to one report, Michael and Chadwick are arrangers for the band, while Messinger, the band's third drummer, is the newest member. The other two, Bill Sleeper and Joseph Kelly, have been drafted and are reportedly "on their way to Vietnam." The band hopes to tour London in the fall.

Also today, the band rehearses for a big fashion show due this Thursday at the Anacacho Room in the St. Anthony Hotel. Michael is interviewed at the rehearsal by reporter Renwicke Cary and says that his band plays a style called folk'n'roll. He further explains that "folk'n'roll is a type of music that has evolved from rock'n'roll. It's pretty new, really. It's something that just had to happen. Don Steele – he's the famous West Coast DJ at KHJ – gave it the name folk'n'roll early this year." Michael mentions that other folk'n'rollers are The Byrds and Sonny & Cher. "It's a combination of the Mersey sound and rhythm & blues and folk music. That's the sound The Beatles developed. Our songs are folk songs – some of them are hundreds of years old. They have more meaning."

Wednesday 11th
PERFORMANCE A further show by Mike's "mod combo" is scheduled for Frost's in downtown San Antonio, Texas, at 11:00am.

Thursday 12th
PERFORMANCE The *San Antonio Light* reports that "Mike Nesmith, up-and-coming young recording star and his Pop-Rock Combo" performs at 12:30pm today at Frost Brothers' 1965 Big Sound College Fashion Show. The event takes place in the St. Anthony Hotel's Anacacho Room and is titled Youthquake. The *Light* also notes that Nesmith is a protégé of singing star Frankie Laine, with recent record releases of 'All The King's Horses' and 'How Can You Kiss Me' on Circa and Columbia Records. (Neither release on these labels is believed to exist. Circa is the name of the distributor of the Mike & John & Bill single.) Michael's combo is now called Mike & John. At 2:30pm the group are scheduled to perform their third and final show at Frost's department store. At 7:00 they have a

further booking at North Star Mall's Fashion Square. Following that show, it is reported that Mike & John return to California, where they are to cut their first album.

It is also reported that the duo has toured such far-off places as Japan and Hawaii. Neither tour is officially documented and no full album by Mike & John is thought to exist.

Saturday 14th
● 'What Are We Going To Do' single by David Jones debuts on the *Billboard* Hot 100 chart. During its three-week chart stay, Davy's second single will make it to #98, though competing trade magazines *Record World* and *Cash Box* will place the disc even higher on their charts.

Tuesday 17th
● Screenwriters Larry Tucker and Paul Mazursky submit their first draft of a half-hour comedy pilot script titled *The Monkeys* to Bob Rafelson and Bert Schneider's production company, Raybert. At this point the script names four characters, Davy, SJ, Rick, and Wendell, confirming that at this early stage Davy Jones is firmly attached to the vehicle.

Wednesday 18th
● Bud Katzel is named chief of Colpix Records, replacing Ward Sylvester. Sylvester will remain Davy's personal manager.

Saturday 21st
● 'What Are We Going To Do' single by David Jones peaks on the *Cash Box* chart at #94.

Thursday 26th
● Bud Katzel fires Colpix Records' A&R head Hank Levine. *Daily Variety* notes that Levine's only charted record in his three-and-a-half years with the company was David Jones's 'What Are We Going To Do' single.

Saturday 28th
● *Cash Box* runs an ad for Davy's 'What Are We Going To Do' declaring that the singer is "moving up the charts with his new hit single," though the song has entirely fallen off the magazine's charts.

LEFT An ad published in July for Davy's second Colpix single, 'What Are We Going To Do?' ABOVE Mike & John – Michael Nesmith and John London – now with electric instruments at a live appearance in San Antonio, Texas, in August.

However, this week's Top Pops chart in *Record World* does place the disc at #77.

● Sunday 29th - Monday 30th

● Michael and Phyllis Nesmith, along with housemate John London, listen to The Beatles perform at the Hollywood Bowl. The duplex they share is just around the corner from the venue.

● Tuesday August 31st - Sunday September 26th

PERFORMANCE The Survivors, featuring Michael, begin a residency at the Duke Of York on Marine Avenue in Manhattan Beach, California. For the next month the group will appear six nights weekly, Tuesday through Sunday. The full line-up is Michael, John London, Owens Castleman, Del Ramos, Nyles Brown, Bill Chadwick, and Carol Stromme.

Randy Sparks gave them their name because, he says, "Everyone else in the folk music business has deserted the ship and gone to rock'n'roll. In view of the fact that these people represent the last of the big folk groups, we've decided on the name The Survivors." A planned album titled *Soul Survivors* will never materialize.

A newsletter related to this booking also reveals that The Survivors were formed and formally educated at a Sparks-owned club called Ledbetter's in West Los Angeles. After two weeks in dry rehearsal, plus another three weeks on stage with an audience, The Survivors were nearly ready to take their place on the concert circuit. However, a fire that destroyed Ledbetter's left the group "homeless" and caused Sparks to seek immediate outside bookings.

SEPTEMBER

'

The New Recruit' / **'A Journey With Michael Blessing'** single by Michael Blessing is released in the USA. Colpix issues this 45 by Michael with a possibly unrelated instrumental on the B-side.
● Davy lands a role on television's *Ben Casey* and films his spot for the series this month. It will be shown on December 27th.

● Wednesday 8th - Friday 10th

● Over these three days both *The Hollywood Reporter* and *Daily Variety* carry a single ad from Raybert Productions seeking "Folk & Roll Musicians Singers for acting roles in new TV series. Running parts for 4 insane boys, age 17-21. Want Spirited Ben Frank's–types. Have courage to work. Must come down for interview." This is for the proposed *Monkees* TV series.

As many as 400 hipsters and hopefuls will answer the call. Raybert's Bert Schneider: "We didn't want the usual type of characters. There are the smart know-it-alls, who know all about cameras and scripts and are kind of professional at playing teenagers. We didn't want this type at all. We wanted a series which would be about the guys we were looking for. They didn't have to play the roles – they just had to be themselves."

Schneider's partner in Raybert, Bob Rafelson: "Davy is the one I had the most doubts about. I'll be honest about that. Davy had the least contact with rock'n'roll than any of the others, and although he had acting experience, I wasn't sure if he would be able to get into the spirit of the thing. I was wrong. Very wrong.

"When we started to do interviews for prospective Monkees, we were literally seeing people hour by hour. It was a lot of fun and we used to do nutty things to see what sort of reaction we got from applicants. We ended up having musical jam sessions in the office. I tell you, the secretary went out of her mind."

Davy recalls the circumstances of these 'interviews' at Raybert. "Mike really cracked me up when he came in," he says, using Michael's Monkee-character forename, and the name that the rest of the group and crew habitually called him. "He walked in with his wool hat, blue jeans and a western shirt, and a laundry bag with his laundry in it – he was afraid to leave it in his car. When Lester [Sill, of Screen Gems] asked him if he had any pictures, he said, 'Yes.' And he was told to go home and get them and come back. He was back in 15 minutes – and he was still hanging on to the laundry bag. He just broke me up."

John London: "At the office, we were filling out a questionnaire and I looked over at Mike's, and where you put down your experience he had written 'LIFE' and drawn a diagonal line through the rest of the sheet. I said, 'You can't do that.' But the producers took a look and said, 'This guy is for us.'"

Davy: "They were also interested in a couple of guys who turned the show down. One was Jerry Yester [see March 16th 1967] and another was Steve Stills of the Buffalo Springfield. They liked Steve very much. He said, 'That's not my bag, it's not what I want to do. But I do have a buddy – a friend of mine is working out at Santa Monica in a coffee shop washing dishes; he plays guitar for his food.'" Bob Rafelson: "I remember I went to great lengths to contact [Peter]. I found him working as a dishwasher – not even a musician – so you can imagine it took a while tracing him. But when I heard him, I knew at once he was right. I was knocked out."

Davy: "So Peter came down in blue jeans that were really dirty, his hair all over the place, and unshaven. Then Bert really flipped for Peter because of something he did. Peter went to sit down and Bert pulled the chair out from under him. So Peter calmly walked over and pulled all the things off the desk. Then he said, as if nothing had happened, 'Do you want to get started now?'"

Micky recalls: "A call went out in the trade [publications], but of course I had already had a [TV] series, so I had a private audition. My agent just set me up for an interview and I went in. I'd been up for like three or four shows that month; it was pilot season. There were three or four other shows about music that were trying to get on the air [but] this was by far the most unique – I thought. I even remember at the time I thought: 'I really want this one, this is kinda cool.'

"The whole thing was different. Whereas most shows at the time were being produced by middle-aged or elderly executives, Bert Schneider and Bob Rafelson were only 30 or something like that. [They] were off the streets themselves, they were part of what was going on at the time: the pop culture. They had a different attitude about it."

● Saturday 18th
● *Record World* reports that Davy recently visited New York City to plug his Colpix single 'What Are We Going To Do'.

● Friday 24th
● With casting underway on the pilot, Lester Sill of Screen Gems sends a memo to the company's Don Kirshner regarding music for *The Monkeys*. The memo states that series co-creator Bert Schneider is seeking two songs: a theme song to be titled 'The Monkeys' and another to be named 'The Chase' "written around and about the last few scenes of the pilot script." Kirshner has suggested Screen Gems staff songwriter Roger Atkins for the job and Sill is requesting demos and lead sheets (written melodies) for the tunes by October 11th.

● Saturday 25th
RECORDING Western Recorders *6000 Sunset Blvd, Hollywood, CA* 6:00-9:00pm. David Gates *prod*; Chuck Britz *eng*; tracking.
1. **'I'll Be Here'**
   unissued master # 10318
2. **'The Girl From Chelsea'**
   Colpix single 789 master # 10319
3. **'Show Me Girl'**
   unissued master # 10320

Personnel Hal Blaine (drums), Glen Campbell (guitar), Al Casey (guitar), David Jones (vocals), Larry Knechtel (bass), Lincoln Mayorga (piano), Ray Pohlman (bass), Julius Wechter (percussion), unknown (backing vocals).
● With Hank Levine now fired from Colpix, Screen Gems staff writer David Gates takes over the production reins for this David Jones session. It will be Davy's last for the label, precipitated by his limited chart success with 'What Are We Going To Do'. Ultimately, only one side is ever released from this date, leaving 'Show Me Girl' (also recorded by Herman's Hermits) and the otherwise unknown 'I'll Be Here' on the cutting room floor.

These outtakes will later be lost, though other Colpix-era acetate recordings will surface on Davy's 1995 release *Just For The Record – Volume One*. (Just for the record, it is unclear where or when these tracks – 'Kiss And Hug,' 'Be My Friend,' 'Let It Happen,' a cover of Ritchie Valens's 'Donna,' 'Never Will I Ever,' 'Boy Can't Win,' 'I Want To Love You,' 'Since I Fell In Love With You,' 'Summertime Is Fun Time,' and 'I Love You Anyway' – were recorded, though it is possible that some may date back to 1964.)

OCTOBER

'The Girl From Chelsea' / **'Theme For A New Love'** single by David Jones is released in the U.S.A. This is Davy's third Colpix single, with an older B-side. Though neither side will chart, Davy will make the promotional rounds for this release.
● Davy is cast to appear on the television program *The Farmer's Daughter* – and the show's set will conveniently be utilized for the *Monkees* screen tests this month. Davy: "They narrowed the field down to ten boys, including myself. We all had to take screen tests. Then they got us down to six, [including] myself, Mike, Peter, Micky, and Bill Chadwick."

Although a memo from Lester Sill at Screen Gems has outlined the need for songs to use in the *Monkees* series pilot by October 11th, this date may have moved since songwriters Tommy Boyce & Bobby Hart have now been assigned to the project in place of Roger Atkins. Some time this month, Boyce & Hart will demo three songs for the program: '(Theme From) The Monkees,' two versions of 'I Wanna Be Free,' and 'Let's Dance On.' At this stage, all feature 'demo' vocals from Boyce & Hart with backing likely provided by the duo's usual crew of musicians – Billy Lewis on drums, bassist Larry Taylor, and Gerry McGee on guitar.

LEFT One of the September ads that prompted hundreds of hopefuls to apply to become one of The Monkees.
ABOVE Michael with John London, Bill Chadwick, Carol Stromme, and others in their group The Survivors. They choose their name to suggest, optimistically, that they are "the last of the big folk groups."

Bobby Hart: "We needed two songs for specific scenes. One was David walking on the beach after having a problem with his love life. So that had to be kind of a romantic ballad. We thought 'I Wanna Be Free' would fit for that. Then they needed an up-tempo song for a dance scene and 'Let's Dance On' filled the bill. Then they needed a theme song. Other than those general requirements they didn't give us any ideas about what they had in mind. Actually we had [previously] written 'I Wanna Be Free,' but we just said this is the perfect song for that slot. Then we wrote the other two specifically."

● Thursday 7th

● Michael's screen test for *The Monkees* is filmed on the set of *The Farmer's Daughter* TV show. In a segment later broadcast in episode 10 of *The Monkees*, Michael is filmed holding a 12-string guitar and harmonica as he discusses his stage name, Blessing, and his time in the Air Force. He admits that he's only been playing music for two years. Bob Rafelson asks what he did before that. "I was a failure," answers Michael candidly, adding: "I think I'm out of work and I hope I get this series."

● Saturday 9th

● *Record World* reviews the first Michael Blessing single among its Four Star Picks, saying: "Fellow sings a sprightly melody. Lyrics are something else again – cynical approach to learning the war game. Watch."

● Tuesday 12th

● Steve Blauner is named vice president of new projects for the Screen Gems television arm of Columbia Pictures. Among his duties will be supervision of the *Monkees* series.

● Friday 15th

RECORDING United Recorders (A) *Hollywood, CA* 8:00-11:00pm. Bob Krasnow & Sam Ashe *prod*; Henry Lewy *eng*; tracking.

1. 'Until It's Time For You To Go' version 1
Colpix single 792 master # 10337

2. 'Thirteen's Not Our Lucky Number' version 1
unissued

Personnel Israel Baker (violin), Arnold Belnick (violin), Dennis Budimir (guitar), Frank Capp (percussion), Jesse Ehrlich (cello), Gene Estes (percussion), Jimmy Getzoff (violin), Bill Kursach (violin), Lincoln Mayorga (harpsichord), Michael Nesmith (vocal), Don Peake (guitar), Lyle Ritz (bass), Joseph Saxon (cello), Ralph Schaeffer (violin), Sidney Sharp (violin), Robert Sushel (violin).

● This session produces Michael Nesmith/Blessing's second and final Colpix single, 'Until It's Time For You To Go.' 'Thirteen's Not Our Lucky Number' is never released and no tapes are known to exist, but Michael will make another attempt at it during a 'Monkees' session in 1969. The song's co-author Michael Cohen will play keyboard for a 1966 Nesmith-produced Monkees session, as well as joining Michael for some post-Monkees solo recordings in the 1970s. (The strings for today's session are arranged by Shorty Rogers and conducted by Kelly Gordon.)

● Tuesday 19th - Thursday 21st

● Davy is employed to act on *The Farmer's Daughter* as Roland, a musician. In an episode named after the character's fictitious group, Moe Hill & The Mountains, Davy sings Boyce & Hart's 'Gonna Buy Me A Dog.' On the first day of filming, Davy's screen test for *The Monkees* is shot on the set of this Screen Gems television program. Davy recalls: "I was really green as far as business goes. I read the script and said yeah, it's great. But, you know, I wasn't thinking about when they'd really do the show; I just read what they had written down."

● Friday 22nd

● 'Thirteen's Not Our Lucky Number' is copyrighted by Randy Sparks's Country Music Inc. for its authors Michael Nesmith and Michael Cohen in preparation for potential release.

● Thursday 28th

● 'Of You' is copyrighted by Country Music Inc. for its authors Bill Chadwick and his brother John Chadwick. It will be recorded during 1966 for The Monkees.

NOVEMBER

● Screen tests for the *Monkees* television series are submitted to Audience Studies, Inc. which runs a 400-seat theater called Preview House located on Sunset Boulevard in Los Angeles, used for testing public response on most Columbia-Screen Gems programs. The process consists of inviting audience members off the street or from supermarkets with the promise of free entertainment. Each audience member is seated at a panel with buttons labeled 'like' and 'don't like' and is encouraged to push or turn these buttons as many times as they feel impelled to do so. Written questionnaires also play a part in the process.

Reportedly, Davy gets the best reaction of all the Monkees screen tests submitted, though his spot in the program is already decided. It is the other actors' ratings that will no doubt pique the interest of *Monkees* production company Raybert, and it is at this point that Davy, Michael, Micky, and Peter are selected as The Monkees.

Jim Frawley, later to become a director on the TV series and the group's improvisation coach, recalls: "They were cast pretty cleverly because their personalities are pretty much what you see. Michael was kind of intuitively the leader – very dry in his attitude and sense of humor. Very clever. Very smart. Micky was the comic, and did a lot of slapstick. We had Peter, who was a quiet, sensitive guy – and he is. Davy [is] the pretty boy, the ladies man. So, if you put them all together they were like one human being endowed with all those qualities. Each one of them was one quarter of the perfect man."

Bob Rafelson: "I often wonder about some of the other guys we said no to and what The Monkees would have been like if we'd had

one or two different people in the group. Maybe they would have fitted well together. Maybe not. When we were making the selection we had to think about that. It's often been said that The Monkees are 'manufactured,' but the term irritates me just a little bit. The Monkees were more like a Japanese marriage: arranged. In America and elsewhere the divorce rate is pretty high, but in Japan things go better."

The four freshly chosen Monkees will appear in Raybert's pilot show, shot this month in order to sell the series idea to a TV network.

● Sunday 7th

PERFORMANCE Michael appears with The Survivors at UCLA's Student Union Coop in Los Angeles, from 7:30 to 9:30pm. Admission is free to the show, part of a series presented under the auspices of a student association at UCLA.

● Tuesday 9th

'Until It's Time For You To Go' / 'What Seems To Be The Trouble Officer' single by Michael Blessing is released in the U.S.A. This is Michael's second Colpix single as Blessing.

● Thursday 11th - Saturday 20th

FILMING During this period the pilot for *The Monkees* is filmed in Los Angeles and San Diego. It will later be broadcast as episode 10 of the series, *Here Come The Monkees*. (It's possible that production stretches to Tuesday 23rd.)

TV Michael appears on TV as Michael Blessing on the syndicated *Lloyd Thaxton Show* on Friday 12th. Likely taped earlier in the week, Nesmith/Blessing is on hand to promote his Colpix single 'Until It's Time For You To Go.' Michael is dressed in his usual blue denim as he lip-synchs (mimes) the song while sitting on a stool. The program also features a brief interview with Nesmith/Blessing in which the single's arranger, Shorty Rogers, is mentioned. In his introduction, host Lloyd Thaxton claims that this is Blessing's television debut.

TV Davy appears on the music program *Shindig!* televised by the ABC network on Saturday 13th. He is seen performing 'What Are We Going To Do' in a *Shindig!* Music Hall segment. The broadcast was taped at an earlier date.

TV Davy appears on the local Los Angeles KCOP Channel 13 dance show *Hollywood Discotheque* on Monday 15th. This too was likely taped before today.

Two views of the November shoots for the pilot show for the proposed *Monkees* TV series. The group (seen with instruments, LEFT) are Davy Jones, Peter Tork, Micky Dolenz, and Mike Nesmith.

DECEMBER

● With their pilot now completed, production company Raybert goes through an agonizing series of edits to assemble a saleable product for the proposed *Monkees* project. But initial testing-scores at the Audience Studies screenings are poor and the producers are unable to secure a deal for the program. Jackie Cooper of Screen Gems will later tell the *Chicago Daily News* that the participants at Audience Studies didn't so much give the show a negative response as no response at all. "They didn't do anything," says Cooper. "They had never seen anything like it before, and they didn't know whether they liked it or not. We noticed that toward the end people were pushing the 'like' button. But the little machine started to add things up, and the number only came out at 600 – and 700 is considered dangerously low."

● Sunday 5th

An article published in today's *Los Angeles Times* reveals that Micky is still on the hunt for work as an actor and recently auditioned for a role in another prospective music-oriented television program. This unnamed project – shockingly similar in form to Raybert's *Monkees* – is according to the *Times* currently casting "three young people to star in a Herb Brodkin-produced television musical-comedy series. The ads [asked] young musicians (they must be able to play and sing as well as act) to apply themselves at Paramount Studios. ... One of

the auditioners was Mickey Braddock who used to be the boy on *Circus Boy*, an almost historic television series."

● Tuesday 7th

TV Davy is seen on Dick Clark's daytime rock show *Where The Action Is* where he lip-synchs (mimes) to both sides of his final Colpix single. The appearance may have been taped last month in Phoenix, Arizona. Davy: "I did a lot of rock'n'roll shows that Screen Gems wanted me to do. [My manager Ward Sylvester] and I were living on North Ivar in Hollywood at the time, in a little apartment with a living room, two bedrooms, and a kitchen as big as a chair."

● Saturday 25th

● Micky invites his new acquaintance Davy Jones to spend the Christmas holiday with the Dolenz family in Los Gatos, California.

● Monday 27th

● Davy's guest appearance as Greg Carter on television's *Ben Casey* is aired on the ABC network at 10:00pm during an episode titled *If You Play Your Cards Right, You Too Can Be a Loser.* Davy recalls that Columbia/Screen Gems have him on retainer "and shipped me out to do spots on different TV shows. On *Ben Casey* I played a married guy who sniffed glue. So I just played myself and then cracked as if I sniffed glue. But I don't want to get out of character like that again really. I don't want to play a glue sniffer that beats his wife."

Two more shots taken of the group during filming in November for the pilot show for the *Monkees* TV series.

1966

Monkees TV series sold to NBC ... filming begins for TV series and continues through year ... music producer is appointed to direct recordings ... instrumental recordings by session players begin at RCA Hollywood for first single and LP; Monkees supply vocals ... producers include Boyce & Hart, Michael Nesmith ... music coordinator Don Kirshner and RCA Records set up special Colgems label for Monkees product ... 'Last Train To Clarksville' first single, makes #1 ... personal appearance tour to promote single and TV show ... weekly *Monkees* show debuts on NBC TV ... first LP *The Monkees*, makes #1 ... some instrumental recording shifts to New York, including 'I'm A Believer' with producer Jeff Barry ... recording for second album starts ... 'I'm A Believer' second single, makes #1 ... first live concerts.

The group pose for a promo photograph to publicize the J.C. Penney line of Monkees clothing.

JANUARY

● The four prospective Monkees scatter this month, with no news from Bob Rafelson and Bert Schneider at the Raybert company regarding the fate of the pilot for their TV series. Davy briefly returns to England while Peter heads back to the East Coast. Meanwhile, Michael acts as master of ceremonies at the West Hollywood Troubadour club's Monday 'hoot' nights, a series of 'open mike' events (or 'open microphone,' where anyone is welcome to get up and do a spot). Micky remains in Los Angeles, probably pursuing non-musical endeavors.

Davy recalls: "We were broke all the time then. I remember I used to take Peter out to lunch and he always used to say, 'One day I'm going to pay you back.' I told him not to worry, that he'd have plenty of opportunity. I had saved a little money from *Oliver!* and that's what I was living off of at the time.

"During the screen test, I would take them all out to lunch – they couldn't get over it. And Mike used to invite us all up to dinner. Phyllis would cook – and she'd cook big. If Mike had ten dollars, he'd go out and buy ten dollars' worth of food. He'd have five or six people and they'd have the best steak, the best vegetables, and a wonderful dessert. Phyllis would manage to make it on that. And then they'd eat canned food for the rest of the week. That's the type of guy Mike is: he'd spend his last dollar on somebody.

"During that time Peter was living at Mike's house. A couple of them borrowed a couple hundred dollars from Screen Gems, but the studio was really tight."

Peter: "Michael was very kind to me at the outset. He put me up through the entire process of shooting the pilot. He and his wife had a wonderful little apartment just big enough for a guest on the day bed."

● Some time this month production company Raybert are able to edit the pilot in a fashion that garners positive audience reaction at the testing theater, Preview House. The real key to their success is adding Davy's screen test to the very beginning of the program. Since he tested the highest in October, the show is now an instant click with the trial audience.

Michael: "When they first tested the show it didn't do well; they came back, stuck the interviews [with us on to it], and it did better. There was no magic to that, it was just that you got to know the characters – you just kind of needed to know who these people were. So they fixed that problem and we were off and running – we got on the air."

● Tuesday 4th
● '(I'm Not Your) Steppin' Stone' by songwriters Tommy Boyce and Bobby Hart is recorded for the first time, by Paul Revere & The Raiders at Columbia Square studio in Hollywood. The Monkees will tape their own, definitive version of the song in July.

● Friday 7th
TV Davy's guest appearance on *The Farmer's Daughter* is aired at 9:30pm on the ABC network.

● Monday 10th
● Casting director Eddie Foy III compiles a final tally of the many contenders who were seriously considered for the *Monkees* pilot, including comments for future reference. 'Monster Mash' hit-maker Bobby 'Boris' Pickett was considered "too old" at 25. Brothers Mark and Matt Andes – later in such groups as Heart, Firefall, Spirit, and Jo Jo Gunne – were of "no interest." Nor was early-'60s hit-maker

Eddie Hodges. Gary Lewis was "not for us." *Shindig* regulars The Wellingtons "Raybert felt all too old." Songwriter Smokey Roberds "did not fit," and Raybert "passed" on Van Dyke Parks, although Foy "liked" this applicant.

● Monday 17th
● With positive test results in hand, *The Monkees* series is sold by Screen Gems to the NBC network.

● Wednesday 19th
● Michael's song 'Don't Wait For Me' is copyrighted by Randy Sparks's Country Music Inc. publishing company.

FEBRUARY

● The group reunites in Los Angeles amid the news that the *Monkees* series has now been sold. Davy: "I had all my things packed, ready to leave for the stables [to continue training as a jockey], and I got a call from Mike: 'Come on Davy, you've got to come back.' But I said no. I'd been waiting for two months for them to contact me and they hadn't. Now I was set on returning to the stables. Then I asked Mike if he was going to do it and he said, 'Yes, it's going to be really fantastic.' He was really excited. So I came back."

Micky: "I didn't even know I had a part until I read about it in *Variety*. No one told me. I called up *Variety* and said, 'Listen, I saw my name in your paper as one of The Monkees, is it true?' And they said, 'Yeah. Didn't they tell you?' I was really happy!"

● Tuesday 8th
● The revised Tommy Boyce and Bobby Hart song 'I Can't Get Her Off My Mind' is copyrighted. It will be recorded in July for the Monkees project.

● Wednesday 9th
● Screen Gems sell two half-hour sitcoms to NBC-TV for next season: *Occasional Wife* and *The Monkees*, reports *Daily Variety*. NBC executives Julian Goodman and Walter D. Scott watch *The Monkees* pilot in total silence, but both men are quietly impressed. "We walked out of the screening room just a couple of squares in the eyes of the producers," Goodman will recall in 1967. "Walter and I sat down and said together: 'I like it.'" The *Monkees* series will begin shooting at the end of May.

● Monday 14th
● *Daily Variety* reports that TV producers David Gordon and David Yarnell have hired an attorney in an effort to establish a claim that they are the originators of *The Monkees*. They claim the show "is a virtual carbon copy of their format, *Liverpool U.S.A.*, which the pair pitched to Screen Gems late in 1964." Formal legal action will be taken when the *Monkees* series debuts in September.

● Wednesday 16th
The Los Angeles Times runs a unique blurb about the sale of the *Monkees* series to NBC. "NBC's new entry is *The Monkees*, a half-hour comedy about an unknown quartet of way-out, impoverished singer-musicians. The series stars are David Jones, Peter Tork, Mike (Wool Hat) Nesmith. Their prototypes are The Beatles, but unlike The Beatles, they are the world's most unknown teen-age idols and at last count their combined wealth totaled $16.87."

An early attempt at a group car is this MG, pictured full of Monkees and a couple of Gretsch promo guitars.

● Friday 18th
● Three of Michael's former bandmates from The Survivors – Michael Murphey, Del Ramos, and Carol Stromme – are now part of another Randy Sparks assemblage called The New Society. The group has a record deal with RCA and today records the songs 'Of You,' '(I Prithee) Do Not Ask For Love' and 'Buttermilk.' Michael will record the first two in a few months for the Monkees project, and while later he is rumored to appear on The New Society's recording of 'Buttermilk,' worksheets show he does not.

● Saturday 19th
● *Record World* carries a news item titled "Colpix' Jones Set For Rock TV Series," the first mention in the music press regarding the upcoming *Monkees* TV series. "There was a time when a rock'n'roll act couldn't get a prime time slot," runs the piece. "That time is so far in the past that NBC is now readying a comedy series for next season called *The Monkees* and dealing with the antics of – guess what? – a rock'n'roll group. It'll star Colpix' David Jones, plus Mickey Braddock and folksingers Peter Tork and Mike Blessing. Surely records will follow if the show clicks." *Record World* is still using Micky and Michael's stage-names.

MARCH

● The Monkees begin a five-week improv and prep course with director Jim Frawley in a 20-by-40-foot cubicle erected on Columbia Studio's Stage #3 near the corner of Sunset Boulevard and Gower in Hollywood. Frawley recalls: "The work I did was really just encouraging them to free up. To be bold and make strong commitments and to trust the fact that they could do no wrong. That was really it, and it was in a way what [series creators Bob Rafelson and Bert Schneider] were telling me as a young, first-time director: you can do no wrong here. Dare to be wrong."
● Michael and family move house to 1611 Sunset Plaza Drive in West Hollywood. Davy lives with the Nesmiths during this period. Davy: "I'd known Mike before *The Monkees* ever went on the air. After

we made the pilot, I lived with him and Phyllis at their house. We had ownership of a dog together. We were great friends. The first car I ever bought was in co-partnership with Mike, a yellow Willis jeep. He was driving an El Dorado at the time and I couldn't imagine how he did it if I couldn't do it. He had about as many pennies to rub together as I did."

● Wednesday 2nd
● Tommy Boyce and Bobby Hart's song 'Whatever's Right' is copyrighted. The duo will record the song for the Monkees project in July.

● Tuesday 15th
● Tommy Boyce and Bobby Hart's song 'She' is copyrighted; they will record it in August for the Monkees project.

● Monday 28th
● The Michael Nesmith song 'Happiness' is copyrighted by Randy Sparks's Country Music Inc. publishing company. It will be the last song of his assigned to Sparks, who will soon sell Michael's compositions back to Screen Gems Music publishing company (see May 27th). No recording of 'Happiness' is known to exist.

APRIL

● The Monkees begin rehearsing as a band to produce music for the upcoming television series and record releases. Although a contract is already struck with RCA Records, who will manufacture and distribute all Monkees recorded product through a new custom label called Colgems, Peter tells *Look* magazine that the band's efforts are "directionless and unproductive, musically speaking." Despite these details, RCA will begin a $100,000 campaign proclaiming "The Monkees Is Coming." Much of the promotional effort is directed at concertgoers for The Beatles' Summer '66 tour until a record is available to supply to disc jockeys.

Davy: "For three months we practiced our music. When you don't know a thing about music, it's a little hard keeping the beat. I had never even picked up an instrument, but Mike, Micky, and Peter were great on guitar. We just played for something to do, and Screen Gems rented the instruments for us. We decided someone would have to play the drums and Micky volunteered, though he couldn't really play them – he couldn't keep rhythm. Peter got to be the bass guitarist because Mike didn't want to play it."

Peter: "I remember having rehearsals before the show started filming. We got back together in March or April of '66 and, among the other things that we were doing, we had a rehearsal room and were starting to play together."

Series co-creator Bob Rafelson: "It was like group therapy. They criticized and laughed at each other, and rehearsed music without supervision. Then the record people were brought in."

Series producer Ward Sylvester tells Peter that Capitol Records would have signed the group even without a TV show, and that Raybert considered getting an established record company – such as Capitol – to release the records before deciding to do it themselves and setting up Colgems. If The Monkees had stayed with the unsuccessful Colpix label they may have flopped, since their indie distribution could not have matched that of RCA, which distributes Colgems. By starting an all-new label, The Monkees have set themselves up as a major operation.

● Sunday 3rd

PERFORMANCE Peter gives a solo performance at West Hollywood's Troubadour. The as-yet-unknown artist opens for Muddy Waters.

MAY

● Friday 27th

● Bob Rafelson and Bert Schneider's company Raybert and TV firm Screen Gems negotiate a fee of $5,000 to buy back the copyrights to 12 early Michael Nesmith songs from Randy Sparks's publishing company. The producers also buy out Michael's management contract from Bob Krasnow for just $2,000.

● Tuesday 31st

FILMING Production on the *Monkees* TV series officially kicks off with the start of production on what will become episode 8, *Don't Look A Gift Horse In The Mouth.* Shooting will continue through June.
● *The Washington Post* runs a remarkably prescient and detailed article, titled "Synthetic Quartet Will Hit Tube Hard." The paper says: "NBC-TV has a secret weapon aimed at Batman and will pull the trigger next fall. It's not a zap gun. It's not even a roadblock for ABC's Batmobile. What it is, is a new show concocted to woo the younger generation away from the dynamic duo.

"The series stars a fearsome foursome in The Monkees, a wholly manufactured singing group of attractive young men who come off as a combination of The Beatles, the Dead End Kids and the Marx Brothers. Critics will cry foul. Longhairs will demand, outraged, that they be removed from the air. But the kids will adore The Monkees; you can bet on it. Screen Gems, which produces the show, interviewed 650 young men and screen-tested 35 of them before settling on the quartet. The stars to-be are David Jones, Peter Tork, Mickey Braddock, and Mike Blessing. Unlike other rock'n'roll groups, the boys had never performed together before. Indeed, they'd never even met.

"Last September they were brought together, presumably by guys in white coats with nets. They shot the pilot show and sent the boys in their several directions with the admonition not to call Screen Gems. Screen Gems would call them. Six months later the show was sold and the boys were corralled once more. Since last January they've been working like slaves to create their own sound, locking themselves on a small sound stage and working away on two guitars, a set of drums, and a tambourine.

"An interview with The Monkees is an impossibility. Ask if any of them are married and Davy immediately claims he and Mike have been married for years. Peter makes the same claim for Mickey. They give their ages variously from 2 to 98 years. They break into off-key singing at the slightest provocation and rather than give straight answers they come up with rehearsed and ad libbed nonsense, most of it hokey. They're an irreverent lot who are certain to offend the press. Their antics, however, are natural and boisterously funny."

JUNE

● With an airdate looming in September, Raybert asks Screen Gems' Don Kirshner to recruit a producer for the Monkees recordings.

Although Raybert love the idea of letting the four cast members create their own music, they now realize the quartet cannot be depended upon to turn out the tunes based on their current rate of progress as a band. Kirshner is a skilled song publisher who recently sold his entire stable of hit-making contract writers – including Goffin & King, Boyce & Hart, and Mann & Weil – to Columbia Pictures.

Series co-creator Bert Schneider: "There were lots of times where I thought what the boys were doing sounded lousy, but there were enough times where I heard them and got gooseflesh. I wanted them to sound upbeat in lyrical content. It was a matter of finding someone to help bring that out."

Don Kirshner tells a reporter: "I heard them. They were loud. It was not the right sound. Not a young, happy, driving, pulsating sound of today. I wanted a musical sex image. Something you'd recognize next time you heard it. Davy was OK – for musical comedy. Mike was the weakest singer as far as I was concerned. Micky was a natural mimic. And he had the best voice for our purposes.

"I went out to California for what was to have been a few days – and stayed months! I found myself in a very exciting situation because, for the first time, RCA went outside to form a record company, Colgems, which they let me run creatively. Now I'm the music supervisor for the series and I'm back in the studio for the first time since Neil Sedaka and 'Who Put The Bomp.'"

Micky recalls: "I'm sure that Bob Rafelson and Bert Schneider said in all honesty, 'Yeah, don't worry. When we start going you're gonna record your tunes and it will be wonderful.' But the thing gets caught up in the inertia of the moment. NBC gets involved. RCA gets involved. Screen Gems gets involved. Millions and millions of dollars are on the line. I think that's kind of what happened. People aren't as forthcoming. Mike's style was very distinct, country-western,

More Gretsch gear from the group's endorsement deal: LEFT sheltering from the California sun, before any regular TV episodes are made; RIGHT with an early attempt at a Monkees logo on the bass drum.

Peter was very folk-rock, neither of which at the time you would have considered mainstream pop. Davy would have done all Broadway show tunes, more or less. I think I ended up singing the leads by default more than anything else. Certainly not because I had any better voice or anything. That was just more my style: pop-rock, as it were."

Lester Sill, West Coast head of Screen Gems Music Publishing, remembers: "There was a deadline to meet. They used Mike's music from the beginning. They did rehearse, they did work, but it took some time. They had to get the show on the air."

Discussions are opened with British producer Mickie Most about working with The Monkees. Most: "It was spring '66 in Los Angeles. They had just made and sold the pilot show, which I saw and I immediately reckoned that the boys were winners. Their producers were looking for a top record producer and offered me the job. I wanted to take it, but it entailed staying over there six months of the year. Family and business commitments didn't allow it. I was willing to fly out regularly to record them, but they needed somebody on the spot."

Lester Sill recalls that the first recording dates were with Snuff Garrett, hit producer of Gary Lewis & The Playboys. "Tommy and Bobby had written the songs," he says, "and Snuff was producing them."

● Thursday 2nd
FILMING Production is in progress on the TV episode *Don't Look A Gift Horse In The Mouth*. Work starts today at 8:00am at Columbia

Studio's Stage #7 for scenes in The Monkees' pad. A normal day of work for the group begins between 7:15 and 7:30am for make-up, with shooting to follow from 8:00am until the early evening. Actors Jerry Colonna, Henry Corden, and Jesslyn Fax are also on set, and four stand-ins are employed who also act as series extras when necessary. They include three of Michael's friends from the San Antonio College days – John London, David Price, and David Pearl – plus a friend of Micky's named Ric Klein.

● Friday 3rd
FILMING At 8:00am the *Monkees* crew arrives on Zuma Beach in Malibu, California, to shoot scenes on the beach for the episode that becomes *Don't Look A Gift Horse In The Mouth*. The crew will also pick up some shots on a nearby playground that are later integrated into the episode *Monkee Vs. Machine*. By the end of the day shooting is officially wrapped on *Gift Horse*. Production on the series will resume after a weekend break.

● Monday 6th
● At 10:00am The Monkees begin a table-read and rehearsal of the episode *Royal Flush* on Stage #7. Actor Theodore Marcuse is also involved. Shooting of this episode probably begins tomorrow.

● Friday 10th
FILMING Production wraps today on what will become episode 1 of the *Monkees* series, *Royal Flush*, after which The Monkees' first official recording session is held.

Fresh-faced Monkees compose themselves for the camera, wearing suits that will not make it to the TV episodes.

RECORDING RCA (B) *6363 Sunset Blvd, Hollywood, CA* 7:00-10:00pm, 10:30pm-1:30am. Snuff Garrett *prod*; tracking.
1. **'Take A Giant Step'** version 1
   unissued master # TPA3-4520
2. **'Let's Dance On'** version 1
   unissued master # TPA3-4519
Personnel Hal Blaine (drums, Latin percussion), James Burton (guitar), Glen Campbell (guitar), Sonny Curtis (guitar), Larry Knechtel (keyboard), Ray Pohlman (bass).
● These earliest professional Monkees recordings are produced by Snuff Garrett, who over the past 18 months has scored seven Top 10 singles for Gary Lewis & The Playboys. Considered a surefire hit-maker, Garrett will soon find that there are an awful lot of people to please in the Monkees hierarchy.

While Rafelson and Schneider at Raybert are aware that the four cast members don't have time to record their own music, they are still willing to hear their opinions of today's productions. Exerting the only control that they have, The Monkees' opinion is predictably negative. Tapes for these sessions are later lost, but those who hear the results describe them as sounding rather like Gary Lewis outtakes. The two tunes are arranged, like all of Lewis's hit recordings, by Leon Russell.

Producer Snuff Garrett says later that his intention to make Davy the lead vocalist on these tracks is unpopular with the group. Garrett is immediately bought out of his production deal for the Monkees project. He will later remark that it is "the most money I'd ever made in a day." Lester Sill of Screen Gems adds: "There was really a frigid atmosphere at the beginning with Snuff. They didn't get along with Snuff from the get go."

● Monday 13th - Friday 17th
FILMING The Monkees are more deeply committed to completing episodes of their TV series following the shaky start to their recording sessions. This week they work on the production of what will become episode 3, *Monkee Vs. Machine*. The entire production will be shot at Columbia Studios on Stages #2, #3, and #7 with the exception of some beach shots captured earlier in the month.

● Monday 20th - Friday 24th
FILMING The *Monkees* crew complete production this week for what will become episode 2 of the series, *Monkee See, Monkee Die*.

● Saturday 25th
● *Cash Box* runs a full-page photo of the music coordinator of the TV series, Don Kirshner, with the vice president of RCA Victor Records, George R. Marek.

The two are pictured signing the pact that establishes The Monkees' brand new record label, Colgems. Kirshner's deal calls for a salary of $35,000 a year or 15 percent of the profits from Colgems Records – whichever is greater.

"Don Kirshner is a dynamic creative talent with a splendid record of success and a reputation for inventive leadership which will assure success for the new label artistically," says Marek. "We intend to see that all of RCA Victor's marketing and promotional facilities are employed to assure maximum success of the label." This amounts to substantial hype for a label that has yet to cut a releasable piece of product. Meanwhile in the studio the second Monkees session is held, with Michael at the helm.
RECORDING RCA (A) *6363 Sunset Blvd, Hollywood, CA* 7:30pm-12:15am. Michael Nesmith *prod*; half-inch 4-track; tracking.
1. **'All The King's Horses'**
   Missing Links 2 master # TZB3-4521

2. **'The Kind Of Girl I Could Love'**
   More Of The Monkees master # TZB3-4522
3. **'I Don't Think You Know Me'** version 1
   Missing Links 1 master # TZB3-4523
Personnel Hal Blaine (drums), James Burton (guitar), Glen Campbell (guitar), Al Casey (guitar), Gary Coleman (percussion), Jim Gordon (percussion), Larry Knechtel (bass, organ 3), Bob West (bass).
● Raybert fulfill their promise to let the cast members create some music for the show by allowing Michael to produce this tracking session. ('Tracking' means the recording of basic instrumentation, before any vocals or other overdubs are added.) It becomes obvious that his country-flavored rock is not going to be an easy sell with Don Kirshner, whose stock in trade is middle-of-the-road pop. Yet it is a testament to the free-thinking spirit of Raybert – and perhaps a sign of their desperate need for soundtrack material – that the songwriter is given his day. The only catch is that while Michael is behind the mixing desk directing the session he is not allowed to play on the tracks. Session tapes from today's recording date are later lost, so no further insight is available on how he sculpts these tracks. On hand to translate Michael's ideas to the musicians on the studio floor is arranger and session musician Don Peake, who will be a fixture at all the tracking sessions that Michael produces this year.

Ultimately, only one song from today's batch of tracks will find original record release, 'The Kind Of Girl I Could Love.' This Latin-tinged composition was created by Michael in collaboration with Roger Atkins, who wrote The Animals' hit 'It's My Life' and was originally slated to provide music for the *Monkees* pilot. The song will appear on next year's *More Of The Monkees* album (and earlier in an episode of the series called *The Spy Who Came In From The Cool*).

As for the other two tracks taped today, 'All The King's Horses,' a holdover from Michael's Mike & John & Bill repertoire, will appear in two early episodes of *The Monkees*, while 'I Don't Think You Know Me,' the first of at least two attempts to capture this song, is never heard during the 1960s. Both will appear much later on Rhino's *Missing Links* series of outtakes and oddities.

The productions for these songs are not fully completed at this single session; overdubs of such crucial elements as lead and backing vocals are added later (see July 16th and July 30th).

● Monday 27th
FILMING Production begins probably today on what will become episode 5 of the *Monkees* series, *The Spy Who Came In From The Cool*. Work on this program will wrap in July.

● Tuesday 28th
RECORDING RCA (A) *Hollywood, CA* 8:00pm start.
● A musicians' union document indicates that a Monkees session takes place at this studio, but no other details are known. It is quite possible that the three Michael Nesmith tracks from the weekend session are at least reviewed if not worked on during this booking.

● Late June
● The Monkees are guests at the Beverly Hills restaurant Chasen's at a dinner held there for NBC network affiliates – the crucial stations that carry the NBC network throughout the country. According to *TV Guide*, this event will prove a turning point that will set back the overall acceptance and ratings of the *Monkees* series. The magazine later quotes a group insider who says that Bert Schneider was against the group going to the event. "He figured it for a square scene and the affiliates wouldn't dig it anyway. But the network insisted; the affiliates had to be won over. The head writers had a sketch for them, and the boys were supposed to kind of come in on

the end of things, make a quick appearance, and get out. But things ran late. They stood outside, tired, nervous, unfed. I said, 'Are you guys going to do the material?' 'Hell, no,' they said. Somebody had dragged along a stuffed peacock [NBC's mascot]. They played volleyball with it, stopping traffic on Beverly Boulevard. Micky got into the restaurant's switch box and turned off all the lights. Finally they were introduced by Dick Clark. Since they didn't have any musical instruments – we were afraid to try and let 'em play – they did 'comedy' material. Micky shaved with a microphone. Davy pretended he was a duck. The jokes began to die. The affiliates were already hostile and what was not needed was a bunch of smart-alec kids. On the way out I heard an affiliate say, 'That's *The Monkees*? Forget it.'"

JULY

● Friday 1st
FILMING Production is completed on the *Monkees* series episode *The Spy Who Came In From The Cool*.

● Monday 4th
● The *Monkees* crew probably enjoys a day off today as the country celebrates Independence Day. The group will not shoot a new episode this week, so focus shifts instead to recording music for the series.

● Tuesday 5th
RECORDING RCA (A) *Hollywood, CA* 2:00-7:30pm. Tommy Boyce, Bobby Hart, Jack Keller *prod*; half-inch 4-track; tracking.
1. **'(Theme From) The Monkees'** version 1
   The Monkees master # TPA3-4607
2. **'Let's Dance On'** version 2
   The Monkees master # TPA3-4519
3. **'This Just Doesn't Seem To Be My Day'**
   The Monkees master # TPA3-4606
Personnel Joseph DiTullio (cello 3), Wayne Erwin (guitar), Gene Estes (percussion including bells), Bobby Hart (organ except 3), Billy Lewis (drums), Gerry McGee (guitar), Louie Shelton (guitar), Larry Taylor (bass).
● The *Monkees* pilot episode filmed back in November featured three songs, written and recorded by Boyce & Hart, and two of these are remade at today's session. Nonetheless, music coordinator Don Kirshner considers the duo only a second or third tier choice as record producers for the project – but when he finds his East Coast stable of writers are nonplussed by the Monkees idea he gives the enthusiastic Boyce & Hart a shot.
Hart: "From the beginning Tommy and I had been led to believe that we were going to be able to produce the music. All this time we had been tugging at [Kirshner's] sleeve, and more specifically talking to Lester Sill, who ran the company on the West Coast, saying, 'Let us do it! We did the sound for the pilot, and we think we know what it should be.' [Kirshner] said, 'We love your sound, but take Jack Keller with you in the studio, because he's had more experience.'"
Keller is a successful songwriter and a veteran Kirshner songsmith, having worked with him on television projects such as *Gidget* and *Bewitched*. Keller will go on to co-produce several sessions for the Monkees project and write a number of songs for the group along the way.

The first track taped today is Boyce & Hart's '(Theme From) The Monkees,' which had originally been demoed by the duo some time late last year for use in test prints of the series pilot. Re-recorded here for record release, the theme is extended to a full-length composition with the addition of a second verse and an instrumental break. Other shorter versions of the song for use on the television series will be taped at subsequent sessions. Today's full-length reading will be featured as the kick-off track to the band's debut album, *The Monkees*.
Also remade today is Boyce & Hart's 'Let's Dance On,' a distant cousin to The Gentrys' late-'65 hit 'Keep On Dancing.' This is in fact the third time the song has been taped for The Monkees, counting both the pilot demo from '65 and Snuff Garrett's abortive version from June 10th. Like the 'Theme,' today's garage-rockin', lo-fi production of the song is also destined for release on the band's first long-player.
Closing out this session is a new and altogether more sophisticated Boyce & Hart song called 'This Just Doesn't Seem To Be My Day.' Modeled after such 'Eastern' influenced tracks as The Rolling Stones' 'Paint It Black,' the tune shows the songwriting duo on the cutting edge of commercial pop. It also employs one of the duo's signature tricks: a frantic verse followed by a slowed-down chorus. Boyce & Hart will later use this formula on songs like 'Sometimes She's A Little Girl.'
● Two of today's producers, Tommy Boyce and Jack Keller, are also listed as musicians on union records for the session. However, their instrumental contributions are not detectable, or were not used in the final productions, so they are omitted from the personnel credits.
● Another version of '(Theme From) The Monkees' featuring vocals by Micky Dolenz, Tommy Boyce, and Bobby Hart and labeled "early version" will appear on the 1994 Rhino CD version of *The Monkees* album. It is unclear exactly when this was recorded, but it's certainly not at today's session.

● Thursday 7th
RECORDING Western Recorders (2) *6000 Sunset Boulevard, Hollywood, CA* 8:00-11:30pm. Michael Nesmith *prod*; J.L.(?) *eng*; half-inch 4-track; tracking and vocals (Davy only).
1. **'Gonna Buy Me A Dog'** version 1 takes 1-10
   unissued master # TPA3-4608
2. **'So Goes Love'** takes 1-5
   Missing Links 1 master # TPA3-4609
3. **'Papa Gene's Blues'** version 1 takes 1-13
   The Monkees master # TPA3-4612
Personnel Hal Blaine (drums), James Burton (guitar), Glen Campbell (guitar), Al Casey (guitar), Gary Coleman (percussion), Jim Gordon (percussion), Jim Helms (guitar), David Jones (vocal 1,2), Bill Pitman (bass), Billy Preston (organ 1, electric piano 2), Peter Tork (guitar).
● Michael's second session as producer kicks off with ten takes of a rocking, bluesy arrangement on Boyce & Hart's 'Gonna Buy Me A Dog.' Michael's choice of this song proves his respect for the duo's pop sensibilities – or at least shows that he thinks he has something to add to them. It is obvious from listening to this version that it is meant as a straight take of the song, unlike the later-released joking take produced by Boyce & Hart. In fact, today's results sound rather like another 'dog' hit from a few years back: Rufus Thomas's 'Walking The Dog.'
Significantly, Michael is able to wrangle Peter a slot as guitarist on this date, making him the first group member to appear musically on a Monkees record release. Admittedly, the employment of five guitarists on this session seems dubious, but it is quite possible

that all of them performed – though they may not all be audible in the final production. Bill Pitman is credited here as a bassist, but is also known for playing guitar. Certainly, Michael gives numerous instructions between takes to James Burton and Glen Campbell, who are the most audible guitarists here.

Jim Gordon and Gary Coleman handle the tambourine and maracas for this track, and Don Peake is once again on the studio floor directing the musicians. Regardless of his efforts, Michael's version of 'Dog' will never be heard by the public. Boyce & Hart will cut their own version of the track on July 23rd.

Michael's next production is another non-original, Goffin & King's 'So Goes Love.' The choice indicates Michael's growing fondness for Goffin/King songs – he selected their 'I Don't Think You Know Me' for his last session – and that they may be his favorites among Kirshner's stable. For 'So Goes Love,' Michael once again involves Peter as well as Davy, who joins the session and sings some rough live vocals. However, the 'final' production, as issued on the outtakes collection *Missing Links* in 1987, features an overdubbed lead vocal and not the live take from this session (see July 16th).

In all, five takes of 'So Goes Love' are taped, with Glen Campbell providing the flamenco guitar runs and James Burton playing the electric guitar backbeats. Meanwhile, Billy Preston moves from organ to tremelo'd electric piano for this track before leaving the session entirely.

Davy remains on the studio floor for Michael's own 'Papa Gene's Blues,' cut under the working title 'Brand X.' Michael instructs Davy to sing into someone's ear – but not on mike. So a version of this song sung by Davy does not truly exist; final vocals will be recorded on July 11th. Jim Gordon and Gary Coleman provide the song's percussion section of cowbell, maracas and vibraslap. Take 1 is mostly acoustic, after which some rehearsal takes place.

All further takes feature the song's trademark guitar introduction played by James Burton. Indeed, it is Burton who Michael implores to "pick it Luther" (a reference to Johnny Cash's lead guitarist Luther Perkins) during the instrumental break. Thirteen takes are made in all, with the last being marked as the master; however, take 5 is later selected as the master to be used as the basis for the song's final backing track.

● Friday 8th

● Composer Stu Phillips begins scoring the incidental music for *The Monkees* series. From 2:00-5:45pm in RCA's Studio C, Phillips along with eight of L.A.'s top session players record cues for the episodes *Monkee Vs. Machine* and *Gift Horse*.

● Saturday 9th

RECORDING RCA (A) *Hollywood, CA.* Tommy Boyce & Bobby Hart *prod*; Hank Cicalo *eng*; half-inch 4-track; overdubs (including vocals).

1. **'This Just Doesn't Seem To Be My Day'**
   The Monkees master # TPA3-4606
2. **'Let's Dance On'** version 2
   The Monkees master # TPA3-4519
3. **'(Theme From) The Monkees'** version 1
   The Monkees master # TPA3-4607
4. **'Take A Giant Step'** version 2
   The Monkees master # TZB3-4520
5. **'I'll Be True To You'** a.k.a. 'Yes I Will'
   The Monkees master # TZB3-4611
6. **'Saturday's Child'**
   The Monkees master # TZB3-4610

Personnel Tommy Boyce (backing vocal 1,2,3,6), Bob Cooper (oboe 4), Wayne Erwin (guitar 4,5,6, backing vocal 1,2,3,6), Gene Estes (percussion including bells 4, glockenspiel 5, tambourine 6), Bobby Hart (organ 6, backing vocal 1,2,3,6), Ron Hicklin (backing vocal 1,2,3,6), Billy Lewis (drums 4,5,6), Gerry McGee (guitar 4,5,6), Michel Rubini (harpsichord 4), Louie Shelton (guitar 4,5,6), Larry Taylor (bass 4,5,6),

● This highly productive session kicks off most likely in the early morning, with producers Boyce, Hart, and Keller occupied all day finishing earlier productions and starting a few new ones. Their first business is to add backing vocals to some of their previously taped backing tracks. First up is 'This Just Doesn't Seem To Be My Day,' which is given a group backing-vocal arrangement led by session pro Ron Hicklin. Nonetheless, in the final production Davy's backing harmonies will dominate the mix. Not coincidentally, Davy's lead and backing vocals are likely added during this period (but not necessarily at this session).

Group vocals are also added to version 2 of 'Let's Dance On' and the album version of '(Theme From) The Monkees.' However, Boyce & Hart will revisit the backing vocals for 'Dance' at a further session on July 16th. Micky's lead vocals will also be added to these tracks during July.

After the vocal session, Boyce & Hart's usual crew of musicians enters the studio to cut some new tracks. 'Take A Giant Step,' a song previously recorded under the direction of Snuff Garrett, is remade during the afternoon, boasting a unique arrangement highlighted by Bob Cooper's oboe and Michel Rubini's harpsichord that add an Eastern flavor. Some unusual guitar parts and echoed percussion also lend a very light psychedelic tinge to this lyrically sophisticated Goffin & King number, which will wind up gracing the flipside of The Monkees' debut single in August.

Gerry Goffin and Russ Titelman's 'I'll Be True To You' has previously been a U.K. hit in January 1965 for The Hollies, who recorded the song under its correct title of 'Yes I Will.' The composition was inspired when Goffin & Titelman saw The Beatles' *A Hard Day's Night* movie (and more specifically the soundtrack song 'If I Fell'). Given that the *Monkees* project is so heavily inspired by that film, it seems only natural that the Goffin/Titelman tune should wind up on The Monkees' debut album. It will never feature in the television series, giving credence to the idea that perhaps Raybert are less enthused by the pure pop music that is Kirshner's specialty. (Michel Rubini does record a harpsichord part today for 'I'll Be True To You' but it will not be featured in the final production of the song.)

Songwriter David Gates produced Davy's last Colpix session in September '65 and is the composer of the next song to be taped, 'Saturday's Child.' Along with Boyce & Hart's 'If You're Thinkin' What I'm Thinkin'' it will be cut by producer Mickie Most for Herman's Hermits around this time, hinting that this was one of the demos Most considered when he was approached to produce The Monkees.

Gates will later claim that 'Saturday's Child' is a serious contender for the group's debut single. It will certainly be featured on the band's debut album as well as appearing on two early episodes of the *Monkees* series. After tracking wraps for this tune, Ron Hicklin and company add group backing vocals to the song, leaving only the taping of Micky's lead vocal to complete the production.

● Monday 11th

FILMING Production probably begins on what will become episode 7 of the *Monkees* series, *Monkees In A Ghost Town*.

● Wednesday 13th

RECORDING RCA (A) *Hollywood, CA* 7:00pm-12midnight. Tommy

Boyce, Bobby Hart, Jack Keller *prod*; half-inch 4-track; overdubs (including vocals), mixdown.

1. 'I'll Be True To You' a.k.a 'Yes I Will'
The Monkees master # TZB3-4611
Personnel Tommy Boyce, Bobby Hart, Ron Hicklin (backing vocal).
● Boyce & Hart return to RCA this evening to work on their production of 'I'll Be True To You.' Activity centers on the addition of backing vocals, once again led by Ron Hicklin, with Boyce and Hart joining in for some three-part harmonies. All backing vocals from this session are combined and dubbed onto a single track of the 4-track tape. American Federation of Television and Radio Artists contracts indicate that this recording is completed in three hours, so the additional studio time is probably used for mixdowns and reductions on this or other songs. Boyce & Hart will resume work on the tune on July 16th, when Davy adds his lead vocal.

● Thursday 14th

FILMING During shooting of episode 7 of the *Monkees* series, *Monkees In A Ghost Town*, pianist Joseph Weiss is employed from 10:00am–12:35pm and 1:35–4:10pm to play tack piano during a saloon scene. (A tack piano is one with specially hardened hammers for a percussive, jangling sound.) Production on this episode will be wrapped tomorrow.

● Saturday 16th

RECORDING RCA (A) *Hollywood, CA* 1:00-4:00pm, 7:00pm-12midnight. Michael Nesmith, Tommy Boyce & Bobby Hart, Jack Keller *prod*; Dave Hassinger *eng*; half-inch 4-track; overdubs (including vocals), mixdown.

1. The Kind Of Girl I Could Love overdubs onto take 10
More Of The Monkees master # TZB3-4522
2. 'All The King's Horses'
Missing Links 2 master # TZB3-4521
3. 'Papa Gene's Blues' version 1 overdubs onto take 5
The Monkees master # TPA3-4612
4. 'I'll Be True To You' a.k.a. 'Yes I Will'
The Monkees master # TZB3-4611
5. 'So Goes Love' overdubs onto take 5
Missing Links 1 master # TPA3-4609
6. 'I Don't Think You Know Me' version 1 overdubs onto take 10
The Monkees master # TZB3-4523
7. 'Let's Dance On' version 2
The Monkees master # TPA3-4519
Personnel Tommy Boyce (backing vocal 7), Micky Dolenz (lead vocal 2,6,7, backing vocal 1,2,3,7, harmony vocal 3), Bobby Hart (backing vocal 7), Ron Hicklin (backing vocal 7), David Jones (lead vocal 4,5, backing vocal 1,2,3,5), Michael Nesmith (lead vocal 1,2,3, backing vocal 1,2,3), Peter Tork (backing vocal 1,2,3,7),
● The Monkees use their day off from filming for vocal overdubs in the studio. First up are some of Michael's recordings from last month. Using take 10 of 'The Kind Of Girl I Could Love' from the June 25th session as a basis, the quartet give a full group performance, adding an impressive four-part vocal background to the song.

The use of all the group members in this arrangement is a further move by Michael to make his productions a group effort. He will return to this recording on July 30th for some final fine-tuning of the master. (At some point between June 25th and today's session

With the fabulous Monkeemobile during a summer TV shoot. The car, one of two made, is a customized Pontiac GTO designed by Dean Jeffries.

a prominent steel guitar overdub has been added to this recording. When later questioned about who plays the part, Nesmith will answer: "It's me.")

Also building on a track from the June 25th session, vocals (including leads) are added to Michael's 'All The King's Horses.' This will be the end of the race for this particular track; it will not find record release until 1990's rarities collection *Missing Links Volume Two*, though it will surface in two early episodes of the *Monkees* series during October '66.

Next today The Monkees add lead and backing vocals to 'Papa Gene's Blues' using take 5 from Michael's July 7th session as a basis. Despite the fact that today's backgrounds are some of the most impressive vocals that The Monkees will ever record, Michael will have a change of heart for the production. At a session on July 30th he will strip them away to leave the simpler lead and harmony parts that he and Micky recorded during that session. The Monkees' group backing vocals will never be heard publicly.

Michael leaves the overdub session after five hours, around 6:00pm, handing over the production reins to Boyce, Hart, and possibly Jack Keller. They supervise the dubbing of Davy's lead vocals onto the nearly completed 'I'll Be True To You.' Davy's voice is double-tracked throughout the song and after four takes (plus five short 'pick-up' pieces) the production is complete.

Boyce & Hart use take 5 from Michael's July 7th session as a basis to complete his production of 'So Goes Love.' Davy adds a new lead vocal, replacing his 'live' one from the original session, plus a simple harmony on the choruses. Despite these efforts, this atmospheric production still sounds unfinished, or at the very least unpolished. As a result it is passed over for record release by music coordinator Don Kirshner, though it is briefly considered for use on the television series. It will finally be exhumed in 1987 for the first volume of the vault-plundering series *Missing Links*.

Next, Boyce & Hart turn their hand to another Michael production, 'I Don't Think You Know Me.' After making a reduction mix of the master backing track, take 10, the duo attempt to dub on a lead vocal from Micky. While Micky sounds good singing just about everything, Michael is obviously dissatisfied when he hears the results and will return and sing the song himself at a session on August 30th. (With the help of some modern re-synching, Micky's vocal performance will later be combined with Michael's final production to create a bonus track for the CD reissue of *The Monkees* album in 1994.)

Boyce & Hart wind up today's lengthy session by teaming with Ron Hicklin to tape the background vocals for 'Let's Dance On,' which may replace or enhance those already recorded on July 9th. Davy has left the session by this point, leaving just Micky and Peter available potentially to join in on the backgrounds. Micky also probably adds his lead vocal to the song at this session, thus completing the production.

● Monday 18th

FILMING Production probably begins today on what will become episode 9 of the *Monkees* series, *The Chaperone*. After a full day of filming, Michael goes on to the studio to start some new recordings.
RECORDING RCA (A) *Hollywood, CA* 8:00pm-12midnight. Michael Nesmith *prod*; Hank Cicalo *eng*; half-inch 4-track; tracking.
1. **'I Won't Be The Same Without Her'** takes 1-7
   Instant Replay master # TPA3-4613
2. **'Sweet Young Thing'** version 1 takes 1-6
   The Monkees master # TPA3-4614
3. **'You Just May Be The One'** version 1 takes 1-31
   Missing Links 2 master # TPA3-4615

Personnel Hal Blaine (drums), Jimmy Bryant (fiddle 2), James Burton (guitar), Glen Campbell (guitar), Al Casey (guitar), Gary Coleman (percussion), Mike Deasy (guitar), Frank DeVito (percussion), Larry Knechtel (piano), Peter Tork (guitar), Bob West (bass).

● This all-night affair begins with the tracking of 'I Won't Be The Same Without Her.' Michael leads his usual studio crew, including fellow Monkee Peter Tork, through seven takes of this Goffin & King tune. Of the five credited guitarists, who play a combination of electric and acoustic instruments, it is only possible to precisely discern that Glen Campbell plays the tremelo'd 12-string guitar part on this track. One of the credited guitarists may in fact be playing a 'dano' bass, a common term for an electric instrument made by Danelectro that, when played with a pick, produces a percussive plucked or 'tic tac' sound. With the addition of lighter strings than normal, a dano bass also produces a slightly higher register sound.

In all, seven takes are made of the song, only three of which are complete passes. The final pass, take 7, is considered the master and Michael will commit further overdubs to this on July 30th.

After a ten-minute break, the musicians return to rehearse and record 'Sweet Young Thing.' This recent collaboration by Michael with songwriters Gerry Goffin and Carole King is a bizarre but rocking confluence of bluegrass fiddle, fuzz guitar, and hard hitting drums. Of the six takes taped, only the first and last are complete. Michael selects the final pass, take 6, for the master, and overdubs will be recorded on July 27th. As on the previous track, a dano bass is used for 'Sweet Young Thing.'

Michael recalls: "I think 'Sweet Young Thing' was a good song. I liked Gerry and Carole quite a bit. It was not the sort of songwriting alliance that I would continue to any great effect. I was not a fan of the writing environment. I didn't like being cast in with some other folks and being told, 'Write with them.' Gerry and Carole had very strong songwriting styles. I really enjoyed working with them; it was just the circumstances that were tough."

Michael will lavish a considerable amount of time on his own 'You Just May Be The One.' Perhaps the best of his early compositions, this song dates from his days with Mike & John & Bill. Using a similar hi-hat pattern to 'I Won't Be The Same Without Her' taped tonight (and the previously recorded 'I Don't Think You Know Me'), Michael leads the musicians through a total of 31 takes of the song. After just three, Michael 'holds the roll,' meaning he deliberately stops the tape so the musicians will get paid overtime fees, probably at 11:00pm since three-hour sessions are a standard. Before take 4, Michael proclaims, "We're in overtime." This good fortune for the studio cats does little to speed up the recording process as they stumble through numerous takes, seemingly having trouble nailing a mistake-free pass of this relatively straightforward tune. Particularly problematic is the song's intro, which requires a regular and a dano bass to play the same figure simultaneously. Take 30 will be considered the master from this session and receives further overdubs on July 27th.

Michael: "'You Just May Be The One' was one of [my] first attempts at writing pop music. But, of course, I still had this sensibility of country and a kind of Latin thing that was going on, to keep the lyrics simple: a very straight-ahead, pop sensibility."

● Tuesday 19th

RECORDING RCA (A) *Hollywood, CA* 2:00-6:00pm, 7:00-10:00pm. Tommy Boyce & Bobby Hart *prod*; Hank Cicalo *eng*; half-inch 4-track; tracking, possibly overdubs.
1. **'I Wanna Be Free'** version 1 take 1
   The Monkees master # TPA3-4616

2. **'I Wanna Be Free'** version 2 takes 1-12
   unissued master # TPA3-4616
3. **'I Wanna Be Free'** version 3 takes 1-5, + pick-up piece 3 takes
   Missing Links 2 master # TPA3/TZRM-4617
4. **'(Theme From) The Monkees'** version 1
   The Monkees master # TZB3-4607

Personnel Micky Dolenz (possibly lead vocal 4), Bonnie Douglas (violin 1,2), Wayne Erwin (acoustic guitar 1,2, guitar 3), Gene Estes (percussion including bells and chimes 2, tambourine 3), Myra Kestenbaum (viola 1,2), Billy Lewis (drums 2,3), Gerry McGee (acoustic guitar 1,2, guitar 3), Michel Rubini (harpsichord 1,2, organ 3), Frederick Seykora (cello 1,2), Louie Shelton (acoustic guitar 1,2, guitar 3), Paul Shure (violin 1,2), Larry Taylor (bass 3).

● Boyce & Hart are the producers at this further tracking session. They concentrate on their composition 'I Wanna Be Free.' The song was first demoed for the *Monkees* TV pilot (see October 1965) and the goal of today's session is to produce master quality takes. Three separate versions are taped, giving the producers some flexibility to use the fast or slow arrangements originally established in the pilot demo arrangements.

Only a single take of version 1 is taped, and this will become the most commonly heard recording of the song. Performed in a slow ballad arrangement with just acoustic guitars, harpsichord, and a string quartet, the production will be completed with a lead vocal from Davy on July 24th. Version 1 will be issued on The Monkees' debut album and featured in two episodes of the series.

Bobby Hart: "'I Wanna Be Free' is one of the few songs in my whole career, certainly with Boyce, that we wrote just because we felt like writing one night. Usually we were writing for projects all the time. This was one evening when Tommy and I were sharing a house in the Hollywood Hills and he just said, 'I have this idea, do you feel like writing something?' He was playing these chords. There was some part of a line in that song that was inspired by a Roger Miller song, a ballad about suicide, basically. It may have had the words in it 'I wanna be free.' We just started with the title and it kind of flowed out really good. He sang me … 'I wanna be free' and I went on into … 'like the bluebirds flying by me.'

"We had the whole thing wrapped up in less than an hour. It was one of those few times when we just did it for the fun of doing it. It was luckily there waiting for us there when we needed a ballad a little later for the pilot."

Next up in the studio, version 2 of 'I Wanna Be Free' differs only slightly from the first attempt. Added to the arrangement are bell and chime accents courtesy of percussionist Gene Estes as well as some brushed snare from drummer Billy Lewis. Boyce & Hart will never complete this particular production – though take 12 is labeled the master – because they will decide that the simpler version 1 is all that is necessary.

Version 3 is a fast, folk-rock-styled arrangement of the tune. The master for this version will consist of the beginning of take 5 and the ending from take 3 of a separately recorded addition, known as a pick-up piece, that starts towards the end of the organ solo. Micky and Davy will add their vocals to this version on July 24th. When completed, this composite take will appear in the revamped-for-broadcast version of the pilot episode, *Here Come The Monkees*, where it replaces Boyce & Hart's original demo from '65. Nonetheless, version 3 is originally passed over for record release and will only later leak out on 1990's *Missing Links Volume 2*.

'(Theme From) The Monkees' also appears on the musicians' union sheet for today's session, though no tapes for the song will survive from this date. The timing on the sheet indicates that the work may be done to the long version of the song, and as studio logs

show extra time is booked, it's possible that vocals such as Micky's lead are dubbed between 7:30 and 10:00pm.

● **Friday 22nd**
FILMING Production wraps on *Monkees* episode 9, *The Chaperone*.

● **Saturday 23rd**
● *Cash Box* runs a 'teaser' ad picturing a pair of dancing feet with the caption "The Monkees is coming." True to the hype, Boyce & Hart record two items for the group's coming long-player.
RECORDING RCA (A) *Hollywood, CA* 2:00-8:00pm. Tommy Boyce & Bobby Hart *prod*; Dave Hassinger, Richie Schmitt *eng*; half-inch 4-track; tracking.
1. **'Jokes'** takes 1-2, + pick-up piece 4 takes
   unissued master # TPA3-4620
2. **'Tomorrow's Gonna Be Another Day'** takes 1-9
   The Monkees master # TPA3-4621
3. **'Gonna Buy Me A Dog'** version 2
   The Monkees master # TPA3-4608

Personnel Wayne Erwin (guitar), Bobby Hart (organ 3), Billy Lewis (drums), Gerry McGee (guitar), Louie Shelton (guitar), Larry Taylor (bass).

● Tommy Boyce & Bobby Hart are now settled in their role as Monkees record producers, no longer teamed with Jack Keller. They start this session with a little extra-curricular activity. 'Jokes' is a 90-second country-styled instrumental that, according to Hart, is intended for use on a Dick Clark program. (Boyce, with and without Hart, has written theme songs for a number of Clark's music programs, including 'Where The Action Is' and its replacement theme 'Action.') The master number for 'Jokes' is later reassigned to the song '(I'm Not Your) Steppin' Stone.'

Next up, Boyce & Hart tape 'Tomorrow's Gonna Be Another Day,' a slightly older composition written in collaboration with his former songwriting partner Steve Venet.

Boyce guides the session from the control room while Hart directs the musicians on the studio floor. In all, nine takes are made, the earliest with a different drum pattern, and it will be the final take that is considered the master for today. Take 9 later receives overdubs of acoustic guitar, harmonica, tambourine, and doubled vocals from Micky (see July 26th).

Series music coordinator Don Kirshner joins the session for the taping of 'Gonna Buy Me A Dog' and offers the following advice: "Bobby, you see the thing is, it's a funny tune. I mean, if we're going to get funny, we might as well be funny and different." Micky and Davy will get their chance to make this song both funny and different at a vocal session tomorrow. Bobby Hart: "We were trying to follow the whole Beatles formula all the way. That's what was happening with the TV show – at least that's what they told us. So we tried to do it musically as well. We wanted to have one novelty number in there like Ringo's obligatory novelty piece on every Beatles record."

● **Sunday 24th**
RECORDING Western Recorders (2) *Hollywood, CA* 11:00am-7:00pm. Tommy Boyce & Bobby Hart *prod*; Henry Lewy *eng*; half-inch 4-track; vocal overdubs.
1. **'I Wanna Be Free'** version 1 overdub onto take 1
   The Monkees master # TPA3-4616
2. **'I Wanna Be Free'** version 3 overdub onto composite take 5
   Missing Links 2 master # TPA3/TZRM-4617
3. **'Gonna Buy Me A Dog'** version 2
   The Monkees master # TPA3-4608

Personnel Micky Dolenz (vocal 2,3), David Jones (vocal 1,2,3).
● Producers Boyce & Hart take advantage of a day off in Micky and

Summer sessions at RCA studios in Hollywood, with Davy at the microphones.

and Davy were one-take or two-take propositions. Usually Micky took a little coaxing. He'd usually come in negative and he'd go out and try one take and say, 'I don't think this song is for me, I don't sound good.' Then Tommy would take him off and give him a little pep talk and he'd come back and sing it in one take usually.

"But this is one of the few times we had more than the one solo singer in the studio at the same time, with the idea of Micky and Davy doing it together."

● Monday 25th

FILMING Production likely begins today on what will become episode 4 of the *Monkees* series, *Your Friendly Neighborhood Kidnappers*. Meanwhile in the studio, Boyce & Hart record instrumentation for the song that will become the band's first single.

RECORDING RCA (B) *Hollywood, CA* 7:00-10:00pm, 12midnight-3:00am. Tommy Boyce & Bobby Hart *prod*; Dave Hassinger *eng*; half-inch 4-track; tracking.

1. **'Last Train To Clarksville'**
   The Monkees master # TZB3-4622
2. **'I Can't Get Her Off My Mind'** version 1
   The Monkees master # TZB3-4623

Personnel Wayne Erwin (guitar), Gene Estes (tambourine 1, marimba 2), Bobby Hart (tack piano 2, autoharp 2), Billy Lewis (drums), Gerry McGee (guitar), Louie Shelton (guitar), Larry Taylor (bass).

● With the *Monkees* television debut only weeks away, Don Kirshner has yet to select a song for the group's first release. At the last minute, Bobby Hart offers up the song recorded today, 'Last Train To Clarksville.' Inspired by the fade of The Beatles' 'Paperback Writer,' which was released as a single in the U.S. on May 30th, the tune is the perfect distillation of Boyce & Hart's pop-meets-folk-rock sound.

Bobby Hart: "As I was pulling into my carport I was punching the radio stations and I heard just the tail end of 'Paperback Writer' for the first time. It had just been released by The Beatles and all I heard was the ending fade-out part. I thought they were saying, 'Take the last train…' to something. Then of course a couple of days later I heard the whole song and I realized it wasn't about a train.

"I was inspired by that phrase and the melodic movement toward the seventh note of the chord. I said, 'Well, since they didn't use it, it's the great start of something else.' So, I just had it in the back of my mind. Then we were coming down to the end of producing the first album and we needed another song or two. So I said I had this idea and Tommy and I got together and did it really quickly.

"There's a little town in northern Arizona I used to go through in the summers on the way to Oak Creek Canyon called Clarkdale. We were throwing out some names and then when we got to Clarkdale we stopped for a minute and thought that sounded pretty good. We thought maybe Clarksville would even be a little better. We didn't know at that time that there is an Air Force base near the town of Clarksville, Tennessee, which would have fit the bill fine."

It's not known when Micky's vocals are added to today's instrumental tracking tapes, but with the release of a single urgently required, they are probably taped soon after this date. Just 22 days after this session 'Clarksville' will be released and on its way to #1.

The second song from this session is far less revelatory. Cast in the Herman's Hermits soft-shoe mode, 'I Can't Get Her Off My Mind' was originally written for a female vocalist to sing as 'I Can't Get Him Off My Mind.' In the end, Kirshner will pass on this song, though Davy obviously likes it – he performs it in The Monkees' upcoming stage show and will re-record it for next year's *Headquarters* album.

Davy's busy schedule by organizing this Sunday session for vocal overdubs. First off, Davy adds his solo lead vocal to version 1 of 'I Wanna Be Free' after which he is joined by Micky for some shared vocals on version 3.

After almost eight hours trapped in the studio and weeks of stressful shooting, the duo finally crack when they are asked to deliver the intentionally banal lyrics of 'Gonna Buy Me A Dog.' Following Don Kirshner's direction given yesterday, Micky and Davy decide to make the song both "funny and different," ad-libbing all the way. To their credit, Boyce & Hart have the good sense to send them home afterwards, as well as the sense of humor to accept and release the results.

Micky: "Originally that was supposed to be done straight. Davy and I just started goofing on it and they ended up using the goof rather than the straight version. That happened an awful lot in the television show too. They would use the outtakes."

Bobby Hart: "They didn't understand the song; they thought it was real stupid. They were just basically making fun of it. That's what usually happened when there were at least two of them in the same room. They would try and outdo each other with cutting up. We thought it was great and we kept the jokes in. They had some input in it. They didn't just walk in and do what they were told. There was some creativity involved.

"How straight can it be? It's true that they contributed the specific little jokes in between and all that was spontaneous. The song itself could hardly be construed as ever being straight. They were pretty spontaneous. Most of the songs that we did with Micky

Meanwhile, simultaneously at a studio only a few blocks east, Michael holds his own recording session.

RECORDING Western Recorders (2) *Hollywood, CA* 8:00pm-12:15am. Michael Nesmith *prod*; Andy R.(?) *eng*; half-inch 4-track; tracking.

1. 'Mary, Mary' takes 1-9
More Of The Monkees master # TZB4-4625
2. 'Of You' takes 1-10
Missing Links 1 master # TZB4-4626
3. '(I Prithee) Do Not Ask For Love' version 1 takes 1-8
Missing Links 2 master # TZB4-4627

Personnel Hal Blaine (drums), James Burton (guitar), Glen Campbell (guitar), Al Casey (guitar), Michael Cohen (keyboard), Gary Coleman (percussion), Mike Deasy (guitar), Jim Gordon (percussion), Larry Knechtel (keyboard), Peter Tork (guitar), Bob West (bass).

● Michael starts his fourth recording session as producer for The Monkees at fever pitch with a very revved-up take of his own 'Mary, Mary,' a song recently covered by The Paul Butterfield Blues Band on their Elektra album *East West*. This first pass lacks most of the drum breaks and stops of the final production.

For take 2 Michael slows down the tempo and instructs Hal Blaine to give the song its rock solid solo drum intro. For takes 5 through 9 the percussion section of maracas and tambourine is added into the new intro section. The final pass made today, take 9, is considered the master.

The keyboards on 'Mary, Mary,' largely inaudible in the final production, consist of organ and piano. The organ track on the next song taped, 'Of You,' is slightly more perceptible. In addition to this ornate Hammond organ part played by Larry Knechtel, the early

takes feature an unusual accented section between the verse and lead break from the whole band, which will be dropped from the final arrangement. The percussion section on this track consists of Jim Gordon on cowbell and Gary Coleman on maracas.

Because of significant rehearsal time for 'Mary, Mary' at the beginning of the session the date runs into overtime at 11:00pm, by which time the band have not yet nailed the arrangement for 'Of You.' Prior to take 6, Michael asks the musicians, "Can everybody go overtime?" Hal Blaine jokes, "That's like asking a blind man if he wants to see!" Take 7 features a double-time pick-up in the choruses and a very off-kilter guitar solo before the take breaks down. Take 8 also features the double-time drumming on the choruses and is still slightly faster than the final version. Everything falls into place for take 10, which is considered the master.

'Do Not Ask For Love' starts off very roughly, with a succession of false starts and several harpsichord fluffs (it's not known which of the two keyboardists is playing this part). Take 6 features an out-of-place double-time speed-up from Hal Blaine on the choruses, making the song sound not unlike 'Of You.' Take 7 is preceded by much discussion about this drum pattern, with Michael even asking Peter's opinion. Things only settle into the standard arrangement with several of the busier elements simplified for the final take 8.

Before the last take, Michael discusses the session going past midnight. He quickly declares that expense is not an issue. "I don't mind that. I'll pay you guys whatever. You all are on overtime, triple time or double million time, whatever you want, right now. I don't care. What do I care? It's only money. Man, I'm not in here to worry about money, I'm here to make records. Fuck money." Hal Blaine quips that Nesmith is a "goddamn communist." With that the crew give a very strong performance on take 8, which is considered the

master and will be used as the basic track for future vocal overdubs. Despite the added expense, 'Do Not Ask For Love' is never originally released.

● Tuesday 26th
RECORDING Western Recorders (1) *Hollywood, CA* 1:00-3:00, 3:30-7:30pm. Tommy Boyce & Bobby Hart *prod*; Henry Lewy *eng*; half-inch 4-track; tracking, reductions, overdubs.
1. **'(I'm Not Your) Steppin' Stone'**
   More Of The Monkees master # TZB3-4620
2. **'Whatever's Right'** test take + take 1
   unissued master # WZB5-5351
3. **'Tomorrow's Gonna Be Another Day'** overdub takes 1A–4A onto take 9
   The Monkees master # TPA3-4621

Personnel Tommy Boyce (acoustic guitar 2,3, vocal 2), Wayne Erwin (guitar 1,2), Bobby Hart (organ 1, autoharp 2), Billy Lewis (drums 1,2), Gerry McGee (guitar 1,2, harmonica 3), Louie Shelton (guitar 1,2), Larry Taylor (bass 1,2), unknown (foot stomps 1, handclaps 1, tambourine 1,3, percussion 2).

● Today sees another full day of recording for Boyce & Hart as the duo work towards completing their contributions to the *Monkees* album and starting a few new productions. Session tapes for one of their best-known compositions, '(I'm Not Your) Steppin' Stone,' are later lost but the final master, take 21, will survive. The instruments on it are spread across two tracks of the 4-track tape with the remaining two tracks saved for lead and background vocal overdubs. It is not known when these overdubs are made, but they are probably not done at today's session. The song was covered earlier in the year by Paul Revere & The Raiders. The Monkees' version will find release on their second single and will spawn even more covers, including one during the '70s by The Sex Pistols.

Bobby Hart: "I think 'Steppin' Stone' was the biggest garage-band song we ever wrote. It seems like a lot of kids cut their teeth on that. It was easy changes," he says, meaning a relatively simple chord sequence. "I don't know what else [made it so popular]. Maybe that was the biggest reason: the changes were easy."

A session tape for the second half of today's date features Tommy Boyce leading his usual crew through a new song called 'Whatever's Right,' a laidback country-like number in the style of The Lovin' Spoonful (and featuring one of the Spoonful's favorite instruments, the autoharp). No recorded vocal is present on the tape, though Tommy Boyce is heard singing very faintly in the background. A Monkees version of this song is probably never completed.

After just one full take of 'Whatever's Right' the focus shifts to finishing 'Tomorrow's Gonna Be Another Day.' The song is treated to 'sweetening,' or final-touch overdubs, in the form of acoustic guitar, tambourine, and harmonica. Also at this session, reductions of these and all previously recorded elements for the song are made. A 'reduction' means that elements of a recording are combined and copied onto another tape in order to make room for other instrumentation or overdubs. Here, the existing recordings are combined to just two tracks of the 4-track tape. 'Tomorrow's Gonna Be Another Day' is now primed for Micky's vocals to be overdubbed, which probably happens within a few days.

● A few blocks west at RCA Studio A, composer Stu Phillips tapes the

incidental music score for episode 1 of the *Monkees* TV series, *Royal Flush*. The session is held from 3:00–7:00pm and features nine top session players.

● Wednesday 27th

RECORDING RCA (B) *Hollywood, CA* 7:00pm-12midnight. Tommy Boyce & Bobby Hart *prod*; half-inch 4-track; mixdown.
● No further details are known about this session, but the most likely candidates for mixing would be the following Boyce & Hart productions: '(Theme From) The Monkees' version 1; 'Let's Dance On' version 2; 'This Just Doesn't Seem To Be My Day'; 'Take A Giant Step'; 'I'll Be True To You'; 'Saturday's Child'; 'I Wanna Be Free' version 1; 'I Wanna Be Free' version 3; 'Tomorrow's Gonna Be Another Day'; 'Gonna Buy Me A Dog' version 2; 'Last Train To Clarksville'; 'I Can't Get Her Off My Mind' version 1; '(I'm Not Your) Steppin' Stone.'

Michael meanwhile works towards completing some of his productions today, holding a session at either Western or United Recorders. The two studios are next door to one another and only about a block from the lot where the *Monkees* series is filmed.

RECORDING United Recorders or Western Recorders *Hollywood, CA*. Michael Nesmith *prod*; Henry Lewy *eng*; half-inch 4-track; reductions, vocal overdubs.
1. **'(I Prithee) Do Not Ask For Love'** version 1 overdub take 1A onto take 8
   unissued master # TZB4-4627
2. **'Of You'** overdub takes 1A-3A onto take 10
   Missing Links 1 master # TZB4-4626
3. **'Mary, Mary'** overdub take 1A onto take 9
   More Of The Monkees master # TZB4-4625
4. **'Sweet Young Thing'** version 1 overdub take 1A onto take 6
   The Monkees master # TPA3-4614
5. **'You Just May Be The One'** version 1 overdub take 1A onto take 30
   Missing Links 2 master # TPA3-4615
Personnel David Jones (lead vocal 1), Micky Dolenz (lead vocal 3, backing vocal 1,4), Michael Nesmith (backing vocal 1,5, lead vocal 2,4,5), Peter Tork (backing vocal 4).
● Michael returns to the last track he taped two days ago, reducing down the session 4-track tape of 'Do Not Ask For Love' to just two tracks of another 4-track tape. Next he overdubs Davy singing lead for the song. The production progresses as Michael dubs himself and Micky singing some background harmonies, although he later decides to scrap this work. After a rethink, he will return to the studio to complete the song with Micky singing lead on October 18th.

Michael next reduces the 4-track tape for 'Of You' take 10 to two tracks on a new tape. He will then add his double-tracked lead vocal to the song. Although he tinkers with the vocals of this song in subsequent years, singing the lead vocal afresh and adding harmonies from himself and Micky, it will remain in the can until 1987's first *Missing Links* release.

Next, Michael makes a reduction mix of 'Mary, Mary,' again combining the existing recording down to two tracks and using the two open tracks this leaves to add a doubled lead from Micky. Although another backing-vocal session will be held for this song on October 18th, the later efforts will probably not be used in the final production.

After a reduction of 'Sweet Young Thing' is made, the song is treated to a double-tracked lead vocal from Michael as well as some backing vocals from Peter and Micky, who sing the song's "sweet young thing" refrain. With this production now complete, the song

is ready for issue on *The Monkees* album. Michael closes out the session by adding his own double-tracked lead vocal and full backing vocal accompaniment (possibly with some unknown others) to version 1 of 'You Just May Be The One.'

This particular version of the song is only heard originally on the television series and will by totally recut in the studio by the group in March next year.

● Friday 29th

FILMING Production wraps on *Your Friendly Neighborhood Kidnappers*.

● Saturday 30th

RECORDING RCA (A) *Hollywood, CA* 2:00-6:00pm. Michael Nesmith *prod*; half-inch 4-track; reductions, vocal overdubs.
1. **'I Won't Be The Same Without Her'** reduction of take 7
   Instant Replay master # TPA3-4613
2. **'The Kind Of Girl I Could Love'** reduction of take 10
   unissued master # TZB3-4522
3. **'Papa Gene's Blues'** version 1 overdub take 1A onto take 5
   The Monkees master # TPA3-4612
Personnel Micky Dolenz (harmony vocal 3), Michael Nesmith (lead vocal 3).
● Michael spends some of his weekend off refining recent productions. In the case of 'I Won't Be The Same Without Her' he reduces take 7 from his July 18th session to two tracks of a new 4-track tape to make room for the song's vocals that will be taped next month.

On 'The Kind Of Girl I Could Love' Nesmith remixes the backing recording so that the steel-guitar part does not occupy a single tape track, and a superior blend of the other instruments is achieved. Nevertheless, he will decide not to redo the vocals from the July 16th session, so this revised backing-track mix is never used.

He does however decide to recut the vocals for 'Papa Gene's Blues.' After remixing the backing track he adds a new lead vocal as well as dubbing on Micky's perfect harmony accompaniment – and dumps The Monkees' original group vocals.

AUGUST

● Monday 1st

● *TV Guide* runs the first in a series of teaser ads for the *Monkees* series. "Dip this page in water. If nothing happens, see *The Monkees* premiere Sept. 12 on NBC ... where something always happens."
FILMING Production begins probably today on what will become episode 12 of *The Monkees* series, *I've Got A Little Song Here*.

● Tuesday 2nd

● The Monkees have a session booked today in RCA's Studio B from 8:00pm until midnight but it is unlikely that any recording actually occurs.

● Friday 5th

FILMING Production wraps on *I've Got A Little Song Here*.

● Saturday 6th

RECORDING RCA (A) *Hollywood, CA* 7:30-10:30pm. Tommy Boyce & Bobby Hart *prod*; Hank Cicalo *eng*; half-inch 4-track; tracking.
1. **'Valleri'** version 1 takes 1-13 (see text) + pick-up piece 1 take
   Missing Links 2 master # TPA3-4624

Precarious positioning during a personal-appearance tour to promote the TV debut and first single, 'Last Train To Clarksville.'

2. '(Theme From) The Monkees' version 2 takes 1-14
The Best Of The Monkees master # TPA3-4607
Personnel Wayne Erwin (guitar), Gene Estes (tambourine), Billy Lewis (drums), Gerry McGee (guitar), Louie Shelton (guitar 1), Larry Taylor (bass).
● Boyce & Hart wrote 'Valleri' after Boyce bragged to music coordinator Don Kirshner that the duo had another surefire hit up their sleeves. Kirshner called his bluff and the duo were forced to compose the song in their car on their way over to see Kirshner. Despite its tenuous birth, there is nothing tentative about today's studio performances of this obvious hit. From take 1 onwards, the band have 'Valleri' well rehearsed, and Louie Shelton's breathtaking guitar solo is intact on every complete pass of the song. The song's fuzz-drenched guitar riff owes a certain debt to The Rolling Stones' '(I Can't Get No) Satisfaction.' Coincidentally, the Stones are present at RCA today, recording next door in Studio B from 4:00pm through the evening.

Only a series of false starts will hamper the early takes of 'Valleri.'. Take 9 features an altered drum pattern in certain sections, which Tommy Boyce instructs drummer Billy Lewis to delete immediately. Boyce, who produces from the control room while Hart is in the studio with the musicians, tells Lewis: "During the solo I don't want you to play real fast. I want you to play back to your same lick." This settles the arrangement and the master is captured only minutes later.

Twelve takes are officially logged but one of these is miscalled and in fact 13 passes are taped. The last pass, officially noted as "take 12," is used as the basis for the master backing track (with some edits). A pick-up piece of the ending is recorded at the close of the session and later integrated into the master. Boyce tells Louie Shelton after this is taped that he can split.

There is just a month to go before the first episode of *The Monkees* is televised, and Boyce & Hart are asked to record a short version of the show's theme song for use in the title sequence. This is not merely an edit of version 1 that was taped in July but rather a unique performance specifically tailored for the opening and closing of the show and lasting a mere 50 seconds. The main difference in the arrangement of the two versions is that 1 fades while 2 has a cold ending. Version 2 also lacks organ and closes with a lyric not heard in 1: "We may be coming to your town." Tight performances are given on every take, which is no surprise since the band have recorded this piece several times.

Boyce is critical of Larry Taylor's bass playing and eventually convinces him to switch from playing with a pick to his fingers for all passes beginning with take 9, which gives the intro a softer tone and mellows out the rest of the track. Take 14 is considered the master backing track and has vocal overdubs added some time this month. (Take 14 will later appear without any overdubs as a karaoke-style bonus track on Rhino's 2003 *The Best Of The Monkees* release, and a variation on the 'Theme' for Italian television, 'Tema Dei Monkees,' is assembled in 1967 using a backing track from this period – see March 11th 1967.)

● **Monday 8th**
● Today's *TV Guide* carries a second teaser ad for the series in the form of a riddle. "What has 8 legs and swings? *The Monkees*. See *The Monkees* premiere, Monday, September 12 on NBC-TV."

● **Tuesday 9th - Friday 12th**
FILMING On the set, the *Monkees* crew shoot what will become episode 11 of the series, *Monkees A La Carte*. The entire production is shot on Stage #7. Scenes filmed on Tuesday include action in a restaurant and an inspector's office, and on Wednesday several dining room shots and some footage of The Monkees' pad. The third day centers on more dining room and restaurant scenes. The final day of production, Friday 12th, is set aside for filming the musical and 'romp' sequences of the show. A romp sequence consists of silent improv action later set to music in post-production or used in brief, non-linear vignette.
● Stu Phillips tapes his scores for two more episodes of the series, working from 2:00–6:00pm in RCA's Studio C with seven session musicians to create the incidental music cues for *Monkee See, Monkee Die* and *Monkees In A Ghost Town*.

● **Saturday 13th**
● The Monkees' first single, 'Last Train To Clarksville,' is scheduled for next Tuesday, and record-trade magazine *Cash Box* runs two teaser ads to promote the group. One reads: "The Monkees are on the hot line," and the other: "There's no business like Monkee business."

● **Monday 15th**
● *TV Guide* carries a third teaser ad for the series: "The Monkees is spelled rong! See *The Monkees* premiere, Monday, Sept. 12 on NBC-TV." To further promote their TV debut, the group have pretaped an interview with Barbara Walters for NBC's *Today* show, which airs today at 8:17am along with a film clip. After the segment, sympathetic show host Hugh Downs remarks to Walters, "You get the damnedest assignments." Meanwhile in the studio, the ever-industrious Boyce & Hart produce two more songs for the group.
RECORDING RCA (A) *Hollywood, CA* 7:00-1:00am. Tommy Boyce & Bobby Hart *prod*; half-inch 4-track; tracking.
1. 'Words' version 1
Missing Links 2 master # TZB3-4723

LEFT **Classic shot of the group, later used for the front of their first LP.**
RIGHT **Michael on the set in August for TV episode 11, *Monkees A La Carte*.**

2. 'She'
More Of The Monkees master # TZB3-4723
Personnel Wayne Erwin (guitar), Bobby Hart (organ 2), Norm Jeffries (tambourine 1,2, chimes 1), Billy Lewis (drums), Gerry McGee (guitar), Ethmer Roten (flute 2), Louie Shelton (guitar), Larry Taylor (bass).
● Boyce & Hart record two of their strongest originals for this session. Both show the duo keeping up with the musical times, with 'Words' even employing a proto-psychedelic backwards tape section. Sadly, the session tapes for this early version of 'Words' are later lost but the final master survives. Production will be completed with a vocal session on August 27th.

The garage-rock-influenced 'She' is the second item taped at this surprisingly lengthy session for just two songs. A master take is selected and then all its instrument recordings are 'bounced' to a single track of another 4-track tape. This gives the producers three open tracks free to use for overdubbing. The final production will feature Bobby Hart doubling his organ part on one of these tracks, with the others reserved for vocals (taped on August 27th).

Hart: "This was another song that we had written ahead of time, before the Monkees project, and just pulled out. I don't know who we were writing for. It was during the period of the groups playing on the Strip in L.A., like The Leaves and Love and several local groups experimenting with psychedelic rock.

"That never really made it nationally. The Doors were the ones that did. We were hanging out on the Strip a lot in those days and kind of being inspired by these psychedelic trends that were happening at the time.

"'Words' too was written ahead of time before the Monkees project was given to us. I was doing it in the nightclubs with [my band] The Candy Store Prophets. We already knew it pretty much and we worked it up and cut it for The Monkees." Hart's Prophets consist of Billy Lewis on drums, Gerry McGee on guitar, Larry Taylor on bass, and Hart on keyboard – the same players who form the core of Hart's regular studio team.

Last Train To Clarksville single

A 'Last Train To Clarksville' (T. BOYCE / B. HART)
B 'Take A Giant Step' version 2 (G. GOFFIN / C. KING)

US release August 16th 1966 (Colgems 1001).
UK release October 1966 (RCA 1547).
Chart high US number 1; UK number 23.

● Tuesday 16th
'Last Train To Clarksville' / 'Take A Giant Step' single is released in the U.S.A. The Monkees' debut 45, issued on Colgems Records, marks the band's first public exposure – the debut of the TV series is still a month away. *Cash Box* calls the A-side "a harddriving, pulsating romantic wailer with catchy repeating riff," while the flip "is a tender, lyrical slow-moving romancer." The lyrical theme of 'Clarksville,' about a soldier shipping off to war, is certainly topical but mostly lost on listeners for now. The song's co-writer Bobby Hart: "That was inherent in the thing: we couldn't be too direct with The Monkees.

We couldn't really make a protest song out of it. We kind of snuck it in subtly. I did a demo of it some time in the '70s that included a recitation about the war." Hart adds: "We cut a follow up to 'Last Train To Clarksville' with a girl named Linda Ball. It was a slight variation of the lyric: 'I'm on the last train to Clarksville … .'"

● Saturday 20th
● *Record World* runs a story about the promotional campaign behind The Monkees' first release and upcoming series. "The RCA Monkees campaign began some weeks ago with teaser ads in the trade papers with such captions as: 'Everybody is going ape for the Monkees,' 'The Monkees is coming,' and 'Monkee business is big business.' These teasers will appear in teen mags. … Teaser mailings to deejays and members of the press have been made, along with a special newspaper-type brochure which includes pictures and biographical information about the group. Advertising and promotion at both the trade and consumer level will coincide with the release of the first single, and continue through the time the series debuts. Ad mats and point-of-sale materials, including blanket mats and miniatures, four-color counterpiece displays, and window streamers are ready for use at the retail level."
● A Boyce & Hart-produced overdub session is scheduled for RCA's Studio B starting at 2:30pm. No further details or tapes survive from the session, but there is no shortage of work to do, from group vocals to Bobby Hart's organ overdub on 'She.'

● Monday 22nd
RECORDING RCA (A) *Hollywood, CA* 9:00-10:00pm. Stu Phillips *prod*; tracking, overdubs.
1. 'New Girl In School'
The Monkees Season 1 DVD
2. 'I Love You Really' versions 1-3
The Monkees Season 1 DVD
Personnel Al Hendrickson (guitar and/or bass), David Jones (vocal 2), Carole Kaye (guitar and/or bass), Lou Morell (guitar and/or bass), Bobby Sherman (vocal 1), unknown (drums).
● Davy and co-star Bobby Sherman pop into RCA tonight in the midst of shooting the TV episode *Monkees At The Movies*, recording a few short musical bursts for the show. Stu Phillips, the regular incidental-music composer, is in charge of this session. The tapes are probably mixed immediately and used for playback during tomorrow's shoot. These performances are never meant for record release, though they will eventually be seen and heard on *Monkees At The Movies*, later part of Rhino's 2003 DVD set *The Monkees Season 1*.

● Tuesday 23rd
FILMING While shooting continues for *Monkees At The Movies*, Boyce & Hart tape two numbers that have the dubious distinction of being responsible for the duo's temporary sidelining from future Monkees productions.
RECORDING RCA (B) *Hollywood, CA* 7:00-10:00pm, 10:30pm-2:00am. Tommy Boyce & Bobby Hart *prod*; Dave Hassinger *eng*; half-inch 4-track; tracking.
1. 'Ladies Aid Society' takes 1-22 + 'Part Two' 3 takes
The Monkees Present master # TZB3-4725
2. 'Kicking Stones' a.k.a. 'Teeny Tiny Gnome' takes 1-13
Missing Links 1 master # TZB3-4726
Personnel Wayne Erwin (guitar), Gilbert Falco (trombone), Bobby Hart (keyboard), Steve Huffsteter (trumpet), Dick Hyde (trombone), Bob Jung (saxophone), Billy Lewis (drums), Don McGinnis (probably saxophone), Gerry McGee (guitar), Emil Richards (percussion, vibes 2), Louie Shelton (guitar), Larry Taylor (bass).

Peter and Micky travel in style and prepare to meet and greet.

● The recording of these two novelty-oriented songs probably contributes to the downfall of Boyce & Hart as chief Monkees producers. Certainly the quality of these songs is an issue for Raybert's Bert Schneider, co-creator of the *Monkees* series, who upon hearing the finished productions writes a memo to Lester Sill at Screen Gems Music Publishing complaining that they are "of dubious value."

A tongue-in-cheek blend of folk protest and Herman's Hermits 'music hall' material, 'Ladies Aid Society' is no worse than, for example, 'Toonerville Trolley' by The Electric Prunes, but it is certainly not one of the duo's top-drawer efforts. Twenty-two cacophonous takes of the song will be taped before Boyce announces the start of a 'Part Two' section, which is recorded in just three takes and consists solely of the song's end chorus played in repetition and wildly off-key. With some edits, take 17 from today's session is considered the overall master backing track. Two further sessions in August and September will be required to complete the production.

'Kicking Stones' – or 'Teeny Tiny Gnome' as it will be titled when finally released on Rhino's *Missing Links* in the late 1980s – was originally just a poem by Boyce & Hart's buddy and sometime hairdresser Lynne Castle. The team's regular studio guitarist Wayne Erwin then set her words to music – and out came a fairytale-like creation.

During the song's recording Hart switches between acoustic and electric piano, and some of the brass players probably thin out or change their set-up. From take 4 onwards, Boyce moves out from the control room to the studio floor to sing with the band so that they can capture the correct 'feel.'

The last pass from today, take 11, becomes the backing track master and will be subjected to further musical and vocal overdubs during August and September.

● Saturday 27th

RECORDING RCA (B) *Hollywood, CA* 3:30pm start. Tommy Boyce & Bobby Hart *prod*; half-inch 4-track; overdubs.

1. **'She'**
   More Of The Monkees master # TZB3-4723
2. **'Words'** version 1
   Missing Links 2 master # TZB3-4723
3. **'Valleri'** version 1 overdubs onto "take 12"
   Missing Links 2 master # TPA3-4624
4. **'Kicking Stones'** a.k.a. 'Teeny Tiny Gnome' overdubs onto take 11
   Missing Links 1 master # TZB3-4726

Personnel Tommy Boyce (backing vocal), Micky Dolenz (lead vocal 1,2,4, backing vocal 1,2,3), Wayne Erwin (backing vocal), Bobby Hart (backing vocal), Ron Hicklin (backing vocal), David Jones (lead vocal 3, backing vocal 1,2), Peter Tork (lead vocal 2, backing vocal 1,2), Unknown (tambourine 1, chimes 2). (It's probable that not all those credited as backing singers on today's union sheet feature on the final tracks, but they are all listed here for the sake of completeness.)

● At this session Boyce & Hart focus on completing masters for four of their recent productions. First up is 'She,' which when finished will open The Monkees' second album. Today the producers add Micky's lead vocal, a group backing vocal, and a tambourine, completing the production.

'Words' features Peter's first lead vocal recording on a Monkees song, performed as a counterpoint to Micky's. Completed today with overdubs of lead and backing vocals plus some chimes, this high-quality song will appear in one episode of the *Monkees* series, *Monkees In Manhattan*. After that one airing, today's version of 'Words' will languish in the vault until 1990's *Missing Links Volume Two*. The Monkees themselves seldom allow a good song to go to waste and will cut a brand new version next year.

Tommy Boyce recalls: "That was one of the first times we thought Peter could actually sing on a record, [and] we thought it would be a good idea to have him come in and sing with Micky. We basically had it narrowed down to Micky singing the fast songs and Davy singing the ballads. Michael was very country in those days and it didn't quite fit the Monkee image of what they wanted for the kids age 3 to 11. Peter was a great musician, great banjo player, but he was mainly from New York, in a different process of thinking about songs, and it didn't quite fit with what we had in mind for the group called The Monkees."

Peter: "I walked into the studio and I said, 'How was that?' Everybody said, 'Pretty good.' I said, 'OK, well what else?' Everybody sort of like faded away and the picture went gray and the next thing you knew somebody else was on the [vocal]. It's like it didn't make a dent. I was infuriated. It was really rough for me because I had these ideas about what it was supposed to be and what you were supposed to do and how it was supposed to go.

"Tommy Boyce, who didn't have a clue about any of that stuff, did it the way he was raised to do it. He just followed his instinct. All he kept saying was, 'You're not The Lovin' Spoonful.' Meaning we hadn't wood-shedded [worked on playing] as a band. That seemed to end the argument as far as Tommy was concerned. Tommy really didn't get it. He just didn't have any idea of what I was up to. What was I on about? What was I carrying on for? What was going on with me? He didn't understand. He didn't have the slightest clue."

Next up at this session is the first version of 'Valleri,' which is completed today with the addition of an apparently triple-tracked Davy lead vocal and some group backgrounds. Like 'Words' version 1, this take of 'Valleri' will be passed over for original release, only appearing on a couple of episodes of the *Monkees* series (*Captain Crocodile* and *Monkees At The Movies*). Unlike 'Words,' 'Valleri' will receive widespread airplay during 1967 by DJs who dub it from the television program. This will force Boyce & Hart to re-record the song for The Monkees in December 1967.

Today's session closes with some vocal work on 'Kicking Stones,' but the production is not completed and Boyce & Hart will return to the song at their very next session, on September 3rd.

● Sunday 28th

The Monkees are among a crowd of 45,000 who turn out to see The Beatles' penultimate live performance at the Dodger Stadium in Los Angeles. The main reason the group attend is to get a taste of what their upcoming live concerts might be like. In fact The Monkees will never play a venue this large in their hometown, and never to an audience of this size.

● Monday 29th

● *TV Guide* carries another teaser ad in the build-up to *The Monkees* TV debut: "Send coupon and 25 cents for a 10 cent picture of *The Monkees*. See *The Monkees* premiere, Monday, Sept. 12 on NBC-TV."

● Tuesday 30th

FILMING Production wraps on what will become episode 6 of the *Monkees* TV series, *Success Story*. After shooting, Michael returns to the studio and revisits two of his productions.

RECORDING RCA (B) *Hollywood, CA* 8:00-12midnight. Michael Nesmith *prod*; Dave Hassinger *eng*; half-inch 4-track; reductions (and possibly overdubs).

1. **'I Won't Be The Same Without Her'** reduction of take 7
   Instant Replay master # TPA3-4613
2. **'I Don't Think You Know Me'** version 1 reduction of take 10
   Missing Links 1 master # TZB3-4523
Personnel Michael Nesmith (vocal).

● Michael makes new 'reduction' mixdowns of these backing tracks and preps them for vocal overdubs. Probably he also overdubs his lead vocal on 'I Don't Think You Know Me,' completing its production. His version of the song never finds original release because during October its composers, Gerry Goffin and Carole King, will cut a new version for The Monkees. Meanwhile, the status of 'I Won't Be The Same Without Her' remains uncertain after this session and the song is most likely completed during preparation of 1969's *Instant Replay* album.

● Wednesday 31st

● Song selection and credits for The Monkees' self-titled debut album are finalized. The album will be officially released in October, though some copies leak out to press and radio early next month.

SEPTEMBER

● Thursday 1st

● TV producers David Gordon and David Yarnell resurface today in the New York State Supreme Court to file an injunction against the *Monkees* TV series. The two claim that over five and a half months they met with Screen Gems about their project *Liverpool U.S.A.* They now seek $6,850,000 in damages from 14 parties including Screen Gems, RCA, Bert Schneider, Bob Rafelson, and *The Monkees* sponsors Kellogg's and Yardley. In November '65 their idea was formally turned down by Screen Gems, and they feel that the company has simply appropriated their concepts and storylines for *The Monkees*. A hearing on this injunction is set for September 7th.

● Columbia-Screen Gems are unperturbed by the action and host a "gigantic block party" to celebrate the imminent debut of the *Monkees* TV series. The reception is held at Screen Gems in Hollywood where two episodes of the series are screened and the group gives a brief musical performance.

● Saturday 3rd

● *Cash Box* reports that the "Monkees have set a whirlwind [personal appearance] tour to capitalize on the initial acceptance of their debut single 'Last Train To Clarksville' on the Colgems logo. Announcement of tour was made by George Parkhill, manager of advertising and promotion for RCA Victor record division, which manufactures and merchandises Colgems. Due to the heavy shooting schedule of their Monkees TV series, which bows on September 12th, the tour will, of necessity, be a short one. The Monkees will be introduced to deejays, members of the trade and consumer press, as well as local distributors and dealers."

● 'Last Train To Clarksville' single this week enters U.S. *Cash Box* Top 100 chart at #68 and U.S. *Billboard* Hot 100 Bound chart at #101. With their television debut just nine days away, the group already have a hit on their hands. Meanwhile, Boyce & Hart are at work in the studio.

RECORDING RCA (B) *Hollywood, CA* 2:00pm-12midnight. Tommy Boyce & Bobby Hart *prod*; half-inch 4-track; overdubs (and possibly mixdown).

1. **'Kicking Stones'** a.k.a. 'Teeny Tiny Gnome' overdubs onto take 11 *Missing Links 1* master # TZB3-4726.
2. **'Ladies Aid Society'** overdubs onto take 17 *The Monkees Present* master # TZB3-4725.

Personnel Tommy Boyce (backing vocal), Micky Dolenz (lead vocal 1, backing vocal 1), Wayne Erwin (backing vocal), Bobby Hart (backing vocal), Ron Hicklin (backing vocal), David Jones (lead vocal 2, backing vocal 2), Paul R. Suter (flute, organ 1).

● Boyce & Hart add vocals and other overdubs to two of their recent productions. From 5:00 to 7:00pm, Paul Suter provides a fuzzed-out flute overdub for the instrumental break on 'Kicking Stones,' according to the union contract consisting of both flute and organ layered together. Then vocals for 'Stones' are either revised or refined from the previous session (August 27th). Now complete, the song is submitted for use on the group's second album or the soundtrack of their series, but there is no interest from the record

Promo shot taken on one of the Columbia movie lots where the *Monkees* TV episodes are made.

label's Don Kirshner or TV production company Raybert. The song will remain in the vault until 1987's *Missing Links* album.

Davy joins the session in the evening and completes his lead vocal for 'Ladies Aid Society' by day's end. Some suitably off-key group backing vocals are also added, wrapping the song's production. This recording too will remain in cold storage, until the 1969 release of the group's penultimate album, *Present*.

● Monday 5th
● *TV Guide* runs yet another teaser ad for the series: "On Sept. 12, 1976 *The Monkees* will celebrate their 10th anniversary on television."

● Tuesday 6th
● *The Hollywood Reporter* announces that plans are already in motion to put The Monkees on the big screen, even though the group's TV series has yet to debut. As part of the seven-year deal that Screen Gems has struck with the group, an option is in place "to produce one or more features, depending on the success of their series. First is being projected for 1967 summer production during series sabbatical." Steve Blauner of Screen Gems says: "We plan to give them the same publicity treatment as The Beatles in every respect. With 30 million people watching them regularly Monday night they should be bigger than The Beatles."

● Evidence of the promotional push is seen today as a second press party is held, at Chicago's Astor Towers Hotel. All four Monkees attend the event, along with show producer Bert Schneider, and an episode is screened for the invited guests. Later this evening the group start an impromptu jam in a hotel suite, with Peter performing one of his favorites, 'If I Could Shimmy Like My Sister Kate.'

● Colgems finalizes plans to issue The Monkees' debut album in October on the relatively new Stereo 8-track format alongside the regular vinyl. The 8-track version will sell at the higher retail price of $6.95 (vinyl will be $3.79 mono, $4.79 stereo). Back home in Hollywood, Boyce & Hart hold a mix session for their recently completed productions.

RECORDING RCA (A) *Hollywood, CA* 2:00pm start. Tommy Boyce & Bobby Hart *prod*; quarter-inch mono; mixdown.

1. **'She'**
   More Of The Monkees master # TZB3-4723.
2. **'Ladies Aid Society'** take 17
   unissued master # TZB3-4725.
3. **'Kicking Stones'** a.k.a. 'Teeny Tiny Gnome' take 11
   unissued master # TZB3-4726.

● While the group are in Chicago, Boyce & Hart mix down three songs to mono for use on future record releases or television programs. Ultimately, only the mono mix of 'She' from this session is used, for the *More Of The Monkees* album. The other two songs will later be remixed in stereo for potential record release. It is likely that Boyce & Hart mix down other tracks at this session, but only a mono tape of these three will survive.

● Wednesday 7th
● The Monkees travel to Boston for another meet-and-greet with assorted industry honchos. Peter: "We mostly just talked to reporters. In one city we did about 20 minutes on stage, but in each city we had special showings of one of the series segments."

● Thursday 8th
● Colgems Records discover they have made an error in printing the album jackets and labels for *The Monkees*. The title of Michael's 'Papa Gene's Blues' has been printed as 'Papa Jean's Blues.' Although the record has yet to hit stores, Colgems has already produced significant quantities of both the mono and stereo versions of the album, and instead of taking the costly measure of scrapping the stock they decide to distribute the record with the mistake intact. After this date, all incorrect label masters are destroyed to eliminate any further costly production errors.

● The group travel to New York City where they undertake another day of promotional activities and prepare for their first genuine public appearance. A banquet is held in their honor at the city's Barbizon Plaza Hotel, attended by Don Kirshner, Bob Rafelson, and Bert Schneider.

● Friday 9th
● The Monkees make a personal appearance from 4:00 to 6:00pm at New York City's Broadway Theatre, located at Broadway and 53rd Street. Although the TV show has yet to debut, 2,000 fans – reported as "too old for Barbie dolls and too young for mini-skirts" – display the first signs of Monkeemania as they attend this free event, which is open to the general public. Micky tells *The Beat*: "We got mobbed in New York. Well, we weren't exactly mobbed, but the girls tried to get us and we had to have guards and the whole bit. It was really groovy!"

Journalist Vincent Canby of *The New York Times* is on hand for this public unveiling, having lunched with TV-series producer Bob Rafelson at the Plaza only hours before. He writes: "The Monkees' appearance at the Broadway was just part of an elaborate campaign designed by RCA and Screen Gems to capture the teenage imagination. The thoroughness of the campaign might prompt renewed debate on the age-old question of free will." Canby asks Rafelson if the teenagers have a chance these days, to which the producer aptly replies: "You can fool some of the kids some of the time."

"These boys," adds an emphatic Don Kirshner, "have scope, interest and color. They are multi-talented." Rafelson says: "I shouldn't say it, but I don't even care if the series is a success. It's been such an enormously satisfying experience working with the boys. We are doing it because we care." Canby notes that RCA hired "76 men around the country promoting the first Monkees record, 'Last Train To Clarksville.' In three weeks about 400,000 records have been sold."

● Saturday 10th
● The Monkees return to Los Angeles to prepare for their final promotional jaunt, a train ride sponsored by a radio station.

● 'Last Train To Clarksville' officially enters *Billboard*'s Hot 100 today at #67, up from last week's 101. Meanwhile in Hollywood

Boyce & Hart produce three more songs intended for The Monkees' next long-player.

RECORDING RCA (A) *Hollywood, CA* 1:00-4:00pm, 5:00-8:00pm, 8:00-9:30pm. Tommy Boyce & Bobby Hart *prod*; half-inch 4-track; tracking.

1. **'Mr. Webster'** version 1
   Missing Links 2 master # TZB3-4728.
2. **'Hold On Girl'** version 1
   Missing Links 2 master # TZB3-4729.
3. **'Through The Looking Glass'** version 1
   Missing Links 3 master # TZB3-4730.

Personnel Norman Benno (oboe 1,2), Tommy Boyce (acoustic guitar 3), Wayne Erwin (guitar), Alan Estes (tympani, tambourine 3), Billy Lewis (drums 2), Gerry McGee (guitar), Michel Rubini (harpsichord 1,2, tack piano 3), Louie Shelton (guitar), Larry Taylor (bass).

● The first item taped today is a slow, brooding, baroque arrangement by Michel Rubini of Boyce & Hart's 'Mr. Webster.' Captured in 21 takes, the song will be given overdubs on September 24th.

Hart describes the song as "our answer to 'Eleanor Rigby.'" Boyce: "'Mr. Webster' was written about a bank detective in Security First National Bank on the corner of Hollywood and Cahuenga. There used to be a guy in there like in *The Bank Dick* [movie with] WC Fields. We used to have our bank account there and there was this guy that used to dress up sort of like WC Fields, actually in a bank detective outfit with a little hat on.

"His job was to stand around and when people wrote a check he'd come over and straighten up the pen-on-the-wire and put it back. We used to watch him do that for a couple of hours, two or three times a week. It was very funny. We decided he was 'Mr. Webster' and he absconded with all the money. Ran away to a place, 'Sorry, stop, cannot attend, I've flown away and taken all your money.' In fact, when the record came out, we actually gave him a few albums and he loved it."

Also in baroque mode is the duo's production of 'Hold On Girl.' The song was composed by Jack Keller (in collaboration with Ben Raleigh and Billy Carr). Keller co-produced The Monkees' first few sessions with Boyce & Hart earlier this year. Recorded in 16 takes, Boyce & Hart give the song a slow, sultry feel. Their production will be completed on September 24th.

Returning to their own material, the duo oversee at least 20 takes of 'Through The Looking Glass,' with Boyce on acoustic guitar. Boyce: "I always liked that song. ... I knew it was a fabulous song and we always thought it should have been a single, but it never was, of course. I think it was an imaginary song we wrote about a couple of girls we knew. Sort of like an *Alice In Wonderland* type of thing: you walk through the mirror, 'Through The Looking Glass' ... and go through this glass into a different world." As with the other material taped today, production of this song will be completed on September 24th.

● Sunday 11th
● Los Angeles radio station KHJ hosts a Monkees promotion from

LEFT NBC TV advertises the debut of the *Monkees* show on September 12th.
ABOVE The group take their nominal places on the set as they prepare to shoot further TV episodes.

12 midday to 7:30pm in which contest winners take a train trip to Del Mar, California. Appropriately, this coastal town is renamed 'Clarksville' by the mayor just for today's event.

The Monkees meet the winners on the beach in Del Mar/Clarksville after arriving in two helicopters. Afterwards they ride back to Los Angeles on the train with their fans. An episode of *The Monkees* television show is screened on the trip and the group give a live musical performance in one of the cars. Their set includes 'Papa Gene's Blues' and Baker Knight's 'She's So Far Out She's In.' The day's activities are filmed in color for use on the KHJ music television program *Boss City* (see September 17th).

At the event, Micky explains that the band are still grappling with their new-found fame. "We really don't know where it's at yet. I mean, like we just got back from the tour and then we got up this morning, flew down to San Diego, took a helicopter to Del Mar, and now we're on a train to L.A.! Picture this. It's six in the morning, right? I'm in bed and the alarm goes off and the radio comes on and they're playing The Monkees' 'Theme.' I think, what? I'm dreaming again! But they're really playing it!"

Peter mentions that their first single was almost called 'Last Train To Home, Girl' instead of 'Clarksville'. "It's good we decided on 'Clarksville,'" quips Peter. "Can't you just see the mayor saying, 'I now proclaim this the city of Home Girl?'"

● Monday 12th

TV The *Monkees* TV series makes its national debut after three months of shooting and a full year's planning. NBC's ads say "Who's putting who on? You'll never know till you see this show!" The corporation airs the program's premiere episode, *Royal Flush*, at 7:30pm tonight. In a perfect tie-in, *TV Guide* carries an ad for The Monkees' first album.

● TV producers David Gordon and David Yarnell, who claim that the *Monkees* series stole their idea, have tried in vain to block tonight's premiere, but New York State Supreme Court Justice Jacob Markowitz decided last Friday to deny their motion for a temporary injunction. He noted that the plaintiffs (Yarnell and Gordon) were aware of the plans for tonight's telecast for some time, but the two waited until substantial promotional money had been spent on the program before they brought their suit. Markowitz infers that Yarnell and Gordon were either waiting to up their claim for damages, or hoping for a speedy settlement. Nonetheless, their suit will drag on through 1967.

TVseries

The Monkees

EPISODE 1: *ROYAL FLUSH*
BROADCAST SEPTEMBER 12TH
The Monkees foil a fiendish plot to assassinate Princess Bettina, the Duchess of Harmonica.
WRITERS: PETER MEYERSON, ROBERT SCHLITT. DIRECTOR: JAMES FRAWLEY.
SONGS 'Take A Giant Step,' 'This Just Doesn't Seem To Be My Day,' 'Last Train To Clarksville.'

● Tuesday 13th

● *The Hollywood Reporter* reviews the start of the *Monkees* series on TV, giving the show faint praise. "Although the plot is thin, the premiere show serves as an intro to this new group of youngsters. They don't get a chance to play their instruments, and whatever singing is done by them is off screen so as not to interrupt the action, or comedy."

● *The New York Times* is more effusive about the group's screen debut. The paper's Jack Gould writes: "At least the attraction on the National Broadcasting Company network is not like every other situation item on the home screen, and this fall even a victory by default is positively to be cherished. Robert Rafelson and Bert Schneider, who recruited the gentlemen named The Monkees (formerly The Inevitables and more recently The Turtles), are savvy chaps. They've played down the rock'n'roll angle to where it's not much more than an incidental sonata and instead have conducted their mop-haired charges through assorted antics suggestive of The Marx Brothers in adolescence. … The Monkees are to be welcomed for joining the pursuit of chuckles rather than orgiastic studio squeals. Progress can turn up in the strangest places."

● Hal Humphrey at *The Los Angeles Times* notes that the new *Monkees* TV show has "moments of ingenuity, something this reviewer hasn't seen yet in a dozen or more of the new season entries. Producers Bert Schneider and Bob Rafelson employed lots of old camera gimmicks, including the slow-motion and speed-up, but blended it all together for some pleasantly startling effects. If one looked for much rhyme or reason in the ensuing shenanigans, he found virtually none. But therein lay most of the charm."

● A recording session scheduled today in Hollywood at RCA's Studio A is cancelled for unknown reasons.

Fooling around for the cameras at Columbia's 'ranch' lot.

● Wednesday 14th

● Today's issue of *Daily Variety* features a further analysis of the TV debut of *The Monkees*. "Run your eye over the credits and there's not one name that strikes a note of familiarity. It's that kind of show, too, newly concepted for TV albeit trading on Beatlemania. But it is asked to rub shoulders with the juggernaut that is CBS' Monday night wrecker of ambitions. To last out the season would be doubly sweet, proof that names do not a show make. … Producers Bert Schneider and Bob Rafelson deserve a footnote for trying to be different. How well they have succeeded remains for the weeks ahead to tell, but it's a frightening prospect. The third Nielsen [audience rating] will tell whether the home viewers like it well enough to come back to."

In the studio, the Monkees machine rolls on for a mix session and a scoring date for the television series.

RECORDING RCA (A) *Hollywood, CA* 12midday-6:00pm. Quarter-inch stereo or mono; mixdown.

● It's not clear if this is a Nesmith or Boyce & Hart session, but it is likely that more material is dubbed down, since the group's first album has already been pressed.

● Also today at RCA Studio C (2:00–6:00pm), composer Stu Phillips completes two more incidental-music scores for the *Monkees* series. Employing eight session musicians, he works on the cues for *Kidnappers* (episode 4) and *The Spy Who Came In From The Cool* (episode 5).

● Saturday 17th

● Local Los Angeles music TV program *Boss City* airs footage at 6:00pm from The Monkees' KHJ 'Clarksville' promotion (see September 11th).

● A recording session scheduled today at Hollywood's RCA is cancelled for unknown reasons.

● 'Last Train To Clarksville' single climbs to #43 in U.S. *Billboard* chart.

TVseries

The Monkees

EPISODE 2: *MONKEE SEE, MONKEE DIE*

BROADCAST SEPTEMBER 19TH

When an eccentric millionaire leaves The Monkees an unexpected legacy, the group must spend the night in the deceased's haunted mansion.

WRITER: TREVA SILVERMAN. DIRECTOR: JAMES FRAWLEY.

SONGS 'Tomorrow's Gonna Be Another Day,' 'Last Train To Clarksville.'

● Monday 19th

TV The NBC television network airs the second episode of *The Monkees* series, *Monkee See, Monkee Die* at 7:30pm.

● A recording session tentatively scheduled at RCA's Studio B in Hollywood is cancelled.

● The group's first album, *The Monkees*, is shipped to distributors. It will be officially released to retailers in October, though copies likely leak out sooner.

● Tuesday 20th

FILMING After a few weeks off for promotion, the group return to production on the *Monkees* TV series, which resumes at the Columbia Pictures lot in Hollywood. During filming of what will become episode 15, *Too Many Girls (Davy & Fern)*, pianist Roger Spiker is employed to provide live piano accompaniment as Davy and actress Kelly Jean Peters (as Fern) perform a song-and-dance routine. The sequence is shot on a 'talent show' set from 8:00am-12:20pm and resumes in the afternoon from 2:00–4:30pm.

● Thursday 22nd

FILMING Production wraps on *Too Many Girls (Davy & Fern)*.

● Friday 23rd

● Production commences on what will become episode 19 of the *Monkees* series, *Find The Monkees (The Audition)*.

Filming today takes place on Stages 2 and 7 at Columbia, including interior scenes in The Monkees' pad, Hubbell Benson's office, and the Department of Missing Persons. Production will resume after the weekend.

● Saturday 24th

● With 'Last Train To Clarksville' now sitting safely inside the Top 40 at #26, Boyce & Hart work to complete three of their recent productions.

RECORDING RCA (B) *Hollywood, CA* 2:00-6:00pm, 7:00pm-12midnight. Tommy Boyce & Bobby Hart *prod*; half-inch 4-track; overdubs.

1. **'Mr. Webster'** version 1 overdubs onto take 21
   Missing Links 2 master # TZB3-4728
2. **'Hold On Girl'** version 1 overdubs onto take 16
   Missing Links 2 master # TZB3-4729
3. **'Through The Looking Glass'** version 1 overdubs onto take 20
   Missing Links 3 master # TZB3-4730

Personnel Maggie Aue (cello 1), Tommy Boyce (backing vocal 2,3), Micky Dolenz (lead vocal 1,3, backing vocal 1,2,3), Bobby Hart (backing vocal 2,3), Ron Hicklin (backing vocal 2,3), David Jones (lead vocal 2, backing vocal 2,3).

● From 2:00 to 5:00pm Boyce & Hart add a cello part performed by Maggie Aue to 'Mr. Webster,' completing the backing track. After this, Micky comes into the studio to record his lead vocal, which in places is doubled in harmony. Although other prospective backing singers are in attendance at this part of the session, none are audible in the final production.

As it turns out, the general public will not hear Boyce & Hart's production of 'Mr. Webster' until 1990 when it is issued on *Missing Links Volume Two*. The Monkees themselves will record and release a new version of the song during 1967.

Boyce & Hart's production of 'Hold On Girl' is put to bed with the addition of Davy's lead voice track and some group backing vocals. Upon hearing the final results, Jack Keller is unhappy with the production and decides to recut the song himself. Boyce & Hart's version also will have to wait for Rhino's *Missing Links Volume Two* for release.

The session ends with vocal overdubs added to take 20 of 'Through The Looking Glass.' Ultimately, Boyce & Hart will decide to completely re-record the song in December 1967, and this early version will not be heard until *Missing Links Volume Three* in 1996.

● Monday 26th

FILMING Production resumes at 8:00am on *Find The Monkees*. In the morning the crew work on Stage #2 shooting scenes in Hubbell

TVseries

The Monkees

EPISODE 3: *MONKEE VS. MACHINE*
BROADCAST SEPTEMBER 26TH
Stan Freberg stars as a headstrong company man, Daggart, who plans to automate an old-fashioned toy company.
WRITER: DAVID PANICH. DIRECTOR: ROBERT RAFELSON.
SONGS 'Last Train To Clarksville,' 'Saturday's Child.'

Benson's office, after which the company moves to Stage #7 for further scenes in The Monkees' pad.
● A *Newsweek* round-up of the fall season's new network shows has *The Monkees* as one of the only programs singled out for total praise. The journal says, "*The Monkees* may be directed at the skateboard set, but if it can keep up its fast lunatic pace, the show may command a lot of adult attention."
TV The NBC television network airs episode 3 of the *Monkees* series, *Monkee Vs. Machine*, at 7:30pm.

● Tuesday 27th

FILMING *The Monkees* crew go on location to Burbank, California, to pick up some shots for the series episode *Find The Monkees (The Audition)*. The shoot, which takes place at the NBC building on Olive Avenue, wraps this production.

● Wednesday 28th

FILMING Production commences on what will become episode 13 of the *Monkees* series, *One Man Shy (Peter And The Debutante)*. Interior shots of the 'game room' are filmed on Stage #10.

● Friday 30th

FILMING Production continues at 8:00am on *One Man Shy* with a location shoot at the Columbia Studios' 'ranch' lot. Various exteriors are filmed today using many of the ranch's street facades. In the studio, Boyce & Hart are also busy.
RECORDING RCA Studio *Hollywood, CA* 8:30pm start. Tommy Boyce & Bobby Hart *prod*; half-inch 4-track; overdubs.
● Boyce & Hart record overdubs to a selection of their productions at their final session of the month. No other details are available.

OCTOBER

The Monkees album is released in the U.S.A. The group's debut LP is officially issued this month on Colgems (although some copies may have been on sale in September).
● Davy goes to New York City to attend the Bar Mitzvah of Jeff Neal, his friend and former cast-mate from *Oliver!*. After the ceremonies, Davy gives an impromptu performance of 'Last Train To Clarksville' with the house band.

● Saturday 1st

● *Billboard* reports that The Monkees are officially a Top 20 item as 'Last Train To Clarksville' ascends to #18.

● Sunday 2nd

● The Monkees' first public interview of sorts is published in *The New York Times* under the banner "Monkees Let Down Their Hair." Writer Judy Stone reveals that it wasn't easy to get any copy on the fellows due to a firm no-interview policy from Screen Gems. "Sometimes the kids aren't very respectful," says their press agent apologetically.

While Peter talks of Vietnam ("The man who said, 'My country, right or wrong,' made a slight error of judgment") and Micky

---

The Monkees album

A1 '(Theme From) The Monkees' version 1 (T. BOYCE / B. HART)
A2 'Saturday's Child' (D. GATES)
A3 'I Wanna Be Free' version 1 (T. BOYCE / B. HART)
A4 'Tomorrow's Gonna Be Another Day' (T. BOYCE / S. VENET)
A5 'Papa Gene's Blues' version 1 (M. NESMITH)
A6 'Take A Giant Step' version 2 (C. KING / G. GOFFIN)
B1 'Last Train To Clarksville' (T. BOYCE / B. HART)
B2 'This Just Doesn't Seem To Be My Day' (T. BOYCE / B. HART)
B3 'Let's Dance On' version 2 (T. BOYCE / B. HART)
B4 'I'll Be True To You' (G .GOFFIN / R. TITELMAN)
B5 'Sweet Young Thing' version 1 (M. NESMITH / C. KING / G. GOFFIN)
B6 'Gonna Buy Me A Dog' version 2 (T. BOYCE / B. HART)

U.S. release October 1966 (Colgems COM-101 mono / COS-101 stereo).
U.K. release January 20th 1967 (RCA SF 7844).
Chart high U.S. number 1; U.K. number 1.

Balancing act: four Monkees gather to shoot the 'I'm A Believer' cover.

discusses long hair ("what matters is inside"), Stone's real angle is other musicians, angry in the wake of the group's runaway success. She asks Davy if he thinks "the big push for The Monkees was fair to *real* rock groups?" He bravely replies: "That's the breaks, but you can't fool the people, you really can't. There's a showdown sometime. Ninety-nine percent of the funny lines come from the guys. The writers do the background things; we take it from there. I played myself in *Pickwick*, I played myself in *Oliver!*, and that's what I'm doing in *The Monkees*. I won't fool anybody."

"I thought you can't fool the kids," adds Michael, explaining that he was reluctant to be involved in Raybert's project from the outset, "but that was not the intention. It was to give the kids something to enjoy. I'm just lucky as I can be, and thankful for whatever reason they picked me."

● Monday 3rd

FILMING On the set, the group film some 'romps' for the episode *One Man Shy*.

● Behind the scenes, Raybert's Bert Schneider sends a memo to Lester Sill at Screen Gems expressing his concern over recent studio expenditures by Boyce & Hart. Schneider feels that the duo's recent material has no commercial value and should therefore not be charged against The Monkees' royalty account. This memo marks the beginning of the end of the duo's exclusive rein as The Monkees' record producers.

By the middle of the month Don Kirshner of Screen Gems will shift the base of music production to his home turf of New York City. This also comes as something of a relief for Kirshner, who suffers from a fear of flying and since the inception of The Monkees has had to suffer many white-knuckle plane trips to the West Coast. He now finds that he has regained any control he may have lost to Boyce & Hart – and does not have to fly.

● Composer Stu Phillips works on music cues for *The Monkees* episode *Success Story*. Twenty-five musicians are employed from 2:00 to 7:00pm for this scoring date, though in truth they are doing double duty since Phillips simultaneously tapes cues for another Screen Gems series, *Iron Horse*. This is ironic since *Iron Horse* airs at the same time as *The Monkees* on a competing network, ABC.

TV Viewers have to choose between *Iron Horse* and *The Monkees* at 7:30pm as NBC airs the fourth episode of the *Monkees* series, *Your Friendly Neighborhood Kidnappers*.

TV series

The Monkees

EPISODE 5: *THE SPY WHO CAME IN FROM THE COOL*
BROADCAST OCTOBER 10TH
The Monkees are cast into the Cold War after Davy purchases a pair of 'red' maracas at a pawnshop.
WRITERS: GERALD GARDNER, DEE CARUSO. DIRECTOR: ROBERT RAFELSON.
SONGS 'The Kind Of Girl I Could Love,' '(I'm Not Your) Steppin' Stone,' 'All The King's Horses,' 'Saturday's Child'

● Wednesday 5th — Friday 7th

FILMING Production commences at 8:00am on Wednesday on what will become episode 30 of the *Monkees* series, *Monkees In Manhattan*. Today's filming includes interior scenes on Stage #2 of a hotel lobby, after which the crew move to Stage #10 for action in the 'Millionaires Club.'

On Thursday the *Monkees* crew travel to the 'ranch' lot for a full day of filming on *Monkees In Manhattan*. Scenes include exterior street shots, interiors of a hotel corridor and Baker's room, and some more action in the 'Millionaires Club.'

Production wraps on Friday with more interiors of Baker's room, the hotel corridor, and a bridal suite, all shot on Stage #34 at the 'ranch.'

● Saturday 8th

● The Monkees climb into the Top 10 for the first time as 'Last Train To Clarksville' sits at #6 on *Billboard*'s Hot 100. Also today, their first album breaks into the charts at #121. It will remain a chart item for the next 78 weeks.

TV series

The Monkees

EPISODE 4: *YOUR FRIENDLY NEIGHBORHOOD KIDNAPPERS*
BROADCAST OCTOBER 3RD
When The Monkees become finalists in a band contest, they are subject to some competitive sabotage.
WRITER: DAVE EVANS. DIRECTOR: JAMES FRAWLEY.
SONGS 'Let's Dance On,' '(I'm Not Your) Steppin' Stone,' 'Last Train To Clarksville'

● Monday 10th

TV At 7:30pm the NBC television network airs episode 5 of *The Monkees* series, *The Spy Who Came In From The Cool*.

● Tuesday 11th

FILMING Production commences on what will become episode 14 of *The Monkees*, titled *Dance, Monkee, Dance*. Today's action takes place on Stage #3 with shots of a reception room and Ranaldo's office.

● Wednesday 12th

FILMING Shooting continues from 8:00am on Stage #7 for *Dance, Monkee, Dance* with dance scenes in the ballroom.

● Army Archerd reports in his 'Just For Variety' column in *Daily Variety* that The Monkees will star in a feature film made by Columbia during their TV show's hiatus. "Last year we couldn't have been able to sell this show – the climate wasn't right," Jackie Cooper of Screen Gems tells the columnist. "The kids buy more toys. I have to keep the adults out of this show, and keep throwing kids out of *Iron Horse* and adding sex and violence! That's one of the problems you face when you have two shows on at the same time."

● The Monkees' first full-length concert appearance is scheduled for Oahu, Hawaii, on December 3rd.

● Thursday 13th

FILMING Production continues on Stage #7 for *Dance, Monkee, Dance*. Scenes shot today include footage of The Monkees' pad and

One of the many promo tie-ins generated by the Monkees machine is an endorsement for shoe manufacturer Thom McAn.

a 'writer's room.' The crew also pick up some footage needed for two episodes already filmed, *Find The Monkees* and *One Man Shy*. Meanwhile in a New York studio, Carole King produces two new tracks for the group.

RECORDING RCA (A) *155 East 24th Street, New York, NY*. Carole King *prod*; half-inch 4-track; tracking.

1. 'Sometime In The Morning' takes 1-13
   More Of The Monkees master # TZB1-7737

2. 'I Don't Think You Know Me' version 2 takes 1-16 + overdub take 17
   More Of The Monkees master # TZB1-7738

Personnel Unknown (two electric guitars, organ, bass, drums, tambourine).

● This session represents the shift away from Boyce & Hart's Hollywood productions towards Don Kirshner's stable of New York songwriter and producers. Today, Carole King has the run of the session. Though also credited, her husband Gerry Goffin and producer/friend Jeff Barry are not audible on the session tape. They may be involved in the production of later overdubs, such as vocals.

The first item taped is the wistful 'Sometime In The Morning.' It is immediately evident that the sound quality or engineering is significantly poorer for these New York sessions, compared to the Hollywood recordings, perhaps due to a different aesthetic approach between East and West Coast studios. More emphasis seems to be placed on squashing everything into a single track, distortion and all. The Hollywood recordings up to this point have had their moments of primitive engineering, but distortion and hiss only creep in as a result of multiple reductions and overdubs. On 'Sometime In The Morning' they are present from the very first take.

Thirteen passes are taped of the song, with the final master a composite of takes 9 and 13. On October 25th, King will return to the studio to record some rough or 'guide' vocals for The Monkees to follow when they later dub on their own voice tracks to these instrumental tracking tapes.

The other song taped at this session is a remake of 'I Don't Think You Know Me.' As previously produced by Michael the song was tried with lead vocals from both Michael and Micky. There was obviously dissatisfaction with the results but still a feeling that the song is right for the group, and so King cuts today's version using the same (unknown) ensemble as 'Sometime In The Morning.'

A total of 16 passes are taped of 'I Don't Think You Know Me' with take 16 considered the master. This take is then immediately overdubbed with a tambourine track and a doubled guitar part, after which it is renamed take 17. Like 'Sometime In The Morning,' this 'sweetened' take will be given a guide vocal overdub on October 25th before being shipped off to Hollywood for further work.

● Friday 14th

'Last Train To Clarksville' / 'Take A Giant Step' single is released in the U.K. The band's debut British record is issued on RCA.

FILMING Production wraps on *Dance, Monkee, Dance* as some 'romp' shots are completed at the Columbia 'ranch.' With some time to spare the crew also pick up romp footage that will later be used in the episode *Captain Crocodile*, production of which will commence properly some time next week. In the recording studio, Jack Keller holds a recording session for two of his compositions intended for The Monkees.

RECORDING American Recording Co. *11386 Ventura Boulevard, Studio City, CA*. Jack Keller & Jeff Barry *prod*; Richie Podolor *eng*; half-inch 4-track; tracking.

1. 'Your Auntie Grizelda'
   More Of The Monkees master # TZB1-4740

2. 'Hold On Girl' version 2
   More Of The Monkees master # TZB1-4729

Personnel David Jones (vocal 2), Peter Tork (vocal 1), unknown (all instruments, but see below).

● Jack Keller cuts two songs for The Monkees' second album at this tracking session, marking his first Monkees recording date since July. No personnel credits will survive for 'Your Auntie Grizelda,' but Billy Lewis later recalls the line-up to include himself on drums, Larry Taylor on bass, and Gerry McGee and Glen Campbell on guitars. The session tape also reveals that the keyboardist for this date is probably Don Randi. In the case of 'Grizelda' all these instruments are recorded onto a single channel of a 4-track tape, after which overdubs are added of fuzz guitar, shaker, tambourine, tom drum, and Peter's vocal. The last item is probably taped at an RCA Hollywood session later this month.

Peter recalls that Jeff Barry got him to sing on this recording. "He had me doin' those funny vocal things in the middle there. I tried it and it worked out, *kind of*. Lester [Sill of Screen Gems] came to me and said, 'We've got a kind of a protest song for you.' It certainly isn't what you call a protest song. That was what they thought a protest song should be for The Monkees."

Jack Keller: "The tracks were recorded at American Studios where Three Dog Night used to record with Richie Podolor, who was the engineer. It's real possible that Glen Campbell played guitar on that. I know [Gerry] McGee played that low part. Then when The Monkees came into town, [Don Kirshner] had to make a choice between what songs were to be recorded, and he liked these two tracks." Keller says that during this period Jeff Barry was The Monkees' key record producer and that if Keller wanted his productions cut he would have to give Barry a cut of the money and let him produce the vocal session. "I didn't know that [Barry] was going to use Peter on 'Your Auntie Grizelda.' We did [the vocals] at the regular studios, probably RCA in Hollywood. The Monkees were based in L.A., so he came out for that stuff.

"I thought The Monkees would cut it like '19th Nervous Breakdown' with Micky singing lead, or Micky and Davy. It turned out to be a total surprise when it came to the session and Jeff said Peter's going to sing it. As it turned out, it was the only lead that I know of that Peter got on. It was a total comedy thing. He did that all in one take. ... He made up the whole thing. I was in a total state of shock when I heard it. '19th Nervous Breakdown' went right out the door."

Keller is dissatisfied with Boyce & Hart's September 24th version and today remakes his 'Hold On Girl,' giving the song a faster, slightly Latin feel. Again, all instruments are recorded on to a single track of the 4-track tape, including an acoustic 12-string guitar (and possibly an electric), harpsichord, drums, and bass. After a basic track is captured – no take numbers are given or called at this session – overdubs of handclaps, Latin style percussion, and muted electric guitar fills are added. Davy's vocal is also present on the final overdubbed take, but as with 'Grizelda' this element is likely added at an RCA session with Jeff Barry later in October. Backing vocals for 'Hold On Girl' are definitely added at a separate session on October 23rd.

Keller: "With 'Grizelda' and 'Hold On Girl,' I did the tracks so I got them exactly the way I wanted – except for Peter's vocal which I didn't expect. But Davy sang 'Hold On Girl' exactly the way I wanted it. Even Peter's vocal turned out where I liked it."

● Saturday 15th

● As the group's 'Last Train To Clarksville' sits at #4 on the U.S. *Billboard* chart, producer Jeff Barry cuts the track that will become the group's next hit single.

RECORDING RCA (B) *155 East 24th Street, New York, NY*. Jeff Barry *prod*; half-inch 4-track; tracking.

1. **'I'm A Believer'** takes 1A-18A
   More Of The Monkees master # TZB1-7744
2. **'Look Out (Here Comes Tomorrow)'** takes 1A-7A
   More Of The Monkees master # TZB1-7739

Personnel Unknown (guitars, keyboards, bass, drums, percussion).

● A pivotal moment, this recording session marks the studio debut of producer Jeff Barry and songwriter Neil Diamond as part of the Monkees project. Not only will it yield The Monkees' next single but also their second #1 and the biggest selling record of their careers: 'I'm A Believer.' In August, Diamond scored his second hit as an artist with a song called 'Cherry Cherry' and since that time Don Kirshner has been anxious to work with the up-and-coming singer-songwriter. Because Jeff Barry is already producing Diamond for Bert Berns's Bang label – and Barry has a standing affiliation with Screen Gems as a songwriter with his wife Ellie Greenwich – Barry and Diamond come as a package to Kirshner.

Neil Diamond: "'Cherry Cherry' was my second chart record, but that was the one that caught Don Kirshner's ear. [He] liked 'Cherry Cherry' very much and asked if I had something The Monkees could do. So I sent them over my version of 'I'm A Believer.' It was originally a song that I just wrote for my album. Kind of a simple, self-expression thing. [A] happy kind of thing. I didn't think too much of it. I just liked the title – that's how the song came. I had written it at about the same time I wrote 'Cherry Cherry' and it was like I had an extra hit."

Although no records will survive to pinpoint who plays on this studio date, a review of the session tape reveals some details of the making of this classic. Jeff Barry guides the musicians from the control room through 18 takes. Neil Diamond is present playing acoustic guitar, and the other instrumentation includes two electric guitars, electric piano, Hammond organ, bass, tambourine, and drums (probably played by Buddy Salzman). The first ten takes are tentative, with several false starts, but by take 11 the track really comes together. The final take from this session, take 18, is considered the best and will be shipped out along with producer Jeff Barry to Hollywood for vocal overdubs next weekend. (The unadorned take 18 backing track will be heard on the 1996 Japanese-only East West-label CD *The Monkees Best!!*.)

Also taped today is Neil Diamond's excellent 'Look Out (Here Comes Tomorrow),' which (with a few exceptions) employs a similar group of musicians and instrumentation. Before take 3, Barry asks Diamond if his guitar is "in tune with the new string." After a quick strum, Barry quips, "That's close enough for The Monkees." Barry

moves to the studio floor to direct the musicians up close for takes 5A through 7A. Despite this extra effort, the master backing track will in fact be derived from take 4A, which will be treated to overdubs in Hollywood on October 23rd.

● **Monday 17th**

TV Episode 6 of the *Monkees* series, *Success Story*, is broadcast at 7:30pm on the NBC television network. In Hollywood, Boyce & Hart are still on the job as producers – at least for the time being.

RECORDING RCA (C) *6363 Sunset Boulevard, Hollywood, CA* 8:00pm-12midnight. Tommy Boyce & Bobby Hart *prod*; half-inch 4-track; overdubs.

● A union log notes that this four-hour date is for overdubs, but no further details or taped evidence of the session will survive.

● **Tuesday 18th**

RECORDING RCA (C) *Hollywood, CA* 4:00pm-12midnight. Michael Nesmith *prod*; Hank Cicalo, Richie Schmitt *eng*; half-inch 4-track; overdubs.

1. **'Mary, Mary'** overdub rehearsal takes 1A-4A + 1A-7A on to take 9
   unissued master # TZB4-4625
2. **'(I Prithee) Do Not Ask For Love'** version 1 overdub takes 1A-3A on to take 8
   Missing Links 2 master # TZB4-4627

Personnel Micky Dolenz (lead vocal 2, backing vocal 1), David Jones (backing vocal 1), Peter Tork (backing vocal 1).

● In a failed attempt to make someone look good – it is unclear exactly who – a recording session is staged today for *Look* magazine reporter Betty Rollin. At this session, held ostensibly to tape vocal overdubs, Michael is put in the producer's chair and the other three Monkees are placed in front of a microphone to sing backgrounds on Michael's 'Mary, Mary.'

It's a recipe for disaster. The Monkees wisecrack their way through a series of rehearsals – labeled 1A-4A and noted on the box as "no good" – and seven 'real' takes. The antics of Davy and Micky are legitimately funny, but after 20 taped minutes, Nesmith says, "Honest to God, no shit – let's cool it." The results do not improve.

On December 27th, *Look* publishes a feature on the group with a photo from the session. With Don Kirshner off to his right, Michael is pictured with his hands cradling his face. A quote below shows his exasperation. "These guys from New York," says Michael, "they bug me." *Look* further describes the session: "With hopes of pacifying him, Kirshner lets Mike conduct a session of a song he wrote himself, 'Mary, Mary.'" Screen Gems' Lester Sill, also pictured, is quoted as saying: "If you gotta girl's name, you gotta lot goin' for you. Think how many Marys there are."

At the 'session,' after dismissing Peter and Davy, Michael makes a brief attempt to get Micky to double-track a lead vocal for 'Do Not Ask For Love.' (Micky's first vocal track for this song, which replaced Davy's of July 27th, was taped at an earlier, undocumented session.) Only take 3A is complete, and though it is good, Micky deems it "terribly out of synch." This will be the last session for this version of the song, and it will be take 3A that is eventually salvaged for release on 1990's *Missing Links Volume Two*. Today's efforts also mark Michael's last documented session as a Monkees producer until November 1967.

According to a union log, Boyce & Hart may also have been a part of today's overdub activity, but the exact details of their work, and whether or not this too is a staged session, is unknown.

● **Friday 21st**

FILMING Production wraps on series episode 23, *Captain Crocodile*.

● Across the ocean, the cover of Britain's *New Musical Express* declares "EXTRA! EXTRA! The Monkees IS 'HEAR'! America's most exciting new group internationally bound with a hit sound." Despite the group's first U.K. release, 'Last Train To Clarksville,' initially failing to chart, Britain too will eventually succumb to Monkeemania.

● Saturday 22nd - Sunday 23rd

RECORDING RCA (B) *Hollywood, CA* 2:00pm start. Jeff Barry *prod*; Hank Cicalo *eng*; half-inch 4-track; overdubs.

1. **'I'm A Believer'** overdubs onto take 18A
   More Of The Monkees master # TZB1-7744
2. **'Look Out (Here Comes Tomorrow)'** overdubs onto take 4A
   More Of The Monkees master # TZB1-7739
3. **'Look Out (Here Comes Tomorrow)'** overdubs onto take 4A
   More Of The Monkees master # TZB1-7739
4. **'Hold On Girl'** version 2
   More Of The Monkees master # TZB1-4729

Personnel Micky Dolenz (lead vocal 1, backing vocal), David Jones (lead vocal 2,4, backing vocal), Peter Tork (narration 3, backing vocal 1,2,3), possibly unknown others (backing vocal 1,3).

● The Monkees, or at least Micky, Davy, and Peter, spend their weekend overdubbing lead vocals with producer Jeff Barry. First up is 'I'm A Believer,' which receives lead and backing vocal overdubs. The final results, which are still possibly a few days off (see 24th and 25th), will be issued as a single in November. An alternative, unused vocal take from today (4A) will later be released as a bonus track on 1994's expanded CD edition of *More Of The Monkees*. (This is in fact the only original multi-track with a vocal of this song that will survive; the original overdubbed master will be lost.)

After 'Believer,' Barry tackles 'Look Out' for which Davy delivers a very confident lead vocal. Micky, Davy, and Peter provide the song's background vocals. The final master, which has to be shortened due to some tape damage, will be issued on January 1967's *More Of The Monkees* album.

However, before finalizing this production, Barry experiments with one further variation. Still trying to find a more prominent place for Peter's vocal contribution, he overdubs a second version of 'Look Out' with Peter giving a joke narration during the song's instrumental sections. This gimmick has barely middling results, and the idea is quickly abandoned. This outtake will only be heard later as a bonus track on the expanded CD edition of *More Of The Monkees*.

Barry also completes Jack Keller's 'Hold On Girl' at this session, definitely adding the song's vocal backgrounds and possibly working on Davy's lead vocal as well. After this session, Barry will spend the

---

TVseries

The Monkees

EPISODE 7: *MONKEES IN A GHOST TOWN*
BROADCAST OCTOBER 24TH
The Monkees get lost on their way to a gig and find their Monkeemobile vehicle out of gas in a seemingly deserted town.
WRITERS: PETER MEYERSON, ROBERT SCHLITT. DIRECTOR: JAMES FRAWLEY.
SONGS 'Tomorrow's Gonna Be Another Day,' 'Papa Gene's Blues.'

---

next few days in the studio further refining this weekend's recordings. (According to internal RCA documents, Sunday may also be the day that Peter records his final lead vocal on 'Your Auntie Grizelda.')

● Monday 24th

● *Newsweek* again covers the band with a full-page feature concerning their creation. The publication describes The Monkees as "direct videological descendants of The Beatles, and the first rock'n'roll group to have its own series." They further note that the band's name was chosen by Bert Schneider but misspelled by Bob Rafelson, who figured that it is "contemporary to distort the names of rock'n'roll groups."

When discussion turns to how their music is created, Davy tells *Newsweek*: "This isn't a rock'n'roll group, it's an act." The article reports that several rural NBC affiliates are refusing to carry the series. "There is a giant resistance to kids with long hair," muses Rafelson. "There's also conservative resistance by adults to the music." *Newsweek* pegs the group members' potential earnings this year at $100,000.

TV The NBC television network broadcasts episode 7 of the *Monkees* series, *Monkees In A Ghost Town*, at 7:30pm. Also this evening, producer Jeff Barry holds an overdub session.

RECORDING RCA (A) *Hollywood, CA* 5:00pm start. Jeff Barry *prod*; *eng*; half-inch 4-track; overdubs.

● A union log notes that Jeff Barry 'sweetens' or embellishes with overdubs the organ tracks on his recent productions. This probably includes 'I'm A Believer' and 'Look Out (Here Comes Tomorrow).' There is no union record of who plays organ at tonight's session. It is quite possible that Barry plays the parts himself.

● Tuesday 25th

RECORDING RCA (A) *New York, NY*. Carole King *prod*; half-inch 4-track; overdubs.

1. **'Sometime In The Morning'** overdubs onto composite take 9 and 13
   unissued master # TZB1-7737
2. **'I Don't Think You Know Me'** version 2 overdubs onto take 17
   unissued master # TZB1-7738

Personnel Carole King (vocal).

● Carole King decides to show the members of The Monkees how she wants her songs sung – but without having to fly to Hollywood to supervise the session. So today in New York she records 'guide' tracks to her two recent productions. Using three tracks of the 4-track tape – the remaining track is taken up with a mono mix of the backing track – she lays down a lead vocal and a two-part backing vocal for each song. Jeff Barry will supervise The Monkees' vocal overdubs for these tracks in Hollywood on Thursday. Barry himself is probably conducting the following session there today.

RECORDING RCA (A) *Hollywood, CA* 7:00pm start. Half-inch 4-track; overdubs.

● No taped evidence of this session will survive but a union log suggests it is a further session to complete Jeff Barry's work on 'I'm A Believer,' 'Look Out (Here Comes Tomorrow),' 'Your Auntie Grizelda,' and 'Hold On Girl' version 2.

● Wednesday 26th

FILMING Production is in progress at 8:00am on what will become episode 16 of *The Monkees*, titled *Son Of A Gypsy*. Shooting today on Stage #7 includes interiors of a ballroom and corridor. Meanwhile in the studio, Boyce & Hart work on three new songs for the group, including a future single.

RECORDING RCA (B) *Hollywood, CA* 1:00-4:00, 4:30-7:30pm, possibly mixing to 1:00am. Tommy Boyce & Bobby Hart *prod*; Dave Hassinger *eng*; half-inch 4-track; tracking, mixdown.

1. **'Tear Drop City'**
   Instant Replay master # TZB3-4731
2. **'Looking For The Good Times'**
   The Monkees Present master # TZB3-4732
3. **'I'll Spend My Life With You'** version 1
   More Of The Monkees master # TZB3-4733

Personnel Tommy Boyce (acoustic guitar 2,3), Wayne Erwin (guitar), Gene Estes (tambourine 1,2, bells 3), Bobby Hart (organ 2), Billy Lewis (drums), Gerry McGee (guitar), Louie Shelton (guitar), Larry Taylor (bass).

● 'Tear Drop City' as taped today is a slow, almost bluesy song and far less the 'Clarksville' carbon copy that it will become when completed. Session tapes for this date will not survive, but the master basic track features Boyce & Hart's usual players performing the song in the key of F-sharp near the tempo of 'Tomorrow's Gonna Be Another Day.' By the time the song finally sees release as a single it will be speeded up electronically to A-flat in a bid to reclaim the magic of 'Clarksville.' However, at this early date 'Tear Drop City' is still just another prospective album track among those that the producers are stockpiling. Little do they know how fierce the competition will be to get even one song on The Monkees' second album.

Tommy Boyce: "We wrote 'Tear Drop City' one day in a park. We were walking down Lankershim Boulevard [in North Hollywood] of all places. We just sat down on a bench with the guitar and started playing this riff. I think it was sort of like the riff to 'She's About A Mover.' I recall explicitly that Bobby [Hart] was having trouble with his girlfriend Francine at the time. Little tears here and there, you know what I'm saying? That was definitely about Bobby and Francine."

Bobby Hart: "We were experimenting along the lines of the seventh chord again, which The Beatles had used in several songs. We thought there was maybe room for another song besides 'Clarksville' using that seventh kind of progression, going from the fifth to the seventh and back, playing around those notes."

Next up in the studio today is 'Looking For The Good Times' featuring the entire Boyce & Hart crew on a rollicking if somewhat slight song. Three further sessions will be held in October and November to complete this production, though the song won't find release until 1969.

The session ends with Boyce & Hart's beautiful 'I'll Spend My Life With You.' The song will be completed next month at a session on November 12th, but like the other songs cut today it will be passed over for release during 1966. Tommy Boyce: "I got that idea about a girl I thought I was in love with, but she left me for another guy. We wrote that in the office.

"In those days, I was a bit confused. I was confused about women in general – like after writing 'I Wanna Be Free' – 'Don't say you love me, say you like me.' This particular girl, she left me for a gangster actually, a New York gangster. I had written the song before that. You know when you're 26 or 27 and totally in love? 'People come and people go, moving fast and moving slow, you're in a crowd, yet you're all alone.' I wrote it for her. Bobby helped me finish it, of course, and I played it for her thinking it would maybe get her to stay with me. Of course she left. Teenage romance!"

It is possible that a separate mix session either follows Boyce & Hart's tracking session or runs concurrently in Studio A with Jeff Barry as producer. The song 'Your Auntie Grizelda' is mentioned on one union document from this date, so Barry may be working on that song this evening.

● **Thursday 27th**

FILMING Production wraps on the *Son Of A Gypsy* episode with shooting on Stage #7 of various interior locations.
● The Recording Industry Association of America (RIAA) awards the group their first gold records for the single 'Last Train To Clarksville' and their album *The Monkees*. RCA's Steve Sholes says of this presentation: "This is the first time in the history of the RIAA that a newly formed label [Colgems] has achieved such success with its debut releases." However, it is unlikely that the group get much chance to celebrate since they are due in the studio directly after today's shooting to record some vocals for their second album.
RECORDING RCA Studio *Hollywood, CA* 7:00pm start. Jeff Barry *prod*; Hank Cicalo *eng*; half-inch 4-track; overdubs (and possibly mixdown).

1. **'Sometime In The Morning'** overdubs onto composite take 9 and 13
   More Of The Monkees master # TZB1-7737
2. **'I Don't Think You Know Me'** version 2 overdubs onto take 17
   unissued master # TZB1-7738
3. **'I Don't Think You Know Me'** version 2 overdubs onto take 17
   More Of The Monkees master # TZB1-7738
4. **'Hold On Girl'** version 2
   More Of The Monkees master # TZB1-4729

Personnel Micky Dolenz (lead vocal 1, backing vocal 1,3), David Jones (lead vocal 2, backing vocal 1,3), Peter Tork (lead vocal 2,3, backing vocal 1,3), possibly unknown others (backing vocal 1).

● Jeff Barry completes the production on Goffin & King's 'Sometime In The Morning.' First he adds a double-tracked lead vocal from Micky on two separate tracks. The producer then overdubs some group backgrounds with Micky, Davy and possibly Peter. (There may be other, unidentified singers involved in these backgrounds.)

The song is mixed soon after and will feature on the group's second album, *More Of The Monkees*. (Micky's double-tracked lead vocal is more prominently heard on the original mono vinyl release of *More Of The Monkees*. See Songography at the back of the book for more about mix variations.)

Barry has admitted defeat on Peter's narration for 'Look Out (Here Comes Tomorrow)' but is seemingly still under pressure to feature more of Peter on the upcoming album. His next, equally unsuccessful plan is to team Peter with Davy for a jointly sung version of 'I Don't Think You Know Me.' The surviving take can only be described as a huge mistake. Although the two give the song their all, they are vocally mismatched for the material. Davy says as much as the track fades: "Miles too high for me man, way out of my range."

So for the third item today Barry makes a new attempt at 'I Don't Think,' deciding to drop the pitch of the backing by slowing down the tape and letting Peter sing it on his own. The results are generally improved, but ultimately the song will be passed over for release by music coordinator Don Kirshner. This original unissued 1966 mix will later find release as a bonus track on 1994's expanded CD edition of *More Of The Monkees*, while a remix is included on 1991's *Listen To The Band* boxed set.

The last song of this session, 'Hold On Girl,' probably receives some final 'sweetening' overdubs before mixdown. Mixing on these and other tracks likely follows this session in either RCA Studio A or B. It is possible that both rooms are used in an urgent bid to complete the second album.

● **Friday 28th**

● The J.C. Penney Company sends a letter to Screen Gems' merchandising kingpin Ed Justin outlining their Monkees clothes promotion, due to start in January. The emphasis of the memo is to persuade Screen Gems to use a photo of the group wearing the J.C. Penney Monkees clothing line on their next album cover. In order to tie in with the campaign, the group's next album must be released in two months. Probably unaware of these specific machinations, Boyce & Hart hold their last Monkees tracking session for 1966.

RECORDING RCA (B) *Hollywood, CA* 1:00-4:00, 4:30-7:30pm, possibly mixing to 1:00am. Tommy Boyce & Bobby Hart *prod*; half-inch 4-track; tracking, mixdown.

1. **'Apples, Peaches, Bananas And Pears'**
   Missing Links 1 master # TZB3-4734
2. **'Don't Listen To Linda'** version 1
   More Of The Monkees master # TZB3-4735
3. **'I Never Thought It Peculiar'**
   Changes master # TZB3-4736

Personnel Tommy Boyce (acoustic guitar 2,3), Wayne Erwin (guitar), Gene Estes (percussion 1,2, tambourine 2, bells 3), Billy Lewis (drums), Gerry McGee (guitar), Jim Seals (saxophone 2), Louie Shelton (guitar), Larry Taylor (bass).

● 'Apples, Peaches, Bananas And Pears' recalls an earlier hit song by Tommy Boyce, 'Peaches And Cream,' which The Ikettes took to #36 in March '65. This new one is not the most inspired song in the Boyce & Hart canon but has the potential to be a decent album track. Two further sessions are held at the end of October to complete its production.

Also taped today is a zippy version of 'Don't Listen To Linda' complete with an oldtimey sax solo from Jim Seals, former member of The Champs and future founder of Seals & Crofts. Boyce & Hart will hold a further session to complete this production on November 6th.

Tommy Boyce: "That was a great little song. It should've been a single too! It was written about Linda Perry [who] married Richard Perry, a great record producer. I got the title from knowing Linda and hanging out with her. Even though it said, 'Don't listen to Linda,' I didn't really mean that when we wrote it. It just was a great title. Of course, I apologized to her later and said I didn't really mean all these things. She liked the song."

Similar in style to 'Linda' is the next song up today, 'I Never Thought It Peculiar,' the perfect Davy Jones music-hall-style ditty. Nevertheless, this will be the only one of today's songs left unfinished this year. Boyce & Hart will return to the tune during 1969 and it will eventually find a home as the last song on the last original Monkees album, *Changes*.

Boyce: "That was kind of an English-oriented song. In the middle we decided to put a Jimi Hendrix guitar solo just for fun. We just sort of did what we felt in those days. We liked to experiment a lot. If we liked it, we figured maybe other people might like it a little bit. I always thought that should have been a single too."

Just as Boyce & Hart are wrapping up tracking and moving into mix mode, Jeff Barry is assembling a session crew to record more new Monkees tracks in Studio A.

RECORDING RCA (A) *Hollywood, CA* 7:00-10:30pm. Jeff Barry *prod*; Hank Cicalo *eng*; half-inch 4-track; tracking.

1. **'Laugh'**
   More Of The Monkees master # TZB3-4737
2. **'I'll Be Back Up On My Feet'** version 1
   Missing Links 2 master # TZB3-4738
3. **'The Day We Fall In Love'**
   More Of The Monkees master # TZB3-4739

Personnel Hal Blaine (drums), Frank Capp (percussion), Al Casey (guitar), Carol Kaye (guitar), Ray Pohlman (bass), Don Randi (keyboard), Michel Rubini (keyboard), Julius Wechter (percussion).

● This evening sees Jeff Barry's one and only Monkees tracking session held in Los Angeles. The date is also notable for featuring most of the key members of Los Angeles's so-called 'wrecking crew' of session musicians. Starting with 'Laugh,' a number penned by East Coast group The Tokens, the assembled ensemble easily tear through a song an hour.

The second item taped could have been one of the best songs on *More Of The Monkees*, had it been included. Nevertheless, music coordinator Don Kirshner's so-called 'golden ear' didn't hear a hit in Sandy Linzer and Denny Randell's composition. However, 'I'll Be Back Up On My Feet' is deemed suitable for inclusion twice during the first season of the TV series, in the episodes *Dance, Monkee, Dance* and *Monkees In The Ring*, and in 1990 this version of the song finally finds legitimate record release, on *Missing Links Volume Two*.

Just the opposite is true of the final track taped today, 'The Day We Fall In Love.' Also penned by Linzer & Randell, this soppy tune will make it onto *More Of The Monkees* but is thankfully never heard in the TV series. These are only a few among the various suspect musical choices that Kirshner will make on the upcoming album. Nevertheless, his judgment will be fully vindicated when it becomes one of the best-selling albums of all time.

Dates for vocal overdubs on these tracks are undocumented but will occur some time during the next few weeks. 'The Day We Fall In Love' is subject to further instrumental sweetening with a string session in New York City on November 23rd. The Monkees obviously enjoy Linzer & Randell's 'I'll Be Back Up On My Feet' because on August 22nd next year they will have Lester Sill request today's master so they can copy the arrangement and recut it. Although they will successfully remake the song in 1968, today's master will be lost in the process and all that will survive is a mono mixdown from November 17th 1966.

● Saturday 29th - Sunday 30th

RECORDING RCA (B) *Hollywood, CA* 2:00-6:00, 7:00pm-12midnight. Tommy Boyce & Bobby Hart *prod*; half-inch 4-track; overdubs.

1. **'Tear Drop City'**
   Instant Replay master # TZB3-4731
2. **'Looking For The Good Times'**
   The Monkees Present master # TZB3-4732
3. **'Apples, Peaches, Bananas And Pears'**
   Missing Links 1 master # TZB3-4734

Personnel Tommy Boyce (backing vocal), Micky Dolenz (lead vocal), Bobby Hart (backing vocal), Ron Hicklin (backing vocal).

● Boyce & Hart are ensconced in Studio B for the weekend to tinker with their recent productions. Saturday's activities are unclear, but on Sunday they manage to corral Micky and session vocalist Ron Hicklin to record vocals for three tunes. It's possible that Micky tries singing on all of these, but the only lead vocal track definitely captured on Sunday is for 'Apples, Peaches, Bananas And Pears.'

Boyce & Hart will resurrect this master of 'Apples' during 1969 when it is remixed for use in the TV series repeats seen on CBS. Though it does turn up in a reconstituted version of the *Royal Flush* TV episode in February 1971, it will never feature on a contemporary record release and will remain in the can until Rhino's 1987 *Missing Links* collection.

● Monday 31st

RECORDING RCA (B) *Hollywood, CA* 2:00-5:00pm. Tommy Boyce & Bobby Hart *prod*; half-inch 4-track; overdubs.

1. **'Tear Drop City'**
   Instant Replay master # TZB3-4731

TVseries

The Monkees

EPISODE 8: *DON'T LOOK A GIFT HORSE IN THE MOUTH*
BROADCAST OCTOBER 31ST
The Monkees are saddled with the responsibility of babysitting a real live horse.
WRITER: DAVE EVANS. DIRECTOR: ROBERT RAFELSON.
SONGS 'Papa Gene's Blues,' 'All The King's Horses.'

2. 'Apples, Peaches, Bananas And Pears'
Missing Links 1 master # TZB3-4734
Personnel Tommy Boyce (backing vocal), Bobby Hart (backing vocal), Ron Hicklin (backing vocal).

● Boyce & Hart spend Halloween refining their backing vocal parts with Ron Hicklin. 'Tear Drop City' will receive further attention at a session on November 6th.
TV At 7:30pm, Monkees fans are treated to a not-so-spooky new episode of their series, *Don't Look A Gift Horse In The Mouth*, on NBC.

NOVEMBER

'I'm A Believer' / '(I'm Not Your) Steppin' Stone' single is released in the U.S.A. This is the group's second 45.
● The recording of the group's second album is nearing completion as they begin a round of nighttime and weekend workouts in preparation for their first concert tour. Choreographer David Winters, formerly of NBC television music show *Hullabaloo*, is on hand for some of these run-throughs and offers advice on what looks good to an audience.
● Peter appears on-stage late this month with the Buffalo Springfield during their stint at Hollywood's Whisky A Go Go club.

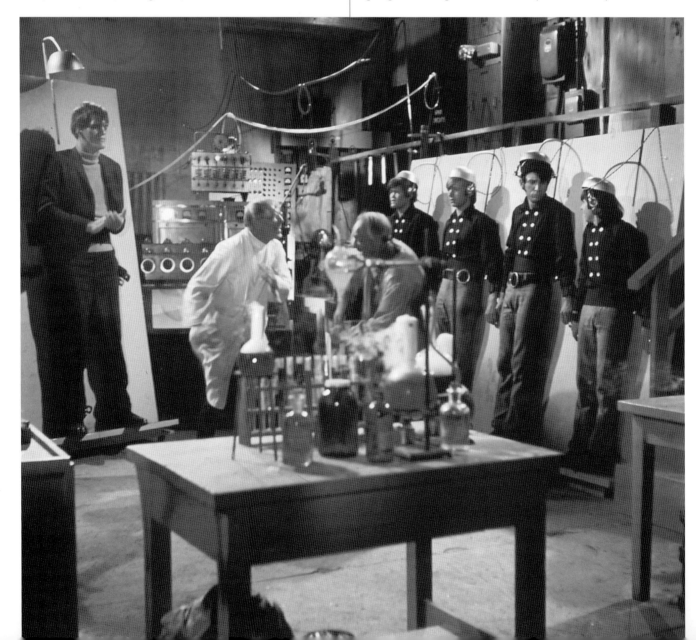

I'm A Believer single

A 'I'm A Believer' (N. DIAMOND)
B '(I'm Not Your) Steppin' Stone' (T. BOYCE / B. HART)

U.S. release November 1966 (Colgems 66-1002).
U.K. release around December 1966 (RCA 1650).
Chart high U.S. number 1; U.K. number 1.

● Tuesday 1st - Thursday 3rd

FILMING On Tuesday production commences at 8:00am on what will become episode 18 of the *Monkees* series, *I Was A Teenage Monster*. Shooting takes place on Stage #7 with interior filming in a study and an exterior shot of a mansion.

The next day shooting again begins at 8:00am, this time on Stage #7 with interior scenes in a lab. The production is wrapped on Thursday with final shots of the lab, plus scenes in the mansion's bedrooms and entrance hall, all on Stage #7. Some stock footage is also employed.

● Also on Thursday composer Stu Phillips works on two incidental music scores for the series. Employing 12 session musicians, Phillips tapes music cues for the programs *I've Got A Little Song Here* and *Monkees A La Carte*.

● Saturday 5th - Sunday 6th

● The group's first number one single is officially registered when 'Last Train To Clarksville' peaks on the *Billboard* chart. Meanwhile its composers and producers, Boyce & Hart, work towards completing further recordings for the group.

RECORDING RCA (B) *Hollywood, CA* 3:00-6:00, 7:00pm-12midnight (but see text). Tommy Boyce & Bobby Hart *prod*; half-inch 4-track; overdubs, mixdown.

1. **'Tear Drop City'**
   Instant Replay master # TZB3-4731
2. **'Don't Listen To Linda'** version 1
   More Of The Monkees master # TZB3-4735
3. **'Looking For The Good Times'**
   The Monkees Present master # TZB3-4732

TVseries

The Monkees

EPISODE 9: *THE CHAPERONE*
BROADCAST NOVEMBER 7TH
When Davy sets his sights on dating the daughter of an uptight military man, Micky is recruited as a chaperone – albeit with a twist.
WRITERS: GERALD GARDNER, DEE CARUSO. DIRECTOR: BRUCE KESSLER.
SONGS 'This Just Doesn't Seem To Be My Day,' 'Take A Giant Step.'

Personnel Tommy Boyce (backing vocal), Micky Dolenz (lead vocal 1, harmony vocal 3), David Jones (lead vocal 2,3), Bobby Hart (backing vocal), Ron Hicklin (backing vocal).

● Boyce & Hart spend their second weekend in a row at RCA's Studio B completing potential tracks for the group's second LP, *More Of The Monkees*. Saturday is probably given over to reductions and mixdowns, while Sunday is specifically noted as a vocal overdub day. From 2:00 to 8:00pm the three songs are treated to lead and backing vocal sweetening. This session marks the completion of 'Tear Drop City,' which will be issued as a single in February 1969. The production for 'Don't Listen To Linda' version 1 is also finalized at this session, but this version will never originally be issued, only appearing as a bonus track on 1994's expanded CD reissue of *More Of The Monkees*. Boyce & Hart will eventually recut the song on December 31st 1967. 'Looking For The Good Times' will be subjected to further refinement at a session on November 12th.

● Monday 7th

TV The NBC television network airs episode 9 of the *Monkees* series, *The Chaperone*, at 7:30pm.

● Thursday 10th

FILMING A recording session scheduled for this evening in RCA Hollywood's Studio B from 8:00pm to 12midnight is cancelled for unknown reasons. The band are probably on the set today filming an episode called *The Case Of The Missing Monkee*.

● Friday 11th

FILMING Production wraps on what will become episode 17 of the *Monkees* series, *The Case Of The Missing Monkee*.

● *Daily Variety* reports that television impresario Dick Clark will be the promoter for The Monkees' upcoming concert dates. Seven gigs are booked so far, including stops in Memphis, St. Louis, Jacksonville, Pittsburgh, Cincinnati, Nashville, and Tulsa.

● Today's *Time* magazine forecasts that Monkees merchandise will gross $20m this year, with J.C. Penney alone accounting for $670,000.

● Tonight in Hollywood demonstrators riot on the Sunset Strip over a newly imposed youth curfew. They ultimately burn down one of their hangouts, Pandora's Box – inspiring Michael Nesmith to write a poem that he will later set to music, 'Daily Nightly.'

● Saturday 12th

● The single 'Last Train To Clarksville' slips to #2 but the album *The Monkees* tops the charts at #1, where it will remain frozen until February 1967. Meanwhile, songwriters Boyce & Hart produce what will turn out be their last Monkees session for a full year.

RECORDING RCA (B) *Hollywood, CA* 5:00-9:00pm. Tommy Boyce & Bobby Hart *prod*; half-inch 4-track; overdubs, mixdown.

1. **'Looking For The Good Times'**
   The Monkees Present master # TZB3-4732
2. **'I'll Spend My Life With You'** version 1
   More Of The Monkees master # TZB3-4733

Personnel Tommy Boyce (backing vocal), Micky Dolenz (lead vocal 2, harmony vocal 1), Bobby Hart (backing vocal), Ron Hicklin (harmony vocal 2, backing vocal), David Jones (lead vocal 1).

● Boyce & Hart's final session of '66 finds them finishing work on the last of their masters for the year. With the exception of vocals for 'I Never Thought It Peculiar,' the duo has so far finished 14 potential productions for the forthcoming second album, *More Of The Monkees*. Of these, only 'She' and '(I'm Not Your) Steppin' Stone' will appear on the LP. Bert Schneider's concerns over the commercial appeal of

TVseries

The Monkees

EPISODE 10: *HERE COME THE MONKEES*

BROADCAST NOVEMBER 14TH

In the pilot episode, The Monkees land a sweet-16 gig that is soon thrown into jeopardy when the birthday girl falls for Davy.

WRITERS: PAUL MAZURSKY, LARRY TUCKER. DIRECTOR: MIKE ELLIOT.

SONGS 'I Wanna Be Free,' 'Let's Dance On.'

Boyce & Hart's material and Don Kirshner's preference for his New York stable of writers will quiet the pair – at least for the time being.

● Monday 14th

TV At 7:30pm this evening the pilot episode of the *Monkees* series is televised by the NBC network. *Here Come The Monkees* has had some sequences reshot and is now officially dubbed episode 10. A true sign of the show's increasing popularity comes when tonight's broadcast wins the most viewers for its time slot for the first time, beating *Gilligan's Island* and *Iron Horse* on other networks and pulling in an audience of more than ten million. This is still a far cry from the 30 million viewers that Steve Blauner at Screen Gems expected before the debut of the series. Meanwhile, the crew for the series are on a break from shooting for the rest of the month. The group probably use this respite to work up their live act.

● Thursday 17th

● Mono masters are compiled of recent recordings for use on The Monkees' upcoming album and future television episodes.

● Friday 18th

● Peter flies to San Francisco this evening with choreographer David Winters and Ward Sylvester, who not only is executive producer on the TV series but also will act as tour manager for the upcoming dates. Their mission is to check out the San Francisco lightshows and see what elements can be incorporated into The Monkees' upcoming stage appearances. They attend a show at the Fillmore by The James Cotton Blues Band, who appear on a bill with Lothar & The Hand People.

TVseries

The Monkees

EPISODE 11: *MONKEES A LA CARTE*

BROADCAST NOVEMBER 21ST

The Monkees monkey with a mobster's plot to take over a string of West Coast restaurants.

WRITERS: GERALD GARDNER, DEE CARUSO, BERNIE ORENSTEIN. DIRECTOR: JAMES FRAWLEY.

SONGS '(I'm Not Your) Steppin' Stone,' 'She.'

After the Fillmore gig they venture to a concert by Quicksilver Messenger Service at the Avalon Ballroom. Peter breaks off to see his folkie friend Lynn Hughes perform at the W.F. Kuh Memorial Auditorium. After a set there by Dino Valenti, Peter takes the stage for an impromptu performance. His set includes 'San Francisco Bay Blues,' 'Take A Giant Step,' and two songs from a musical his mother and brother have written called *Tippy The Toiler*. Peter, Sylvester, and Winters board a return flight at 12:55am. Rehearsals for The Monkees' stage show continue over the weekend.

● Monday 21st

● Composer Stu Phillips records two more incidental scores for the *Monkees* series. Working with 11 musicians from 10:00am–1:00pm he tapes the cues for the programs *Dance, Monkee, Dance* and *Too Many Girls*.

TV The NBC network airs episode 11 of the *Monkees* series, *Monkees A La Carte*, at 7:30pm. For the second week in a row the show tops its time slot, attracting almost 11 million viewers.

● Wednesday 23rd

● Work shifts back to New York City for the final tracking session for the forthcoming *More Of The Monkees* album.

RECORDING RCA (A) *New York, NY* 9:30am-1:30pm. Neil Sedaka & Carole Bayer *prod*; Ernie Oelrich *eng*; half-inch 4-track; tracking.

1. **'The Girl I Left Behind Me'** version 1
   Instant Replay master # TZB1-8689
2. **'When Love Comes Knockin' (At Your Door)'**
   More Of The Monkees master # TZB1-8690

Personnel Maurice Bialkin (cello 1), Al Gafa (guitar), Leo Kahn (violin 1), Herb Lovelle (drums), Russ Savakus (bass), Neil Sedaka (keyboard), Julius Schachter (violin 1), Willard Suyker (guitar), Don Thomas (guitar), unknown (percussion).

● Songwriters Neil Sedaka and Carole Bayer (later known as Carole Bayer Sager) produce this final session of new material for The Monkees' second album. Sedaka and Bayer first tape a version of their song 'The Girl I Left Behind Me,' which will eventually turn up on 1969's *Instant Replay* album. Over the next two years, at least two further Monkee recordings will be made of this composition.

The second song taped is the duo's charming 'When Love Comes Knockin' (At Your Door).' This likable tune easily finds a place on *More Of The Monkees*, though it will never feature on the television series. Davy probably dubs his lead vocals onto these tracks within a day of this session.

Neil Sedaka: "Don Kirshner asked Carole Bayer Sager and I to go into the studio with Davy Jones and produce a couple of sides for the *More Of The Monkees* album. What sticks out in my mind [is] a phrase I've come to hate over the years, when people told you years ago, 'If not this album, the next album.' I'll explain that. Don Kirshner heard the two songs … and said, 'Well, we're going to put 'When Love Comes Knockin' (At Your Door)' on the album, but we'll reserve 'The Girl I Left Behind Me' for the next album.' That has stuck with me through the years. I was so discouraged because it was left off the album. As a result I lost a lot of money. I don't think it ever came out."

Meanwhile, across the hall in Studio B, Jeff Barry puts the finishing touches on his last production for *More Of The Monkees*.

RECORDING RCA (B) *New York, NY* 10:00am-1:00pm. Jeff Barry *prod*; Ray Hall *eng*; half-inch 4-track; overdubs.

1. **'The Day We Fall In Love'**
   More Of The Monkees master # TZB3-4739

Personnel Seymour Barab (cello), Louis Haber (violin), David Sackson (viola), Murray Sandry (viola), Irving Spice (violin), Louis Stone (violin).

A frame from a November photoshoot that will later make the front cover of the group's 1967 album *Headquarters*.

● Jeff Barry uses this three-hour session to overdub a string arrangement by Artie Butler onto 'The Day We Fall In Love.' Davy flies into New York City to work with Barry and adds his recitation to the track soon after the string date is wrapped.

Aside from some mixing, this work officially concludes the *More Of The Monkees* sessions – and indeed all recording sessions for the rest of the year. In a matter of days The Monkees will make their live concert debut.

● Friday 25th

● After recording his vocals in New York City, Davy celebrates Thanksgiving with Don Kirshner and Kirshner's family. When the traditional meal is complete, he departs from New York's JFK Airport and travels to San Antonio, Texas, where he will enjoy the rest of the holiday with Michael, Phyllis, and some of the Nesmith clan. Although Davy misses his initial flight – inspiring a pointed letter from Don Kirshner to Braniff Airlines – he probably catches another plane the same evening. During the visit to Texas he meets an old friend of Michael's, Steve Pitts. Davy and Pitts begin a songwriting collaboration during 1967.

● Monday 28th

● The Monkees are awarded a gold record by the RIAA for outstanding sales of their second single 'I'm A Believer.'
TV At 7:30pm, episode 12 of the *Monkees* series, *I've Got A Little Song Here*, is broadcast by the NBC television network.

TVseries

The Monkees

EPISODE 12: *I'VE GOT A LITTLE SONG HERE*
BROADCAST NOVEMBER 28TH
An unscrupulous music publisher tries to take Mike Nesmith for a ride until The Monkees turn the tables.
WRITER: TREVA SILVERMAN. DIRECTOR: BRUCE KESSLER.
SONGS 'Gonna Buy Me A Dog,' 'Mary, Mary.'

DECEMBER

● Michael probably attends a performance this month by The Turtles, possibly in Cerritos, outside of Los Angeles, on the 17th. He is a fan of the band's current bass player, Chip Douglas, a former member of an outfit known as the MFQ or Modern Folk Quartet. More recently Douglas was a part of The Gene Clark Group, but since that venture quickly folded he found almost instant employment with The Turtles. Douglas first met Michael last year when he saw a performance by Michael and Bill Chadwick at The Troubadour. After watching Douglas play with The Turtles, Michael asks him if he's interested in working with The Monkees in the recording studio.

● Local Los Angeles publication *TV Week* features The Monkees on the cover. Inside, series co-creator Bob Rafelson is interviewed at length and provides interesting insights into *The Monkees*. Marian Dern of *TV Week* writes: "The keynote of the show, according to Rafelson, was something rare in television – creativity, freedom and non-phoniness. ... Now sadly, the show has not done well in the ratings. ... Certain factors, such as the fact that the program airs only in 160 markets (as opposed to the usual 200 for a network show) are involved. Some observers have opined that stations were reluctant to buy a show about rock and rollers."

The fact that the *Monkees* series has won its time slot on a number of occasions is not the same thing as achieving high ratings. It is like a record that receives a lot of airplay but does not chart. Many people watch the *Monkees* shows, but because of the way in which the ratings are compiled, many other shows come out way ahead of *The Monkees*. It airs at 7:30pm on Mondays – not the prime day or time for a maximum audience.

"In any case, one thing is certain," Dern continues in *TV Week*. "There has been a gaping lack of publicity about the boys. ... The producers themselves are the ones who put the clamp on publicity interviews with The Monkees. ... Sometimes an interview is granted and the writer gets only as far as the second question. 'We had one representative from a big magazine whom we threw bodily out of the office,' says Rafelson. 'His attitude and line of questioning were impossible.'

"Just why the four Monkees must be protected so carefully is a question the answer to which has ranged from the suggestion that they might be asked embarrassing questions about their musical prowess (Rafelson assures they do all their own playing of instruments and singing) to the hint that they are so outspoken that they might say something unconventional (it has been rumored that a remark on Vietnam by one of The Monkees, during the summer, led to a news ban). When asked, Rafelson explains the ban in rather vague terms having to do with preserving a certain 'uniqueness' characteristic of the show and the boys.

"'We're doing something new, avoiding the status quo,' [Rafelson] says. 'We're probably the only show with a technical crew built around the content. I interviewed lighting men, cameramen, and sound men. Writers and directors too. Most of them are young, but the main thing is they had to be 'involved,' had to have an eagerness to swing with the inventive style of the show. We interviewed several hundred guys. We didn't want professional actors – they're too concerned with image and acting technique. We finally settled on Peter, Mike, Micky, and one Englishman, Davy. They hadn't met before; they were all musicians. The one quality above all else was that they came over as original people.

"'Take those interviews at the end of some episodes. Those interviews are strictly unedited. I don't touch them. I don't want to.

The minute I have to edit them, out they go. I can tell you damn well they're not puppets. They're sensitive and intelligent – they have opinions on everything – they can speak for themselves. Only an in-depth interview would do them justice – I want a writer to spend some time, find out what they're really saying, what we're really doing. Those quick, on-the-set, instant-quote type interviews can turn out as silly, distorted stories. Look what happened to John Lennon's recently misunderstood remark.

"'Of course, in-depth interviews are practically impossible,' [Rafelson continues.] "The boys work a staggering schedule – sometimes 12 hours on the set and then four hours recording. They're rehearsing for a concert tour, and some weekends they're making personal appearance tours. They love the singing, and it makes them some money.'" The writer adds: "Presumably they are also making money for their producers, and Screen Gems."

● Thursday 1st

● The Monkees depart from Los Angeles International Airport on a United Airlines flight bound for Honolulu, Hawaii, with an entourage that includes series co-creators Bob Rafelson and Bert Schneider, Steve Blauner, of Screen Gems, choreographer David Winters, and stand-in and extra Ric Klein. After the five-hour flight the group is greeted by around 2,500 fans at the airport, some of whom rip their way through a wire fence to reach the band. During the fracas, Davy is poked in the eyes. Once safely away from the fan frenzy, the boys stay at the Royal Hawaiian Hotel and enjoy authentic

LEFT The four Monkees perform as a group at the TV studios for a series episode.
ABOVE Davy in the studio with Monkees music coordinator Don Kirshner.

Hawaiian music and dancing at the Queen Surf night club.
● Composer Stu Phillips completes his music cues for the episode *Son Of A Gypsy*. Employing just three session musicians, from 4:30 to 7:30pm, the taping concludes Phillips's incidental scoring this year on *The Monkees*.

● Friday 2nd

● In Hawaii, The Monkees stage the first of what will become a tradition for the group on tour. They visit the concert's radio sponsor, KPOI, and proceed to 'take over' the station. This entails the various members playing DJ, taking live call-ins from fans, and a Michael Nesmith 'farm report.'

Micky tells the *Honolulu Advertiser's* Wayne Harada that the group's success is connected to the current social climate. "I think it has a lot to do with the bag that the whole country is in at the moment," says Micky. "There's so much hate and prejudice, fights, wars, killings on TV. I think we're giving them pure entertainment and humor."

● Saturday 3rd

● The Monkees hold last-minute rehearsals starting at 8:00am at tonight's venue, in preparation for their first full-length concert. Two full run-throughs are staged until the rehearsal is finally concluded at 6:15pm.
PERFORMANCE Honolulu International Center Arena *Honolulu, HI* 9:00pm, *Miss K-POI Pageant*
● The Monkees' perform their first live show before an audience of 8,364 fans, a reported sell-out crowd. After a pre-recorded burst of '(Theme From) The Monkees' the group, dressed in black suits with white shirts and paisley ties, open with 'Last Train To Clarksville.' The first set continues with Baker Knight's 'She's So Far Out, She's In' (sung by Michael); 'You Just May Be The One'; 'I Wanna Be Free' (accompanied by rear-screen still projections of various world leaders and a 'freedom group'); 'Mary, Mary'; Michael Murphey's '(I Prithee) Do Not Ask For Love'; 'Sweet Young Thing'; and the as-yet-unissued 'I Can't Get Her Off My Mind'.

Following a short intermission, the show picks up with '(I'm Not Your) Steppin' Stone'; a solo performance by Peter of 'East Virginia'; Willie Dixon's 'You Can't Judge A Book By The Cover' (performed by Michael solo with accompaniment by an unidentified back-up band – not the other Monkees); Anthony Newley's 'The Joker' from the Broadway play *The Roar Of The Grease Paint* (performed by Davy with the back-up band); Ray Charles's 'I Got A Woman' (performed by Micky in mock James Brown fashion with the back-up band); 'If I Could Shimmy Like My Sister Kate' (sung by Peter and backed by the rest of The Monkees, who have now all returned to the stage); 'Take A Giant Step'; and a finale of 'I'm A Believer.'

The *Honolulu Advertiser's* Wayne Harada reviews this first show. "The Arena was jammed when the Monkees took the stage," he writes. "Even a Russian poet, Yevgeny Yevtushenko, was there to see what The Monkees could do. ... Talk about energy! I admit I had my doubts about a foursome formed after would-be Monkees answered an ad in *Variety*, but these guys are out-of-sight (translation: so way out, they're in).

"They're highly compatible with the flair of seasoned pros. Yet they're new to the rock game, but theirs is a swift-paced review of 16 songs that are simply fascinating to watch. I refer to the grab bag of visual gimmicks The Monkees use – things never before seen or done in a rock'n'roll show. And I've seen quite a few over the last couple of years.

"Colored slides are flashing onto huge screens above the stage while there's some hilarious Monkee business, both chatter and musical patter, in the foreground. Like their hit TV show, the staccato technique results in an audio video pop art effect. Ever see a quick change rocker? Each Monkee left the stage before garb changes – mostly mod, curiously colorful – in between songs.

"'We're not like most singing groups today,' Mike said when The Monkees' 'solo recital' started. And how true. Most groups – The Beatles included – are just that: groups. They sing and appear as groups. The Monkees hurled that tradition aside as each guy had a few minutes alone on stage. Micky's take-off on Negro soul singer James Brown – and remember those gaudy aloha shirts that were used? – featured some fancy footwork and from-the-heart wailing. It, easily, was the evening's highlight. Perhaps the favorite Monkee, David, with puppy dog eyes and long flowing hair, was the best overall performer. His Broadway stage experience – he was in *Oliver!* – was very much in evidence when he belted out 'The Joker' and 'I Wanna Be Free.' Peter, too, was a sensation when he plucked his banjo and chanted a folk tune. He had a Ringo-like naiveté, and looked like Dutch Boy on the cleanser.

"Mike, unfortunately, gets into the act too infrequently. He has the makings of a real charmer – he's a funny fellow – but he lets his buddies take the spotlight. Most of The Monkees' hits are recreated: 'Last Train To Clarksville,' 'I'm A Believer,' 'Steppin' Stone.' If you listened carefully, you'd have recognized 'If I Could Shimmy Like My Sister Kate,' too. The fans were most responsive (my ears are still ringing) and well behaved, with one exception: someone hurled a flare-type fire cracker toward the stage."

The show grosses $36,000 for promoters Arena Associates, making The Monkees the second most popular draw at Honolulu International Center. (The 'gross' is the total amount of money taken at the box office.) The most successful artist the venue has showcased is The Rolling Stones, who beat The Monkees' gross by $3,000. Promoter Tom Moffatt says The Monkees were a faster sell-out than the Stones. "We sold out The Monkees in six days," he explains, "two days before the show."

● Sunday 4th
● The Monkees enjoy a rare day off, which they spend sightseeing in Hawaii.

● Monday 5th
● Before the group's afternoon departure from the islands they take over a local Hawaiian radio station for several hours and play their favorite records.
TV At 7:30pm episode 13 of the *Monkees* series, *One Man Shy*, is broadcast on the NBC television network.

TVseries

The Monkees

EPISODE 13: ***ONE MAN SHY (PETER AND THE DEBUTANTE)***
BROADCAST DECEMBER 5TH
When Peter falls for a debutante The Monkees come to the rescue with a plot to win her heart.
WRITERS: GERALD GARDNER, DEE CARUSO, TREVA SILVERMAN. DIRECTOR: JAMES FRAWLEY.
SONGS 'You Just May Be The One,' 'I'm A Believer.'

● Tuesday 6th
FILMING The *Monkees* series goes back into production after several weeks off. At 8:00am the crew begin shooting what will become episode 20, *Monkees In The Ring*, as The Monkees, fresh from their jaunt to Hawaii, return to the confines of Stage #7 for various interior shots.

● Wednesday 7th
FILMING At 8:00am production continues on *Monkees In The Ring*, with more interiors on Stage #7, including a gym, boxing ring, dressing room, booth, and Sholto's office.
● Behind the scenes, song selection and publishing information are finalized for the group's second album *More Of The Monkees*. The record will be released in January.

● Thursday 8th
FILMING The final day of shooting on *Monkees In The Ring* starts once more at 8:00am.
Today's filming again takes place on Stage #7 with more interiors of the gym, the Monkees' pad, and some exterior street shots on Beachwood Drive, just outside the Columbia lot.

● Friday 9th
FILMING Today production starts at 8:00am on what will become episode 22 of *The Monkees*, titled *Monkees At The Circus*. Shooting today takes place on Stage #9 with interior shots of a circus tent and an exterior of a wagon.
● *Daily Variety*'s Army Archerd reports that The Monkees are already talking about their movie. Micky says, "We want it to be as different a movie as the series was to TV. And we want to bring back a lot of the old Hollywood glamour and excitement with it. I think we had it tougher than The Beatles: we had to be a hit in three media at one time – TV, records, and [personal appearances]. And we had no experience together in any."

Despite the group's stunning success in Hawaii, their homecoming wasn't particularly special for Michael, who is refused entrance at Hollywood's venerable Italian restaurant Martoni's. "I agree, I looked kinda scruffy in a blue jean jacket and with this long hair," he tells Archerd. "That's why I asked if we could come in. When they said no, we went to Villa Capri." In August last year Sonny Bono had been similarly barred from Martoni's for his unacceptable appearance. Bono instantly composed the folk protest song 'Laugh At Me,' which made the Top 10. Michael will not be similarly inspired.

● Saturday 10th
● The Monkees occupy four spaces on the *Billboard* charts. The *Monkees* album holds at #1 while 'Last Train To Clarksville' descends to #27. The group's new single 'I'm A Believer' debuts this week at #44, and its flipside, '(I'm Not Your) Steppin' Stone,' receives sufficient airplay to register on *Billboard*'s Hot 100 Bound chart at #120.
Billboard comments on the group's phenomenal record sales. "For RCA Victor, who manufactures and distributes the Colgems label, this represents the warmest distributor reception ever gained with the exception of certain Elvis Presley records."
Micky recalls: "I knew nothing about the industry. Tommy Boyce tells a great story. He says he came up to me and said, 'Micky, you have three records in the top ten in *Billboard*.' I said, 'What's *Billboard*?' I did! He couldn't believe it and that's true. I was the innocent naïÔve artist just singing the stuff. It was great. I had a great time."

TVseries

The Monkees

EPISODE 14: DANCE, MONKEE, DANCE
BROADCAST DECEMBER 12TH
A lifetime contract of dance lessons keeps The Monkees on their toes until the group tap into a scheme of their own.
WRITER: BERNIE ORENSTEIN. DIRECTOR: JAMES FRAWLEY.
SONGS 'I'll Be Back Upon My Feet,' 'I'm A Believer.'

● Monday 12th
FILMING After a weekend break, production resumes on Stage #9 for *Monkees At The Circus*.
TV Episode 14 of *The Monkees* series, *Dance, Monkee, Dance*, is aired by the NBC television network at 7:30pm. This broadcast will win its time slot, pulling in just over ten million viewers.

● Tuesday 13th
FILMING Production wraps on *Monkees At The Circus* with a final day of shooting on Stage #9. The crew will start a new episode, *The Prince And The Pauper*, later this week.

● Saturday 17th
● 'I'm A Believer' single leaps into *Billboard's* Top 10, placing at #8. The group also hold position 43 with 'Last Train To Clarksville,' #77 with '(I'm Not Your) Steppin' Stone,' and, of course, #1 on the album charts with *The Monkees*.
● Later rumors will suggest that The Monkees are guests today on Dick Clark's *American Bandstand* but it is highly unlikely that the group materialize in person on the program. In America they are generally barred by Raybert from appearing on television programs other than their own. Raybert justifiably fear the group's overexposure.

● Sunday 18th
The *Newark News* publishes an article about Don Kirshner titled "Video Music Flows From 'Golden Ear.'" The highlight is a picture of Kirshner with his wife Sheila posed in front of a huge photo of The Monkees that bears the inscription, "To Donnie, the man who made it all possible." The paper's Tom Mackin notes: "An odd aspect of

TVseries

The Monkees

EPISODE 15: TOO MANY GIRLS (DAVY AND FERN)
BROADCAST DECEMBER 19TH
A scheming stage mom plots to place her doe-eyed daughter alongside Davy in a dynamic duo.
WRITERS: GERALD GARDNER, DEE CARUSO, DAVE EVANS. DIRECTOR: JAMES FRAWLEY.
SONGS 'I'm A Believer.'

this situation is the fact that The Monkees – four unknowns who individually answered an ad in a trade paper – have been less than outstanding as a TV series.

In the most recent Nielsen ratings, the Monday night NBC situation comedy was #47, its highest peg to date. It has been as low as #65. Kirshner has no explanation for this, and indeed the series is not his responsibility."

● Monday 19th
FILMING The final day of production commences at 8:00am for what will become episode 21 of the *Monkees* series, *The Prince And The Pauper*. Filming today on Stage #7 includes interior scenes in the Monkees' pad, the 'throne' room, 'fencing' room, and dungeon. Local scenester Rodney Bingenheimer is on the set today to act as Davy's body double in some sequences. He doesn't normally act as Davy's stand-in on the series: the job is handled regularly by one of Michael's San Antonio folk buddies, David Price.
TV At 7:30pm the NBC network televises episode 15 of the *Monkees* series, *Too Many Girls*.
● The group's second album, *More Of The Monkees*, is shipped to distributors. It will officially be available from retailers next month. As with the first LP, more mono copies are produced than stereo, reflecting current public demand, and stereo copies are priced a dollar more than mono.

● Tuesday 20th
FILMING Production starts on what will become episode 25 of *The Monkees*, titled *Alias Micky Dolenz*. Filming today includes work on Stages #7 and #10. Davy is written out of most of this program so that he can visit Britain, although he will later film a post-show interview to explain his absence to viewers. He departs from Los Angeles at noon and will arrive tomorrow in London.

● Wednesday 21st
● Davy arrives in Britain at 7:30am for a brief family visit and some promotional duties, including photo sessions, a solo press conference, and a few brief television appearances. He will return to the States in time for the group's next live engagement.
FILMING Back on the set, production continues on *Alias Micky Dolenz* with filming on Stage #7 of a police station scene, plus exteriors outside on Beachwood Drive for a parking lot sequence.

● Thursday 22nd
Thursday 23rd
FILMING Production wraps on *Alias Micky Dolenz* with interior scenes of a night club and 'den of thieves,' after which the *Monkees* crew break for the Christmas holiday.

● Sunday 25th
● Micky spends Christmas day with his family in Los Gatos, California, but must leave after just a few hours in order to make the group's concert in Denver tomorrow. Denver's *Rocky Mountain News* announces today that Monkees-inspired fashion lines are now available from J.C. Penney's.

● Monday 26th
● At 9:00am The Monkees and their crew leave Los Angeles as they fly to Denver, Colorado, for the group's second concert performance. Upon their arrival the group are greeted by more than 400 fans. Most of The Monkees' day will be spent holed up at the Hotel Cosmopolitan. At 6:00pm they hold a brief press conference to award a guitar in a local contest for Vox instruments.

PERFORMANCE **Auditorium Arena** *Denver, CO* with Jewel Akens, The Apollos, Bobby Hart's Candy Store Prophets; sponsored by radio station KIMN
● Later this evening the group perform their second live concert, in 17 degree weather.

Support act The Apollos are female singers; Akens had a hit in 1965 with 'The Birds And The Bees.' Bobby Hart's Candy Store Prophets – Boyce & Hart's regular session crew – serve as openers and also back The Monkees on their individual solo spots. During tonight's show closer, '(I'm Not Your) Steppin' Stone,' several young fans rush the stage.

Jackie Cooper of Screen Gems flies in from Hollywood to catch the performance and later says, "The kids in the audience never stop screaming. The [group] can't even hear each other. I sat in the first row. If you sit in the first four or five rows, you can hear the bass guitar and the drums, and that's about it. The rest of it is screaming. They all go to hear each other scream." The gross take for this concert is $31,726.

The group's set tonight includes 'Last Train To Clarksville,' 'She's So Far Out She's In,' 'You Just May Be The One,' '(I Prithee) Do Not Ask For Love,' 'I Wanna Be Free,' 'Sweet Young Thing,' 'I Can't Get Her Off My Mind,' 'Take A Giant Step,' 'Mary, Mary,' 'You Can't Judge By The Cover,' 'I Got A Woman,' 'I'm A Believer,' and '(I'm Not Your) Steppin' Stone.'

The Monkees leave for the airport directly after the show, but their flight to Memphis is delayed and the airport is besieged by fans. Because of the cold weather, the group decide to sign

TVseries
The Monkees

EPISODE 16: *SON OF A GYPSY*
BROADCAST DECEMBER 26TH
A band of jealous gypsies kidnap Peter after The Monkees purloin their party gig.
WRITERS: GERALD GARDNER, DEE CARUSO, TREVA SILVERMAN. DIRECTOR: JAMES FRAWLEY.
SONGS 'I'm A Believer.'

autographs for fans who would otherwise be stuck in the cold outside the terminal. The Monkees eventually arrive in Memphis and go directly to their accommodations at the Sheraton Peabody.
TV Episode 16 of the *Monkees* series, *Son Of A Gypsy*, is televised at 7:30pm on the NBC television network.

● **Thursday 27th**
● This afternoon Davy is interviewed by the *Memphis Commercial Appeal*. He tells the paper's Larry Williams that the group "dig

touring. It is really what we want to do and we believe we can make it big on the road.

"We are concerned with putting on a good show. I can promise you we will not come into town and do 15 minutes and shag off. We will be out there 55 minutes to an hour, and we will pour ourselves into it. I promise you that."

PERFORMANCE Mid-South Coliseum *Memphis, TN* 8:00pm, with The Blossoms, The Montellas; sponsored by radio station WMPS

● The Monkees pour themselves into a performance at the Coliseum in front of an audience reported at 8,000 fans. The gross take for this concert is $39,028. After their performance, the group fly to Louisville, Kentucky.

● *Look* magazine publishes its feature on the group. It is an honest take on the Monkees phenomenon in which TV series co-creator Bert Schneider aptly credits the group with their own success. "Hollywood has thrown too many things out and said, 'This is for you, kids,' and it isn't. We wanted four guys who kids would watch and say, 'Yeah.'"

Journalist Betty Rollin also notes that Schneider and Rafelson's production company Raybert was able to find "a cameraman and crew willing to shoot 75 kaleidoscopic setups a day."

When talk turns to the music, Peter says: "We have the potential, but there's not time to practice."

Micky adds: "We're advertisers. We're selling Monkees. It's gotta be that way."

Michael feels differently. "They're in the middle of something good and they're trying to sell something," he says. "They want us to be The Beatles, but we're not. We're us. We're funny." Peter, who *Look* says has been scolded for talking about Vietnam, remarks: "It's the game. It's a crummy game. But I signed a contract, so I'll play along. What can I do? There are better games ahead."

The article features several photos, including one in which Micky is having his hair combed by one of the crew, Sally Berkeley. *Look* says Berkeley makes about $450 a week, while each Monkees makes $400. A crummy game indeed.

● Wednesday 28th

PERFORMANCE Freedom Hall *Louisville, KY* sponsored by radio station WKLO

● During the day the group relax at the Sherwin Hotel in Louisville and tonight perform at the Freedom Hall in a show that grosses $25,329.

● *Weekly Variety* publishes an article titled "Kirshner Has Monkees On His Back And It's A Great Way To Be Hooked." The piece notes that The Monkees are currently selling faster than The Beatles did at their launch.

Three million copies of the debut album have been sold so far, while singles of 'Clarksville' and 'Believer' have both topped a million. The mechanical royalty take from the first album – meaning earnings from reproduction of copyright material on that record – is expected to be about $750,000, and good things are expected from the yet-to-be-released *More Of The Monkees*, which has already received more than a million advance sales.

The article also reports that Kirshner's latest protégés are Denny Randell and Sandy Linzer. He plans TV and film assignments for the team, and Randell will even get a shot to produce some sides for The Monkees next year. Kirshner is in no rush to develop any other artists for the Colgems label.

● Thursday 29th

● The Monkees travel to Winston-Salem, North Carolina, to tape an interview for the town's local NBC affiliate, television station WSJS.

They are pictured with reporter Anne Parrish during the taping and the photo is eventually published in *Billboard*.

The touring party spends the day at the Robert E. Lee Hotel, where Davy and Peter talk to reporter Luix Overbea. Overbea will write: "All four Monkees are salaried actors. They do not get extra pay from the current personal-appearance tour taking them to ten cities on one-night stands." Davy tells Overbea: "We collect for ourselves only on records." After the interview, the group are whisked away for a tour of a local tobacco plant.

PERFORMANCE Memorial Coliseum Winston-Salem, NC 9:10pm, with Jewel Akens, The Apollos, Candy Store Prophets; sponsored by radio station WTOB

● Forty policeman are on hand tonight to hold back from the stage a crowd reported to be 8,200 strong.

The Monkees' set includes 'Last Train To Clarksville,' 'I Wanna Be Free,' 'Sweet Young Thing,' 'I Got A Woman' (during which Micky hurts his back due to his stage antics), and the standard 'Happy Birthday' sung for Davy and Michael who will officially celebrate their birthdays tomorrow. The Winston-Salem *Journal* calls the show "delightful fun for those who could stand the noise," and the gross take is $33,489. After the performance the group head straight for the airport.

● Friday 30th

PERFORMANCE Civic Arena *Pittsburgh, PA* 8:00pm; sponsored by radio station KQV

● During the day, Michael and Davy celebrate their joint birthday in Davy's suite at the Hilton in Pittsburgh – Michael is 24, Davy 21 – and tonight the group's performance includes another rendition of 'Happy Birthday.' The show grosses $47,020.

● Saturday 31st

● *Billboard* reports that The Monkees have the #1 single across the nation, 'I'm A Believer,' and the #1 album, *The Monkees*. Additionally, their B-side '(I'm Not Your) Steppin' Stone' jumps to #32.

● Now in Cincinnati, Ohio, the group stay on the 19th floor of the Terrace Hilton. For an hour from 2:00pm they entertain winners of radio station WSAI's 'Meet The Monkees' contest with an early copy of their yet-to-be-released album, *More Of The Monkees*, playing the record in their hotel room. Davy tells the fans that The Monkees may shoot a film in Southern France during March. Michael declines a meeting since he has a bad cold.

PERFORMANCE Cincinnati Gardens *Cincinnati, Ohio* with The Candy Store Prophets, Jewel Akens, The Apollos. sponsored by radio station WSAI

● One reporter says that the show, performed before an audience of 8,000, "was like taking a trip without the benefit of LSD." Tonight's 45-minute-plus set includes 'Last Train To Clarksville,' 'Gonna Build A Mountain,' and 'I Got A Woman.' The gross take is $38,000, of which The Monkees' fee is reportedly $15,000 plus a percentage.

After the show the group fly on to Nashville, Tennessee, where they attend singer Brenda Lee's masquerade party. During the event, held in the basement of an electrical store, Peter sits in on guitar with the hired band, followed by Micky and Davy who each perform their solo spots from the band's concert act.

After the party, the group retire to the Dinkler Andrew Jackson Hotel in Nashville.

● The *Monkees* series makes its British debut on BBC television today. The group's second single, 'I'm A Believer,' was issued in Britain yesterday, and the coming weeks will see the U.K. gripped by its own bout of Monkeemania.

Attired in more J.C. Penney clothes to help promote the retail store's Monkees gear.

1967

More Of The Monkees second LP, makes #1 ... more concerts ... TV series continues on NBC ... more TV series filming ... first recording sessions with Monkees as self-contained band, Chip Douglas producing ... Jeff Barry continues New York sessions ... London visit, meeting various Beatles, Kinks, Stones ... TV show achieves biggest audience, 12 million plus ... tussle over inclusion of 'group' side on new single leads to dismissal of Don Kirshner ... third single 'A Little Bit Me, A Little Bit You' with group-recorded B-side 'The Girl I Knew Somewhere,' makes #2 ... concerts in Canada ... shooting starts of second TV series as first nears end ... *Headquarters* third LP, makes #1 ... first TV series reruns with some new music ... more U.S. concerts ... 'Randy Scouse Git' released as 'Alternate Title' single in U.K., makes #2 ... TV episode shot in Paris, France ... concerts in London, England ... fourth single 'Pleasant Valley Sunday,' makes #3 ... long U.S. summer concert tour; Jimi Hendrix quits after seven shows ... last rerun of first TV season; second season debuts ... fourth LP *Pisces, Aquarius, Capricorn & Jones Ltd.* and fifth single 'Daydream Believer' both make #1 ... Michael records *The Wichita Train Whistle Sings* ... group members record separately ... Boyce & Hart remake 'Valleri.'

Seeing the world: Michael and Micky in Paris to film a special edition of the TV series.

JANUARY

More Of The Monkees album is released in the U.S.A. The group's second LP finds instant commercial success, even eclipsing the sales of the first album. Yet the group are incensed by the entire package, from the front cover, where they are pictured in tacky J.C. Penney's clothing, to the rear, which features a set of self-aggrandizing Don Kirshner liner notes, and on to the record inside, some of which they claim they have never even heard.

Peter: "The second record was so angering, because [of] Donnie Kirshner. He was almost militantly out to cut us out of the process. It was like he was angry at us. They designed the J.C. Penney clothes that we had to wear on the cover. Then the album came out without our having heard it and on the back of it is nothing but Donnie Kirshner congratulating himself for having hired all these other good musicians. We were playing our music on-stage, and we were righteously pissed.

"We obviously did parts of it and they put it together, but the fact that it was out there without our having heard it … . We had to buy the album to hear it. Somebody went across the street to the mall and bought the album."

Davy: "So Donnie Kirshner showed up all pleased and all great and said, 'Look guys, here's your second album,' with us dressed in J.C. Penney's clothes – which we thought was just a promotion we were going to get paid two thousand for. [We got] a thousand dollars … to sell their clothes and for Thom McAn shoes, all the shoes we could wear. Anyway, they all went bloody mad. Mike Nesmith and Peter Tork especially. 'What do you mean this is our album? They told us we were going to be doing our own album!'"

Micky: "To me, these were soundtrack albums to the show and it wasn't my job. My job was [as] an actor and to come in and sing the stuff when I was asked to do so. I had no problem with that. When I'd get an album I'd go, 'Wow, hey look, another album!' It wasn't until Mike and Peter started getting so upset about it that Davy and I started defending them and siding with them and getting concerned on their behalf. They were very upset about it because it wasn't the way that they were used to making music. The artist is the bottom line. The artist decides what songs are gonna go on and in what order and who writes 'em and who produces 'em. So they, right from the beginning, were in a very, very difficult situation. They were always compromising all the time."

A meeting with Kirshner does little to cool the situation. Although the group members will each receive substantial royalty checks for recent record sales, Michael insists that the method in which the records are released must change. Herb Moelis, head of business affairs at Colgems, reminds Michael that he is under contract and has no say in the matter. In a fit of anger, bravado, or both, Michael puts his fist through a wall and exclaims, "That could have been your face."

Don Kirshner recalls: "The incident when Mike Nesmith put his fist through the wall at the Beverly Hills Hotel is very vivid and near and dear to my heart. I had flown out to the Beverly Hills Hotel to give the boys a quarter of a million dollars apiece from some of the royalties on the first album. I was there with my wife Sheila, and my mother-in-law, Joyce, and we thought we were gonna celebrate.

"Mike had given me a lot of heat that he didn't like the records and he didn't like the albums. He wanted to do it his way. It was a little disconcerting to me because every album and single I put out was number one, but he had a right to his opinion.

"I handed each of them a check and I would have respected them if they hadn't taken the money. They all took the money, and

Mike proceeded to put his hand through the wall – which amazed me because I thought they were pretty solid walls – and said, 'We're not recording for you any more. We want to do our own thing.' And again, had he not taken the money, I would have had a lot of respect. But they all took the money, then went crying back to Bert [Schneider] and Bob [Rafelson]. Don't forget Bert's father was the president of Columbia Pictures, so he had a lot of clout. They said, 'We want to get rid of Donnie Kirshner.'

"I think the main problem with The Monkees at that time is a couple of 'em were really spoiled," Kirshner continues. "I think they were of modicum talent compared to the superstars of the days; they certainly weren't writers like Lennon & McCartney. I think they had a good thing going with the royalties they were getting. They wanted to have creative control and they thought they had more talent than they really had."

Despite the bruised feelings, a truce of sorts is struck with Kirshner. He agrees to meet with Chip Douglas, whom Michael recently approached about working with the band. Up to this point, Douglas has never produced a record on his own, but did recently arrange The Turtles' recording of 'Happy Together.' The single, which becomes one of the top hits of 1967, will reach the national charts in February and will be The Turtles' most successful record. Kirshner will give the go-ahead for Douglas to produce a session with The Monkees this month.

Chip Douglas: "They needed somebody to produce the group. A fifth Monkee, so to speak, a leader of the group. They didn't have a leader because they were all assembled – and it was wise for them to stay without one too."

More Of The Monkees album

A1 'She' (T. BOYCE / B. HART)
A2 'When Love Comes Knockin' (At Your Door)' (N. SEDAKA / C. BAYER)
A3 'Mary, Mary' (M. NESMITH)
A4 'Hold On Girl' version 2 (J. KELLER / B. RALEIGH / B. CARR)
A5 'Your Auntie Grizelda' (J. KELLER / D. HILDERBRAND)
A6 '(I'm Not Your) Steppin' Stone' (T. BOYCE / B. HART)
B1 'Look Out (Here Comes Tomorrow)' (N. DIAMOND)
B2 'The Kind Of Girl I Could Love' (M. NESMITH / R. ATKINS)
B3 'The Day We Fall In Love' (S. LINZER / D. RANDELL)
B4 'Sometime In The Morning' (G. GOFFIN / C. KING)
B5 'Laugh' (H. MEDRESS / P. MARGO / M. MARGO / J. SIEGEL)
B6 'I'm A Believer' (N. DIAMOND)

U.S. release January 1967 (Colgems COM-102 mono / COS-102 stereo).
U.K. release March 25th 1967 (RCA SF 7868).
Chart high U.S. number 1; U.K. number 1.

● **Sunday 1st**
PERFORMANCE Municipal Auditorium *Nashville, TN* 8:00pm; arena floor tickets $5; sponsored by radio station WKDA
● New year's day, and the group continue their first tour – that began late last year – with this concert at Nashville's Municipal Auditorium, grossing $36,820.

Sammy Davis Jr. visits the group in the TV studio during the making of episode 24, *Monkees A La Mode*, in January.

● Monday 2nd
PERFORMANCE Civic Center Arena *Tulsa, OK* reserved-seat tickets $4; sponsored by radio station KAKC
● The group performs tonight to 8,500 fans in Oklahoma with a set that includes 'I Wanna Be Free' accompanied by rear-projected scenes of a freedom march in Montgomery, Alabama. The group stay at the Mayo Hotel. The concert gross is $38,119.

● Thursday 5th
FILMING The *Monkees* crew are in production on what will become episode 26 of series, *Monkees Chow Mein*.
● Meanwhile in Britain the group finally crack the charts today with 'I'm A Believer.' During its 17-week British chart run the single will peak at #1.

● Friday 6th
FILMING Production wraps on *Monkees Chow Mein*.
● Overwhelming advance orders earn the group a gold record award for the *More Of The Monkees* album.

● Saturday 7th
● *New Musical Express* reports that The Monkees will make their first visit to Britain in February. This will be primarily a promotional trip, though a three-week concert tour in August with The Troggs is currently in the works. Troggs manager Larry Page will fly to America next week to hold discussions with what the *NME* describes as "Monkees management." The first UK pressing of 'I'm A Believer' has already sold out, and another 150,000 copies are due in the shops next week.

● Monday 9th
TV The NBC television network airs episode 17 of the *Monkees* series, *The Case Of The Missing Monkee*, at 7:30pm.

TVseries
The Monkees

EPISODE 17: *THE CASE OF THE MISSING MONKEE*
BROADCAST JANUARY 9TH
Peter stumbles into a plot to kidnap an esteemed professor and shortly thereafter stumbles out of sight.
WRITERS: GERALD GARDNER, DEE CARUSO. DIRECTOR: ROBERT RAFELSON.
SONG '(I'm Not Your) Steppin' Stone'

● Tuesday 10th
FILMING Sammy Davis Jr., currently filming a guest appearance on the Screen Gems TV show *I Dream Of Jeannie*, visits the set of *The Monkees* where production is in progress on what will become episode 24 of the series, *Monkees A La Mode*. Although Davis reportedly performs a quick cameo, no footage materializes in the final program.

● Wednesday 11th
● *Daily Variety* notes that the *Monkees* series now "boasts a healthy 18.5 Nielsen rating." (One rating point equals one percent of the 'TV households' in the U.S.A. according to the Nielsen calculations.)

● Thursday 12th
FILMING Production wraps on *Monkees A La Mode* as the group prepare for another weekend of concerts.

● Saturday 14th

PERFORMANCE Olympia Stadium *Detroit, MI* 7:30pm; tickets $5.50 seats, $3.50 standing; sponsored by radio station WKNR
● The group perform a sold-out concert to an audience of 15,573. Reportedly, 13 tactical mobile units are lined up outside just in case fan frenzy overwhelms the stadium. The concert will gross $74,707. (The 'gross' is the total amount of money taken at the box office.) After the performance the group are rushed off to Metropolitan Airport where they fly on to their next stop, Cleveland.
● *New Musical Express* reports that The Monkees are likely to film an episode of their series in Britain during their February visit. Over half a million copies have now been sold of 'I'm A Believer' in the UK, and the BBC claims that over five million homes tuned in to watch the TV series last week.

● Sunday 15th

PERFORMANCE Public Hall *Cleveland, OH* with Freddy Scott & The Go-Go-lets, Bobby Hart's Candy Store Prophets; sponsored by radio station WIXY
● The group perform for an hour to an audience of 10,255, and the gross take for this extravaganza is $50,718. The set includes 'I Wanna Be Free.'

● Monday 16th

● The Monkees, fresh from a weekend of concerts, hold their first recording session as a fully functioning, self-contained band. While the newly hired Chip Douglas essentially produces the session, Lester Sill attends the first half of the date to ensure that the combined efforts of Douglas and The Monkees are productive.
RECORDING RCA (A) *6363 Sunset Boulevard, Hollywood, CA* 10:00am-1:00pm, 2:00-6:00pm. Chip Douglas *prod*; Dick Bogert, Richie Schmitt *eng*; half-inch 4-track; tracking.
1. **'She's So Far Out, She's In'** takes 1-2
   Headquarters Sessions master # UPA3-8184
2. **'The Girl I Knew Somewhere'** version 1 takes 1-25
   Headquarters master # UPA3-8185
3. **'All Of Your Toys'** takes 1-20
   Headquarters master # UPA3-8186

Personnel Micky Dolenz (drums), David Jones (maracas 1, tambourine 2,3), John London (bass 2,3), Michael Nesmith (electric 12–string guitar), Peter Tork (bass 1, acoustic guitar 2, harpsichord 3).
● The session gets off to a bumpy start with Baker Knight's 'She's So Far Out, She's In.' Although the group have performed this song live at all of their concerts so far it is obvious that they have not really settled on an arrangement for the recording or even what instruments to play.
First, Peter asks to play bass in place of Michael's buddy John London. Then he announces: "Davy's instrument is maracas," although Davy is not playing them at this point. After several untaped rehearsals, take 1 is a false start and take 2 barely complete. During take 2 the tone and volume of Michael's guitar changes drastically from the intro to the body of the performance. Producer Chip Douglas comments that Peter's bass isn't cutting through. Seemingly, no satisfactory takes will ever be made of this song and no vocal overdubs are attempted (though Michael is probably the most likely to have sung the lead). The surviving tape of this song will be included on the limited-edition *Headquarters Sessions* set released in 2000.
For the first version of Michael's 'The Girl I Knew Somewhere' Peter switches to acoustic guitar, Davy to tambourine, and John London settles in on bass. The group loosens up considerably for this song and by take 16 they are, to use Chip Douglas's word, cookin'. In all, 25 takes are made, though only four of these are complete passes. Take 22 is considered the best and will be used as the basis for the final master. An excerpt from the session will be released on *Headquarters Sessions*, while a completed version of the song appears as a bonus track on 1995's expanded edition of the *Headquarters* CD.
Bill Martin's 'All Of Your Toys' is the last song attempted at this session and the recorded results are perhaps the best of the three songs taped today. From take 1 onwards the band sound well-rehearsed, playing with a beautiful, relaxed feel. A total of 20 takes are made in all, and takes 1, 3, 11, 17, 19 and 20 are full passes of the song. Take 20 is marked the best and is edited together with portions of takes 11, 15 and 17 to create the final master backing track. An excerpt from this session will later be found on *Headquarters Sessions* while the completed version of the song will appear as a bonus track on the regular *Headquarters* CD.
Chip Douglas: "We thought ['All Of Your Toys'] was going to be a great single. That was when I first became involved. I got real excited about the song when Bill Martin showed it to me. I didn't realize at the time that it didn't have a chorus. It was a song that didn't quite finish off right: it goes into this rip-off of the 'Paperback Writer' build-up in the middle, but it never had a chorus to it. And that's probably why it didn't ever get any excitement as a single. It was supposed to be a single: they were thinking about it, but they couldn't grab the publishing [rights], so it got canned."
TV It is possible that The Monkees finish today's session in time to catch episode 18 of their series, *I Was A Teenage Monster*, which is broadcast at 7:30pm this evening on the NBC network.

● Thursday 19th

FILMING Production wraps on what will become episode 27 of the *Monkees* series, *Monkee Mother*. Meanwhile at RCA Studios work continues on The Monkees' new 'group' recordings.
RECORDING RCA Studio *Hollywood, CA*. Chip Douglas *prod*; Hank Cicalo *eng*; half-inch 4-track; remixes, reductions.
1. **'All Of Your Toys'** reduction takes 1-5
   Headquarters master # UZB3-8186

Arriving in Detroit in January (ABOVE) for their performance at the city's Olympia Stadium.

Live at Cleveland's Public Hall. Rear-projection screens will be a part of nearly all Monkees concerts, featuring images of the show and other special clips. The group often stop to watch themselves on the screen.

TV series

The Monkees

EPISODE 18: *I WAS A TEENAGE MONSTER*
BROADCAST JANUARY 16TH
When a mad scientist creates a mod monster he hires The Monkees to make him rock'n'roll.
WRITERS: GERALD GARDNER, DEE CARUSO, DAVE EVANS. DIRECTOR: SIDNEY MILLER.
SONG 'Your Auntie Grizelda'

2. **'The Girl I Knew Somewhere'** version 1 reduction takes 1-5
Headquarters master # UZB3-8185
● Chip Douglas along with engineer Hank Cicalo prepares these two songs for overdubs and completion. First off, the basic track for 'All Of Your Toys' is reduced down to one track of a 4-track tape, at the same time adding equalization and compression. A total of five attempts are made at this process with the fifth marked best, and this will be used to create the final multi-track master. Identical treatment is given to 'The Girl I Knew Somewhere,' again with the fifth reduction being marked as best for the multi-track master. It is not clear if any overdubs are attempted by the group or if they are even present in the studio.

● **Friday 20th**
The Monkees album is released in the U.K. A belated release for the group's debut LP in Britain, where 'I'm A Believer" will reach #1 in the *NME* charts tomorrow.
● This evening The Monkees fly from L.A. to Phoenix's Sky Harbor Airport. Their arrival is filmed for an upcoming TV episode. This evening they take over radio station KRUX for two hours of records and mayhem (scenes of which are also featured in the TV series).

● **Saturday 21st**
PERFORMANCE Memorial Coliseum *Phoenix, AZ* sponsored by radio station KRUX
● The Monkees draw a crowd of 13,789 resulting in a gross take of $54,375.25, a house record. The original contract for this date has been ruled illegal because it calls for expenditures of state money for advertising. The contract is duly renegotiated to fit recent rulings by the Arizona attorney general's office, and the State Fair Commission receives 15 percent of the gross after taxes. The show is also subject to The Monkees' first 'remote' or live-location recording session.
LIVE RECORDING Memorial Coliseum *Phoenix, AZ* evening; half-inch 4-track.
1. **'Last Train To Clarksville'** live version 1
The Monkees Season 1 DVD
2. **'She's So Far Out, She's In'** live version
unissued
3. **'You Just May Be The One'** live version 1
unissued
4. **'I Wanna Be Free'** live version 1
The Monkees Season 1 DVD
5. **'Take A Giant Step'** live version
unissued

6. **'Sweet Young Thing'** live version 1
The Monkees Season 1 DVD
7. **'Papa Gene's Blues'** live version
unissued
8. **'I Can't Get Her Off My Mind'** live version
unissued
9. **'Mary, Mary'** live version 1
The Monkees Season 1 DVD
10. **'Cripple Creek'** live version 1
The Monkees Season 1 DVD
11. **'You Can't Judge A Book By The Cover'** live version 1
The Monkees Season 1 DVD
12. **'Gonna Build A Mountain'** live version 1
unissued
13. **'I Got A Woman'** live version 1
The Monkees Season 1 DVD
14. **'I'm A Believer'** live version 1
unissued
15. **'(I'm Not Your) Steppin' Stone'** live version 1
The Monkees Season 1 DVD

Personnel Micky Dolenz (vocal, drums), Bobby Hart (organ 11,12,13), David Jones (vocal, percussion, bass 14, drums 9), Billy Lewis (drums 11,12,13), Gerry McGee guitar 11,12,13), Michael Nesmith (vocal, guitar), Larry Taylor (bass 11,12,13), Peter Tork (vocal, bass, organ 14, banjo 10).

● Tonight's entire performance is professionally taped and filmed for use in the *Monkees* TV series. Although the show is captured on 4-track tape, no vocal performances are directly recorded. The short sections of the songs used for the television broadcast will have vocals overdubbed at a separate session (most likely during this month; dates and location unknown). No complete overdubbed versions of these songs with vocals are known to survive. The raw tape without vocals will circulate later among collectors.

● During the day, members of the group are also filmed at the Mountain Shadow riding stable, among other locations. Also today, producer Jeff Barry works back on the East Coast to prepare some new tracks for the Monkees project.

RECORDING RCA (B) *155 East 24th Street, New York, NY* 11:00am-2:30, 3:00-7:00pm. Jeff Barry *prod*; Ray Hall *eng*; half-inch 4-track; tracking.
1. **'Love To Love'** takes 1-14
Missing Links 3 master # UZB1-4403
2. **'You Can't Tie A Mustang Down'** takes 1-5
Daydream Believer And Other Hits master # UZB1-4401
3. **'Gotta Give It Time'** takes 1-4
unissued master # UZB1-4405
4. **'99 Pounds'** takes 1-7
Changes master # UZB1-4402
5. **'A Little Bit Me, A Little Bit You'** takes 1-4
Greatest Hits master # UZB1-4406
6. **'She Hangs Out'** version 1 takes 1-2
Missing Links 3 master # UZB1-4406

Personnel Artie Butler (organ 4 [except take 1]), Tom Cerone (tambourine), Stan Free (clavinet 1,4 [except take 1],5,6), Al Gorgoni (guitar), Herb Lovelle (drums), Lou Mauro (bass), Hugh McCracken (guitar), Don Thomas (guitar).

● This tracking session is Jeff Barry's first recording date for the group since November 1966, and he cuts six new songs as potential choices for their next single. The first song taped is Neil Diamond's moody but rocking 'Love To Love.' The studio musicians perform takes 1 through 5 in the key of B-flat and the remaining takes (6 through 14) in C minor. Barry does this so that he will have a choice of which Monkee to use to sing the lead. When a Monkee does attempt a vocal (in this case Davy) take 6 in B-flat is used as the master backing track for his overdubs. Although never used, take 14 is considered the best of the C minor takes.

Neil Diamond recalls: "It was just another one of the songs I was writing at the time. I never heard them do it. I haven't heard it in years. That goes way back. You know honestly, I don't ever remember sending it to The Monkees or The Monkees ever recording it. It may have been one of the songs I was writing for one of my albums that Jeff tried with them."

Jeff Barry's composition 'Mustang' is in a similar vein to Wilson Pickett's late 1966 hit 'Mustang Sally,' but more bubblegum than soul. After a brief rehearsal, five takes of the song are taped. The first three are performed in the key of F while the last two are played in G, again to provide options when it comes to choosing a vocalist. Take 3 will eventually be used when Davy overdubs a lead vocal.

After a loose rehearsal and jam session, the studio musicians next settle in to recording Joey Levine's promising 'Gotta Give It Time,' not coincidentally co-written with today's session producer Jeff Barry. Only four takes are made of this garage-styled rock number, the final one being marked as the master. Had The Monkees ever completed the recording it could have been another '(I'm Not Your) Steppin' Stone.'

Another Barry tune is the similarly rocking '99 Pounds.' No keyboards are heard during a guitar-dominated take 1 but Stan Free and Artie Butler return to play clavinet and organ respectively for all the remaining takes. By this point in the session Barry has left the control room and is leading the musicians from the studio floor where, off-mike, he sings and claps the musicians through the feel of each take. In all, seven takes are made of '99 Pounds,' with the last being marked as best.

For Neil Diamond's 'A Little Bit Me, A Little Bit You' two of the guitarists on the session switch to acoustic instruments, a six-string and a 12-string. The change helps to capture the classic Everly Brothers-style feel of the song's strummed introduction. Only four takes are taped of the tune, which will become The Monkees' next single. The last take is marked the best and used for all future overdubs.

The final song of the session is another Jeff Barry tune, this one co-written with his ex-wife Ellie Greenwich. It's captured in just two takes, of which the first isn't even complete, and Barry quickly puts the wraps on a highly successful session. With six songs tracked in little more than six hours, the producer has not only taped the next Monkees single but also several potential album tracks.

(Although RCA's original recording sheet for today's date lists two bassists for every song – Louis Mauro and James Tyrell – a review of the session tapes reveals only one audible bassist. Producer Jeff Barry is heard speaking with bassist Mauro on several occasions, so he is the musician credited here. It is possible that Tyrell does play at some point but he is certainly not present throughout the entire session.)

● Sunday 22nd

PERFORMANCE Cow Palace *San Francisco, CA* sponsored by radio station KFRC

● The group perform in concert for an audience of 15,283, resulting in a gross take of $72,362. Davy is made an honorary fire chief for the day by the Daly City Fire Department and poses for a series of photos at their station. Portions of tonight's performance may be professionally filmed and integrated into the edited footage for *The Monkees On Tour* episode of the television series. Most of the production crew of the *Monkees* series are on hand to experience their first in-person taste of Monkeemania.

TV series director Jim Frawley: "That same weekend they played two places and we shot both; we intercut the two of them. We had four or five cameras. It was really a revelation for me because [we] worked on this very insular soundstage. … Their records were selling and you knew they had fans, but you didn't really get the full impact of their popularity until you put a camera on your shoulder and shot one of their concerts. You really got a sense of their personalities and their music."

RECORDING RCA (B) *New York, NY* 1:00-7:30pm. Denny Randell *prod*; Ray Hall *eng*; half-inch 4-track; tracking, overdubs.

1. **'I Wanna Be Your Puppy Dog'** takes 1-10
   unissued master # UZB1-4415
2. **'Love Is On The Way'** takes 1-7
   unissued master # UZB1-4413
3. **'I Didn't Know You Had It In You Sally, You're A Real Ball Of Fire'** takes 1-4
   unissued master # UZB1-4414
4. **'Sugar Man'** takes 1-6
   unissued master # UZB1-4416

Personnel Artie Butler (tambourine 1, percussion 2,3, drums 4, percussion 4), Don Butterfield (tuba 3), Ralph Casale (guitar 1,2,4), Dom Cortese (accordion 2), Stan Free (clavinet 1, percussion including mallets 2,4, tack piano* 3), Al Gorgoni (guitar 1,2,4), Joseph Grimaldi (saxophone 3), Artie Kaplan (soprano saxophone 3), Joe Macho (bass), Charlie Macy (guitar 1,2,4, banjo 3), Seldon Powell (saxophone 3), Bob Rand (guitar 1,2,4), Buddy Salzman (drums). (* A 'tack' piano is one with specially hardened hammers for a percussive, jangling sound.)

● Don Kirshner's recent signing Denny Randell, who has provided the group with such songs as 'I'll Be Back Up On My Feet' and 'The Day We Fall In Love,' gets a crack at producing The Monkees. While Jeff Barry's last New York recording session was earmarked by RCA for working on single releases, it is quite possible that today's activities are aimed at generating album tracks. Kirshner admits that, based on the popularity of 'I'm A Believer,' he has already promised Jeff Barry and Neil Diamond the follow-up single release. Certainly the songs generated by Randell – and to a lesser extent his production work – are not of the same caliber as Jeff Barry's.

Randell and Sandy Linzer's 'Puppy Dog' is a straightforward rock'n'roll tune, rather outdated for 1967. Tracking for the song is completed in ten takes, with the last marked best. ('Tracking' means the recording of basic instrumentation, before any vocals or other overdubs are added.) Jazzman Jimmy Wisner is the arranger for this session and conducts the band from the studio floor, but does not play any instrument.

After a break the musicians return to record another Linzer & Randell tune, 'Love Is On The Way.' This is a mid-tempo pop ballad with accordion by Dom Cortese thrown in for color. It's taped in seven takes with the last cut marked as the master. During the entire session two tape machines are run simultaneously. On one of the resulting tapes an additional guitar part is experimentally added to the intro of 'Love Is On The Way' take 7 but this effort is later marked "DO NOT USE."

The session takes a musical left turn when the musicians veer from MOR pop into 1920s nostalgia with 'I Didn't Know You Had It In You Sally, You're A Real Ball Of Fire.' It's probably inspired by the late-'66 success of The New Vaudeville Band's 'Winchester Cathedral' and could make a passable song-and-dance number for Davy. So it is surprising that more than two years after today's session – on September 15th 1969 – Micky will overdub a lead vocal onto take 4. Though this recording is not released, it will be the only song from today's session to come into close contact with an actual Monkee.

The date closes with six takes of Linzer & Randell's 'Sugar Man,' a Bo Diddley/Strangeloves-styled stomp similar to 'I Want Candy.' A slightly edited take 6 is marked as the master. In later years Kirshner and others will often remark that during the infamous wall-busting Beverly Hills Hotel meeting Kirshner offered The Monkees a demo of Jeff Barry and Andy Kim's 'Sugar, Sugar,' later a hit for The Archies. It is more likely that he offered the band 'Sugar Man,' given that he is currently hot on Linzer & Randell.

● Monday 23rd
● The Monkees, back from their concert in San Francisco, set about completing their 'group' recordings.
RECORDING RCA (A) *Hollywood, CA* 10:00am-1:00, 2:00-7:00, 8:30pm-12midnight. Chip Douglas *prod*; half-inch 4-track; reductions, overdubs.
1. **'All Of Your Toys'**
   Headquarters master # UZB3-8186
2. **'The Girl I Knew Somewhere'** version 1
   Headquarters master # UZB3-8185
● Though no tapes will survive from this session, it's probably today that The Monkees begin the process of overdubbing their vocals and additional instruments onto these two songs. American Federation of Musicians documents reveal that John London is present at this session from 1:00 to 3:00pm and may have participated musically in the overdubs.
TV At 7:30pm the NBC network airs episode 19 of the *Monkees* series, *Find The Monkees*. The broadcast occurs during a break in tonight's session, so the group possibly stop to watch their program.

TVseries

The Monkees

EPISODE 19: *THE AUDITION (FIND THE MONKEES)*
BROADCAST JANUARY 23RD
The Monkees try to impress TV producer Hubbell Benson who is looking for a group to star in his show.
WRITERS: GERALD GARDNER, DEE CARUSO. DIRECTOR: RICHARD NUNIS.
SONGS 'Sweet Young Thing,' 'Papa Gene's Blues,' 'I'm A Believer'

● Tuesday 24th
RECORDING RCA (A) *Hollywood, CA* 1:00-9:00pm. Chip Douglas *prod*; half-inch 4-track.
● Very few details exist for this session but it is probably a continuation of the work started yesterday for 'All Of Your Toys' and 'The Girl I Knew Somewhere' version 1.
● Elsewhere, Stu Phillips employs 11 session musicians from 10:00am to 1:00pm to tape the incidental music score for *The Monkees* episodes *Captain Crocodile* and *Monkees At The Circus*.

● Wednesday 25th
● *Weekly Variety* runs the headline "No Biz Like 'Monkees' Biz" and has the facts and figures to back up this claim. The accompanying article by Jack Pitman lays out the details of Screen Gems earnings on The Monkees empire and reveals it to be quite a racket.

The Monkees' two albums have now sold well over five million copies while their singles have surpassed four million sales.
Putman writes: "Screen Gems pockets the big loot, picking up a production fee of 10-15 percent per disc" plus the publishing at 25 cents per song. The series meanwhile is quite a steal at only $75,000 per show, "the result of well-pared costs all around – talent production, script, etc."
The Monkees take home only $400 a week, while the scripts are assembled by a staff of writers also on a flat weekly rate and not a per-script fee, which is the current industry norm.
The band's concert appearances also represent something of a financial first. "Arena managements get no more than a flat 10 percent of the gate (they do better than that, even with The Beatles), while Screen Gems and Dick Clark Productions, producer of the tours, divvy the big remainder."
Astonishingly, the band members are only paid their weekly fee as 'actors.' No additional recompense comes to them for travel. Advertising and promotional outlays are also low since each show has a radio sponsor, who will plug the show and themselves incessantly for free, just to be a part of the bonanza. Screen Gems' only other expense is to give away some free records.
The pending suit by TV producers David Yarnell and David Gordon is also discussed in the *Weekly Variety* piece. In pre-trial depositions the two now claim they presented their idea for a *Monkees*-style show directly to Bert Schneider in October or November of 1964. They say a few months later he teamed with Bob Rafelson to launch Raybert. This rather sticky allegation will not disappear quietly, and depositions will continue through the summer.

● Thursday 26th
FILMING Production is in progress on what will become episode 20 of *The Monkees*, titled *Monkees Get Out More Dirt*. From 11:00am to 7:15pm a string quartet is hired to perform on set while Peter acts out a scene where he conducts a piece of classical music. Meanwhile in the studio Jeff Barry and Chip Douglas are active as the race to complete new Monkees material continues.
RECORDING RCA (B) *New York, NY* 11:00am-2:00pm, 3:00-6:30pm. Jeff Barry *prod*; Ray Hall *eng*; half-inch 4-track; tracking.
1. **'Poor Little Me'** takes 1-14
   unissued master # UZB1-4408
2. **'If I Learned To Play The Violin'** takes 1-5
   Hey Hey We're The Monkees CD-ROM master # UZB1-4409
3. **'Black And Blue'** takes 1-6
   unissued master # UVB1/UZB1-4411
4. **'Eve Of My Sorrow'** takes 1-7
   unissued master # UZB1-4410
5. **'The Love You Got Inside'** takes 1-9
   unissued master # UZB1-4412
Personnel Artie Butler (organ), Tom Cerone (tambourine 1,2), Sal DiTroia (guitar), Stan Free (clavinet), Herb Lovelle (drums), Hugh McCracken (guitar), Don Thomas (guitar), James Tyrell (bass).
● Jeff Barry tapes five new recordings today. From the three New York sessions held this month alone there is enough material to fill another Monkees album.
The first instrumental backing taped today is Barry's 'Poor Little Me,' a country and western tinged number he co-wrote with Andy Kim. A total of 14 takes are made of the song with the last marked as the master.
After this, Artie Resnick and Joey Levine's sugary ballad, 'If I Learned To Play The Violin,' is committed to tape. Despite its suspect quality, the song (recorded in five takes) is the only one

recorded today that will ultimately be given a Monkees lead-vocal overdub. Davy will do the honors on take 5 next month.

For 'Black And Blue' Jeff Barry moves from the control room to the studio floor to conduct the musicians. The song is a collaborative effort between Neil Diamond and songwriting legends Jerry Leiber and Mike Stoller. This is the last Neil Diamond song ever recorded for or by The Monkees and is taped in six takes, of which take 6 is marked as the master.

Barry returns to the control room for his composition 'Eve Of My Sorrow,' a slow ballad he has co-written with Joey Levine and Leiber & Stoller. The song is completed in seven takes, with lucky take 7 taking the prize for master. The final song taped today is the most promising of the bunch. A creation by Barry, Andy Kim, and Leiber & Stoller, 'The Love You Got Inside' is recorded in nine passes. Sadly, this upbeat pop number will never receive a Monkee vocal overdub. Meanwhile, another session is taking place over in Los Angeles.

RECORDING RCA (B) *6363 Sunset Boulevard, Hollywood, CA* 2:00-5:00pm. Chip Douglas *prod*; half-inch 4-track.
No further details are available.

● Friday 27th
● The first 'Monkees Club' is officially opened by Greg Merhige in West Caldwell, New Jersey. The idea is to showcase new talent "in a theatre environment" where teenagers are easily admitted – no alcoholic is to be sold – and there is to be no dancing. Thirty-four more of these clubs are apparently planned though it is unclear if any are ever opened. (Certainly more are solicited – see entry for March 25th.)

The Monkees' record label, Colgems, will have first right of refusal on any talent discovered at the clubs, which hold auditions on Sundays. *Record World* says: "The Monkees themselves won attention after talent auditions [and] this Monkees discovery pattern will now be adapted at the Monkees Clubs." Winners of the contests will play a circuit of the other clubs. It is unknown if any talent is actually discovered at this venue.

This first club has been open for several weeks prior to tonight's grand opening and the organizers now plan to open regularly from 7:00pm to 12midnight on Fridays and Saturdays and 2:00 to 6:00pm on Sundays. The menu consists of soft drinks and "elaborate ice cream concoctions." Admission is $1 per person before 9:30pm.

FILMING Back in tinsel town, the group continue work on episode 29 of the *Monkees* series, *Monkees Get Out More Dirt*. The same string quartet from yesterday is employed (from 9:00am–6:00pm) to complete their scene with Peter. Shooting probably wraps on this program at day's end. Meanwhile in the studio Denny Randell holds his second recording session for The Monkees.

RECORDING RCA (B) *New York, NY* 11:00am-2:00pm, 3:00-7:00pm. Denny Randell *prod*; Ray Hall *eng*; half-inch 4-track; reductions, overdubs.

1. **'I Wanna Be Your Puppy Dog'** overdub takes A-J onto take 10
   unissued master # UZB1-4415
2. **'Love Is On The Way'** overdub takes A-P onto take 7
   unissued master # UZB1-4413
3. **'Sugar Man'** overdub takes A-C onto take 6
   unissued master # UZB1-4416

Personnel Ralph Casale (guitar), Stan Free (clavinet 1, percussion 2,3), Al Gorgoni (guitar), Don Thomas (guitar), unknown (handclaps 1, lead and backing vocal 1 [take 1 only], percussion 3).
● Denny Randell returns to the studio to make additions and improvements to three of the tracks from his January 22nd session. He works with arranger Jimmy Wisner and engineer Ray Hall to

make reduction mixes of the previous work to two tracks of a fresh 4-track tape while adding new overdubs. This leaves two tracks open for vocals.

'Puppy Dog' features added handclaps, clavinet fills, and guitars. Take I (marked as the master from this session) also features the lead and backing vocal work of an unknown group of singers (probably including Randell) who fill all the remaining tape tracks. This version gives a glimpse of what a finished product could be, revealing the song to be a rather trite, Everly Brothers-influenced bit of pre-teen fluff. Mercifully, no Monkees version of the song is ever completed.

Some additional guitar and percussion are added to take 7 of 'Love Is On The Way' from the January 22nd session. Take P is the new master for today but will be soon be superseded by take R recorded tomorrow. 'Sugar Man' is sweetened with tambourine and shaker among other things. Only one successful reduction/overdub take is made today – take C – but work will resume tomorrow.

● Saturday 28th
● *The Saturday Evening Post* publishes an in-depth exposé on The Monkees and the powers behind their collective entity. Michael talks candidly about the phenomenon, leaving nothing to the imagination. "The music had nothing to do with us," he tells the *Post*. "It was totally dishonest. Do you know how debilitating it is to sit up and have to duplicate somebody else's records? That's really what we're doing. The music happened in spite of The Monkees.

"It was what Kirshner wanted to do. Our records are not our forté. I don't care if we never sell another record. Maybe we were manufactured and put on the air strictly with a lot of hoopla. Tell the world we're synthetic because, damn it, we are. Tell them The Monkees are wholly man-made overnight, that millions of dollars have been poured into this thing. Tell the world we don't record our own music. But that's us they see on television. The show is really a part of us. They're not seeing something invalid." Michael's candor will earn The Monkees little added respect within the industry or the general public.

He recalls later: "The press decided they were going to unload on us as being somehow illegitimate, somehow false. That we were making an attempt to dupe the public, when in fact it was me that was making the attempt to maintain the integrity. So, the press went into a full scale war against us. Talking about 'The Monkees are four guys who have no credits, no credibility whatsoever, who have been trying to trick us into believing that they are a rock band.'

"Number one, not only was it not the case, the reverse was true. Number two, [for] the press to report with genuine alarm that The Monkees were not a real rock band was loony tunes. It was one of the great goof ball moments of the media, but it stuck. So that, by the time '67 rolled around, we were completely into the target window of the press and, which was even worse, we were wildly successful.

"The records were going number one. We were sellin' millions of 'em. We were doin' record-setting stadium shows and the people who had somehow got it into their minds The Monkees weren't a real rock band – which of course is just absurd, because they never were a rock band – decided that this was some kind of great hoax that was being perpetrated. The rabid element and the hatred that was engendered was almost impossible to describe. It lingers to this day among people my own age."
● On BBC Radio in Britain the group are featured in a ten-minute interview with DJ Chris Denning on *Where It's At*. Their conversation is interspersed with music from their latest album to complete a 30-minute show. Meanwhile in New York, Denny Randell continues his studio sessions for The Monkees.

RECORDING RCA (B) *New York, NY* 4:30-7:30pm. Denny Randell *prod*; Ray Hall *eng*; half-inch 4-track; reductions, overdubs.
1. **'Love Is On The Way'** takes Q-R onto take 7
   unissued master # UZB1-4413
2. **'Sugar Man'** takes D-H onto take 6
   unissued master # UZB1-4416
3. **'I Didn't Know You Had It In You Sally, You're A Real Ball Of Fire'** takes A-E onto take 4
   unissued master # UZB1-4414
Personnel Don Thomas (guitar 2 [take G only]), unknown (drums 1, vocal 1,2,3 [take E only], percussion 2, organ 2, tambourine 3).
● Continuing yesterday's work, producer Denny Randell makes two further reductions of 'Love Is On The Way.' Today's master (take R) features additional drums and guide vocals from unknown singers, probably including Randell. Though a Monkees vocal version of this song will never surface, Linzer & Randell will record their own take in a few months, releasing it as a single on Columbia in August this year.

The already percussive 'Sugar Man' is given some added punch with shaker and tambourine overdubs. On take G an organ and guitar solo are taped alongside guide vocals from singers (undocumented but probably including Randell again).

The last song of the session, 'Sally,' is given a tambourine overdub and, on take E only, some guide vocals. Micky will dub a vocal onto this 4-track master – but not for another 31 months! This song brings the Denny Randell sessions to a close. Over on the West Coast, meanwhile, the tapes are just starting to roll.
RECORDING RCA (B) *Hollywood, CA* 2:00-5:00pm. Chip Douglas *prod*; half-inch 4-track.
● Few details are known about this four-hour session, though it's probably called for final overdubs on 'All Of Your Toys' and 'The Girl I Knew Somewhere' version 1.

● **Monday 30th**
RECORDING RCA (B) *Hollywood, CA* 10:00-1:00, 2:00-4:00, 5:00-7:00pm. Chip Douglas *prod*; Hank Cicalo *eng*; half-inch 4-track; demo.
1. **'Seeger's Theme'** demo takes 1-3
   Headquarters Sessions master # UZB3-8187
2. **'All Of Your Toys'**
   Headquarters master # UZB3-8186
3. **'The Girl I Knew Somewhere'** version 1
   Headquarters master # UZB3-8185
Personnel Peter Tork (acoustic guitar, whistling 1).
● Amidst work on the group's next single Chip Douglas encourages the band members to find songs they like and demo them on acoustic guitar (see also February 24th, October 28th). This first example of these informal recordings is Peter's demo version of 'Seeger's Theme.' Ultimately he will tape multiple arrangements of this simple melody penned by his folk mentor, Pete Seeger, but today's sparse run-throughs are perhaps the best ever committed to tape. Take 3 will later be included on 2000's *Headquarters Sessions* set. On October 28th this take, along with the other acoustic oddities from the year, will be compiled into a fascinating odds-and-ends reel of performances.

Unspecified work also continues on two other songs, with Chip Douglas, Michael Nesmith, and John London all present. The session breaks up at 7:00pm, after which the participants rush home

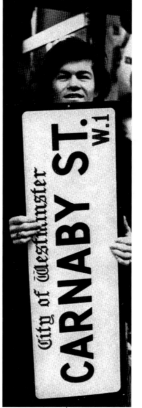

TVseries

The Monkees

EPISODE 20: *MONKEES IN THE RING*
BROADCAST JANUARY 30TH
A shady promoter enters Davy into the ring as an unlikely boxing champion.
WRITERS: GERALD GARDNER, DEE CARUSO. DIRECTOR: JAMES FRAWLEY.
SONGS 'Laugh,' 'I'll Be Back Up On My Feet'

to catch episode 20 of the *Monkees* series, *Monkees In The Ring*, which airs at 7:30pm on NBC.

● **Tuesday 31st**
● RCA (B) *Hollywood, CA* 2:00-6:00, 7:00pm-12midnight. Chip Douglas *prod*; Hank Cicalo *eng*; half-inch 4-track; overdubs, mixdown.
1. **'All Of Your Toys'**
   Headquarters master # UZB3-8186
2. **'The Girl I Knew Somewhere'** version 1
   Headquarters master # UZB3-8185
● At this session masters are finalized for The Monkees' recent 'group' recordings, vocals for which have been recorded over the last few days. Musicians' union records indicate that between the hours of 3:00 and 6:00pm Michael, Peter, and John London are present at this session in addition to producer Chip Douglas.

FEBRUARY

● Britain's Beat Publications publishes the premiere issue of *Monkees Monthly*, the world's first Monkees-only magazine – but not the last.
● The Challenge label releases a pre-Monkees recording by Micky called 'Don't Do It.' The disc is a successful attempt to cash in on his recent popularity and will enter the charts in March. Challenge have cleverly coupled 'Don't Do It' with a non-Dolenz track on the flipside, giving the label an option for a spin-off single with a second track they have purchased. This follow-up, 'Huff Puff,' will appear later this year (see July 6th).

● **Thursday 2nd**
FILMING Production wraps on the *Monkees* first season with the completion of what will become episode 28 of the series, *Monkees On The Line*. This leaves the group free to travel (and record) through April.
RECORDING RCA (B) *Hollywood, CA* 8:00-10:00pm. Chip Douglas *prod*; Hank Cicalo *eng*; quarter-inch mono; mixdown.
● This brief two-hour session probably produces the final mono

mixes from the completed multi-tracks of 'All Of Your Toys' and 'The Girl I Knew Somewhere' version 1, intended for Kirshner's review and potential single release.

● Saturday 4th

● With filming and recording commitments now wrapped, the group members take well-deserved vacations. Michael and his wife Phyllis along with Micky and producer Chip Douglas fly to New York City for the weekend. Micky and Michael are due in England for a promotional visit at the beginning of next week.

During this evening in New York, Micky visits the Night Owl club for a performance by The Flying Machine, after which he returns to his hotel, the Sherry-Netherlands, to pick up Davy, who has apparently flown to New York in advance of Michael and Micky. Davy and Micky, alongside several members of Paul Revere's Raiders, take in a performance of The Daily Flash at Ondine's. Earlier today, Davy joined Jeff Barry in the studio to overdub his voice onto several of the producer's recent productions.

RECORDING RCA (B) *New York, NY*. Jeff Barry *prod*; Ray Hall *eng*; half-inch 4-track; reductions, overdubs.

1. **'A Little Bit Me, A Little Bit You'** overdub takes A-G + pick-up endings onto take 4
   Greatest Hits master # UZB1-4406
2. **'You Can't Tie A Mustang Down'** reduction takes 1-4 of take 3
   Daydream Believer & Other Hits master # UZB1-4401
3. **'If I Learned To Play The Violin'** overdub takes 1-6
   Hey Hey We're The Monkees CD-ROM master # UZB1-4409
4. **'Love To Love'** reduction takes 6 and 14
   Missing Links 3 master # UZB1-4403
5. **'She Hangs Out'** version 1 reduction take 2
   Missing Links 3 master # UZB1-4406
6. **'99 Pounds'** reduction take 7
   Changes master # UZB1-4402

Personnel David Jones (vocal 1,3,5,6), unknown (backing vocal 5,6).

● Under the guidance of producer Jeff Barry, Davy dubs his voice onto Barry's recent round of Kirshner-approved material not performed by the group. Davy is the most reluctant to upset Kirshner's proven hit-making formula with the non-group productions. While Davy's involvement in this session shows a certain lack of solidarity with his bandmates – who now wish to make their own records – it is probably a simple case of Davy keeping his options open.

Barry begins the session by making a reduction mix of the 4-track tape of 'A Little Bit Me, A Little Bit You' from January. (In a 'reduction' all the instrumental tracks are combined to a single track of a new 4-track tape, allowing maximum space for overdubs.) After Davy's first complete vocal is recorded (take B) Barry immediately begins taping Davy doubling this vocal. These recordings, with a new vocal alongside the take B vocal, are marked as takes C, D and E.

Take E is an almost complete doubled vocal, so Barry has Davy record a third vocal onto the remaining open track of tape. The tripled vocal takes are labeled takes F and G. Davy's first vocal (take B) was a rather off-the-cuff affair, and Barry seems comfortable rushing through the overdubs. This means that Davy has to try several takes of the ending (coming out of the organ solo) to get the vocal ad-libs to 'synch' or match up. After the three vocals are fully taped, Davy does quite a bit of vocal clean-up to try to improve the early passes and harmonize some of the lyrics. These efforts are 'punched in' on top of portions of earlier vocals, and so no new take numbers are documented. More work will be done to finalize this production later in the month.

For 'Mustang' Barry bounces the session 4-track of take 3 down to a single track of a second 4-track tape. Four passes are made until he is satisfied with the mix of the backing track, but no Davy vocals are recorded today. Davy will eventually record his vocals for 'Mustang' at another session some two-and-a-half years later (see August 5th 1969).

A similar pattern is followed for 'If I Learned To Play The Violin.' A single bounce-down to a new tape achieves a master onto which Davy can overdub his vocals. The session tape box officially logs only takes 1 through 6 as vocal overdubs, but several more attempts at are made by Davy. One can sympathize with the vocalist on this number, since he is rushed through the proceedings and can do little to save this lamentable composition. Ultimately, Davy dubs a total of three acceptable vocals onto the master tape, but the song will never be originally issued. (During the 1990s, while reviewing this session tape, this author will make a rough mix of the song. This mix is released in 1996 on a Monkees CD-ROM, *Hey Hey We're The Monkees*. Thus far, this is the song's only official release.)

Next, reductions are made of both master takes of 'Love To Love,' one in C minor, the other in B-flat. Nevertheless, Davy will not record any vocals for it today. As with 'Mustang' he will dub his vocals at a session on August 5th 1969.

After a reduction mix, 'She Hangs Out' version 1 is not only given a lead vocal overdub from Davy but the singer also participates in a backing-vocal session with another unnamed vocalist (possibly Jeff Barry). Two tracks of the 4-track tape remain open for further overdubs (see February 6th).

For his final performance of the day, Davy busts out his best soul shout and turns in a very confident performance on Jeff Barry's '99 Pounds.' The final master features a double-tracked vocal from Davy on two separate tape tracks. Further 'sweetening' will be added at a session on February 6th.

● Sunday 5th

● Micky spends Sunday shopping in Greenwich Village in New York

LEFT Taking home a piece of Swinging London. **ABOVE** Micky enjoys a day hanging out with Paul McCartney in February and the two are pictured together at the Beatle's house in St John's Wood, north London.

City but soon finds the crowds too unruly to enjoy himself freely. After a quick carriage ride through Central Park he prepares for his 7:45pm flight to London. Davy will also leave New York today, flying to Nassau in The Bahamas. Around this time Peter will venture back east to visit his old haunts in the Village. All the while, Jeff Barry works towards completing his recent productions.

RECORDING RCA (B) *New York, NY*. Jeff Barry *prod*; Ray Hall *eng*; half-inch 4-track; reductions.

1. **'Love To Love'**
   Missing Links 3 master # UZB1-4403
2. **'She Hangs Out'**
   Missing Links 3 master # UZB1-4404
3. **'99 Pounds'**
   Changes master # UZB1-4402
4. **'If I Learned To Play The Violin'**
   Hey Hey We're The Monkees CD-ROM master # UZB1-4409
5. **'A Little Bit Me, A Little Bit You'**
   Greatest Hits master # UZB1-4406

● Jeff Barry and engineer Ray Hall clean up their work from yesterday, making reductions so that more overdubs can be added. A later report in the *New Musical Express* reveals that Micky may have stopped by this session on the way to the airport today. But his musical involvement is highly unlikely since the drummer has now fully sided with Michael and Peter and no longer wishes to be involved in Kirshner's productions.

● Monday 6th

● Micky flies to England. After a brief stopover at Shannon Airport in Ireland he arrives in London for an eventful day, kicking off with a reception from 300 fans who mob him at the airport. Breaking free, he handles a throng of reporters eager to interview him. Later in the evening he meets Paul McCartney at a London disco and is invited to McCartney's house in St. John's Wood, London.

McCartney is enjoying a day off from filming promo clips for The Beatles' forthcoming single and plays Micky a preview of 'Penny Lane,' 'Strawberry Fields Forever' and one other song. The landmark single will not be issued to the public for a further 11 days.

Towards the early hours of the morning McCartney entertains Micky by playing a special left-handed sitar. At 2:00am Brian Epstein invites Micky, McCartney and their entourage to his flat to watch films of The Spencer Davis Group and Cream. Two and a half hours later McCartney drives Micky back to his hotel in the Beatle's Aston Martin.

Micky: "We just sat around listening to the tracks from his next LP and he played us 'Penny Lane' and 'Strawberry Fields.' They're both beautiful numbers, but I prefer 'Strawberry Fields' – it's more progressive. It's the kind of music I want to do."

● Michael and Phyllis Nesmith depart from New York City for London. Another celebrity present on their flight is Cass Elliot of The Mamas & Papas. A recording of Michael discussing his interaction with Cass on this flight made during a Monkees overdub session on March 9th will be released much later on *Headquarters Sessions*. Meanwhile in the same city Jeff Barry does some final 'sweetening' on his sessions.

RECORDING RCA (B) *New York, NY*. Jeff Barry *prod*; Ray Hall *eng*; half-inch 4-track; reductions, overdubs.

1. **'If I Learned To Play The Violin'**
   Hey Hey We're The Monkees CD-ROM master # UZB1-4409

2. **'She Hangs Out'** version 1
Missing Links 3 master # UZB1-4404
3. **'A Little Bit Me, A Little Bit You'**
Greatest Hits master # UZB1-4406
4. **'99 Pounds'**
Changes master # UZB1-4402
Personnel Neil Diamond (backing vocal 3, handclaps 3), unknown (backing vocal 2,3,4, handclaps 3,4).
● Attempts are made to combine Davy's triple-tracked vocals on 'Violin' but no further improvements can be made and the production of this rather weak ballad goes no further. However, producer Jeff Barry does add some backing vocals from a group of uncredited session singers to 'She Hangs Out,' thus completing the song's production. It will be mixed on February 10th.

After some editing of the vocal performances on 'A Little Bit Me' Barry decides to dump one of Davy's three vocal tracks in favor of backing vocals from the same singers. Neil Diamond is on hand for this portion of the session and, in the process of adding claps and vocals, discusses the tan he got on a recent vacation.

At this stage the master consists of one track of backing vocals, two tracks of Davy's lead vocal, and an instrumental backing on one track. In 1969, this incomplete multi-track will be used to prepare a stereo mix of 'A Little Bit Me, A Little Bit You' for the *Monkees Greatest Hits* album. This will remain the only available 'true' stereo mix of the song. Despite the fact that it lacks the strength – and handclaps – of the final single mix, the version will appear on countless compilations until the discovery in the late 1980s of the final overdub session master. After that, a mono remix from the session tape will be used.

Barry completes this production by overdubbing the handclaps. Lacking an open track on which to record them, engineer Ray Hall makes a copy of the tape and simultaneously mixes the claps onto the same track as the backing vocals. 'A Little Bit Me' will be mixed on February 8th.

To complete '99 Pounds,' backing vocals and handclaps are added to the final master. Again lacking an open track on which to dub the claps, Hall makes a copy of the tape and simultaneously adds the claps to the same track as the backing. Although the song is completed today, it will be left in the can until 1970 when The Monkees reunite with Barry as producer for their *Changes* album. For now, a mono mix will be made on February 8th.

TV At 7:30 this evening the NBC network televises episode 21 of the *Monkees* series, *The Prince And The Pauper*. This broadcast will win its time slot for viewership, attracting an audience of nearly 12 million, the best rating for the series so far.

TVseries

The Monkees

EPISODE 21: *THE PRINCE AND THE PAUPER*
BROADCAST FEBRUARY 6TH
Davy comes to the aid of a lovelorn Prince Ludlow – who just happens to be Davy's doppelganger.
WRITERS: GERALD GARDNER, DEE CARUSO, PETER MEYERSON. DIRECTOR: JAMES KOMACK.
SONGS 'Mary, Mary'

● **Tuesday 7th**
● Michael and Phyllis Nesmith arrive in London. Meanwhile, Micky makes an early-morning shopping trip to Carnaby Street where he buys six new suits at the Lord John shop. He later appears on two BBC programs, *Pop-Inn* and *24 Hours*.

On *24 Hours* he is interviewed by Cliff Michelmore, who asks: "Does it worry you that you are, in effect, a manufactured pop star?" Micky replies: "No, not a bit, because we weren't. I was discovered going to school, L.A. Trade Tech. Mike was discovered in The Troubadour singing to 15 people every night. Peter was discovered in Greenwich Village singing to two people every night. And Davy was discovered trying to get a job singing to anybody in L.A.. Yes, we were discovered. No, we're not a manufactured group. Where do you draw the line?"

Rounding off a hectic day, Micky attends a show at the Marquee club by his current favorite band, The Spencer Davis Group, and will end the night at the Scotch Of St. James club. Both the Nesmiths and Micky stay at the Grosvenor House Hotel in plush Park Lane.

● **Wednesday 8th**
● At 10:30am a BBC crew films Micky at Regents Park Zoo for about an hour and a half. He returns to the Grosvenor for a lunch date with Spencer Davis and, later, does some more shopping on Carnaby Street.
● Elsewhere in London, it's possibly today that Michael and Phyllis Nesmith attend a recording session by The Kinks at Pye Recording Studios in ATV House, Marble Arch.
● In the evening, Michael and Phyllis meet up with Micky and Paul McCartney at the Bag O' Nails club in London. Meanwhile, Davy travels to Kingston, Jamaica from The Bahamas.
● *Weekly Variety* runs a piece titled "Monkees Pace Biz Recovery" about the group's recent U.K. successes. Roger Watkins reports that 'I'm A Believer' could reach a million sales in Britain. "The previously issued 'Last Train To Clarksville,' which flopped without the exposure their vid-show affords them, has picked up and is now a runaway hit, too. And it's not too much to suggest that this could touch the million mark here also. Monkees have achieved this volume of business during a period when a single could hit top with a sale as low as 70,000 copies. Indeed, the 250,000 seller – an average advance order during the full flush of Beatlemania – had become a rarity."
● In the studio, Jeff Barry and Ray Hall mix the Monkees' next single.
RECORDING RCA (B) *New York, NY*. Jeff Barry *prod*; Ray Hall *eng*; quarter-inch mono; mixdown.
1. **'A Little Bit Me, A Little Bit You'**
Greatest Hits master # UZB1-4406
2. **'99 Pounds'**
Changes master # UZB1-4402
● Don Kirshner has appeased The Monkees by allowing them to record on their own – but has no intention of releasing their wares. Not only does his contract guarantee him total creative control on Colgems releases, but when 'I'm A Believer' was released he made a promise to Jeff Barry and Neil Diamond that he would give them the follow-up if the single hit #1. In other words, it's payback time. Little does Kirshner know where this promise will lead him.

Mono mixes are made of these two songs for use on The Monkees' next release. However, '99 Pounds' will not be selected by Kirshner and another mix session will be held on the 10th for the single's flipside. Today's mix of 'Little Bit Me' is later lost when an attempt is made on April 21st to insert it into the master for The Monkees' third album. In fact 'A Little Bit Me, A Little Bit You' will

Michael and his wife Phyllis are in London too, mixing with The Beatles and seen here shopping in a hip boutique.

never appear on any regular Monkees album and is forever consigned to a run of Greatest Hits-type releases.

● Thursday 9th

● After a trip to the trendy London shop Biba, Micky joins Michael for an appearance on BBC television's *Top Of The Pops*. During the program the two Monkees accept a British silver-disc award from DJ Jimmy Savile for outstanding sales of their 'I'm A Believer' single. Also at this taping Micky reconnects with model Samantha Juste, whom he first met earlier this week. Juste, a regularly featured personality on *Top Of The Pops*, is simply part of the studio audience for this particular telecast. After the taping, the two enjoy a small dinner party in Micky's suite with his guest Spencer Davis. Later, Micky visits the Bag O' Nails club with Juste and singer Sandie Shaw.

● Friday 10th

● After dinner with the ubiquitous Spencer Davis, Michael and Phyllis Nesmith attend a five-hour evening recording session at Abbey Road's studio 1 for The Beatles' song 'A Day In The Life.' They arrive two hours into the proceedings at approximately 10:30pm.

The Beatles' session centers on recording a 40-piece orchestra for eventual overdub on to the song's climactic finale. In addition to the audio recording, the session is filmed by seven handheld cameras (two manned by professional operators, the other five by Ringo Starr and guests such as Keith Richards, Mick Jagger, and Klaus Voormann). A brief clip of Michael sitting with John Lennon is later included in a promo film for 'A Day In The Life.' However, because the BBC bans the song prior to release, the accompanying clip is never widely shown (excerpts will be seen much later in The Beatles' *Anthology* documentaries). Michael also reportedly participates in an unused recording of several people singing the notes A and E. After the session, most of the participants continue to party at London clubs including the Bag O'Nails and the Scotch Of St. James.

Michael: "The only thing I can remember about the sessions was Marianne Faithfull. I thought, 'This is the rock'n'roll mama of all time.' I was just unabashedly stricken. When she wandered into the room, I thought oh, this is what the fuss is all about. She was some stone fox, I'll tell you." Meanwhile, Micky is due to fly to Berlin, Germany but cancels his plans in order to stay in London with Samantha Juste for just a few more days.

● In New York City, Peter reunites with some of his old buddies at the Tin Angel on Greenwich Village's Bleecker Street. In the studio, Jeff Barry mixes the flipside to the group's next release.

RECORDING RCA (B) *New York, NY*. Jeff Barry *prod*; Ray Hall *eng*; quarter-inch mono; mixdown.

1. 'She Hangs Out' version 1

Missing Links 3 master # UZB1-4404

● Mixing this track completes work on The Monkees' third single. Although the group had requested that one of their 'group' sides be included, neither 'All Of Your Toys' or 'The Girl I Knew Somewhere' version 1 is deemed suitable by Don Kirshner. Without the group's knowledge he uses their absence to press ahead with plans for the single. He will have picture sleeves printed for the U.S. release with the titles 'A Little Bit Me, A Little Bit You' and 'She Hangs Out' and will deliver masters of these songs to RCA in Canada, who zealously press product immediately.

● Saturday 11th

● *New Musical Express* publishes an interview with Micky conducted in London. "We have several tracks in the can," he says of the

group's recent sessions, "but [we] would like the next single to be an all-Monkee production. … Last week we almost passed out from fatigue – and what's more, I was annoyed with the recording set-up." He also mentions the group's upcoming feature film. "We still do not have a story line – we're looking around and we're hoping a suitable script turns up in time." Today, Micky rents a Triumph car and cruises to Stratford-upon-Avon with Samantha Juste.

● Michael and Phyllis Nesmith stay at John and Cynthia Lennon's house in Weybridge, Surrey. John plays them unfinished tracks from the forthcoming *Sgt. Pepper's Lonely Hearts Club Band* album. It is also reported by *Flip* magazine that Michael is invited to contribute to some musical experiments that Lennon has generated on his Mellotron Mark II tape-replay keyboard. An impressed Michael will later buy his own Mellotron.

Michael recalls: "[Lennon] would come home and play the acetates from the day's sessions. 'What do you think of that sound? Do you think there's too much bass on there?' Of course, I just didn't have any way to talk to him because he was rearranging my musical realities at the time. I said, 'This is just miraculous. This is some of the most innovative and creative and interesting stuff I've ever heard.'"

● Back in the States, *Billboard* reports that the group are "Top Banana Globally." In the U.S. alone their two albums have now sold in excess of six million copies, while their singles, 'Clarksville' and 'Believer,' have passed the five million mark.

In the U.K. 'I'm A Believer' has sold in excess of 600,000 copies. The single also reached #1 in both Holland and Sweden, as well as making the Top 10 in Belgium, Norway, Japan, and Australia. Strong sales have been reported in Canada, Germany, and The Philippines. The *Billboard* album chart shows that the group currently hold the #1 and #2 slots with their first and second albums respectively, while 'I'm A Believer' remains the #1 single this week in the U.S.A., the U.K., and Holland.

● Sunday 12th

● Davy flies from Jamaica in the West Indies back to New York City. He will then travel to London, England.

● Micky attends the Pop Disc Awards at London's Hilton, mingling with Spencer Davis, Cliff Richard, Cat Stevens, Brian Epstein, Del Shannon, Samantha Juste, and others.

● Monday 13th

● Peter receives an 11-foot homemade card from a fan to mark his 25th birthday.

● Davy arrives in London from New York and Mike and Phyllis Nesmith return to the U.S. from Britain. Davy spends the evening

---

TV series

The Monkees

EPISODE 22: *MONKEES AT THE CIRCUS*

BROADCAST FEBRUARY 13TH

When an old-fashioned circus company faces extinction The Monkees step in to save the day.

WRITER: DAVE PANICH. DIRECTOR: BRUCE KESSLER.

SONGS 'She,' 'Sometime In The Morning.'

clubbing at such spots as the Cromwellian, the Scotch Of St. James, and the Bag O' Nails, where he bumps into Sonny & Cher, Mick Jagger, and Brian Jones.

Micky does more clothes shopping at Lord John and Dudley Edwards, while he spends the evening in the company of Spencer Davis, Del Shannon, and 'Mama' Cass Elliot.

TV Episode 22 of the *Monkees* series, *Monkees At The Circus*, is televised at 7:30pm by the NBC network. For the second week in a row the series attracts the most viewers in its time slot. With over 12 million viewers tuned in, this will be the largest single television audience that *The Monkees* series will ever reach.

● Tuesday 14th

● Peter returns to Los Angeles from his East Coast sojourn. In England, after a full day of press interviews Davy travels to Middleham, Yorkshire to visit some old haunts. Micky attends a fashion show at the Carlton Towers where Samantha Juste is modeling. Impressed by her dress, he purchases the original for her to keep as a gift. Not to be outdone, he goes on another clothes-buying bonanza at shops including Granny Takes A Trip, Biba, Susan Lockes, and Dandi's. He then dines with Juste and hits the clubs once again before he has to leave town.

● Wednesday 15th

● Micky flies to Copenhagen, Denmark. He hosts a press conference at a discotheque called The Club 6. In the evening he visits the Hit Club.

● In Middleham, Yorkshire Davy visits the stables owned by his former boss Basil Foster. He will also stop at the White Swan pub to pull a pint in a photo op for the assembled press.

● An agent from Brian Epstein's NEMS firm, Vic Lewis, flies to America today to meet with Bert Schneider and discuss bringing The Monkees to Britain for some concert dates.

● Thursday 16th

● Micky appears on Jorgen Mylius's radio show in Denmark. In England, Davy tells reporters he's headed for Manchester to see his dad, but instead goes sightseeing at nearby Bolton Castle.

● Friday 17th

● Micky flies from Copenhagen to Stockholm, Sweden. Upon arrival he appears at a press conference at the Apollonia Hotel and takes part in a snow-laden photo session. Later he travels 20 miles north of Stockholm to Svavelsö^n island so that he can be filmed by the Swedish Broadcasting Corporation for an insert for the *Drop In* TV show. Meanwhile, Davy does an interview in Manchester for Granada Television with his former *Coronation Street* co-star Violet Carson.

● Saturday 18th

● Micky flies from Stockholm to Copenhagen and then back to London. Davy, who has returned to London, makes an appearance on BBC television's *Rolf Harris Show* singing 'Consider Yourself' and tapes an interview for a pirate radio station.

● In Canada tickets for The Monkees' April 2nd appearance at Toronto's Maple Leaf Gardens are put on sale. All 17,000 seats are sold within four hours to fans who line up in zero-degree weather. Reported sales are in excess of $91,000 setting a new one-night record for a Monkees concert gross.

● *Billboard* reports that radio station WEIF in Moundsville, West Virginia, is now providing an Instant Monkees Service. Listeners can call a hotline on which a DJ will ask their name, school, and favorite Monkees record, after which their choice will be instantly broadcast.

● Sunday 19th

● Micky's flight from Copenhagen makes an unpublicized stop at London's Heathrow airport to allow him an easy getaway. He will spend the remainder of his London jaunt staying at the apartment of Screen Gems' London chief Jack McGraw and shares his time with Samantha Juste.

● Monday 20th

TV The NBC network airs episode 23 of the *Monkees* series, *Captain Crocodile*. Once again the series wins its slot for viewership, though the audience slips below the 12 million mark. The program features The Monkees improvising a story for a flock of angry kids, the first words of which are: "Once upon a time in the land of Kirshner … ." Behind the scenes, a real-life story is developing around Don Kirshner in the boardrooms of Screen Gems and Columbia Pictures – and there will be no fairytale ending.

TVseries

The Monkees

EPISODE 23: *CAPTAIN CROCODILE*
BROADCAST FEBRUARY 20TH
The Monkees find themselves at odds with an egomaniacal children's show host, Captain Crocodile.
WRITERS: GERALD GARDNER, DEE CARUSO, PETER MEYERSON, ROBERT SCHLITT.
DIRECTOR: JAMES FRAWLEY.
SONGS 'Valleri,' 'Your Auntie Grizelda'

● Tuesday 21st

● Micky attends a Beatles overdub and mixing session for 'Fixing A Hole' at EMI's Abbey Road studio 2.

● In the U.S.A. *Daily Variety* notes that Screen Gems have set a six-month profit record. Company president Abe Schneider, father of Monkees co-creator Bert Schneider, quotes a figure of $2,593,000. The only project singled out in the article for responsibility in this windfall is *The Monkees*. The Monkees have established the Colgems label as one of the most successful platteries and made the wax division a profitable operation," reports *Variety*.

● Wednesday 22nd

● Micky returns to the United States from London, barely recovered from his Beatles experience.

● Thursday 23rd

● NBC renews the *Monkees* series for a second season, to start on September 11th. In the studio, three Monkees reunite with Chip Douglas to make a second version of Michael's 'The Girl I Knew Somewhere.'

RECORDING RCA (A) *Hollywood, CA* 2:00-5:30, 6:00-9:00pm. Chip Douglas *prod*; Hank Cicalo *eng*; half-inch 4-track; tracking, reductions, overdubs.

1. 'The Girl I Knew Somewhere' version 2 takes 1-15 + 3 takes of a remix + takes 1A-14A
　Greatest Hits master # UZB3-8185

2. 'Sunny Girlfriend'
　Headquarters master # UZB3-8373

Personnel Micky Dolenz (drums 1,2), John London (bass 1,2, tambourine 1), Michael Nesmith (electric 12-string guitar 1,2, acoustic 12-string guitar 1), Peter Tork (electric six-string guitar 2, harpsichord 1).

● The group are unaware that masters for their next single have already been shipped to Canada and that a U.S. single isn't far behind, so they forge ahead with plans to tape a releasable 'group' side.

With Chip Douglas they have found that the publishing for Bill Martin's 'All Of Your Toys' cannot be purchased by Screen Gems, and decide that their best shot at a 'group' single is Michael's 'The Girl I Knew Somewhere.'

The hang-up with the version 1 they've already recorded is the vocal. Michael is deemed acceptable as an album-track vocalist by the powers that be, but in order to realistically snare a single release, either Micky or Davy will have to be the lead vocalist. In this case Micky is chosen, and judging by the impromptu singing that opens take 1 he is well-prepared for the job.

This remake is a big improvement over the previous version, especially the drumming. Fifteen takes of the song are recorded, with take 14 marked the master. This take is then reduced to two tracks of a new 4-track tape, while simultaneous overdubs are added of 12-string acoustic guitar (Michael), tambourine (John London, substituting for a still-vacationing Davy) and harpsichord (Peter). The best elements of these overdubs, including a doubled harpsichord solo piece from Peter, are edited together to create the master take, marked 13A. (Percussionist Gene Pello is credited on the session contract for 'Somewhere' but the original session tape has no indication that he performed on the final recording. Producer Chip Douglas recalls later that Pello may have played tambourine, if anything.)

Peter says that 'The Girl I Knew Somewhere' is "one of Mike's better ones of the era. I remember the harpsichord solo. I was playing around with it. I had the general idea for it for a while, and then Mike was in my dressing room and I played him what I had for it. I was noodling around with it. Then we hit that thing at the end where it hits the discord on the downbeat, at the end of the solo, and I hadn't meant to do that. I said, 'What was that?' Mike said, 'I heard it, I heard it!' So, that was great. We were tickled to death to have this funny note. It disappeared in the record. Young kids hearing a note that excites them!

"You know, the harpsichord did not work terribly well in pop music," Peter continues. "It was just something that I wanted to do because I am partly a classicist. I love the classic stuff. It was really just that this is an instrument I want to play on a record. I want to hear how it sounds. I just want to put it on a record. I believe in the old stuff. Bach was already, by that time, my favorite composer, so harpsichords were the thing. I had one on the TV show with Julie Newmar; they mounted it on a bicycle."

Later at the session a new Michael Nesmith song, 'Sunny Girlfriend,' is tracked. No session tapes will survive, but a version of the master (take 7, as heard on *Headquarters Sessions*) reveals the group performing live with Michael singing a rough 'guide' vocal. Of particular note is Peter's electric six-string guitar part, essentially the lead instrument at this early stage of the production.

● **Friday 24th**
RECORDING RCA (A) *Hollywood, CA* 1:00-6:00, 6:30-7:30pm. Chip Douglas *prod*; Hank Cicalo *eng*; half-inch 4-track; tracking, demo.
1. **'Mr. Webster'** version 2
Headquarters master # UZB3-8374
2. **'She'll Be There'** demo
Missing Links 3 master # UZB3-8375

3. **'Midnight Train'** demo
Missing Links 3 no master #
Personnel Coco Dolenz (harmony vocal 2,3), Micky Dolenz (guitar, vocal 2,3), David Jones (tambourine 1), John London (bass 1), Michael Nesmith (steel guitar 1), Peter Tork (piano 1).
● This session marks the return of Davy to the fold as work focuses on recutting 'Mr. Webster,' Boyce & Hart's previously rejected song from September 1966. Chip Douglas and The Monkees rearrange the track, stripping away some of the more dramatic elements of the previous version and giving the song a country flavor with Peter's piano and Michael's steel guitar. No session tapes will survive from today, but take 28 (with some edits) is marked as the master version.

Over the weekend, discussions will be held to determine the fate of Monkees Music Supervisor Don Kirshner, who deems the group's recent efforts as "rather ordinary."

Peter recalls later that he liked 'Mr. Webster' a lot. "As I look back on it, I see that it's a little easy, but it was fun and it was great to do. It's like so crazy: you look back and it seems such a big deal to say, 'Sorry, stop.' The song stops right there! We fought for a while before that was decided on, [as well as] stopping the song's tempo in the middle and then slowly building it back up to full tempo. ... When we finally decided that, it was like the second take or something after we had decided. It just came up to the right tempo right away, right on the money I think. There were some pleasant surprises for me on that." Tommy Boyce: "I actually liked our version a little better, but they were both quite good. [The group's] was a little different than the one we did. It was a little more country."

Around this time – but not necessarily at this session – Micky and his sister Coco cut two fantastic acoustic demos at RCA with Chip Douglas presiding over the board. Never intended for official release, 'She'll Be There' and 'Midnight Train' were later included on the 1996 rarities set, *Missing Links Volume Three* (as well as the 2000 set titled *Headquarters Sessions*). Micky will record a full-blown version of his 'Midnight Train' during 1969.

● **Saturday 25th**
● *New Musical Express* publishes a candid interview with Davy. He tells Keith Altham that the group have yet to receive much income from their success. "So far we really haven't seen a penny of it. A great deal of money has to be deferred over several years because of taxes, and things like record royalties just take time. The only one of us who has really had any big money is Micky, who got a fat check when he was 21 for *Circus Boy*, under that child-actors' law which holds so much money in trust until you are of age."

As for the bad press and word-of-mouth the band have received, Davy says: "I can only speak for myself. I am an actor and I have never pretended to be anything else – the public have made me into a rock'n'roll singer. No one is trying to fool anyone! People have tried to put us down by saying we copy The Beatles. So, all right, maybe *The Monkees* is a half-hour *Hard Day's Night*. But now we read that The Who are working on a TV series around a group. Now who's copying who?" On January 28th the *NME* indeed reported that The Who were planning a series along the lines of *The Monkees*. The venture, produced by Brian Epstein's Subafilms, will never go past the planning stage.

Davy says the shooting schedule for their TV series has changed considerably since last year. "Originally the show took five days to film," he reports. "Now we've got it down to two-and-a-half. But people still have no idea how hard we work or they'd never put us down."

The paper also notes that The Monkees' next single will couple 'A Little Bit Me, A Little Bit You' and 'She Hangs Out.' Canadian

The group are determined to make the third album, *Headquarters*, their own way. Peter is pictured at the Hammond organ at RCA in March.

copies of this pairing have probably leaked out by now. With the group trying hard to create their own music, Kirshner will pay a heavy price for his lack of interest in their efforts.

● Monday 27th
● Today, Don Kirshner is officially dismissed as Music Coordinator for the Monkees project and head of Colgems Records. A series of events have led to this action, most important among which is Kirshner's handling of the group's third single.

Using his contract's stipulation of total creative control, Kirshner overruled requests from Raybert and The Monkees to issue a 'group' performance on the flipside of the release. In Canada, singles with the non-group recording 'She Hangs Out' on the B-side not only made it to radio but, according to *Weekly Variety*, turned up in stores outside of Toronto.

Adding to the group's embarrassment, many U.S. disk jockeys were able to beg copies for airplay of the 'A Little Bit Me, A Little Bit You'/'She Hangs Out' single from their friends in the great white north. Despite The Monkees' claims to the press that they would create their own music, their new single is now on the air and they are not a part of it.

Peter: "We did not ask for creative control. We did not ask to replace Kirshner. He released the record in Canada. Fired! Bam! Just like that. I think [the people at Columbia who fired him] were getting sick of him for reasons of their own."

TVseries

The Monkees

EPISODE 24: *MONKEES A LA MODE*
BROADCAST FEBRUARY 27TH
A haughty style rag selects the group as 'the typical young Americans of the year.'
WRITERS: GERALD GARDNER, DEE CARUSO. DIRECTOR: ALEX SINGER.
SONGS 'Laugh,' 'You Just May Be The One'

Lester Sill will replace Kirshner as Music Coordinator for The Monkees television programs and as head of the Colgems label. Kirshner does remain employed as president of the Screen Gems-Columbia music division – at least for the time being. With a contract entitling him to 15 percent of the world's current #1 group, he will not go quietly. He is even less likely to be watching the television this evening as NBC broadcasts episode 24 of the *Monkees* series, *Monkees A La Mode*, at 7:30pm. Nevertheless, it will top its time slot for the fourth week running, attracting close to 12 million viewers.

MARCH

'A Little Bit Me, A Little Bit You' / 'The Girl I Knew Somewhere' single released in the U.S.A. Following Don Kirshner's dismissal, The Monkees' revised third single is issued, now featuring the group's recording of Michael's song 'The Girl I Knew Somewhere.' Advance orders total 1.5 million copies. The Recording Industry Association of America (RIAA) simultaneously audits these sales and awards a gold single to the group. Since August 16th last year The Monkees have sold a combined 12 million albums and singles in the United States alone.

● *16* magazine reports that Monkee Pads will soon be opening in big cities across the States. The 'Pads' are said to be "a cross between a discotheque and an ice cream parlor." J.C. Penney's department stores will have a Monkee Corner with a full Monkees fashion line of clothes for guys and a matched Mary Quant-designed set for girls.

A Little Bit Me, A Little Bit You
single

A 'A Little Bit Me, A Little Bit You' (N. DIAMOND)
B 'The Girl I Knew Somewhere' version 2 (M. NESMITH)

U.S. release March 1967 (Colgems 1004).
U.K. release March 31st 1967 (RCA 1580).
Chart high U.S. number 2; U.K. number 3.

● **Thursday 2nd**
● Davy attends the 1966 Grammy awards at the Beverly Hilton Hotel's International Ballroom in Beverly Hills. Unexpectedly he is asked to stand in for a scheduled but mysteriously absent presenter, comedian Bob Newhart. Davy winds up presenting two of the night's biggest awards, Song Of The Year and Record Of The Year. Although The Monkees are nominated in two categories for their 'Last Train To Clarksville' single (for Best Contemporary Group Performance

and Best Contemporary Group Recording) Davy goes home empty-handed. Also this evening, sessions officially begin for the group's third album, to be titled *Headquarters*.

RECORDING RCA (A) *Hollywood, CA* 7:00pm-12midnight. Chip Douglas *prod*; Hank Cicalo *eng*; half-inch 4-track; set-up, rehearsals, tracking.

1. **'Randy Scouse Git'**
   Headquarters master # UZB3-8371
2. **'Band 6'**
   Headquarters master # UZB3-8378

Personnel Micky Dolenz (drums), Chip Douglas (bass 1), Michael Nesmith (electric 12-string guitar 1, steel guitar 2), Peter Tork (piano 1, electric guitar 2).

● With Kirshner now out of the picture, The Monkees prepare for a full month of 'group' recordings at RCA. The first order of business is to find a drum sound for Micky that they can use for the duration of the sessions. They also work out soundchecks of Michael on 12-string guitar, Peter on piano, and Chip Douglas on bass.

Throughout the evening Michael, Micky, Peter, and Chip run through a new song of Micky's that was written during and about his recent trip to London. Micky: "It was the morning after The Beatles had thrown us a party at some club. I had some girl with me and my friend was in the room and we were just sittin' around. I was literally just making it up as I went along. It's not very significant but it mentions The Beatles, and it mentions this girl that I was with at the time who later on was to become my first wife. She's the girl in the limousine.

"I mean, all this stuff is really stupid. It was just about my experiences. It was like word association, really. Mama Cass is in there, who I knew at the time. The Monkee experience of the limos and black darkened windows and black leather naugahyde. It's absolutely diddly shit, but it works! Then there was a social comment about having long hair and being abused for having long hair. 'Why don't you cut your hair, why don't you live up there.' It was like a bit of social commentary about young long-haired hippies at the time being abused by the establishment.

"Well, I'd written the song in England and when I got back we were just sitting around in the studio doing *Headquarters* and I started playing it. I don't recall specifically how we managed to put the arrangement together, but it was a pretty collaborative effort at the time with Chip Douglas."

The arrangement gradually evolves from Micky's basic idea into what becomes the album's closing song, 'Randy Scouse Git.' After several unnumbered rehearsals, 25 takes are committed to tape. After take 25 engineer Hank Cicalo switches the take names to 1A, 2A and 3A (actually 26 through 28), but the total number of takes is unknown, and it's not clear which take or takes are ultimately used to compile the final album master. Excerpts from this evening's recording set-up and tracking will be heard on 2000's *Headquarters Sessions*.

Also tonight, Micky, Michael, and Peter fool with a rendition of the Warner Bros. *Merrie Melodies* cartoon theme. This piece of studio mayhem is originally logged as 'Band Three' but when take 3 of the session goof is eventually issued on *Headquarters* it is retitled 'Band 6.'

Peter: "I'm pleased to say that was my contribution. I don't know whose idea it was to keep the tape running at all times. We tried to get them to keep the tape running so that we would catch this stuff. My idea was the start and stop points. But that whole take, beginning to end, is right as it happened. That's live, you know! If people are willing to cut loose, these kinds of things happen generally. I think 'Band 6' really was like a peak moment. I think that one of the things

Michael's interest in country music is growing, and here he plays pedal steel guitar during the Headquarters *sessions.*

about the decision to put that on the record was that that's why we wanted to make this record ourselves. We didn't know how to do better at the outset. We certainly didn't know enough about making records to begin with to make the first records."

● Friday 3rd

● Micky Dolenz's pre-Monkees recording, 'Don't Do It,' is issued in Britain by the London-American label. Meanwhile in Hollywood the group holds another *Headquarters* session.

RECORDING RCA (B) *Hollywood, CA* 7:30-12midnight. Chip Douglas *prod*; Hank Cicalo *eng*; half-inch 4-track; tracking.

1. **'You Told Me'** version 1
   Headquarters master # UZB3-8380
2. **'Zilch'**
   Headquarters master # UZB3-8381

Personnel Micky Dolenz (drums 1, spoken word 2), Chip Douglas (bass 1), David Jones (tambourine 1, spoken word 2), Michael Nesmith (electric 12-string guitar 1, spoken word 2), Peter Tork (banjo 1, spoken word 2).

● During this evening The Monkees record a new Michael Nesmith number called 'You Told Me.' No session tapes will survive, but take 15 from this session is marked as the master, and musicians' union documents suggest that Davy probably adds his tambourine to this track as an overdub at a later date. Also added later will be the song's mock 'frantic' count-in, which lampoons the kick-off to The Beatles' 1966 *Revolver* album, 'Taxman.'

Peter: "The opening is satirical of 'Taxman.' Very interesting use of banjo on that cut; I thought it really kicked it. I suppose anybody listening to it would automatically throw that into a country bag, but I always thought that it was just a pretty rocky use of the banjo. My friends all said, 'That's your ax, buddy.' It really kills when the banjo comes in and the band hits with that nice bass drop. I think in terms of what you want to make happen on pop records, that one moment whips the other two albums to hell. Tommy and Bobby were really experts at what they did, and [Kirshner] was an expert at doing what he did, but none of those guys were really interested in how music is just exciting in and of itself. That's what music's supposed to be."

Probably also taped around this time is the *Headquarters* spoken interlude, 'Zilch.' It's constructed from four spoken phrases and spotlights The Monkees' esoteric sensibilities.

Peter: "'Zilch' was constructed, obviously. We'd been collecting these rhythmic nonsense things. 'China clipper calling Alameda' was from the movie called *China Clipper*. 'Mr. Dobolina' somebody actually heard in an airport, one of the mini-Monks I think, Charles Rockett, or David Pearl, one of those guys. ['Monks' is an in-phrase among group insiders, an abbreviation for Monkees; 'mini-Monks' are the hangers-on and general entourage around the group.] We climbed into the studio to do ['Zilch'] on purpose. Not like 'Band 6,' which we extracted from life. We had enough separation so that we weren't leaking too badly into each other's mikes and we just heard each other on the earphones. There were the two sections: we did it a while and then assembled the slow and the fast one, and the laughter."

● Saturday 4th

● Micky Dolenz's pre-Monkees recording 'Don't Do It' hits the *Billboard* singles chart today. Over the next six weeks it will peak at #75 – not bad for a genuine missing link.

● *New Musical Express* reports that The Monkees will perform three British concerts in July. The paper also publishes more of Davy's chat with Keith Altham from last month, with much discourse on The Beatles. "A reporter came up to me in the U.S. and asked what

I thought about John Lennon's 'Jesus' quote, when he said he thought The Beatles were more popular. I said that there was some talk about us being more popular than The Beatles at the moment, so where does that put us! I can imagine this guy going away now and writing: 'Davy Jones says he's God.' Young people are bored with the Church as an establishment. There are too many conflicting dogmas. They should all put their heads together and come up with a new, more acceptable religion."

● The Monkees move permanently into RCA's Studio C where the remainder of the *Headquarters* sessions will be recorded. So much for all the time they have spent "getting sounds" in Studio B. In all, today's session runs a full 12 hours as The Monkees record 'I'll Spend My Life With You' and add overdubs to 'Randy Scouse Git.' Peter: "I like that studio. I mean, what are you gonna do? You got a little tiny rock band and you're going to be in there for three or four weeks. When you consider [we were] rehearsing and creating arrangements in the studio, when you think that albums now take three or four months with the arrangements and the rehearsals all done … wow, intense! Do you have any idea how much it cost to produce that album? I'll bet you anything that it came in for something like $8,000 for the whole album."

RECORDING RCA (C) *6363 Sunset Boulevard, Hollywood, CA* 12midday-3:00, 3:30-8:00, 8:30pm-1:00am. Chip Douglas *prod*; Hank Cicalo *eng*; half-inch 4-track; tracking, overdubs.

1. **'I'll Spend My Life With You'** version 2
   Headquarters master # UZB3-8382
2. **'Randy Scouse Git'**
   Headquarters master # UZB3-8371

Personnel Micky Dolenz (electric six-string guitar 1), Chip Douglas (bass 1), David Jones (tambourine 1), Michael Nesmith (steel guitar 1), Peter Tork (acoustic 12-string guitar 1, organ 1, celeste 1).

● 'I'll Spend My Life With You' becomes another Boyce & Hart reject revamped for *Headquarters*, with The Monkees' faster re-recording made today featuring many fine dynamics absent from the original late-'66 version. No session tapes will survive, so it is unclear how elaborate the tracking process is for this tune. It is quite possible that Peter's organ and celeste parts are added as overdubs at a later session. The surviving (empty) tape boxes have today's take 9 marked as master.

Peter: "I liked 'Spend My Life With You.' I managed to talk to Tommy [Boyce] about that. It was one of the few real songs he wrote, because there really was somebody, he really was thinking about a specific person when he wrote that song. You can tell: the song is sort of real heartfelt. Something about it is not jacked up and it's not forced. Did you notice, incidentally, there were no traps on that song? There's not a drum kit on it. The rhythm section is Micky playing backbeats on guitar and David on the tambourine. Michael was just taking a few pedal-steel lessons. I would not like to have seen us be a country music band, but I love the idea of Michael playing pedal steel. In some ways he's a very powerful guy."

Surviving musicians' union documents and tape boxes indicate that Micky's 'Randy Scouse Git' receives its first round of overdubs today, but with no session tapes surviving it is unclear exactly what is done. Records indicate that John London is present, but the extent of his involvement is also unclear.

● Monday 6th

● A session scheduled to commence at midday in RCA's Studio C is canceled.

TV At 7:30pm NBC airs episode 25 of the *Monkees* series, *Alias Micky Dolenz*. For the sixth straight week *The Monkees* wins its time slot, pulling a viewing audience of more than 11 million.

TVseries

The Monkees

EPISODE 25: *ALIAS MICKY DOLENZ*
BROADCAST MARCH 6TH
Micky's resemblance to a vicious killer causes calamity.
WRITERS: GERALD GARDNER, DEE CARUSO, DAVE EVANS. DIRECTOR: BRUCE KESSLER.
SONGS 'The Kind Of Girl I Could Love,' 'Mary, Mary'

● Tuesday 7th

● *Daily Variety* publishes the National Nielsen television ratings showing that *The Monkees* is currently one of the top-rated shows, coming in at #30. In the studio Chip Douglas's song contribution to *Headquarters*, 'Forget That Girl,' is taped.
RECORDING RCA (C) *Hollywood, CA* 12:30-5:30, 6:00pm-12 midnight. Chip Douglas *prod*; Hank Cicalo *eng*; half-inch 4-track; tracking, overdubs.
1. **'Forget That Girl'**
   Headquarters master # UZB3-8379
2. **'Where Has It All Gone'** version 1 take 1 + takes 1-4
   Headquarters Sessions master # UZB3-8377
3. **'Memphis Tennessee'**
   Headquarters Sessions no master #
4. **'Twelve-String Improvisation'**
   Headquarters Sessions no master #
5. **'Where Has It All Gone'** version 2 takes 5-16
   Headquarters Sessions master # UZB3-8377
Personnel Micky Dolenz (drums), Chip Douglas (bass 1), David Jones (tambourine 2,3,4,5), John London (bass 2,3,4,5), Michael Nesmith (electric 12-string guitar), Peter Tork (electric piano 1, electric six-string guitar 2,3,4, organ 5), unknown (acoustic guitar 1).
● Chip Douglas's 'Forget That Girl' was first introduced to the group in January 1967. Although some early rehearsals will survive from that date, session tapes from today will not, so it is unclear how many takes are made.

Peter: "'Forget That Girl' had I think Wurlitzer [electric piano] though it might have been a Rhodes. It has the sound. I thought that was a pretty good song, actually. Chip [is] a pretty sophisticated musician, or at least he was for the time, but I've heard places where his sophistication just totally ran away with him. This was not a case where that happened. I like the changes. Kind of nice idea to the lyric, too."

Chip Douglas: "They said, 'Well, do you have a song?' I said, 'Yeah, well, I have this one song.' Actually I'd showed it to Kirshner too and his comment was, 'It has a negative message, don't you think?' I was really taken aback. I'd never thought about it that way. It was advice to myself. I was crazy about a girl who had this other guy that she was crazy about. I knew it was never going to work out. It was a childhood sweetheart who lived next door in Hawaii.

"I had real mixed feelings when we did it because no one could pick up on the original riff that I had worked out. I had done a demo with Mark Volman [of The Turtles] and I think he probably sang it. It sounded really neat with the bass parts, which I doubled. It had an entirely different riff. It was more like 'Rescue Me' from Fontella

Bass: I had become fascinated with that record. I just got hung up on that particular style of bass playing, the Motown thing. I was hoping it would sound Motown.

"Nobody could get the hang of that riff because of the way it started. It didn't start on the downbeat; it was a couple of beats before the downbeat. For some reason no one could get that, so we had to compromise. Which I really wasn't crazy about, because the whole song was built on this other little Motown-sounding thing. I remember being kind of bummed out as we did that. The way it turned out was a lot more bubblegum than I had hoped."

The Monkees also tackle a song by Michael at this session, 'Where Has It All Gone.' Early attempts feature both Michael and Peter playing electric guitar, but only one take is made before the group stop for a break. Upon their return they slip into a quick jam on Chuck Berry's 'Memphis Tennessee' and a Michael-dominated 12-string guitar improvisation (later issued on the *Headquarters Sessions* under the speculative title 'Twelve-String Improvisation'). The group then return to 'Where Has It All Gone,' making four more passes of the song that are marked as takes 1–4, discounting the earlier take 1.

At Chip Douglas's suggestion the group then try recording a different arrangement, beginning with take 5. The main difference is that Peter switches from guitar to Hammond organ for the remainder of the nine recorded takes. The take closest to being marked master is the final one for today, take 16. But the group will never return to this intriguing tune and it will remain incomplete, with no further instrumental or vocal overdubs ever attempted. The very first take 1 plus take 12 will later be included on 2000's *Headquarters Sessions* set.

● Wednesday 8th
RECORDING RCA (C) *Hollywood, CA* 12:30-5:30, 6:00pm-12midnight. Chip Douglas *prod*; Hank Cicalo *eng*; half-inch 4-track; overdubs.
1. **'Forget That Girl'**
   Headquarters master # UZB3-8379
2. **'Randy Scouse Git'**
   Headquarters master # UZB3-8371
● No tapes will survive from today's session, but union records indicate that Douglas along with Michael, Peter, and Micky spend 11 hours in the studio recording overdubs.

● Thursday 9th
● The Monkees are the big winners at the National Association of Record Merchandisers (NARM) awards ceremony held at the Century Plaza Hotel in Los Angeles. For the last three years The Beatles have dominated these awards but tonight they barely make a showing. Awards are based strictly on calculated sales. The Monkees nab top honors for best-selling album and single, and American vocal group. It is unlikely that they attend this ceremony as they are otherwise occupied in the studio.
RECORDING RCA (C) *Hollywood, CA* 12:30-5:30, 6:00pm-12midnight. Chip Douglas *prod*; Hank Cicalo *eng*; half-inch 4-track; reductions, overdubs.
1. **'You Told Me'** version 1
   Headquarters master # UZB3-8380
2. **'I'll Spend My Life With You'** version 2
   Headquarters master # UZB3-8382
● The first round of overdubs for these two songs are taped at today's session, and union documents indicate that Michael, Peter, and Micky are present for the first portion. It is very possible that the second half is given over to reduction 'bounce-downs' of the new

Micky with headphones and headgear at a session for *Headquarters*.

overdubs to make space for future embellishments such as vocals. (A conversation from today's session for 'You Told Me' will be excerpted on the 2000 *Headquarters Sessions* CD set as 'Monkee Chat.')

● **Friday 10th**
RECORDING RCA (C) *Hollywood, CA* 2:00-5:00pm. Chip Douglas *prod*; Hank Cicalo *eng*; half-inch 4-track; demo, reductions, overdubs.
1. **'I Had A Dream Last Night' demo** takes 1-2
   unissued master # UZB3-8385
2. **'I'll Spend My Life With You'** version 2 test take + takes 1A-9A
   Headquarters master # UZB3-8382
3. **'Forget That Girl'**
   Headquarters Sessions master # UZB3-8379
Personnel Micky Dolenz (backing vocal 3), Chip Douglas (unknown 1, backing vocal 3), David Jones (backing vocal 3), Peter Tork (backing vocal 3).
● Chip Douglas records a solo demo of 'I Had A Dream Last Night' to start this session. Douglas co-wrote the effort with Bill Martin. There is no Monkees involvement and the group will never attempt their own version of the song.
    Next, take 12 of the backing 4-track tape for 'I'll Spend My Life With You' is remixed and reduced down to two tracks of a new 4-track tape. A total of ten attempts will be made, with the seventh pass (called take 7A) resulting in the final master. (A letter is added to the end of a take number to indicate overdubs. The letter A usually indicates that only one overdub – using one or more instruments – has been made on a song; B indicates two overdubs; C means three; and so on.)
    Also at this session Micky, Davy, Peter, and Chip Douglas record background vocals for 'Forget That Girl.' The process is a little shaky, with Micky insisting that he doubles his voice alone without the others to achieve correct pitch. Regardless of Micky's suggestion, the final master features his voice alongside Davy, Peter, and Douglas, indicating that they managed to get it right after all. (A humorous work-in-progress take will be presented on disc 2 of 2000's *Headquarters Sessions* set.)
    Peter: "At one point, Micky called Tommy Boyce and Bobby Hart the 'wizards of ahhs' because of their backing vocals. Chip Douglas was probably the inheritor of the mantle."

● **Saturday 11th**
● *Billboard* publishes a three-page article detailing the rapturous response for the group's discs in Europe. In Norway 'I'm A Believer' has now earned a silver disc with a reported 25,000 copies sold. The group still have to break Italy, the paper reports, but there are plans afoot to change that. Reporter Germano Ruscitto says that later this month RCA Italiana representative Gian Piero Ricci will supervise an Italian-language recording session with the group in Hollywood. The only known result from the Italian session will be a version of '(Theme From) The Monkees.' Using a Boyce & Hart backing track recorded during 1966, Micky records a phonetically-sung triple-tracked Italian-language lead vocal for 'Tema Dei Monkees.' (The recording will be issued as a single in Italy and on a rare 1970 album, *I Monkees In TV*, though it will be more easily found later on the 1996 collection *Missing Links Volume Three*.)
● The *NME* talks with and about The Monkees in today's edition. Del Shannon has some insightful comments on the band's recent activities. "They're proud: they want respect from people in the business. Right now they're only for teenyboppers. They want recognition to come from the other side, the creative side. I think what The Monkees are trying to do will surprise a lot of people. I hope they succeed for their own self respect. There's gonna be a lot

of changes." In the studio, The Monkees are hard at work on those very changes.
RECORDING RCA (C) *Hollywood, CA* 12midday-12midnight. Chip Douglas *prod*; Hank Cicalo *eng*; half-inch 4-track; tracking, reductions, overdubs.
1. **'Forget That Girl'**
   Headquarters Sessions master # UZB3-8379
2. **'East Virginia'**
   Headquarters Sessions master # UZB3-8386
3. **'Forget That Girl'**
   Headquarters master # UZB3-8379
4. **'I'll Spend My Life With You'** version 2
   Headquarters master # UZB3-8382
5. **'Jericho'**
   Headquarters no master #
Personnel Micky Dolenz (vocal 2,3,4,5), Chip Douglas (vocal 3,4,5), David Jones (vocal 3,4,5), Peter Tork (vocal 2,3,4,5, banjo 2).
● Some additional instrumental overdubs are attempted on 'Forget That Girl.' Since Davy's lead vocal has already been recorded and an open track is required for the final background vocals, Michael, Micky, Peter, Davy, and Douglas try to perform these new overdubs live at the same time as the master is reduced to two tracks of another 4-track tape. Unfortunately they are unable to synch their piano, guitar and percussion parts with the existing tracks. The overdubs are considered abortive and never used. (An excerpt from this work-in-progress will be presented on disc 2 of the *Headquarters Sessions* set.)
    Peter and Micky make a few attempts to record the folk standard 'East Virginia.' One abandoned idea is to tag a performance of the song onto the end of 'Randy Scouse Git' in place of the final piano discord. An edit is made on an early multi-track master, but the concept will not reach the final album. ('East Virginia,' sometimes known as 'East Virginia Blues,' will appear as 'I Was Born In East Virginia' on the *Headquarters Sessions* set.) During this session Peter and Micky also run through a bit of Tom Paxton's oft-covered 'The Last Thing On My Mind.'
    Towards the end of the session Micky, Peter, Davy, and Douglas record vocal overdubs for 'Forget That Girl' and 'I'll Spend My Life With You.' During the process Micky lapses into a story about the walls of Jericho as Davy clowns around on a horn left in the studio. Two different edits of Micky's banter – both labeled 'Jericho' – will later become available: on 1995's regular-issue *Headquarters* CD and 2000's limited-edition *Headquarters Sessions* set.

● **Monday 13th**
● A session scheduled for today in RCA's Studio C is canceled.

TVseries

The Monkees

EPISODE 26: *MONKEES CHOW MEIN*
BROADCAST MARCH 13TH
During a visit to a Chinese restaurant The Monkees get tangled up in a plot to unleash the dreaded Doomsday bug.
WRITERS: GERALD GARDNER, DEE CARUSO. DIRECTOR: JAMES FRAWLEY.
SONGS 'Your Auntie Grizelda'

TV NBC airs episode 26 of the *Monkees* series, *Monkees Chow Mein*, at 7:30pm. The series remains a strong draw, beating out all other programs for this time slot for the seventh straight week. Tonight's audience is estimated to exceed 11.5 million viewers.

● Tuesday 14th

● *Daily Variety* publishes an article about the group's current activities titled "Monkees Biz (And Battle) Thickens." The journal notes that Davy along with his personal manager Hal Cone has formed several companies of his own, totally independent of the group. Among them are a vanity label, Davy Jones Records Ltd., a music publishing firm, Synchro Music, and a managerial set-up, Jon-Con. All are straight 50/50 splits with manager Cone. Davy's label is headed on the East Coast by former Ember and Harold labels executive Jack Angel while the West Coast office is run by ex-drummer Lee Young in Beverly Hills.

The band have spent the last several weeks recording their future releases from scratch, but the negative publicity stemming from their inorganic origins will not cease. Now the press are propagating the idea that they do not even sing (let alone perform) on their releases. Axing Kirshner has clearly done nothing to stop these rumors.

Daily Variety writes: "The Monkees, hurting from sundry recent reports, both printed and otherwise, that voices other than their own have been responsible for end product on many of their Colgems recordings, are anxious to groove their own material. Therefore, the group has complicated the bad feelings that have existed between Don Kirshner and Bert Schneider over the past several weeks.

"According to [Davy's manager Hal] Cone, The Monkees, with the exception of Jones, want Schneider and partner Bob Rafelson to A&R all their Colgems wax without interference from Kirshner. At the heart of the Kirshner-Schneider conflict is the fact that Kirshner does not want to alter the existing formula.

"Kirshner, now incommunicado in the east, reportedly has retained D.C. attorney Edward Bennett Williams to file suit against Screen Gems. Kirshner's current contract has eight years to run."

As the legal plot thickens, Micky meanwhile enjoys a carefree day experimenting in the studio.
RECORDING RCA (C) *Hollywood, CA* 12midday start. Chip Douglas *prod*; Hank Cicalo *eng*; half-inch 4-track; tracking, overdubs.
1. '**Pillow Time**' version 1
Headquarters no master #
2. '**Mickey In Carlsbad Caverns**'
Headquarters Sessions no master #
● Micky records vocals for an undefined group of *Headquarters* tracks, straying from the task to experiment with different types of reverb and tape effects. Engineer Cicalo does his best to keep up with the antics, recording an item that he writes on one tape box as 'Mickey In Carlsbad Caverns,' as well as several eerie unnumbered takes of 'Pillow Time.' This lullaby, co-written by Micky's mother, will be re-recorded in 1969 for the *Monkees Present* album. Micky recalls: "My mother and father used to sing that to me from as early as I can remember. I sang it to my daughters too." Another tape from this session consists of speeded-up drum effects.

None of these experiments will make it to the *Headquarters* album, though two different edits of this early take on 'Pillow Time' will be made available later on the standard issue *Headquarters* CD and the *Headquarters Sessions* set. The *Sessions* set also features an excerpt of 'Mickey In Carlsbad Caverns' subtly retitled as 'Micky In Carlsbad Cavern.'

● Wednesday 15th

● In New York City, Don Kirshner files a $35.5m lawsuit against Columbia Pictures, Screen Gems, Columbia Pictures' President Abe Schneider, Screen Gems' Executive Vice President Jerry Hyams, and *Monkees* show creator Bert Schneider. Kirshner's claims include breach of contract and conspiracy directly leading to his February 27th discharge. He is seeking $17m in compensatory damages alone.

Daily Variety says the "crux of litigation is the head-on clash between Kirshner and Bert Schneider. … It's not only a clash over executive billing, but a matter of dividing up the monies earned by The Monkees."

Variety further notes that Davy has signed the first act to his own label, blind drummer/singer Vinnie Basile. *Variety* also mentions that Jones is the only Monkees member siding with Kirshner. Meanwhile, a studio session is scheduled – but perhaps the band are too busy consulting their attorneys to attend.
RECORDING RCA (C) *Hollywood, CA* 12midday start. Chip Douglas *prod*; Hank Cicalo *eng*; half-inch 4-track.
No further details survive for this session.

● Thursday 16th

RECORDING RCA (C) *Hollywood, CA* 12:30-3:30, 4:00-7:00pm. Chip Douglas *prod*; Hank Cicalo *eng*; half-inch 4-track; tracking.
1. '**Shades Of Gray**'
Headquarters master # UZB3-8383
2. '**Masking Tape**' takes 1-18
Headquarters Sessions master # UZB3-8388
3. '**You Just May Be The One**' version 2 takes 1-4
Headquarters master # UZB3-8372
4. '**Peter Guns Gun**'
Headquarters master # UZB3-8387
Personnel Micky Dolenz (drums 1,2,3,4), Chip Douglas (bass 4*), David Jones (tambourine 1,2,3,4, maracas 1), Michael Nesmith (steel guitar 1,4, electric 12-string guitar 2,3), Peter Tork (piano 1,4, electric six-string guitar 2, bass 3), Jerry Yester (bass 1,2,3,4*). *Douglas or Yester on bass.
● The Monkees begin recording one of the highlights of *Headquarters*, Barry Mann and Cynthia Weil's 'Shades Of Gray.' No session tapes will survive, so it is unclear how this lovely production takes shape, although the song's cello, French horn, and vocal parts are certainly overdubbed at a separate session.

Peter: "Great song. We were just thrilled to death with that. I was really pleased with that little piano introduction I wrote. We created the arrangement ourselves from scratch. I don't remember what kind of a demo they gave us, except that it had verse, verse, instrumental, half-verse and out – no bridges."

Producer Chip Douglas, who has recently been playing bass in the studio, wants to remain focused in the control room and so recruits his friend and former bandmate Jerry Yester to play bass for this session. Yester was once in The Modern Folk Quartet with Douglas, recently produced The Association (which includes his brother Jim), and later this year will join The Lovin' Spoonful. The Spoonful were once considered for *The Monkees* series and, according to Davy, Yester was also a prospective Monkee (see September 8th 1965).

Next, Michael switches back to his trusty 12-string and Peter picks up an electric six-string guitar for 'Masking Tape.' Session tapes will survive for takes 6 to 18 and capture the band laying into a Stax-like groove with great enthusiasm. Despite their eagerness, 'Masking Tape' never develops beyond this basic rhythm track. The song's composer is unknown. (A composite of takes 6 through 8 will be heard on 2000's *Headquarters Sessions* set.)

To close out the session Peter switches to bass for Michael's 'You

Just May Be The One.' The four takes taped are perhaps the most solid group sounds ever produced by The Monkees. They are obviously confident with the tune, having played it live, and soar during its brief two-minute duration.

Peter: "It has two bars of five [time] in the middle of it, which Mike didn't know he'd written. I mean, I told him that and he just didn't take it in because he never listened to me. Somebody else told him and he came at me yelling, 'Look what I did!' It was a good Mike song."

Chip Douglas recalls seeing Michael and Bill Chadwick performing live at The Troubadour a few years earlier. "That's when I first got to know him. In particular they were doing 'You Just May Be The One.' That is the one song that I remember that they did that I was real impressed with. I remember those harmonies – Bill hitting that high A note [on the bridge]. I thought wow, that sounds neat. So when the song came up for suggestion to put on the album I said yeah, that's great, can we do that same harmony on there and everything, like you guys used to? Mike said, 'Sure, Micky will do it.'"

Around this time, but possibly not at this session, The Monkees jam an improvisation based on Henry Mancini's theme for the 1958-61 television series *Peter Gunn*. Written on the tape box as 'Peter Guns Gun,' this loose bit of musical meandering will later be included as a bonus track on the CD reissue of *Headquarters* (and *Headquarters Sessions*) as 'Peter Gunn's Gun.'

● **Friday 17th**
RECORDING RCA (C) *Hollywood, CA* 12:30-3:30, 4:00-7:00pm. Chip Douglas *prod*; Hank Cicalo *eng*; half-inch 4-track; tracking.
1. **'I Can't Get Her Off My Mind'** version 2

Headquarters master # UZB3-8389
2. **'Two-Part Invention In F Major'** version 1
Headquarters Sessions no master #
3. **'No Time'** version 1 take 1
unissued master # UZB3-8390
4. **'Blues'** take 1
Headquarters Sessions master # UZB3-8391
5. **'No Time'** version 1 takes 2-5
Headquarters Sessions master # UZB3-8390
6. **'Banjo Jam'** take 1
Headquarters Sessions master # UZB3-8391
7. **'Cripple Creek'** take 1
Headquarters Sessions master # UZB3-8391
Personnel Keith Allison (guitar 3-7), Micky Dolenz (drums 1, 3-7), David Jones (percussion 1), Gerry McGee (guitar 3-7), Michael Nesmith (electric 12-string guitar, steel guitar 4), Peter Tork (tack piano 1, piano 2-7, banjo 6,7), Jerry Yester (bass 1, 3-7).
● The first part of today's studio date is used to remake Boyce & Hart's 'I Can't Get Her Off My Mind.' The song was first taped by the songwriters in July 1966 and performed by the group on early tour dates, but has so far remained in the can. Today's resurrection, probably suggested by Davy who will be the song's lead vocalist, will find release on *Headquarters*. Peter's tack piano is doubled for the final production and may be added as an overdub after this initial tracking session.

Also taped around this time is Peter's impromptu rendition of Bach's 'Two-Part Invention.' The recording, never intended for release, will appear on *Headquarters Sessions*. When today's session picks up again at 4:00pm guitarists Keith Allison and Gerry McGee

Davy chats to tireless Monkees engineer Hank Cicalo during the making of *Headquarters* at RCA's Hollywood recording studios.

join the crew to spice up the simple Chuck Berry-inspired 'No Time.' The group will give their long-suffering recording engineer Hank Cicalo the writer's credit for this song as a gift. The results are desultory and after one take the band veer into an overly long jam simply titled 'Blues.' After that musical detour the musicians lumber through another four takes of 'No Time.'

Later at the same session, Peter switches from piano to banjo and leads the group through the standard 'Cripple Creek' and the speculatively titled 'Banjo Jam.' Excerpts from this session – including portions of 'No Time,' 'Blues,' 'Banjo Jam' and 'Cripple Creek' – will be heard on 2000's *Headquarters Sessions* (and unedited versions of 'Blues' and 'Banjo Jam' will be posted on the Rhino Handmade website).

After this crew clears out, Harry Nilsson enters the studio to record a private demo session for Chip Douglas. In 1965, Nilsson wrote 'This Could Be The Night' for Douglas's group MFQ. Though they recorded it with producer Phil Spector, who featured it in the 1966 movie *The Big T.N.T. Show*, the song remains unissued on record and Nilsson's songwriting prowess is still relatively unknown.

At Douglas's behest, Nilsson today tapes more than ten potential songs for The Monkees to record, including 'This Could Be The Night,' 'Cuddly Toy,' 'The Story Of Rock And Roll,' and 'Good Times.' The composer just happens to be at RCA studios today to begin recording sessions for his own album, *Pandemonium Shadow Show*. As it turns out, Nilsson will have a long and varied association with The Monkees.

● Saturday 18th

RECORDING RCA (C) *Hollywood, CA* 12:30-3:30, 6:00pm-2:30am. Chip Douglas *prod*; Hank Cicalo *eng*; half-inch 4-track; tracking, overdubs.

1. **'The Story Of Rock And Roll'** version 1 takes 1-23
   Headquarters Sessions master # UZB3-8394
2. **'Cantata & Fugue In C&W' a.k.a. 'Six String Improvisation'**
   Headquarters Sessions no master #
3. **'I'll Spend My Life With You'** version 2
   Headquarters master # UZB3-8382

Personnel Micky Dolenz (drums 1, instrument unknown 3), Chip Douglas (bass 1), John London (instrument unknown 3), Michael Nesmith (electric six-string guitar 1, instrument unknown 3), Peter Tork (piano 1, instrument unknown 3).
● Chip Douglas is immediately sold on the talent and songs of Nilsson (see yesterday) and attempts to lead Michael, Micky, and Peter through the tunesmith's 'The Story Of Rock And Roll.' Twenty-three takes are made in all, though only three of these are complete passes. None of today's recordings is deemed successful enough to be considered a master and the crew will return to the song tomorrow. (Today's take 23 of 'The Story Of Rock And Roll' will be heard on *Headquarters Sessions*.)

During a lull in the proceedings Michael busts out the instrumental 'Cantata & Fugue In C&W' (misidentified on Rhino Handmade's *Headquarters Sessions* of 2000 as 'Six-String Improvisation'). He will record the instrumental properly some six years later, on February 11th 1972, at a post-Monkees Michael Nesmith session. That recording will remain unissued until 2001 when it appears as a bonus track on the British Camden-label CD *Nevada Fighter & Tantamount To Treason*.

After a two-and-a-half-hour break, all four Monkees plus John London return to the studio to put the finishing touches to 'I'll Spend My Life With You.' No tapes will survive to tell exactly what is added, but musicians' union records indicate that the final master is completed at this session.

● Sunday 19th

RECORDING RCA (C) *Hollywood, CA* 2:00-6:00, 6:30-11:00pm. Chip Douglas *prod*; Hank Cicalo *eng*; half-inch 4-track; tracking, overdubs.

1. **'The Story Of Rock And Roll'** version 2 takes 1-31
   Headquarters Sessions master # UZB3-8394
2. **'Don't Be Cruel'** take 1
   Headquarters Sessions no master #
3. **'I Can't Get Her Off My Mind'** version 2
   Headquarters master # UZB3-8389

Personnel Micky Dolenz (drums 1,2, instrument unknown 3), Chip Douglas (bass 1), Davy Jones (instrument unknown 3), John London (instrument unknown 3), Michael Nesmith (electric six-string guitar 1, instrument unknown 3), Peter Tork (piano 1,2, instrument unknown 3).
● Pressure is mounting on the group to complete their album and so they return to the studio for a rare Sunday session. They make a second attempt at recording 'The Story Of Rock And Roll' and tape 31 takes. Although the results are superior to the previous version, no take is deemed good enough to be marked as a master.

While recording the song, Peter and Micky slip into the Elvis classic 'Don't Be Cruel' and the entire group takes time for an aimless jam, marked on the tape box as 'Jim's Blues No. 2.' After this jam, Michael performs his song 'Hollywood' for the group but unfortunately this solo rendition is not properly recorded. (Take 5A of 'The Story Of Rock And Roll' as well as 'Don't Be Cruel' from today's session will be heard on *Headquarters Sessions*. A third version of 'The Story Of Rock And Roll' will be cut in April.)

During the second half of today's session all four Monkees are present for overdubbing and completion of Boyce & Hart's song 'I Can't Get Her Off My Mind.' Union documents also indicate that John London is present but the extent of his involvement is unclear. No tapes of this portion of today's session will survive.

TVseries

The Monkees

EPISODE 27: *MONKEE MOTHER*
BROADCAST MARCH 20TH
When The Monkees can't pay the rent, their landlord moves a more mature tenant (played by Rose Marie) into their pad.
WRITERS: PETER MEYERSON, ROBERT SCHLITT. DIRECTOR: JAMES FRAWLEY.
SONGS 'Sometime In The Morning,' 'Look Out (Here Comes Tomorrow)'

● Monday 20th

TV NBC televise episode 27 of the *Monkees* series, *Monkee Mother*, at 7:30pm. Also today, The Monkees have vague plans to record at RCA Studios, but it is unclear if any session takes place.

● Wednesday 22nd

● *Weekly Variety* publishes a few articles about Kirshner's legal dispute. The journal questions just how long Kirshner can remain president of Screen Gems-Columbia while suing them "in a most unusual case of corporate schizophrenia." Kirshner's presidential deal still has nine years to run and offers the executive $70,000 or 7.5 percent of pre-tax net profit. It is an entirely separate contract to his Colgems pact, which delivers $35,000 or 15 percent of net receipts, whichever is greater. The journal also comments on the Yarnell/Gordon lawsuit that claims origination of the *Monkees* series. *Variety* reports that the suit is still in pre-trial hearings and notes that the *Monkees* series cautiously carries no "created by ..." credit in its end-of-show title roll but only a "developed by ..." mention for Paul Mazursky and Larry Tucker.

In Los Angeles, The Monkees spend morning, noon, and night in the studio.
RECORDING RCA (C) *Hollywood, CA* 9:00am-12:30, 1:00-6:00, 6:30pm-1:00am. Chip Douglas *prod*; Hank Cicalo *eng*; half-inch 4-track; tracking, overdubs.
1. **'Early Morning Blues And Greens'**
   Headquarters master # UZB3-8393
2. **'Shades Of Gray'**
   Headquarters master # UZB3-8383
3. **'No Time'** version 1
   Headquarters Sessions master # UZB3-8390
Personnel Vincent DeRosa (French horn 2), Micky Dolenz (drums 1), Chip Douglas (bass 1), David Jones (maracas 1), Michael Nesmith (electric 12-string guitar 1), Frederick Seykora (cello 2), Peter Tork (electric piano 1, organ 1),
● This marathon 15-hour session comes as The Monkees rush to complete *Headquarters*. Today is the first session listing for the moody Jack Keller/Diane Hilderbrand song 'Early Morning Blues And Greens,' though work tapes indicate that it may have been tracked four days ago, on March 18th.

Peter recalls: "I love that record. I should have sung it – that's what I always thought, because I think it was right up my alley. But Davy did a good job singing it. He certainly acted out the setting very well. I remember there were no chord changes [in the original demo]. The second verse was in the same key as the first. I said, 'We have to go see if we can't change the key.' [The others in the studio] said, 'We can change the key.' I said, 'We have to go ask the authors.' They said, 'Peter, for Christ's sake, we can change the key, we can do anything we want.' I said, 'No, no. We have to ask the authors.' So I call up Keller and Hilderbrand and they both said, 'Sure, what do we care? We're just staff writers.' Here I was, all caught up in the sanctity of the authorship and that kind of thing. Nobody else had the slightest concern about it."

Jack Keller: "I got a call from Lester Sill, a panicked call. 'They're in the studio and they're cutting the song, but they want to make a change in the music.' So I said, 'It's OK, go ahead.' And they did – and it's different than the original. It wasn't much different. They wanted to go 'up' sooner in the music. I had kept it on one level for quite a while and then I went into the bridge and really went high. They couldn't hear it staying at that level all of the way to the bridge. They wanted it to kind of rise up a little bit. So I said, 'Go ahead and do it.'"

Also today, cello and French horn overdubs are placed onto the majestic 'Shades Of Gray' (most likely take 9B). Peter: "Mike wrote the horn and cello parts and I notated them. Mike wrote the two of 'em in his head and sang them to me. It was great to have him do that and to know how to tell a French horn player what to do. At one point later on the French horn player goes, 'Buh buh buh.' I had to coach him; it's a diminuendo. He'd never heard that kind of pop phrasing; I had to coach him carefully and sing it to him. It was really thrilling to have that stuff change. The horn player said, 'How about one of these – bah bah bada.' I said, 'Sure, go ahead.' By the time I got it done, I thought: this is one of my favorite things I've ever done."

Union contracts indicate that some work is done to 'No Time' version 1 but it is unclear exactly what, since no embellished tapes exist and version 1 is soon scrapped in favor of an all-new recording.

● **Thursday 23rd**
RECORDING RCA (C) *Hollywood, CA* 1:00-6:00, 7:30pm-2:30am. Chip Douglas *prod*; Hank Cicalo *eng*; half-inch 4-track; tracking, overdubs.
1. **'For Pete's Sake'**
   Headquarters master # UZB3-8490
2. **'Shades Of Gray'**
   Headquarters master # UZB3-8383
Personnel Vincent DeRosa (French horn 2), Micky Dolenz (drums 1), Chip Douglas (bass 1), David Jones (tambourine 1), Michael Nesmith (electric 12-string guitar 1), Frederick Seykora (cello 2), Peter Tork (electric six-string guitar), unknown (electric guitar 1).
● Another lengthy session is held today as The Monkees record a Peter Tork original, 'For Pete's Sake.' The song is co-written by Joey Richards, a friend of Peter's from Greenwich Village. (Richards will later become involved in a religious group with Byrds leader Roger McGuinn and co-write a 1969 single for The Byrds, 'Bad Night At The Whiskey.') Session tapes of 'For Pete's Sake' will not survive so it is unclear who performs one of the electric guitar overdubs on the final master, but it is most likely a Monkee.

Peter: "The lyrics [on 'For Pete's Sake'] were out of thin air. It was basically just me playing these chords at my house and my then-roommate Joey Richards threw in a couple of odds and ends of lines as I was going along. It just fell right into place. There was no particular reference, we weren't thinking about anything much. The lyrics sound a little silly to me now, but it was OK. Mike played the seventh changes on the organ. The thing about it that I remember is that one note is an added fourth, it's not a suspended. It was so weird and it sounds so funky. I was really pleased with that. It just fell out of my hands, you know? It was one of those things where my hands just wrapped around the guitar and that's what they did. It was my first song on a Monkees record and my first song that I had written. There *was* one song that I wrote before that in ... oh god, I don't know ... '62 or something like that."

Union contracts indicate that further 'sweetening' is possibly done today to the cello and horn parts on 'Shades Of Gray.'

● **Saturday 25th**
More Of The Monkees album is released in the U.K. The group's second LP gets its British release.
● Davy appears at the Miss Teen International Pageant at the Hollywood Palladium. The program is telecast live on the ABC Television network and features as hosts actress Sally Field and musician/actor Noel Harrison, currently seen as Mark Slate in *The Girl From U.N.C.L.E.*.
● *Billboard* reveals more details about the first artist on Davy's record label. Vinnie Basile is a 21-year-old self-taught drummer and singer who has been blind since the age of eight. His single for the label, 'Gypsy Girl,' has been issued previously under the band name The Staccatos on the Synchro label. Davy will eventually release four singles on his label, including sides from Dickie Goodman, Randy Johnson, and The Relations, none of which will chart.
● *Billboard* also features a full-page ad for The Monkees' 'Stage To Stardom,' also known as Monkees Clubs. The pitch seeks a $15,000 minimum from each potential investor – and those who look at today's charts might just bite. The Monkees' new single 'A Little Bit Me, A Little Bit You' enters the Hot 100 today at #32 and will remain on the charts for the next ten weeks, peaking at #2. *More Of*

The *Monkees* is the best-selling album, while the debut *Monkees* LP runs a close third. The group's own musical effort, 'The Girl I Knew Somewhere,' B-side of 'A Little Bit Me,' debuts on the charts thanks to significant airplay. Over the next five weeks it will rise to a respectable #39.

● The *Monkees* series makes its debut on Swedish television. 'I'm A Believer' is still a Top 10 item in Australia, Denmark, Holland, Mexico, New Zealand, Norway, The Philippines, Singapore, and South Africa.

● In an article relating to Kirshner's lawsuit *Record World* notes that the group's success in records still far out-strips their television ratings. "The TV show has never been extremely high in the national ratings, whereas the first two Monkees singles and albums quickly achieved number one chart spots, and the third single, out last week, is on the way."

TVseries

The Monkees

EPISODE 14: *MONKEES ON THE LINE*
BROADCAST MARCH 27TH
The group is pressed into service as unlikely operators of an answering service.
WRITERS: GERALD GARDNER, DEE CARUSO, COSLOUGH JOHNSON. DIRECTOR: JAMES FRAWLEY.
SONGS 'Look Out (Here Comes Tomorrow)'

● Monday 27th

TV Episode 28 of the *Monkees* series, *Monkees On The Line*, is aired at 7:30pm on NBC. Following a week behind *Gilligan's Island* the series returns to the top viewership of its time slot, reaching an audience of close to 12 million.

● Tuesday 28th

RECORDING RCA (C) *Hollywood, CA* 12midday start. Chip Douglas *prod*; Hank Cicalo *eng*; half-inch 4-track; tracking, overdubs.
1. **'No Time'** version 2 takes 1-7
   Headquarters master # UZB3-8390
2. **'Just A Game'** version 1 takes 1-3
   Headquarters Sessions master # UZB3-8491
Personnel Micky Dolenz (drums 1, vocal 2, electric 6-string guitar 2), Chip Douglas (bass), David Jones (tambourine 1, percussion 2), Michael Nesmith (electric guitar 1), Peter Tork (piano 1, percussion 2), unknown (electric guitar 1).
● This is the final tracking session for *Headquarters*. 'No Time' is remade, with superior results. Of the seven takes, the final one, take 7, is used as the master with an additional rhythm guitar part immediately added as an overdub (and it is unclear which Monkee performs this).

At the end of the session Micky debuts a new song, 'Just A Game.' It is logged under the working title of 'There's A Way' and will later be recut in a more elaborate production next year. The version recorded today is rudimentary and merely work in progress. Micky recalls 'Just A Game' as "one of the first songs that I had written. I was not nearly as prolific as Mike and everybody. I think I

played it for Mike on the guitar once and he encouraged me to record it."

Excerpts from the tracking session for 'No Time' version 1 and all three takes of 'Just A Game' version 1 will later be included on the *Headquarters Sessions* CD set.

● Wednesday 29th

RECORDING RCA (C) *Hollywood, CA* 1:00pm start. Chip Douglas *prod*; Hank Cicalo *eng*; half-inch 4-track; reductions, overdubs, possibly mixdown.
● Douglas and Cicalo do some clean-up work on an undisclosed group of *Headquarters* tracks.

● Thursday 30th

● In Britain, Davy features in a BBC radio program called *Pop Goes A Person* ("a potted history of the pop scene over the last decade"). In Hollywood, the *Headquarters* sessions come to a close.
RECORDING RCA (C) *Hollywood, CA* 1:00pm start. Chip Douglas *prod*; Hank Cicalo *eng*; half-inch 4-track; reductions, overdubs, mixdown.
● The productions for all of the tracks to be included on *Headquarters* are finalized at this session. A multi-track master reel of all the album tracks is compiled and it is likely that most of the album is also mixed down to mono and stereo.

● Friday 31st

'A Little Bit Me, A Little Bit You' / 'The Girl I Knew Somewhere' single is released in the U.K.
● The Monkees plus full entourage, including bodyguards, fly to Canada for a brief tour. Their first stop is Winnipeg, where they will stay on the sixth floor of the Fort Garry Hotel.

APRIL

● The first issue is published of *Tiger Beat*'s official Monkees-only magazine, *Monkees Spectacular*.
● *16* magazine reports that the Monkee Pads they detailed last month are in reality the proposed Monkees 'Stage to Stardom' clubs (see also March 25th). *16* says that local up-and-coming groups who make it at the 'Stage to Stardom' will not only be awarded a Colgems recording contract but also have a chance to appear on the *Monkees* TV series.
● Following the revival of early material by Micky ('Don't Do It' released by the Challenge label) and Davy (his '65 Colpix album), Michael's recording of 'Just A Little Love' from around 1965 is given a low-key re-release this month on the Edan label. The song is coupled with an apparently non-Nesmith instrumental, 'Curson Terrace,' hinting that Edan are perhaps hoping to follow Challenge's game plan by releasing as a follow-up at a later date another early Nesmith track, 'How Can You Kiss Me,' coupled with a further non-Nesmith instrumental on the B-side. But the single meets with little response, so there are no more releases.

● Saturday 1st

PERFORMANCE Arena *Winnipeg, MB, Canada*
● The Monkees perform an afternoon concert at a venue normally seating 12,000, but an extra 500 standing-room-only tickets have been added to meet demand for this already sold out show.

Today's set reportedly includes 'Last Train To Clarksville,' 'The

Kind Of Girl I Could Love,' the yet-to-be-released 'Sunny Girlfriend,' 'Your Auntie Grizelda' with Davy on keyboard bass to allow Peter to take the front of the stage without an instrument, and '(Look Out) Here Comes Tomorrow' performed as Davy's solo spot. Micky, Davy, and Mike's solo spots are backed by Bobby Hart's Candy Store Prophets. Peter performs solo with only his banjo.

Spooked by a prediction that The Monkees will be killed, Michael hires David Price, Charlie Rockett, and Michael's brother-in-law Bruce Barbour to make sure that items thrown at the stage are immediately thrown back to the audience. One policeman will be hurt during the show when zealous fans push over a wire fence. After the concert The Monkees and crew fly to their next date in Toronto amid a blizzard.

● In Britain the *NME* reports that three London concert dates have been confirmed for June 30th and July 1st and 2nd. The paper also mentions that Davy will have no part in the upcoming feature film version of *Oliver!*. Davy is not pleased with this news.

Saturday 2nd
● At the King Edward hotel in Toronto thousands of fans hold vigil below The Monkees' eighth-floor window. Meanwhile, Michael does a live phone interview with radio station CHUM-FM.

TVseries
The Monkees

EPISODE 29: *MONKEES GET OUT MORE DIRT*
BROADCAST APRIL 3RD
A soap opera develops when Mike, Micky, Davy, and Peter all fall for the same woman, a luscious laundromat owner (played by Julie Newmar).
WRITERS: GERALD GARDNER, DEE CARUSO. DIRECTOR: GERALD SHEPARD.
SONGS 'The Girl I Knew Somewhere'

PERFORMANCE Maple Leaf Gardens *Toronto, ON, Canada*
● The group perform in concert this evening for 18,200 fans with a set that reportedly includes 'Last Train To Clarksville.' After the show The Monkees' touring party flies back to Los Angeles where production will begin next week on season two of the *Monkees* TV series.

● Monday 3rd
TV Episode 29 of the *Monkees* series, *Monkees Get Out More Dirt*, is aired at 7:30pm on the NBC network. The series continues its winning streak by gaining most viewers in this time slot, reaching an estimated audience of more than 10 million.

● Tuesday 4th
RECORDING RCA (A) *Hollywood, CA* 7:30pm start. Chip Douglas *prod*; half-inch 4-track.
● The Monkees reconvene tonight for their first post-*Headquarters* recording session; further details unknown.

● Wednesday 5th
● British Davy Jones fanatic Linda Hards is joined by 150 like-minded supporters in a march protesting Davy's possible involuntary enlistment into the United States Army. The march in central London's Marble Arch, Hyde Park, and Church Street culminates in a visit to the American Embassy in Grosvenor Square. Hards reportedly hands a 2,000-signature petition to the embassy addressed to President Lyndon Johnson. The protest is filmed by newsmen and footage will survive. Tomorrow the group's latest single, 'A Little Bit Me, A Little Bit You,' enters the British charts. Over the course of the next 12 weeks it will peak at #3.
FILMING Back in California production commences on the second season of *The Monkees* for what will become episode 34, *The Picture Frame*.

● Friday 7th
FILMING Production wraps on *The Picture Frame*.

● Saturday 8th
● With the press still abuzz with talk of Kirshner's dismissal and lawsuit, the *NME* asks Micky if there is a rift between Davy, who supports Kirshner, and the rest of the group. "I don't really know about Davy's opinion of this matter," he says. "I believe he wanted to continue as we had been, but the rest of us are determined to do all our own work in the future. Our new producer, Chip Douglas, is working us hard and we will be working exclusively for him in the future. I'm very pleased with what he's doing because I think that having so many producers in the past marred some of our recordings. There is no split in the group. We will stay together and we haven't even discussed the situation. Chip Douglas is our producer and we are all very happy with our new recordings."

● Monday 10th
TV At 7:30pm, episode 30 of the *Monkees* series, *Monkees In Manhattan*, is aired on the NBC network. The show once again tops this time slot, though the size of the audience shows a slight decline as tonight's program pulls in just over 10 million viewers.
● Peter most likely misses the broadcast since he is spotted giving a solo performance at The Troubadour's regular 'hoot' night. The *NME* reports later that his 15-minute set includes 'If I Could Shimmy Like My Sister Kate' and some Boyce & Hart songs from The Monkees' next album. For an encore he sings "a beautiful ballad written by a close friend of Mike Nesmith's," which may well be '(I Prithee) Do Not Ask For Love'.

On the road again: The Monkees on stage in Canada in early April.

TVseries

The Monkees

EPISODE 30: *MONKEES IN MANHATTAN*

BROADCAST APRIL 10TH

At the urging of a would-be producer The Monkees hit the Big Apple to star in his rock'n'roll musical.

WRITERS: GERALD GARDNER, DEE CARUSO. DIRECTOR: RUSSELL MAYBERRY.

SONGS 'The Girl I Knew Somewhere,' 'Look Out (Here Comes Tomorrow),' 'Words'

● Friday 14th

FILMING Production wraps on what will become episode 37 of the *Monkees* series, *Art For Monkees Sake*.
● In Britain a golden oldie from Davy's Colpix past, 'It Ain't Me Babe,' is issued as a single.

● Saturday 15th

● The *NME* reports that The Monkees' movie planned for this year has been cancelled. "It's simply because we have such a tight schedule on other commitments," explains Micky. "Plus the fact that we can't find the right script. We want to do something completely different from the TV show, and not make a film as merely an extension of what we are doing already. The TV series is keeping us fully occupied – besides which we have a visit to London and a possible nationwide tour of America later this year."
RECORDING RCA (C) *Hollywood, CA* 12midday start. Chip Douglas *prod*; half-inch 4-track.
● No further details about this session are available.

The band's former producers, Tommy Boyce and Bobby Hart, are booked into the adjacent RCA studio A today and tomorrow. They now have a recording contract with the A&M label: Boyce & Hart's first single 'Out And About,' which was inspired by Bobby Hart's recent Canadian tour with The Monkees, will hit the charts later this year, in July.

● Monday 17th

TV Episode 31 of the *Monkees* series, *Monkees At The Movies*, is aired

TVseries

The Monkees

EPISODE 31: *MONKEES AT THE MOVIES*

BROADCAST APRIL 17TH

The group is cast as extras in a teen-exploitation beach party flick ...Ö until Davy is cast into the spotlight.

WRITERS: GERALD GARDNER, DEE CARUSO. DIRECTOR: RUSSELL MAYBERRY.

SONGS 'A Little Bit Me, A Little Bit You,' 'Valleri,' 'Last Train To Clarksville'

---

at 7:30pm on the NBC network. The group take the day off from filming and hold a recording session instead.
RECORDING RCA (C) *Hollywood, CA* 12midday start. Chip Douglas *prod*; half-inch 4-track.
● Another mysterious session. The group probably work out new ideas and rehearse. It is unlikely that any serious attempts to record are made.

● Tuesday 18th

RECORDING RCA (C) *Hollywood, CA* 11:00am-12midday. Chip Douglas *prod*; half-inch 4-track; overdubs.
1. 'Sunny Girlfriend'
probably unissued master # UZB3-8373
● This brief one-hour session is held weeks after work has wrapped on *Headquarters*. Nonetheless, a union document notes that Chip Douglas brings in friends John London, Jerry Yester, and another MFQ member, Eddie Hoh, to sweeten 'Sunny Girlfriend.' The session tapes do not indicate that any overdubs attempted today are either successful or are included in the final mix of the song.

● Thursday 20th

FILMING Production wraps on what will become episode 57 of the *Monkees* series, *Monkees Blow Their Minds*. An intro sequence for this program featuring Frank Zappa and Michael will be filmed later in the year.

● Friday 21st

RECORDING RCA (C) *Hollywood, CA* 12midday-12midnight. Chip Douglas *prod*; Richie Schmitt *eng*; half-inch 4-track; tracking.
1. 'The Story Of Rock And Roll' version 3 takes 1-10
unissued master # UZB3-8394
Personnel Micky Dolenz (drums), Chip Douglas (bass), David Jones (percussion), Harry Nilsson (piano).
● Chip Douglas tries for a third time to cut a suitable track for Nilsson's 'Story.' Nilsson himself is on hand to play piano but the results are only mildly better than the recordings made in March. Today's version suffers particularly from Micky's tentative drumming and Nilsson's unfamiliarity with the arrangement that Chip has cooked up for The Monkees. A number of takes are taped but only ten are logged, and the final pass from today's session is the only fully acceptable run-through of the song. Despite the uneven results, Douglas will remain eager to cut this song, eventually convincing his former band The Turtles to tape their own version next year. Michael will also maintain an interest in the tune, cutting a fourth version for The Monkees (with Nilsson) on January 10th next year.

Also at today's session a mono master reel for the *Headquarters* album is assembled. Prior to its May release, the long-player will go through a few changes of sequence, and the single sides 'A Little Bit Me, A Little Bit You' and 'The Girl I Knew Somewhere' will be dropped entirely.

● Saturday 22nd

● Davy is featured as host of a BBC radio program, *Be My Guest*. The show features some of his favorite records – including discs by Harry Secombe, Max Bygraves, and Lonnie Donegan – alongside some patter taped during Davy's last British visit.
● Due to overwhelming demand two more concerts have been added to the group's U.K. itinerary. Lulu has been named as opening act and British Rail will be operating a series of Monkee Expresses to transport fans to the concerts.
RECORDING RCA (C) *Hollywood, CA* 12midday-12midnight. Chip Douglas *prod*; half-inch 4-track; tracking.

● The Monkees are booked for another full day of recording today but their precise activities are unknown. It's likely that no new songs are seriously recorded.

TVseries

The Monkees

EPISODE 32: *MONKEES ON TOUR*
BROADCAST APRIL 24TH
A mini-documentary showing a day in the life of The Monkees during their first concert tour.
WRITER: ROBERT RAFELSON. DIRECTOR: ROBERT RAFELSON.
SONGS 'The Girl I Knew Somewhere,' 'Last Train To Clarksville,' 'Sweet Young Thing,' 'Mary, Mary,' 'Cripple Creek,' 'You Can't Judge A Book By The Cover,' 'I Wanna Be Free,' 'I've Got A Woman,' '(I'm Not Your) Steppin' Stone,' 'I'm A Believer.'

● Monday 24th

TV At 7:30pm the NBC network airs the last episode (#32) in the *Monkees* first season, *The Monkees On Tour*. This broadcast will win its time slot, snaring more than 11 million viewers – an improvement over the last few weeks. Next week NBC will begin a rerun of revised first-season episodes.

Although *The Monkees On Tour* is undoubtedly a series highlight, *Daily Variety*, perhaps missing the point, gives the program only scornful notice.

"Gee – mom – look – how – good – I – am was the modest theme of this half hour blurb about how popular the longhairs are. ... One of The Monkees in a rare moment of candor thanked The Beatles for their success. They should have paid NBC-TV for this commercial, instead of vice versa. Promo was produced by series producers Robert Rafelson and Bert Schneider, with Rafelson given a writing credit. For what?"

Bob Rafelson: "Everybody in Hollywood is old. They don't understand. You wouldn't realize half the trouble we have trying to get people there to accept new ideas. At first people didn't like that documentary show we did on The Monkees' concert because it broke with tradition. I didn't even have permission when, in the end, I went out and did it myself."

In the studio, Chip Douglas produces a session with Micky and possibly some outside musicians.
RECORDING RCA (C) *Hollywood, CA* 12midday start. Chip Douglas *prod*; Richie Schmitt *eng*; half-inch 4-track; tracking.
1. 'I Don't Know Yet' takes 1-2
    unissued master # UZB3-5431
Personnel Micky Dolenz (drums), unknown (electric guitar, bass).
● 'I Don't Know Yet,' as it is labeled on the tape box, is a rock'n'roll styled number of unknown origins.

Micky is the only identifiable player on the session tape and may have written the piece since he can be heard faintly singing some of the song's lyrics off-mike. Producer Chip Douglas is definitely not playing bass – he is present in the control room, directing the session – and the guitarist's playing is not particularly in the style of Peter or Michael. Seemingly we are all in the same boat as the person who titled this number.

● Wednesday 26th
RECORDING RCA Studio *Hollywood, CA*. Chip Douglas *prod*; half-inch 4-track.
1. 'Cuddly Toy'
    Pisces, Aquarius... master # UZB3-8392
Personnel Micky Dolenz (drums), Chip Douglas (bass), David Jones (tambourine), Edgar Lustgarten (cello), Ted Nash (brass/woodwind), Michael Nesmith (acoustic guitar), Tom W. Scott (brass/woodwind), Bud Shank (brass/woodwind), Peter Tork (piano, electric piano).
● Today's session yields the first song destined for the group's fourth album, to be titled *Pisces, Aquarius, Capricorn & Jones Ltd*. This Nilsson tune was demoed for the group last month and is much more suited to their style than the previous choice, his anachronistic 'Story Of Rock And Roll.'

Michael: "I loved 'Cuddly Toy' when I heard it. I said oh, man, we gotta do this." Peter: "There's something great about that one. It was great to meet Harry. He was so talented and so clearly, obviously good, right away, you know?"

Overdubs are recorded of cello and brass/woodwind instruments from 9:30 to 11:00pm. (Only the cello performance will be audible in the final production; the horns and woodwinds will be only very faintly heard doubling the backing vocal pattern in the song's second and third verses.) Today's overdubs are integrated into the multi-track with some very deft reduction mixing. The cello part is mixed directly with the piano and bass track, and a second cello part is mixed in passages with the backing vocals, which is where the brass/woodwind overdubs also find their home.

● Thursday 27th
FILMING Production wraps on what will become episode 35 of the *Monkees* series, *Everywhere A Sheik, Sheik*.

● Saturday 29th
● *Billboard* reports that Dick Clark will emcee three concerts by The Monkees at Forest Hills Tennis Stadium in New York City. The performances are set to take place from July 14th to 16th. Clark has also rented the outdoor venue from July 17th-19th in case rainy weather postpones any of the shows.
● The *NME* says that The Monkees may spend three weeks filming their series on location in Britain. The shooting is set for the month of June and would entail the group flying back to Los Angeles on June 24th for a recording session and then returning to the U.K. for

On the set filming TV episode 35, *Everywhere A Sheik, Sheik*.

their concert dates on the 29th. The Monkees are also expected to appear on the July 1st edition of the British television program *Juke Box Jury*. Furthermore, there is now talk of the group's concerts at Wembley, north London being filmed for a television special, contingent upon the group's approval of "the Wembley Pool acoustics."

● Rumors are still in circulation about Davy's imminent U.S. Army call-up. The *NME* says he could be replaced in the group by the "very mod" Tim Rooney, son of Mickey Rooney and brother of Mickey Rooney Jr. who was very seriously considered for *The Monkees* series. For the time being Davy is embroiled in a vocal session for the group's latest recording, 'Cuddly Toy.'

RECORDING RCA (C) *Hollywood, CA* 8:00pm-12midnight. Chip Douglas *prod*; half-inch 4-track; reductions, overdubs.

1. 'Cuddly Toy'
   Pisces, Aquarius ... master # UZB3-8392
Personnel Micky Dolenz (lead vocal, harmony vocal, backing vocal), Chip Douglas (possibly backing vocal), David Jones (lead vocal, backing vocal), Peter Tork (backing vocal).

● This is more than likely the date when vocals are completed on 'Cuddly Toy.' The performances are mixed and reduced to a new 4-track tape: Davy's lead voice is combined with Micky's lead harmony on track two, and backing vocals from Micky, Davy, and Peter on track three.

MAY

Headquarters album is released in the U.S.A. is issued. *The Los Angeles Times* will publish a favorable review of The Monkees' third LP under the headline "Monkees Upgrade Album Quality." Pete Johnson writes: "The Monkees are getting better. *Headquarters* has more interesting songs and a better quality level than have their

Headquarters album

A1 'You Told Me' version 1 (M. NESMITH)
A2 'I'll Spend My Life With You' version 2 (T. BOYCE / B. HART)
A3 'Forget That Girl' (D. F. HATELID)
A4 'Band 6' (D. JONES / M. NESMITH / P. TORK / M. DOLENZ)
A5 'You Just May Be The One' version 2 (M. NESMITH)
A6 'Shades Of Gray' (B. MANN / C. WEILL)
A7 'I Can't Get Her Off My Mind' version 2 (T. BOYCE / B. HART)
B1 'For Pete's Sake' (P. TORK / J. RICHARDS)
B2 'Mr. Webster' version 2 (T. BOYCE / B. HART)
B3 'Sunny Girlfriend' (M. NESMITH)
B4 'Zilch' (D. JONES / M. NESMITH / P. TORK / M. DOLENZ)
B5 'No Time' version 2 (H. CICALO)
B6 'Early Morning Blues And Greens' (D. HILDERBRAND / J. KELLER)
B7 'Randy Scouse Git' (M. DOLENZ)

U.S. release May 1967 (Colgems COM-103 mono / COS-103 stereo).
U.K. release June 1967 (RCA SF 7886).
Chart high U.S. number 1; U.K. number 2.

previous two LP's. ... The album shines in comparison to its predecessors. None of the tracks is a throwaway to fill the record, none was released previously as a single, and the quartet has undertaken some experiments. The improvement trend is laudable."

● **Monday 1st**
● Nominations for Emmy awards – which are presented for "prime-time television excellence" – are announced today with *The Monkees* singled out for two potential honors: Outstanding Comedy Series (for show creators Bert Schneider and Bob Rafelson) and Outstanding Directorial Achievement in Comedy (for series director Jim Frawley). The awards presentation is scheduled for June 4th.

TV At 7:30pm the *Monkees* series begins a cycle of first-season reruns with a repeat of episode 2, *Monkee See, Monkee Die*. In fact these repeats are unique because the soundtracks have been updated to include the group's newer recordings. For this episode the original's 'Tomorrow's Gonna Be Another Day' is replaced by the single 'A Little Bit Me, A Little Bit You.' The broadcast will barely beat out *Gilligan's Island* in the ratings, with an audience of close to nine million viewers.

RECORDING RCA (C) *Hollywood, CA* 12midday start. Chip Douglas *prod*; Richie Schmitt *eng*; half-inch 4-track; tracking, overdubs.

1. 'Come On In' version 1 takes 1-6
   unissued master # UZB3-5432
2. 'Come On In' version 2 takes 1-5
   unissued master # UZB3-5432
Personnel Micky Dolenz (drums 1 [take 6 only], 2), Michael Nesmith (guitar 2), Stephen Stills (bass), Peter Tork (electric piano, guitar 1 [takes 4-6 only]),

● Peter recruits Buffalo Springfield's Stephen Stills to work on today's recordings, foreshadowing his future experimental solo sessions. The song at hand is 'Come On In,' a number written by a femme fatale of Fifties folk, Jo Mapes. Peter has been playing around with the song for some time but the other musicians are less familiar with it.

Peter's first attempt features just electric piano set against a rhythmic, offbeat bass part from Stills. Starting at take 4, Peter tries overdubbing guitar parts (one electric and one acoustic) to the already taped track of keyboard and bass. Unfortunately these new parts are wildly out of synch and rhythmically awkward.

For take 6 Peter starts afresh, laying down a basic track on electric guitar and then adding overdubs of himself on electric piano, Micky on drums, and Stills on bass.

Though the results are flawed, this is the most satisfying pass yet. Obviously dissatisfied, Peter starts a new recording of the song almost immediately.

Peter is unsure if version 1 is "the one" and so tapes a slower, more settled arrangement of 'Come On In.' The results are similar to take 6 of version 1 but with a more confident overall feeling.

Producer Chip Douglas gives positive feedback throughout the five occasionally shambolic takes, imparting suggestions on how to solidify the arrangement.

Nevertheless, it is obvious that the group are rushed for time. In the end, no truly successful recording is made of this version.

After take 5, which is incomplete, producer Douglas announces: "Boys, I'm afraid that's it for the evening." Obviously this session has run overtime and the staff union engineer is anxious to get home. Peter will tape a further version of this song on February 8th 1968.

● **Wednesday 3rd**
● *Daily Variety* announces that The Monkees will begin a 30-city U.S. tour with a date at the Hollywood Bowl on June 9th.

● Thursday 4th

FILMING Production wraps on what will become episode 52 of the *Monkees* series, *The Devil & Peter Tork*. Censorship problems with its content will delay airing until next year (see January 1968 entry).

● Friday 5th

This evening The Monkees start their tour as they fly from Los Angeles to Wichita, Kansas, where they will be greeted by some 300 fans.

● Saturday 6th

PERFORMANCE W.S.U. Field House *Wichita, KS* 8:00pm, compère DJ Peter Rabbitt

● The Monkees perform to an audience of over 10,000 tonight at a show that grosses $40,000. The set reportedly includes 'Last Train To Clarksville.' *Billboard* magazine writes that the group spend more than ten hours as guest DJs at Peter Rabbitt's local radio station KFH-FM.

● *The Beat* magazine says that a deal has been struck between Columbia Pictures and Screen Gems for The Monkees' movie, which is presumably back on again. In exchange for use of the group in the film, Columbia is allowing Screen Gems to make a television series out of *The Professionals* movie.

● Today's *NME* mentions that the Marquis of Bath has offered the group every filming facility at his west-of-England stately home, Longleat House, during the planned shoot for their series in England in June. The group are said to be very enthusiastic about this offer. They will not, however, undertake any 'outside' TV appearances during their stay, so the projected *Juke Box Jury* special is now out of the question.

● Monday 8th

● *Daily Variety* reports that Don Kirshner will officially leave his post as head of Screen Gems-Columbia Pictures Music today. Kirshner has instructed his attorneys to begin action involving his final exit from the company. *Variety* says: "Kirshner charged his superiors with instituting a 'program of harassment designed to force me out of the music division.'" Further details of Kirshner's exit will be revealed in the coming days.

TV Another updated repeat from the first season of *The Monkees* is aired at 7:30pm on NBC. For this broadcast, the two original songs from *Royal Flush*, 'This Just Doesn't Seem To Be My Day' and 'Take A Giant Step,' are replaced by newer recordings, 'You Told Me' and 'The Girl I Knew Somewhere.' This rerun is more successful than the original airing, drawing more than ten million viewers. The first-run audience was just over eight million.

Meanwhile at RCA, Chip Douglas supervises the recording of demos for The Monkees by an uncredited songwriter.

RECORDING RCA (C) *Hollywood, CA* 3:00-6:00, 7:00pm-1:00am. Chip Douglas *prod*; Richie Schmitt *eng*; half-inch 4-track; demos, tracking.

1. **'Symphony Is Over' demo** take 1
   unissued master # UZB3-5433
2. **'She Said To Me' demo** takes 1-3
   unissued master # UZB3-5434
3. **'A Man Without A Dream'** version 1
   unissued master # UZB3-5435

Personnel Micky Dolenz (instrument unknown 3), Chip Douglas (harmony vocal 2, instrument unknown 3), David Jones (instrument unknown 3), Larry Taylor (instrument unknown 3), Peter Tork (instrument unknown 3), unknown (vocal 1,2, guitar 1,2),

● An anonymous tunesmith performs the first two demos here,

accompanying himself on guitar with Douglas assisting on vocals during the second. The Monkees will not record either song. After the two tunes are taped, an elongated piano rehearsal is recorded, but the player is not documented.

Also apparently taped today is the band's first attempt at Goffin & King's 'A Man Without A Dream.' Tapes for today's version will not survive. This version may be performed by Peter, who has been working on an arrangement of the song with Chip Douglas. Peter will tape both piano and guitar versions at subsequent sessions. Musicians' union records indicate that the other musicians involved include Micky, Davy, Chip Douglas, and one-time Boyce & Hart session man Larry Taylor. Next month, Taylor will make a big splash with his new group Canned Heat at the Monterey International Pop Festival.

● Thursday 11th

FILMING Production wraps on what will become episode 38 of the *Monkees* series, *I Was A 99lb. Weakling*.

● Friday 12th – Saturday 13th

● It is possible that The Monkees are booked to record in RCA's Studio C this weekend, starting at 7:00pm each evening.

● Monday 15th

TV Another repeat from the first season of *The Monkees* – episode 4, *Your Friendly Neighborhood Kidnappers* – is aired at 7:30pm on NBC. As usual now, the soundtrack has been updated with a different line-up of songs. This broadcast wins its time slot, pulling in almost nine and a half million viewers.

● A further recording session is booked tonight in RCA's Studio C, starting at 7:00pm, but it is unclear if it goes ahead.

● Tuesday 16th

● Copies of The Monkees' third album, *Headquarters*, are shipped to distributors. The album will also be available on 8-track tape cartridges.

● Thursday 18th

FILMING Production wraps on what will become episode 40 of *The Monkees* series, *Monkees Marooned*.

● Friday 19th – Monday 22nd
Another series of evening sessions are booked for this weekend in RCA's Studio C but again it is unclear what Monkees activity occurs, if any.

● Saturday 20th
● *Billboard* reports that The Monkees' new album *Headquarters* has been awarded a gold record for more than a million dollars in sales a week in advance of its official release by the RIAA (the Recording Industry Association of America, a record manufacturing trade association). RCA, which manufactures and distributes The Monkees' records, received more than a million pre-orders for the disc and made an early request to the RIAA.

● Monday 22nd
TV A further updated repeat from the first season of *The Monkees* is aired at 7:30pm on NBC. Tonight's episode – number 3, *Monkee Vs. Machine* – is revised to include the *Headquarters* track 'You Told Me' in place of 'Saturday's Child.' The program once again wins its time slot, pulling in some eight million viewers.

● Tuesday 23rd
● Michael is admitted to Cedars Of Lebanon Hospital in Los Angeles for a tonsillectomy. Davy recalls: "Mike had a problem for the first year and half of our relationship. He was singing like it was coming out of his nose. During the course of The Monkees' first year he had his tonsils out. That was why he had a different [vocal] quality when he went on to do his later stuff. If you listen to it, it's very nasal, very throaty. He had his tonsils out. Can you believe that: a 24-year-old man? But he did. That's why he sounded like he did. It all sounded as if he had a cushion in his throat. After he had 'em out his vocal presentation changed."

● Friday 26th
FILMING Production wraps on what will become episode 49 of the *Monkees* series, *Monkees Watch Their Feet*. Michael is absent from this program since he is recovering from his tonsillectomy. Later this year he will film a 'wrap-around' segment for the program with personality Pat Paulsen. (A 'wrap-around' is a segment shot separately and designed to introduce a show's main segments or give them context.)

● Saturday 27th
● A concert scheduled for 8:00pm at Spartan Stadium in San Jose,

California, is cancelled due to Michael's illness.
● The Monkees' British filming schedule is also in jeopardy, though today's *NME* notes that no firm decision has been made. "Quite honestly, we don't know what we're doing," Davy tells the paper. "We have been told that we might arrive in Britain on June 15th for filming before our concerts, but it depends on whether we can complete our Hollywood filming schedule in sufficient time."
● Today's *Billboard* reveals more details behind Don Kirshner's legal fracas with Columbia/Screen Gems. There is now a countersuit, and Columbia/Screen Gems have made public a list of allegations that directly led to Kirshner's dismissal. They include Kirshner's threat to withhold recording master tapes on the eve of the debut of the *Monkees* series (in September 1966) unless show producers Raybert refrained from taking a piece of the publishing royalties from songs performed by the group.

Also under attack is Kirshner's self-aggrandizing publicity, which the company felt erroneously implied that The Monkees' lack of talent was covered by Kirshner's use of modern recording techniques.

Further cited is Kirshner's refusal to release 'The Girl I Knew Somewhere,' which led to, among other things, a $25,000 printing cost for unusable picture sleeves that featured the title of the Kirshner-selected song 'She Hangs Out.' Lastly, a charge is made that Kirshner secretly recorded telephone conversations with various executives from the company.
● Also in today's issue, *Billboard* reports that Davy and his manager Hal Cone have set up another new company, Davy Jones Publications, in London. The magazine's album charts show the group holding strong with four Monkees-related placings. The second album, *More Of The Monkees*, clings to #1, while last year's *The Monkees* is still impressively placed at #7. Davy's Colpix album *David Jones*, now on re-release, debuts at #188, and *The Monkees Song Book*, a long-player of instrumental interpretations of the group's songs performed by The Golden Gate Strings, holds down the bottom of the chart at #200.

● Sunday 28th
● Davy makes an appearance on the British television program *Secombe And Friends* fronted by his former *Pickwick* co-star, Harry Secombe.

● Monday 29th
TV The next revised repeat from the first season of *The Monkees* is aired at 7:30pm on NBC. Tonight's version of episode 6, *Success Story*, features 'Shades Of Gray' in place of 'I Wanna Be Free.' Also today sessions begin for the fourth Monkees album.
RECORDING RCA (C) *Hollywood, CA* 2:00-5:00, 7:00pm-1:00am. Chip Douglas *prod*; half-inch 4-track; tracking.
1. 'The Door Into Summer' version 1
    unissued master # UZB3-5436
Personnel Micky Dolenz (drums), Chip Douglas (acoustic guitar), Larry Taylor (acoustic guitar), Peter Tork (keyboards).
● Chip Douglas leads Micky, Larry Taylor, and possibly Peter through this Bill Martin song. Martin's last composition submitted to the band, 'All Of Your Toys,' was canned due to a publishing dispute, among other issues. Martin is now writing for Screen Gems proper and so is free to submit as many tunes as he likes to the group, though 'Summer' will be the only one they will record.

Micky is surprised by the strength of his own drumming performance on this first version of the song, leading him to quip at the end of the best take: "Hey, he was recording!" Peter is listed on the musicians' union work sheet for both the afternoon and evening

---

Work goes on in the TV studio during May for episode 38, *I Was A 99lb Weakling* (LEFT), and episode 40, *Monkees Marooned* (ABOVE).

sessions of this song, but his clavinet and piano parts are probably added after the initial tracking is completed.

It is possible that today's version is used as the basis for the final work heard on the *Pisces* album, but the significant amount of production placed on the final recording makes this impossible to verify. The final released version will be edited and speeded up from the original (recorded in the key of D) to a peppy E-flat, and additional drums, probably played by Eddie Hoh, are incorporated into the production to strengthen Micky's original performance. Chip Douglas will attempt an entirely new backing track for the song on June 22nd.

JUNE

● *16* magazine reports that a new duo called The Boomer Boys will soon appear on Colgems Records. The group includes two of Michael's former bandmates from The Survivors, John London and Owens 'Boomer' Castleman, as well as songwriter and friend Michael Murphey. Colgems' Lester Sill will eventually rename them The Lewis & Clarke Expedition.
● Michael is 'sponsoring' another band, The Penny Arkade, which includes Chris Ducey, Craig Smith, Don Glut, and Bobby Donaho. Smith, who auditioned for *The Monkees* and was seriously considered, is responsible for 'Salesman' which Michael will record with The Monkees this month. Currently, The Penny Arkade are performing gigs at the Spectrum club on Sunset Strip in Los Angeles. Prior to Michael's patronage, Ducey and Smith recorded for Capitol Records as Chris & Craig and were to be stars of a failed Monkees-like series for ABC, *The Happeners*.

● Friday 2nd
FILMING Production wraps on what will become episode 33 of the *Monkees* series, *It's A Nice Place To Visit*, which will screen as the debut episode for the second season of the series.

● Saturday 3rd
● The *NME* says that Micky's 'Randy Scouse Git' may be left off British editions of *Headquarters* because of the offensive title and that a previously unissued track may be substituted in its place. The paper also notes that the group may do some filming in Paris for their series, though they are still eager to shoot in Britain.
● *Billboard* reports that Jack Angel, vice president of Davy Jones Records, is on a global trek to secure worldwide distribution for the label. Angel and Davy are also mounting a radio contest called *Why Davy Jones Is Your Favorite Monkee* that will produce 50 winners from across the country.
● A Monkees-related recording session is scheduled in RCA's Studio C from 8:00pm to midnight, but no further details are available.

● Sunday 4th
● The group along with Bert Schneider and Bob Rafelson attend the National Academy of Television Arts and Sciences' annual presentation of Emmy Awards, given for excellence in television performance and production.

Series creators Schneider and Rafelson win the award for Outstanding Comedy Series and director Jim Frawley takes home the Outstanding Directorial Achievement In Comedy award for his work on *Royal Flush*, episode 1 of *The Monkees*. The awards presentation is telecast live in color.

● Thursday 8th
FILMING Production wraps on what will become episode 36 of the *Monkees* series, *Monkee Mayor*. (Afterwards, Davy travels on an evening flight to New York City.) The series will go on hiatus for the summer as the group prepare for a tour and complete recordings for their fourth album. Production of the TV series will resume in September.
● 'Barbary Coast' and 'Doomed To War' are copyrighted by Kelton International music publishers on behalf of Micky. He used to perform at least the second song live with his sister Coco at a Los Angeles club prior to The Monkees' debut. It is unusual that these songs are registered at this late date since all of Micky's current songs are published and controlled by Screen Gems Music. Perhaps they exist in recorded form and the publisher is hoping to get them issued as a single.

● Friday 9th
PERFORMANCE Hollywood Bowl *Los Angeles, CA* 8:00pm, with Ike & Tina Turner & The Ikettes; tickets $4-$8; sponsored by radio station KHJ
● The Monkees perform a hometown concert to an audience exceeding 17,000. Twelve hundred and fifty of the box seats have been reserved for VIPs from Screen Gems, RKO General (affiliated with RCA), and other corporations. Davy returns to Los Angeles from New York just prior to the show, which will gross in excess of $115,000.

The band's 65-minute set reportedly includes (in no specific order): 'Last Train To Clarksville,' 'I'm A Believer,' '(I'm Not Your) Steppin' Stone,' 'I've Got A Woman' (during which Micky will jump into the three-feet-deep fountain pool at the front of the stage – a Hollywood Bowl no-no), 'Your Auntie Grizelda,' 'Pick A Bale Of Cotton' (performed by Peter solo), 'Shades Of Gray' (the show's finale, which is accompanied by a colored light show), 'I Wanna Be Free' (accompanied by film clips of freedom marches, anti-war demonstrations, and the Sunset Strip riots), 'Gonna Build A Mountain' (with Davy backed by The Sundowners, a club band who have recorded for Decca), 'Sunny Girlfriend,' 'You Just May Be The One,' and 'You Can't Judge A Book By The Cover.'

LEFT Peter in costume for his role in TV episode 49, *Monkees Watch Their Feet*. ABOVE At the Emmy Awards bash in June where the *Monkees* television series wins prizes for the two producers and a director.

Pete Johnson reviews the show for the *Los Angeles Times*. "They have been criticized for not playing their instruments on the first Monkees records and for leaning heavily on other people's talent to produce their music," he writes. "But each member soloed and played several instruments during the evening, showing that they can support themselves and are willing to accept the responsibility of their popularity."

After the event, The Monkees host an 11:00pm party at PJs club on Santa Monica Boulevard in West Hollywood.

● Saturday 10th
● Jackie Cooper of Screen Gems tells the *Chicago Daily News*: "I think *The Monkees* is going to be the most popular show in the history of television. It's been one of the best kept secrets in the world," he says, alluding to NBC's strange decision to compete with itself by scheduling *The Monkees* opposite their own *Iron Horse* show on another network. Cooper reports that the show's major network competition next season will shift from *Gilligan's Island* and *Iron Horse* to *Gunsmoke* and *Cowboy In Africa*.

Thus far the group's sales of records and merchandising have far outstripped their TV show's ratings. "The Monkees are selling more records than anybody in the history of RCA," states Cooper. "Last year we grossed $1.5m in the merchandising division – Monkee stove pipe pants, Monkee gum, Monkee wool caps, Monkee suede boots – and the boys were unknowns till September."

Although the group are increasingly outspoken, Cooper is still enforcing a 'no press' rule. "They are primitive talents," he explains. "They don't conduct themselves like you expect a professional to act. They've learned a helluva lot in the past year, but a lot they say is misinterpreted. Don't forget, they are part of that youth [culture] which is quite rebellious against all us old fuddie-duddies who expect them to cut their hair and all this and that. These kids are very politically aware of what's going on in the world. They are quarreling with us as to what kind of world we have left them. They are quarreling with us as to what kind of parents we are. And they have opinions that are not ours. They can be right, and I can be right, we both can be right, but that's not the kind of stuff that I as a studio head want these kids to sit down and be discussing with the press."

● The *NME* says that the group will spend four days filming in Davy's hometown of Manchester in northern England, beginning June 21st, and that Davy is now exempt from the U.S. draft.

● A proposed second concert in Los Angeles scheduled for this evening never gets past the planning stages. Instead, the group begin recording their next single at RCA.

RECORDING RCA (A) *Hollywood, CA* 7:00-11:30pm. Chip Douglas *prod*; half-inch 4-track; tracking.

1. **'Pleasant Valley Sunday'**
   Pisces, Aquarius... master # UZB3-5437
2. **'Peter Percival Patterson's Pet Pig Porky'**
   Pisces, Aquarius... master # UZB3-9832

Personnel Micky Dolenz (possibly acoustic guitar 1), Chip Douglas (bass 1), Eddie Hoh (drums 1), Michael Nesmith (electric guitar 1), Peter Tork (piano 1, spoken word 2).

● Gerry Goffin & Carole King's 'Pleasant Valley Sunday' is one of Chip Douglas's most complex productions for The Monkees. Sadly, session tapes will not survive for this landmark date so it is impossible to follow this wonderful creation step-by-step. The basic track is most likely recorded with Chip Douglas and Eddie Hoh

forming the rhythm section of bass and drums while Michael and Peter perform on electric guitar and piano. Union documents indicate that Micky is also present for this session, and it is quite possible that he contributes some acoustic guitar to the track. Additional guitar overdubs will be recorded tomorrow.

Chip Douglas: "Mike played the lead guitar. That was my riff that I threw in there and taught to Mike. Not many guitar players can play it the right way. ... It's kind of an offshoot of the Beatles song 'I Want To Tell You' but in a different tempo and with different notes.

"I wish I could hear the original demo, because I can't recall if I got a [lyric] line right or not. It's in the bridge, 'creature comfort goals can only numb my soul and make it hard for me to see.' For 'make it hard for me to see,' for some reason I had the impression that I didn't do the right line in there, or changed it possibly. I couldn't understand that line, or something like that. One of those great mysteries.

"I do remember seeing Carole King up at the Screen Gems office from across the room after we did 'Pleasant Valley Sunday.' She kind of gave me this dirty look. I thought, 'Was it that line that I got wrong, perhaps? Or didn't she like the guitar intro?' It was faster, definitely, than the way she had done it. She had a more laidback way of doing stuff."

Michael: "I remember that we went after the guitar sound. Everybody was trying to get that great big present guitar sound – nobody knew quite how to do it. I think I used like three [Vox] Super Beatle [amplifiers] in the studio, playing really loud trying to get the sound, and it just ended up sounding kind of ... like it does. Kind of wooden. There was a tube-type of limiter/compressor called a UREI 1176, and boy you could really suck stuff out of the track. That was the first time that we really could do it. I think everybody got a little carried away with the 1176 on that record."

Also reportedly taped this evening is Peter's spoken piece 'Peter Percival Patterson's Pet Pig Porky.' He learned this brief nursery rhyme from friend and future bandmate Judy Mayhan. Peter's performance will later be edited on to the beginning of 'Pleasant Valley Sunday' for its album release.

Douglas: "He just did it sometime in the studio, for people that were there, maybe; there were always a couple of girlfriends. That was one of his little bits of some sort. So I said, 'Let's record it.' My tendency was to do anything that was slightly entertaining, be it music or talking."

● Sunday 11th

● Monkees series producer Bob Rafelson leaves Los Angeles at midday to fly to London on Pan Am flight 120. He will arrive in England tomorrow to publicize the series and prepare for filming an episode in Paris. Back in Los Angeles, work continues on The Monkees' next single.

RECORDING RCA (A) *Hollywood, CA* 2:00-6:30pm. Chip Douglas *prod*; half-inch 4-track; reductions, overdubs.
1. **'Pleasant Valley Sunday'**
   Pisces, Aquarius... master # UZB3-5437
Personnel Bill Chadwick (acoustic guitar), Eddie Hoh (shaker, congas), Michael Nesmith (electric guitar).
● 'Pleasant Valley Sunday' gets its first round of overdubs at this session. It is likely that the original 4-track session master is 'bounced' to a second machine and that the overdubs are added at the same time. Michael doubles his electric guitar part while Bill Chadwick adds an additional acoustic guitar. Eddie Hoh adds shaker to the song's verses and congas to the bridge section. Chip Douglas: "We may have compressed the guitars a lot, because there were

several guitars in there. I think Bill Chadwick played rhythm and Mike did the lead live and then overdubbed it and fattened it up. We did it with his Vox amp and probably a Gretsch guitar."

● Monday 12th

TV Another repeat from the first season of *The Monkees* – episode 16, *Son Of A Gypsy* – is aired at 7:30pm on NBC, but on this occasion no changes to the soundtrack are made. The airing still wins its time slot, though only with a relatively meager audience of six and a half million viewers. Show producer Bert Schneider will not be watching tonight since he too has flown to London to meet up with Bob Rafelson and make preparations for The Monkees' European visit.

● Tuesday 13th

RECORDING RCA Studio *Hollywood, CA* 3:00-6:00pm. Chip Douglas *prod*; half-inch 4-track; reductions, overdubs.
1. **'Pleasant Valley Sunday'**
   Pisces, Aquarius... master # UZB3-5437
Personnel Micky Dolenz (lead vocal, backing vocal), Chip Douglas (possibly vocal), Eddie Hoh (percussion), David Jones (backing vocal), Michael Nesmith (electric guitar, vocal), Peter Tork (backing vocal).
● The final session is held to complete the production of 'Pleasant Valley Sunday.' The first part is attended by Michael and Eddie Hoh, who are on hand to do last-minute clean-up on their guitar and percussion parts respectively, after which the song's vocal tracks are probably added. These feature Micky on lead with a harmony from Michael. All four Monkees (possibly with the help of Chip Douglas) sing the song's complex backing vocal arrangement, which is recorded in sections and then edited together. The stunning results will be issued next month as the group's fourth single.

● Wednesday 14th

● One of the more productive sessions of The Monkees' career takes place today. Proving that they have truly hit their stride in the studio, they cut three superb tracks at this session, including the band's next #1 single.
RECORDING RCA (A) *Hollywood, CA* 6:00-9:00, 9:30pm-12midnight. Chip Douglas *prod*; half-inch 4-track; tracking.
1. **'Words'** version 2
   Pisces, Aquarius... master # TZB3-4723
2. **'Daydream Believer'**
   The Birds, The Bees... master # UZB3-5438
3. **'Salesman'**
   Pisces, Aquarius... master # UZB3-5439
Personnel Chip Douglas (bass, nylon-string guitar 3), Eddie Hoh (drums), Michael Nesmith (electric guitar 1,3, electric 12-string guitar 2, shaker 3), Peter Tork (organ 1, piano 2, possibly acoustic guitar 3).
● First off, the group set about re-recording Boyce & Hart's 'Words.' It was originally taped in August '66; today's updated version retains the original's arrangement (and master number). The only real difference is that the instrumental section will feature an organ break from Peter in place of the original's flute solo. The track is captured in nine takes. Percussion parts heard in the song's final production are added at a separate session, some possibly by Michael since he can be heard commenting: "You play the chimes, I'm tired of playing the bell." He may also play a second electric guitar part that is later overdubbed.

Chip Douglas: "We tried to do it as close to the original one, which was [recorded] by Boyce and Hart. We just duplicated what was on the original. The only difference is there's Monkees in the

Another day, another recording session: Micky calmly prepares for a take at RCA. He will later explore his Native American heritage in the song 'Mommy And Daddy.'

background instead of Boyce and Hart. Peter did the solo."

Tracking for the classic 'Daydream Believer' is basic. Peter plays piano and Michael does some very subtle picking and harmonics on his 12-string. Meanwhile, Douglas and Hoh lay down the bass and drums. The song will be given extensive overdubs in the future and will eventually be transferred to a new recording format for the group: one inch 8-track tape.

'Salesman' was composed by Michael's protégé from The Penny Arkade, Craig Smith, and features a rather sly lyric. However, at this session the group concentrate on the song's backing track. No session tapes will survive so it is not known how many takes are required to complete it to everyone's satisfaction. There are two acoustic guitars on the final production: one playing rhythm throughout, and a nylon-string guitar played by Chip Douglas, adding twangy fills. Given Peter's presence for the rest of this session he is most likely playing the first acoustic. Douglas's nylon-string part and Michael's shaker track are overdubs that may be added at a later session. Work on the track will resume in July.

● Thursday 15th
RECORDING RCA (C) *Hollywood, CA* 7:00pm-12midnight (possibly later). Chip Douglas *prod*; Hank Cicalo *eng*; half-inch 4-track; overdubs.
1. **'Words'** version 2 overdubs onto take 9
   Pisces, Aquarius... master # TZB3-4723
Personnel Micky Dolenz (vocal 1), Peter Tork (vocal 1).
● During this session Micky and Peter record their lead vocals for version 2 of this song (and it's possible that vocals for other songs are also attempted). During run-throughs of 'Words' Micky, Peter, Douglas, and engineer Hank Cicalo discuss recording a joke commercial for the upcoming album, as well as lampooning The Beatles' 'A Day In The Life' by singing "I'd love to turn you ... off."

Micky has recently returned from a trip to Mexico and tells the group of the wild DJs south of the border. He is especially fond of the amount of reverb they use down there. Micky is very complimentary of Peter's vocal performance on 'Words,' though he is insecure about his own singing and the session breaks off sometime after midnight so that Micky can get some coffee for his throat. When Micky and company return the session resumes, but it is not clear if the vocals for 'Words' are completed in the early morning hours.

● Friday 16th
'**Alternate Title**' / '**Forget That Girl**' single is released in the U.K. This is Micky's 'Randy Scouse Git' from *Headquarters* with a new title, backed with Chip Douglas's 'Forget That Girl,' also from the new album. Micky picked up the phrase 'randy scouse git' from a British TV program *Till Death Us Do Part*, which he saw during his February trip to London. He was unaware that it might be offensive. Roughly

---

Alternate Title single

A '**Alternate Title**' (M. DOLENZ)
B '**Forget That Girl**' (D. F. HATFIELD)

U.K. release June 16th 1967 (RCA 1604).
Chart high U.K. number 2.

---

translated, the phrase means 'lecherous Liverpudlian jerk.' When told that the title would have to be changed for successful single release, he flippantly renames it 'Alternate Title.' In the U.S.A. no single will be pulled from the *Headquarters* album. Still unavailable in Britain, the LP is due for release there at month's end to tie in with the group's Wembley concerts.
● Micky and Peter travel to Northern California to attend the Monterey International Pop Festival. Peter will act as MC for part of tonight's program, introducing performances by Buffalo Springfield and Lou Rawls. Micky tells Keith Altham of the *NME* that The Monkees' movie "won't be this year. The TV series is coming along real nice so the film will have to wait till next year."
● Back in Los Angeles, Chip Douglas has the whole weekend booked to work on the group's album at RCA studios. However, it is unclear what exactly is accomplished and if these sessions actually take place in the absence of Peter and Micky.

● Saturday 17th
● The *NME* says that The Monkees will shoot portions of their movie in Britain during February 1968. "I want to make a movie here because I believe film people are more creative in Britain," says Bob Rafelson. "They have freedom. Deciding on a storyline and treatment is giving me a lot of problems. I do not want the movie to be just an extension of the TV show. Neither must it be like a Beatles production, or a piece of rock'n'roll exploitation. I may base the script on some incidents from my own life as a boy – many of my own experiences have already inspired several of the TV shows."

Rafelson has also scheduled The Monkees' first ever 'group' press conference for June 29th, but their proposed series-shoot in Manchester is now cancelled. "I am afraid we are having to change our plans almost hourly," he tells the *NME*. "Last week we intended that The Monkees should spend four days filming on location in Britain for a future TV show. I now realize this is impossible: they are too well known here, and the fans would swamp every shot. Apart from this, The Monkees are now working day and night in America on their fourth album. ... They have so much work, I am amazed they have not cracked up by now. Because of this, they will not be able to leave for Europe until the last possible moment."
● *Billboard* reports that The Monkees' upcoming summer tour has a potential box office gross of $2.25m. The largest potential gross is for their three-day stint at New York's Forest Hills Tennis Stadium, which is pegged to earn $307,000.
● Today at the Monterey International Pop Festival, Micky visits a booth set up to demonstrate a relatively new keyboard instrument called the Moog synthesizer. Instantly impressed by the sounds produced by this invention of Robert Moog's, Micky places an order for one. He will own one of the earliest production models and will use it at some of the group's sessions later this summer.

● Sunday 18th
● Still in Monterey, Micky attends an afternoon performance by sitar master Ravi Shankar. He affords Shankar's set a rapturous response and can be seen cheering wildly in the film of this event (released in December 1968 as *Monterey Pop*). This evening Micky and Peter witness a performance by The Jimi Hendrix Experience. Micky is so impressed by Hendrix that he begins plotting a way to get the guitarist onto the bill of The Monkees' summer tour.

● Monday 19th
TV At 7:30pm the NBC network repeats episode 5 from *The Monkees*, *The Spy Who Came In From The Cool*. The soundtrack is updated to include 'Randy Scouse Git' in place of 'Saturday's Child.' Meanwhile

in the studio the group record two overtly psychedelic songs for their fourth album.

RECORDING RCA (C) *Hollywood, CA* 2:00-5:00, 8:00pm-12:30am. Chip Douglas *prod*; half-inch 4-track; tracking.

1. **'Daily Nightly'**
   Pisces, Aquarius... master # UZB3-5440
2. **'Love Is Only Sleeping'**
   Pisces, Aquarius... master # UZB3-5441

Personnel Chip Douglas (bass 1,2, acoustic guitar 2), Eddie Hoh (drums 1,2), David Jones (tambourine 2), Michael Nesmith (electric guitar 1,2), Peter Tork (organ 1,2).

● During the afternoon the group concentrates on recording Michael's poem set to music, 'Daily Nightly.' Lyrically it is vaguely inspired by last November's curfew riots on Los Angeles's Sunset Strip. Michael: "It's the Hollywood street scene. I wrote it because I had bought a Hammond B3 [organ]. That guitar line – do, do, ba, dudly, dee, da, da – that's a keyboard lick and I'm not sure how it got over into the guitar. I may have done it, or Chip may have done it. It was just a kind of a rambling comment on the Hollywood street scenes of the time.

"Somewhere around that time [the club] Pandora's Box had burned down. It was at the intersection of Crescent Heights and [Sunset Boulevard]. Something happened one night. The people – the street scene – would congregate, and that was a very important corner, West. They had gotten a bus and caught a bus on fire. Which had then in turn I think burned down Pandora's Box. That was the first real time that those crazy kids got out of control. I was amused by the obvious inability of the press to digest this information: they just didn't have any sense of what was going on at all. Completely lost. So, I just wrote it down in that poem."

Although today's recording will eventually find its way onto 8-track tape for further overdubs, including Micky's Moog effects, no details or dates will survive for any further 'Daily Nightly' sessions and the final 8-track master will be lost. (As The Monkees switch formats to 8-track it will be harder for future researchers to get a clear picture of how the group's productions develop. From this time onwards more emphasis will be placed on piecing together a collection of overdubs rather than capturing a performance and then perfecting it.)

After a three-hour break, today's session resumes at 8:00pm. The next song at hand is 'Love Is Only Sleeping,' an epic by Barry Mann and Cynthia Weil. After this initial tracking work the song will receive a myriad of overdubs, though most of the details (along with the tapes) will be lost. Probably taped on another, undisclosed date are Peter's organ part, heard only in sections of the song's final mix, and the lead vocal overdub by Michael – with Micky providing a harmony and an almost identical double of Michael's performance during the first half of the song. Also at another session Douglas, Davy, and Micky will provide the song's heavily 'treated' backing vocals and percussion. As with 'Daily Nightly,' the final tracks for 'Love Is Only Sleeping' will be transferred to an 8-track tape for final production touches such as handclaps and the song's fading sound of Peter's Hammond organ being switched off.

Michael: "I remember when they would send me Barry and Cynthia's songs. We were always looking for songs to record. I just remember liking ['Love Is Only Sleeping'] quite a bit in the demo." Chip Douglas: "It was a demo and became one of the keepers. We all listened to the demos and we all said, 'This one sounds good, let's do this.' It was a group effort when it came to the demos; we'd all listen down. I'd kind of go through them and find the ones that I thought they might like. Then I would play them for them. Mostly all of the stuff that came in we listened to, I think."

● **Tuesday 20th**

● Four hundred journalists, including foreign press, have requested seats for The Monkees' London press conference and 18 camera crews are slated to capture the event. The group's concerts in Wembley, north London are now expected to gross $85,000. As a follow-up, Rafelson has announced that the group will tour the Far East in February, with a further world tour next summer. Rafelson says that *The Monkees* is now the most widely circulated 'teleseries' in the history of Screen Gems. He also admits that he has so far "tossed away" five scripts for The Monkees' upcoming feature film.

Meanwhile at RCA in Los Angeles two of Michael's selections for the group's fourth album are taped.

RECORDING RCA (A) *Hollywood, CA* 2:00-6:30pm. Chip Douglas *prod*; half-inch 4-track; tracking.

1. **'What Am I Doing Hangin' 'Round'**
   Pisces, Aquarius... master # UZB3-5442
2. **'Don't Call On Me'**
   Pisces, Aquarius... master # UZB3-7314

Personnel Doug Dillard (electric banjo 1), Chip Douglas (bass 1,2, acoustic guitar 2), Eddie Hoh (drums 1,2, claves 2), Michael Nesmith (electric guitar 1,2), Peter Tork (organ 2).

● This session produces The Monkees' groundbreaking foray into country-rock, 'What Am I Doing Hangin' 'Round.' Though Michael had certainly cut other country flavored numbers for the group, most prominently 'Papa Gene's Blues,' this recording will be seen by many as a landmark in the fusion of country and rock.

The song is taped under the working title of 'Yankee Loudmouth' and the recording appears to be a straightforward affair. The most prominent feature is the electric banjo played by guest musician Doug Dillard, a longtime Chip Douglas cohort. At a later date Michael will overdub his lead vocal and Micky, Davy, and Douglas will provide background harmonies on the choruses. The song is written by Michael Murphey and Owens 'Boomer' Castleman but credited under their Colgems stage names of Lewis & Clarke.

Michael: "One of the things that I had really felt was honest was country-rock. I wanted to move The Monkees more into that because I felt like gee, you know, if we get closer to country music, we'll get closer to blues, and country blues, and so forth. [Murphey and Castleman] were writers at Screen Gems and they just wrote all kinds of really wonderful little songs, and 'Hangin' 'Round' was one of them. I think Mike Murphey was more of the architect of that song than 'Boomer' Castleman, but I don't know: they may have written it equally. It had a lot of un-country things in it: a familiar change from a I major to a VI minor – those kinds of things. So it was a little kind of a new wave country song. It didn't sound like the country songs of the time, which was Buck Owens."

Next up at the session is 'Don't Call On Me,' a revived Michael Nesmith/John London composition dating back to their folk duo days as Mike & John. Here it's updated for the *Pisces* sessions in an arrangement not too far from Michael's pre-Monkees demo of the song and is taped in a total of 28 takes. Although Peter tracks his organ part live with the other musicians, it will later be redone – along with Michael's lead vocal – at a session in Nashville during August.

Chip Douglas: "When we were doing *Pisces* Mike would come in with three songs; he knew he had three songs coming on the album. He knew that he was making a lot of money if he got his original songs on there. So he'd be real enthusiastic and cooperative and real friendly and get his three songs done.

"Then I'd say, 'Mike, can you come in and help on this one we're going to do with Micky here?' He said, 'No Chip, I can't, I'm busy.' I'd say, 'Mike, you gotta come in the studio.' He'd say, 'No Chip, I'm afraid I'm just gonna have to be ornery about it, I'm not comin' in.' That's when I started not liking Mike as much any more. Even though he was the one that got me into it in the first place.

"Then I began to kind of hang out with Peter – there wasn't quite as big a crowd over at Peter's house as everybody else's. So I could hang out and talk about things – philosophy and whatnot. Mike, he'd get his stuff done and then be of no help to anyone else. *Headquarters* [had been] different. Once *Headquarters* was done and they proved they could play their own stuff, Mike didn't care about anything except getting his songs on the album.

"I had a hell of a time trying to get him to come in and do background things, which I was always really adamant about. I wanted it to only be them singing. I didn't even like putting all the [non-Monkees] on there, but I got used to it after it went down on tape and sounded great. My whole philosophy was the *Headquarters* edict: only [The Monkees] get to play on this stuff and sing, especially sing."

● Wednesday 21st

● Producers Bob Rafelson and Bert Schneider fly to Paris from London. Back in Los Angeles sessions for the group's fourth album are continuing.

RECORDING RCA (A) *Hollywood, CA* 4:30-7:30pm. Chip Douglas *prod*; half-inch 4-track; tracking.

1. **'She Hangs Out'** version 2
   Pisces, Aquarius... master # UZB3-7313
2. **'Goin' Down'**
   Greatest Hits master # UZB3-7315

Personnel Chip Douglas (bass 1,2), Eddie Hoh (drums 1,2), Michael Nesmith (electric guitar 1,2), Peter Tork (organ 1, electric guitar 2).

● Today sees a return to the rather innocuous song that caused such discord in the Monkees organization just six months ago, Jeff Barry's 'She Hangs Out.' It is now unavailable in its Barry-produced take, which briefly appeared as a single B-side in Canada only. Now the group – or at least Michael and Peter – get to perform a backing track themselves for this new version. It will take several sessions to complete the production, and today's results on 4-track tape will eventually be transferred to 8-track.

Chip Douglas: "I guess Davy liked the song and we were just looking for songs, and somebody said, 'Well, what about that one we did?' Of course everybody said, 'Well, we can't use what we did before, we've got to do it again.' So we redid it. I liked the song, so I figured it was good."

'Goin' Down' develops out of a jam at the end of 'She Hangs Out' and is originally meant to be The Monkees' version of Mose Allison's 'Parchman Farm,' a blues number that has been recorded under a variety of subtly different titles over the years. After the track is completed, Michael will suggest that since the results don't actually sound much like Allison's song, some new lyrics could be written to make it a Monkees original. Diane Hilderbrand, who earlier penned 'Your Auntie Grizelda' and 'Early Morning Blues And Greens' for the group, will do the honors, and the song is thus credited to the whole group plus Hilderbrand. Micky will overdub his lead vocal for the song after the lyrics are composed and impressive brass arrangements will be added to both 'Goin' Down' and 'She Hangs Out' later this year.

Peter recalls: "Somebody gave me an arrangement of 'Parchman Farm' that a friend of theirs had sort of generated – the real folk process at work. I had played that version around for a while in the group amongst the guys. We'd sort of all known it. I don't remember why we started playing it that day, but we just jammed it … like

unrehearsed. We just started to play that tune.

"It's a funny thing, it doesn't sound like Mike on guitar. I listened to it just the other day. It sounded a little looser and a little bit more sort of frolicy than Mike's guitar playing was as I recall. In any case, I think we just started with bass, guitar, and drums. Maybe a couple of guitars and we just jammed. We broke into that I-IV-I-IV jam spontaneously too, I remember. Next thing I knew Lester [Sill] came to us and said, 'Listen, we've written some lyrics for that song and we're gonna overdub some horns and get Micky to go in and do it.' That was 'Goin' Down.' It was one of the things that can only come up if you're engaged in the record-making process on a regular basis. You can't do that by yourself."

Michael: "Peter had always loved to jam 'Parchman Farm' and started off on this thing. We just headed off into la-la land. Then Micky started riffing this thing over the top of it. Yeah, that's how it worked – I remember now. It actually doesn't work bad! And then I think Chip [Douglas] went and put horns on it. I think I introduced [the horns arranger Shorty Rogers] to Chip."

● Thursday 22nd

● Micky's 'Alternate Title' enters the British singles chart where it will peak at #2 during its 12-week chart run. 'Alternate Title' is 'Randy Scouse Git' renamed in order to avoid offending any pop pickers. Meanwhile, just prior to leaving for Europe, the group hold their last session of the month at RCA's Studio A.

RECORDING RCA (A) *Hollywood, CA* 2:00-5:00, 8:00pm-12midnight. Chip Douglas *prod*; Hank Cicalo *eng*; half-inch 4-track; tracking.

1. **'Yours Until Tomorrow'**
   unissued master # UZB3-7318
2. **'The Door Into Summer'** version 2 rehearsals + takes
   unissued master # UZB3-7318
3. **'I've Got Rhythm'** take 1
   unissued no master #
4. **'Sixty-Nine'** take 1
   unissued no master #
5. **'Can You Dig It'** demo takes 1-11
   Headquarters Sessions no master #
6. **'Tear The Top Right Off My Head'** demo take 1
   unissued no master #
7. **'The Bells Of Rhymney'** demo take 1
   unissued no master #
8. **'Untitled'** demo takes 1-9
   unissued no master #
9. **'A Man Without A Dream'** demo takes 1-3
   unissued no master #
10. **'Star Collector'**
    Pisces, Aquarius... master # UZB3-7319

Personnel Chip Douglas (bass 1*,2,10 guitar 2, piano 2, shaker 2, vocal rehearsal 2, possibly electric guitar 10) Eddie Hoh (drums 1,2,3,4, 10), Michael Nesmith (electric guitar 1,10), Peter Tork (bass 1*, acoustic guitar 5,6,7,8,9,10 organ 10). * Tork or Douglas on bass.

● To start this busy and varied session just one take is made of the promising Goffin & King song 'Yours Until Tomorrow'. The bass playing is somewhat less self-assured than Chip Douglas's normal style so it is possible that Peter plays it. Regardless of the line-up, this single take is as far as The Monkees will go with the tune. Although the song is cut by countless other artists – including Gene Pitney, Engelbert Humperdinck, and Alan Price – a Monkees version is never publicly heard.

Next up is a second version of 'The Door Into Summer.' The difference to the version from May 29th is that Douglas today performs it virtually solo, playing everything save for the drums. After a number of run-throughs on acoustic guitar and a brief vocal rehearsal, he builds up a master backing track piece by piece. The Monkees are not keen on this version, so no vocals will ever be added.

Douglas: "It had a real good feel to it, but we had to redo it for some reason. Someone didn't like it, one of the guys or something. The same key and everything, but for some reason we had to do the whole thing again. I was always a little disappointed in the newer version of it."

Drummer Eddie Hoh kills some time during a lull in the session by taping two drum improvisations. These recordings are never intended for release, though they will survive on the session tape. Next, Peter tapes a series of demos. The first item recorded, for now titled 'Tentatively,' is an instrumental version of his song 'Can You Dig It.' Take 2 is marked as the master and pulled to a separate reel of odds and ends. (In 2000 it will be issued on the *Headquarters Sessions* set because it is assumed that it dates from earlier in 1967.)

As the session proceeds Peter confesses that he is feeling a little "uptight" but disregards Douglas's joking suggestion that he get stoned again. A few takes later Douglas tells Peter that they are all alone; Peter then seriously suggests that perhaps the producer could leave too. Douglas says he thinks that maybe the best take of 'Tentatively' was captured earlier in the session, so Peter moves on to a run-through of his 'Tear The Top Right Off My Head.'

Although Peter feels like singing the song – and briefly breaks into 'The Bells Of Rhymney' – Douglas wants him to stick to instrumentals, so Peter plays an otherwise unknown piece that he appropriately calls 'Untitled.' Douglas thinks the song is "really groovy" and asks Peter to extend it. After playing around with the structure, Peter segues into his arrangement of Goffin & King's 'A Man Without A Dream.' Douglas is quite impressed by his reading of the song but no further work is done on the piece at this session.

From 8:00pm until midnight work centers on tracking yet another Goffin & King song, 'Star Collector.' The song features a rather risqué lyric about the era's groupies and will develop into a free-form jam that, even after editing, lasts well over four minutes. It is possible that producer Douglas, in addition to playing bass on this track, adds a repeating electric guitar lick, barely audible in the final production, at this or another session. Certainly this 4-track recording is ripe for further overdubs. Vocals, Moog synthesizer, and other recorded elements will be added to the song when it is later transferred to 8-track tape.

The *NME's* Keith Altham attends the session and files a report a few days later. "When I arrived at 10:00pm, Peter, Micky and Mike were completing the last track for their fourth album, 'Star

Collector'. … There were ten or 12 takes before the group and Lester Sill were satisfied with the track. 'Star Collector' was supposed to run for about two and a half minutes, but ran out of control as they improvised their way into six minutes of playing time, with Micky 'buh-by-ooing' his way into infinity. Dolenz was particularly gratified by the playback. 'That's great, you guys,' he shouted. 'I can do some fantastic things with my sound synthesizer in there!' This electronic machine is Micky's latest plaything.

"The group went back to tape some dialogue, and the conversation wheeled around to what they could have on the album cover. Mike suggested, 'I thought we might have this gigantic organ grinder thing which goes up right out of the picture so you can just see the handle and a huge hand turning it. Then the four of us in monkey suits, with shackles and chains around our necks, attached to the giant wrist.' Dolenz suggested: 'How about a huge monkey foot with just us squatting beside it?' Dolenz decided the muse was upon him, and further expounded: 'Black! That's what I want. I want the whole sleeve black – black, black, black!' Nobody seemed terribly enthusiastic about the idea and they all went home."

● **Friday 23rd**
● At 9:30pm The Monkees depart from LAX airport in Los Angeles on Air France flight 004 bound for Paris.

● **Saturday 24th**
● The group touch down in Paris, France at 4:20pm for some filming and a few brief moments of relaxation. Since show producers Raybert have opted to shoot footage for the TV series in Paris instead of Britain, a group of models is employed to chase the group around – because they are still relatively unknown in France. The group stay at the George V Hotel.
● A *Billboard* report underlines that it would be unnecessary to hire anyone to chase the group around in the United States since they have hit #1 with the *Headquarters* album. Although it will be replaced next week by The Beatles' *Sgt. Pepper's Lonely Hearts Club Band*, The Monkees still have further cause to celebrate since today's chart places *More Of The Monkees* at #7, their debut *The Monkees* at #16, and Davy's Colpix album, *David Jones*, at #190. Internationally, 'A Little Bit Me, A Little Bit You' still holds allure, with Top 10 placings in Argentina, Australia, New Zealand, The Philippines, and South Africa. A single of '(Theme From) The Monkees' also rates in the Top 5 in Mexico, Norway, and Sweden.

● **Sunday 25th**
TV In Britain episode 32 of the *Monkees* series, *The Monkees On Tour*, is aired on the BBC in advance of the group's London concerts next week.
● The *Chicago Sun-Times* column 'The Stagg Line' reports that Davy has been reclassified 2-A by the U.S. draft board. The board is giving special consideration to Davy since he provides the sole financial support for his father.
● In Paris The Monkees enjoy a rare day off and go sightseeing.
● Los Angeles radio station KRLA broadcasts a special that looks back on the recent Monterey Pop Festival. Reportedly included are interviews with Micky and Peter taped during the event.

● **Monday 26th**
FILMING At 6:30am production commences in Paris on an episode of the TV series to be called *Monkees In Paris*. Today's shoot includes scenes at a flea market and around the famed Arc de Triomphe. 'Wrap-around' segments for this episode will be filmed in Hollywood later this year.

Europe in June: ABOVE with TV series co-creator Bob Rafelson in France to shoot *Monkees In Paris*; RIGHT in London amid the first 'group' press conference.

TV Back in the States another repeat from the first season of *The Monkees* – episode 12, *I've Got A Little Song Here* – is aired at 7:30pm on the NBC network. The soundtrack is revised to include 'For Pete's Sake' in place of the original 'Mary, Mary.'

● Tuesday 27th
FILMING Production continues on *Monkees In Paris* in the French city as the crew films the group in vintage swimming outfits as well as during visits to a cemetery, a fairground, and the Eiffel Tower. The crew stops traffic in the Champs-Elysees as the group rides through the area in an open-top jeep.

Michael: "It was funny not being recognized. We filmed around the Eiffel Tower and caused a three-hour traffic jam in the Champs-Elysees. I got out of the car and lifted the bonnet and it came off in my hand. It was a bit of an anti-climax when we discovered our cameraman had run out of film while I had this gendarme jumping up and down with absolute fury."

● In Britain the TV program *As You Like It* airs what is described as "an exclusive film clip" to promote the single 'Alternate Title.'

● Wednesday 28th
● The group take a French canal trip, filmed for *Monkees In Paris*, and a meal at Maxim's, and then fly out of Paris at 10:35pm on Air France flight 860. They arrive at London's Heathrow Airport at 11:30pm where they are greeted by 300 fans perched atop the balcony of the airport's Queen's Building. One lucky fan will get Davy in a headlock before he is allowed to escape with the rest of the group. Another 200 fans are waiting for them at their hotel in Kensington, central London. The group eludes their fervent admirers by entering the hotel through a side door.

● Thursday 29th
● The Monkees hold their first 'group' press conference, staged in the Buckingham Suite of the Royal Garden Hotel in Kensington, London. According to a tongue-in-cheek press report, the event is "better attended than Winston Churchill's address on World War II."

Davy tells the press that he has recently produced a session in Hollywood for Texan rock group The Children. The group, who hail from Michael's old stomping grounds in San Antonio, had originally approached Michael for help, but found Davy and his new record label more receptive. Reportedly, Davy cuts three tracks with the group but the project will fail when the label hits the skids.

One reporter asks Micky if it is "necessary for pop groups to take drugs," to which he replies, "Do you like The Beatles' album? Well?"

● Micky tapes an appearance on BBC television's *Top Of The Pops* chart show, which is broadcast this evening.

● Friday 30th
PERFORMANCE Empire Pool *Wembley, north London, England* with Lulu, compère: Jimmy Savile

The summer of love, Monkees style.

● After a full afternoon spent in rehearsal, the group arrive late for their debut concert performance in England at the 9,597-capacity Empire Pool.

Michael spent the late afternoon test driving his custom-ordered Radford Mini car.

The group is backed during their solo spots by Dusty Springfield's regular backing band, The Echoes, who have been renamed The Epifocal Phringe for this series of shows following a naming contest in the *NME*.

During the band's performance of 'I Wanna Be Free' images are shown of Mick Jagger, who has just been convicted of drug offences and sentenced to three months in jail. "The audience booed," Michael later tells *NME*'s Keith Altham. "I can't tell you how miserable that made me. I can only hope they were booing authority and not the Stones."

After tonight's performance a member of the audience who closely resembles Davy is hired by the touring party to pose as a decoy so that the band can leave the venue safely.

JULY

● This month's issue of *Tiger Beat* features a guest editorial from Michael that consists of an early draft of the lyrics for his song 'Tapioca Tundra,' which will be recorded in November.
● The Monkees appear on the cover of British magazine *Music Maker*.

'Pleasant Valley Sunday' / 'Words' single is released in the U.S.A. This is the group's fourth official 45.

Pleasant Valley Sunday single

A 'Pleasant Valley Sunday' (G. GOFFIN / C. KING)
B 'Words' version 2 (T. BOYCE / B. HART)

U.S. release July 1967 (Colgems 1007).
U.K. release August 1967 (RCA 1645).
Chart high U.S. number 3; U.K. number 11.

Saturday 1st
● Micky spends the morning on London's Kings Road shopping for mod fashions.
PERFORMANCE Empire Pool *Wembley, north London, England* 3:00pm & 7:45pm, with Lulu
● The group perform a further two shows before a combined audience of 20,000 at Wembley. After the concert they are whisked away in a catering van, while Davy's double stays behind to confuse fans. Brian Jones pays a post-show visit to The Monkees' hotel, the Royal Garden, bringing with him a barrage of guitars, sitars, and dulcimers.
● The *NME* publishes an exclusive interview with Michael by Keith Altham. The conversation probably took place on June 23rd, just prior to the group's departure for France. "I'm convinced that our comedy TV series is a classic and will be regarded as such in years to come," says Michael. "We've taken a Marx Brothers approach and

given it a contemporary twist. The concept of The Beatles, or four guys in a group, gave us the excuse to have four young people doing things together. Someone decided we could not just be four actors standing there holding instruments. We had to be a pop group as well. So between designing our own clothes, merchandising, personal appearances, we made records.

"Then everyone expected us to be as creative as The Beatles. We would like to spend more time on our records, but we just do not have it. I regard the *More Of The Monkees* album as probably the worst album in the world. We are now putting more effort and time into our discs, but it's still not enough time. ... We have to be content to produce music that makes people happy, while The Beatles create music to make people think.

"It's impossible to continue at the present pace, and by the end of the year we will have to stop. It's making old men out of us before our time. I've got the first sign of gray hairs. And little cherubic Davy has even got the beginnings of worry lines! Just to give you some idea of the pace things are going, it has been estimated that we have trebled The Beatles' earnings. In the last eight months the Monkees organization has earned $180m. That is just 16 million less than all the people in the U.S."

Michael goes on to discuss the differences between the Los Angeles and London pop scenes. "The really significant people are those like Frank Zappa, of The Mothers Of Invention, a 60-year-old sculptor called Vito, who borders on a genius here, Timothy Leary, and The Beatles. These are the people responsible for making people think in new directions. The people out here don't really have the status they do in England. For example, if Ray Davies says something in print in England, then the public might well listen to it. But we're just regarded as pop millionaires, and nobody listens to us.

"On my first trip to England I did not make many friends. I upset a few people. ... The only person I really got on with was John Lennon. The reason I liked him so much is that he's a compassionate person. ... I know he has a reputation for being caustic, but it is only a cover for the depth of his feeling.

"I've written three books, but I'll never publish them under my own name, or people will think I'm copying John. I've written a 300-page-long poem which was really just an exercise in rhyme to see if I could do it. The story concerns a boy who falls through the eye of a camera into a world where all the values are reversed – black is white and white is black. Eventually he becomes a photograph in the sky without dimension. One of the other books is simply an observation on society and the rules we live by. The real satisfaction for me was simply in having written them – if they are ever published it will be under another name."
● The *NME* also reports that Jimi Hendrix has been added as one of the opening acts on The Monkees' U.S. summer tour.

Sunday 2nd
PERFORMANCE Empire Pool *Wembley, north London, England* 3:00pm & 7:45pm, with The Epifocal Phringe, Lulu; compères: Rick Dane (3:00), Pete Murray (7:45)
● The group perform their final shows at Wembley. Following the afternoon show the Red Cross is called to revive Michael, who collapses from exhaustion. The evening show is opened by sets from The Epifocal Phringe, whose songs include 'Knock On Wood' and 'Sweet Soul Music,' and Lulu, rocking through 'Shout' and Neil Diamond's 'Boat That I Row.'

The Monkees' evening set kicks off with 'I'm A Believer' (featuring Davy on bass) followed by 'Last Train To Clarksville.' Other songs include 'You Just May Be The One,' 'Sunny Girlfriend' (not performed at the other four Wembley concerts), 'Your Auntie Grizelda,' 'I Wanna Be Free' (again with a rear-projected still of Mick Jagger), 'Sweet Young Thing,' 'The Girl I Knew Somewhere,' and 'Mary, Mary.'

There's a brief burst of 'Happy Birthday' for a member of the crew, and then 'Cripple Creek' (performed by Peter solo), 'You Can't Judge A Book By The Cover' (performed by Michael with The Epifocal Phringe), 'Gonna Build A Mountain' (Davy with the Phringe), 'I Got A Woman' (Micky's turn with the Phringe), 'Alternate Title' (a.k.a. 'Randy Scouse Git'), and '(I'm Not Your) Steppin' Stone,' which closes the show.

Michael and Micky wear black armbands in a show of solidarity or sympathy for the embattled Mick Jagger and Keith Richards, recently convicted and sentenced to jail for drug offences. Davy also feels for the Stones. "The Rolling Stones' sentences get me down," he tells Alan Smith after the show. "Do you know that in that room next door I have pills twice as strong as those that got Mick Jagger in trouble? I haven't got a prescription for them either. I've got a swollen throat, and a guy gave them to me to ease it off."

A post-concert party is held at the Royal Garden Hotel in Kensington, central London. Among those in attendance are Spencer Davis and Keith Moon, who both graced The Monkees' evening performance (Moon riling the crowd with a chant of "We want The Who!"). Michael heads to the Speakeasy club where he bumps into Lulu and George Harrison. Plans are made for a grand get-together tomorrow evening.

● **Monday 3rd**
● This afternoon Peter, Micky, Samantha Juste, and Lulu take a trip to Chelsea in central London to see the antique market and boutiques of Kings Road. After a quick Indian meal the gang prepares for this evening's big soirée. Meanwhile, Phyllis Nesmith arrives in London just in time to see Michael pick up their custom Mini Cooper car that cost the couple some £3,600 (equivalent to $8,640 at the time).
● Brian Epstein's NEMS Enterprises hosts a party for The Monkees at London's hippest nightclub, the Speakeasy. Festivities kick off at 10:30pm. An hour later the club's clientele includes Eric Clapton, The Who, all the members of Manfred Mann, and Jonathan King, as well as DJs Kenny Everett and Rick Dane. Micky and Samantha Juste soon appear alongside Michael and Phyllis Nesmith. As a live group performs, Paul McCartney and Jane Asher arrive, joined shortly thereafter by John and Cynthia Lennon.

By midnight the club is packed. Joining the festivities are producer Mickie Most, producer/songwriter Vicki Wickham, Frank Allen of The Searchers, Patsy Ann Noble, Lulu, Dusty Springfield, and the members of Procol Harum. Late attendees include George and Pattie Harrison, as well as Peter, who spent the earlier part of this evening visiting Ringo and a pregnant Maureen Starr at their home.

By 3:30am George Harrison has broken out his ukulele for a jam with Peter on banjo and Keith Moon who drums on a table. The party finishes some time around 6:00am. Davy has to miss the whole event because he has rushed to visit his family who have traveled to Norfolk to elude fans.
● Back in Los Angeles, Chip Douglas begins a series of sessions to prepare the fourth album's work-in-progress tracks for further overdubs.
RECORDING RCA (A) *Hollywood, CA* 7:00-11:30pm. Chip Douglas *prod*; half-inch 4-track; reductions, overdubs.
1. **'She Hangs Out'** version 2
    Pisces, Aquarius... master # UZB3-7313

● No taped evidence of this session will survive, though union records specify that work was done on this particular song. A union official attends the session and notes that one guitarist was employed for the date, and the contract lists both Chip Douglas and songwriter/musician Bill Martin, so it is very possible that one of them played a role in tonight's activities, possibly contributing the additional electric guitar, handclaps, tambourine, or shaker parts that are added prior to the song's transfer from 4-track to 8-track tape. Davy's lead vocal and backing vocals from Davy, Micky, and Chip Douglas are also added before the transfer.

● **Tuesday 4th**
● Returning from the previous night's party, Micky is escorted by a throng of adoring fans as he takes an early morning jaunt through London's Hyde Park.

● **Wednesday 5th**
● The Jimi Hendrix Experience are presently on the East Coast playing a series of warm-up concerts in preparation for their big shows with The Monkees. On Monday night (3rd) the group appeared at New York's Scene discotheque and today they are scheduled to perform with The Young Rascals in Central Park. Meanwhile on the West Coast, Chip Douglas works on in the studio.
RECORDING RCA (A) *Hollywood, CA* 7:00pm-12:30am. Chip Douglas *prod*; half-inch 4-track; reductions.
1. **'Goin' Down'**
    Pisces, Aquarius... master # UZB3-7315
● Although this is logged as a 'sweetening' date there is very little to add at this stage in the production (the song's lead vocal and horn overdubs are taped at later sessions). Yet both Chip Douglas and Bill Martin are paid quite handsomely for working on the track this evening and it cannot be ruled out that they did attempt some additional work to the song's instrumentation.

● **Thursday 6th**
● The Monkees return to the United States from London in the early morning, arriving in New York City for a press conference at the Warwick Hotel. As a farewell, BBC television's *Top Of The Pops* airs a recap of their stay in Britain. Footage includes excerpts from the June 29th press conference coupled with music from their British single 'Alternate Title.'
● Micky has another single in the works, though probably without his involvement or approval. Today, the Challenge label prepares the master of their remaining pre-Monkees Micky recording, 'Huff Puff,' at Hollywood Sound Recorders for a release later this month. The song will be coupled with a non-Dolenz track, 'Fate' (originally titled 'Big Ben'). Unlike the label's 'Don't Do It' this release will not chart. A few blocks north, Chip Douglas is working at RCA studios.
RECORDING RCA (A) *Hollywood, CA* 7:00pm-1:00am. Chip Douglas *prod*; half-inch 4-track; reductions, overdubs.
1. **'Star Collector'**
    Pisces, Aquarius... master # UZB3-7319
● This session is logged by the union as a 'sweetening' session, though it is unclear what work Chip Douglas and Bill Martin perform. The Monkees are presently in New York City preparing for their summer tour.

● **Friday 7th**
● The group's summer tour is scheduled to kick off today at Braves Stadium in Atlanta, Georgia – but they are in New York City suffering from exhaustion after their European jaunt and are given an extra day off. This evening they will dine at the Volsin and later

venture to the Electric Circus in Greenwich Village. Meanwhile in Los Angeles, Chip Douglas preps 'Don't Call On Me' for further overdubs.

RECORDING RCA (A) *Hollywood, CA* 7:00pm-12:30am. Chip Douglas *prod*; Hank Cicalo *eng*; half-inch 4-track; reductions, overdubs.

1. 'Don't Call On Me'
  Pisces, Aquarius... master # UZB3-7314

Another sweetening session, and again both Chip Douglas and Bill Martin are paid for adding unknown elements to the song's production. Most importantly, this session finds Douglas and engineer Hank Cicalo compiling all of the master takes of the songs for the *Pisces* album that have been recorded up to this point. Douglas will soon shuttle these reels to sessions in New York, Nashville, and Chicago before final mixing and overdubs are completed in Hollywood.

● Saturday 8th

PERFORMANCE The Coliseum *Jacksonville, FL* 8:00pm, with The Jimi Hendrix Experience, The Sundowners, Lynne Randell; sponsored by radio station WAPE

● The Monkees' summer tour officially begins at this 10,828-seat venue. Openers are Australian hit maker Lynne Randell, Decca label artists The Sundowners, and special guest stars The Jimi Hendrix Experience. The Sundowners also provide instrumental backing for Lynne Randell and accompany Michael, Davy, and Micky on their solo spots.

  The Monkees and entourage stay at the Heart Of Jacksonville hotel. After tonight's performance the touring party board the group's rented DC-6 airplane, emblazoned with their famed guitar logo, bound for Miami airport. They are due to arrive some time after 1:30am and have a whopping 21 rooms reserved at the Eden Roc hotel.

● Today's *NME* mentions that, just prior to the tour, Jimi Hendrix was staying at Peter's house when Peter was in London. Hendrix was involved in an auto accident while driving Peter's Pontiac GTO. Reportedly, Jimi's ankle was injured, and "he will have to be strapped up" for his concert appearances. The paper says that Peter's car was "severely damaged." Pontiac, makers of the GTO, a car that is the basis for the group's Monkeemobile vehicle, provided each member of the group with a complimentary car last year.

● Britain's *Disc & Music Echo* reports that the UK-only 'Alternate Title' single has climbed to #3 on the charts. A guest reviewer in the paper, Hollies lead singer Allan Clarke, says: "'Alternate Title' is a load of rubbish. I've nothing against the boys, but the song is terrible." The paper also notes that *The Monkees* TV series is seen in over 33 countries.

● Sunday 9th

PERFORMANCE Miami Convention Hall *Miami Beach, FL* 8:00pm, with The Jimi Hendrix Experience, The Sundowners, Lynne Randell; sponsored by radio station WQAM

● The Monkees perform in concert at this 12,086-seat venue. Despite sponsorship by radio station WQAM, its chief competitor WFUN also gets in on the act by buying a block of tickets for giveaways. Prior to the show The Monkees charter a yacht moored across from their hotel. A party with the entire crew is held on board in honor of Experience drummer Mitch Mitchell's 21st birthday.

● Monday 10th

● The group enjoy a day off in Charlotte, North Carolina.

TV At 7:30pm another repeat from the first season of *The Monkees* is

aired by NBC: episode 23, *Captain Crocodile*. The soundtrack is updated to include the group's current single, 'Pleasant Valley Sunday,' in place of the original soundtrack's 'Your Auntie Grizelda.' Meanwhile in the studio, Chip Douglas prepares another song for future overdubs.

RECORDING RCA (A) *Hollywood, CA* 7:00pm-1:00am. Chip Douglas *prod*; half-inch 4-track; reductions, overdubs.

1. 'Love Is Only Sleeping'
  Pisces, Aquarius... master # UZB3-5441

● Union contracts indicate that Bill Martin and Chip Douglas are paid to 'sweeten' this recording tonight, though it is more likely that only reductions take place. However, given the elaborate production that will result, it is impossible to rule out their involvement. The pair will be present at a further session for the track on September 7th.

● Tuesday 11th

PERFORMANCE The Coliseum *Charlotte NC* 8:00pm, with The Jimi Hendrix Experience, The Sundowners, Lynne Randell; tickets $4-$6; sponsored by radio station WAYS

● The Monkees perform to a crowd of 11,573. The touring party stays at the Red Carpet Inn.

● In Britain, Granada television reruns *A Man And A Dog* from 1961 featuring a young David Jones.

● In the studio in California, Chip Douglas has another Monkees session booked at RCA's Studio A at 7:00pm but it is unclear if any work does take place.

● Wednesday 12th

● Abandoning their plane in favor of a tour bus for the short 60-mile hop from Charlotte to Greensboro, The Monkees travel to North Carolina in the early morning hours to avoid any fan frenzy. The touring party stays in 22 rooms at the Oaks Motel.

PERFORMANCE Greensboro Coliseum *Greensboro, NC* 8:00pm, with The Jimi Hendrix Experience, The Sundowners, Lynne Randell; sponsored by radio station WCOQ

● Tonight's performance is at a 9,327-seat venue, but modest ticket sales dictate a less than capacity crowd. Good seats for this show are priced at $6. In the end about 7,000 people will attend the concert resulting in a take of $40,000. After the performance the touring party flies to New York City.

● Also tonight, Chip Douglas has another session scheduled in RCA's Studio A, from 7:00pm-12midnight. It is possible that he does some last minute assembling of tracks since sessions are due to shift over to RCA's Studios in New York City tomorrow.

● Thursday 13th

RECORDING It is possible that overdubs for The Monkees' fourth album are recorded at RCA's New York City studios today.

● Friday 14th

PERFORMANCE Forest Hills Tennis Stadium *New York, NY* 8:00pm, with The Jimi Hendrix Experience, The Sundowners, Lynne Randell; compères: WMCA 'Good Guys' DJs; sponsored by radio station WMCA

● The Monkees perform at the 14,174-seat Tennis Stadium with radio station WMCA's 'Good Guys' DJs as MCs for the three-night stand in place of the previously reported Dick Clark. The touring party stays at the Warwick Hotel where a press conference is also held today (a brief clip of which will be seen on Rhino's 2003 *The Monkees Season Two* DVD boxed set). Sometime today Micky's friend Samantha Juste will take a plane for the journey from London to New

York to join the group's entourage for the rest of their tour dates.
● The Monkees are awarded a gold record for outstanding sales of their single 'Pleasant Valley Sunday' in the U.S.A.

● Saturday 15th

PERFORMANCE Forest Hills Tennis Stadium *New York, NY* 9:15pm, with The Jimi Hendrix Experience, The Sundowners, Lynne Randell; compères: WMCA 'Good Guys' DJs; sponsored by radio station WMCA
● *The New York Times* reports that almost all 14,174 seats are filled for this hour-long show, the group's largest audience during the three-night stint here. Reviewer Murray Schumach writes: "No one profiting from the millions being brought in on television, radio, gadgets, and costume manufacture need have worried about the investment in The Monkees. The audience protected them beautifully. From the moment the four personable young men bounced on the stage at 9:15 until they left an hour later, amid a psychedelic display on a screen and swinging giant spotlights on the audience, a shrill, ear-shattering stream of adulation pierced the air."
RECORDING During the day the group work on overdubs at RCA Studios in New York City. Full details will not survive, but tape boxes indicate that the master 4-track tape of 'Salesman' is combined to two tracks of a new tape at this session by engineer Ray Hall. It is also possible that some work is done on vocal tracks.

● Sunday 16th

● *Weekly Variety* reports that Davy has been subpoenaed while in New York City in the Yarnell/Gordon suit, where the TV producers claim the *Monkees* TV concept as their own. Davy is considered a material witness in the case since he was allegedly referred to by Screen Gems as a potential cast member for Yarnell and Gordon's *Liverpool U.S.A.* concept in late 1964. He was certainly under contract to the company at that time. Depositions are expected to be completed in August, after which a trial will be requested. The lawsuit will allegedly be settled out of court. Ironically, David Yarnell later serves as producer on the television series *Don Kirshner's Rock Concert*.
PERFORMANCE Forest Hills Tennis Stadium *New York, NY* 8:00pm, with The Jimi Hendrix Experience, The Sundowners, Lynne Randell; compères: WMCA 'Good Guys' DJs; sponsored by radio station WMCA
● The Monkees make their final appearance at Forest Hills, with gross income for the venue reported at over $307,000 for the three nights. Audience turnout for the three shows is less than capacity (an estimated 36,192) due to harsh weather conditions.
● During the stay in New York City, The Jimi Hendrix Experience will leave the tour. On July 22nd Hendrix's single of 'Purple Haze' will break into the *Billboard* Hot 100 Bound charts at #132, providing the Experience with some new opportunities.

Micky: "What happened was [Hendrix] broke his record and he got an offer to headline. It was weird, as you can imagine. Any opening act has a problem when they're in front of a big name act. He was so different than we were. We loved it, we had a great time. He was a fan of ours, that's why he went on the tour. He liked what we were doing. I think he recognized the kind of show business carnival atmosphere. The kids I think quite liked it. It's probably the mothers that objected the most when he started pissing on his guitar and stuff like that. They probably thought that was a bit strange."

A few weeks later, Hendrix himself discusses the decision to leave the tour. "Firstly, they gave us the 'death' spot on the show – right before The Monkees were due on," he tells the *NME*. "The audience just screamed and yelled for The Monkees! Finally, they agreed to let

us go on first and things were much better. We got screams and good reaction, and some kids even rushed the stage. But we were not getting any billing – all the posters for the show just screamed out MONKEES! Then some parents who brought their young kids complained that our act was vulgar. We decided it was just not the right audience. I think they're replacing me with Mickey Mouse!

"There was no tension between us and The Monkees whatever. And all the rumors about being segregated on the plane were just nonsense. I got on well with both Micky and Peter and we fooled around a lot together. There was this fantastic girl singer on the tour – an Australian girl called Lynne Randell. She's got a record out in Britain, so you may be hearing more of her. In New York, we all went out to the Electric Circus club in the Village, which just completely blew my mind. There was a group called The Seeds playing there."

● Monday 17th – Wednesday 19th

RECORDING RCA (B) *New York, NY*. Chip Douglas *prod*; half-inch 4-track; reductions, overdubs.
● The Monkees overdub various portions of previously recorded tracks for their forthcoming *Pisces, Aquarius, Capricorn and Jones Ltd.* album in New York City. Reportedly vocal work is done on 'Star Collector' and 'She Hangs Out' version 2. A session may also occur on Thursday 20th prior to the group's evening concert in Buffalo, New York.
TV On Monday 17th another repeat from the *Monkees* first season – episode 7, *Monkees In A Ghost Town* – is aired at 7:30pm. The soundtrack is updated to include 'Words' version 2 in place of 'Tomorrow's Gonna Be Another Day.'

● Thursday 20th

PERFORMANCE **Memorial Auditorium** *Buffalo, NY* 8:30pm, with The Sundowners, Lynne Randell; sponsored by radio station WKBW
● Tonight's venue is an 11,514-seater, and the touring party stays at the Statler Hilton Hotel. A 'secret' trip to Niagara Falls is disrupted when a local radio station divulges the group's plans.

● Friday 21st

PERFORMANCE **Civic Center** *Baltimore, MD* 8:30pm, with The Sundowners, Lynne Randell; sponsored by radio station WCAO
● The group perform in concert at this 13,309-seat venue to a reported crowd of 10,000. Tickets run as high as $7.50. The touring party stays at the Sheraton-Baltimore. Michael tells one paper that the crowd for this show could have been larger but the show was poorly promoted. He also begins a spate of solo press interviews to unload his pent-up views on life as a Monkee.

During an interview in Baltimore he says: "We could always play, but the man who was responsible for the first two albums and the first singles preferred to have others do the playing. And I didn't mind that. What I did mind was the publicity releases saying we did our own playing when we did not. Now we do. We do our own playing on the third album and on the fourth which is not yet released. And we'll do all our own playing from here on."

As for Michael's new-found openness, he says: "I just started this yesterday. I want to talk to the press. So far I'm the only one to do it this way. I've talked to the [other Monkees] but they haven't done it yet."

● Saturday 22nd

PERFORMANCE **Boston Garden** *Boston, MA* 9:00pm, with The Sundowners, Lynne Randell; tickets $4-$6; sponsored by radio station WBZ
● On the day that their latest single, 'Pleasant Valley Sunday,' enters

the charts the group perform to a crowd here of 12,000. The touring party stays at the Sheraton-Boston.

● *Billboard* reports that Jack Angel, Vice President of Davy Jones Records, is completing plans for a 50-state talent search. The trek is set to include stops at schools and churches and will kick off in September. Winners or signees will receive cash awards and a trip to Hollywood or New York.

● Today's *Billboard* also shows several Monkees chart placings. 'Pleasant Valley Sunday' debuts at #51 while strong airplay boost's the single's flipside, 'Words,' to #78. The *Headquarters* album sits at #2, behind The Beatles' *Sgt. Pepper's*, *More Of The Monkees* is at #10, and their debut album slips to #30. In Mexico, The Monkees have three Top 10 singles: 'She,' 'I'm A Believer,' and the group's theme song. Elsewhere they have Top 10 items in Britain, New Zealand, Norway, Spain, Sweden, and The Philippines.

● Sunday 23rd

PERFORMANCE Convention Hall *Philadelphia, PA* 8:30pm, with The Sundowners, Lynne Randell; sponsored by radio station WFIL
● The Monkees continue their summer tour with a concert at this 12,009-seat venue. The touring party stays at the Warwick Hotel.

● Monday 24th

● The touring party travels back to New York City this afternoon. Davy has left in advance of the group in order to make an early-morning appointment in the city.
TV NBC airs at 7:30pm a further repeat from the first season of *The Monkees*: episode 17, *The Case Of The Missing Monkee*. The soundtrack is updated to include their new single, 'Pleasant Valley Sunday,' in place of '(I'm Not Your) Steppin' Stone.' Tonight's broadcast wins its time slot, pulling in more than six million viewers.

● Tuesday 25th

RECORDING The Monkees return to RCA studios in New York City for unspecified recording. The working title for their upcoming album is currently *At Random.*

● Wednesday 26th

RECORDING A proposed concert in Indianapolis, Indiana, never occurs. Instead recording continues at RCA. During the session Peter presents Davy with a new Guild six-string acoustic guitar to replace an instrument that Davy has recently broken. The Monkees fly to Rochester, New York, later this evening.

● Thursday 27th

PERFORMANCE War Memorial Auditorium *Rochester, NY* 8:30pm, with The Sundowners, Lynne Randell; sponsored by radio station WBBF
● The Monkees perform in concert at the 9,442-seat Auditorium. The touring party stays at the Townhouse Motor Inn (though the group will fly directly to Cincinnati after tonight's performance). A concert originally scheduled to take place today at the Public Hall in Cleveland, Ohio, is cancelled by the city's mayor, Ralph S. Locher, because of concerns over crowd control. "We aren't banning The Monkees from Cleveland," says Locher. "They can use the [3,000-seat] Music Hall." Despite the mayor's invitation, the group will never perform in Cleveland.
● *Billboard* reports that Don Kirshner is back "in show business again." Kirshner, who is still locked in a lawsuit with Columbia-Screen Gems over the Monkees project, has launched the Kirshner Entertainment Corporation. Herb Moelis, former head of Colgems business affairs, is once again at Kirshner's side for this new venture.

● Friday 28th

PERFORMANCE Cincinnati Gardens *Cincinnati, OH* 9:30pm, with The Sundowners, Lynne Randell; sponsored by radio station WSAI
● The Monkees perform to a crowd of 10,300, and the touring party stays at the downtown Holiday Inn.

● Saturday 29th

● Today's scheduled Monkees concert at Olympia Stadium in Detroit, Michigan, is canceled due to rioting and an enforced curfew. A daytime performance is rescheduled for August 13th. With no gig, the group fly on to their next scheduled stop, Chicago. At 12:30am The Monkees' DC-6 arrives at Chicago's Midway Airport and about 75 fans are on hand to great them. After arriving at their hotel, the Astor Tower, some of the group check out the establishment's discotheque, Maxim's, while the others retire to bed. Reportedly the band members insist that only Beatles records are played, and the venue's manager, Carmine Gibbs, is happy to comply.

By dawn, Micky is up and taking pictures of the lakefront sunrise. At 3:30pm the group are due at the studio of radio station WLS on Wacker Drive where they are on air for just 20 minutes before being whisked off to meet a group of fan club presidents.

During their Chicago sojourn the group hang out with members of Buffalo Springfield and The Association, and pay a visit to Hugh Hefner's *Playboy* mansion. Micky and Davy also stop by the city's Museum of Science and Industry.

● Sunday 30th

● Michael grants an interview to the *Chicago Daily News* from the easy chair of his Astor suite. The outspoken musician discusses his firm opposition to the war in Vietnam among other topics. "At heart I'm still a fan," he says. "I feel a part of this generation. This Monkee thing will be good as long as the four of us can understand our responsibility, our influence, and if we sincerely keep our interest in the kids.

"I think The Monkees have formed sort of a mutual admiration society with the kids. You do your thing, and we'll do ours. You grow up your own way, and we won't interfere.

"And when we're up there, on stage, there is a deafening roar. It's a drag. We give them two numbers to get it out of their systems, and then we say there's an hour to go in the show. Don't blow it. Cool it. We're not running away. We'll entertain you; you'll respond better if you can hear us. And they do quiet down, until Davy waves at them."
PERFORMANCE Chicago Stadium *Chicago, IL* 7:15pm, with The Sundowners, Lynne Randell; tickets $5–$7
● The Monkees hit the stage of the 18,348-seat Stadium to a reported capacity crowd. According to the *Chicago Daily News* tonight's set includes 'Zilch,' 'I'm A Believer,' 'Forget That Girl,' and a finale of '(I'm Not Your) Steppin' Stone.'

● Monday 31st

RECORDING RCA Studio *Chicago, IL.* Chip Douglas *prod*; half-inch 4-track; overdubs.
● The Monkees record more overdubs for their fourth album at the RCA studios in Chicago. Reportedly work is done on 'Salesman' and 'Cuddly Toy,' most likely vocal overdubs. These two tracks will be mixed in September.
● After the session the group attend a Buffalo Springfield concert at the Big Top Historyland (an Indian Reservation) in Old Hayward, Wisconsin. Micky joins the Springfield on-stage towards the end of their set.
TV Also this evening another repeat from the first season of *The*

Monkees is aired – episode 26, *Monkees Chow Mein*. The soundtrack is updated to include 'Words' version 2 in place of 'Your Auntie Grizelda.'

AUGUST

● Tuesday 1st
● *The Milwaukee Journal* reports that tomorrow night's Monkees concert at the Arena has been postponed indefinitely because of a riot emergency. A youth curfew is currently in force and, despite hopes that the concert can be rescheduled, the group will not perform in this city until June 22nd 1969. With no gig, the group probably returns for some further recording at RCA studios in Chicago today, though no details are available.

● Wednesday 2nd
● With an opening in their schedule because of the cancellation of their Milwaukee show, the group film musical segments at Fred Niles Film Studios in Chicago for their second-season show endings. These feature two different backdrops. First is a 'rainbow room' for clips of 'Daydream Believer,' 'Love Is Only Sleeping,' 'No Time,' 'Pleasant Valley Sunday,' 'Randy Scouse Git,' and an early mix of 'She Hangs Out.' The second setting is a 'Southwest' backdrop for a lip-synch performance of 'What Am I Doing Hangin' 'Round.'

● Thursday 3rd
RECORDING RCA (B) *Hollywood, CA* 7:00pm-12midnight. Chip Douglas *prod*; half-inch 4-track.
● Chip Douglas returns to Los Angeles with overdubbed masters from the New York and Chicago sessions. He uses RCA's Studio B – because Henry Mancini has booked Studio A – probably for a simple playback or reduction session.
● Around midnight tonight The Monkees fly to St. Paul, Minnesota, for their next tour stop. Their arrival at Twin Cities International airport is covered by radio station KDWB, who also set up a broadcasting rig in the group's hotel, the Capp Tower. This location is called "secret city" for the broadcast and Michael, Micky, and Peter all take turns playing guest DJ. They spin their favorite records into the early-morning hours and even give some off-color treatments to the station's commercials. After a lighthearted claim that any listener who can guess the location of secret city will be given $85,000, KDWB is flooded with phone calls correctly guessing the group's hotel. Some listeners plan to pursue the matter in court. The group also manage to play a little of rival station WDGY over the air on KDWB, an apparent violation of Federal Communications Commission regulations.

● Friday 4th
PERFORMANCE St. Paul Auditorium Arena *Minneapolis, MN* 9:30pm, with The Sundowners, Lynne Randell; tickets $4–$6; sponsored by radio station KDWB
● The Monkees perform a capacity show at this 10,874-seat venue (with a set including 'Last Train To Clarksville') and the estimated gross is $55,000. It is the largest seated audience for any event so far in the Auditorium. The touring party stays at the Capp Tower Motel. After the show, a female fan stows away on the group's private plane. Her father threatens to press charges against everyone on board, claiming that they have committed a felony by transporting a minor across state lines.

● In St. Paul, Michael speaks to the Associated Press and makes a statement on the group's recorded output. "Don't buy us if you want good music. Our music is sort of inane, banal. The Beatles give the kids the good stuff. Do you remember our second album? That was all tripe. We're limited in musical ability. We have to overdub."

● Saturday 5th
PERFORMANCE Kiel Auditorium *St. Louis, MO* 8:30pm, with The Sundowners, Lynne Randell; sponsored by radio station KXOK
● The group play at the 10,574-seat Auditorium, and the touring party stays at the Hilton Inn. *Billboard* reports that among the instruments the group are using on stage during their tour are an Ode banjo, a Baldwin banjo, a Gretsch bass, a Gretsch 12-string guitar, a Guild bass, and a Rickenbacker 12-string guitar. No mention is made of the brand of maracas Davy Jones is currently using.

● Sunday 6th
● The group arrive in Iowa and spend the afternoon relaxing poolside at Johnny & Kay's Motor Hotel. Micky briefly signs autographs for fans before shooting some 16mm film of Davy golfing. Peter is interviewed by James Beaumont of the *Iowa Register*.
PERFORMANCE Veterans Memorial Auditorium *Des Moines, IA* 8:00pm, with The Sundowners, Lynne Randell; tickets $4-$6; sponsored by radio station KIOA in conjunction with Dick Clark Productions
● On the continuing summer tour, tonight the group perform in concert to 9,000 fans at a venue with a capacity of 11,448. The $6 tickets are for the 'good' main floor or balcony while $5 and $4 will get you into the upper balcony. The performance this evening includes 'Last Train To Clarksville,' 'I Wanna Be Free' (accompanied by rear-projected still images of a civil rights march in Montgomery, Alabama), and Micky's solo 'I've Got A Woman.'

● Monday 7th
TV At 7:30pm the NBC network airs another repeat from the *Monkees* first season, episode 10, *Here Come The Monkees*. The soundtrack is updated to include 'Shades Of Gray' in place of the slow version of 'I Wanna Be Free.' It is likely that the two other

Monkees music cues – 'I Wanna Be Free' (fast version) and 'Let's Dance On' – are left intact. This broadcast will win its time slot, attracting more than six million viewers.

● Tuesday 8th
● The Monkees' 30-member touring party flies from Des Moines, Iowa, to Dallas, Texas.

● Wednesday 9th
● Michael is interviewed by the *Dallas Times Herald*. "The Beatles, they're classics," he says. "They opened the door and we walked through. The Beatles started it all, but while they're a singing group, we're a television one. Our music is to play at a party and not to pay attention to. We're pointedly inane. Television makes no sense, a vast wasteland and all that, so why pretend? Once somebody told me The Monkees would make no lasting impression. 'Good,' I said. We don't want to. … We want to let the kids grow up."

Michael still sees his membership in the group as a magical opportunity. "That was the first big break for any of us. It was more than a break: it was a fantasy. In one year we've made $2.5m each. We closed out the season as number 21 out of the Top 100 on television. This year, I think we'll make it into the Top 10.

"We'll be tied up in television for five or six years yet. NBC offered us a blanket, 15-year contract but we turned it down. Who wants to see a bald group? I guess the show will run another year or so. And after that there will be Saturday morning reruns. I imagine we'll be around for quite a while."

PERFORMANCE Memorial Auditorium *Dallas, TX* 8:30pm, with The Sundowners, Lynne Randell; sponsored by radio station KVIL
● During the day before tonight's performance at the 10,131-seat Auditorium the group take over radio-station sponsor KVIL for their own special show – leaving just a little bit of time for a shopping trip to the Neiman Marcus store. The touring party stays at the Cabana Hotel. After the concert the group attends a jam session with The Sundowners at a local club. Meanwhile back home in Los Angeles horn and string overdubs are recorded using RCA's recently installed 8-track tape machine.

RECORDING RCA (A) *Hollywood, CA* 7:30-11:30pm. Chip Douglas *prod*; Hank Cicalo *eng*; one-inch 8-track; overdubs.
1. **'She Hangs Out'** version 2 remix takes 1-2
   Pisces, Aquarius... master # UZB3-7313
2. **'Daydream Believer'** remix takes 1-3
   The Birds, The Bees... master # UZB3-5438
Personnel Pete Candoli (trumpet), Nathan Kaproff (violin 2), George Kast (violin 2), Dick Leith (bass trombone), Bill Martin (bell 2), Alex Murray (violin 2), Erno Neufeld (violin 2), Dick Noel

Filming special ending segments (LEFT AND ABOVE) for the second season of *The Monkees*, in Chicago, early August.

(trombone), Al Porcino (trumpet), Manny Stevens (trumpet, piccolo trumpet 2), Phil Teele (bass trombone).

● Arranger Shorty Rogers leads a six-piece brass section through overdubs for 'She Hangs Out.' The first take is a false start but the second is complete and used as the master. The group are recorded onto two tracks of the spacious new one-inch 8-track tape. Prior to this session, the song's original instrumental and vocal tracks have been transferred to this new tape from the 'old' 4-track master. In the end, two whole tracks are left blank on the 8-track as no further overdubs are required to complete this production, which is now ready for mixing.

'Daydream Believer' is remixed three times for transfer to 8-track. The first two takes are short false starts, while take 3 is a full pass and is used as the final master for all further overdubs. Four violins are added playing a two-part arrangement onto two separate tracks, and the brass arrangement is dubbed onto a single track. Manny Stevens also overdubs a solo piccolo trumpet part on a separate track for the song's ending section. Stevens's solo shares its tape track with the sound of a dinner bell played by Bill Martin, who acts as the song's "six o'clock alarm." The completed production will be released in November as The Monkees' next single.

● Thursday 10th
PERFORMANCE Sam Houston Coliseum *Houston, TX* 8:30pm, with The Sundowners, Lynne Randell; tickets $5-$7; sponsored by radio station KNUZ

● Tonight's concert sees the group at the 11,421-seat Coliseum. (Their set includes 'I Wanna Be Free.') The touring party stay on the seventh floor of the Shamrock Hotel.

● Before the show Michael gives an interview to the *Houston Chronicle*. "People say that 20 years from now these kids won't even remember what The Monkees were," he muses. "They probably won't, but what they will remember is that they had a good 14th year. A very groovy 14th year – and they won't remember just exactly why.

"That's the idea not to put so many work words on the [TV] show, but kind of a vibration. A good vibration. It's not the show itself. Good lord, there's no plot. No sense. The dialogue is gibberish, we act like nebbishes. They say the whole TV bag is a wasteland. Well, we're the only ones who admit it. You know, we come on at 6:30 and say, 'Here we are kiddies, welcome to the wasteland.' That is the way all of it is. I think there's some justice in the fact that we were given two Emmys for it.

"The music is innocuous. It neither hurts nor helps. It brings no reaction. That's the whole idea of The Monkees. It's important we don't get in the way of what the kids think, get in the way of their growing up. It's not a responsibility we shirk. We have it, but we're careful not to use it. And people put us down for it. They say we're totally manufactured, totally nebulous, have nothing to do or say. But no statement *is* a statement, you see. Absolutely. Not doing anything is doing something, man."

● Davy is interviewed by Casey Fowler of the Houston *Post*. He tells Fowler that the group have a big hand in the scripts for their series. "We all write stories and scenes," says Davy. "Then sometimes the show's writers rewrite them into scripts. A lot of our shows are just a skeleton script anyway. We ad-lib and polish them up. We have no idea what we're going to do next season. For all I know, right now, we could dissolve the format and make it into some crazy interview show or something ridiculous like that."

● Friday 11th
PERFORMANCE State Fair Coliseum *Shreveport, LA* 8:00pm, with The Sundowners, Lynne Randell; sponsored by radio station KEEL

● The Monkees' set tonight includes 'Last Train To Clarksville.' The touring party stays at the Shreveporter.

● Due to heavy airplay of a U.S. copy of 'Pleasant Valley Sunday' on British pirate station Radio London, RCA decides to release the single ahead of schedule in the U.K. to meet listener demand. Advance orders already exceed 150,000 copies.

● Saturday 12th
PERFORMANCE Municipal Auditorium *Mobile, AL* 8:00pm, with The Sundowners, Lynne Randell; sponsored by radio station WABB

● The group perform in concert at the 9,927-seat Auditorium tonight on their continuing summer tour. The touring party stays at the Town House Motor Hotel.

Tonight's set features the following songs: 'Last Train To Clarksville,' 'You Just May Be The One,' 'The Girl I Knew Somewhere' (with Davy on bass guitar and Peter playing organ), 'I Wanna Be Free,' 'Sunny Girlfriend,' 'Your Auntie Grizelda,' 'Forget That Girl,' 'Sweet Young Thing,' 'Mary, Mary,' 'Cripple Creek' (performed solo by Peter), 'You Can't Judge A Book By The Cover' (performed by Michael with backing from The Sundowners), 'Gonna Build A Mountain' (performed by Davy with backing from The Sundowners), 'I Got A Woman' (performed by Micky with backing from The Sundowners), 'I'm A Believer,' 'Randy Scouse Git,' and '(I'm Not Your) Steppin' Stone.'

A mono recording is made of most of this performance directly from the mixing desk. But this mix merely captures a feed from the public address (PA) system and so lacks most of the amplified instruments heard by the audience, including guitar, bass and organ. This primitive recording will later be made available on the limited-edition Rhino Handmade 2001 release *The Monkees Summer 1967*. (Tonight's recording is of a non-professional standard so a full breakdown of personnel is not included here. However, since the recording has been commercially released, full details are included in the Songography at the rear of this book.) After tonight's performance, the entire crew flies directly to Detroit.

● Sunday 13th
● At 3:30am The Monkees' private plane arrives at the Executive Terminal of Detroit Metropolitan airport where it is greeted by just seven die-hard fans. In the early morning a reporter from *Teen News And Views* interviews Peter and Davy. Peter tells them: "We're better than The Beatles. They're just a musical group; we're individual musical stars. One of us produced an album without his name on it and another bought a recording studio. And next year we'd like to discontinue our one-night concert appearances and perform in only ten cities, staying about a week in each city."
PERFORMANCE Olympia Stadium *Detroit, MI* 3:30pm, with The Sundowners, Lynne Randell; tickets $4-$6; sponsored by radio station WKNB

● This afternoon the group make up for the cancelled appearance here from July 29th. It will be the only daytime show of the tour. The touring party stays on the 20th floor of the Pontchartrain Hotel. The set today reportedly includes 'Last Train To Clarksville,' 'Forget That Girl,' 'Sweet Young Thing,' 'You Can't Judge A Book By Its Cover,' 'I Got A Woman,' 'Mary, Mary,' and 'I'm A Believer.'

Detroit's *News Tempo* reports that ticket sales for the concert have been slow when compared with the frenzy elicited by the band's show here back in January. Only 12,500 fans turn out at this 16,000-seat venue, and the gross take is $63,000. Refunds of $2,500 went to parents who refused to let their kids go to this show in the still riot-torn town. Support artist Lynne Randell: "We'd missed out Detroit on the tour earlier, because of riots. But everything's OK now – the curfew is cancelled. So we traveled back Sunday and did a concert, even though it was miles out of the way for us. The audience went out of its mind – it was a year to the day since The Beatles appeared there, so it was like a happy anniversary or something! One girl went so wild, she ran along a ramp and fell off a balcony right on to Micky. It was a miracle nobody got hurt."

Immediately after the concert the group fly to Nashville, Tennessee, for further recording work on their fourth album.

● A proposed concert to be held on this date in Montgomery, Alabama, never gets past the initial tour plans.

● Monday 14th

RECORDING RCA (B) *800 17th Avenue South, Nashville, TN*. Chip Douglas *prod*; half-inch 4-track; overdubs.

1. 'A Man Without A Dream' version 2 takes 1-20
   unissued master # UZB3-5435
Personnel Peter Tork (piano).

● Sessions are booked for the next three days at RCA's legendary studio, home of the 'Nashville Sound.' Chet Atkins will attend one of these sessions and talk extensively with Michael.

Chip Douglas: "I think Peter put a Hammond organ part on that song of Mike's, the real laidback one, 'Don't Call On Me.' I think Mike did the vocal there [too]. I think it was just overdubs. Anything that has a Hammond organ on it was probably done down there."

In addition to overdubs, at least one new recording is tried as Peter runs through several piano takes of Goffin & King's 'A Man Without A Dream.' It is possible that this attempt at an all-new recording is in response to a recent review of the recording from May 8th, which was briefly transferred to an 8-track tape on August 9th before being abandoned altogether.

Throughout the session Peter plays to a rhythmic guide 'click track,' something previously unheard on a Monkees session. Producer Chip Douglas is obviously eager for the group to record this quality song and, based on his comments during the session, he and Peter have developed today's arrangement together. Despite some later attempts at overdubbing, this particular version will remain unreleased.

TV NBC airs another repeat from the first season of *The Monkees* – episode 13, *One Man Shy*. The soundtrack is updated to include 'Forget That Girl' in place of 'I'm A Believer.' The show will draw more than seven million viewers, beating out all competition in its 7:30pm time slot.

● Tuesday 15th

RECORDING As the group's sessions in Nashville continue, composer Stu Phillips holds a scoring date for their television series in Los Angeles. He employs 13 top session players and conducts them through the cues for the episodes *It's A Nice Place To Visit* and *The Devil And Peter Tork*.

● Wednesday 16th

RECORDING The group wrap up recording in Nashville. Their album is now very nearly complete and all further work will be done at their home base in Los Angeles.

● Thursday 17th

● The group travel to Memphis, Tennessee, where Michael, Peter, and Micky attend a Booker T. & The MGs session at Stax recording studio. A plaque commemorating this visit will later be fixed to the studio's museum wall and will include the comment "they just wouldn't leave."

PERFORMANCE Mid-South Coliseum *Memphis, TN* 8:00pm, with The Sundowners, Lynne Randell; sponsored by radio station WMPS

● The group do leave Stax – to perform at the town's 12,045-seat Coliseum. The touring party stays at the Admiral Benbow Inn. Although the group and their entourage are invited to Elvis Presley's Graceland estate they decline because the King is currently in Los Angeles.

● Friday 18th

PERFORMANCE Assembly Center *Tulsa, OK* 8:00pm, with The Sundowners, Lynne Randell; sponsored by radio station KAKC

● The Monkees perform to some 9,000 fans at what is probably a sell-out show. The touring party stays at the Mayo Hotel.

● Saturday 19th

PERFORMANCE Coliseum *Denver, CO* 8:00pm, with The Sundowners, Lynne Randell; sponsored by radio station KIMN

● For this concert at the 10,858-seat Coliseum, Michael plays a Fender 12-string acoustic fitted with a pickup after difficulties with his Gretsch electric 12-string guitar. Most of Micky's immediate family are specially flown in to see this date of the tour. The touring party stay at Writers Manor.

● The group were originally booked to perform at the State Fair Arena in Oklahoma City this evening. That concert was cancelled for unknown reasons and the band's Denver booking – originally scheduled for August 20th – has been moved forward by one day.

● Sunday 20th

● The Monkees return to Los Angeles for a week off.

● Monday 21st

TV NBC screens a further repeat from the first season of *The Monkees*: episode 32, *The Monkees On Tour*. The non-live musical portions of the soundtrack are revised for this airing, with 'The Girl I Knew Somewhere' replaced by 'Pleasant Valley Sunday' and 'I'm A Believer' by 'Words' version 2.

RECORDING Chip Douglas holds a recording session from 10:00am to 6:00pm in RCA's Studio B in Hollywood but any Monkees involvement is speculative.

● Tuesday 22nd

RECORDING As yesterday, Chip Douglas has RCA's Studio B booked from 10:00am until 6:00pm but no specific work is documented.

● Wednesday 23rd

● A final tracking session is held to start new recordings and refine others for the band's upcoming album. These are the group's most drawn-out sessions so far for any project.

RECORDING RCA (B) *Hollywood, CA* 12midday-3:00, 4:00-7:00, 9:00pm-1:00am. Chip Douglas *prod*; Hank Cicalo *eng*; one-inch 8-track, half-inch 4-track; tracking, overdubs.

1. 'The Door Into Summer' version 3?
   Pisces, Aquarius... master # UZB3-5436
2. 'Hard To Believe'
   Pisces, Aquarius... master # UZB3-7322
3. 'Jam #1' rehearsal
   unissued no master #
4. 'I'll Be Back Up On My Feet' version 2 take 1
   unissued master # TZB3-4738
5. 'You Just May Be The One' version 3 rehearsal
   unissued no master #
6. 'I'll Be Back Up On My Feet' version 2 take 2
   unissued master # TZB3-4738

7. 'Jam #2' rehearsal
unissued no master #
8. 'I'll Be Back Up On My Feet' version 2 takes 3-4
unissued master # TZB3-4738
Personnel Michael Nesmith (guitar 3-8), Kim Capli (guitar 2, drums 2, shaker 2, bass 2, piano 2, cowbell 2, claves 2, other percussion 2), unknown (bass 3-8, drums 3-8).
● Today's session was originally booked to start at 10:00am, but possibly due to a cancellation by Elvis Presley, who was scheduled to start work in Studio B at 7:00pm this evening, the group are allowed to begin later and record through the day and night.

Chip Douglas returns to Bill Martin's 'The Door Into Summer' for the third time at this session, but it is unclear if a 'new' third version of the song is recorded from scratch or if version 1 from May 29th is simply revisited and refined. Session tapes will not survive for this portion of the day so it is impossible to verify personnel. However, if today's session does indeed produce a brand new version of the song, then Chip Douglas plays bass and Eddie Hoh drums (the May 29th version featured Micky). Doug Dillard is hired for this session, but it is unlikely that he participates in the final recording of this song. It is quite possible that the original May 29th track was merely augmented today with further overdubs – for example Eddie Hoh doubling Micky's original drumming in sections – but it is impossible to say for sure. Whatever happens today, the results of the work will be developed at a further session tomorrow.

Today's recording of Davy's 'Hard To Believe' is certainly brand new. The song was composed on tour with the help of Sundowners Eddie Brick and Kim Capli as well as Michael's San Antonio cohort Charlie Rockett and marks Davy's first songwriting credit for The Monkees not shared with other group members.

The song's tracking session lasts from 4:00 to 7:00pm and centers on multi-instrumentalist Kim Capli, who amazes all by using RCA's 8-track facilities to record virtually the entire song by himself, although some of the elements listed above are probably added at two further sessions in September. Eddie Hoh and Chip Douglas are on hand to provide support, but it is clearly not needed.

Douglas: "Kim Capli did all the instruments on that, starting with the drums. I was never crazy about that song. I had to sit there and [record] all his parts – and I was real cranky when I did it, too. I thought, 'Oh god, if we could just do this together with the guys and try to make it nice,' but it came out well for what he did and sounded like a real track.

"I'd never done that with anybody before – I didn't like anyone but The Monkees in there, really. Kim Capli had a Beatle imitation group called The Sundowners, he was the drummer. They went on tour, then Davy and Kim started hanging out and writing songs. Then they'd come in and talk to me about what they wanted to do. Kim was an alright guy. It was just a distraction to me to have them sort of collaborating with anyone but themselves. Anyone on the outside that they collaborated with was like kind of pulling it apart, to me, instead of them collaborating together on something. That's what I was always wishing for."

The final part of today's session runs from 9:00pm till midnight and is given over to taping a new version of 'I'll Be Back Up On My Feet.' The song was first recorded in October 1966 as a possible contender for the *More Of The Monkees* album, and today's recording is probably an attempt to capture a 'group'-led recording of the song suitable for release. After a jam featuring Michael on electric 12-string guitar, the ensemble (unidentifiable other than Michael) attempt to play the song. After one abortive pass, Douglas asks Michael if he could make his guitar a little "brighter." Michael replies: "Let me tell you a little secret," and proceeds to read

Douglas his amp settings, noting that his treble is at 10 and his brightness switch is on.

After being told to turn down by engineer Cicalo, Michael goes directly into a brief run-through of his song 'You Just May Be The One,' but soon stops to say, "Let me tell you about this guitar." Chip suggests the word Michael needs to describe it "begins with an 's'," but Michael is more concerned with finding a way to leave the session and to not play on 'I'll Be Back.' He suggests they do "Davy's song," hinting that perhaps he intends to play on 'Hard To Believe' – or knows he doesn't have to and can leave the studio.

Douglas asks if someone can be sent to collect one of Michael's other guitars. Michael says it's up at his house in the back of the car. After another half-hearted run-through, Michael asks: "What's the story with my guitar? I can't play with this thing." Douglas says, "I think we've gotta go with what we got," to which Michael replies, "I don't even know this song." After suggestions about looking at a lead sheet (written music for the song's melody) or listening to a dub of the old version, another brief jam takes place. Following this they try two more takes of 'I'll Be Back Up On My Feet' but these are incomplete passes with the musicians barely finding their way through the song. The tune will be cut for a third time, without Michael or Douglas, on March 9th 1968.

● **Thursday 24th**
RECORDING RCA (B) *Hollywood, CA* 12midday-6:00pm. Chip Douglas *prod*; Hank Cicalo *eng*; one-inch 8-track, half-inch 4-track; reductions, overdubs.
1. 'The Door Into Summer' version 3? remix take 2A
Pisces, Aquarius ... master # UZB3-5436
2. 'Riu Chiu' version 1
The Monkees Season 2 DVD master # UZB3-7321
Personnel Micky Dolenz (vocal), Chip Douglas (bass 1), David Jones (vocal), Michael Nesmith (vocal), Peter Tork (vocal).
● Chip Douglas bounces the backing track of 'Summer' from 4-track to 8-track and then records his bass part for the final released version. The finished take also receives a plethora of overdubs, possibly including an abortive lead vocal from Davy. Other instrumentation on this final tape includes a clavinet keyboard, pianos, rhythm guitar, two sets of drums, percussion, organ, and a further guitar. It is possible that some of these items are added during a further session for the song on September 7th.

According to television cue sheets, today the four Monkees also record the traditional Spanish song 'Riu Chiu' for the Christmas episode of their series. An abortive overdub session using today's take as a basis will be held on September 7th.

● **Friday 25th**
● The Monkees resume their summer tour with three final shows, all of which are professionally recorded for use as part of a potential live album (see joint entry for 25th-27th following the 27th).
PERFORMANCE Seattle Center Coliseum *Seattle, WA* 8:00pm with The Sundowners, Lynne Randell, compères: KJR DJs; sponsored by radio station KJR
● Today the group journey to Washington where they perform at the 14,139-seat Coliseum. The touring party stay at the infamous Edgewater Inn, renowned among musicians for bawdy activities. The group do indeed take the opportunity to fish from their hotel windows.

The concert starts with sets from The Sundowners, who run through a Beatles medley, a Dave Clark Five medley, and brief covers of The Lovin' Spoonful's 'Do You Believe In Magic,' The Association's 'Cherish,' The Four Tops' 'Reach Out I'll Be There,'

The Four Seasons' 'Dawn (Go Away),' Tom Jones's 'It's Not Unusual,' and Gene Pitney's 'I'm Gonna Be Strong.' Next, Lynne Randell performs a set backed by The Sundowners and including 'Goin' Out Of My Head,' 'That's A Hoedown,' 'Ciao Baby,' 'Heart,' and 'Shout.'

The Monkees perform their regular set of the period (see joint entry for 25th-27th), all of which is recorded and later included on Rhino Handmade's limited-edition release of 2001, *The Monkees Summer 1967*. A different mix of '(I'm Not Your) Steppin' Stone' from tonight's show will be featured on Rhino's *Live 1967* CD released in 1988.

● Saturday 26th
PERFORMANCE Memorial Coliseum *Portland, OR* 8:00pm with The Sundowners, Lynne Randell, compère: KISN 'Good Guys' DJs Mike O'Brien Roger W. Morgan, Don Kennedy; sponsored by radio station KISN
● The group travel to Oregon to perform a concert to almost 9,000 fans here, a less-than-sell-out crowd. The touring party stays at the Benson Hotel. After an introduction from the 'Good Guys,' The Sundowners kick things off at 8:10pm, duplicating their set from last night with the addition of their current Decca single 'Always You.' Lynne Randell's set includes her 1965 debut single, 'Hold Me.' The Monkees' set (which begins at 9:10pm) remains unchanged from last night (see joint entry for 25th-27th), though Michael will croon a bit of 'Singin' In the Rain' before the band perform 'Mary, Mary.'

As with last night (and tomorrow) the entire show is recorded on 4-track by engineer Hank Cicalo and later will be officially issued on the limited-edition Rhino Handmade 2001 release *The Monkees Summer 1967*. Several of tonight's performances will appear in unique mixes on the 1988 Rhino CD *Live 1967*. They are: 'Last Train To Clarksville,' 'You Just May Be The One,' 'The Girl I Knew Somewhere,' 'I Wanna Be Free,' 'Sunny Girlfriend,' 'I'm A Believer,' and 'Randy Scouse Git.' An alternative mix of this evening's '(I'm Not Your) Steppin' Stone' will be featured on the 1991 boxed set *Listen To The Band*.

● Sunday 27th
PERFORMANCE The Coliseum *Spokane, WA* 7:30pm with The Sundowners, Lynne Randell, compère: KJRB DJs Gary Taylor, Mike Dalton, Jim Simms, Charlie Brown; tickets $6; sponsored by radio station KJRB
● The Monkees fly into Washington at 2:30am and are greeted by about 75 fans. Prior to the final show of the summer tour a press conference is held at the Ridpath Hotel. The show gets underway before 7,300 fans with The Sundowners who play their usual set (including 'Always You') and then Lynne Randell, who varies her act slightly to feature 'Goin' Out Of My Head,' 'Hold Me,' her current single 'Ciao Baby,' 'Heart' and 'Shout.'

The Monkees' full set is once again taped (see following joint entry for 25th-27th) and will appear on the limited-edition Rhino Handmade 2001 release *The Monkees Summer 1967*. Appearing in different mixes on 1988's *Live 1967* CD will be the same Spokane performances of 'Your Auntie Grizelda,' 'Forget That Girl,' 'Sweet Young Thing,' 'Mary, Mary,' 'Cripple Creek,' 'You Can't Judge A Book By The Cover,' 'Gonna Build A Mountain,' and 'I Got A Woman.'

Before 'You Just May Be The One' Micky sings a bit of 'There's No Business Like Show Business' as a wry comment on the poor set-up of his drums. Similarly, Davy throws in a snatch of Buck Owens's 'Act Naturally' before 'Forget That Girl.' After the concert Michael donates an estimated $7,000 worth of equipment from the tour to an undisclosed local group.

● Friday 25th – Sunday 27th
● The entire show from each of these three dates in Seattle, Portland, and Spokane (see previous individual entries) are recorded on 4-track by engineer Hank Cicalo and in 2001 will be officially issued on the limited-edition Rhino Handmade release *The Monkees Summer 1967*. Some of the recordings will also appear in different mixes on the 1988 Rhino CD *Live 1967*.
LIVE RECORDING Seattle Center Coliseum *Seattle, WA*; Memorial Coliseum *Portland, OR*; The Coliseum *Spokane, WA*. Chip Douglas *prod*; Hank Cicalo *eng*; half-inch 4-track.
1. **'Last Train To Clarksville'** live versions 3-5
   The Monkees Summer 1967
2. **'You Just May Be The One'** live versions 3-4
   The Monkees Summer 1967
3. **'The Girl I Knew Somewhere'** live versions 2-4
   The Monkees Summer 1967
4. **'I Wanna Be Free'** live versions 3-5
   The Monkees Summer 1967
5. **'Sunny Girlfriend'** live versions 2-4
   The Monkees Summer 1967
6. **'Your Auntie Grizelda'** live versions 2-4
   The Monkees Summer 1967
7. **'Forget That Girl'** live versions 2-4
   The Monkees Summer 1967
8. **'Sweet Young Thing'** live versions 3-5
   The Monkees Summer 1967
9. **'Mary, Mary'** live versions 3-5
   The Monkees Summer 1967
10. **'Cripple Creek'** live versions 3-5
    The Monkees Summer 1967
11. **'You Can't Judge A Book By The Cover'** live versions 3-5
    The Monkees Summer 1967
12. **'Gonna Build A Mountain'** live versions 3-5
    The Monkees Summer 1967
13. **'I Got A Woman'** live versions 3-5
    The Monkees Summer 1967
14. **'I'm A Believer'** live versions 3-5
    The Monkees Summer 1967
15. **'Randy Scouse Git'** live versions 2-4
    The Monkees Summer 1967
16. **'(I'm Not Your) Steppin' Stone'** live versions 3-5
    The Monkees Summer 1967
Personnel Kim Capli (drums 11,12,13), Dom DeMieri (guitar 11,12,13), Bobby Dick (bass 11,12,13), Micky Dolenz (vocal, drums), David Jones (vocal, percussion [also occasional bass, organ, drums]), Michael Nesmith (vocal, electric 12-string guitar), Eddie Placidi (guitar 11,12,13), Peter Tork (vocal, banjo 10, bass, organ). Capli, DeMieri, and Dick are The Sundowners.
● Producer Chip Douglas recalls: "We recorded them live at these three concerts performing the act they did on that summer tour. Some things came out good; some things didn't come out so good. The big appeal in a live album is in between the numbers: all the clowning around. The excitement with all the kids screaming is groovy, but it's not that great sound-wise."

Engineer Hank Cicalo: "We were trying to put together a live album. The problem was there was so much noise on stage and so much noise from the audience. I mean, the screaming started before they got on and just went on and on. So from a technical standpoint the recordings were barely usable. I didn't feel there was anything performance-wise and there wasn't any new material either. So doing a live album, although we [recorded] it in a couple of places, was a bit weird. Even though we had a good truck and good equipment and everything else, I mean ... boy, it was horrendous on-stage."

● Monday 28th
TV At 7:30pm the NBC network airs its final primetime rerun of the *Monkees* first season, episode 27, *Monkee Mother*. It dominates its time slot, attracting nearly eight million viewers, but this is the last time it will achieve such success. When the show returns for its second season in September it will run against the Western series *Gunsmoke*, which proves an unbeatable foe.

● Tuesday 29th
● A union log notes that The Monkees may have a session booked at some point today in RCA's Studio A.

Thursday 31st
RECORDING RCA Studios *Hollywood, CA* 10:00am-1:00, 2:00-6:00, 8:00-11:00pm. Chip Douglas *prod*.
● A slightly more elaborate session listing appears today in a union log but details of the group's activities are still relatively sketchy. The first two blocks of time are spent in Studio B before a session booked for Jefferson Airplane in that studio causes The Monkees to shift work to Studio C for the remainder of the evening.

SEPTEMBER

● Micky makes a surprise TV appearance on the *Joey Bishop Show* this month to introduce Buffalo Springfield performing their new single 'Rock & Roll Woman.'

● Friday 1st
● In Britain, the London-American label issues a single of Micky's pre-Monkees recording 'Huff Puff.'

● Saturday 2nd & Sunday 3rd
● Two proposed concerts slated to take place on these dates in the Los Angeles area never occur.

● Tuesday 5th
RECORDING RCA Studios *Hollywood*. Chip Douglas *prod*; quarter-inch mono; mixdown.
1. **'Salesman'**
   Pisces, Aquarius... master # UZB3-5439
2. **'Don't Call On Me'**
   Pisces, Aquarius... master # UZB3-7314
3. **'What Am I Doing Hangin' 'Round?'**
   Pisces, Aquarius... master # UZB3-5442
4. **'Daily Nightly'**
   Pisces, Aquarius... master # UZB3-5440
5. **'Cuddly Toy'**
   Pisces, Aquarius... master # UZB3-8392
6. **'Love Is Only Sleeping'**
   Pisces, Aquarius... master # UZB3-5441
7. **'She Hangs Out'** version 2
   Pisces, Aquarius... master # UZB3-7313
8. **'Hard To Believe'**
   Pisces, Aquarius... master # UZB3-7322
9. **'Daydream Believer'**
   The Birds, The Bees... master # UZB3-5438

10. **'The Door Into Summer'** version 3
    Pisces, Aquarius... master # UZB3-5436
● A great deal of mixing is done of the masters intended for the group's fourth album, but due to the complexity of these productions this will be the first of several mix sessions to complete the project.
Today's mix of 'Salesman' features an alternative ending with a rap from Nesmith about an automatic cigarette-rolling machine, an allusion to the song's obvious drug connotations. This mix will later be featured as a bonus track on the 1995 *Pisces* CD (see the Songography at the rear of this book for more information about mix variations).
The mix made today of 'Don't Call On Me' will be used on the mono pressings of the *Pisces* album, though it has yet to have the song's special beginning and ending pieces edited on to the master. These bits will be added on October 9th. Likewise, the mono master for record release of 'What Am I Doing Hangin' 'Round?' is also captured during this session.
'Daily Nightly' as mixed today is still missing the prominent Moog synthesizer sound effects that will feature on the final released version as Micky will not receive the Moog he bought in June for another ten days. This mix of 'Cuddly Toy' also differs considerably to the released master in that it features an alternative and extended ending.
Today's mixes of 'Love Is Only Sleeping,' 'She Hangs Out' version 2, and 'Hard To Believe' are all deemed unusable and will be remixed on September 23rd. But the mix made today of 'Daydream Believer' is probably the one used as the single master when the song is released in November. (A stereo mix of this song will not be made until 1968.) Finally, this mix of 'The Door Into Summer' will feature later as a bonus track on the expanded CD release in 1995 of the *Pisces* album. It will not find contemporary release because the group decides to recut Nesmith's lead vocal in October.

● Wednesday 6th
RECORDING RCA Studios *Hollywood, CA* 7:30-11:00pm. Chip Douglas *prod*; one-inch 8-track; overdubs.
1. **'Hard To Believe'**
   Pisces, Aquarius... master # UZB3-7322
● A mono mix was made of this track at yesterday's session, indicating that it is probably nearing completion, but work continues to refine the production today. Whatever augmentation occurs is likely performed by Kim Capli who, aside from Davy's vocals, is responsible for all the elements heard on the track. At least two further sessions will be held in September to complete it.

● Thursday 7th
RECORDING RCA Studios *Hollywood, CA* 3:30-6:30pm. Chip Douglas *prod*; Hank Cicalo *eng*; one-inch 8-track, half-inch 4-track; tracking, overdubs.
1. **'Hawaiian Song'** take 1
   unissued no master #
2. **'Riu Chiu'** version 1 takes 1-11
   The Monkees Season 2 DVD master # UZB3-7321
3. **'The Door Into Summer'** version 3
   Pisces, Aquarius... master # UZB3-5436
4. **'Love Is Only Sleeping'**
   Pisces, Aquarius... master # UZB3-5441
Personnel Micky Dolenz (vocal 1,2, sleigh bells 1), unknown (drums 1).
● The piece labeled as 'Hawaiian Song' is merely Micky chanting to his own accompaniment of sleigh bells. He goes through several different vocal movements, though it is unclear if these are

improvised or based on traditional Hawaiian songs. After four minutes, Micky starts singing "Get your drums…" and an unidentified participant briefly joins in on drums.

After chanting, Micky attempts to dub a counterpoint vocal onto the recording of 'Riu Chiu' from August 24th. A rhythmic 'click track' and a tuning tone are used to help him with his timing and pitch. But he is all giggles and freely admits that he is stoned. Producer Chip Douglas jokes that a copy of the tape will cost him "ten thousand." After several takes, none of which is too bad, Douglas calls an end to the session, saying that it's very difficult to sing on pitch when you're stoned. Micky asks if it's really that bad, to which Chip says: "I'm not even stoned, but I can't tell at this point." The group will cut a new version of this song on October 3rd.

At some point during today's session the productions of 'The Door Into Summer' and 'Love Is Only Sleeping' are examined. On hand to assist in this process are friends Bill Martin and Harry Nilsson, and they may or may not contribute some final musical augmentation to these masters.

● Saturday 9th
RECORDING RCA Studios *Hollywood, CA* 12:30-4:30pm. Chip Douglas *prod*; one-inch 8-track; overdubs.
1. 'Hard To Believe'
Pisces, Aquarius… master # UZB3-7322
● Today sees a third session for 'Hard To Believe,' probably just involving producer Douglas and multi-instrumentalist Kim Capli. The song's final overdub session of brass and strings will take place next Friday.

● Monday 11th
● Stu Phillips works with 13 musicians on the incidental scores for the *Monkees* TV episodes *Everywhere A Sheik, Sheik* and *Monkee Mayor* at United Recorders Studio A in Hollywood between 9:30am and 12:30pm.
TV Tonight at 7:30pm the *Monkees* second season premieres on the NBC network with the broadcast of episode #33, *It's A Nice Place To Visit*. A reviewer from *Daily Variety* writes: "As *The Monkees* begin a second season, it's a new ball game, because the competition is different. Opposite the delight of the screamers is *Cowboy In Africa* on ABC-TV and *Gunsmoke* on CBS-TV. But the wild ones who flocked to see The Monkees on those [personal appearances] will probably remain loyal to the American version of The Beatles." Or will they?

● Friday 15th
● Production resumed earlier this week on the *Monkees* TV series after a two-month hiatus. Today, production wraps on what will become episode 39, *Hillbilly Honeymoon*.

TVseries

The Monkees

EPISODE 33: *IT'S A NICE PLACE TO VISIT*
BROADCAST SEPTEMBER 11TH
A trip to Mexico goes south when the evil El Diablo captures Davy.
WRITER: TREVA SILVERMAN. DIRECTOR: JAMES FRAWLEY.
SONG 'What Am I Doing Hangin' 'Round?'

● Micky takes delivery of his Moog modular keyboard synthesizer system and, probably in the next few weeks, adds it to 'Daily Nightly.'
Peter: "I went to a party at Micky's house once with a friend. I said: 'And there is the famous Moog synthesizer. Micky's one of the better Moog players around.' Micky came by at that moment and he said, 'Yeah, but it's even better if it plays itself.' He pushed a few knobs and turned the thing on and then walked away from it. It honked and did things on an absolutely random basis, never repeated itself. It was so interesting. You know he was really out there, Dolenz. One of my great regrets is that he wasn't able to credit himself for his own creativity. That to me is one of the great tragedies of the history of The Monkees. Maybe the greatest single tragedy – aesthetically, anyway."
In the studio, 'Hard To Believe' and 'Goin' Down' are sweetened with brass and string overdubs.
RECORDING RCA Studios *Hollywood, CA* 10:00am-1:30, 2:00-5:00pm. Chip Douglas *prod*; one-inch 8-track; overdubs.
1. 'Hard To Believe'
Pisces, Aquarius… master # UZB3-7322
2. 'A Man Without A Dream' version 2
unissued master # UZB3-5435
3. 'Goin' Down'
Greatest Hits master # UZB3-7315
Personnel Leonard Atkins (violin 1,2), Arnold Belnick (violin 1,2), Lou Blackburn (trombone 3), Bud Brisbois (trumpet 3), Buddy Collette (saxophone 3), Vincent DeRosa (French horn 1,2), Virgil Evans (trumpet 3), Bill Hood (saxophone 3), Jim Horn (baritone saxophone 1,2), Plas Johnson (saxophone 3), Nathan Kaproff (violin 1,2), Bobby Knight (bass trombone 1,2), Dick Leith (trombone 3), John Lowe (bass saxophone 3, bass clarinet 3), Ollie Mitchell (flugelhorn 1,2), Dick Nash (trombone 3), Wilbert Nuttycombe (violin 1,2), Uan Rasey (trumpet 3), Jerome Reisler (violin 1,2), Tom Scott (trumpet 3), Phil Teele (trombone 3), Tony Terran (flugelhorn 1,2), Darrel Terwilliger (violin 1,2).
● During the first part of the session arranger George Tipton – best known for his work with Nilsson – conducts a 12-piece brass and string ensemble for overdubs on 'Hard To Believe' and the probably incomplete second version of 'A Man Without A Dream.'
This concludes the production of 'Hard To Believe,' which will be mixed on the 23rd. However there is no evidence that today's version of 'A Man Without A Dream' is ever mixed. It will certainly never be heard again, and the masters will be lost, but the song will be re-recorded at least twice during 1968.
In the afternoon arranger Shorty Rogers works with a 12-piece brass section to complete the track for 'Goin' Down.' This remarkable arrangement featuring some of the city's foremost jazz musicians will be mixed on the 28th.

● Saturday 16th
● *Billboard* reports that Don Kirshner has a new record label modeled after Colgems. As with Colgems, RCA will manufacture and distribute this new venture, of which Kirshner will again have sole creative control. RCA's previous business enterprise with Kirshner – in other words Colgems – is said to have added $20m to RCA's coffers during Kirshner's eight-month reign.
● Germany's ZDF network debuts the *Monkees* TV series under the title *Die Monkees sind Amerikas Beatles* (which roughly translates as *The Monkees Are America's Beatles*).

● Monday 18th
TV The NBC network broadcasts episode 34 of the *Monkees* series, *The Picture Frame*, at 7:30pm.

TVseries

The Monkees

EPISODE 34: *THE PICTURE FRAME*
BROADCAST SEPTEMBER 18TH
Peter labors to clear the name of his bandmates after they unwittingly rob a bank.
WRITER: JACK WINTER. DIRECTOR: JAMES FRAWLEY.
SONGS 'Pleasant Valley Sunday,' 'Randy Scouse Git.'

● **Thursday 21st**
● Stu Phillips works in RCA's Studio A from 9:00am to 12midday with eight musicians to tape the incidental scores for the *Monkees* episodes *Art For Monkees' Sake* and *I Was A 99lb. Weakling* (known for now as *Physical Culture*).

● **Friday 22nd**
FILMING Production wraps on what will become episode 43 of the *Monkees* series, *A Coffin Too Frequent*.

● **Saturday 23rd**
● The Monkees appear on the cover of *TV Guide* for a second time. The magazine runs a lengthy exposé of the group's creative struggles, headlined "The Great Revolt Of '67."
The band's battle with Kirshner is the centerpiece, though this once-sensational story now seems like old news. Meanwhile at RCA studios in Hollywood, Chip Douglas remixes three songs for the band's next album.
RECORDING RCA Studios *Hollywood, CA*. Chip Douglas *prod*; Hank Cicalo *eng*; quarter-inch mono; mixdown.
1. **'Love Is Only Sleeping'**
   Pisces, Aquarius... master # UZB3-5441
2. **'She Hangs Out'** version 2
   Pisces, Aquarius... master # UZB3-7313
3. **'Hard To Believe'**
   Pisces, Aquarius... master # UZB3-7322
● Although these songs were mixed on the 5th, all are deemed suitable for further refinement today. 'Hard To Believe' benefits from brass and strings, missing from the September 5th mix, and today's best mix will be featured on the mono release of the *Pisces,*

TVseries

The Monkees

EPISODE 35: *EVERYWHERE A SHEIK, SHEIK*
BROADCAST SEPTEMBER 25TH
Davy's hand in marriage becomes the object of desire for a wealthy Arabian princess.
WRITER: JACK WINTER. DIRECTOR: ALEX SINGER.
SONGS 'Love Is Only Sleeping,' 'Cuddly Toy.'

Aquarius album, as will today's mix of 'She Hangs Out.' Today's work on 'Love Is Only Sleeping' is still unacceptable and the song will be dubbed down for a third time on October 1st.

● **Monday 25th**
TV At 7:30pm the NBC network broadcasts episode 35 of the *Monkees* series, *Everywhere A Sheik, Sheik*.

● **Wednesday 27th**
FILMING Production is in progress on what will become episode 41 of the *Monkees* series, *The Card Carrying Red Shoes*. Shooting will wrap on Friday.

● **Thursday 28th**
RECORDING T.T.G., Inc. *1441 North McCadden Place, Hollywood, CA*. Chip Douglas *prod*; Jack ? *eng*; quarter-inch mono; mixdown.
1. **'Goin' Down'**
   Pisces, Aquarius... master # UZB3-7315
● Chip Douglas shifts studios today for the first-ever Monkees session at T.T.G. studio (nicknamed by some as 'Two Terrible Guys'). Nothing from this mix session will ever see contemporary release, and 'Goin' Down' will be mixed for a second time on October 3rd. Nevertheless, a unique and significantly longer mono mix of the song from this session will later appear as a bonus track on the expanded 1995 CD reissue of the *Pisces, Aquarius, Capricorn & Jones Ltd.* album.

● **Friday 29th**
FILMING Production wraps on *The Card Carrying Red Shoes*.

● **Saturday 30th**
● BBC television premieres the second series of *The Monkees* in Britain.

OCTOBER

● The *Monkees* series debuts on Japanese television station TBS and proves a phenomenal success. For these broadcasts the group's voices are dubbed by Japanese actors Yasushi Suzukt (Micky), Hiroyuki Ohta (Peter), Jun Nagasawa (Mike), and Gentaro Takahashi (Davy).

● **Sunday 1st**
RADIO In Britain BBC Radio 4 airs the 1961 radio play *There Is A Happy Land* featuring Davy Jones. Meanwhile in Los Angeles, Chip Douglas mixes 'Love Is Only Sleeping' for the third time. The song is currently under consideration as The Monkees' next single release.
RECORDING RCA Studios *Hollywood, CA*. Chip Douglas *prod*; Hank Cicalo *eng*; quarter-inch mono; mixdown.
1. **'Love Is Only Sleeping'**
   Pisces, Aquarius... master # UZB3-5441
● Today's session probably produces the final mono mix heard on discs of 'Love Is Only Sleeping.' A stereo mix is likely produced later this month. 'Love Is Only Sleeping' is being considered for single release this month but will wind up as an album track.

● **Monday 2nd**
TV At 7:30pm the NBC network broadcasts episode 36 of the *Monkees* series, *Monkee Mayor*.

Micky enjoys sonic explorations with his new acquisition, a Moog synthesizer.

TVseries

The Monkees

EPISODE 36: *MONKEE MAYOR*
BROADCAST OCTOBER 2ND
Mike runs for mayor in a bid to save the group's groovy pad.
WRITER: JACK WINTER. DIRECTOR: ALEX SINGER.
SONGS 'No Time.' 'Pleasant Valley Sunday.'

● **Tuesday 3rd**

RECORDING RCA Studios *Hollywood, CA*. Chip Douglas *prod*; Hank Cicalo *eng*; one-inch 8-track, quarter-inch mono; tracking (vocals), mixdown.

1. **'Riu Chiu'** version 2 takes 1-21
   Missing Links 2 master # UZB3-7321
2. **'Goin' Down'**
   Pisces, Aquarius... master # UZB3-7315
3. **'The Door Into Summer'** version 3?
   Pisces, Aquarius... master # UZB3-5436

Personnel Micky Dolenz (vocal 1), Chip Douglas (vocal 1), Michael Nesmith (vocal 1), Peter Tork (vocal 1).

● Micky, Michael, and Peter make another attempt at recording the

yuletide traditional 'Riu Chiu.' For this second version, Chip Douglas fills in for Davy Jones on vocals. The session begins with numerous rehearsals sung in deep voices in a less than serious manner. Douglas is seldom in control of the proceedings at this stage. When proper takes start they slow the tempo considerably, but the group are still mostly joking around. Peter mentions an idea for their upcoming film in which they enter a tunnel and take the tunnel with them. Micky and Michael are unimpressed.

By take 3 – and several partial rehearsals – the group have settled down and the arrangement starts to take shape. Douglas suggests singing the song in a higher key and adding handclaps. Meanwhile the group splits up and Peter begins playing a version of the song on harpsichord.

After some technical problems are sorted out the session continues. Instead of splicing together an acceptable take they continue to sing in the hope of capturing a complete performance that is satisfactory. But they make very few complete takes and no truly great ones. One of the few full passes, take 15, will later be mixed for the 1990 *Missing Links Volume Two* collection. But none of today's recordings is given a contemporary release. At 11:00pm Peter notes that it is getting late and reminds everyone that The Monkees have an 8:00am call on the set in the morning, bringing this session to a close.

After the session, Douglas combs through the 'Riu Chiu' performances and splices together an acceptable take featuring The Monkees clapping and singing. The producer then subjects the song to several overdubs, completing the production and placing it alongside other tracks on a master reel for the upcoming *Pisces* album. However, the lead voice on this composite master is that of

Douglas himself rather than Micky, so this creation is never truly considered for release.

Also at today's session both 'Goin' Down' and 'The Door Into Summer' are remixed in mono for the second time. None of today's mixes will used for anything, and both songs will be mixed again tomorrow at a different studio. The version of 'The Door' mixed today still features Michael's original lead vocal but this will be re-recorded and replaced on the multi-track probably during the next few days.

● Wednesday 4th
RECORDING RCA Studios *Hollywood, CA* 11:00am-3:00pm. Chip Douglas *prod*; one-inch 8-track; overdubs.
1. 'Star Collector'
  Pisces, Aquarius... master # UZB3-7319
Personnel Paul Beaver (Moog synthesizer).
● Douglas has already taped Micky making some spacey Moog noises on 'Daily Nightly' but now recruits the man who sold Micky his synth to perform some relatively straightforward overdubs for 'Star Collector.' The song will be mixed in mono and stereo later this month.

Douglas: "'Star Collector' was done by the guy who was *the* synth session musician at the time, Paul Beaver, but 'Daily Nightly' was Micky. Micky bought a new Moog and he had no idea how to run it or anything. We just kind of turned on the track and turned on Micky's input, plugged him in, and he just kind of fiddled around there on several different tracks.

"We just put the best little bits in there that we could. After Micky experimented with his synthesizer I thought well, let's find a real synthesizer player. I'd heard about Paul Beaver; Micky had told me about him. So I met him through Micky and he was a good player. He knew what to do."

Peter: "That was Beaver on Moog. I always thought that he didn't know what he was doing. As far as he was concerned it was just a monophonic musical keyboard. He played it for the musicality. I thought Micky's Moog part on 'Daily Nightly' was brilliant. Another example of his intense creativity when he was into it. I thought he just made the Moog stand up and speak in a way that Paul Beaver didn't have a clue. It was like Paul thought it was a flute or something. He was kind of out there musically, but it was still within the normal harmonic bounds. Micky just went out there with this stuff; it was about screeches and swoops."

After this session, Douglas takes the multi-tracks for several of the fourth album's songs to another studio for an evening of mixing.
RECORDING Western Recorders (1) *6000 Sunset Boulevard, Hollywood, CA* evening. Chip Douglas *prod*; Eddie Brackett *eng*; quarter-inch mono; mixdown.
1. 'Star Collector'
  Pisces, Aquarius... master # UZB3-7319
2. 'Goin' Down'
  Pisces, Aquarius... master # UZB3-7315
3. 'Daily Nightly'
  Pisces, Aquarius... master # UZB3-5440
4. 'The Door Into Summer' version 3
  Pisces, Aquarius... master # UZB3-5436
5. 'Peter Percival Patterson's Pet Pig Porky'
  Pisces, Aquarius... master # UZB3-9832
● Teamed with ace engineer Eddie Brackett, Chip Douglas rips through six mono mixdowns of these songs, all of which supersede the previous mixes (except for 'Peter Percival' which has never been mixed before). All today's mixes will be featured in the album assembly that Douglas will compile on Monday.

● Friday 6th
FILMING Production wraps on what will become episode 42 of the *Monkees* series, *The Wild Monkees*.

TVseries
The Monkees

EPISODE 37: *ART FOR MONKEES SAKE*
BROADCAST OCTOBER 9TH
Peter gets caught in a plot to counterfeit and steal a priceless Rembrandt.
WRITER: COSLOUGH JOHNSON. DIRECTOR: ALEX SINGER.
SONGS 'Randy Scouse Git,' 'Daydream Believer.'

● Monday 9th
TV The NBC network broadcasts at 7:30pm episode 37 of the *Monkees* series, *Art For Monkees Sake*. In the studio, The Monkees and friends tape some tongue-in-cheek links for their upcoming long-player.
RECORDING RCA Studios *Hollywood, CA*. Chip Douglas *prod*; Hank Cicalo *eng*; half-inch 4-track; tracking, overdubs, mixdown, assembly.
1. 'Don't Call On Me' intro and fade
  Pisces, Aquarius... master # UZB3-7314
2. 'Special Announcement'
  Pisces, Aquarius... no master #
Personnel Micky Dolenz (spoken chatter 1), David Jones (spoken chatter 1), Bill Martin (spoken chatter 1), Steve Pitts (dog barks 2), Bob Rafelson (piano 1, dog barks 2), Charlie Rockett (spoken chatter 1), Peter Tork (spoken word 2, dog barks 2), unknown others (spoken chatter 1).
● In an effort to create some 'atmosphere' for Michael's 'Don't Call On Me' a session is held to record some clatter, chatter, and piano patter that can be spliced onto the beginning and end of the song. Bob Rafelson is on hand to tinkle the ivories and also gives some direction to the incidental background conversations.

Between takes Micky mentions that the previous night he was at Rafelson's house, very stoned, admiring some of Bob's old sheet music. Micky proceeds to run through the first lines of some of his favorites. With Douglas's help, Micky, Davy, and assorted guests eventually provide some accurate loungey patter and applause with which to segue Michael's performance.

Douglas: "I think that was done in the little Studio B. There were people in there for some other overdub, I think, that required a lot of folks, or maybe we were just celebrating something. It was a little get-together. Everyone happened to be there and it was an idea that came up."

An idea for the opening of the *Pisces* album is to parody the machine-alignment tapes that help maintain proper playback with a series of tone frequencies, used as a standard in all recording studios. The joke is that only a dog could hear the highest frequencies. While The Beatles employed a tone especially for animals in the run-out groove of U.K. versions of their *Sgt. Pepper's* album, The Monkees' more nuanced in-joke is probably too obscure for anyone but a recording engineer to appreciate. Nevertheless, with Peter as the

Davy watches Bob Rafelson at the piano in RCA recording studios, Hollywood, early October, for some incidental work on the Pisces, Aquarius album.

announcer, recordings are made of various human dog imitations intended for editing.

With these interstitial pieces complete, Douglas compiles a master reel for the *Pisces* album. It has the following line-up: Side One: 'Special Announcement' / 'She Hangs Out' / 'Salesman' / 'Cuddly Toy' / 'Words' / 'Don't Call On Me' / 'Goin' Down.' Side Two: 'The Door Into Summer' / 'Hard To Believe' / 'What Am I Doing Hangin' 'Round?' / 'Peter Percival Patterson's Pet Pig Porky' / 'Pleasant Valley Sunday' / 'Daily Nightly' / 'Star Collector.'

● Tuesday 10th
RECORDING RCA Studios *Hollywood, CA.* Chip Douglas *prod*; one-inch 8-track; demo.
1. 'I'm A Man' demo take 1
unissued master # UZB3-7539
Personnel Chip Douglas (vocal), unknown (bass, piano, organ, drums).
● When Douglas's band the MFQ was recording with Phil Spector a few years ago Spector played him this song by Barry Mann and Cynthia Weil. Douglas, now a producer himself, feels it might be right for Davy Jones to sing. Today Douglas tapes a full demo of the song – with no Monkee involvement – in an arrangement to suit the group. On November 4th he will record a fuller version.

● Friday 13th
● 'Love Is Only Sleeping' is tentatively scheduled for release as a single in Britain but its release in America is scrapped by RCA.
FILMING Production wraps on what will become episode 44 of the *Monkees* series, *Hitting The High Seas*. Some of the action for this program took place aboard a real life boat – which the group briefly consider purchasing. During the week Michael became sick and asked to leave the production. He will be absent from most of the finished episode.

● Saturday 14th
● Davy tells the *NME* that his latest business venture is a boutique in New York City named Zilch after a track from *Headquarters*. "I'm going to sell only Indian gear, beads and shoes," explains Jones. "Everything is going to be just unique. We are just going to have one garment of each design and then customers can select any buttons or trimmings, which the girls in the shop will sew on while they wait. It's being managed by Herb Neal, a very good friend in New York, and I am going to commute back and forth and spend as much time in the shop as possible."

TVseries

The Monkees

EPISODE 38: *I WAS A 99LB. WEAKLING*
BROADCAST OCTOBER 16TH
Micky's pride is at stake when a muscle man steals his chick.
WRITERS: GERALD GARDNER, DEE CARUSO, NEIL BURSTYN, JON C. ANDERSEN.
DIRECTOR: ALEX SINGER.
SONGS 'Sunny Girlfriend,' 'Love Is Only Sleeping'

● Monday 16th
TV At 7:30pm the NBC network broadcasts episode 38 of the *Monkees* series, *I Was A 99lb. Weakling*. In the studio Chip Douglas works on mixing the band's fourth album.
RECORDING United Recorders (A) *6050 Sunset Boulevard, Hollywood, CA* 2:00-5:00pm. Chip Douglas *prod*; Eddie Brackett *eng*; quarter-inch stereo and mono; mixdown.
1. 'Star Collector'
Pisces, Aquarius... master # UZB3-7319
● A complete reshuffle of the *Pisces* album begins today with the remix of 'Star Collector' (mono and stereo). Over the course of this week Chip Douglas works with engineer Eddie Brackett to remix, re-sequence, and, in some cases, entirely drop some items from the October 9th master. However, today's mono and stereo mixes of 'Star Collector' are indeed the finals.

● Thursday 19th
FILMING Production wraps on what will become episode 45 of the *Monkees* series, *Monkees In Texas*, after which Davy and Peter travel to New York City. In the studio Chip Douglas completes the production of the *Pisces* album.
RECORDING United Recorders *Hollywood, CA.* Chip Douglas *prod*; quarter-inch stereo and mono; mixdown, assembly.
● Douglas assembles the final mono and stereo masters destined for pressing of The Monkees' fourth album, *Pisces, Aquarius, Capricorn & Jones Ltd.* The title consists of the band's astrological signs, with 'Jones' added at the end since Davy and Michael are both Capricorns.

'She Hangs Out,' 'Cuddly Toy,' and 'Star Collector' are edited for length while 'Goin' Down' is dropped from the sequence entirely, along with the spoken intro 'Special Announcement.' 'Love Is Only Sleeping,' once under consideration as The Monkees' next single, is now added to the album and will never be issued as a 45. ('Daydream Believer' coupled with 'Goin' Down' will be issued as a companion release to the album in November.) Finally, 'The Door Into Summer' now features Michael's final vocal.

The album is now sequenced as follows. Side One: 'Salesman' / 'She Hangs Out' / 'The Door Into Summer' / 'Love Is Only Sleeping' / 'Cuddly Toy' / 'Words.' Side Two: 'Hard To Believe' / 'What Am I Doing Hangin' 'Round?' / 'Peter Percival Patterson's Pet Pig Porky' / 'Pleasant Valley Sunday' / 'Daily Nightly' / 'Don't Call On Me' / 'Star Collector.' With the album's release only days away, these masters probably go into the record manufacturing process next week.

● Friday 20th
● Davy opens his own boutique, Zilch, in Greenwich Village, New York City. The two-story shop at 217 Thompson Street features an exclusive line of Davy-designed his-and-her clothing and accessories. Some 2,000 fans gather to witness the opening along with Peter Tork, actress Sally Field, and recent tour support Lynne Randell. Zilch catalogs are due to be available by mail at 25 cents apiece. During 1968 a weekly radio show for Chicago's WEAW-FM called *Neal Deals With The Stars* will be taped from the shop. The 15-minute broadcast will be heard on Friday nights from 11:45pm to 12midnight hosted by Davy's teenage pal Jeff Neal, whose parents run the Zilch shop for Davy.
● Back in Hollywood, Stu Phillips works with pianist Pearl Kaufman to tape some incidental cues for the *Monkees* series episode 41, *Card-Carrying Red Shoes*, in a session lasting from 9:30am to 12:30pm.

● Saturday 21st
● Davy's Zilch shop attracts such large crowds that only five people are let into the establishment at a time.

● **Sunday 22nd**
● *16* magazine shoots a photo spread at Davy's boutique, Zilch. During the early evening Davy flies back from New York to Los Angeles.

TVseries
The Monkees

EPISODE 39: *HILLBILLY HONEYMOON*
BROADCAST OCTOBER 23RD
Davy is caught in the middle of a family feud and once again threatened with the prospect of marriage.
WRITER: PETER MEYERSON. DIRECTOR: JAMES FRAWLEY.
SONG 'Papa Gene's Blues.'

● **Monday 23rd**
TV The NBC network broadcasts episode 39 of the *Monkees* series, *Hillbilly Honeymoon*.
● Michael submits three new songs to Screen Gems for copyrights: 'Magnolia Simms' (a collaboration with his San Antonio pal Charlie Rockett) and two that will go unrecorded, 'The Coffee Table' and 'Soul-Writer's Birthday.' Meanwhile in the studio Chip Douglas starts a brand new song for The Monkees.
RECORDING RCA Studios *Hollywood, CA* 6:00-10:30pm. Chip Douglas *prod*; one-inch 8-track; demo, tracking.
1. **'We Were Made For Each Other'** demo
   unissued no master #
Personnel Rodney Dillard (instrument unknown), Doug Dillard (instrument unknown), Chip Douglas (instrument unknown), Eddie Hoh (instrument unknown), Bill Martin (instrument unknown).
● Only days after completing work on The Monkees' fourth album Douglas is back in the studio cutting a new song for the group. He tapes a two-minute version of this song by Carole Bayer and George Fischoff, though this recording is probably just a demo for another version that he will record on November 4th. No tapes will survive of this demo so it is unclear what instrumentation is featured today. All four Monkees were paid for their attendance at the first three hours of this date but their presence is highly unlikely. It will become virtually standard practice in the coming months for them to be credited for attendance and payment on musicians' union sheets even if they are not at the session, to make it seem that they still play on everything – which they don't.

● **Tuesday 24th**
● The release of 'Love Is Only Sleeping' as a British single is officially canceled. Instead plans are announced to issue 'Daydream Believer' and 'Goin' Down' as a single there in mid November.

● **Friday 27th**
FILMING Production wraps on what will become episode 46 of the *Monkees* series, *Monkees On The Wheel*.

● **Saturday 28th**
RECORDING RCA Studios *Hollywood, CA*. Chip Douglas *prod*; Hank Cicalo *eng*; half-inch 4-track; assembly.

1. **'Nine Times Blue'** demo
   Headquarters no master #
2. **'Until It's Time For You To Go'** version 2
   Headquarters Sessions no master #
3. **'Until It's Time For You To Go'** version 3
   unissued no master #
4. **'Fever'**
   Headquarters Sessions no master #
5. **'Instrumental #1'**
   unissued no master #
6. **'Instrumental #2'**
   unissued no master #
Personnel Micky Dolenz (drums 4), Chip Douglas (bass 4,5,6), Eddie Hoh (drums 5,6), David Jones (vocal 3, tambourine 4), Michael Nesmith (vocal 1,2, acoustic guitar 1,2,3,5,6), Peter Tork (piano 4, organ 5,6), unknown (electric guitar 5,6).
● Chip Douglas and Hank Cicalo assemble a 4-track tape reel of odds and ends featuring outtakes from their various 1967 sessions with The Monkees.
   All the items were recorded before today, but only scant information is written on the tape box.
   Many of the masters will later feature on Rhino Handmade's *Headquarters Sessions* in 2000, including 'Mickey In Carlsbad Caverns' (sic), 'Peter Gun's Gun' (sic), 'Fever,' 'Seeger's Theme' demo, 'She'll Be There,' 'Midnight Train' demo, 'Can You Dig It' demo, 'Nine Times Blue' demo, 'Jericho,' and the Michael-sung take of 'Until It's Time For You To Go.'
   Some of the more interesting items are detailed here. Michael's acoustic versions of 'Nine Times Blue' and 'Until It's Time For You To Go' probably date from early '67, as does an unreleased performance of the same song sung by Davy (and accompanied by a very out-of-tune guitar).
   The speculatively titled 'Fever' is a jam from the *Headquarters* era, most likely March 1967. The untitled jams listed here as 'Instrumental #1' and 'Instrumental #2' sound like June '67 outtakes from the sessions for 'Salesman' or 'Star Collector.'
   As if wrapping up this era with a nice bow, Douglas's reel of oddities signals the end of his partnership with The Monkees. Although they will continue to work together occasionally, the

TVseries
The Monkees

EPISODE 40: *MONKEES MAROONED*
BROADCAST OCTOBER 30TH
When Peter trades his guitar for a treasure map the group goes in search of buried booty.
WRITER: STANLEY RALPH ROSS. DIRECTOR: JAMES FRAWLEY.
SONGS 'Daydream Believer,' 'What Am I Doing Hangin' 'Round?'

creative spirit and group energy with which they approached the sessions from February through October 1967 are gone forever.

● **Monday 30th**
TV At 7:30pm NBC airs series episode 40, *Monkees Marooned*.

● **Tuesday 31st**
RECORDING RCA Studios *Hollywood, CA* 7:30pm-12:10am. David Jones *prod*; one-inch 8-track; tracking.
1. **'The Girl I Left Behind Me'** version 2
   Music Box master # UZB3-9780
Personnel David Jones (vocal), Charlie Smalls (piano).
● Closing out the month, Davy returns to the Neil Sedaka song that he recorded almost a year ago at the *More Of The Monkees* sessions but which remains unreleased. With accompaniment from his friend Charlie Smalls (soon to film a guest appearance on the *Monkees* series), Davy begins building a new version today, using the space of RCA's 8-track machine to compile a master piece by piece. Probably the only elements captured at this session are Smalls's piano and a rough vocal from Davy, but work will resume on November 7th.

Davy recalls: "I met Charlie back in New York when I was doing *Oliver!*. I used to go to improvisation and sort of hang out with him. He was a good buddy. He came to see me in '66, said he had this idea for a show called *The Wiz*, a black *Wizard Of Oz*, and I said, 'It's an incredible idea.'"

NOVEMBER

Pisces, Aquarius, Capricorn & Jones Ltd. album is released in the U.S.A.
'Daydream Believer' / **'Goin' Down'** single is released in the U.S.A.
The group's fourth LP and fifth single are issued in America this month. These are the last recordings produced in partnership with Chip Douglas because the individual band members will, with only a few exceptions, produce their own sessions over the coming months. Peter: "We couldn't find a producer that we liked. I mean, I liked Chip Douglas on the first album he did with us, *Headquarters*, but [*Pisces*] was not a true Monkees album. It was a Chip Douglas album

Pisces, Aquarius, Capricorn & Jones Ltd. album

A1 'Salesman' (C.V. SMITH)
A2 'She Hangs Out' version 2 (J. BARRY)
A3 'The Door Into Summer' version 1 or 3 (C. DOUGLAS / B. MARTIN)
A4 'Love Is Only Sleeping' (B. MANN / C. WEIL)
A5 'Cuddly Toy' (H. NILSSON)
A6 'Words' version 2 (T. BOYCE / B. HART)
B1 'Hard To Believe' (D. JONES / K. CAPLI / E. BRICK / C. ROCKETT)
B2 'What Am I Doing Hangin' 'Round?' (T. LEWIS / B. CLARKE)
B3 'Peter Percival Patterson's Pet Pig Porky' (P. TORK)
B4 'Pleasant Valley Sunday' (G. GOFFIN / C. KING)
B5 'Daily Nightly' (M. NESMITH)
B6 'Don't Call On Me' (M. NESMITH / J. LONDON)
B7 'Star Collector' (G. GOFFIN / C. KING)

U.S. release November 1967 (Colgems COM-104 mono / COS-104 stereo).
U.K. release December 1967 (RCA SF 7912).
Chart high U.S. number 1; U.K. number 5.

Daydream Believer single

A 'Daydream Believer' (J. STEWART)
B 'Goin' Down' (D. HILDERBRAND / P. TORK / M. NESMITH / M. DOLENZ / D. JONES)

U.S. release November 1967 (Colgems 1012).
U.K. release November 1967 (RCA 1645).
Chart high U.S. number 1; U.K. number 5.

performed by The Monkees. I don't think the *Pisces* album was as groovy to listen to as *Headquarters*. Technically it was much better, but I think it suffers for that reason."

● **Thursday 2nd**
● The Monkees are awarded a gold record for outstanding U.S. advance sales of their album *Pisces, Aquarius, Capricorn & Jones Ltd*.
FILMING Production wraps on what will be broadcast as the 50th episode of the *Monkees* series, *Monstrous Monkee Mash*.

● **Saturday 4th**
RECORDING RCA Studios *Hollywood, CA* 10:00am-1:30pm and beyond. Chip Douglas *prod*; Hank Cicalo *eng*; one-inch 8-track, half-inch 4-track; tracking.
1. **'I'm A Man'** takes 1-11
   unissued master # UZB3-9781
2. **'We Were Made For Each Other'** version 1
   unissued master # UZB3-9779
3. **'Carlisle Wheeling'** version 1 takes 1-13
   Music Box master # UZB3-9782
Personnel Al Casey (guitar 1,2), Gary Coleman (percussion 1,2, tympani 1, vibes 2), Henry Diltz (banjo 2), Eddie Hoh (drums 1,2,3), Milt Holland (percussion 1,2, tympani 1, vibes 2), Larry Knechtel (piano 1, bass 2), Neil Levang (guitar 1,2), Michael Melvoin (organ 1,2), Michael Nesmith (guitar 3), Bill Pitman (guitar 1,2), Ray Pohlman (bass 1,2).
● Producer Chip Douglas attempts to cut master versions of the two songs he demoed for The Monkees during October. No Monkees are involved, signaling a shift from the group music-making that was once Douglas's trademark. George Tipton, arranger of 'Hard To Believe,' returns to lead the studio musicians, who are spot on for virtually every take of 'I'm A Man.'

In what will become a new custom at RCA, two recorders – a 4-track and an 8-track – are run simultaneously. However, all future overdubs will be made on the 8-track reels. The 4-track is run merely as a safety or back-up tape.

The final pass of 'I'm A Man' from this session, take 11, is marked as the master and is pulled to another reel for potential overdubs, though none will ever be made. The Monkees have begun to assert their musical individuality and no longer want to make records that they do not produce themselves. Nonetheless, Douglas will make another attempt to interest the band in 'I'm A Man' during 1969.

Today's version of 'We Were Made For Each Other' shows just how much the group will lose when they part company with Douglas. In his hands this otherwise schmaltzy ballad is transformed into a dramatic pop stunner with some country flavor, courtesy of Henry

1967

Diltz's banjo. The master take (11) for this song will survive even though the session tape does not, and this George Tipton arrangement is clearly superior to the second version that will be recorded for the group next year. Sadly, no further overdubs will be made to this excellent track, which is left incomplete after today. Douglas will occasionally play bass on some upcoming Monkees sessions, but he will not produce anything more for the group until May 1969.

Douglas: "Things were kind of falling apart and there was less and less time. Everybody was more and more frustrated and wanting to do their own ideas. They didn't want to have to go through a central interpreter like me. Peter had his little group and in a way he was really the one who drifted away first. I don't know – he lost enthusiasm for me somewhere along the line and just wanted to do his own thing. Then everybody did. Everybody wanted to do these songs and produce them the way they wanted to hear them. Then they said: 'Chip, we're not working with you any more. We're going to do our own thing.'"

An example of this new direction comes today with Michael's recording of a song he calls 'Carlisle Wheeling And The Effervescent Popsicle.' This is his first self-produced session since October 1966 and the first official step in The Monkees moving off in four different directions. Michael still uses drummer Eddie Hoh, who worked on all of Douglas's recent productions, but now has the freedom to work without his bandmates. The final take from this session, number 13, will be used as the basis for further overdubs of vocals, organ, banjo, and various percussion.

Michael will tap Peter to add a banjo part at some point, but it's likely that Michael plays everything else, and he takes full advantage of the new ability to overdub more widely on the 8-track recorder. Although the results are excellent, for unknown reasons the completed version 1 of this song is left in the can. The song will be recorded again during 1968 (as well as in Michael's post-Monkees days as 'Conversations') but today's take will later be exhumed for Rhino's 1987 *Missing Links* collection and a more complete mix will be made available on the 2001 *Music Box* set. (See Songography at the rear of this book for more about different mixes.)

Engineer Hank Cicalo recalls: "Michael was wonderful, extremely creative. He'd bring in two or three guys – a drummer, a bass player – on a Saturday morning or a Saturday afternoon. As a record progressed, he'd have a good idea. We'd put a basic [track] down, we'd overdub, and by the time we finished in the evening we'd have a nice sounding record. Michael was creative and welcomed my input and the players' input – everybody was open. He was dynamite. I was available to Davy or Michael or Peter whenever they wanted me, but Michael was the one who was the most creative and had the ability to go into the studio with a song. He could write a song; he could hear a good tune. So we actually worked more with him, only because he was more attuned to doing it and more interested in making music."

● **Monday 6th**
TV At 7:30pm the NBC network broadcasts episode 41 of the *Monkees* series, *Card Carrying Red Shoes*.

● **Tuesday 7th**
RECORDING RCA Studios *Hollywood, CA* 7:30pm-1:00am. David Jones *prod*; tracking.
1. **'The Girl I Left Behind Me'** version 2
   Music Box master # UZB3-9780
Personnel Eddie Hoh (drums), David Jones (vocal), Charlie Smalls (piano).
● Davy picks up work on this track from October 31st. Smalls is once again on hand, and today's line-up includes Eddie Hoh who probably adds a drum part to the basic tape that Davy and Smalls have started. The production will be further fleshed out at a session on November 21st.

● **Friday 10th**
FILMING Production wraps on what will become episode 48 of the *Monkees* series, *Fairy Tale*.

● **Saturday 11th**
● *Billboard* reports that The Monkees have sold nearly ten million albums and almost seven million singles. This week their latest single, 'Daydream Believer,' debuts at a mild #101 on the *Billboard* Hot 100 Bound chart, though it will quickly ascend to #1 and becomes the group's second biggest selling single. Meanwhile today in the studio Michael cuts a track that will become The Monkees' strangest Top 40 single.
RECORDING RCA Studios *Hollywood, CA*. Michael Nesmith *prod*; Hank Cicalo *eng*; one-inch 8-track; tracking (and possibly overdubs).
1. **'Tapioca Tundra'** version 1
   The Birds, The Bees... master # UZB3-9783
Personnel Eddie Hoh (drums), Michael Nesmith (vocal, guitar).
● Michael probably uses RCA's 8-track recorder to build up this unlikely concoction of abstract poetry and Latin rhythms, captured in seven takes. He will eventually augment the basic guitar and drums taped today with vocals, whistling, percussion, bass, and additional guitar. The results will be released next year as the flipside to The Monkees' sixth single.
Michael: "I wonder if 'Tapioca Tundra' and 'Daily Nightly' came out of the same thing? I have always enjoyed writing poetry. Standalone poetry. As a matter of fact, one of the ways I got into songwriting was to find poems by great poets and see if I could put them to music. I did that in high school and college. In English class I would set some of these poems we were studying to music. It was

TVseries

The Monkees

EPISODE 41: *CARD CARRYING RED SHOES*
BROADCAST NOVEMBER 6TH
A Druvanian prima ballerina involves the group in a plot to smuggle microfilm.
WRITER: LEE SANFORD. DIRECTOR: JAMES FRAWLEY.
SONG 'She Hangs Out.'

Faceless ad for the group's fourth album.

from there that I decided that I would enjoy writing poetry. I wrote poetry routinely.

"About the time that 'Tapioca Tundra' and 'Daily Nightly' came along I had been writing my own poetry for a while. The poems tend to be fairly complex and we were fourth album in at that point, the second year on the series and all that stuff.

"I realized that I couldn't continue to write pop tunes of the type that Neil Diamond and Gerry Goffin & Carole King and Boyce & Hart were writing. I just thought I probably ought to go ahead and put my own imprimatur on things and write those songs. If they tend to be metaphorical and they tend to be more imaginative and complex, that was from the poetry I was writing. They weren't really designed as songs at all."

● **Sunday 12th**
RECORDING RCA Studios *Hollywood, CA*. Peter Tork *prod*; Hank Cicalo *eng*; one-inch 8-track, half-inch 4-track; tracking, overdubs.
1. **'Lady's Baby'** version 1 takes 1-3
   unissued master # UZB3-9784
2. **'Crow On The Cradle'** take 1
   unissued no master #
3. **'Lady's Baby'** version 1 takes 4-9
   unissued master # UZB3-9784

4. **'Seeger's Theme'** version 1 takes 1-5
   unissued no master #
5. **'Unknown #1'** take 1
   unissued no master #
6. **'The Dolphins'** take 1
   unissued no master #
7. **'The Water Is Wide'** take 1
   unissued no master #
8. **'Lady's Baby'** version 1 takes 10-26
   unissued master # UZB3-9784
Personnel Karen Harvey Hammer (backing vocal), Peter Tork (lead vocal, acoustic guitar, whistling 4).
● Today marks Peter's first attempt at recording 'Lady's Baby,' his composition that will become a musical obsession over the next several months. Today's simple acoustic-based version is recorded in the presence of the song's inspiration, his friend Karen Harvey Hammer, who accompanies Peter occasionally on vocals. The lady's baby, Justin, is also briefly audible on some takes.

Monkees assistant Brendan Cahill brings pillows into the studio to attain the ultimate laidback vibe, and Peter presumably performs cross-legged on the floor. After nine takes of 'Lady's Baby' and a brief duet on the Sydney Carter folk tune 'Crow On The Cradle' Peter tells Hammer that it is too early in the acid trip to be playing.

Peter in full period gear for the making of TV episode 48, Fairy Tale.

When taping resumes, Peter plays through a few takes of 'Seeger's Theme,' then an unidentified song that he only hums. Next is Fred Neil's 'The Dolphins' and a folk traditional, 'The Water Is Wide.' He also discusses The Beatles' recent 'I Am The Walrus,' saying that he thinks the lines about climbing up the Eiffel Tower and singing Hare Krishna refer to "us," meaning The Monkees. At Peter's request, engineer Cicalo does not give take numbers to any of today's work. But for the purposes of this book we have noted the takes – and take 20 is initially considered a potential master for this song. As the day wears on, opinions change and a later performance (take 26) is transferred to 8-track where the session picks up again.

Using take 26 as a basis, Peter and Hammer overdub their vocals in four passes, with the final performance marked as the master, at least for today. (A new version will be cut on November 16th.) After work is wrapped, Brendan Cahill joins Peter in the studio for a brief acoustic moment in which Cahill sings and plays a brief version of a traditional song, 'Bobby Shaftoe.'

TVseries

The Monkees

EPISODE 42: THE WILD MONKEES

BROADCAST NOVEMBER 13TH

The group pose as tough bikers to win the hearts of four motorcycle mamas.

WRITERS: STANLEY RALPH ROSS, COREY UPTON. DIRECTOR: JON C. ANDERSON.

SONGS 'Goin' Down,' 'Star Collector'

● Monday 13th

TV At 7:30pm the NBC network broadcasts episode 42 of the *Monkees* series, *The Wild Monkees*.

● Tuesday 14th

● The RIAA awards The Monkees a gold record for outstanding U.S. sales of their 'Daydream Believer' single. In the studio today Davy produces another session with some friends, including The Sundowners and Charlie Smalls.

RECORDING RCA Studios *Hollywood, CA* 7:30pm-12:30am. David Jones *prod*; Hank Cicalo *eng*; one-inch 8-track, half-inch 4-track; tracking.

1. **'The Ceiling In My Room'** takes 1-30
I'm A Believer And Other Hits master # UZB3-9787
Personnel Kim Capli (drums), Dom DeMieri (guitar), Bobby Dick (bass), Eddie Placidi (guitar), Charlie Smalls (piano).
● Members of The Sundowners join Charlie Smalls to record a version of the band's Davy-sponsored composition 'The Ceiling In My Room.' Davy produces the song from the control room, guiding the musicians through 30 takes.

A fight with Peter earlier this afternoon landed Davy in Cedars Of Lebanon hospital for stitches, and he sounds rather subdued throughout the session. Peter will claim that the fight broke out because the two were "getting on each other's nerves."

A combination of takes 19 and 27 are edited together to create the master backing track. Vocals will be overdubbed at a later recording session but 'Ceiling' is never given contemporary release.

In 1997 it will turn up on a budget compilation, *I'm A Believer And Other Hits*.

● Wednesday 15th

FILMING As production wraps on episode 51 of the *Monkees* series, *The Monkees Paw*, the group's latest single, 'Daydream Believer,' enters the British chart. Over the next 17 weeks it will peak at #5.

● Thursday 16th

RECORDING RCA Studios *Hollywood, CA*. Peter Tork *prod*; Hank Cicalo *eng*; one-inch 8-track; tracking, overdubs.
1. **'Lady's Baby'** version 2 takes 1A-4A
unissued master # UZB3-9784
Personnel Karen Harvey Hammer (harmony vocal, backing vocal), Peter Tork (lead vocal, acoustic guitar, bass, clavinet).
● Peter makes a second and much improved attempt at recording his 'Lady's Baby.' Takes 1A through 3A feature him simply playing acoustic guitar with no other accompaniment. For take 4A he is joined again by Karen Harvey Hammer on backing vocals. Peter then overdubs bass, clavinet, and a lead vocal onto this take, making it complete (though it is possible that some of these overdubs are added on December 1st). The results from this session alone are excellent, but Peter will feel the need to alter today's recording substantially during a session on December 3rd.

For the band's longtime engineer, Hank Cicalo, today marks his final session with Peter since he no longer feels any empathy for Peter's methods or songwriting. Cicalo: "'Lady's Baby' was a very weird and ridiculous situation. To accommodate Peter at the time ... he wanted to do this thing, and he wanted it to be real spacey. So we set up the studio and brought rugs in and made a little room with pillows. He would bring his friends in and they'd sit around and he'd play a little bit. It was pretty outrageous. Days and days of doing the same piece of material that wasn't that good.

"I think that Lester [Sill of Screen Gems] had given them all a good hunk of latitude to do their things, and he had to accommodate Peter in some way. And so Peter had this thing about this tune. So here was Peter and this entourage of hippies. They would just sit around for hours and drink wine and carry on, and try to get takes of this tune. Maybe we would make one or two takes.

"I think after doing this on and off for about two weeks, I said: 'I gotta move on.' I don't know if it was ever finished or what. It shouldn't have been released. If you heard it you'd know what I mean. We must have done a hundred takes on that thing.

"Peter got to be very difficult towards the end. Plus there were problems with the guys at that time. He sort of went off on his own in a lot ways, and there was a little resentment between the guys in not working together. There was a difference between Peter working on his own and Michael working on his own."

● Saturday 18th – Sunday 19th

RECORDING RCA Studios *Hollywood, CA*. Michael Nesmith *prod*; Hank Cicalo *eng*.
1. **'Nine Times Blue'** version 1
The Wichita Train Whistle Sings no master #
2. **'Carlisle Wheeling'** version 2
The Wichita Train Whistle Sings no master #
3. **'Tapioca Tundra'** version 2
The Wichita Train Whistle Sings no master #
4. **'Don't Call On Me'** version 2
The Wichita Train Whistle Sings no master #
5. **'Don't Cry Now'**
The Wichita Train Whistle Sings no master #

6. **'While I Cried'** version 1
The Wichita Train Whistle Sings no master #

7. **'Papa Gene's Blues'** version 2
The Wichita Train Whistle Sings no master #

8. **'You Just May Be The One'** version 4
The Wichita Train Whistle Sings no master #

9. **'Sweet Young Thing'** version 2
The Wichita Train Whistle Sings no master #

10. **'You Told Me'** version 2
The Wichita Train Whistle Sings no master #

Personnel John Audino (trumpet), Israel Baker (violin), Robert Barene (violin), Arnold Belnick (violin), Chuck Berghofer (bass), Milt Bernhart (trombone), Lou Blackburn (trombone), Hal Blaine (drums), Bud Brisbois (trumpet), James Burton (guitar), Frank Capp (percussion including mallets), Jules Chaikin (trumpet), Buddy Childers (trumpet), Gene 'Cip' Cipriano (woodwind), Gary Coleman (percussion including mallets), Jim Decker (French horn), Vincent DeRosa (French horn), Joe DiFiore (viola), Doug Dillard (banjo), Jesse Ehrlich (cello), Victor Feldman (percussion including mallets), Jimmy Getzoff (violin), Justin Gordon (woodwind), Bill Hinshaw (French horn), Jim Horn (woodwind), Joe Howard (trombone), Harry Hyams (viola), Dick Hyde (trombone), Jules Jacob (woodwind), John Kitzmiller (tuba), Manny Klein (trumpet), Larry Knechtel (piano), Ray Kramer (cello), John Lowe (woodwind), Edgar Lustgarten (cello), Leonard Malarsky (violin), Lew McCreary (trombone), Ollie Mitchell (trumpet), Alex Neiman (viola), Jack Nimitz (woodwind), Barrett O'Hara (trombone), Earl Palmer (drums), Dick Perissi (French horn), Don Randi (piano), Red Rhodes (steel guitar), Sam Rice (tuba), Ralph Schaeffer (violin), Sid Sharp (violin), Kenny Shroyer (trombone), Tommy Tedesco (guitar), Tony Terran (trumpet), Tibor Zelig (violin), Jimmy Zito (trumpet).

● Michael in a fit of artistic and financial extravagance decides to bankroll two full-blown sessions filled with the city's top musicians. The purpose is to record instrumental interpretations of ten of his compositions without thoughts of commercial release. With Shorty Rogers on board to arrange the musicians, Michael puts a quirky spin on many of the renderings, with styles ranging from big-band to muzak.

Today marks the first professional recordings of 'Nine Times Blue,' which was demoed earlier this year, 'While I Cried,' which will be recorded for The Monkees next year as 'While I Cry,' and a song unique to this project, 'Don't Cry Now.'

To cap it all, Michael has L.A.'s exclusive eatery Chasen's cater the entire weekend. "I've been writing for a year and a half and I did not want to be blinded by dollar signs or tied down to what is commercially acceptable," A little later Michael will tell Keith Altham of the *NME* about these sessions. "I wanted to find something new. This is it. It cost me approximately $50,000 to do it."

Drummer Hal Blaine is the musicians' union contractor or organizer for these dates and later writes about them in his 1990

book *Hal Blaine And The Wrecking Crew*. "Michael called me and laid out plans for a super session, the likes of which had never been seen in Hollywood," wrote Blaine, "a session that would be done on Saturday and Sunday, known as 'golden time' for union members. It was a date that we'd never forget – catered with Chasen's silver service and a gathering of musicians that was unbelievable. Shorty Rogers was doing the arrangements. ... It sounded like World War III. In fact, Nesmith was going to call it that, but changed it to *The Pacific Ocean* and ultimately called it *The Wichita Train Whistle*.

"The town was buzzing with excitement about the session; no one could believe that it could get on tape. I was the envy of all the major contractors in town; many of them called and made nice offers to take over the job. Everyone wanted to be on the session. ... Shorty had worked his ass off and came up with brilliant arrangements. Earl Palmer and I were on cloud nine, because it was a drummer's dream to be able to kick this gigantic band in the butt. We all took a lot of breaks during the recording to stuff our faces with gourmet chow. Gene Cipriano, the saxophone/oboist, got his reeds jammed with caviar. We were like kids in a candy store. Two of the 'wrecking crew' trumpet players came close to exploding.

"Finally, I asked Michael why he had called for such a costly session. He explained that Uncle Sam was about to remove 50 grand from his pocket and, instead of paying the taxes, he decided to spend it on a raucous write-off.

"The Nesmith dates came off without a hitch. It was the greatest party I've ever been invited to. Two days of Chasen's food, and more music than you could expect in a lifetime.

"It was fun and games all the way through, and when the last note was played, Tommy Tedesco threw his guitar up in the air (about 40 feet), and we all stood frozen as it crashed down on the floor of the studio and splintered to bits. He had the pieces mounted and framed."

TV series

The Monkees

EPISODE 43: *A COFFIN TOO FREQUENT*
BROADCAST NOVEMBER 20TH
The group's pad becomes the scene of a spooky séÈance.
WRITER: STELLA LINDEN ROSS. DIRECTOR: DAVID WINTERS.
SONGS 'Daydream Believer,' 'Goin' Down.'

● Monday 20th
TV NBC airs episode 43 of *The Monkees* second series, *A Coffin Too Frequent*, at 7:30pm.

● Tuesday 21st
RECORDING RCA Studios *Hollywood, CA* 7:30pm-12midnight. David Jones *prod*; one-inch 8-track; overdubs.
1. Medley: 'The Girl I Left Behind Me' version 2 / 'Girl Named Love'
  Music Box master # UZB3-9780
Personnel Israel Baker (violin), Robert Barene (violin), Red Callender (bass), Vincent DeRosa (French horn), Elliott Fisher (violin), John Gross (bass), Milt Holland (percussion), David Jones

(vocal), Red Mitchell (bass), Dick Noel (trombone), Frederick Seykora (cello), Charlie Smalls (piano), unknown (acoustic guitar).
● Davy and Charlie Smalls make adjustments and amendments to their recording of 'The Girl I Left Behind Me' from the end of October. One of today's major changes is the addition of a lengthy tag piece to incorporate their own song 'Girl Named Love' into the master. This will bring the running time of the track up to nearly seven minutes.

They also experiment with different bass parts, electric and acoustic, though not all three credited players' work will appear in the final production. Davy does record a fine vocal for the first section of the song but will never complete his vocal for 'Girl Named Love.' The piece is left unfinished and unreleased, and an entirely new version of 'The Girl I Left Behind Me' will be taped in February 1968.

A portion of today's recording is later made available as a bonus track on 1994's expanded CD reissue of *The Birds, The Bees & The Monkees*, though a more complete and better sounding mix will surface on the 2001 *Music Box* collection. As for 'Girl Named Love,' no formal studio recording of the song will ever be completed, but Davy and Smalls can been seen and heard performing the song during episode 56 of the *Monkees* TV series, *Some Like It Lukewarm*.

● Wednesday 22nd
FILMING Production wraps on what will become episode 47 of the *Monkees* series, *The Christmas Show*. Before The Monkees shoot their next episode they probably take a few days off to work on the script for their upcoming movie. Traveling north to the coastal town of Ojai, California, the group tape their ideas for a screenplay. In addition to the four Monkees a number of others participate in these brainstorming sessions for the script, including series co-creators Bob Rafelson and Bert Schneider, actor Jack Nicholson, and Monkees assistant Brendan Cahill.

Peter: "The main thing I remember about the movie was retiring to Ojai. For three or four days we talked about what we did and didn't want. Just hung out and talked about things. We sort of found a common ground. All that we wanted was just to do something special. Something a little extraordinary. Something not quite normal. What exactly that was, we wound up leaving to Bob and Jack. The exact script of the movie was basically their idea. I think what they really wanted from us was to do something off the wall. We really were glad to do that. We didn't want to do any of the conventional stuff."

● Saturday 25th
● *Billboard* reports that a new line of temporary tattoos featuring The Monkees will be launched in January by the Huckleberry Tomorrow Company.
● Today's *Billboard* also shows that the group's self-penned 'Goin' Down' has picked up enough airplay as a B-side to tickle the charts at #104. In Mexico, a single of 'She' that has been in the charts since July sits at #5. The Mexican Top 10 also features 'Gonna Buy Me A Dog' at #3 and '(Theme From) The Monkees' at #6. In The Philippines a single of 'Shades Of Gray' charts at #8. The group's latest album, *Pisces, Aquarius, Capricorn & Jones Ltd.*, enters the U.S. Top LPs chart at #29, their best first-week showing for an album ever. By next week it will be #1.

● Monday 27th
TV The NBC network broadcasts at 7:30pm episode 44 of the *Monkees* series, *Hitting The High Seas*.
FILMING Meanwhile on the set, Micky makes his directorial debut

TVseries

The Monkees

EPISODE 44: *HITTING THE HIGH SEAS*
BROADCAST NOVEMBER 27TH
When the group take jobs on a shady ship, thoughts of mutiny are bountiful.
WRITER: JACK WINTER. DIRECTOR: JAMES FRAWLEY.
SONGS 'Daydream Believer,' 'Star Collector.'

with what will become the finale of the second series of *The Monkees*, an episode titled *Mijacgeo* (also known as *The Frodis Caper*). Production on this episode will wrap some time later this week.

DECEMBER

● *Monkees Monthly* magazine reports that the group will take January off before shooting commences on their first motion picture. Bob Rafelson is writing the script for the feature and has recently moved offices so that he may fully concentrate on the job. Rafelson says the basic idea of the film will be somewhat similar to the television series. He will select a series of incidents that the members will handle in their usual crazy fashion.
● Michael submits a new song, 'I Remember,' to Screen Gems for copyright purposes. The song is a collaboration with George Fischoff, the co-writer of the recently taped 'We Were Made For Each Other,' but this one will never be recorded.

● Friday 1st
RECORDING RCA *Hollywood, CA* 7:00-11:00pm. Peter Tork *prod*; one-inch 8-track.
1. 'Lady's Baby' version 2
  unissued master # UZB3-9784
● Peter probably reviews the results of his last session for this song. It is possible that some of the overdubs credited to the November 12th date are added this evening. Nevertheless, Peter will substantially alter this recording at a further session the day after tomorrow.

● Saturday 2nd
● This week The Monkees hold the #1 slot on both the album and single charts with *Pisces, Aquarius, Capricorn & Jones Ltd.* and 'Daydream Believer.' The group's first three albums also remain impressively situated in the charts. Meanwhile in the studio Michael records two new songs at two studios.
RECORDING T.T.G. *Hollywood, CA* 12midday-3:00, 5:00-8:00pm. Michael Nesmith *prod*.
1. 'St. Matthew' version 1
  unissued no master #
Personnel Chip Douglas (bass), Eddie Hoh (drums), Michael Nesmith (vocal, guitar).
● At Michael's first session of the day he works with Chip Douglas and Eddie Hoh on his new song inspired by Bob Dylan. No tapes will

survive of this session so it is not known how successful or elaborate are today's recordings, but he will record at least two further versions of the song during 1968.
  Michael: "It's a song about Bob Dylan. The 'steal' and 'kneel' is a reference to 'She Belongs To Me.' ['You will start out standing / Proud to steal her anything she sees ... But you will wind up peeking through her keyhole / Down upon your knees.'] The ['her'] in that is the 'St. Matthew' that I'm referring to, and the 'St. Matthew' that I'm referring to is biblical. It refers to the biblical sense of the holy ghost as the central character in 'She Belongs To Me.'
  "As I think about that song many times – and I have many times – I realize that it was prescient to Dylan's born-again phase. 'Cos I could see what he was doing was wandering into the areas of biblical representations of the holy ghost, and I was convinced at the time that he did not know that he was doing that. It was interesting to me. So, that was what the song was about. But you know, that's so totally obscure that I didn't ever expect anybody to understand it or try and communicate anything with it. It was just a song, a little note that I wrote to myself in a way."
  After a three-hour break, Michael heads east on Sunset to RCA studios for a further session.
RECORDING RCA *Hollywood, CA* 11:00pm-12:30am. Michael Nesmith *prod*; Hank Cicalo *eng*; one-inch 8-track; tracking, overdubs.
1. 'Magnolia Simms'
  The Birds, The Bees... master # UZB3-9788
Personnel Max Bennett (bass), Jim Horn (woodwind), Lew McCreary (trombone), Ollie Mitchell (trumpet), Michael Nesmith (vocal, guitar), Jack Nimitz (woodwind), Earl Palmer (drums), Paul Smith (tack piano).
● Shorty Rogers arranges and contracts these fine jazz musicians for a late-night session and in a mere hour-and-a-half they will knock out Michael's ode to 1920s simplicity. In an effort to make it sound like the 'real thing' their playing will be buried under a scratchy swath of noise during mixing, "to more realistically capture the sound of the 1920-30 yippees" as the sleevenote will describe it. Michael will further thwart technological progress by placing everything in the left channel for the song's stereo mix. His music will go in ever more eccentric and eclectic circles at future sessions.

● Sunday 3rd
● Leonard Feather, respected jazz critic and author of the seminal *Encyclopedia Of Jazz*, writes in *The Los Angeles Times* about the *Wichita Train Whistle* sessions, gushing over Michael's collaboration with Shorty Rogers. "Verbally and musically," says Feather, "Mike Nesmith is one of the most articulate spokesmen for the new and literate breed of pop musicians who have sprung from the loins of primitive rock. The *Wichita Train Whistle* signals the advent of a new kind of locomotion. This train, with its carriage trade of symphony, rock, country, western, and swing, and with jazz riding in the caboose, may well indicate where contemporary popular music will be situated in the early 1970s."
● In what will become something of a trend for the group, two members are in the studio today, in the same building, recording music – without one another. Although all the band's record releases from this point on will bear the collective credit "Produced by The Monkees," with few exceptions they are now solo recording artists.
RECORDING RCA Studios *Hollywood, CA* 3:00-10:00pm. Michael Nesmith *prod*; Hank Cicalo *eng*; one-inch 8-track; tracking, overdubs.
1. 'Writing Wrongs'
  The Birds, The Bees... master # UZB3-9789

Personnel Rick Dey (bass), Eddie Hoh (drums), Michael Nesmith (vocal, piano, organ, electric guitar).

● Having rested and regrouped from last night's 1920s jazz exploration, Michael re-enters the studio this afternoon to cut his rather angular 'Writing Wrongs.' This idiosyncratic piece, which features a long instrumental break, is captured in 24 takes with some edits and will be the second lengthiest Monkees track ever issued. On bass is Rick Dey, a musician involved with such groups as The Merry-Go-Round and The Vejtables. Dey will fill the bass role on several of Michael's upcoming dates. Meanwhile, across the hall, The Monkees' 'bass player' is conducting a session of his own.

RECORDING RCA Studios *Hollywood, CA*. Peter Tork *prod*; Pete Abbott *eng*; one-inch 8-track, half-inch 4-track; tracking, overdubs.

1. **'Who Will Buy'** takes 1-26
   unissued master # UZB3-9790
2. **'(I Prithee) Do Not Ask For Love'** version 2 takes 1-5
   unissued no master #
3. **'You Can't Judge A Book By The Cover'** take 1
   unissued no master #
4. **'(I Prithee) Do Not Ask For Love'** version 2 take 6
   unissued no master #
5. **'You Can't Judge A Book By The Cover'** take 2
   unissued no master #
6. **'Two-Part Invention In F Major'** version 2 takes 1-5
   unissued no master #
7. **'Lady's Baby'** version 3 take 4A
   unissued master # UZB3-9784
8. **'(I Prithee) Do Not Ask For Love'** version 3 takes 1-2
   unissued no master #

Personnel Karen Harvey Hammer (harmony vocal 7, backing vocal 7), Stephen Stills (guitar 7,8), Peter Tork (electric guitar 1,2,3,4,5, clavinet 6, lead vocal 7,8, acoustic guitar 7, bass 7, harpsichord 7, guitar 8).

● Before Peter's stint as director on the *Monkees* TV series starts he spends his Sunday recording at RCA. His choice of 'Who Will Buy' from Lionel Bart's *Oliver!* is inspired and unusual, but the 26 takes are fragmentary at best. Tuning and amp problems plague him. Most takes last less than 20 seconds and none of the 26 passes of the song is a complete performance. The song is obviously deemed a total failure and its master number will soon be reallocated to a new version of 'Seeger's Theme' taped at a later session.

Peter then switches to Michael Murphey's '(I Prithee) Do Not Ask For Love' and is at last successful at performing a complete track as his efforts turn from aimless to inspired in a matter of moments. Between takes he breaks into a couple of brief bits of Willie Dixon's 'You Can't Judge A Book By The Cover.' Although Peter has some useable performances here that he can build upon, he will tape a second, more elaborate version of 'Prithee' later in the session.

Moving over to clavinet, an electric keyboard, Peter tapes a few rehearsals and then makes five takes of Bach's 'Two-Part Invention In F Major.' He previously put a version of this piece on tape during the *Headquarters* sessions but today's recording is a more serious attempt at capturing a performance. After take 5 he says, "OK, let's cool it on that and move onto the 8-track." Up to now they have been working on 4-track tape.

Switching to the 8-track machine, Peter resumes work on version 2 of his 'Lady's Baby.' He dumps the bass, clavinet, and some of the vocals from the November 16th recording of take 4A in favor of new bass, lead, and backing vocals, and adds a harpsichord in place of the clavinet. Stephen Stills adds two new guitar parts in his trademark Buffalo Springfield 'twang' style. (Because the resulting recording is substantially altered from the November 16th take we

have renamed it here as version 3.) However, Peter is still unsatisfied with the song in its present state and will continue to tinker with it at a session on the 17th.

Peter's second version of 'Prithee' from today's session features guitars played by himself and Stills with heavy delay effects. He also adds a solo lead vocal onto take 2. This particular production will go no further, and in November 1968 producer Bones Howe will cut a new version of 'Prithee' for Peter to sing in The Monkees' television special.

TVseries

The Monkees

EPISODE 45: *MONKEES IN TEXAS*
BROADCAST DECEMBER 4TH
The group comes to the rescue of Mike's Aunt Kate, whose ranch is under siege.
WRITER: JACK WINTER. DIRECTOR: JAMES FRAWLEY.
SONGS 'Words,' 'Goin' Down.'

● **Monday 4th**
TV At 7:30pm NBC airs episode 45 of the *Monkees* series, *Monkees In Texas*.

● **Tuesday 5th – Thursday 7th**
FILMING Production is in progress on what will become episode 55 of the *Monkees* series, *Monkees Mind Their Manor*. Peter Tork, billed as Peter H. Thorkelson, serves as director on this episode.

● **Saturday 9th**
● *Billboard* reports that Colgems is planning a total expansion. In addition to information about new personnel at the label, the article mentions that The Monkees' sales are approaching 15 million albums and ten million singles. In the studio, meanwhile, Michael tapes a brand new song.

RECORDING RCA Studios *Hollywood, CA* 7:00-8:30pm. Michael Nesmith *prod*; Hank Cicalo *eng*; one-inch 8-track, half-inch 4-track; tracking, overdubs.

1. **'Circle Sky'** takes 1-7
   Head master # UZB3-9792

Personnel John S. Gross (bass), Eddie Hoh (drums), Michael Nesmith (electric guitar).

● This is one of Michael's most rocking compositions, a simple, straight-ahead tune destined for use in The Monkees' upcoming film project. This rendition, featuring Michael and session players, is the first musical piece recorded for the project, although the movie will feature a live take from The Monkees – but by some stroke of fate the version taped today is the one that will be released on the film's soundtrack album. Later this will cause some friction within the group, who see it as a slight by Nesmith. Despite the fact that his bandmates are not involved in today's date, they are apparently the musical inspiration behind his song.

From take 1 onwards 'Circle Sky' is fully arranged and very close to the final recording, albeit with electric guitar and drums only. Take 6 is marked as the master and will receive several overdubs, including a bass part from John S. Gross, who does not track live with Nesmith and Hoh.

Michael: "'Circle Sky' was a song that I wrote while I was in the band with The Monkees: playing with The Monkees, thinking of what would be a good, simple, aggressive rock'n'roll tune that The Monkees could play. It was written around the concept of the band playing as a band. 'Hamilton smiling down,' one of the lyric lines in it, refers to the name on the music stand that I was sitting in front of. They were made-up lyrics to represent a collage of the times of The Monkees playing as a band. It's one of the reasons it's one of the best things that The Monkees do as a band. Very simple, straight-ahead, power-trio stuff."

TVseries

The Monkees

EPISODE 46: *MONKEES ON THE WHEEL*
BROADCAST DECEMBER 11TH
Micky 'Magic Fingers' Dolenz meddles with the mob when The Monkees land in Las Vegas.
WRITER: COSLOUGH JOHNSON. DIRECTOR: JERRY SHEPPARD.
SONGS 'The Door Into Summer,' 'Cuddly Toy.'

● **Monday 11th**
TV The NBC network broadcasts at 7:30pm episode 46 of the *Monkees* series, *Monkees On The Wheel*.

● **Tuesday 12th**
● Stu Phillips records incidental scores for *Monkees* episodes *The Christmas Show* and *Fairy Tale*, working from 1:30 to 5:45pm at Western Studio 2 in Hollywood.

● **Wednesday 13th**
FILMING Production wraps at the end of the day as the crew finish work on what will become episode 56 of the *Monkees* series, *Some Like It Lukewarm*.

● **Friday 15th**
● Bob Rafelson and Jack Nicholson's final draft script for The Monkees' movie *Changes* is now complete. Prior to and during shooting, the script will be subject to numerous changes, not least of which is the title.

● **Sunday 17th**
RECORDING RCA Studios *Hollywood, CA* 12:30-3:30, 4:30-7:30, 8:30-11:30pm. Peter Tork *prod*; Pete Abbott *eng*; one-inch 8-track; tracking, overdubs.
1. **'Merry Go Round'** version 1 takes 1-2
   unissued master # UZB3-9791
2. **'Lady's Baby'** version 3
   unissued master # UZB3-9784

Personnel Peter Tork (lead vocal 1, acoustic guitar 1, unknown 2), Lance Wakely (unknown 2).
● Peter spends virtually all of his Sunday in the studio focused on two of his recent compositions. Most importantly he lays down a very simple acoustic version of a new song called 'Merry Go Round,' the result of a collaboration with Diane Hilderbrand, who co-wrote 'Your Auntie Grizelda' and 'Early Morning Blues And Greens' for the group. Peter will record a more elaborate take on this song on January 20th.

Peter: "Diane and I began to visit socially just through the songs. She was there in the Screen Gems building on the West Coast. We became friends somewhat, 'cos I loved her lyrics for 'Goin' Down,' and I thought 'Early Morning Blues and Greens' was a good song, which she wrote with Jack Keller.

"At one point when we met together I played her the music for the verses [of 'Merry Go Round'] and she said, 'This is what it sounds like,' and she wrote those lyrics. Then she gave it to me and said, 'Well, now it needs a bridge.' So I walked to the piano and what flew out of my fingers was the bridge. It's one of those things where you just watch it happen. You go, 'My God … this seems to be working out OK.' She had written the lyric for the bridge in the same rhythm so that it was easy. Music just flew out of me like that and there it was. Presto. Instant song."

Peter with the help of his friend Lance Wakely also reviews version 3 of 'Lady's Baby' at today's studio session, but the existence or extent of their work is undocumented. Wakely and Peter will attempt a new version of the song on December 21st. Meanwhile, down the hall from Peter, Michael is sweetening one of his recordings.
RECORDING RCA Studios *Hollywood, CA* 2:00-5:00, 7:00-10:00pm. Michael Nesmith *prod*; Hank Cicalo *eng*; one-inch 8-track; overdubs.
1. **'Circle Sky'** overdubs onto take 6
   Head master # UZB3-9792
Personnel Eddie Hoh (percussion), Michael Nesmith (vocal, electric guitar, acoustic guitar, organ, percussion).
● Michael overdubs his recent 'Circle Sky,' adding his vocal, a second electric guitar part, an acoustic guitar track, some organ, and percussion (with Eddie Hoh on hand to assist). Two further sessions in January 1968 will augment and complete this production.

● Wednesday 20th
FILMING Production wraps on what will become episode 53 of the *Monkees* series, *Monkees Race Again*, a.k.a. *Leave The Driving To Us*. Also this week, inserts are filmed of The Monkees and some hand-picked guests to be used in the opening or closing spots of some upcoming episodes. Inserts include Micky introducing Tim Buckley; Michael and Frank Zappa destroying a car; and Davy's friend Charlie Smalls explaining rhythm while performing their song 'Girl Named Love.' A planned segment featuring Peter with his hero Pete Seeger is evidently never shot.

● Thursday 21st
RECORDING United Recorders *Hollywood, CA* 8:00-10:30pm. Peter Tork *prod*; possibly tracking.
1. **'Lady's Baby'** version 3?
   unissued master # UZB3-9784
Personnel Peter Tork (unknown), Lance Wakely (unknown).
● The Monkees are now officially on hiatus from television shooting, even though post-production work will continue without them on the second season of their series. The individuals will be doing a certain amount of traveling, but for the most part the break means a lot of recording. Peter is back in the studio today, possibly to tape an all-new version of his 'Lady's Baby.' No tapes will survive from this date, and it is quite possible that no takes are made today. Peter will return to the song in January.

● Friday 22nd
● The *Los Angeles Times* reports that The Monkees recently "entertained" at the annual Operation Bootstrap Christmas Party "attended by thousands of Negro youngsters."

● Saturday 23rd
TV Davy departs Los Angeles's LAX airport for a trip to visit his family in Britain. There, in a first for the series, episode 47 of *The Monkees*, titled *The Christmas Show*, is shown today in advance of its U.S. airing. American audiences will have to wait until Christmas day to see this special episode.
● *Billboard* reports that Columbia-Screen Gems has been hit with another lawsuit stemming from the Monkees project. The suit was filed by a production company called BB&D who claim that members of Boyce & Hart's studio band – bassist Larry Taylor, drummer Billy Lewis, and guitarist Gerry McGee – were under exclusive contract to their organization when they began cutting tracks for The Monkees and refused to honor other commitments to BB&D. They claim that Boyce & Hart, Screen Gems, Columbia Pictures, and Raybert Productions purposely induced the three to breach the agreement. Taylor, Lewis, and McGee were part of a group called The New Order which recorded for Warner Bros. Records in early 1966, and were signed through BB&D. Although they have not recorded a track for The Monkees in more than a year, Lewis and McGee will return to work for the group in a few days.

● Sunday 24th
FILMING Production officially wraps on season two of *The Monkees* as the show's crew completes post-production on what will become episode 54 of the series, *The Monkees In Paris*. This show was filmed on location in France during June but requires significant editing and additional opening and closing segments. Most of the crew for the series will find employment on The Monkees' motion picture, which begins shooting early next year.
● Davy arrives in Manchester (via London) for Christmas. He visits with his family and later attends a television taping involving The New Vaudeville Band, which includes Davy's friend, guitarist Mick Wilsher. Davy will also sneak into a football match at Old Trafford to watch his team, Manchester United.
● Micky and Samantha Juste travel to Northern California to visit the Dolenz family.

TVseries

The Monkees

EPISODE 47: *THE CHRISTMAS SHOW*
BROADCAST DECEMBER 25TH
The group try to instill the spirit of Christmas in a cynical rich kid (played by Butch Patrick).
WRITERS: DAVE EVANS, NEIL BURSTYN. DIRECTOR: JON ANDERSON.
SONG 'Riu Chiu.'

Micky welcomes the driver in TV episode 53, Monkees Race Again.

Monday 25th

TV The NBC network broadcasts at 7:30pm the special holiday installment of the *Monkees* series, episode 47, *The Christmas Show*. Meanwhile in Britain the band's fans enjoy a brief glimpse of the group in a special taped message for the show *Meet The Kids*. This BBC-1 program is screened live from Queen Mary's Hospital, Carshalton, Surrey in south-east England.

● Today the group are spread around the globe. Micky spends Christmas with Samantha Juste and his family in Saratoga, California. Davy is back home with his family in Manchester, England. Peter heads east to Connecticut, and Michael stays in Los Angeles with Phyllis who is expecting another child. The couple have recently moved into the luxury home they purchased in June. This showplace at 15221 Antello Place in Bel Air features a 360-degree view of the city and will be the location of a grand Christmas party.

Tuesday 26th

● Micky travels to Honolulu, Hawaii, to spend time at Chip Douglas's parents' house. In Manchester, Davy enjoys The Beatles' *Magical Mystery Tour* film which he watches on TV. And back in Hollywood, Tommy Boyce and Bobby Hart mark a surprising return as producers for The Monkees.

RECORDING United Recorders (B) *6050 Sunset Boulevard, Hollywood, CA* 8:30-11:30, 12:30pm-3:30am. Tommy Boyce & Bobby Hart *prod*; Henry Lewy *eng*; one-inch 8-track; tracking.

1. **'P.O. Box 9847'** takes 1-25 + pick-up pieces
   The Birds, The Bees... master # WZB3-0183
2. **'Valleri'** version 2 takes 1-13
   The Birds, The Bees... master # TZB3-4727
3. **'Me Without You'** take 1
   Instant Replay master # WZB3-3511

Personnel Bobby Hart (tack piano 1, keyboard 3), Billy Lewis (drums), Gerry McGee (guitar), Joe Osborn (bass), Louis Shelton (guitar).

● A stroke of pure fate returns Boyce & Hart to their roles as producers. The duo last worked for the group back in November 1966 but since their song 'Valleri' first aired earlier this year on the *Monkees* episodes *Captain Crocodile* and *Monkees At The Movies* Screen Gems has been deluged with requests for a record release of the song. Some DJs have even played good quality dubs from the TV and the song has received significant airplay.

Now that The Monkees are each exploring their own individuality in the studio, the only central force is their music supervisor, Lester Sill. He feels that 'Valleri' can still be a hit for the group, so he brings back Boyce & Hart to recut their song that they first recorded in August 1966 – but under one condition. They will not be credited for their work. Instead these new productions, like all the others now, will bear the credit "Produced by The Monkees." Having sat on the sidelines for more than a year, Boyce & Hart are well aware that it is better to have a song on a Monkees record without credit than nothing at all.

But the first song taped at today's session is a newer composition inspired by Bob Rafelson, 'P.O. Box 9847.' Although Rafelson's name will later be removed from the writing credits due to a Screen Gems policy, he gave Boyce & Hart the rough idea knowing that they could fashion something from it. Musically, the song is heavily influenced by The Beatles, sounding like an outtake from *Magical Mystery Tour*. The basic tracks are dominated by some McCartney-like bass from Joe Osborn, who now replaces Canned Heat's Larry Taylor in the regular Boyce & Hart crew. Take 21 (with some slight edits) is marked as the master from this session and is used for future overdubbing. These additions – Micky on lead vocals, as well as

strings, marxophone (a sort of mandolin-zither), tabla (Indian drum), additional drums, handclaps, and an experimental Moog synthesizer part – will be taped next year. Boyce & Hart will also release their own version of the song next year on A&M – with Rafelson's name restored to the credits.

Bobby Hart: "It was Bob Rafelson's idea to do a song about a classified ad. It wasn't his title or anything. He said, 'I have a great idea for a song worded the way a classified ad would be worded, in the abbreviated style.' So we wrote 'P.O. Box 9847' and gave him a third of the song for his inspiration and original idea. The powers that be would not let him have a writer's credit. I don't know why. I guess it was some sort of conflict of interest with him being producer on the TV show."

Boyce & Hart next focus on cutting the new version of 'Valleri.' The arrangement for this second recording retains the original's flavor but eventually features more augmentation than the '66 version. As with the original version, 13 takes are taped, with the last marked as the master. Production will continue on December 28th and the results will be issued as The Monkees' next single, in February 1968.

Hart: "We had cut the song just prior to the point where we were dismissed as producers. Over a year later, Lester Sill came back to us and said they wanted to do 'Valleri' but couldn't use the original track because the musicians' union contracts were filed with us as producers, and we can't have producers' credit. He said, 'We want you to go back in and do it again, making it sound as close to the original as possible and not take producer's credit on it.' So that's what we did. We wrote the song [in 1966] in the car going up Mullholland from Woodrow Wilson and Laurel Canyon over to the house that [Don Kirshner] was renting in the suburbs."

The final song recorded at this session is 'Me Without You,' taped in just one take. With a melody not unlike The Beatles' 'Your Mother Should Know,' the song will turn into a Boyce & Hart classic when the production is completed next year. Nevertheless, this master will not see the light of day until 1969's *Instant Replay* album.

Tommy Boyce: "That should have been a single too! Absolutely. I think we had probably been listening to The Beatles that day and ['Your Mother Should Know'] came on. I always had a book of song titles with me, you know? Sometimes when we got stuck for an idea I'd say to Bobby, 'Look, I have these 25 ideas for songs. What do you think? "Me Without You." What do you think about that for a song?' He said, 'Yeah, that's a good idea for a song. Who should we write it about?' I remember at the time there was a couple of our friends that were splitting up, that shouldn't have been splitting up. I forget who they were, of course. So we wrote this song about them. Then we finally told them later, 'This song is about you.' Then after they heard the song they totally split up!"

Thursday 28th

RECORDING United Recorders *Hollywood, CA* 7:00-10:00pm. Tommy Boyce & Bobby Hart *prod*; Henry Lewy *eng*; one-inch 8-track; overdubs.

1. **'Valleri'** version 2 take 13
   The Birds, The Bees... master # TZB3-4727

Personnel Roy Caton (trumpet), Jim Horn (saxophone), Billy Lewis (tambourine), Lew McCreary (trombone), Jay Migliori (saxophone), Ollie Mitchell (trumpet), Louis Shelton (fuzz guitar, guitar solo).

● Boyce & Hart have given themselves a day to recover and now return to their new take of 'Valleri.' They further augment the song with a Don McGinnis brass arrangement, among other things. The production will be completed in a few weeks when Davy returns from England and tapes his double-tracked lead vocals.

● Friday 29th

● In England, Davy flies from Manchester to London to meet up with Peter who has just arrived from the East Coast. The two will stay at the Mayfair Hotel, and sometime during this sojourn The Beatles hold a party for them at their hotel. Entertainment will be provided by a folk group, The MacPeakes, whose use of bagpipes apparently entrances John Lennon.

● Back in Hollywood, *Daily Variety* announces that the *Monkees* TV series has a new acting-producer, though in fact it is the band's longtime associate Ward Sylvester. "Ward Sylvester, at 26 the youngest producer Screen Gems ever has had, takes over reins of SG's *The Monkees* NBC-TV series," reports *Variety*, "succeeding Bert Schneider and Bob Rafelson. Sylvester's promotion, SG coast chief Jackie Cooper notes, is part of his policy of upping personnel within the ranks. Sylvester has been production exec on series since inception."

● Saturday 30th

RECORDING United Recorders (B) *Hollywood, CA* 2:00-5:00, 7:00-10:00pm. Tommy Boyce & Bobby Hart *prod*; Henry Lewy *eng*; one-inch 8-track; tracking.

1. **'Through The Looking Glass'** version 2 takes 1-20
   Instant Replay master # WZB3-3512
2. **'Nashville'** takes 1-6
   unissued no master #

Personnel Keith Allison (guitar), Tommy Boyce (vocal 2, acoustic guitar 2), Wayne Erwin (guitar), Bobby Hart (tack piano), Billy Lewis (drums), Gerry McGee (guitar), Joe Osborn (bass), Louis Shelton (guitar).

● Boyce & Hart return to another of their 1966 leftovers, 'Through The Looking Glass.' In keeping with the musical mode of the last few sessions, this new arrangement has a distinct Beatles flavor. Back on board is guitarist Wayne Erwin (probably on fuzz guitar) as well as Keith Allison augmenting the regular guitar line-up of Shelton and McGee. Twenty takes are taped with the last being marked as the master ready for overdubs. Production on this version of the song will be completed next year, though it will not see release until early '69.

Boyce & Hart were dismissed as producers in '66 partly because they were accused of using Monkees studio time for recordings of dubious value. Ironically, after only a few days back on the job, the duo are again taking liberties. Today they record a song for their own amusement, 'Nashville.' It is absolutely not intended for The Monkees and will never even grace any of Boyce & Hart's own A&M releases. In fact it is a special piece that the duo will perform in an appearance at the Grand Ole Opry – and it is impossible to guess how this parody of the country music idiom goes down in that hallowed hall. Today, all six takes feature Tommy Boyce on lead vocal and acoustic guitar. Take 6 is marked as the master and features Boyce's impersonations of various A&M employees among other irreverent banter.

● Sunday 31st

● In England, Davy and Peter attend a New Year's Eve party at London's Speakeasy club. They are joined in the festivities by Jimi Hendrix, Jeff Beck, Eric Burdon, Tommy Steele, *Oliver!* creator Lionel Bart, and actress Adrienne Posta. Back in Los Angeles, Boyce & Hart are at work on the final Monkees recording session of the year.
RECORDING United Recorders *Hollywood, CA* 12midday-3:00pm. Tommy Boyce & Bobby Hart *prod*; Henry Lewy *eng*; one-inch 8-track; tracking.

1. **'Don't Listen To Linda'** version 2 takes 1-3 + tag piece 2 takes
   Instant Replay master # WZB3-0187
Personnel Tommy Boyce (guitar), Billy Lewis (drums), Gerry McGee (guitar), Joe Osborn (bass), Louis Shelton (guitar).
● Today sees another recut of a Boyce & Hart reject from 1966, and in this case the producers turn the jaunty 'Don't Listen To Linda' into a love ballad. They need just three takes to nail this new arrangement. Take 2 is marked as the master and will be given several overdubs next year. Additionally, two takes of a separately recorded tag piece are taped and then spliced on to the end of the master to give the song a 'cold' ending.

Peter arrives at Heathrow Airport, London, with 'Lady' (Karen Harvey Hammer) and 'Baby' (Justin) in tow. Justin's father is Peter's business partner, Bob Hammer.

1968

Davy, Michael, Micky, and Peter recording self-produced sessions separately ... second season TV series continues on NBC ... script developed for forthcoming Monkees movie *Changes* ... 'Valleri' sixth single, makes #3 ... filming starts on *Changes* movie ... NBC says no to third TV season ... movie name changed to *Untitled* ... TV reruns start as second season ends ... *The Birds, The Bees & The Monkees* fifth LP, makes #3 ... Michael's instrumental *Wichita Train Whistle Sings* LP released ... Michael records in Nashville ... 'D.W. Washburn' seventh single, makes #19, the first 'flop' ... rare meeting of four Monkees in studio, for spoken-word piece ... movie name changed to *Head* ... final primetime TV episode of *The Monkees* shown ... concerts in Australia, Japan ... 'Porpoise Song' eighth single, makes #62 ... Bones Howe is new Monkees record producer ... *Head* sixth LP, makes #45 ... *Head* movie is (briefly) released ... recording and filming for TV special ... Peter leaves The Monkees.

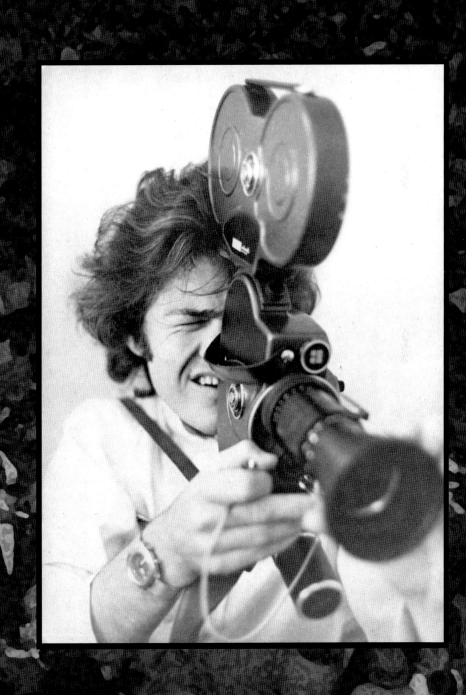

Micky points his 16mm camera at a year of movie-making.

1968

JANUARY

● Peter visits The Beatles' Apple boutique while still on his trip to London and eventually reconnects with George Harrison, whom he met last July. Harrison is in the midst of scoring the film *Wonderwall* and invites Peter over to the studio where he is working. Peter is soon recruited to play some five-string banjo at the session on an instrument borrowed from Paul McCartney, and the result is some incidental music that later appears in the film and soundtrack album. When Peter expresses interest in seeing the recently televised *Magical Mystery Tour*, Harrison makes arrangements for a screening at Peter's hotel. Like Davy, Peter loves the film, asking to see it several times and taking color slide photographs while the screening is in progress.
● During his London visit Peter holds a press conference during which he discusses the future of the group's TV series. "We thought the present shows were losing their impetus," Peter says. "They were getting harder to act. We felt yoked by their plots. We want our shows to be fun, simple … but inventive, fresh, and interesting. Did you see *Magical Mystery Tour*? That's what we like. We must go as far afield as possible on the lines of *Magical Mystery Tour*. We also have in mind five-minute interviews with someone we respect. Some have already been filmed. I want to do Pete Seeger. Davy has spoken to a guy he admires called Charlie Smalls. We also plan Tim Buckley and Frank Zappa."
● This month's issue of *Hit Parader* reports that "an episode of The Monkees' TV series, *The Devil And Peter Tork*, was rejected by the network because one of the songs, 'Salesman,' was thought to contain veiled references to drugs. The song was taken out and the episode was rescheduled." In fact, the program will air this February with the song intact.

Peter recalls: "NBC said we're not putting that song out. We said, 'How come?' They said, 'Because "Salesman's" got drug references in it.' In fact, it sort of does, but it's not direct and it's not approving by any stretch of the imagination. What it really says is, 'Salesmen are so sleazy, they'll sell anything.' [That's] the basic thrust of that song. Bert Schneider was convinced that the reason [NBC] didn't want that episode out was that we were challenging the notion that you can't say 'hell' on television. I don't know if you remember that part of [the episode]. That was the whole joke. 'Wow, so that's what "bleep" is like?' 'What's worse is you can't say "bleep" on television!' Of course it seems like an awfully tame controversy today. You can say 'shit' on television under certain circumstances. I think I've even heard 'fuck' on commercial cable television some place. So, it seems a little weird and a little tame now, but I think Bert felt they didn't want to put the show on because they were having their ideas of what's right and wrong challenged."

● **Tuesday 2nd**
● Davy flies to Zurich, Switzerland for a few days skiing.

● **Thursday 4th**
● Still in London, Peter appears on BBC television's *Top Of The Pops*, after which he attends a party thrown at the Revolution club by Clive Donner for the film *Here We Go Round The Mulberry Bush*. Peter mingles with other guests including actor Michael Caine.
● Back in California, composer Hugo Montenegro uses 16 session musicians from 1:00 to 4:00pm to record the incidental score for episode 54 of the *Monkees* series, *The Monkees In Paris*. This is a one-off for Montenegro; most of the other cues for the series are provided by Stu Phillips.

● **Saturday 6th**
● The *NME* reports that The Monkees will spend the next four months shooting their feature film after which they plan to mount a summer tour. Meanwhile in the studio Michael works on two tracks destined for upcoming album releases.
RECORDING RCA *6363 Sunset Boulevard, Hollywood, CA* 12midday-3:00, 4:00-8:30pm. Michael Nesmith *prod*; Hank Cicalo *eng*; one-inch 8-track; tracking, overdubs.
1. **'Circle Sky'** overdubs onto take 6
   Head master # UZB3-9792
2. **'Auntie's Municipal Court'**
   The Birds, The Bees… master # WZB3-0107
Personnel Keith Allison (guitar 1*,2), Bill Chadwick (guitar 1*,2), Rick Dey (bass 1*,2), Eddie Hoh (percussion 1*, drums 2), Michael Nesmith (guitar 2). * = possible work.
● From noon until 3:00pm Michael revisits his production of 'Circle Sky.' It's possible that the four musicians listed contribute the asterisked overdubs, perhaps replacing parts that were taped at the two previous sessions for the song in December last year. A further session this month will complete the production (see January 8th).

The second half of this date produces 'Auntie's Municipal Court,' one of the best tracks featured on The Monkees' next album, *The Birds, The Bees & The Monkees*. The song is a mélange of Michael's poetry-style lyrics and a Keith Allison country-rock guitar riff. Captured in ten takes, the song will go through a few title changes – 'Sound Of The Sunset, Sound Of The Sea' and 'Auntie And The Municipal Court' among them – before settling on the obscure 'Auntie's Municipal Court,' a titular reference to nothing in particular. Two further sessions this month will complete the dense production.

● **Sunday 7th**
• Over-enthusiastic fans break a plate glass window at Peter's hotel in London, forcing him to move accommodation to the Royal Lancaster. Back in the studio in California, Micky begins his production of Bill Chadwick's anti-war epic 'Zor And Zam.'
RECORDING RCA *Hollywood, CA* 3:00-6:00pm. Micky Dolenz *prod*; one-inch 8-track; tracking.
1. **'Zor And Zam'**
   The Birds, The Bees… master # WZB3-0108
Personnel Keith Allison (guitar), Bill Chadwick (guitar), Rick Dey (bass), Eddie Hoh (drums).
● 'Zor And Zam' is the first in a series of ambitious productions that Micky will commit to tape over the next year, this one written by group confidant Bill Chadwick with his brother John. Though The Monkees previously taped Chadwick's 'Of You' back in 1966, 'Zor And Zam' will be the first of his songs for The Monkees to find record release.

After today's basic tracking session the production will be built up with numerous layers of overdubs added over the next two months. The next session for 'Zor And Zam' will be held on January 13th.

Bill Chadwick recalls: "Originally my brother John and I had written a treatment for a television series that was to be called *The Friendship*. John was a former Disney animator and it was to be live action and animation. It was very fantasy oriented. [The scenario was that] some guys were sailing on a ship and the ship went into a whirlpool. Imagine *Yellow Submarine* with live action and animation – except about three or four years earlier. There were two kings – Zor and Zam – and 'Zor And Zam' was to be one of the songs in the pilot. We never did anything with it. We got bogged down in the creative end of it. I got involved with the Monkees thing and I used the song

In London, Peter meets up with George Harrison during sessions for the Beatle's Wonderwall soundtrack album. Guitarist on the left is Colin Manley of The Remo Four.

TVseries

The Monkees

EPISODE 48: *FAIRY TALE*

BROADCAST JANUARY 8TH

The group put their own twist on a classic fairy tale.

WRITER: PETER MEYERSON. DIRECTOR: JAMES FRAWLEY.

SONG 'Daily Nightly.'

there. It was basically about two kings that gave a war and nobody came. We all had friends going off to Vietnam and nobody was real happy about the way things were being handled, the way that guys were going over there and weren't getting any support. It was: if you're not going to get support from your own country, why the hell should you go?"

Micky: "'Zor And Zam' was a great tune. I remember hearing Bill Chadwick singing it at a party. We used to hang out. He was one of the sidekicks/bodyguards/stand-ins. I said, 'God, wow man, I'd really like to do that song.' So we brought it in and we did it."

● **Monday 8th**

TV Episode 48 of the second series of *The Monkees*, titled *Fairy Tale*, is broadcast at 7:30pm on the NBC network. Also today Michael

holds the final session for his studio version of 'Circle Sky.'

RECORDING RCA *Hollywood, CA* 1:00-4:00pm. Michael Nesmith *prod*; one-inch 8-track; overdubs.

1. **'Circle Sky'** overdubs onto take 6
   Head master # UZB3-9792

Personnel Rick Dey (probably bass), Eddie Hoh (probably percussion).

● Work is completed today on Michael's 'Circle Sky.' It is likely that, some time between the last session and this one, Rick Dey has replaced the bass track originally taped by John Gross in December 1967. Eddie Hoh is also present at this session and may contribute some of the percussion – cowbell, shaker and so on – heard on the final production. This studio version of 'Circle Sky' will be mixed later this month, though The Monkees themselves will tape an all-new live version of the song in May.

● **Tuesday 9th**

● An Australian newspaper reports that negotiations are underway for a Monkees concert tour down under.

● Peter returns to the U.S.A. from Britain. In Los Angeles, Mike records a song for Davy.

RECORDING RCA *Hollywood, CA* 1:00-4:00, 5:00-8:00pm. Michael Nesmith *prod*; Hank Cicalo *eng*; half-inch 4-track, one-inch 8-track; tracking, overdubs.

1. **'My Share Of The Sidewalk'** version 1 takes 1-43
   Missing Links 1 master # WZB3-0109 formerly UZB3-9795

Personnel Rick Dey (bass), Eddie Hoh (drums), Michael Nesmith (vocal, piano, tack piano [take 43 only], guitar [take 43 only]).

● Michael makes another stylistic shift as he delves into the world of

show tunes with this unique concoction. Singing and playing piano along with all 43 takes, he never quite pulls off a polished performance, though he seems to enjoy the effort. The final take is considered the master and additional tack piano and guitar are immediately overdubbed on the 8-track tape only, probably by Michael himself. Further overdubs, including a lead vocal from Davy, will be taped soon (the next session will be on January 19th).

Michael recalls: "I wrote it with the idea that Davy would sing it for The Monkees, a kind of Broadway-ish send-up that I thought he would like. It was late in the show as I recall, and he did like it and wanted to sing it, but things were falling apart by then, and there wasn't much support for the tune from 'the powers.'"

● **Wednesday 10th**
● Davy returns to London following a side trip to Paris and takes a few more days vacation. In Hollywood, Michael records a session featuring Harry Nilsson.
RECORDING RCA *Hollywood, CA* 1:00-5:00, 7:00-10:00pm. Michael Nesmith *prod*; Pete Abbott (1:00pm start), Hank Cicalo (7:00pm start) *eng*; half-inch 4-track, one-inch 8-track; tracking.
1. **'Daddy's Song'** takes 1-21
   Head master # WZB3-0110
2. **'Good Times'** takes 1-6
   unissued master # WZB3-0111
3. **'The Story Of Rock And Roll'** version 4 takes 1-4
   unissued master # WZB3-0112
Personnel Rick Dey (bass), Eddie Hoh (drums), Michael Nesmith (acoustic guitar 1, vocal 1 [take 21 only], electric guitar 1 [take 21 only], 2,3), Harry Nilsson (piano, vocal 2 [takes 5 and 6 only]).
● Michael tapes three Harry Nilsson songs today, with the composer on hand to play piano and do a little singing. Until 5:00pm Michael and his usual studio crew record 21 takes of 'Daddy's Song.' The first five are merely false starts, with some instruction by Michael to Hoh on how to begin the song. Before take 16, Hoh suggests that they add an intro to the front of the song, missing on all the takes to this point. This provides the musicians with an easier way of falling into the groove and also provides a 'hook' to the arrangement. The last take taped, 21, is marked as the master and pulled to another reel for Michael to add a lead vocal and an additional electric guitar, probably during the next session for this song on January 16th.

After a two-hour break work resumes at 7:00 as Michael's group tapes another Nilsson song, 'Good Times.' Nilsson recorded the song for the Tower label in 1966 and demoed it for The Monkees the following year (see March 17th 1967). Lacking the heavy Beatles influence of the writer's more recent RCA recordings, the song is really an old-fashioned Nilsson composition and relatively outdated for 1968. It is an especially anachronistic choice to cut considering that The Monkees have never really been known as purveyors of good-time, boogie-woogie rock'n'roll.

After take 4, Nilsson asks if they can record his vocal. Engineer Hank Cicalo tells him that is fine if they don't mind having the piano and guitar on the same track. So Nilsson vocalizes for the final two takes, although take 5 is incomplete. Take 6 is marked as the master from this session, though no further work will be done, leaving it as an unfinished outtake with no Monkees vocals.

To close out this date, Nilsson's 'The Story Of Rock And Roll' is attempted for the fourth and final time at a Monkees session. Today's rendition is more or less the same as the three 1967 versions but with steadier drumming. As with all previous recordings, no vocals are taped for this version, which is left incomplete after today's session. Like 'Good Times,' 'The Story Of Rock And Roll' is out of step with The Monkees' current style. In May, both The

Turtles and The Collage will issue singles of their versions of the song. The Chip Douglas-produced Turtles recording will reach a mild #48 during June, indicating that big success was probably never on the cards for the song.

● **Thursday 11th**
● Davy is scheduled to tape an appearance on British TV show *Top Of The Pops* today but cancels due to illness. In Hollywood, Michael records another session with Harry Nilsson.
RECORDING RCA *Hollywood, CA* 2:00-5:00pm. Michael Nesmith *prod*; Hank Cicalo *eng*; half-inch 4-track, one-inch 8-track; tracking.
1. **'Mr. Richland's Favorite Song'** takes 1-19
   unissued master # WZB3-0113
Personnel Rick Dey (bass), Eddie Hoh (drums), Michael Nesmith (electric guitar), Harry Nilsson (piano, vocal).
● Following on from yesterday's session, Michael records a fourth Nilsson track, this one with a title that refers to RCA promo man Tony Richland. It is a more recent Nilsson composition, featuring his vocal and piano accompaniment on every take, and could be quite well suited to the group. But as with yesterday's 'Good Times' and 'The Story Of Rock And Roll' no further work will be done by The Monkees on this recording. In fact none of the takes recorded at this session is marked as a master – or is even complete.

● **Saturday 13th**
● *The Beat* magazine reports that Davy is suing his ex-manager, Hal Cone, for $150,000. Davy claims that his contract with Cone is invalid because he was underage when he signed. He is also asking for an accounting of his various business ventures including his now defunct record label.
● In Britain, Davy travels to Caesar's Palace in Dunstable to see Lulu perform. He is briefly filmed there, and the footage later turns up in the BBC documentary *All My Loving*. Back in the studio in Hollywood Micky works on 'Zor And Zam.'
RECORDING RCA *Hollywood, CA* 8:00-11:00pm. Micky Dolenz *prod*; one-inch 8-track; overdubs.
1. **'Zor And Zam'**
   The Birds, The Bees... master # WZB3-0108
Personnel Bill Chadwick (instrument unknown), Henry Diltz (instrument unknown), Chip Douglas (bass).
● It is not clear what is attempted during this session, though it is very likely that former Monkees producer Chip Douglas adds a second bass part to 'Zor And Zam.' Douglas's work will augment the part already recorded by Rick Dey and both will be heard on the final production. It is also probable that Henry Diltz and the song's composer, Bill Chadwick, add further musical embellishments. Work on 'Zor And Zam' will continue on January 18th.

● **Sunday 14th**
Davy returns to Los Angeles from London. In the studio, Peter and Michael hold separate recording sessions.
RECORDING Western Recorders (2) *6000 Sunset Boulevard, Hollywood, CA* 11:00am-2:00pm, 10:30pm-1:30am. Peter Tork *prod*; Joe ? *eng*; one-inch 8-track; tracking.
1. **'Lance's'** takes 1-8
   unissued no master #
2. **'Lady's Baby'** version 4 takes 1-51
   unissued master # UZB3-9784
3. **'Long Title: Do I Have To Do This All Over Again'** version 1
   unissued no master #
4. **'Seeger's Theme'** version 2
   unissued master # UZB3-9790

5. '?' takes 1-3
unissued no master #
Personnel Buddy Miles (drums 2,3,4,5), Stephen Stills (electric guitar 2,5, electric guitar or bass 3,4), Peter Tork (bass 1,2,5, vocal 2 [take 24 only], acoustic guitar 2 [take 24 only], electric guitar 3,4), Lance Wakely (acoustic guitar 1, electric guitar 2,5, electric guitar or bass 3,4).
● Peter, fresh from his London vacation, starts his first recording session of 1968 with an instrumental by Lance Wakely, his Greenwich Village pal and current house guest. Eight takes are taped of the appropriately titled 'Lance's' with Wakely on guitar and Peter on bass. Although this is a structured piece of music, no further work is done. It is probably just considered a warm-up.

The main focus of today's session is yet another version of 'Lady's Baby,' which Peter began recording last November and has since become his musical obsession. Today's rendition is a departure from the previous acoustic-based takes of the song, with the tune now arranged for a full rock band. After some rehearsals, Peter and Wakely along with Stephen Stills and Buddy Miles ramble through 51 takes, though many of these are merely false starts and not full passes.

The reel containing takes 30 through 45 will be lost (though its box will survive) so it is unknown what occurred during a lengthy part of today's session. After take 15 the group breaks into a jam, which somehow meanders into a version of the Stones' 'Satisfaction.' The relatively successful take 24 is marked not as master but rather "BEST YET!!" and Peter will later overdub a vocal and acoustic guitar on to it. Takes 46 through 51 are taken at a slower tempo, but the arrangement is fairly consistent throughout the date. The final take from this session, 51, is marked "choice," though it will not be given any further overdubs. These recordings will be reviewed and evaluated at a session on January 19th.

After their lengthy bout with 'Lady's Baby' Peter and friends jam through several unnumbered takes of Peter's recently composed 'Long Title' along with some free-form meanderings. Buddy Miles offers some musical direction: "Peter … it sounds good. But it would sound good if you did it at half that tempo. It would sound better. 'Cos it'd be awful funky." The band take note and jam on at a slower pace before moving to something else entirely. Peter will tape a second version of the song on January 20th.

Following a lengthy drum freak-out from Miles, Peter revisits 'Seeger's Theme.' On this occasion the song sounds like pure chaos with all the musicians going in different directions. After a reel change, the group get it together, though aimless jams overwhelm most of today's unnumbered takes. There are no useable passes of 'Seeger's Theme' from today's session. Peter will cut a third version of the song on January 20th.

The date ends with three pointless jams labeled '?' on the tape box. Sadly, the music recorded is as questionable as the title.

(According to musicians' union records it is likely that David Getz, drummer for Big Brother & The Holding Company, attends Peter's session, but it is not known if he contributes to any of the music recorded today.)

Meanwhile, a few blocks west on Sunset, Michael is busy with his own recording date.
RECORDING RCA *Hollywood, CA* 3:00-6:00, 7:00-10:00pm. Michael Nesmith *prod*; one-inch 8-track; tracking.
1. 'While I Cry' version 2
Instant Replay master # WZB3-0114
Personnel Rick Dey (bass), Eddie Hoh (drums), Michael Nesmith (guitar).
● This piece was first taped as an instrumental for Michael's *Wichita*

Train Whistle project under the title 'While I Cried' (see November 18th 1967) but today he remakes it as a lovely ballad for The Monkees. All tapes for this session including the multi-track master will be lost, so there are no further details. Another session tomorrow will complete the song's production. Michael: "It has kind of a rolling guitar intro. It's slow. It's a ballad. It's me playing guitar, a guitar lick that I was just foolin' around with and wrote a song around the lick. Not an uncommon move."

TVseries

The Monkees

EPISODE 49: *MONKEES WATCH THEIR FEET*
BROADCAST JANUARY 15TH
Smothers Brothers star Pat Paulsen narrates this bizarre tale of alien abduction.
WRITER: COSLOUGH JOHNSON. DIRECTOR: ALEX SINGER.
SONG 'Star Collector.'

● **Monday 15th**
TV Episode 49 of the second series of *The Monkees*, titled *Monkees Watch Their Feet*, is broadcast at 7:30pm on the NBC network. In the studio, Michael adds overdubs to two of his recent productions.
RECORDING RCA *Hollywood, CA* 1:00-4:00, 5:00-8:00pm. Michael Nesmith *prod*; one-inch 8-track; overdubs.
1. 'Auntie's Municipal Court'
The Birds, The Bees… master # WZB3-0107
2. 'While I Cry' version 2
Instant Replay master # WZB3-0114
Personnel Keith Allison, Bill Chadwick, Michael Nesmith, Harry Nilsson (all instruments unknown).
● According to a union worksheet some overdub work is done to these songs at this session. The roles of the personnel are not defined, but as vocals are certainly added around this time it is likely that they contribute to the massed backing vocals heard on the released tracks. It is also possible that Bill Chadwick and Keith Allison supply some additional guitar.

● **Tuesday 16th**
RECORDING RCA *Hollywood, CA* 1:00-4:00, 5:00-8:00pm. Michael Nesmith *prod*; one-inch 8-track; overdubs.
1. 'Auntie's Municipal Court'
The Birds, The Bees… master # WZB3-0107
2. 'Daddy's Song' overdubs onto take 21
Head master # WZB3-0110
Personnel Keith Allison, Bill Chadwick, Michael Nesmith (all instruments unknown).
● Much like yesterday's session, Michael tinkers with two of his recent productions, adding or subtracting musical elements. Chadwick and Allison are once again in attendance, potentially contributing to the process. At this stage Michael is the lead vocalist on 'Daddy's Song' and his performance is electronically filtered, giving a megaphone-like quality to his vocals. This vocal performance will later be heard as a bonus track on 1994's expanded CD reissue of *Head*.

● Thursday 18th

RECORDING RCA *Hollywood, CA* 2:00-5:00, 6:00-9:00, 10:00pm-12midnight. Micky Dolenz *prod*; Pete Abbott *eng*; one-inch 8-track; tracking, overdubs.

1. 'Zor And Zam'
The Birds, The Bees... master # WZB3-0108
2. 'Title' take 1
unissued master # WZB3-0115

Personnel Micky Dolenz (conga 2), unknown (Moog synthesizer 2, tack piano 2, tympani 2).

● This lengthy session for 'Zor And Zam' probably includes the addition of Micky's lead vocal. An early mix will be dubbed down this month and used in the 'romp' sequence of the Micky-directed TV episode *The Frodis Caper*. The mix is unique since many elements of the song's production will soon be revised, making way for some heavy orchestral overdubs. A further session for 'Zor And Zam' will take place on February 14th. A jam at the end of the session produces an oddity that Micky calls 'Title.' The other participants on Moog, piano, and tympani are unidentified. There is nothing musically significant about the piece.

● Friday 19th

RECORDING RCA *Hollywood, CA* 10:00am-1:00pm, 8:00-11:00pm. Micky Dolenz *prod*; one-inch 8-track; tracking.

1. 'Shorty Blackwell'
Instant Replay master # WZB3-0116

Personnel Micky Dolenz (piano 1).

● Micky begins the process of recording his first self-written song for almost a year. Although he found immediate success with 'Randy Scouse Git' he is nowhere near as prolific as his bandmates and will make very slow progress in producing his own material. Nevertheless, the results of his writing are always entertaining, unusual, and in some respects the most captivating of the group.

Today's composition was inspired by Micky's pet cat, Shorty Blackwell, and like his 'Zor And Zam' will be built up over time. It becomes the biggest (and longest) Monkees production ever committed to tape. Before any studio wizardry can take place, Micky must first lay down a basic track, which in this case consists of a single piano, played by Micky. Production will continue over the next six months.

Micky: "That was just me again being incredibly self-indulgent and writing about things that were happening in my life. That's just a typical kind of 1960s spaced-out ... my feeble attempt at something to do with *Sgt. Pepper*."

While Micky takes a break from his session, Peter enters RCA with his recent tapes from Western Recorders.

RECORDING RCA *Hollywood, CA* 2:00-5:00pm. Peter Tork *prod*; one-inch 8-track.

1. 'Lady's Baby' version 4
unissued master # UZB3-9784

Personnel Peter Tork (vocal, acoustic guitar).

● In reviewing various takes of 'Lady's Baby' Peter adds some vocals and acoustic guitar to take 24 from January 14th. Nevertheless, nothing from today's session will ever be issued commercially, and Peter will decide to cut a fifth version of the song next week.
Meanwhile, just down the hall from both Micky and Peter, Michael sweetens two of his recent productions with the help of arranger Shorty Rogers.

RECORDING RCA *Hollywood, CA* 1:00-4:00pm. Michael Nesmith *prod*; one-inch 8-track; overdubs.

1. 'My Share Of The Sidewalk' version 1 overdubs onto take 43
Missing Links 1 master # WZB3-0109 formerly UZB3-9795

2. 'Daddy's Song' overdubs onto take 21
Head master # WZB3-0110

Personnel Pete Candoli (trumpet), Buddy Childers (trumpet), Justin DiTullio (cello), Ray Kramer (cello), Dick Leith (trombone), Lew McCreary (trombone), Emmet Sargeant (cello), Eleanor Slatkin (cello), Tony Terran (trumpet).

● With today's addition of trumpets, trombones, and cellos these productions are nearly complete, save for Davy's lead vocals. 'Sidewalk' will be mixed on March 13th. 'Daddy's Song' will receive further augmentation and attention over the next several months and is eventually selected for use in The Monkees' upcoming feature film.

● Saturday 20th

● *Billboard* publishes a photo of Peter taken during his recent London visit. The caption reveals that he was given a special reception at the offices of Decca Records, which distributes The Monkees' records in Britain.

● The Monkees have won a poll in Norway, scoring six of 1967's most popular singles there ('I'm A Believer,' '(Theme From) The Monkees,' 'Alternate Title,' 'A Little Bit Me, A Little Bit You,' 'Pleasant Valley Sunday,' and 'Daydream Believer'). The Beatles and local artist Sven Ingvars tied for second place. Meanwhile in the studio, Peter tapes new versions of three of his previously recorded tracks and one new piece.

RECORDING Western Recorders (2) *Hollywood, CA* 2:00-5:00, 7:00-11:00pm. Peter Tork *prod*; Joe ? *eng*; one-inch 8-track; tracking.

1. 'Merry Go Round' version 2 takes 1-3
unissued master # UZB3-9791
2. 'Alvin' takes 1-8
The Birds, The Bees... master # WZB3-0124
3. 'Seeger's Theme' version 3 takes 1-5
unissued master # UZB3-9790
4. 'Long Title: Do I Have To Do This All Over Again' version 2 takes 1-3
unissued master # WZB3-0117

Personnel Peter Tork (piano 1, bass 1 [take 3 only], 3 [take 5 only], vocal 1 [take 3 only], 2, acoustic guitar 3,4, whistling 3 [take 5 only], handclaps 3 [take 5 only]).

● A week after his super-session with Stephen Stills and Buddy Miles, Peter returns to the studio for a less star-studded but more lucid date.

The first item taped is a second version of his 'Merry Go Round,' first recorded in December last year. Today's arrangement results in a more sophisticated arrangement featuring (on take 3) two piano tracks, bass, and a lead vocal. This take will be removed from the session reel on January 31st for further production work and, much later, is lost. Peter will tape a third version of 'Merry Go Round' on Monday (see 22nd).

The one new track at this session is Peter's a cappella rendition of his brother Nick's nursery rhyme about Alvin the alligator, similar in style to last year's 'Peter Percival Patterson's Pet Pig Porky.' Take 8 of this short vocal piece will be seriously considered for release on The Monkees' next album. The master take will be removed from the session reel on January 31st for mixing and it too is later lost. An alternate take from today's session will eventually be issued as a bonus track on Rhino's expanded 1994 CD reissue of *The Birds, The Bees & The Monkees*.

Peter then fingerpicks his way through another five takes of 'Seeger's Theme' that mark his third formal version of this instrumental. The final take from this session, take 5, will receive further musical embellishment at a session on January 22nd.

Michael at a January recording session in RCA studios, Hollywood.

Peter closes out this productive date by laying down a second embryonic version of his 'Long Title,' first taped on January 14th. Take 3 is marked as the master from this session, though no further overdubs will be made. He will record a third version of the song on Monday (see 22nd).

TVseries

The Monkees

EPISODE 50: *MONSTROUS MONKEE MASH*
BROADCAST JANUARY 22ND
When Davy falls for a mysterious woman, The Monkees enter a spooky scene with Dracula, a Wolfman, and the Mummy.
WRITERS: NEIL BURSTYN, DAVID PANICH. DIRECTOR: JAMES FRAWLEY.
SONG 'Goin' Down.'

● Monday 22nd

TV Episode 50 of the *Monkees* series, *Monstrous Monkee Mash*, is broadcast at 7:30pm by the NBC network. Directly after this airing, Peter begins an all-night recording session at RCA.
RECORDING RCA *Hollywood, CA* 8:00-12midnight, 1:00-5:00am. Peter Tork *prod*; Pete Abbott *eng*; one-inch 8-track; tracking, overdubs.
1. **'Seeger's Theme'** version 3 take 5
   unissued master # UZB3-9790
2. **'Merry Go Round'** version 3 takes 1-12
   unissued master # UZB3-9791
3. **'Long Title: Do I Have To Do This All Over Again'** version 3
   unissued master # WZB3-0117
Personnel Peter Tork (piano 2, vocal 2, bass 2 [take 12 only], electric guitar 3), Lance Wakely (bass 3).
● After a day off, Peter starts this session with some overdubs on his recording of 'Seeger's Theme' from Saturday. Exactly what this involves is undocumented but may include guitar, bass, handclaps, or whistling. Still unsatisfied with the results, Peter will tape a new, more rock-oriented version of this instrumental on February 12th.

Abandoning his take of 'Merry Go Round' from Saturday, Peter next tapes 12 new takes of the song, accompanying himself on piano. Much like Saturday's recording, the final take from today (12) will be treated to additional piano and vocals, plus a bass track. The results are respectable; nevertheless, Peter will feel artistically moved to record a fourth version on January 31st.

Peter completes a triangle with his third song of the day, a third attempt at 'Long Title.' This time he and Lance Wakely work their way through numerous rehearsals before committing anything to tape. Take 17 is the only complete pass captured, but it's likely that no further overdubs are made to this rendition of the song. Tapes of takes 1 through 17 will be the only survivors from this date. It's probable that further versions are recorded today, but the second reel will be lost. In any event, Peter is unsatisfied with any results and will start a fourth version of the song on Thursday.

● Tuesday 23rd

RECORDING RCA *Hollywood, CA* 4:00-7:00, 9:00pm-12midnight. Michael Nesmith *prod*; Hank Cicalo *eng*; half-inch 4-track, one-inch 8-track; tracking.

1. **'No Title'** version 1 takes 1-19
   unissued master # WZB3-0118
2. **'War Games'** version 1 takes 1-13
   unissued master # WZB3-0119
Personnel Keith Allison (guitar 1 [takes 5-19 only], electric guitar 2), Kim Capli (drums 1), Eddie Hoh (drums 2), Michael Nesmith (organ 1, acoustic guitar 2), Joe Osborn (bass 1,2*), Bob Ray (bass 2*). * Osborn or Ray on bass.
● For the first half of the session Michael works through 19 takes of his soul-infused rock piece labeled as 'Untitled' (on musicians' union contracts) or 'No Title' (on original session reels). He conducts from a Hammond organ, which he plays on every take. The performances of the Blood, Sweat & Tears-like workout vary only slightly from take to take. From take 5 onwards guitarist Keith Allison joins in and performs on all the remaining passes. Take 18 is marked as the master and is later pulled to a separate reel for overdubbing. However, no further work will be done on this take of the song as a new version will be recorded on Thursday.

From 9:00pm Michael focuses his energies on taping a Davy Jones song, 'War Games,' which is aimed for inclusion in The Monkees' movie. It is a collaboration between Davy and one of Michael's buddies from Texas, Steve Pitts, whom Michael introduced to Davy in November 1966. Both Davy and Pitts are in the studio's control room to offer their two cents on the production of their song.

Bob Rafelson is also in attendance and makes several enthusiastic comments about the music. Prior to take 12 he describes the visual image he is getting from the track. "It sounds to me like four spade chicks all dressed in American flags and all wigglin' their asses at the same time, goin' down the street. You dig what I mean? If you just start thinkin' on that, it sounds awful good." Michael replies, with some reserve: "Thanks Bob. That's very groovy. That's what we are playin', right?"

"That's what you're playin'," confirms Rafelson, "and that's what I'm hoping you're playin', you dig?" Michael jokingly bats back: "You bet your ass, baby. We understand each other. Religion's not everything."

The final take from today's session, take 13, is marked as the master and is pulled to another reel for overdubbing. It will eventually receive a lead-vocal overdub by Davy as well as some Hammond organ, probably from Michael. But this version will never surface commercially. Davy will tape a new, slower arrangement of the song on February 6th. Davy: "Steve Pitts and I sat down to write some tunes originally for the movie *Head*. We were told that we were all going to be writing some stuff. So I wrote with the themes of whatever they wanted in regards to the movie. We also had written some other tunes during that particular session. Lester Sill was kind enough to buy me a Gibson Dove guitar. I sat down with it and that was one of the songs [that came]."

● Wednesday 24th

● The script for The Monkees' upcoming movie, currently titled *Changes*, is subject to a number of additions and revisions today. These include the film's opening bridge sequence, some war-helmet dialogue, Peter's exit from the battlefield and interaction with Ray Nitschke, and a long sequence to be shot in Japan involving The Monkees and Godzilla (which will be omitted entirely). There is also Micky's desert odyssey, a studio commissary sequence, Vito Scotti's sales pitch on merchandising, Davy's sequence leading up to his fight with Sonny Liston, Peter's punch, and the group's trip through the vacuum cleaner. Also added to and/or revised are a showcase for Michael singing 'Magnolia Simms' (which is rewritten as a spotlight for Davy singing 'Daddy's Song'), the band's interaction with a cop (and the cop's dream), Mike's birthday party, the black box being dropped from a helicopter, and most of the picture's ending.

Meanwhile in the studio, Michael cuts a demo and plays a game of pinball.

RECORDING RCA *Hollywood, CA* 12midday-3:00, 4:00-7:00pm. Michael Nesmith *prod*; Hank Cicalo *eng*; quarter-inch mono, half-inch 4-track, one-inch 8-track; tracking.

1. 'Tears Of Joy' demo take 1
unissued master # WZB3-0120

2. 'Pinball Machine'
unissued master # WZB3-0121

Personnel Eddie Hoh (drums 1), Michael Nesmith (electric 12-string guitar 1, pinball player 2), Bob Ray (bass 1),

● Michael records a single take of 'Tears of Joy,' the most straightforward musical piece he has produced in months. It is probably not one of his compositions – the tape box labels this recording specifically as a demo – and is possibly a Leiber & Stoller song published by Screen Gems. The Monkees will record a few Leiber & Stoller songs in the coming weeks. Whatever the case, it is not known what Michael's intentions are for this song – or the next piece he records today.

For some reason, Michael decides to professionally record not only the noise of a pinball machine's motor but also a few full games on the machine. RCA even allocates this dubious piece its own master number. Engineer Hank Cicalo is pretty much game for anything at this point. Except, that is, for recording with Peter, who instead has a session booked a few blocks away at Sunset Sound to once again tape his 'Lady's Baby.'

RECORDING Sunset Sound Recorders *6650 Sunset Boulevard, Hollywood, CA* 5:00-8:00, 9:00pm-12midnight, 1:00-2:00am. Peter Tork *prod*; Brian ? *eng*; one-inch 8-track; tracking.

1. 'Just Another Dream' demo takes 1-10
unissued no master #

2. 'Song #2' demo takes 1-8
unissued no master #

3. 'My Song In #7' takes 1-8
unissued master # WZB3-0185

4. 'Lady's Baby' version 5
The Birds, The Bees... master # UZB3-9784

Personnel Dewey Martin (drums 4), Stephen Stills (electric guitar 4), Peter Tork (vocal 1, piano 1, instrument unknown 2, guitar 3, electric guitar 4), Lance Wakely (bass 4).

● Sadly, almost all of today's recordings will be lost. However, by some miraculous accident the engineer's worksheet detailing the contents of the missing reels is mistakenly wedged in a box of outtakes from the session, revealing the information listed here. No further versions of 'Just Another Dream,' the speculatively titled 'Song #2,' and Peter's 'My Song In #7' will ever be taped.

As for 'Lady's Baby,' Peter begins his fifth, full-fledged version of the song this evening and is finally able to capture an arrangement that fulfills his musical vision. Nevertheless, the recorded saga of 'Lady's Baby' will stretch on through March.

Davy: "Hey listen, fair is fair. They laugh and joke about that. OK, it cost as much to do I think as 'Good Vibrations.' They were laughing about Peter Tork, but that [song] is a true-to-life thing. He was living with a woman at the time and she had a little baby and that changed his life, you know? That gave him something to think about. He was being downtrodden by the studio in regards to his recording and his playing and his songs and everything else, but the guy was the salt of the earth. It wasn't just Hare Krishna, waterbeds, and brown rice. That guy was a very, very accomplished musician. He needed magic to be able to get in and do 'Lady's Baby.' It's a nice

song. It's true. It's got the warmth and everything of what he was living. 'Lady's Baby' touches me, lets me know that I am free, whatever it is. I remember it so well. It's a real tune, you know? I love it."

● **Thursday 25th**

RECORDING RCA *Hollywood, CA* 10:30am-6:00pm. Michael Nesmith *prod*; Hank Cicalo *eng*; half-inch 4-track, one-inch 8-track; tracking.

1. 'Empire' takes 1-15
unissued master # WZB3-0122

2. 'No Title' version 2 takes 1-48
unissued master # WZB3-0118

Personnel Ron Brown (bass 1,2, tambourine 1 [take 14 only]), Michael Nesmith (electric guitar 1, organ 2), Earl Palmer (drums 1,2, percussion 1 [take 14 only]), Charles Wright (electric guitar 1,2, organ 1 [take 14 only]).

● Michael takes another stylistic detour with a funky R&B number dubbed 'Empire.' Flanked by an all-black band – foreshadowing his 1969 work with Sam & The Goodtimers – he tapes 15 fairly consistent takes of this groove. Take 14 is marked as the master and is almost immediately treated to overdubs of percussion and organ by the guest musicians. However, no vocal tracks will ever be taped. At the time of writing this unusual soul excursion has never been publicly heard.

Continuing in the soul vein, Michael tapes a further 48 takes of his 'No Title' first recorded on the 23rd. Aside from a difference in personnel, there is little musical variation between today's arrangement and version 1. In fact, today's recordings reflect only the slightest improvement over the earlier rendition. Around take 30, drummer Earl Palmer comes up with a new intro for the song, but it doesn't substantially change the composition. Take 47 is marked as the master from today, but no further work will ever be done on this recording or the song.

Meanwhile at Sunset Sound, Peter holds his own recording session.

RECORDING Sunset Sound Recorders *Hollywood, CA* 4:30-7:30, 8:30-11:30pm, 12midnight-1:00am. Peter Tork *prod*; one-inch 8-track; tracking, overdubs.

1. 'Lady's Baby' version 5
The Birds, The Bees... master # UZB3-9784

2. 'Long Title: Do I Have To Do This All Over Again' version 4
Head master # WZB3-0117

Personnel Dewey Martin (drums 2), Stephen Stills (electric guitar 2), Peter Tork (electric guitar 2), Lance Wakely (bass 2).

● Having captured the desired take during last night's session, Peter makes unspecified amendments to the master of 'Lady's Baby.' Further augmentation will occur on February 2nd. Using the same line-up as last night's session, with Buffalo Springfield members Stephen Stills and Dewey Martin, Peter finally manages to nail a great rock arrangement of his 'Long Title.' Now that he is relatively satisfied with the production of 'Lady's Baby,' 'Long Title' will become his musical obsession for the rest of this month – and most of February.

Peter: "The funny thing is that the lyric [to 'Long Title: Do I Have To Do This All Over Again'] just came to me right out of the air. I was playing those chord changes on the guitar and I just opened my mouth and that's what popped out. Once I had the first verse, the second verse followed the theme for the first. The weird thing is that the song has been prophetic. I had no idea when I wrote the song that that was going to be my attitude about anything to do with music. It just came out that way. It just fell out of my mouth. I think I wrote the lyric in London. I was on that famous trip [to

London this month] with Karen Harvey Hammer and Justin Hammer, who are Lady and Baby respectively."

● **Friday 26th**
RECORDING Sunset Sound Recorders *Hollywood, CA* 2:00-5:00, 6:00-7:00pm. Peter Tork *prod*; one-inch 8-track; overdubs.
1. **'Long Title: Do I Have To Do This All Over Again'** version 4
   Head master # WZB3-0117
Personnel Stephen Stills, Peter Tork, Lance Wakely (all instruments unknown).
● Using an unspecified master take captured at yesterday's session, Peter alongside Stills and Wakely makes musical amendments to 'Long Title.' Work on the piece will continue tomorrow.

● **Saturday 27th**
RECORDING RCA *Hollywood, CA* 2:00-6:30pm. Peter Tork *prod*; one-inch 8-track; overdubs.
1. **'Long Title: Do I Have To Do This All Over Again'** version 4
   Head master # WZB3-0117
Personnel Peter Tork (instrument unknown), Lance Wakely (instrument unknown).
● Peter takes his tape of 'Long Title' back to The Monkees' usual home base, RCA studios. For four-and-a-half hours he and Wakely work on further refining the production. Another session at a different studio will follow tomorrow.

● **Sunday 28th**
RECORDING Western Recorders *Hollywood, CA* 1:00-4:00, 5:00-8:00, 10:00pm-1:00am. Peter Tork *prod*; one-inch 8-track; tracking, overdubs.
1. **'Long Title: Do I Have To Do This All Over Again'** version 4
   Head master # WZB3-0117
2. **'Can You Dig It'**
   Head master # WZB3-0123
Personnel Michael A. Glass, Dewey Martin, Buddy Miles, Peter Tork, Lance Wakely (all instruments unknown 2).
● Peter shifts operations to Western studio and continues his production work on 'Long Title.' Towards the end of this date he will also begin a new recording of 'Can You Dig It.' He first demoed 'Can You Dig It' last year on June 22nd as an acoustic instrumental but today tapes the song in an Eastern-influenced arrangement with a full set of lyrics appropriately inspired by the Tao philosophical system. The original session tapes will become lost and thus all other details of the recording process for this track are a mystery. Further adding to the confusion, three conflicting musicians' union contracts are filed for this one date and make personnel credits speculative at best. Work on 'Can You Dig It' will continue tomorrow.

Peter: "'Can You Dig It' is about the Tao. I wrote the hookline in my dressing room on the set. I'd written the chords for the chorus in college and they had just stuck with me. I hadn't been able to do a thing with them until I was sittin' there just writin' on a scrap of paper with ideas, and I wrote: 'Can you dig it, do you know, would you like to let it show.' Those three as a triplet – as opposed to a couplet. I just looked at them and went, 'Wow!' I grabbed a pencil and circled those three. They were part of a quatrain. I said, 'Wait a minute, no, this works best as a little three-line chorus there.' I was very happy with myself. In those days, I thought songs fell out of me without my having to do any work."

● **Monday 29th**
TV Episode 51 of the second series of *The Monkees*, titled *The Monkees' Paw*, is broadcast on NBC at 7:30pm. In the studio, Peter continues his work on 'Can You Dig It.'

TVseries

The Monkees

EPISODE 51: *THE MONKEES' PAW*
BROADCAST JANUARY 29TH
Micky buys a mystical monkey's paw from a malicious magician.
WRITER: COSLOUGH JOHNSON. DIRECTOR: JAMES FRAWLEY.
SONG 'Words,' 'Goin' Down.'

RECORDING RCA *Hollywood, CA* 5:00-8:00, 9:00pm-12midnight. Peter Tork *prod*; one-inch 8-track.
1. **'Can You Dig It'**
   Head master # WZB3-0123
Personnel Michael A. Glass, Dewey Martin, Peter Tork, Lance Wakely (all instruments unknown).
● This evening's session represents either a continuation of last night's production process on a take selected from that session or possibly the beginning of an entirely new recording of 'Can You Dig It.' No tapes will survive, but it is reasonably certain that between this session and the last a master take of 'Can You Dig It' is captured on tape. An overdub session for the song will be held tomorrow night.

● **Tuesday 30th**
RECORDING RCA *Hollywood, CA* 7:30-10:00pm. Peter Tork *prod*; one-inch 8-track; overdubs.
1. **'Can You Dig It'**
   Head master # WZB3-0123
Personnel Peter Tork (instrument unknown), Lance Wakely (instrument unknown).
● Peter and Wakely refine elements of 'Can You Dig It.'

● **Wednesday 31st**
RECORDING RCA *Hollywood, CA* 9:00am-12midday, 1:00-5:00pm. Peter Tork *prod*; one-inch 8-track; overdubs.
1. **'Can You Dig It'**
   Head master # WZB3-0123
2. **'Merry Go Round'** version 4
   Missing Links 3 master # UZB3-9791
Personnel Peter Tork (instrument unknown), Lance Wakely (instrument unknown).
● Peter continues the production process on 'Can You Dig It' but also likely begins a new, fourth version of his 'Merry Go Round' during this session. It is probably this new version of the song that will form the basis of the only commercially available version, issued on the 1996 rarities collection *Missing Links Volume Three*.

FEBRUARY

'Valleri' / 'Tapioca Tundra' single is released in the U.S.A. This is The Monkees' sixth 45.
● *Monkees Monthly* reports that sales of 'Daydream Believer' have exceeded the half million mark, making it the group's second-

***Valleri* single**

A '**Valleri**' version 2 (T. BOYCE / B. HART)
B '**Tapioca Tundra**' version 1 (M. NESMITH)

U.S. release February 1968 (Colgems 1019).
U.K. release April 1968 (RCA 1673).
Chart high U.S. number 3; U.K. number 12.

biggest selling single in the U.K. The 'zine also notes that Micky is planning to record a children's album with his Moog synthesizer.

● Thursday 1st
Composer Stu Phillips possibly does some last minute clean-up work today on his incidental scoring for the second season of *The Monkees*. Since production on the series has now wrapped, this will mark Phillips's final day of employment on the show. Meanwhile in the studio, Peter continues the production process for 'Can You Dig It' and 'Long Title.'
RECORDING Western Recorders *Hollywood, CA* 6:00-9:00, 10:00pm-12midnight. Peter Tork *prod*; one-inch 8-track; overdubs.
1. '**Can You Dig It**'
   Head master # WZB3-0123
2. '**Long Title: Do I Have To Do This All Over Again**' version 4
   Head master # WZB3-0117
Personnel Peter Tork (instrument unknown), Lance Wakely (instrument unknown).
● Moving to Western studio, Peter alongside Wakely clocks in another six hours of overdub time on these two pieces. Work will continue on Friday.

● Friday 2nd
RECORDING RCA *Hollywood, CA* 12:00-4:30, 7:30-9:00pm. Michael Nesmith *prod*; Pete Abbott *eng*; half-inch 4-track, one-inch 8-track; tracking.
1. '**Nine Times Blue**' version 2 takes 1-18
   unissued master # WZB3-0125
2. '**Seasons**' takes 1-8
   unissued master # WZB3-0126
Personnel Keith Allison (electric guitar 1), Justin DiTullio (cello 2), John Ethridge (bass 1), Sam Freed (violin 2), Eddie Hoh (drums), Nathan Kaproff (violin 2), Pearl Kaufman (harpsichord 2), Edgar Lustgarten (cello 2), Jacqueline Lustgarten (cello 2), Joe Mondragon (bass 2), Michael Nesmith (acoustic guitar 1,2), Erno Neufeld (violin 2), Emmet Sargeant (cello 2), Bud Shank (flute 2).
● From noon to 4:30pm Michael returns to 'Nine Times Blue,' a song that he recorded twice during 1967, first as an informal demo and later in the year for the *Wichita Train Whistle* project. Today's rendition more closely resembles the demo from last year. Michael tapes at least 18 takes of the song but is dissatisfied with the results. He says after the last take: "Somehow, I don't think we have it. Let's come back tomorrow and do it again." Actually, he will begin a new version next Thursday.
   After a three-hour break Michael tapes a lovely baroque piece called 'Seasons.' It features an exquisite string arrangement by Shorty Rogers and a melody carried by famed flautist Bud Shank. However, according to the musicians' union contract the session is cut short by an engineer's strike and "NO SUCCESSFUL TAKES WERE MADE." Seemingly, Michael will never return to complete this recording, though it is reminiscent of his oft-recorded tune 'Carlisle Wheeling.' Meanwhile, Peter's musical efforts at the same time but at a separate studio are not hampered by this engineer's strike, suggesting that perhaps it was confined to RCA's studios.
RECORDING Western Recorders *Hollywood, CA* 5:30-10:30pm. Peter Tork *prod*; one-inch 8-track; overdubs.
1. '**Lady's Baby**' version 5
   The Birds, The Bees & The Monkees master # UZB3-9784
Personnel Peter Tork (instrument unknown), Lance Wakely (instrument unknown).
● Peter and Wakely clock in a further five hours on 'Lady's Baby.' By the end of this evening the production is very close to completion. One further recording session will be held for the song, next Wednesday, before mixing begins. After this session Peter performs solo for an audience of 7,000 at an anti-war rally held at the Los Angeles Sports Arena. Other artists appearing include Nina Simone, Steppenwolf, Blue Cheer, and The Collage.

● Saturday 3rd
RECORDING Western Recorders *Hollywood, CA* 2:00-7:30, 8:30pm-12:30am. Peter Tork *prod*; one-inch 8-track; overdubs.
1. '**Long Title: Do I Have To Do This All Over Again**' version 4
   Head master # WZB3-0117
2. '**Can You Dig It**'
   Head master # WZB3-0123
Personnel Chester Anderson (instrument unknown 2), Peter Tork (instrument unknown), Lance Wakely (instrument unknown).
● Peter and Wakely make unspecified amendments to these productions, which are now close to completion. Most future sessions for the two songs will consist merely of fine-tuning and mixing, but a considerable amount of time will be lavished on these minor tweaks. Simultaneously at a studio next door, Boyce & Hart conduct their first 'Monkees' session of '68.
RECORDING United Recorders *6050 Sunset Boulevard, Hollywood, CA* 2:00-5:00pm. Tommy Boyce & Bobby Hart *prod*; one-inch 8-track; overdubs.
1. '**Me Without You**' overdub onto take 1
   Instant Replay master # WZB3-3511
Personnel Gerry McGee (guitar).
● This simple overdub adds some guitar to 'Me Without You,' a track recorded in December last year. Ultimately the song will be passed over for release on The Monkees' next album, but Boyce & Hart will resume production on the track at the end of this year (see December 20th).

● Sunday 4th
● At 10:45pm Michael Nesmith's wife Phyllis gives birth to the couple's second child, Jonathan Darby Nesmith, at Hollywood Presbyterian Hospital. In the studio, both Micky and Peter are actively working on their self-composed material.
RECORDING United Recorders *Hollywood, CA* 8:00-11:00am, 12midday-1:30pm. Micky Dolenz *prod*; Henry Lewy *eng*; one-inch 8-track; overdubs.
1. '**Shorty Blackwell**'
   Instant Replay master # WZB3-0116
● Micky returns to his song that he began recording last month and puts in four and a half hours on overdubs. However, the song is still in embryonic form, lasting only a mere two minutes and ten seconds. It will eventually grow in length to well over five minutes. Sessions will continue for the track on February 15th.

RECORDING Western Recorders *Hollywood, CA* 2:00-5:00, 6:00-9:00, 10:00pm-12midnight. Peter Tork *prod*; quarter-inch stereo, one-inch 8-track; overdubs, mixdown.

1. **'Long Title: Do I Have To Do This All Over Again'** version 4
   Head master # WZB3-0117

● Peter goes through all Lance Wakely's lead-guitar overdubs for 'Long Title' and selects the best for the final master. At this stage the vocals are not quite finished so they too will likely be revised at a later date. It is also possible that during this session Peter mixes a version of 'Can You Dig It' in which he features as lead vocalist and that will eventually appear as a bonus track on 1994's expanded CD reissue of *Head*. The decision to have Micky sing lead on 'Can You Dig It' is yet to be made.

TVseries

The Monkees

EPISODE 52: *THE DEVIL & PETER TORK*

BROADCAST FEBRUARY 5TH

Peter sells his soul to the Devil (Monte Landis) during a lesson in music and morality.

WRITERS: GERALD GARDNER, DEE CARUSO, ROBERT KAUFMAN. DIRECTOR: JAMES FRAWLEY.

SONGS 'Salesman,' 'No Time.'

● **Monday 5th**

TV Episode 52 of the second series of *The Monkees*, titled *The Devil & Peter Tork*, is broadcast at 7:30pm on the NBC network. In the studio, Peter begins taping a new song and does further work on 'Long Title.'

RECORDING Western Recorders *Hollywood, CA* 2:00-6:00, 8:00pm-12midnight. Peter Tork *prod*; one-inch 8-track; tracking, overdubs.

1. **'Tear The Top Right Off My Head'**
   Missing Links 3 master # WZB3-0184
2. **'Long Title: Do I Have To Do This All Over Again'** version 4
   Head master # WZB3-0117

Personnel Dewey Martin (drums 1), Peter Tork (guitar or bass 1), Lance Wakely (guitar or bass 1).

● Most of Peter's material is now nearing fruition and the first part of today's session finds him starting a new track, 'Tear The Top Right Off My Head.' It was first aired during a Monkees session on June 22nd last year as a mere acoustic demo, mostly instrumental, and then in October of that year Peter performed a bit of the song with Micky on the TV episode *Hitting The High Seas*. It is now finally complete and ready to record, and today's arrangement features a full band with Buffalo Springfield's Dewey Martin on drums and Peter and Wakely playing either bass or guitar. Sessions for the song will continue tomorrow. Union records indicate that during the second part of the session Peter reviews his production of 'Long Title' and maybe adds further unspecified overdubs.

● **Tuesday 6th**

● The March issue (#11) of *Monkee Spectacular* goes on sale and reports that some of the group's forthcoming movie "will have Davy, Micky, Mike, and Peter zooming across the country on motorcycles."

Although this idea will not be employed for The Monkees' feature it will become the backbone of Bert Schneider's next film project, *Easy Rider*. In the studio, meanwhile, six new backing tracks are cut in just seven hours.

RECORDING RCA *Hollywood, CA* 2:00-5:00, 10:00pm-2:00am. David Jones, Lester Sill, Shorty Rogers *prod*; Hank Cicalo *eng*; half-inch 4-track, one-inch 8-track; tracking.

1. **'War Games'** version 2 takes 1-5 + pick-up piece 2 takes
   Missing Links 1 master # WZB3-0119
2. **'Dream World'** takes 1-4
   The Birds, The Bees & The Monkees master # WZB3-0127
3. **'Changes'** takes 1-4
   Missing Links 2 master # WZB3-0128
4. **'The Girl I Left Behind Me'** version 3
   unissued master # UZB3-9780
5. **'We Were Made For Each Other'** version 2
   The Birds, The Bees & The Monkees master # UZB3-9779
6. **'It's Nice To Be With You'**
   Greatest Hits master # WZB3-0129

Personnel Max Bennett (bass), James Burton (guitar 4,5,6), Mike Deasy (guitar), Al Hendrickson (guitar), Milt Holland (tambourine 2*,6*, percussion 3,4, percussion including mallets 5), Gerry McGee (guitar), Michael Melvoin (harpsichord 4,5, keyboard 6), Earl Palmer (drums), Don Randi (harpsichord 1,2, piano 3), Jerry Williams (tambourine 2*,6*, percussion 3,4, percussion including mallets 5). *Holland or Williams on tambourine.

● This is the most productive albeit bland session of the year. The fit of industry is brought on by the nearing release date of The Monkees' fifth album, *The Birds, The Bees & The Monkees*, and the fact that the group are not truly producing the session (though Davy is present). Instead, Monkees music supervisor Lester Sill sits in the control room offering advice and arranger Shorty Rogers is right in the studio, putting the hired musicians through their paces.

The first song taped is a remake of Davy's 'War Games,' which was cut under Michael's direction on January 23rd but not quite to Davy's satisfaction. Today's rendition is a considerably slower arrangement by Rogers set to a steady marching rhythm. After a few slight edits, take 5 is marked as the master and will be treated to further overdubs on Thursday.

The second song tackled is another Davy original, 'Dream World,' which will become the kick-off song for The Monkees' fifth album. Taped easily in four takes – only the first and last of which are full passes – the final rendition is marked as the master and it too will receive further overdubs on Thursday.

Davy: "I think the idea of 'Dream World' was a bit of a cop-out or a bit of a steal, in a sense. I'd done a song called 'Dream Girl' years before with Colpix Records. 'Dream World' was a song that I wrote with [Steve Pitts] and I wanted to try to incorporate some of the violins and all that early-'60s stuff on it. We were very restricted to our studio time and budget availability. Prior to that, people like Tommy Boyce & Bobby Hart, and Jeff Barry, had carte blanche with our money. This was our opportunity to go in, and it was one of the first things I'd gone in to do and produce."

The third and final Jones/Pitts composition cut today is 'Changes,' still at this stage the title for The Monkees' upcoming movie. It's possible therefore that it's being submitted as a potential song for the project, and even features a lyrical allusion to the movie's plot of The Monkees being trapped: "Seasons may change / We stay the same. / We always stay the same." Captured in just four takes, the last being marked as the master, 'Changes' will be treated to further overdubs at Thursday's session.

After a five-hour break and a slight reshuffle of personnel work

---

Micky listens to a playback during a vocal session at RCA, probably for 'Porpoise Song' or 'D.W. Washburn.'

resumes with a third recorded version of 'The Girl I Left Behind Me,' previously taped in both 1966 and '67 but still unissued on record. During most of take 2 Davy is heard singing the song off-mike, but his lead vocal for this track will likely be added at a later date. It is unknown how many takes in total are recorded today because the session tapes for everything after take 4 will later be lost. The song is subjected to further overdubs at a session on Friday.

'We Were Made For Each Other' is also remade today, for the second time. The song was recorded twice late last year under the guidance of producer Chip Douglas, once as a demo and then as a full-fledged master, but it is today's 'Produced By The Monkees' version that will ultimately find release. The session tapes for this song will become lost, so few details are available on the recording process. However, the final multi-track master will survive. The song will be subjected to further overdub work tomorrow.

The last song taped today is Jerry Goldstein's 'It's Nice To Be With You,' and when completed it will feature as the flipside of The Monkees' next single. Unfortunately, the session tapes for this song too will be lost, so there are few details about the recording process. It will be given further overdubs tomorrow.

Peter is also in the studio today, holding a session only a few blocks east of RCA.

RECORDING Western Recorders *Hollywood, CA* 2:00-6:30, 7:30pm-12midnight. Peter Tork *prod*; one-inch 8-track; tracking, overdubs.
1. **'Tear The Top Right Off My Head'**
   Missing Links 3 master # WZB3-0184
Personnel Ron Brown (bass), Dewey Martin (drums), Peter Tork (guitar), Lance Wakely (guitar).
● Today's session may produce an all-new recording of Peter's song, or it could be an extension of yesterday's production. The second half of the session is certainly used only for overdubs, a process that will continue on Thursday.

● **Wednesday 7th**
RECORDING Western Recorders *Hollywood, CA* 3:00-6:00pm. Peter Tork *prod*; one-inch 8-track; overdubs.
1. **'Lady's Baby'** version 5
   The Birds, The Bees & The Monkees master # UZB3-9784
Personnel Peter Tork (instrument unknown), Lance Wakely (instrument unknown).
● Something of a landmark in Monkees history, today sees the final recording session to complete Peter's work on 'Lady's Baby.' This version, number five, was completed in just four sessions, but another seven sessions have been dedicated to the four (now scrapped) early versions. Mixing on 'Lady's Baby' will begin on March 13th.
RECORDING RCA *Hollywood, CA* 7:00-8:00pm. David Jones, Lester Sill, Shorty Rogers *prod*; *eng*; one-inch 8-track; overdubs.
1. **'We Were Made For Each Other'** version 2
   The Birds, The Bees & The Monkees master # UZB3-9779
2. **'It's Nice To Be With You'**
   Greatest Hits master # WZB3-0129
Personnel Gerry McGee (guitar).
● Monkees studio veteran Gerry McGee is drafted in to add some simple strummed acoustic guitar to each of these productions, giving them a mellow texture. After an hour, both tracks are primed for a more significant overdub session set for Friday.

● **Thursday 8th**
● In one very busy day of recording, four sessions are held at three different studios for seven songs. The Monkees' recent studio activity has come at a cost. From January 11th through early February the

group have spent more than $10,000 just in union recording payments to session musicians. This figure does not include the bills for use of the various studios, which are likely to be in the same league.

RECORDING Western Recorders *Hollywood, CA* 9:00am-1:30pm. Peter Tork *prod*; one-inch 8-track; tracking.
1. **'Come On In'** version 3
   Missing Links 2 master # WZB3-0180
Personnel Dewey Martin (drums), Peter Tork (bass), Lance Wakely (guitar).
● Peter starting at an early hour to return to a song he taped twice in May of last year. Those takes featured Buffalo Springfield guitarist Stephen Stills but today's rendition has that band's drummer, Dewey Martin. Peter's pal Lance Wakely is also on hand to participate musically. The production – at this point quite sparse – will be built up over the course of February, with work continuing at a session tomorrow. Just as Peter's first session of the day ends, musicians are filing into RCA for a date with Michael.

RECORDING RCA *Hollywood, CA* 2:00-6:00pm. Michael Nesmith *prod*; Pete Abbott *eng*; half-inch 4-track, one-inch 8-track; tracking.
1. **'St. Matthew'** version 2 takes 1-4
   unissued master # WZB3-0135
2. **'Nine Times Blue'** version 3 takes 1-11
   unissued master # WZB3-0125
Personnel Keith Allison (electric guitar), Bill Chadwick (electric guitar 2), John Ethridge (bass), Eddie Hoh (drums), David Jones (vocal 2 [take 11 only]), Michael Nesmith (vocal 1,2 [take 11 only], acoustic guitar).
● During this four-hour session Michael records his Dylan-inspired 'St. Matthew' for the second time. Today's rendition is still very rough in form and is really just a work in progress: Michael's vocals are not properly recorded and are sung only to guide the other musicians. After four takes, none of which is considered a master, Michael remarks, "Wasn't that ever terrible?" and decides to put the song aside for several months. A third version will be recorded on June 2nd.

He instead returns to 'Nine Times Blue' and quickly completes 11 takes. Although the final pass is marked as a master and treated to lead vocals from both Michael and Davy, this respectable recording is never commercially released. Michael will record a fourth version on April 5th. As the musicians pack up, RCA prepares to host a 16-piece brass-and-string ensemble.

RECORDING RCA *Hollywood, CA* 7:30-10:30pm. David Jones, Lester Sill, Shorty Rogers *prod*; one-inch 8-track; overdubs.
1. **'War Games'** version 2 overdubs onto take 5
   Missing Links 1 master # WZB3-0119
2. **'Dream World'** overdubs onto take 4
   The Birds, The Bees & The Monkees master # WZB3-0127
3. **'Changes'** overdubs onto take 4
   Missing Links 2 master # WZB3-0128
Personnel John Cave (French horn), Buddy Childers (trumpet), David Duke (French horn), Marie Fera (cello), Sam Freed (violin), Nathan Kaproff (violin), George Kast (violin), Marvin Limonick (violin), Edgar Lustgarten (cello), Jacqueline Lustgarten (cello), Arthur Maebe (French horn), Alex Murray (violin), Erno Neufeld (violin), George Roberts (trombone), Frederick Seykora (cello), Jack Sheldon (trumpet).
● Brass and string overdubs are added to these three recent tracks under the direction of Shorty Rogers. All will eventually receive lead-vocal overdubs from Davy but only one, 'Dream World,' will be given a contemporary release. 'War Games' version 2 and 'Changes' will be issued on Rhino's *Missing Links* (1987) and *Missing Links Volume Two*

Davy relaxes at home for the benefit of a magazine photographer.

(1990). Meanwhile, today's fourth recording session is held almost simultaneously at Western Recorders.

RECORDING Western Recorders *Hollywood, CA* 8:00-11:00pm. Peter Tork *prod*; one-inch 8-track; overdubs.

1. 'Tear The Top Right Off My Head'
Missing Links 3 master # WZB3-0184

Personnel Peter Tork (instrument unknown), Lance Wakely (instrument unknown).

● Following a lengthy break after his earlier session ended at 1:30pm, Peter continues apace with some further unspecified overdubs on his song. Another session for this track will be held next Monday.

● Friday 9th

● Davy's former manager, Hal Cone, is found guilty of grand theft, forgery, conspiracy, and receiving stolen goods. In the studio, Michael, Davy, and Peter each supervises a recording session.

RECORDING Western Recorders *Hollywood, CA* 10:00am-1:00, 7:00-9:00pm. Peter Tork *prod*; one-inch 8-track; overdubs.

1. 'Come On In' version 3
Missing Links 2 master # WZB3-0180

Personnel Peter Tork (instrument unknown), Lance Wakely (instrument unknown).

● Peter presumably picks up where he left off yesterday morning refining the production of 'Come On In.' After three hours, Peter and Wakely take a six-hour break but will resume their work this evening. In the middle of their break time, Michael holds a session at RCA for a mysterious, untitled recording.

RECORDING RCA *Hollywood, CA* 2:00-5:30pm. Michael Nesmith *prod*; tracking.

1. 'Untitled'
unissued no master #

Personnel Keith Allison, Bill Chadwick, Bobby Donaho, John Ethridge, Eddie Hoh (all instruments unknown).

● Michael employs most of his usual session crew (as well as Penny Arkade drummer Bobby Donaho) to cut a track lasting a mere 1:37. The musicians' union contract refers to the piece as 'Untitled,' and as all recorded evidence will seemingly be lost, no further information is available. Two hours after this session ends, another overdub date begins in the same building.

RECORDING RCA *Hollywood, CA* 7:30-10:30pm. David Jones, Lester Sill, Shorty Rogers *prod*; one-inch 8-track; overdubs.

1. 'The Girl I Left Behind Me' version 3
unissued master # UZB3-9780

2. 'We Were Made For Each Other' version 2
The Birds, The Bees & The Monkees master # UZB3-9779

3. 'It's Nice To Be With You'
Greatest Hits master # WZB3-0129

Personnel Buddy Childers (trumpet), Vincent DeRosa (French horn), David Duke (French horn), Marie Fera (cello), Sam Freed (violin), Nathan Kaproff (violin), George Kast (violin), Marvin Limonick (violin), Jacqueline Lustgarten (cello), Lew McCreary (trombone), Alex Murray (violin), Erno Neufeld (violin), Dick Perissi (French horn), Kurt Reher (cello), Jack Sheldon (trumpet), Eleanor Slatkin (cello).

● This is more or less a continuation of yesterday's sweetening

process led by Shorty Rogers, today with a very similar 16-piece brass and string ensemble to augment another three backing tracks. All these songs will be given a lead vocal by Davy, though not at this session.

'We Were Made For Each Other' version 2 will be mixed next month for The Monkees' upcoming album, while the forecasted single side, 'It's Nice To Be With You,' will receive further brass augmentation at a session on March 14th. 'The Girl I Left Behind Me' version 3 is never completed or mixed. Davy's lead vocal for the track is nearly complete, but in attempting to fix the first verse and chorus with a 'punch-in' he falls short of his desired goal and gives up on the production. (A 'punch-in' is a short, inserted piece recorded within an existing take.) This leaves one of the choruses incomplete, and this version will never be publicly heard. When the song is eventually given a commercial airing on the early-1969 *Instant Replay* album, the powers-that-be return to Neil Sedaka's original production from November 1966.

● **Saturday 10th**
RECORDING Western Recorders *Hollywood, CA* 10:00am-1:00, 6:00-9:00pm. Peter Tork *prod*; one-inch 8-track; overdubs.
1. **'Long Title: Do I Have To Do This All Over Again'** version 4
   Head master # WZB3-0117
2. **'Seeger's Theme'** version 3
   unissued master # UZB3-9790
Personnel Peter Tork (instrument unknown), Lance Wakely (instrument unknown).
● Peter heads another session to review recent productions. 'Long Title' is now nearly ready for final mixing, but he decides to scrap 'Seeger's Theme' version 3 from last month in favor of a new take that he will produce on Monday. Meanwhile at United Recorders next door a sweetening session is wedged in during a break in Peter's activities.
RECORDING United Recorders *Hollywood, CA* 2:00-5:00pm. Tommy Boyce & Bobby Hart *prod*; Henry Lewy *eng*; one-inch 8-track; overdubs.
1. **'P.O. Box 9847'** overdubs onto take 21
   The Birds, The Bees & The Monkees master # WZB3-0183
Personnel Victor Arno (violin), Philip Goldberg (viola), Ray Kelley (cello), Jack Pepper (violin).
● Over the course of this three-hour date arranger Don McGinnis leads a string quartet through a series of overdubs for Boyce & Hart's 'P.O. Box 9847,' recorded late last year. Today's work will erase an experimental Moog synthesizer part that was added to the track earlier in the year (and later heard in rough-mix form as a bonus track on 1994's CD reissue of *The Birds, The Bees & The Monkees*). The production of the song is probably complete now and very soon it will be mixed down for release on The Monkees' next album.

● **Sunday 11th**
● The *Chicago Sun Times* publishes a phone interview with Davy concerning the group's recent activities. "Mike had a baby Monday and I've got a groovy new girlfriend," he boasts. "She's Linda [Haines], with long blond hair, also a suntan, a little chubby, and 5 feet 6 inches tall. Cool. We've been going steady a bit for three months, and that's a long time for me. Weird. She can clean a house, but I can cook. Like the other night, I see some carrots. Chop, chop. Celery, meat, and potatoes and I've got groovy stew at home.

"That's 'Dream World' you hear [in the background]. I wrote it with a friend. The Monkees want to go the way of 'What Kind Of Fool Am I,' Broadway rock, if you know what I mean. The Beatles are still groovy, but they're on the wrong side of tomorrow. Funky stuff that's too heavy for my old man."

The article reveals that Davy and Michael (who Davy refers to as "skinny the snide") are negotiating for the purchase of the Monkees name and hope to form their own business. "We are shipshape now," reckons Davy. "All settled in our new homes and playing softball on Sundays and basketball on Wednesdays and doing all the normal things." As is normal for Peter these days he spends his Sunday in the studio.
RECORDING Western Recorders *Hollywood, CA* 2:00-5:00, 6:00-9:00, 10:00pm-12midnight. Peter Tork *prod*; one-inch 8-track; overdubs.
1. **'Come On In'** version 3
   Missing Links 2 master # WZB3-0180
Personnel Peter Tork (instrument unknown), Lance Wakely (instrument unknown).
● Over the next three days Peter will complete his production of Jo Mapes's 'Come On In.' Another session for the song will take place at RCA tomorrow.

TVseries
The Monkees
EPISODE 53: *MONKEES RACE AGAIN*
BROADCAST FEBRUARY 12TH
The group come to the rescue of a friend whose race car is the victim of sabotage.
WRITERS: DAVE EVANS, ELIAS DAVIS, DAVID POLLACK. DIRECTOR: JAMES FRAWLEY.
SONG 'What Am I Doing Hangin' 'Round?'

● **Monday 12th**
TV At 7:30pm episode 53 of the second series of *The Monkees*, titled *Monkees Race Again*, is broadcast on the NBC network. In the studio Peter records yet another version of 'Seeger's Theme,' and others.
RECORDING RCA *Hollywood, CA* 1:00-6:00, 8:00pm-1:00am. Peter Tork *prod*; Pete Abbott *eng*; one-inch 8-track; tracking, overdubs.
1. **'Seeger's Theme'** version 4 takes 1-9
   Missing Links 2 master # UZB3-9790
2. **'Come On In'** version 3
   Missing Links 2 master # WZB3-0180
3. **'Long Title: Do I Have To Do This All Over Again'** version 4
   Head master # WZB3-0117
4. **'Tear The Top Right Off My Head'**
   Missing Links 3 master # WZB3-0184
Personnel Buddy Miles (drums), Peter Tork (bass 1), Lance Wakely (electric guitar 1).
● Peter tapes his fourth and final attempt at Pete Seeger's 'Seeger's Theme.' The session produces a master version that Peter will build upon and complete tomorrow. He also addresses various production concerns on his other tracks in progress. All will be completed in the next few days and, remarkably, this will mark Peter's last intensive day of 'Monkees' recording for the remainder of 1968.

● **Tuesday 13th**
RECORDING Western Recorders *Hollywood, CA*. Peter Tork *prod*; one-inch 8-track; overdubs.
1. **'Seeger's Theme'** version 4 overdubs onto take 9
   Missing Links 2 master # UZB3-9790

2. 'Come On In' version 3
Missing Links 2 master # WZB3-0180
Personnel Stephen Stills (electric guitar 2), Peter Tork (guitar 1, banjo 1, whistling 1, vocal 2, tack piano 2), Lance Wakely (electric guitar 2).
● Peter completes his production of 'Seeger's Theme' with the addition of more guitars, banjo, and some whistling. Though the resulting recording is quite exciting – and short – Peter will be unable to interest anyone in releasing the instrumental. Long after the event, it will be exhumed for 1990's *Missing Links Volume Two*.

Peter also puts the wraps on his rendition of Jo Mapes's 'Come On In' but, as with 'Seeger's Theme,' he is unable to secure a contemporary release for the song. It will also appear eventually on Rhino's *Missing Links Volume Two*.

Davy recalls: "There's one song that Peter Tork sings on that *Missing Links* album where he sounds absolutely super. He sounds great; he's right on the button. Sings it good and he wasn't supposed to be a singer. The other guys were always pushing him out and Mike Nesmith was always sort of like threatening him: putting his fist through the wall, doing all this kind of shit. I'm sure Peter could kick his ass if he wanted to, but he never did. Unbelievable."

● **Wednesday 14th**
RECORDING RCA *Hollywood, CA* 9:00am-1:00pm. Micky Dolenz *prod*; one-inch 8-track; reductions, overdubs.
1. 'Zor And Zam'
The Birds, The Bees & The Monkees master # WZB3-0108
Personnel Bill Chadwick (instrument unknown), Micky Dolenz (instrument unknown).
● Micky and Bill Chadwick work this morning to prepare 'Zor And Zam' for a grand orchestral score by Shorty Rogers, the final production element that will be added on February 17th. Later at Western, Peter once again tinkers with his 'Long Title.'
RECORDING Western Recorders *Hollywood, CA* 6:30-9:30, 10:30pm-12:30am. Peter Tork *prod*; one-inch 8-track; overdubs.
1. 'Long Title: Do I Have To Do This All Over Again' version 4
Head master # WZB3-0117
● This is Peter's tenth recording session for 'Long Title' version 4, the recorded saga of which will almost come to a close at a mix session tomorrow.

● **Thursday 15th**
● Principal photography is due to commence today on the group's movie, *Changes*, but work is delayed when Micky, Davy, and Michael strike for an advance against the film's gross profits. Peter will stay on the sidelines of this action, remaining loyal to the film's producers Raybert.

Meanwhile, more additions and revisions are made to the shooting script, including the 'look in the mirror' (after a kissing contest), Mike and Micky's scene with Teri Garr, and the dialogue in the vacuum cleaner, among other minor tweaks. In the studio, three Monkees hold three separate recording dates.
RECORDING RCA *Hollywood, CA* 1:00-5:30pm. Micky Dolenz *prod*; one-inch 8-track; overdubs.
1. 'Shorty Blackwell'
Instant Replay master # WZB3-0116
Personnel Bill Chadwick (instrument unknown), Micky Dolenz (instrument unknown).
● Micky and his pal Bill Chadwick review and possibly overdub just a small portion (lasting 1:56) of 'Shorty Blackwell' during this date. The song consists of a series of musical movements and so Micky is building it up section by section. However, after today's session work

will stall on the piece until April 9th. Following a two-hour break, sessions resume at RCA with the recording of three new Davy Jones tunes.
RECORDING RCA *Hollywood, CA* 7:30-10:30pm. David Jones, Shorty Rogers *prod*; Hank Cicalo *eng*; half-inch 4-track, one-inch 8-track; tracking.
1. 'The Poster'
The Birds, The Bees & The Monkees master # WZB3-0136
2. 'The Party' takes 1-3
Missing Links 1 master # WZB3-0137
3. 'I'm Gonna Try' takes 1-5
The Birds, The Bees & The Monkees master # WZB3-0138
Personnel Hal Blaine (drums), Al Casey (guitar), Gary Coleman (tambourine, glockenspiel 1, marimba 2,3), Michael Deasy (guitar), Gene Estes (tambourine, glockenspiel 1, marimba 2,3), Don Randi (organ 1,2, harpsichord 3), Lyle Ritz (bass), Howard Roberts (guitar).
● Davy wrote 'The Poster' after his winter vacation in Europe, and as with all his tunes of the period (and this session) it is a collaboration with Steve Pitts. The inspiration for the song comes from another uncredited collaborator, and when it appears on the Monkees' next album, *The Birds, The Bees & The Monkees*, Davy will get some legal heat as a result. A further session for the song will take place on Saturday.

Davy recalls going to Manchester and meeting Edith Sidebottom. "She was an old lady of maybe 86 years old and we discussed some things. She showed me some song lyrics and this, that and the other. She showed me one song that she had about a circus. I think the only line that I took from her was 'The circus is coming to town.' It was the end of it, 'bum di bum di bum di … and the circus is coming to town.' She named that 'Why Are We Forever Weaving New Ties To Bind Us To The Earth.'

"She gave me this quote – it wasn't hers, but it was like some person from yester-decade. 'Why are we forever weaving new ties to bind us to the earth.' I put that on the back of the *Birds, The Bees & The Monkees* album and [underneath] I put 'Edith Sidebottom.'

"When the album came out in America I actually sent her a copy. All of a sudden I got a letter from her lawyer saying she is claiming you stole this and did that. But the only line I took was 'And the circus is coming to town.' Not to make an old lady unhappy, I think I sent her about 3,000 bucks at the time, which was probably more than she'd seen in a long, long time."

Davy says that circuses always seemed fun to him. "A family sort of a place to be. I remembered that so much, so I wrote mostly the lyrics. I collaborated with Steve [Pitts] once again. He was the guy that actually sang, or put down the notes that went along with my singing the tune and my lyrics. So we collaborated, and once somebody writes one line then they're part of the tune. I think we gave Edith part of the tune and gave her some money and that was the end of that.

"I like to write stories and that was just a story. If you can't get to the circus, read the lyrics. You know you'll feel as if you're there. 'I feel like I'm already there, I must see her fly through the air.' I try to paint a picture with my lyrics."

Davy's soul-oriented number, 'The Party,' paints more of an adult lyrical picture and is captured at today's session in just three takes. Take 3 is marked as the master and will receive further overdubs on Saturday. The breezy 'I'm Gonna Try' is next, completed in five takes. As producer, Davy makes only one minor adjustment, requesting that the musicians speed the song up a bit. Take 5 is marked as today's master and will be used for further overdubs, also on Saturday.

Davy: "All this stuff was just sitting around. I think it was all written in about four minutes. Along with, 'Did you buy your tickets for the war games,' and a couple of other things that were written around about that time. I have loads of tapes on a lot of other material that never even got it, but it's only 2-track and it's not even worth thinking about. 'I'm Gonna Try' was just a throwaway thing, really. Those are my first songs I'd ever written. I wasn't technical about it, I just wrote down whatever came out at the time. They're not very sophisticated, but they're very sort of youthful and Monkee oriented."

Also in the studio today, Peter mixes down his production of 'Long Title.'

RECORDING Western Recorders (2) *Hollywood, CA* 6:30-9:30, 10:30pm-12:30am. Peter Tork *prod*; one-inch 8-track; overdubs.

1. 'Long Title: Do I Have To Do This All Over Again' version 4
unissued master # WZB3-0117

● This track now seems to be complete, and both mono and stereo mixes are dubbed down at this session. The mixes, which feature a prominent backing vocal from Davy, will be seriously considered for release on the band's next album, *The Birds, The Bees & The Monkees* (see March 19th), but the song will later be remixed when it is decided instead to include it in the band's film. Ultimately, none of today's mixes will ever be released.

● Friday 16th

● In the studio, two mysterious sessions are held with no Monkee involvement.

RECORDING RCA *Hollywood, CA.* Pete Abbott *eng*; quarter-inch stereo; tracking.

1. 'Games' demo takes 1-2
unissued master # WZB3-0119

Personnel David Crosby (vocal, guitar).

● Peter's pal David Crosby tapes one of his songs as a submission for The Monkees. Crosby is now solo, having been recently asked to leave his band, The Byrds. The Monkees will never work on a full-fledged version of the track, and Crosby himself will put the song aside for four years until his April 1972 album with Graham Nash, *Crosby Nash*. In any event, since Crosby is not a Screen Gems-published writer, it is doubtful that the group would be allowed to release 'Games.' The tape box confirms this with a scrawled comment of "not ours." Meanwhile at a studio east of RCA another intriguing session takes place.

RECORDING California Recorders *5203 Sunset Boulevard, Hollywood, CA* 6:00-9:00, 10:00pm-1:00am. Gerry Goffin *prod*; tracking.

1. 'Dear Marm'
unissued master # WZB4-3514

Personnel Ken Bloom (guitar), Danny 'Kootch' Kortchmar (guitar), Doug Lubahn (bass), Michael Ney (drums, percussion), John Raines (drums, percussion).

● Sadly, no tapes will survive for this unheard Goffin & King song. Gerry Goffin will use the same studio and personnel in a few days to cut his 'Porpoise Song,' which he wrote with Carole King. 'Dear Marm' is arranged by Clark Gassman and the band is led by Russ Titelman, who co-wrote The Monkees' 1966 recording 'I'll Be True To You.' A guitar overdub session for 'Dear Marm' will be held on April 2nd.

● Saturday 17th

● *NME* reports that on Monday shooting will finally commence on The Monkees' feature film. The paper lists both America and Japan as likely locations and claims that the script is "centered around The Monkees traveling across America on motorcycles and the

adventures they encounter en route." The film is now set for late summer release, but the title is up in the air since *Changes* is attached to another feature already in progress.

As for a third season of the group's TV series, *NME* reports that Bert Schneider has tried to persuade NBC to accept eight hour-long specials in lieu of a weekly series. NBC "was not prepared to accept this suggestion." Show producers Raybert are currently slated to produce another 26 half-hour episodes this year.

● *Billboard* publishes an ad hyping Michael's as-yet-unreleased project *The Wichita Train Whistle Sings*. Under the heading "The Organized Accident" the full-page blurb features an excerpt of Leonard Feather's December 3rd 1967 article for *The Los Angeles Times* and closes with the information that *Wichita Train Whistle* is represented by Perenchio Artists Ltd., Michael's personal managers. (See also Michael's recording session today, details below.)

● This evening The Jimi Hendrix Experience perform at the Shrine Auditorium in Los Angeles, after which they attend a party at Peter's house. Other guests include David Crosby, Jim Frawley, Micky Dolenz and Samantha Juste, and Graham Nash. Peter treats them all to health food as well as prospective tracks from The Monkees' next album such as 'Tapioca Tundra' and 'Can You Dig It.'

Meanwhile the group are still hard at work on the forthcoming long-player. Today three separate sessions are held, one of which produces The Monkees' next single.

RECORDING RCA *Hollywood, CA* 1:00-4:00, 5:00-8:00pm. Lester Sill, Micky Dolenz *prod*; one-inch 8-track; tracking.

1. 'D.W. Washburn'
Greatest Hits master # WZB3-0130

Personnel Keith Allison (guitar), Bill Chadwick (guitar), Henry Diltz (banjo), Chip Douglas (bass), Jim Gordon (drums).

● Lester Sill, an old-school music man of the first order, believes that this Leiber & Stoller song, cut and rejected by The Coasters vocal group in October last year, can somehow work for The Monkees.

Despite Sill's unquestioned experience, his concept for The Monkees to turn back the clock musically is rather suspect. Nonetheless, he has the ultimate power to see this song issued as a single. The assembled crew do a reasonable job of arranging 'D.W. Washburn' in the style of The Lovin' Spoonful's early-'66 hit, 'Daydream.' However you slice it, 'D.W. Washburn' is a little outdated for the pop market of 1968 and quite an odd choice for the group. A further session will be held for the track on March 1st.

Sill recalls: "I loved the feel of the song. I loved the sound of the demo that I heard. Then I realized after we did it and it came out that it was really a downer. It was a story about a guy in the gutter, about a bum. I thought there was kind of a comical, Dixieland feel to it, that I felt was rather different. In hindsight I realized it was an awful mistake." While Sill is returning to the early days of rock, Michael assembles more than 20 musicians to tape an instrumental jazz odyssey that is without doubt far less commercial than 'D.W. Washburn.'

RECORDING RCA *Hollywood, CA* 6:30-9:30pm. Michael Nesmith *prod*; Hank Cicalo *eng*; half-inch 4-track, one-inch 8-track; tracking.

1. 'Impack' Parts 1, 2 & 3 takes: see text
unissued master # WZB3-0139

Personnel Milt Bernhart (trombone), Hal Blaine (drums), Max Bennett (bass), Al Casey (guitar), Buddy Childers (trumpet), Gene 'Cip' Cipriano (woodwind), Mike Deasy (guitar), Al Hendrickson (guitar), Milt Holland (conga, tambourine), Jim Horn (woodwind), Jules Jacob (woodwind), Dick Leith (trombone), Stanley Levey (conga, tambourine), John Lowe (woodwind), Lew McCreary (trombone), Michael Melvoin (keyboard), Clyde Reasinger (trumpet), Mac Rebennack [a.k.a. Dr. John] (keyboard), Frank Rosolino

Micky, director Bob Rafelson, and, behind Peter, Jack Nicholson – all on the movie set in February discussing the group's forthcoming feature film, eventually to be titled Head.

(trombone), Jack Sheldon (trumpet), Tony Terran (trumpet).

● 'Impack' is a lengthy horn-driven instrumental in three movements and clearly an extension of Michael's November '67 *Wichita Train Whistle Sings* sessions. It is arranged by Shorty Rogers, who secures many of L.A.'s top jazz musicians for the date, and is recorded in sections and then edited together.

Part 1 is captured in two takes, with take 2 being used for the master. Part 2 is captured in four takes, and take 4 is edited to take 2 of Part 1. Lastly, two takes of Part 3 are recorded, with the second edited onto the master.

According to today's musicians' union contract the composition may have some relation to Michael's January 24th recording, 'Pinball Machine,' but as the song will never be released or worked on after this date, a connection cannot be verified. However, it is possible that Michael has some intention to include this piece on the *Wichita* album since the ad in today's *Billboard* refers to "a new extended instrumental work recorded in five sections." Whatever the intention, the public will never hear the adventurous 'Impack.'

Half an hour after this session wraps, many of the 'Impack' musicians participate in a lengthy overdub date with Shorty Rogers.
RECORDING RCA *Hollywood, CA* 10:00pm-2:00am. Shorty Rogers *prod*; Hank Cicalo *eng*; one-inch 8-track; overdubs.
1. **'Zor And Zam'**
   The Birds, The Bees & The Monkees master # WZB3-0108
2. **'The Party'** overdubs onto take 3
   Missing Links 1 master # WZB3-0137
3. **'The Poster'**
   The Birds, The Bees & The Monkees master # WZB3-0136
4. **'I'm Gonna Try'** overdubs onto take 5
   The Birds, The Bees & The Monkees master # WZB3-0138
Personnel Max Bennett (bass 1), Milt Bernhart (trombone), Hal Blaine (drums 1, percussion including tympani & gong 1), Buddy Childers (trumpet), Milt Holland (drums 1, percussion including tympani & gong 1), Nathan Kaproff (violin), George Kast (violin), Dick Leith (trombone), Stanley Levey (drums 1, percussion including tympani & gong 1), John Lowe (woodwind), Marvin Limonick (violin), Lew McCreary (trombone), Michael Melvoin (piano 1), Alex Murray (violin), Erno Neufeld (violin), Clyde Reasinger (trumpet), Frank Rosolino (trombone), Ambrose Russo (violin), Jack Sheldon (trumpet), Tony Terran (trumpet).
● Although four sessions have been held for 'Zor And Zam' this year, it isn't until this evening that the song's production takes shape. Shorty Rogers builds on a basic track of electric guitars, bass, and percussion, adding eight pieces of brass and a low woodwind part to the mix. This is complimented by a raft of violins and a plethora of percussion, including two sets of marching snares, tympani, and a gong. Now completed, this grandiloquent track will be mixed for release on March 13th.

After that elaborate arrangement is captured on tape Rogers adds more mundane brass and string textures to three of Davy's recent tracks. Except for some vocal dubbing that may remain, this will complete these productions, of which only 'The Poster' is destined for wide release – on The Monkees' next album. Both 'The Party' and 'I'm Gonna Try' will be passed over for contemporary release. 'The Party' will eventually appear on 1987's *Missing Links* set, while the 1994 CD reissue of *The Birds, The Bees & The Monkees* will feature 'I'm Gonna Try' as a bonus track.

● **Sunday 18th**
RECORDING RCA *Hollywood, CA* 4:00-7:00pm; tracking.
1. **'Untitled?'**
   unissued no master #

Personnel Keith Allison, Bill Chadwick, Henry Diltz, Chip Douglas, Jim Gordon (all instruments unknown).
● Today's session has an identical line-up to the one assembled yesterday to cut 'D.W. Washburn' and it is possibly a continuation of that work. The other possibility is that the session may be called to produce a new Micky original titled 'Rose Marie' (see also tomorrow's entry).

● **Monday 19th**
TV At 7:30pm episode 54 of the *Monkees* second series, *The Monkees In Paris*, is televised on the NBC network.
FILMING Shooting at last begins on The Monkees' feature film. The schedule is set to run for 30 to 40 days, but on the first two the crew focus on scenes in The Monkees' pad, including a kissing contest with Jack Nicholson's girlfriend I.J. Jefferson and the 'look in the mirror.' Meanwhile off the set it is possible that Micky cuts a new song, 'Rose Marie.'
RECORDING RCA *Hollywood, CA*. Micky Dolenz *prod*; Hank Cicalo *eng*; one-inch 8-track; tracking.
1. **'Rose Marie'**
   Instant Replay or *Missing Links 1* master # WZB3-0140
Personnel Keith Allison (electric guitar), Micky Dolenz (vocal, acoustic guitar), Chip Douglas* (bass), Jim Gordon* (drums), Peter Tork (acoustic guitar). * possibly Douglas and Gordon on bass and drums.
● This R&B-infused number by Micky has something of a sketchy recording history. It is definitely started around this time by Micky and Keith Allison and will go through a bewildering series of lyrical and instrumental changes over the next year. At this point the lyrics are mostly unfinished, with Micky singing "dadadadadadadada" through major sections. Peter will also step in at some point during the next few days to add a quarter-time acoustic guitar overdub to certain sections of the song. The track will receive further augmentation at a session on March 1st.

● **Tuesday 20th**
● A day after shooting starts on the group's film, NBC announces their new fall line-up – and *The Monkees* is surprisingly absent from their Monday-night schedule. It is one of six shows cancelled by NBC, including the far higher rated *I Spy* (which earns a 19.2 Nielsen rating). *The Monkees* by comparison holds only a 17.5 rating but is by no means at the bottom of the pack. (One rating point equals one percent of the 'TV households' in the U.S.A. according to the Nielsen calculations.) In fact the show's following isn't strong

enough to satisfy its sponsors, Kellogg's and Yardley. Raybert and The Monkees offset news of the cancellation by claiming that they are reluctant to shoot a third season of the series. The show *I Dream Of Jeannie* will take the *Monkees* Monday-night slot in the fall.

Don Kirshner: "The TV show never got great ratings, which surprised me. It was the records that were really the big, big hit and got most of the notoriety. Bert Schneider and Bob Rafelson are very talented people. They were bored with doing a mundane, zany, Beatles type of show. Being creative and being innovative, they probably wanted to be different, more bizarre … and change. I think that change eventually hurt the group, because if you're happy watching The Three Stooges or The Beatles, there's a formula that's working. If you put in a drastic change, whether it's musically or TV-wise, you're gonna lose audience."

● Wednesday 21st

FILMING The Monkees' movie crew moves out of the confines of Columbia's lot to shoot on location in Bronson Canyon in Los Angeles. It is here that many of the picture's war scenes will be captured.

● Thursday 22nd

FILMING Shooting on the movie today includes sequences in which The Monkees are inmates in a jail cell and one where Peter listens to the Swami in a steam room.

● Saturday 24th

● The *NME* reports that Hollies member Graham Nash was a recent visitor to Micky's home where the host demonstrated his Colortron machine. This apparatus is valued at £700 (about $1,700 at the time) and "flashes lights in relation to sound."

Nash watched the Colortron interpret The Hollies' *Butterfly* album and found it to shine brighter for this than for *Sgt. Pepper*.

Davy, Mike, and Micky all attended one of The Hollies' recent gigs at the Whiskey A-Go-Go on West Hollywood's Sunset Strip. Micky even took to the stage to introduce one of The Hollies' performances.

During this period, Peter will host a historical get-together for Nash with his pals Stephen Stills and David Crosby, who will soon form Crosby Stills & Nash.

Meanwhile in the studio Micky eschews his original songs to record some more Brill Building material proffered by Lester Sill.
RECORDING T.T.G. (2) *Hollywood, CA* 4:00-7:00, 8:00-10:30pm. Micky Dolenz *prod*; Jack ? *eng*; one-inch 8-track; tracking, overdubs.

1. **'Shake 'Em Up And Let 'Em Roll'** takes 1-20 + insert ending takes 1-8
   Missing Links 3 master # WZB3-0181
2. **'Don't Say Nothin' Bad (About My Baby)'** takes 1-2
   unissued master # WZB3-0182
Personnel Keith Allison (electric guitar 1 [takes 4-21 only], 2), Bill Chadwick (acoustic guitar 1), Henry Diltz (clarinet 1), Micky Dolenz (vocal 1 [take 20 only], 2), Chip Douglas (bass), Eddie Hoh (drums), unknown (piano 1 [takes 1-4 only]).
● Micky produces Leiber & Stoller's 'Shake 'Em Up' on a weekend break from shooting the group's movie, probably at the suggestion of Lester Sill, music coordinator of The Monkees' record releases. Micky conducts the musicians from the control room of T.T.G.'s studio 2, but the early takes are a shambolic affair. For the most part, the assembled players are confused about exactly what kind of performance Micky requires from them.

After numerous false starts Micky is quite willing to halt the entire session, but Keith Allison and Bill Chadwick quickly step in to help arrange the song. Ultimately, take 20 is marked as the master and Micky adds a lead vocal to the song right on the spot. Excited by this final take he moves to the studio floor to direct the band through some potential endings that might be edited onto the tail.

After Leiber & Stoller's 'D.W. Washburn' flops for the group, 'Shake 'Em Up' will be left on the cutting-room floor and will only be made available much later, on Rhino's 1996 *Missing Links Volume Three*. (Ironically, The Coasters' contemporary version of the song, cut at New York's Bell Sound on February 13th, will share a similar fate, being issued posthumously on Rhino in 1992.)

Back at the session, after some untaped rehearsals, Micky leads his studio crew through an old Cookies hit from 1963, Goffin & King's 'Don't Say Nothin' Bad (About My Baby).' Singing live with the musicians, Micky completes just two takes of the song. Take 1 is merely a discussion while the second is a complete and respectable reading of the song. Despite the rough quality of the overall performance, which is little more than a run-through, Micky's voice is quite impressive. Nevertheless, the track is soon abandoned and never publicly heard.

TV series

The Monkees

EPISODE 55: *MONKEES MIND THEIR MANOR*
BROADCAST FEBRUARY 26TH
The group travel to England to sort out Davy's inheritance of Sir Malcolm Kibee's estate.
WRITER: COSLOUGH JOHNSON. DIRECTOR: PETER H. THORKELSON.
SONG 'Star Collector.'

● Monday 26th

● The Monkees are awarded a gold record by the RIAA for outstanding U.S. sales of their single 'Valleri.'
● *The Los Angeles Times* reports that "Bert Schneider will play a policeman in the Monkees film for Columbia." Ultimately, Schneider does not perform the role, which is taken by Logan Ramsey.
TV At 7:30pm episode 55 of the second series of *The Monkees*, the

Peter Tork-directed *Monkees Mind Their Manor*, is broadcast by the NBC network. Also during this evening Gerry Goffin produces the main theme for the group's motion picture.

RECORDING California Recorders *Hollywood, CA* 6:00-9:00, 10:00pm-1:00am. Gerry Goffin *prod*; one-inch 8-track; tracking.

1. 'Porpoise Song'
   Head master # WZB4-3513

Personnel Ken Bloom (guitar), Bill Hinshaw (French horn), Jules Jacob (oboe), Danny 'Kootch' Kortchmar (guitar), Doug Lubahn (bass), Michael Ney (drums, percussion), John Raines (drums, percussion), Leon Russell (keyboard), Ralph Schuckett (keyboard).

● 'Porpoise Song' is a striking example of the astonishing way in which popular music progressed so rapidly during the 1960s. In 1963 Gerry Goffin & Carole King were writing veritable teen throwaways like 'Don't Say Nothin' Bad (About My Baby)' but only five short years later they produced sophisticated gems like the lyrically obtuse and musically mind-blowing 'Porpoise Song.'

The session for this astounding track was directed with great majesty (and mystery) by its co-writer Goffin. Russ Titelman, who conducts the musicians for this piece, recalls later that California Recorders "was a divey little studio that Gerry knew about."

Although a few incomplete takes are heard on the session reel, probably none of the real-time tracking recordings will survive. All the energy is placed into building up a single master take through overdubbing. The main tracking occurs this evening between 6:00 and 9:00pm and then French horn and oboe parts are added from 10:00pm to 1:00am by Bill Hinshaw and Jules Jacob. The final production features these particular performances heavily processed through a filter, giving them an almost synthetic sound quality. The production process on 'Porpoise Song' will continue on February 28th.

● Tuesday 27th

FILMING Shooting continues on The Monkees' feature. Further war sequences are filmed on location in Bronson Canyon as well as shots of Micky falling down a mountain. Studio shots likely filmed this week include the group betting on a girl's suicide, Davy looking into a bathroom mirror, and some factory/black box sequences. Towards the end of the week the group travel to the Olympic boxing ring in Los Angeles to shoot boxer Sonny Liston's cameo appearance in the film.

● Wednesday 28th

FILMING The Monkees and a full film crew spend the day shooting on location at the Hyperion Sewage Treatment Plant in Playa Del Rey, a suburb of Los Angeles, where most of the feature's factory sequences are captured. Meanwhile in the studio Gerry Goffin adds brass and strings to 'Porpoise Song.'

RECORDING California Recorders *Hollywood, CA* 9:30pm-2:30am. Gerry Goffin *prod*; one-inch 8-track; overdubs.

1. 'Porpoise Song'
   Head master # WZB4-3513

Davy's performances will be recorded with the tape running at slower than normal speed and then played back at standard pitch, giving a mild speeded-up effect. Without a doubt this is the most elaborate production ever for a Monkees recording and a true landmark in studio manipulation.

MARCH

● *Monkees Monthly* reports that Michael has sold the rights for his independently produced *Wichita Train Whistle Sings* album to the Warner/Reprise label. However, this deal will never reach fruition and several more months will pass before the album appears in the marketplace.

● Davy sends a letter to his fans to let them know that catalogs are not yet available for his Zilch boutique. He signs off with: "Thanx 2 U my groovy fan 4 being so cool and understanding."

● Lulu is in Los Angeles on a promotional jaunt and to visit Davy. She drops by the set of The Monkees' film, which now bears the enigmatic moniker *Untitled*. She tells the *NME*: "I went to the film set with Davy, and Frank Zappa was there and he's so nice. I couldn't believe it. I was dead scared of him and I kept away on purpose from where he was. It was like the first time I met Jimi Hendrix. I was scared of him, but he's really polite and nice. Davy called me over to where he was talking with Frank Zappa, and Frank told Davy that The Monkees were the only group of that type that he liked. He's sweet. Isn't that strange?

"When I was in Los Angeles," Lulu continues, "Davy just sort of took care of me like a big brother. He was so sweet. It sounds silly to say we're just good friends, but we are. He's such a friendly guy and he's not ready to get involved with any one girl and I don't want to get involved with any one guy. What I love about Davy is that he's really humane. He's not pretentious, he's not phoney … he's him! Now I understand why all the kids go mad for him, because his real self does come over. I think he's adorable!"

Personnel Gregory Bemko (cello), Max Bennett (upright bass), David Filerman (cello), Bill Hinshaw (horn, woodwind), Clyde 'Whitey' Hoggan (upright bass), Jim Hughart (upright bass), Jules Jacob (horn, woodwind), Jan Kelley (cello), Jacqueline Lustgarten (cello), Jerry Scheff (upright bass).

● During this further session for the centerpiece of *Head*, Jack Nitzsche's stunning orchestral arrangement is committed to an already brimming master. Nitzsche is a musical jack-of-all-trades who has already worked with Phil Spector, The Rolling Stones, and Buffalo Springfield, among others. His score features a double quartet of cellists and bassists conducted by Russ Titelman. The results are split – cellists on one track, bassists on the other – but still carry a remarkable aural thickness. Bill Hinshaw and Jules Jacob are on hand once again to augment their parts from Monday's session. The final track features both French and English horns that are very likely overdubbed today. A further session will be held for the piece tomorrow.

● Thursday 29th

● Michael and Phyllis Nesmith, Micky and Samantha Juste, and Davy with his date Linda Haines attend the Grammy Awards dinner at the Century Plaza Hotel in Los Angeles. Tonight's awards represent the best in song from 1967. The Monkees are up for two awards for 'I'm A Believer,' in the Group Vocal Performance and Contemporary Vocal Group categories, but they lose in both cases to The Fifth Dimension's 'Up Up And Away.' When Davy is called upon to present the award for Best Spoken Word, Documentary Or Drama Recording he commits a Grammy gaffe. As he announces nominee Victor Lundberg's 'An Open Letter To My Teenage Son' he interjects the off-script comment: "I hope it doesn't win." Meanwhile in the studio, production continues on 'Porpoise Song.'

RECORDING Wally Heider Recording *6373 Selma Avenue, Hollywood, CA*. Gerry Goffin *prod*; Chris Hinshaw *eng*; one-inch 8-track; reductions, overdubs.

1. 'Porpoise Song'
Head master # WZB4-3513
Personnel Russ Titelman (cymbals), unknown (chimes).

● Producer Gerry Goffin moves to Wally Heider's studio for some further sweetening, but first bounces down the tracks from his previous two sessions for 'Porpoise Song.' This is a rather daunting task given the amount of instrumentation previously taped, but he succeeds in creating a new 8-track master tape. Even after taking this step to create more space, Goffin must use whatever open tracks he can find to add overdubs of cymbal crashes (courtesy of pal Russ Titelman), chimes, or tubular bells, and some genuine aquatic sound effects.

In April Goffin will overdub three vocal tracks from Micky and some background vocals from Davy. To add another subtle texture,

● Friday 1st

RECORDING RCA *Hollywood, CA* 8:00-11:00pm. Shorty Rogers *prod*; one-inch 8-track; overdubs.

1. 'D.W. Washburn'
Greatest Hits master # WZB3-0130
2. 'Rose Marie'
Instant Replay or *Missing Links 1* master # WZB3-0140
3. 'Daddy's Song' overdub onto take 21
Head master # WZB3-0110

Personnel Lou Blackburn (trombone 1,2), Larry Bunker (glockenspiel 1, tambourine 2), Herbie Harper (trombone 1,2), Bill Hood (saxophone 1,2), Cappy Lewis [Carroll Lewis] (trumpet 1,2, flugelhorn 3*), Michel Rubini (tack piano 1, piano 2), Stu Williamson (trumpet 1,2, flugelhorn 3*). * Lewis or Williamson on flugelhorn; more likely Lewis.

● The production of the group's next single, 'D.W. Washburn,' is fleshed out with some punchy horn charts from Shorty Rogers, a little glockenspiel from jazz veteran Larry Bunker, and a touch of tack piano courtesy of Michel Rubini. (A tack piano is one with specially hardened hammers for a percussive, jangling sound.) Micky's vocal will be added on April 3rd and the completed production mixed on April 23rd.

Key overdubs such as piano, tambourine, and brass are added to Micky's 'Rose Marie,' but the production of the song is still in flux.

Further brass augmentation will occur on March 14th. The master for Nilsson's 'Daddy's Song' is also revised at this session to include a prominent flugelhorn. The song is now slated for inclusion in The Monkees' movie and so will go through a number of edits and transfers later this month.

● Sunday 3rd
FILMING The group – along with a 110-member film crew – travel to Palm Springs, California, to shoot desert sequences for their motion picture. The company stays at the Erawan Arden Hotel. The first day of shooting is close to a bust when a tank that Micky is scripted to drive breaks down. New treads are brought in for the vehicle from Los Angeles this afternoon but it is too late in the day to continue filming.

● Monday 4th
FILMING Day two of the group's Palm Springs desert shoot focuses solely on Micky, leaving the other Monkees to enjoy a day off.
TV At 7:30pm the crew assemble to watch episode 56 of the *Monkees* second series, *Some Like It Lukewarm*, broadcast by NBC. Micky is so exhausted from standing out in the hot sun all day that he falls asleep well before the program begins.

TVseries

The Monkees

EPISODE 56: *SOME LIKE IT LUKEWARM*
BROADCAST MARCH 4TH
When the group enters a mixed-gender 'rockathon' Davy learns that band contests can be a drag.
WRITERS: JOEL KANE, STANLEY Z. CHERRY. DIRECTOR: JAMES FRAWLEY.
SONGS 'The Door Into Summer,' 'She Hangs Out.'

● Tuesday 5th
● Davy's former business manager, Hal Cone, is placed on two years' probation and fined $900 on his conviction of 15 felony counts stemming from the sale of stolen blank airline tickets. This will not prevent Cone from suing Davy for $5m next month (see April 12th).
FILMING Micky's tank scenes and the surrender of the Italian army are completed by 10:00am on this third day of movie shooting in the desert. After a break all four Monkees are filmed being approached by a band of Arabs, and then being fired at with arrows by Native Americans. Shooting wraps at 4:30pm due to an impending sandstorm. Davy recalls: "It was terribly hot. The temperature went up to 105 degrees at times. On the third day we had a sandstorm, which really caused a panic. We were OK though as everyone put on goggles and face masks until it blew itself out."

● Friday 8th
RECORDING RCA *Hollywood, CA* 8:00-11:00pm. Peter Tork *prod*; one-inch 8-track; overdubs.
1. 'Can You Dig It'
   Head master # WZB3-0123
Personnel Eddie Hoh (instrument unknown), Dom DeMieri (instrument unknown).
● Peter holds a short sweetening date more than a month after his last session for this song. It seems unlikely that Hoh and DeMieri provide any significant instrumentation for the final production since rough mixes from last month showed the track to be virtually complete save for Micky's lead vocal. Whatever the circumstances, this will be the final recording session for 'Can You Dig It,' which will be mixed for use in the group's movie on August 1st.

● Saturday 9th
● The Los Angeles *Herald-Examiner* recently sent reporter Harrison Carroll to the set of the group's *Untitled* movie and his lengthy report on the peculiar nature of the film is published in the paper today. "The scene today is a street at the Columbia studio," writes Carroll. "On top of a building, a pretty girl in a bikini, June Fairchild, is threatening to jump. There is a crowd of people watching her. Included are the four Monkees … nobody is doing anything about the girl's threats to jump. They are just watching.

"I ask director Bob Rafelson what is the meaning of the scene. 'It shows people's complete disinterest in each other,' he says. 'The boys are not worried about what will happen to the girl. They are just betting among themselves as to whether she will jump.' What audience will the picture appeal to? 'Young teenagers,' [Rafelson] replies. 'We also are including some anti-war and anti-brutality sequences. [Which] may win the interest of older fans.'

Carroll continues: "Like the rest of the crowd I stand waiting for the girl to jump. Presently, the four Monkees get bored. They go to a nearby men's room. There, I am told, they hear the roar of the crowd, indicating that the bikini-clad beauty has made the leap. They pay off the bets. But when they come out for the next scene, June Fairchild, the leaper, is standing there unharmed."

Carroll later approaches Michael for clarification of the scene and gets an entirely different story. It seems that the director and actors may be working from two different scripts. "Well," says Michael, "when the four of us are in the men's room, we open up a cabinet and see the head of Victor Mature. One of the biggest sequences in the movie takes place in Victor Mature's hair."

Carroll asks Michael if there is a plot to this movie. "A very deep plot," he answers, "but it won't be readily apparent if you see the picture only once." Michael feels that revealing the film's plot for Carroll's article "wouldn't be fair."
● In the charts The Monkees' latest single 'Valleri' debuts at an impressive #24 while *Billboard's* Top LPs chart includes the group's first four albums. Meanwhile in the studio the final tracking session is held for the band's fifth long-player.

RECORDING RCA *Hollywood, CA* 4:30-7:30, 8:30-11:30pm. Lester Sill, Shorty Rogers, Jack Keller *prod*; Pete Abbott *eng*; half-inch 4-track, one-inch 8-track; tracking.

1. **'Wasn't Born To Follow'** takes 1-3
   unissued master # WZB3-0144
2. **'I'll Be Back Up On My Feet'** version 3 takes 1-5
   The Birds, The Bees & The Monkees master # WZB3-0141
3. **'The Shadow Of A Man'** takes 1-2
   unissued master # WZB3-0142
4. **'A Man Without A Dream'** version 3 takes 1-11
   unissued master # WZB3-0143
5. **'If I Ever Get To Saginaw Again'** takes 1-2
   Missing Links 2 master # WZB3-0178
6. **'All The Grey Haired Men'** takes 1-12
   unissued master # WZB3-0179

Personnel Max Bennett (bass), Dennis Budimir (guitar), Al Casey (guitar), Mike Deasy (guitar), Milt Holland (percussion including mallets 1, tambourine 2,3,4,5,6, quica* 2, vibes* 3,4,5,6), Stan Levey (percussion including mallets 1, tambourine 2,3,4,5,6, quica* 2, vibes* 3,4,5,6), Michael Melvoin (harpsichord 1,2,5,6, organ 3, piano 4), Earl Palmer (drums). * Holland or Levey on quica and on vibes.

● Six songs in six hours – and not a Monkee in sight. Lester Sill and Shorty Rogers return to the production formula of 1966 as they work today to cut some pop tracks to help fill out what is shaping up to be The Monkees' most stylistically chaotic album. Since the group are now consumed with making their movie, *Untitled*, this session garners little interest from The Monkees or at the very least falls well beneath their radar. If they had been in attendance they might have taken issue with the first track cut, Goffin & King's lovely rolling 'Wasn't Born To Follow.'

Just three takes are made with only the final pass complete and considered a potential master. The song is undoubtedly a fine composition but its selection is unusual given that little more than a month ago The Byrds issued the same song on their *Notorious Byrd Brothers* album. Raybert are without doubt aware of this version since it will feature prominently in their next movie production, *Easy Rider* (released in 1969). In response to the success of that film The Byrds' version will be issued as a single. But this 'Monkees' version will go no further than take 3 and will remain unissued and largely unadorned.

'I'll Be Back Up On My Feet' is another song that would be familiar to The Monkees (and their fans) since it was featured in the first season of their TV series. But it has yet to be included on any of the group's record releases. An attempt to revive the song in August 1967 proved a total failure, but today's rendition is easily captured and completed for the next album. The Latin-flavored arrangement by Shorty Rogers is dominated by the curious 'rubbing' sound of the quica percussion instrument but also features three guitars (two electric and one acoustic). Of the five surprisingly similar takes, take 4 is considered the master and will be transferred to another reel so that in the next few days Micky's lead vocal can be

added along with vocal backgrounds from an uncredited group of singers. A brass arrangement will also be added to the track, on March 14th.

'The Shadow Of A Man,' highlighted by vibes and organ, might be ideal for The Monkees but apparently does not develop beyond the two takes made today. It is possible that this recording is deemed unsuccessful as the only complete version – take 2 – is marked merely "hold" rather than "master."

After an hour-long break the crew resume with a new, third version of Goffin & King's 'A Man Without A Dream.' Today's arrangement closely resembles version 2 of the song taped during the latter half of '67. The final take here will be marked as a master, but no further overdubs will be made to the recording, which is left incomplete after this session. An all-new fourth version will be taped on November 7th by producer Bones Howe.

During the tracking of 'A Man Without A Dream' songwriter Jack Keller joins the session to rib the studio musicians with a few jokes. His real role is to supervise the taping of the next two songs, which are his compositions (in collaboration with Bob Russell). After a few run-throughs, the Glen Campbell-like 'If I Ever Get To Saginaw Again' is recorded in just two takes. Keller instructs the musicians to "attack it with the same fervor in which you just rehearsed it and it will be a smash." The musicians nail the song immediately, with take 2 marked as the master, but nothing further will be done with the track until next year (see January 31st 1969).

The intriguing 'All The Grey Haired Men' will also sit in the can for a year before a string arrangement is added on that same day in January 1969. In the meantime vocal group The Lettermen will issue a version as a single in May on Capitol which enters the *Billboard* chart on June 8th but disappears after just two weeks, going no higher than #109.

● **Monday 11th**
TV Episode 57 of the second series of *The Monkees*, titled *Monkees Blow Their Minds*, is broadcast at 7:30pm by the NBC network.

LEFT **Davy enjoys a visit from British pop singer Lulu on the** *Head* **set.** ABOVE **Micky and Michael plan a movie scene with June Fairchild, whose character is threatening to jump off a building.**

● Wednesday 13th

FILMING Shooting for *Untitled* continues in Los Angeles with a canteen sequence and marching-band footage. Meanwhile in the studio most of the group's next album is mixed.

RECORDING Western Recorders (3) *6000 Sunset Boulevard, Hollywood, CA.* Henry Lewy *eng*; quarter-inch mono and stereo; mixdown.

1. **'We Were Made For Each Other'** version 2
   The Birds, The Bees & The Monkees master # UZB3-9779
2. **'Dream World'**
   The Birds, The Bees & The Monkees master # WZB3-0127
3. **'Rose Marie'**
   unissued master # WZB3-0140
4. **'Zor And Zam'**
   The Birds, The Bees & The Monkees master # WZB3-0108
5. **'I'll Be Back Up On My Feet'** version 3
   unissued master # WZB3-0141
6. **'Alvin'**
   unissued master # WZB3-0124
7. **'The Poster'**
   The Birds, The Bees & The Monkees master # WZB3-0136
8. **'Tapioca Tundra'** version 1
   The Birds, The Bees & The Monkees master # UZB3-9783
9. **'Writing Wrongs'**
   The Birds, The Bees & The Monkees master # UZB3-9789
10. **'My Share Of The Sidewalk'** version 1
    Missing Links 1 master # WZB3-0109 formerly UZB3-9795

● Ten songs are mixed for potential use on The Monkees' upcoming album, *The Birds, The Bees & The Monkees*. These will be the final released mono and stereo mixes of 'We Were Made For Each Other,' 'Dream World,' 'Zor And Zam,' and 'The Poster.'

Today also sees production for the album of a new stereo mix of Michael's 'Tapioca Tundra' (the recent single release of this song featured a unique mono mix) and 'Writing Wrongs,' which was probably mixed in mono at an earlier session. Mono and stereo rough mixes are also made of Micky's 'Rose Marie,' which is still relatively unfinished. It will receive further brass augmentation at a session tomorrow.

Another recording due for a brass overdub is 'I'll Be Back Up On My Feet,' which is mixed in mono and stereo today without that crucial element. A further oddity produced today is a stereo mix of 'My Share Of The Sidewalk,' complete with a Davy lead vocal. This won't make it to *The Birds...* and is not released until 1987's *Missing Links* compilation. Similarly, Peter's 'Alvin' will not find contemporary release but at this point is still a serious contender for the album (see March 19th). Peter is hoping that another of his songs, 'Lady's Baby,' will be included on the LP. He holds his own mix session for it today at another studio.

RECORDING Sunset Sound Recorders (2) *6650 Sunset Boulevard, Hollywood, CA* 2:00-5:00pm. Peter Tork *prod*; Gene Shiveley *eng*; quarter-inch mono; mixdown.

1. **'Lady's Baby'** version 5
   unissued master # UZB3-9784

● This session apparently produces the first serious mix of Peter's long-in-the-works 'Lady's Baby,' and the resulting mono mixdown will probably be submitted along with the other tracks mixed today for *The Birds, The Bees & The Monkees*. Predictably, given the convoluted history of this song's recording, Peter is dissatisfied with the initial results and will hold a further mix session for the song on Sunday. Today's mix will go unused and is never heard publicly. Significantly, it lacks the 'real life baby' sound-effects that were once a part of Peter's aural master plan.

● Thursday 14th

RECORDING RCA *Hollywood, CA* 9:00am-1:30pm. Shorty Rogers *prod*; Pete Abbott *eng*; one-inch 8-track; reductions, overdubs.

1. **'I'll Be Back Up On My Feet'** version 3 overdubs onto take 4
   The Birds, The Bees & The Monkees master # WZB3-0141
2. **'It's Nice To Be With You'**
   Greatest Hits master # WZB3-0129
3. **'Rose Marie'**
   Instant Replay or Missing Links 1 master # WZB3-0140

Personnel Lou Blackburn (trombone), Buddy Childers (trumpet), Bill Hood (saxophone), Lew McCreary (trombone), Ollie Mitchell (trumpet).

● The primary purpose today is to commit to tape Shorty Rogers's brass arrangement for 'I'll Be Back Up On My Feet.' After this session the song is probably mixed down to mono and stereo for inclusion on *The Birds, The Bees & The Monkees* – making yesterday's mixes of the song redundant.

Rogers also supplements his previous arrangements for 'It's Nice To Be With You' and 'Rose Marie.' It is possible that only trumpeters Ollie Mitchell and Buddy Childers are involved in this part of the session.

'Rose Marie' certainly goes through a few significant changes today as it is bounced to another 8-track tape to create a new master. During this process Peter's acoustic-guitar fills as well as some of Micky's acoustic work is dumped to make room for additional vocal tracks from Micky and for today's horn overdubs.

'Rose Marie' will meander through further changes at a session on June 7th.

An hour into today's session, another Monkees recording date is getting underway at the nearby T.T.G. studio for a Carole King song, 'Look Down.'

RECORDING T.T.G. *Hollywood, CA* 10:00am-1:00, 2:00-5:00pm. possibly Gerry Goffin *prod*; tracking.

1. **'Look Down'** version 1
   unissued no master #

Personnel Danny 'Kootch' Kortchmar (guitar), Doug Lubahn (bass), Michael Ney (drums, percussion), Ralph Schuckett (keyboards), Dallas Taylor (drums, percussion).

● Given the musicians involved in this session it is likely that Gerry Goffin produces the date. The song at hand is composed by his wife Carole King (in collaboration with Toni Stern). Much like another Goffin production from this period, 'Dear Marm,' no tapes will survive of today's recording. A guitar and brass overdub session will follow tomorrow.

● Friday 15th

RECORDING T.T.G. *Hollywood, CA* 10:00am-1:00pm. possibly Gerry Goffin *prod*; overdubs.

1. **'Look Down'** version 1
   unissued no master #

Personnel Ken Bloom (guitar), Lew McCreary (trombone), Ollie Mitchell (trumpet), Stu Williamson (trumpet).

● A sweetening session is held for yesterday's recordings. Again, no tapes will survive, but a second version of 'Look Down' with entirely different personnel will be taped on April 6th.

● Saturday 16th

● Today's *NME* says that The Monkees' film, *Untitled*, will feature 100 minutes of sight gags, 11 songs, and 20 totally different plots. Each Monkee will wear 11 different costumes in the film.

Ever since last month's shoot with Sonny Liston (see February 27th) Davy has kept in touch with the boxer and tonight some of the

group travel to Reno, Nevada, to see their *Head* co-star Liston fight Bill McMurray at the Centennial Stadium.

The group are due to be more active on other fronts now that their TV series has definitely been cancelled, reports *NME*. In addition to filming three television specials for next season, Jackie Cooper of Screen Gems says that the group will now go out on two concert tours a year. He says they will also increase their recorded output. *NME*: "Another revolutionary idea in the works is that The Monkees are recording two albums at the same time and are hoping to release one on a Monday and another seven days later. This would be a record-industry first."

● Michael has reportedly sold his instrumental *Wichita Train Whistle* album to MGM-Verve, with a release due in three months.

● Micky's girlfriend Samantha Juste is hoping to open a clothing boutique in Hollywood.

● *Billboard* reports that the group have received their tenth gold record award from the RIAA, this one for outstanding U.S. sales of their latest single, 'Valleri.' The record hit sales of a million within three days of release.

● Sunday 17th
RECORDING Sunset Sound Recorders (2) *Hollywood, CA*. Peter Tork *prod*; Gene Shiveley *eng*; quarter-inch mono; mixdown.
1. 'Lady's Baby' version 5
    Missing Links 1 master # UZB3-9784
● Peter works again with engineer Gene Shiveley to create a second series of mono mixes of 'Lady's Baby,' featuring a new vocal track probably recorded in the last four days. The recording will be submitted for consideration on the group's next album, but is passed over. Nevertheless, one of today's mixes will surface a full 20 years later on the CD version of Rhino's *Missing Links* compilation.

● Monday 18th
TV The NBC television network reruns episode 39 of the *Monkees* series, *Hillbilly Honeymoon*.

● Tuesday 19th
FILMING Shooting continues for The Monkees' *Untitled* movie at Columbia's 'ranch.' Today's footage includes the group driving in a Dean Jeffries customized yellow dune buggy, and a hanging sequence. When filming wraps for the day Micky hosts a screening of The Beatles' *Magical Mystery Tour* at his home.

● In the studio, engineer Pete Abbott assembles a stereo master for the group's next album, which becomes *The Birds, The Bees & The Monkees*, with the following line-up: Side One: 'Through The Looking Glass' / 'We Were Made For Each Other' / 'Writing Wrongs' / 'I'll Be Back Up On My Feet' / 'Valleri' / 'Long Title: Do I Have To Do This All Over Again.' Side Two: 'Dream World' / 'P.O. Box 9847' / 'Tapioca Tundra' / 'The Poster' / 'Alvin' / 'Daydream Believer' / 'Zor And Zam.'

Over the next week the album will be recompiled and resequenced, resulting in a number of musical casualties. 'Through The Looking Glass' will be dropped from the album and eventually remixed for its appearance on next year's *Instant Replay*. (The mix of the song intended for *The Birds…* is later included as a bonus track on 1995's expanded CD reissue of *Instant Replay*).

Today's master also features 'I'll Be Back Up On My Feet' and 'Valleri' in some form of quasi-medley probably achieved through editing. They will be completely separated and resequenced on the final release. Likewise 'The Poster' and 'Alvin' are edited together in Abbott's compilation to form a medley. Not only will they be separated for the final release but 'Alvin' will be dropped entirely and the master tapes for this spoken track lost in the process.

More shooting for the presently *Untitled* movie, here at Columbia's 'ranch' lot. The group's dune buggy was customized by Monkeemobile designer Dean Jeffries.

Not lost but certainly dropped is Peter's 'Long Title: Do I Have To Do This All Over Again,' which will later be remixed for inclusion on the group's next album, *Head*. The musical reshuffle for *The Birds, The Bees & The Monkees* will leave Peter with no material on the album. Instead, two more of Michael's songs will be added to the disc, 'Auntie's Municipal Court' and 'Magnolia Simms,' making him the best represented composer on the set with four songwriting credits. Davy will snag two credits with 'The Poster' and 'Dream World' while Micky will have no songwriting credits but at least the inclusion of his production of 'Zor And Zam.' A recompiled master will be assembled the week after next (see April 4th).

● Friday 22nd
'Valleri' / 'Tapioca Tundra' single is released in the U.K.

● Saturday 23rd
● *Billboard* publishes a second ad hyping Michael's *Wichita Train Whistle Sings* project – which despite prior reports to the contrary has yet to find a home. The full-page ad is paid for by Michael's management and reads: "From the creative genius that is Mike Nesmith comes the musical brilliance that is The Wichita Train Whistle." Meanwhile in the studio engineer Pete Abbott works on 'Daddy's Song.'
RECORDING RCA *Hollywood, CA*. Pete Abbott *eng*; one-inch 8-track; transfers.
1. 'Daddy's Song'
   Head master # WZB3-0110
● Abbott makes two copies of the final multi-track of this recording. They will be used in conjunction with the filmed performance of the song for the group's movie and/or will be dubbed into the soundtrack.

● Monday 25th
TV The final first-run primetime episode of the second series of *The Monkees*, titled *Mijacogeo (The Frodis Caper)*, is broadcast at 7:30pm by the NBC network.
FILMING The group near the end of their six-week shooting schedule for the *Untitled* movie this week.

   Footage probably made now includes some unusual shots of The Monkees who, suspended by wires, are dressed in white to appear as particles of dandruff that will then be sucked through a vacuum cleaner's hose.

● Tuesday 26th
● *The Hollywood Reporter* says that two days of filming for The Monkees' movie is now completed and that there will be a ten-day respite while Davy rehearses a musical dance number set to 'Daddy's Song.' Production will resume on April 8th at Columbia. *Untitled* is currently planned for a mid-summer release.

● Wednesday 27th
● The group wrap filming on *Untitled* for a few weeks, supposedly to concentrate on the movie's soundtrack. Sporadic shooting on the feature will continue through April, including a trip to Paramount Studios where a set from *Rosemary's Baby* is used for a birthday-party sequence. One hundred extras are brought in for this event along with pop artist Edward Keinholz and his 1964 sculpture *Back Seat Dodge '38*. (The piece will later go on display at the Los Angeles County Museum Of Art.)

● Friday 29th
RECORDING RCA *Hollywood, CA*. One-inch 8-track; transfers.
1. 'Daddy's Song'
   Head master # WZB3-0110
● At this final session of the month another set of copies are made of 'Daddy's Song' for use in Davy's dance number in the movie. The song will be mixed for record release later this year.

● Saturday 30th
● *NME* reports that the group are now more than half way through the shooting schedule of their movie. Completion is set for April 29th, though further scenes might still be shot in Japan. When filming wraps, Davy is planning a visit to Britain to see his father and to make some television appearances, including one for Lulu's upcoming television series.
● In the charts 'Valleri' peaks at #3 on *Billboard's* Hot 100 this week. The single's flipside, 'Tapioca Tundra,' which has earned a remarkable amount of airplay considering its off-beat nature, also peaks this week at a respectable #34.

   In Britain 'Valleri' entered the charts last Wednesday (27th) and the single will have a mild eight-week run, peaking at #12. This is the band's lowest 45 placing so far in the U.K. since the 'Last Train To Clarksville' single.

   Elsewhere in the world 'Daydream Believer' is a Top 10 item in

A bizarre Head sequence has the group dressed in white suits as particles of dandruff, while the large cigarette in the foreground is the movie's only overt drug reference.

Japan, Malaysia, and The Philippines, where Davy's 'Hard To Believe' currently places at #5. Meanwhile, Mexico is still seemingly gripped by the early sounds of the group, with '(Theme From) The Monkees' at #6 and a single of 'Look Out (Here Comes Tomorrow)' at #4.

APRIL

The Birds, The Bees & The Monkees album is released in the U.S.A. This is the group's fifth LP, and in America it will be their last issued in separate mono and stereo editions. Later albums will appear in mono for various other territories, but these will simply feature the normal stereo mix combined to a single channel. In fact most of the group's earlier foreign albums used this technique and do not feature the exclusive mono mixes that were issued in the U.S.A., Canada, and South America.
● *Monkees Monthly* reports that Jackie Cooper of Screen Gems is more than pleased with the decision to abandon the *Monkees* TV series in favor of three hour-long specials. "The Monkees grossed $2m on their last tour," says Cooper. "They've sold 21 million records. Now that's more than we're going to make in a 26-week half-hour series that ties you up for so much time."

The Birds, The Bees & The Monkees album

A1 'Dream World' (D. JONES / S. PITTS)
A2 'Auntie's Municipal Court' (M. NESMITH / K. ALLISON)
A3 'We Were Made For Each Other' version 2 (C. BAYER / G. FISCHOFF)
A4 'Tapioca Tundra' version 1 (M. NESMITH)
A5 'Daydream Believer' (J. STEWART)
A6 'Writing Wrongs' (M. NESMITH)
B1 'I'll Be Back On My Feet' version 3 (S. LINZER / D. RANDELL)
B2 'The Poster' (D. JONES / S. PITTS)
B3 'P.O. Box 9847' (T. BOYCE / B. HART)
B4 'Magnolia Simms' (M. NESMITH)
B5 'Valleri' version 2 (T. BOYCE / B. HART)
B6 'Zor And Zam' (B. CHADWICK / J. CHADWICK)

U.S. release April 1968 (Colgems COM-109 mono / COS-109 stereo).
U.K. release July 5th 1968 (RCA 7948).
Chart high U.S. number 3; U.K. none.

● **Monday 1st**
TV At 7:30pm the NBC television network reruns episode 34 of the *Monkees* series, *The Picture Frame*.

● **Tuesday 2nd**
RECORDING California Recorders *Hollywood, CA* 7:00pm-1:00am. Gerry Goffin *prod*; overdubs.
1. **'Dear Marm'**
   unissued master # WZB4-3514

Personnel Lowell George (guitar).
● This follow-up to an earlier session for the song on February 16th has guitarist Lowell George adding overdubs to the mysterious 'Dear Marm,' probably under the direction of Russ Titelman. It's the final stop for what becomes a lost Goffin & King-composed Monkees track, reported to run for approximately two-and-a-half minutes. Later this year George will reappear to play on some of Peter's self-financed non-Monkees sessions. (In the 1970s George will form cult band Little Feat.)

● **Wednesday 3rd**
RECORDING RCA *Hollywood, CA*. One-inch 8-track; overdubs.
1. **'Porpoise Song'**
   Head master # WZB4-3513
2. **'D.W. Washburn'**
   Greatest Hits master # WZB3-0130
Personnel Micky Dolenz (vocal).
● Micky enjoys some time off from shooting *Untitled* and adds his voice to The Monkees' next two single A-sides. 'D.W. Washburn' will be mixed for release on April 23rd.

● **Thursday 4th**
● Final masters for The Monkees' fifth album, *The Birds, The Bees & The Monkees*, are assembled at RCA with the revised track listing and copied for the various non-U.S. territories where the record will now be issued. In the same building, Davy amends the multi-track for 'Daddy's Song.'
RECORDING RCA *Hollywood, CA* 6:30-10:00pm. One-inch 8-track; overdubs.
1. **'Daddy's Song'** overdubs onto take 21
   Music Box master # WZB3-0110
Personnel David Jones (vocal), Michel Rubini (piano).
● Amid the shooting of his dance spotlight for *Untitled*, Davy returns to the studio to tweak the featured tune, 'Daddy's Song.' It is now planned to have Davy sing a verse of 'Daddy's Song' live – with some string accompaniment from arranger Ken Thorne, to be added during final scoring for the movie – and so tonight he adds a similar section to the version due to be issued on the accompanying soundtrack album. The short insert – beginning with the passage "The years have passed, and so have I…" – is taped with simple piano accompaniment from studio regular Michel Rubini. But the insert will never be used. (In 2001 it will be mixed and integrated into the regular released version of 'Daddy's Song' for Rhino's *Music Box* collection.)

● **Friday 5th**
RECORDING RCA *Hollywood, CA* 7:30-10:00, 10:00pm-1:30am. Michael Nesmith *prod*; Pete Abbott, Pat Iaerci *eng*; one-inch 8-track; tracking.
1. **'Carlisle Wheeling'** version 3 takes 1-4
   Instant Replay master # UZB3-9782
2. **'Nine Times Blue'** version 4 takes 1-17
   Missing Links 1 master # WZB3-0125
Personnel Chip Douglas (bass), Michael Nesmith (electric 12-string guitar), Red Rhodes (pedal steel guitar).
● This is a new recording of 'Carlisle Wheeling,' even though it retains the master number of Michael's previous 'Monkees' version of the song from November 1967. In comparison to that take (and the instrumental *Wichita Train Whistle* cut) today's version is performed in a stripped-down arrangement with a slower, laidback country feel, and no drums. The song is perfected in just four takes, with Michael adding a lead vocal and an additional acoustic guitar

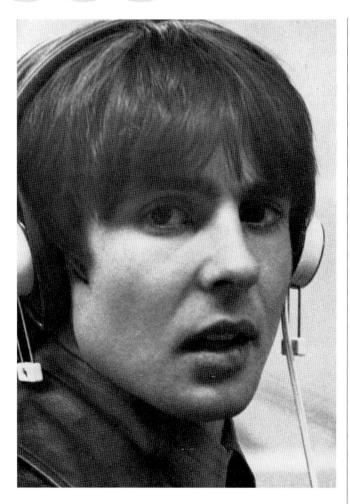

part to the final take at this or another recording session. The track will be mixed on April 11th.

The second half of Michael's session tonight is given over to recording 'Nine Times Blue' for a fourth time. The resulting recording is the best yet, and Michael will treat the final performance from this session, take 17, to further overdubs of lead and harmony vocals, as well as acoustic guitar. Nevertheless, it will never find contemporary release and only creeps out years later on Rhino's 1987 *Missing Links* collection. Michael will cut a fifth version of the song during 1970.

● Saturday 6th
● The *NME* publishes a report by Ann Moses from the set of *Untitled*. After watching some shooting and rehearsals she quizzes Peter on the script's incomprehensible dialogue. "Actually there are several levels of understanding and a couple of levels of meaning," he explains. "It's not going to be funny," admits Michael. "We are not the stars. The movie stars Victor Mature and Annette Funicello. We won't even be billed as stars."

"What we're doing is not a comedy," says director Bob Rafelson, "but it's funny. It sounds campy, but it's the enemy of camp. It opens with one of The Monkees committing suicide. It's kind of a trip." Davy tells Moses that the film's incidental score may be composed by Michael. As for the group's new album, *The Birds, The Bees & The Monkees*, which will precede the movie, Peter notes that it represents a major change for the group. "I felt much more involved in the music that I wrote for [that] album," he says. "The only trouble with

the ... LP is that it's going to be too scattered. It's not going to have a unifying factor. Like Mike's things will be all Mike. He's the producer on those cuts. We did almost no collaboration."

Davy feels the group are making an error by penning all their own material. "Everybody makes the mistake of putting all their own songs on an album," he says. "In fact, when The Beatles first started they had other people writing; now they're doing all their own stuff. I think there are too many good songwriters around today to put all our own things on an album. There are songwriters better than The Beatles around – Gerry Goffin & Carole King, Howard Greenfield, people like that. They all write unbelievable songs. So if you use all your own songs, you're really cutting your own throat. For the next album we have a couple of monologues by Peter and we have some different endings and different beginnings. There will be some very weird chord changes and songs that are not ultra-commercial like most have been. I just hope the kids go into this new phase of music [and] accept it for what it is – The Monkees growing."

For the kids who don't follow, *NME* reports that Don Kirshner has a new television series planned. Kirshner is said to be forming a new four-piece group, and British songwriters Tony Macaulay and John Macleod have been approached to provide the music. "My new group – which I haven't named yet – will comprise two American boys and two British lads," says Kirshner. "Although they won't actually be seen performing in the series, I shall put them out as an attraction in their own right as soon as the TV shows hit the screen." Kirshner has already sold the series (without a group) in America, Japan, and Australia. The records will be available through Kirshner's link with RCA. "Once the TV series is established, we shall make a live, full-length cinema film starring the group," adds Kirshner. "It will be produced by [James Bond filmmaker] Harry Saltzman." Kirshner is now in London ironing out the details.

Meanwhile in the studio Carole King's 'Look Down' is cut for a second time.

RECORDING T.T.G. *Hollywood, CA* 10:00am-1:00pm. Lester Sill *prod*; Jack ?, Angel ? *eng*; one-inch 8-track; tracking.

1. 'Look Down' version 2 takes 1-6
Missing Links 3 master # WZB4 -3515
Personnel Hal Blaine (drums), Dennis Budimir (guitar), Al Casey (guitar), Jules Chaikin (trumpet), Jim Horn (saxophone), Larry Knechtel (bass), Lew McCreary (trombone), Jay Migliori (saxophone), Michel Rubini (piano), Tommy Tedesco (guitar), Tony Terran (trumpet), Ken Watson (percussion).
● Artie Butler arranges today's version of 'Look Down,' which is taped easily in six takes by many of L.A.'s key 'wrecking crew' of musicians. The song is an upbeat contrast to much of the Carole King material recently cut for the group, which has ranged from the super-slow 'Porpoise Song' to the mild, mid-tempo 'Wasn't Born To Follow.' Caught somewhere between bubblegum and soul, 'Look Down' is an obvious candidate for Davy to sing. And he will do just that, probably adding his vocal to today's track at a session next month. King obviously has a direction in mind for the singer and will tape a full guide vocal for Davy to follow. A rough mix of today's take 6 will be made on the 25th of this month.

● Sunday 7th
● Michael works at Wally Heider's studio from 1:00 to 4:00pm with The Penny Arkade on their recordings 'Give Our Love (To All The People)' and 'Odds And Ends.' Since last summer he has produced a dozen or more tracks with the band for his American Wichita Corp., none of which will find contemporary release. (In 2004 many of these recordings will be featured on a Sundazed-label CD released by the band, *Not The Freeze*, but 'Odds And Ends' is not included on the set.)

● Monday 8th

TV At 7:30pm the NBC television network reruns episode 35 of the *Monkees* series, *Everywhere A Sheik, Sheik*.
● At the Columbia lot Davy films his dance sequence for the *Untitled* movie.

● Tuesday 9th

RECORDING Western Recorders (1) *Hollywood, CA* 7:30-11:30pm. Micky Dolenz *prod*; Henry Lewy *eng*; one-inch 8-track; tracking, overdubs.
1. **'Just A Game'** version 2 takes 1-3
   Instant Replay master # WZB5-5311
2. **'Shorty Blackwell'**
   Instant Replay master # WZB3-0116
Personnel Max Bennett (bass), George Berres (violin), Bud Brisbois (trumpet), Buddy Childers (trumpet), Vincent DeRosa (French horn), Justin DiTullio (cello), Micky Dolenz (acoustic guitar 1, vocal 1 [take 3 only]), David Duke (French horn), Jim Gordon (drums, percussion 2), Anatol Kaminsky (violin), Armand Kaproff (cello), Bernard Kundell (violin), Ronnie Lang (flute), Edgar Lustgarten (cello), Ollie Mitchell (trumpet), Ted Nash (flute), Erno Neufeld (violin), Dick Perissi (French horn), Joe Porcaro (percussion 1, percussion including tympani and mallets 2), George Roberts (trombone), Nathan Ross (violin), Michel Rubini (harpsichord 1, piano 2), Bud Shank (flute), Joseph Stepansky (violin), Tommy Tedesco (acoustic guitar 1, electric 12-string guitar 2), Ray Triscari (trumpet).
● Strangely, Micky's 'Just A Game' is announced by engineer Henry Lewy as 'French Song' – a title later used by Davy for one of his songs. But it is actually a remake of a number that Micky first aired at the tail end of the *Headquarters* sessions under the working title 'There's A Way.' The song, with its new official name, carries the same simple melody of the '67 version but now boasts a lovely score arranged by Shorty Rogers. Micky performs all three takes live with the full ensemble. The final take, number 3, is marked as the master and will be treated to further overdubs on June 7th.
   Micky next returns to work on his mini-opera 'Shorty Blackwell,' adding today's huge ensemble to his fascinating suite of musical movements. The production, now too with an expert arrangement by Shorty Rogers, is virtually complete by the end of the session. Nevertheless, even more musical embellishments will be added to the track at a session on April 30th.

● Thursday 11th

FILMING The group resume shooting of their movie at Columbia's 'ranch' lot. Footage shot includes some underwater sequences (likely in a pool) and action on the 'old West' set. Meanwhile in the studio Michael mixes 'Carlisle Wheeling.'
RECORDING Location unknown. Michael Nesmith *prod*; quarter-inch mono; mixdown.
1. **'Carlisle Wheeling'** version 3 take 4
   Instant Replay master # UZB3-9782
● Some time after his filming obligations are complete, Michael makes a mono mix of his latest version of 'Carlisle Wheeling.' Although today's mix is briefly considered for release on the *Instant*

Replay album (see January 10th 1969) it will be superseded by a stereo version featuring a new lead vocal track from Michael, dubbed down on August 21st. Before that, yet another variation of the song will be taped on May 3rd. Despite all this activity, the only version of 'Carlisle Wheeling' issued in the 1960s will be the instrumental version on *Wichita Train Whistle Sings*.
   Michael: "[I was] trying to get it right and not realizing until after I had tried several times that the problem was not in the recording. The problem was in the song. Early in life as an artist, and certainly before The Monkees ever came along, I was casting about for native design keys – native meaning native to myself – that I could work in. One of the ones that I came up with that was most satisfying and very easy for me was delight. Another one I came up with was whimsy, and they have served me well as I have gotten more and more into them.
   "But the problem is that when you work in delight and whimsy and things like that, you are beset on all sides. It's a razor-edge line to walk and the foment is poignancy, sentimentality, maudlin, and all of the things that take those dandy little notions and just cast them into the worst elements of sentimentality and shallowness.
   'I'm afraid that as I was making an attempt to write this song I got knocked off the straight and narrow, because this was a song of reverie and of retrospection and contemplation. Those dynamics are just as subject to poignancy and sentimentality as anything else. That's what happened to this song: it just got cratered. I started to torture the metaphors and torture the similes, that's what happened to it. 'The phoenix of our love' – I mean, please! We're just right off into 'excuse me' land. All of us have got to do one of those I suppose.
   "'So forgive me my dear if I seem preoccupied.' I know that we're both old and settled in now and we don't say much to each other, but that doesn't mean that I still don't love you. Now that's a nice, sweet dynamic for a song. Unfortunately, I managed to murder it pretty good. It's written from the first person. I'm using 'he' like they used to use the author in the '40s and '50s when they wrote books."

● Friday 12th

● *The Hollywood Reporter* says that Davy's ex-manager and business partner Hal Cone has filed a $5m suit against Davy. The suit asks for damages stemming from a breach of contract among other things.

● Saturday 13th

● The *NME* publishes an interview with Michael by Keith Altham. "Our film is going to astound the world," he boasts. "I think it is fair to say that not even The Beatles would be able to duplicate what we are doing in this film. It's not like our TV series. It doesn't go 'bang, bang, bang;' it has more liquid composition and we stick to the script.
   "Everyone is in it from the mayor of Los Angeles and Annette Funicello to Sonny Liston, who beats up Davy in the film. He follows that with a scene in which the midliner from the Green Bay Packers throws body blocks at him. Davy is going to have a tough time.
   "We've just finished a scene in which Micky is in the desert dying of thirst when suddenly he sees a coke machine in the middle of all

Davy in the studio (LEFT) and performing his song-and-dance sequence to 'Daddy's Song' for The Monkees' movie (ABOVE).

the sand. He can't get his 30-cent piece in the machine because the only one he has is bent. When he does finally get the machine to accept it a little light comes on saying that the machine is empty. Then an Arab on a camel arrives from nowhere and whispers in his ear. Next minute the entire Italian army comes over the hill and surrenders to him!"

As for the war scenes, Michael admits: "We don't really say, 'War is hell,' but we imply it in the film. There is another sequence in a sewage factory where we get shut in a black box."

The black box represents The Monkees' career, and Michael makes his usual candid statements about the state of their union. "The Monkees are dead," he says. "We've been gently moving away from the prefabricated image of the four of us in the last few TV episodes. That's why we put in the little ad lib pieces on the end of the stories. We want to be thought of as real people. We are still largely victims of the monsters we helped to create, and people still expect us to act our TV parts in real life.

"Our next record is a reflection of that – in my opinion 'Valleri' is the worst record I have heard in my entire life! It isn't a step forward – it's a step back. 'Tapioca Tundra' on the flipside is the kind of musical progression we are trying to make." Furthermore, Michael sees the musical shift away from the psychedelia of *Pisces* as an obvious move. "I think flower power smoked itself to death, and the only thing that the rock'n'roll revivalists are doing is to underline the event of its death! 'Lady Madonna' is a type of rock'n'roll, of course, but the brilliant Beatles have done it again by giving it an entirely new twist. I'm hoping to do something similar with the *Wichita Train Whistle*, which will go out as an 18-piece big-band playing a fusion of rock'n'roll, country & western, and jazz. We could start the big-band

era rolling over again. I'm hoping to play concerts in some big cities – Chicago, New York, San Francisco – and conduct and direct the band myself."

Asked about the future of The Monkees on the small screen, Michael says: "At present we are negotiating on the basis of several [hour-long] spectaculars with NBC, but we've gone as far as we can with the series. We can't go on forever on the same line and we can't go on forever working as hard as we have. Now is the time for new directions."

● Sunday 14th
● *The New York Times* runs a piece about the title of The Monkees' film. "Later this summer Columbia plans to release a comedy called simply *Untitled*. Seems that the previous titles dreamed up for the first feature starring The Monkees, of TV and pop fame, just weren't appropriate to cover their bag of individuality. 'They are involved in a series of quick, anti-war, anti-establishment or just plain comedy vignettes, somewhat in the manner of the Beatles films,' said a Columbia spokesman. 'And director Bob Rafelson didn't think any of the titles suggested fit. Someone suggested *Untitled* and we all agreed pronto. Why not?' Why not indeed."

● Monday 15th
TV At 7:30pm the NBC television network reruns episode 36 of the *Monkees* series, *Monkee Mayor*.

● Wednesday 17th
● The group are awarded a gold record for outstanding sales of their album *The Birds, The Bees & The Monkees* – although it will take some

time for them to collect their plaques.
FILMING Work continues on the movie, including a ribbon-cutting segment shot on a bridge.

● Friday 19th
● *The Hollywood Reporter* notes that filming is due to wrap on The Monkees' film. Nevertheless, further filming and post-production on the feature will continue over the next several months.

● Saturday 20th
● The *NME* reports that Don Kirshner now plans to form two new groups. One will be for an animated cartoon series and the other will appear in a live-action film he is planning with James Bond producer Harry Saltzman. The animated series, *The Archies*, is to be based on a group of comic-book characters and will debut later this year. The motion picture group will be called Toomorrow: production on their feature is scheduled to commence in August. Kirshner's new RCA-distributed label is called Calendar Records, and he has already signed Steve Lawrence & Eydie Gorme.

● Monday 22nd
TV NBC reruns episode 37 of the *Monkees* series, *Art For Monkees' Sake*, at 7:30pm.

● Tuesday 23rd
RECORDING United Recorders *Hollywood, CA*. Henry Lewy *eng*; quarter-inch mono and stereo; mixdown.
1. **'D.W. Washburn'**
   Greatest Hits master # WZB3-0130
● Engineer Henry Lewy mixes The Monkees' next single A-side into both mono and stereo today. The song will not appear on any of the group's original albums so today's stereo mix will never find a contemporary release; much later it appears on several compilations issued by Rhino.

● Thursday 25th
RECORDING United Recorders (B) *6050 Sunset Boulevard, Hollywood, CA*. Henry Lewy *eng*; quarter-inch mono and stereo; mixdown.
1. **'It's Nice To Be With You'**
   Greatest Hits master # WZB3-0129
2. **'Look Down'** version 2 take 6
   Missing Links 3 master # WZB4 -3515
3. **'Daddy's Song'** take 21
   Head master # WZB3-0110
● More mixing from engineer Henry Lewy, who today works on the flipside of The Monkees' next single, 'It's Nice To Be With You,' mixing it into both mono and stereo at this session. Like 'D.W. Washburn,' 'It's Nice To Be With You' never appears on one of the group's original albums so today's stereo mix does not find a contemporary release, but will later appear on several compilations issued by Rhino.
   The version of 'Look Down' mixed just to mono today will never find release at all since it is just a mix of the backing track with no vocals (likely added to the track some time after this session). 'Daddy's Song' is also mixed in mono only, and parts of this

particular mix may be used in the film soundtrack – but not on the soundtrack album, which will feature a stereo mix made later this year.

● Monday 29th
TV At 7:30pm the NBC network reruns episode 38 of the *Monkees* series, *I Was A 99lb. Weakling*.

● Tuesday 30th
RECORDING Western Recorders *Hollywood, CA* 2:00-6:30pm. Micky Dolenz *prod*; Henry Lewy *eng*; one-inch 8-track; overdubs.
1. **'Shorty Blackwell'**
   Instant Replay master # WZB3-0116
Personnel Bud Brisbois (trumpet), Vincent DeRosa (French horn), Victor Feldman (percussion), Emil Richards (percussion), Kenny Shroyer (trombone).
● This is a further sweetening session for Micky's ambitious 'Shorty Blackwell.' Production will continue with dubbing of vocal tracks at a session on Thursday.

MAY

FILMING Micky and a special film crew travel to Paradise Island in The Bahamas some time this month to shoot underwater sequences for the opening segment of the group's movie.

● Thursday 2nd
RECORDING Western Recorders *Hollywood, CA* 9:00pm-12midnight. Micky Dolenz *prod*; Henry Lewy *eng*; one-inch 8-track; overdubs.
1. **'Shorty Blackwell'**
   Instant Replay master # WZB3-0116
Personnel Coco Dolenz (vocals), Micky Dolenzy (vocal).
● Micky and his sister Coco add lead and backing vocals to his 'Shorty Blackwell' this evening. It is also possible that pianist Michel Rubini attends this session to fix his piano parts on the track, but his name is later struck from the union contract, so perhaps no amendments are made. The production will be further refined at a session on June 7th.

● Friday 3rd
RECORDING Wally Heider Recording (3) *6373 Selma Avenue, Hollywood, CA* 1:00-4:00am, 5:00-8:00am; tracking.
1. **'Carlisle Wheeling'** version 4
   unissued no master #
Personnel Ken Bloom (guitar), Denny Bruce (percussion), Charles Larkey (bass), John Raines (drums), Neil Young (guitar).
● Sadly, no taped evidence will survive of this tantalizing session that includes Neil Young on guitar. Studio and personnel credits imply that this is either a Gerry Goffin or Carole King production of Michael's song. The musicians' union contract reveals that the recordings made at this middle-of-the-night-into-early-morning session are intended for The Monkees' movie. A sweetening date will occur on Monday.

● Sunday 5th

● Michael spends this Sunday at Wally Heider's studio in Hollywood with Shorty Rogers, adding brass, string, and percussion overdubs to his production of The Penny Arkade's 'Give Our Love (To All The People).' Thirty-six years later the track will be issued on the Sundazed CD *Not The Freeze*.

● Monday 6th

TV NBC reruns episode 41 of the *Monkees* series, *Card-Carrying Red Shoes*, at 7:30pm. And in the studio, version 4 of 'Carlisle Wheeling' is treated to some overdubs.

RECORDING Wally Heider Recording (3) *Hollywood, CA* 1:00-4:00am. overdubs.

1. 'Carlisle Wheeling' version 4
   unissued no master #

Personnel Bill Hinshaw (French horn), Ray Kelley (cello), Jacqueline Lustgarten (cello), John Raines (percussion), Herb Steiner (steel guitar).

● This second middle-of-the-night session for the Goffin or King produced version of 'Carlisle Wheeling' probably has Russ Titelman conducting the unusual group of players. Also attending and providing the arrangement is the legendary Jack Nitzche. The union contract notes that the recording is for The Monkees' movie – but the song will not appear in the film, and this version will never be released. Carole King will use the same studio and some of the same personnel to record a new song, 'As We Go Along,' at the end of May.

● Friday 10th

RECORDING Wally Heider Recording (3) *Hollywood, CA* 8:00pm-12:30am. David Jones *prod*; Henry Lewy *eng*; one-inch 8-track; tracking.

1. 'You And I' takes 1-2
   Instant Replay master # WZB3-5307

2. 'That's What It's Like Loving You' takes 1-4
   unissued master # WZB3-5308

3. 'Smile' takes 1-3
   Instant Replay master # WZB3-5309

Personnel Hal Blaine (drums), Larry Knechtel (organ 1,2, electric piano 3), Gerry McGee (guitar 1,3, acoustic guitar 2), Joe Osborn (bass), Neil Young (guitar 1,3, electric guitar 2).

● Three compositions by Davy the budding songwriter are cut at this session, which he leads. The majority of 'You And I' was written some time earlier by Bill Chadwick but is completed with Davy's help. The song has a prescient set of lyrics regarding the fleeting nature of fame. Its shining moment today comes with a blistering guitar solo from Neil Young – now a former member of the Buffalo Springfield, who played their final gig on Sunday 5th.

Young's solo is overdubbed onto the master, take 2, in addition to a second organ track from Larry Knechtel, some more guitars,

and eventually a lead vocal from Davy. The next session for this production will take place on June 19th.

Bill Chadwick: "I originally wrote the lyrics. It was kind of a poem to a friend. We were both moving up in the entertainment business and realized that it's not a lasting thing, to say the least. One day you're at the top and the next day you're at the bottom. That's what it was about. Davy's contribution [came when] we edited some of the lyrics together and we created the melody and arrangement together. Davy was always great to work with because he wouldn't work with somebody unless he had a lot of respect for them."

Davy recalls later: "It was just the old story: all of a sudden we were being pushed under the mat because The Partridge Family and that crew were coming along. 'You and I have seen what time does, haven't we / We've both had time to grow / You know we've got more growing to do / Me and you and the rest of them too. / In a year or maybe two / We'll be gone and someone new will take our place / Another song, another voice, another pretty face.' That was basically what it was: we were just about to be moved aside and they were gonna go and spend their money somewhere else. They got a better deal down the road. It's such an unbelievably tragic shame, you know? I'm sure they would have wished in the early 1970s we all croaked – and now we'd probably be folk heroes. It didn't work out that way. We're all still working."

The second song taped, 'That's What It's Like Loving You,' is a promising mid-tempo track co-written by Davy and Steve Pitts. Four takes are made of the breezy tune with the last marked as the master. Neil Young later adds a second electric guitar overdub, but no lead vocal is ever dubbed on the song and work will stall on the production after today. In 1970 it will be sent to producer Jeff Barry for consideration as a song to complete for the *Changes* album. When Barry passes, it is left unfinished and unreleased.

The lilting 'Smile' is a very good solo composition from Davy. The final take of the three passes will receive further overdubs of more guitars and (at a separate session) lead and backing vocals from Davy. Despite the song's quality it will be left in the can – and then it too is sent to Jeff Barry for consideration for The Monkees' *Changes* album. In 1995 it will finally find release as a bonus track on the Rhino CD reissue of *Instant Replay*.

● Saturday 11th

● Davy flies in to Sky Harbor Airport in Phoenix, Arizona, to visit an ailing fan, Rhonda Cook. The 11-year-old was crossing the street with a friend when she was struck by a pick-up truck. She lost a leg. The girl had been clutching a Monkees album and was trying to pick up her record player from the repair shop. Her father appealed to Davy to write her a letter, but instead he has come today for a personal visit. He gives Rhonda a new stereo record player (hers was only mono) and a slide projector, and offers to buy her any records she might like. He also promises to send her his personal tambourine and gives her his phone number to call him any time she likes.

● Davy has been hoping to get to Manchester, England to see his dad but post-production of the group's film has prevented him from traveling so far. The *NME* reports: "Columbia and Screen Gems are unhappy with the prospect of Davy making solo appearances in Britain and that the filming schedule has been prolonged to overcome this." Jack McGraw, head of Screen Gems' London office, denies this: "It is simply that he and Micky are needed for extra production sequences, as often happens in a major film." The group are scheduled to shoot some more footage this Friday during a specially scheduled concert in Salt Lake City. The prospect of Davy

making his planned appearance on Lulu's British television series is now slim, says *NME*. Concert promoter Vic Lewis is still hoping to bring The Monkees to Britain to play there "in the late summer or autumn."

● *The Birds, The Bees & The Monkees* has only just entered the *Billboard* charts this week, at #80. *Pisces, Headquarters* and *More Of The Monkees* remain chart staples. In The Philippines a single of last year's 'Hard To Believe' spends its second week at #1, while 'Valleri' is a Top 20 item in Australia, Britain, and Norway.

● Monday 13th

TV At 7:30pm the NBC network reruns episode 40 of the *Monkees* series, *Monkees Marooned*.
● At Western Recorders in Hollywood engineer Henry Lewy compiles the mono masters mixed last month for the group's next single. The 45, featuring 'D.W. Washburn' and 'It's Nice To Be With You,' will be issued in June.

● Wednesday 15th

● *The Salt Lake Tribune* reports that The Monkees will fly to Salt Lake City on Thursday night to film a portion of their upcoming film, which according to this paper is now called *The Monkees*. The shooting is scheduled to begin on Friday afternoon at the city's amusement resort known as the Lagoon, specifically at the Patio Gardens. The event is described as not a formal concert. The group will travel with a crew of 30 and the finished film, says the *Trib*, is now scheduled for release in August. Micky: "I think they picked Salt Lake City 'cos they had a big RCA contingent there. And a lot of fans and a good venue. They knew they could fill it with a lot of screaming kids."

● Thursday 16th

● At 3:00pm The Monkees fly to Salt Lake City, Utah, on Western Air Lines. Later they make a guest appearance on radio station KCPX as DJs, clowning around on the Bob Barnett show (8:00pm to 12midnight). After that, Micky, Bob Rafelson, Henry Diltz, and Jack Nicholson hit local clubs including the Crow's Nest and Big Jim's. The group and their entourage stay overnight at the Ramada Inn.

● Friday 17th

LIVE RECORDING Valley Music Hall *Salt Lake City, UT* 1:00-7:00pm; one-inch 8-track; remote recording.
1. **'Circle Sky' rehearsal** take 1
   unissued master # UZB3-9792
2. **'You Just May Be The One' rehearsal** take 1
   unissued no master #
3. **'Rehearsal Jam #1'** take 1
   unissued no master #
4. **'Rehearsal Jam #2'** take 1
   unissued no master #
5. **'Sunny Girlfriend' rehearsal** take 1
   unissued no master #
6. **'Circle Sky' rehearsal** take 2
   unissued master # UZB3-97927
7. **'Two-Part Invention In F Major' rehearsal** take 1
   unissued no master #
8. **'Circle Sky' rehearsal** takes 3-5
   unissued master # UZB3-97927
9. **'Bo Diddley' rehearsal** takes 1-2
   unissued no master #
10. **'Last Train To Clarksville' rehearsal** take 1
    unissued no master #

Underwater photography is one of many technical innovations in *Head* – though few will notice as the movie will not be widely seen.

11. 'Circle Sky' rehearsal takes 6-7
unissued no master #
12. 'Circle Sky' live version 1 take 1
unissued no master #
13. 'You May Just Be The One' live version 6
unissued no master #
14. 'I Wanna Be Free' live version 6
unissued no master #
15. 'Sunny Girlfriend' live version 5
unissued no master #
16. 'Circle Sky' live version 1 take 2
unissued no master #
17. 'Cuddly Toy' live version 1
unissued no master #
18. 'Forget That Girl' live version 5
unissued no master #
19. 'The Girl I Knew Somewhere' live version 5
unissued no master #
20. 'You Told Me' live version 1
unissued no master #
21. 'Circle Sky' live version 1 take 3
Head master # UZB3-9792
22. 'Mary, Mary' live version 6
unissued no master #

Personnel Micky Dolenz (drums, vocal), David Jones (percussion, organ, vocal), Michael Nesmith (guitar, vocal), Peter Tork (bass, organ, banjo, vocal). See Songography at the rear of the book for song-by-song instrumentation.

● At 1:00pm The Monkees arrive at Salt Lake City's Valley Music Hall to rehearse, film, and record a performance for their motion picture *Untitled*. The event was originally scheduled for the Lagoon's Patio Gardens but has shifted to better accommodate the film-crew's lighting needs.

Four-thousand tickets are given away for this event by radio station KCPX. The lucky winners see the group perform Michael's 'Circle Sky' three times. Along the way they throw in a few requests to appease the restless crowd. Micky explains: "We haven't played a concert in quite a while so we're brushing up on some of our old songs," and Peter leads the audience through the film's 'War Chant.'

Despite the group turning in some decent renditions of such rarely performed numbers as 'You Told Me' and 'Cuddly Toy,' today's tapes are very poorly engineered. Most of the vocals are barely audible. Because of this, take 3 of 'Circle Sky,' which is to be used as the basis for the film version, will be given a newly recorded vocal by Michael (see 21st).

Prior to the group's appearance on stage KCPX DJ Bob Barnett tells the crowd that the group's movie *Untitled* "will be released sometime around Thanksgiving."

Many fans went to the Patio Gardens instead of Valley Music Hall and so the group perform a 30-minute set at the Gardens at 8:00pm. Five thousand fans attend this unique concert, which is not filmed or taped. The group arrive early and decide to take a roller-coaster ride prior to their set. After the performance – which will turn out to be their last as a foursome in the United States – the group board a plane bound for Los Angeles at 9:50pm.

● Saturday 18th

● *Billboard* reports that Michael's management has finally found a home for his *Wichita Train Whistle* project. Though he was "hawking the LP to a number of labels" Dot's Dick Pierce offered the best deal.

The label is set to launch "its most expensive merchandising campaign" for the album. The article also notes that "albums sold to the public will not have any bands" but that DJ copies will have track separations. This may be the initial plan, but stock copies of the album do indeed have track separations or 'bands.'

● In Britain BBC television airs its final original broadcast of the *Monkees* second series. The Hollies' Graham Nash has invited the group to perform at a royal Gala Of Pop at the London Palladium on December 8th. He has also approached Donovan, The Seekers, and Paul McCartney. A member of the royal family has also tentatively agreed to attend the show. The concert will benefit under-privileged children and is to be recorded and filmed in color.

● Monday 20th

TV At 7:30pm the NBC television network reruns episode 44 of the *Monkees* series, *Hitting The High Seas*.

● Tuesday 21st

RECORDING RCA *Hollywood, CA*. Michael Nesmith *prod*; one-inch 8-track; overdubs.

1. 'Circle Sky' live version 1 take 3
Head master # UZB3-9792
Personnel Michael Nesmith (vocal).

● Michael combs through seven taped performances of 'Circle Sky' – four full rehearsal takes and three passes in front of a live audience – to select the final take for use in the film. To compensate for the poorly recorded live vocal on the tape, today he adds a new lead vocal to the chosen performance. Although the original live vocal will not be used at all in the released mix, no other doctoring or overdubbing takes place; everything else is just as it was heard a few days ago in Salt Lake City. However, this 'live' rendition will originally appear only in the film. On the soundtrack album, issued later this year, Michael's studio version of 'Circle Sky' will be substituted in place of the live Monkees take.

Michael: "I don't have any idea how that happened. I think that The Monkees always played it better. I can't remember a studio version being better than the way we played it live, 'cos live it was just pure unbridled energy." Peter: "It was my understanding that it was Mike's doing that his studio version went on the album. I'm pretty sure Michael did that. In fact I'm positive. How else could it have gotten out if he hadn't pumped and pushed for it?"

● Wednesday 22nd

● Micky travels to London to visit Samantha Juste, whose expired visa has forced her to return to Britain. This evening he attends a concert by Eric Burdon at London's Revolution club.

● Thursday 23rd

● Micky shops at The Beatles' Apple boutique in London, purchasing some Adam and Eve sheets, pillowcases, and some frilly shirts. Afterwards he travels to BBC Studios at Lime Grove to appear on television's *Top Of The Pops*. During the program he and host Jimmy Saville display paintings made by young viewers in Bristol Children's Hospital. After the show Micky invites *Top Of The Pops* producer Johnny Stewart to dinner at Nick's Diner in Chelsea. He finishes off the evening with a quick visit to Big Ben.

Today during the *Top Of The Pops* taping *NME* journalist Alan Smith corners Micky to discuss the band's film and future. "There is really no plot," Micky says of the film. "Part of the story concerns an itinerant parrot salesman in Florida who tries to get us to buy a warehouse. And it also involves square basketballs. Anyway, we're hoping to have the movie out in August in the States – I don't know

when it will be out here; I notice they often seem to release our stuff later in Britain; I wonder why? – but they're still undecided about the title. Originally we were going to call it *Changes*, but I'm trying to stick out for an idea of my own. I'd like to see it called *The Monkee Movie Starring Victor Mature, Annette Funicello and Sonny Liston*."

Asked about the cancellation of the *Monkees* on TV, Micky says: "I'm not particularly distressed at the ending of our TV series as it stood. We ended it ourselves, because we wanted to. Davy was still in love with the same little girl – it wasn't changing. We wanted the show to be different every week. It was a question of format. We wanted to be fresh and inventive, and just to come up with new things without having to consult sponsors and everybody else. But it just couldn't be done.

"We came up against the establishment. They couldn't understand how we couldn't go on doing the same thing. The kids aren't fools. A tree doesn't stop growing.

"Another thing is that The Monkees never existed as a group like The Beatles. That's why we don't socialize very much outside of our work. We were always much more individuals from the start, in four different directions.

"We take this situation one step further on our next album. Each track is individually produced by one of us. Also, all of us are moving more and more into our own separate scenes. Mike is on the big-band scene. Peter is into hard rock, and Davy is doing what Davy likes: ballads, and orientating again towards Broadway shows. I am heading towards electronics. In the past, none of us has been free. But it's getting different."

● Friday 24th

● Micky purchases a Rolls Royce and a Bentley from a vintage car dealer in Paddington, west London. This evening he attends a concert by The Hollies, Paul Jones, and The Scaffold at Lewisham, south London. Other celebrities in attendance are Paul McCartney, Jane Asher, David Frost, and Bobbie Gentry.

● Saturday 25th

● Micky visits Jaeger's of Regent Street in central London to purchase a special outfit to go with his new cars.

● Sunday 26th

● Micky along with Samantha Juste and her father travels to Scotland for some salmon fishing.

● Monday 27th

● Michael and Phyllis Nesmith host a party at their home to commemorate the release of his *Wichita Train Whistle Sings* album. Jazz legend Stan Kenton is in attendance.

TV The NBC network reruns episode 45 of the *Monkees* series, *The Monkees In Texas*, at 7:30pm.

● Tuesday 28th

Michael travels on American Airlines flight 1131 to Nashville to realize a long-held ambition to cut some of his 'rock' songs with backing from authentic Nashville country musicians.

RECORDING RCA (B) *800 17th Avenue South, Nashville, TN* 10:00pm-1:00am. Michael Nesmith *prod*; Al Pachucki *eng*; one-inch 8-track; tracking.

1. 'Propinquity (I've Just Begun To Care)' version 1
Missing Links 3 master # WZA4-3070
Personnel David Briggs (organ), Kenny Buttrey (drums), Lloyd Green (steel guitar), Wayne Moss (acoustic guitar), Sonny Osborne (banjo), Norbert Putnam (bass).

● The Monkees taped portions of their *Pisces* album in Tennessee, but this is Michael's first chance to work with non-Monkee musicians outside of Hollywood. With the help of RCA's Nashville A&R man/producer Felton Jarvis, Michael has some of the town's finest players at his disposal for the next several days.

Michael: "I could just feel this happening that there was this 'thing.' So, I headed off to Nashville to see if I couldn't get some of the Nashville country thing into the rock'n'roll, or vice versa."

Only one song is taped on this first night of recording, Michael's fairly straightforward country number 'Propinquity' – perhaps a nod to the immediate kinship he feels towards the Nashville cats. Some time between this session and when the song is mixed on August 21st Michael will add lead and harmony vocals to the track. The pitch of the backing track is lower than he wants so his vocals will be recorded at a higher pitch with the help of a device called a variable speed oscillator. The final mixes of this song will be sped up so that his vocals do not sound unnaturally slow.

● **Wednesday 29th**
● Day two of Michael's Nashville sessions is decidedly more productive as he cuts four full tracks over the course of a 12-hour studio day.
RECORDING RCA (B) *Nashville, TN* 10:00am-1:00, 2:00-5:00, 6:00-9:00, 10:00pm-1:00am. Michael Nesmith *prod*; Al Pachucki (10:00am start), Bill Vandevort (6:00pm start) *eng*; one-inch 8-track; tracking.
1. **'The Crippled Lion'** version 1
   Missing Links 2 master # WZA4-3071
2. **'Don't Wait For Me'**
   Instant Replay master # WZA4-3072
3. **'Some Of Shelly's Blues'**
   Missing Links 2 master # WZA4-3073
4. **'Hollywood'** version 1
   unissued master # WZA4-3074
Personnel Willie Ackerman (drums 3,4), Harold Bradley (acoustic guitar 1,2), David Briggs (organ 1,2), Larry Butler (organ 3,4), Jerry Carrigan (drums 1,2), Bobby Dyson (bass), Lloyd Green (steel guitar), Sonny Osborne (banjo), Billy Sanford (acoustic guitar 3,4).
● A couple of Michael's relatively new compositions are taped during the first two blocks of this session.

The lovely 'Crippled Lion' is a slow, simple country tune; today's results will be mixed on August 21st.

The even slower 'Don't Wait For Me' is destined for release on The Monkees' first album of 1969, *Instant Replay*, and will become a part of Michael's on-stage repertoire during that year.

Michael: "It's just a pop tune. No particular inspiration at all. It's just me noodling on the guitar, playin' a song."

After an hour-long break and a slight shuffle of personnel the session resumes with two of Michael's songs from his pre-Monkees folk days.

'Some Of Shelly's Blues' will be treated to further overdubs on June 2nd, but tonight's rendition of 'Hollywood' is deemed unsuccessful and the song will be remade at Michael's next session. Sadly, no tapes containing version 1 of 'Hollywood' will survive. Michael: "'Hollywood' came out of the 'Different Drum,' 'Nine Times Blue' period. It was written well before The Monkees."

● **Thursday 30th**
● After yesterday's marathon session Michael takes a kind of day off. He goes to Nashville airport to pick up a Leslie organ speaker – and spontaneously hops on a plane bound for New York City so that he can enjoy the nightlife. Arriving at 5:00pm, he checks into the

Warwick Hotel, ventures out to Greenwich Village's Dugout for dinner, and later goes to the Electric Circus for some music. Meanwhile in Hollywood, Carole King records a song destined for The Monkees' movie soundtrack.
RECORDING Wally Heider Recording *Hollywood, CA* 1:00-4:00, 5:00-7:00am. Carole King *prod*; one-inch 8-track; tracking.
1. **'As We Go Along'**
   Head master # WZB5-5342
Personnel Denny Bruce (percussion), Ry Cooder (guitar), Carole King (guitar), Danny 'Kootch' Kortchmar (guitar), Harvey Newmark (bass), Earl Palmer (drums), Neil Young (guitar).
● Carole King produces and performs a song she wrote for The Monkees with Toni Stern, 'As We Go Along,' starting in the early-morning hours and recording through the night. It is without doubt one of the most wistful and hypnotic waxings made for the group and is captured in just nine takes, with King providing a guide vocal for the session musicians.

Some time between now and a reduction session for this production on July 31st Micky will replace King's voice with his own lead vocal track.

Micky: "I remember that because it was a bitch to sing. It was in 5/4 time or some bizarre signature. I had a lot of trouble kind of picking it up. Typically we didn't have a lot of time to rehearse this stuff. We were filming. I'd go in and they'd play the song a few times. I remember that was a tough song to sing, but I loved it. I still love it. It's actually one of my favorites."

● **Friday 31st**
● Davy flies to London while Michael returns to Nashville from New York City. Michael takes advantage of the evening start time of his next session and squeezes in a trip to the Country Music Hall Of Fame and the Sho-Bud pedal steel guitar factory where he orders a custom instrument with his name inlaid on the neck in mother-of-pearl.
RECORDING RCA (B) *Nashville, TN* 6:00-9:00pm. Michael Nesmith *prod*; Al Pachucki *eng*; one-inch 8-track; tracking.
1. **'How Insensitive'**
   Missing Links 3 master # WZA4-3075
2. **'Hollywood'** version 2
   Missing Links 3 master # WZA4-3074
Personnel Harold Bradley (guitar), David Briggs (piano), Kenny Buttrey (drums), Lloyd Green (steel guitar), Michael Nesmith (vocal, guitar), Norbert Putnam (bass), Buddy Spicher (fiddle), Bobby Thompson (banjo).
● Michael resumes his Nashville musical experiment with a style uniquely his own: Latin country.

In his topsy-turvy arrangement of Antonio Carlos Jobim's 'How Insensitive' he attempts to turn a trademark bossa nova into a country ballad. The drunken sound of the fiddle and pedal steel adds to this track's eerie quality, and Michael's somber triple-tracked vocals complete the aural picture.

Despite its potential, 'How Insensitive' will instantly be deemed unsuccessful. It is labeled "no master," indicating that it is not suitable for release, and unlike the rest of Michael's Nashville cuts won't even be mixed during the 1960s. During the 1990s, however, it will finally be rescued from the original 8-track master, given a first-time stereo mix, and eventually issued on 1996's *Missing Links Volume Three* CD.

Also this evening Michael re-records 'Hollywood.' The primary difference between this and Wednesday's version is probably today's use of Buddy Spicher on fiddle. Further overdubs will be added to this version 2 on Sunday.

JUNE

'**D.W. Washburn**' / '**It's Nice To Be With You**' single is released in the U.S.A. This is The Monkees' seventh single.

The Wichita Train Whistle Sings album by Michael Nesmith is released in the U.S.A.

● *Monkees Monthly* reports that the group are renegotiating their contracts with Screen Gems and that this will prevent them from undertaking a summer tour this year.

● *Monkees Monthly* also mentions that Michael is sponsoring a blues band by the name of Armadillo. Actually it is not exclusively a blues group but rather a new version of The Penny Arkade. Armadillo features Arkade members Chris Ducey, Don Glut, and Bobby Donaho alongside John Andrews, Bob Arthur, and former *Monkees* series stand-in David Price. Michael put the two factions of musicians together when they fell at a loose end with their respective projects. According to Price's later recollection, the union is shortlived and Armadillo will split after performing a two-week residency at a club in the San Fernando Valley, a suburb of Los Angeles.

● Peter vacations in Carmel, California. Some time between the 7th and the 18th he is visited at his new home – 3615 Shady Oak Road in Studio City, California – by George Harrison and Ringo Starr.

● In London Davy makes various TV appearances and also attends

D.W. Washburn single

A '**D.W. Washburn**' (J. LEIBER / M. STOLLER)
B '**It's Nice To Be With You**' (J. GOLDSTEIN)

U.S. release June 1968 (Colgems 1023).
U.K. release June 21st 1968 (RCA 1706).
Chart high U.S. number 19; U.K. number 17.

a Beatles recording session for 'Revolution.' A photograph taken by Tony Barrow shows Ringo playing the latest Tiny Tim record for Davy and Lulu.

● Micky and Samantha Juste take a vacation in Britain.

● Saturday 1st

● *Cash Box* record-trade magazine reports that reruns of the *Monkees* series have been scheduled for Saturday morning broadcasts in 1969.

● The *NME* says that the group's forthcoming movie will be released

Michael records sessions in Nashville with some of Music City's best players, pictured here, including bassist Norbert Putnam, pianist David Briggs, and harmonica king Charlie McCoy.

in Britain at Christmas and in the United States during the Thanksgiving holiday weekend.

● In Britain Davy appears on the BBC television program *Dee Time* hosted by Simon Dee. Meanwhile Michael is still in Nashville and today cuts two future Monkees singles.

RECORDING RCA (B) *Nashville, TN* 10:00am-1:00, 2:00-5:00, 6:00-9:00, 9:00pm-12midnight. Michael Nesmith *prod*; Al Pachucki *eng*; one-inch 8-track; tracking.

1. **'Good Clean Fun'**
   The Monkees Present master # WZA4-3077
2. **'Listen To The Band'** version 1
   The Monkees Present master # WZA4-3086

Personnel Harold Bradley ("additional" guitar 1*, 2*), David Briggs (piano), Jerry Carrigan (drums), Lloyd Green (steel guitar), Wayne Moss (guitar), Michael Nesmith (guitar 2), Norbert Putnam (bass), Billy Sanford ("additional" guitar 1*,2*), Buddy Spicher (fiddle 1), Bobby Thompson (banjo 1), unknown (percussion 1,2, organ 2). * Bradley or Sanford on "additional" guitar.

● 'Good Clean Fun' is perhaps the most upbeat and commercial track that Michael lays down in Nashville. It's labeled on one tape box as 'Here I Am' in reference to the final line – and it might have been a good idea to add this to the title for record release of the song, which doesn't feature the lyric "good clean fun" anywhere. But Michael is intent on proving a point about perceived commerciality. He says: "That's poetic license. That was a direct insult to a songwriter publisher who had told me that in order to have successful tunes I had to write music that was 'good clean fun' and that had a recurring theme or hookline. Of course I just rejected that out of hand. So that was: OK, I'll write a song called 'Good Clean Fun' – but I just won't put it in there anywhere."

The second song taped is Michael's anthemic 'Listen To The Band.' He cuts it here under the working title of 'Bonnie Jean And The Psychedelic Car' and will build it into a production tour de force during this year. But for today he has yet to pen the song's lyrics. He'll make up words for this inspiring track in short order, and will add a great bass harmonica overdub to the production tomorrow.

Michael: "When I went to Nashville to record, one of the things I wanted to do was to experiment with pure Nashville players playing a type of rock'n'roll sensibility. 'Listen To The Band' is 'Nine Times Blue' backwards. I just took the chords to 'Nine Times Blue' and played them backwards and used it as a point of departure. And then the lyrics were made up in the studio just in order to give me something to sing to it, to see whether the band could play at that type of pace, that type of rhythm. Just to see where it would all get."

● **Sunday 2nd**

● Pete Johnson contributes a lengthy piece to *The Los Angeles Times* about Michael's solo album (and its launch party) under the heading "Evolution Of A Musical Monkee." Johnson starts with a quote from Michael. "'I don't know if this is significant or not,' Mike Nesmith said. 'It may be an enormous failure. This is probably the first pop album in a long time which doesn't claim to be a milestone.' A lot of the 'milestones,' of course, have proved to be millstones, and the sideburned member of The Monkees does not want to be cubbyholed with the artificial experimenters who have pandered to the rock-is-art school.

"He was discussing *The Wichita Train Whistle Sings* (Dot DLP-25861), a rollicking album which unites his songs with a [big-]band conducted by Shorty Rogers (with some help during the stranger moments from Nesmith). Nesmith produced the album and collaborated with Rogers on the arrangements, which included such non-traditional band instructions as 'Freak Out.' He was talking

between the handshakes and civilities of a press party in his home to introduce the album, which was finished several months ago but had been held up by negotiations with record companies (The Monkees record for Colgems but this was Nesmith's own project, financed by him).

"Despite the title of the LP, there are no vocals on it, just the energetic big-band which mixes good music, humor, and insanity for a thoroughly enjoyable excursion outside of tradition. Nesmith's ideas blend country & western, folk, a collage of sounds borrowed from various big-bands, and rock music into a loudly spirited romp. Rock tunes, including those of The Monkees, have been orchestrated and big-banded on numerous occasions, but never before under the guidance of a totally independent rock musician (after all, it was his money).

"The result is resoundingly successful, enough so that some of the jaundiced partygoers who had expected nothing significantly musical from a Monkee expressed their surprise unprompted. ... The Monkees have been attacked for shallowness and lack of initiative in their music, but a Monkee has offered a convincing rebuttal to generalizations that they have no talent with a complex, innovative album."

RECORDING RCA (B) *Nashville, TN* 12midday-3:00, 4:00-7:00, 7:30-10:30, 10:30pm-1:30am. Michael Nesmith *prod*; Al Pachucki *eng*; one-inch 8-track; tracking, overdubs.

1. **'St. Matthew'** version 3
   Instant Replay master # WZA4-3076
2. **'Listen To The Band'** version 1
   The Monkees Present master # WZA4-3086
3. **'Hollywood'** version 2
   Missing Links 3 master # WZA4-3074
4. **'Some Of Shelly's Blues'**
   Missing Links 2 master # WZA4-3073

Personnel Harold Bradley (guitar 1), David Briggs (piano 1), Jerry Carrigan (drums 1), Lloyd Green (steel guitar 1), Charlie McCoy (harmonica 2,3,4), Wayne Moss (guitar 1), Michael Nesmith (guitar), Norbert Putnam (bass), Buddy Spicher (fiddle), Bobby Thompson (banjo), unknown (organ, percussion).

● Michael's final Nashville session features 'St. Matthew,' a song he has previously recorded twice in Hollywood with uneven results. Today's take will not only meet his expectations but will result in the most progressive and rocking music produced at these sessions. Michael will make great use of the Leslie speaker that he picked up at the airport last Thursday. Once an acceptable backing track is selected, many of the instruments as well as Michael's vocal track are filtered through the rotating speaker. Further production work today includes the doubling of Buddy Spicher's fiddle part and of one of the electric guitar parts. Michael will make further amendments and adjustments to the song at a session back in Hollywood on the 12th. Today's session also sees overdubs added to three songs by legendary harmonica player Charlie McCoy, who has worked with everyone from Elvis to Dylan. From 4:00 to 7:00pm he augments 'Listen To The Band' (to be mixed on October 29th), 'Hollywood,' and 'Some Of Shelly's Blues' (both mixed on August 21st).

Michael finishes his Nashville sessions at 1:30 in the morning and must feel elated with this incredible musical expedition, even though these groundbreaking sessions will go largely unheard. The style he pioneers will be more successfully mined by The Byrds, The Eagles, and Linda Ronstadt, who follow a similar musical path by melding country and rock.

Michael: "What I found out was that Nashville country was not the country that was going to be the basis of country rock." Country rock, he says, was largely influenced by Southern California musicians, particularly in Bakersfield. "But I ended up with a lot of, you know, dobro and mandolin and banjo and things, which were hardcore mountain music stuff that didn't really work. 'Listen To The Band' worked pretty good, 'St. Matthew' worked pretty good, but the Nashville cats were so blown out by playin' this kind of music. They loved it, for one thing. As a matter of fact, I think David Briggs and Norbert Putnam and a few of those guys went on and played a little bit of it in [their band] Area Code 615, or at least they started as an ensemble during that time."

● Monday 3rd
● Micky travels with Samantha Juste from Scotland to Manchester in northern England to meet Davy who is currently visiting with his father.
● Michael probably returns to Los Angeles from Nashville today.

● Tuesday 4th
● Micky and Samantha Juste return to Los Angeles.

● Wednesday 5th
● Columbia Pictures sends out an industry mailer regarding The Monkees' movie *Untitled* that reproduces portions of a recent *16* magazine feature on the film.

● Thursday 6th
● Davy appears on BBC-TV's *Top Of The Pops* in Britain. At Lime Grove studios where the show is taped he is interviewed by the *NME's* Keith Altham. Commenting on the group's future, Davy says: "We'll do another film and then maybe split. It will probably always be 'Davy of The Monkees,' but we are already doing things on our own in the recording field. Micky produced and sang 'D.W. Washburn,' and I produced and sang the other side, 'It's Nice To Be With You.' The only other Monkee who plays on that side is Peter. I had studio cats in to do the rest exactly how I wanted it – but as long as it has one of us, it's The Monkees."

● Saturday 7th
RECORDING Western Recorders *Hollywood, CA* 5:00-7:30, 10:00pm-2:30am. Micky Dolenz *prod*; Henry Lewy *eng*; one-inch 8-track; overdubs.
1. **'Rose Marie'**
   Instant Replay or *Missing Links 1* master # WZB3-0140
2. **'Shorty Blackwell'**
   Instant Replay master # WZB3-0116
3. **'Just A Game'** version 2 take 3
   Instant Replay master # WZB5-5311
Personnel Micky Dolenz (vocal).
● Micky, fresh from his British vacation, spends this evening making some adjustments to his productions of these three songs. From 5:00 to 7:30pm he focuses specifically on 'Rose Marie,' probably adding a new vocal track which possibly fleshes out the lyrics. For the second half of the session he concentrates on adding a lead vocal – possibly with assistance from his sister Coco – to version 2 of 'Just A Game.' Musicians' union records indicate that Micky also fine-tunes the master of 'Shorty Blackwell' late this evening, though any adjustments are probably minor. 'Just A Game' and 'Rose Marie' will be mixed next Wednesday.

● Saturday 8th
● In Britain Davy appears on the BBC program *Junior Choice* with presenter Ed Stuart. In today's *NME* he says that the group are about to mount a long concert tour. "The Monkees will be going out in

July," reports Davy. "We plan to visit Hawaii, South America, Japan, Australia, New Zealand, Holland, Germany, and Sweden, as well as Britain. We shall play concerts in Glasgow, Edinburgh, Birmingham, and my hometown of Manchester. They would be some time in August."
The band's UK agent, Vic Lewis, quickly refutes Davy's itinerary, claiming: "I have heard nothing from the band's management in Hollywood – and, in any case, I would think it is too late to book venues for August concerts." Lewis says the group will more likely appear in Britain during November.
Nevertheless, Davy hints that no appearances will take place until a lawsuit is resolved with Screen Gems involving the group's name. He tells the *NME* that The Monkees would like to break away from Screen Gems if this matter can be resolved (and they can keep their name). He mentions also that he may make a solo appearance in Lulu's upcoming movie, which is slated to be directed by Jim Frawley.
● The Monkees' new single 'D.W. Washburn' debuts on *Billboard's* Hot 100 Bound chart at #101. Meanwhile 'Valleri' is still Top 10 in Australia, Japan, New Zealand, Singapore, and The Philippines. *The Birds, The Bees & The Monkees* peaks this week at #3 on *Billboard's* Top LPs chart. Excepting *Pisces*, which clings to #106 this week, the group's other albums have all left the U.S. charts.

● Monday 10th
TV At 7:30pm the NBC television network reruns episode 46 of the *Monkees* series, *The Monkees On The Wheel*.

● Tuesday 11th
● Davy has his handprints cast in concrete for posterity in his hometown of Manchester.

● Wednesday 12th
● Davy travels to his old haunt, Basil Foster's stables in Suffolk, southern England, to visit his horses Chicomono and Pearl Locker. Meanwhile, over in Hollywood Michael works in the studio on his recent Nashville production of 'St. Matthew.'
RECORDING Wally Heider Recording *Hollywood, CA*. Michael Nesmith *prod*; Chris Hinshaw *eng*; half-inch 4-track, one-inch 8-track; reductions, overdubs.
1. **'St. Matthew'** version 3
   Instant Replay master # WZA4-3076
Personnel Michael Nesmith (vocal).
● Michael takes his final recording from Nashville into Wally Heider's and makes a simple reduction of the backing track, combining all the musical elements of the Nashville 8-track to three tracks of a new 4-track tape. After this process is completed he adds a single lead vocal to the song on the one open track of the new 4-track. However, this performance is only temporary. It features some unique lyrics, such as "standing in a lunch line" as opposed to the later "standing in a landslide." It will be superseded by a new vocal performance on August 5th.

● Wednesday 13th
● Davy returns to Hollywood from London. In the studio, Micky mixes two of his recent productions.
RECORDING Wally Heider *Hollywood, CA*. Micky Dolenz *prod*; Henry Lewy *eng*; quarter-inch mono; mixdown.
1. **'Just A Game'** version 2 mixdown takes 1-5
   unissued master # WZB5-5311
2. **'Rose Marie'** mixdown takes 1-3
   unissued master # WZB3-0140

● Micky works with engineer Henry Lewy to make mono mixes of these two songs, but none of the work will ever be heard publicly. Both tracks will be mixed again at a session on December 28th.

Sunday 16th
● Michael spends part of this Sunday (from 3:00 to 5:00pm) at The Monkees' current studio of choice, Wally Heider. He will work on a song called 'A Walk In The Park' expressly for his American Wichita Co. production outfit. Musicians are John London (Michael's former stand-in on the TV series), keyboardist Michael Cohen (who co-wrote a song with Michael in 1965), Don Glut (ex-Penny Arkade, currently in Armadillo), and orchestrator John Neufeld. Nothing more is known about the song or what becomes of Michael's production of the track.

Monday 17th
TV NBC reruns episode 51 of the *Monkees* series, *The Monkees' Paw*, at 7:30pm.

Wednesday 19th
RECORDING Sunset Sound Recorders *Hollywood, CA* 12midday-3:00, 4:00-7:00pm. David Jones *prod*; one-inch 8-track; overdubs.
1. **'You And I'** overdubs onto take 2
Instant Replay master # WZB3-5307
Personnel Bill Chadwick (guitar), Neil Young (guitar).
● Davy, now returned from Britain, works with Bill Chadwick to add more guitars to their song 'You And I,' including a double of Neil Young's blistering solo. Around this time Davy adds his lead vocal to the song, and a further session will be held for it on Friday.

Friday 21st
'D.W. Washburn' / 'It's Nice To Be With You' single is released in the U.K. Meanwhile in America, Davy does some more work in the studio to 'You And I.'
RECORDING Sunset Sound Recorders *Hollywood, CA* 9:00pm-12midnight. David Jones *prod*; one-inch 8-track; overdubs.
1. **'You And I'** overdubs onto take 2
Instant Replay master # WZB3-5307
Personnel Bill Chadwick (guitar), Neil Young (guitar).
● The master for this song is further refined with some guitar touch-up work from Young and Chadwick. Additional guitar augmentation will be overdubbed on September 10th.

Saturday 22nd
● *Billboard* runs an article regarding Michael's recent recording sessions in Nashville. He is referred to as "the musically talented member of The Monkees." According to *Billboard* the new tracks are to be included on a "24-cut double" Monkees album. Each of the four members will be featured on six cuts of the record, with Michael's tracks culled from his Nashville sides.
Michael tells the industry magazine: "Nashville is the best place for music; it's that simple. I like the [RCA Nashville] studio, but the musicians are the greatest. The rest of the album will be recorded in various places, though, including Houston." The article says that two albums' worth of material are already "in the can" and will precede this epic release. Michael calls his new music "weird." *Billboard* says "it will be up to Colgems to give it a name."
● In Britain the *NME* publishes more of Davy's chat with Alan Smith (probably done on May 31st). In response to Micky's claims that The Monkees are growing apart, Davy says: "Man, Micky says we're now beginning to go our separate ways, but we've been that way for three years. Originally we were four actors together; then we were two actors and two musicians; now we're four actors and four musicians.

We've all developed in different ways. I tell you, as long as I keep the beat on my tambourine, we have an act. And that's what matters. "Man, the Screen Gems contract means nothing to me. When I split, I split. We have a seven-year contract, and it's now in its third year – but for me, it ran out. It just ran out. I'm tired of working for nothing. We're four different personalities. It's not all lovey-dovey and cuddly-cuddly. It's been that way for two and a half years and we've all been just a little unhappy. And it's not gonna continue, man. It's not."

Monday 24th
TV At 7:30pm the NBC network reruns episode 48 of the *Monkees* series, *Fairy Tale*.

JULY

● According to *Monkees Monthly* a rough cut of the group's film, *Movee Untitled*, is screened for 100 people this month "at a small cinema in Los Angeles." According to the publication "the audience reaction was mixed. Some of them said that they didn't understand parts of the film – others thought it was great." Surprisingly, the movie's director Bob Rafelson is said to be "quite satisfied" by this reception, which is "just what he expected." The magazine also reports that Peter has formed his own production organization called the Breakthrough Influence Company or BRINCO, and that Michael recently spent time traveling to various radio and television stations around the U.S. to promote his *Wichita Train Whistle* album.

Monday 1st
TV At 7:30pm the NBC network reruns episode 53 of the *Monkees* series, *The Monkees Race Again*.

Thursday 4th
● On this national holiday Peter holds a party for New York musician and producer Harvey Brooks, who is currently a member of Electric Flag. Peter's party guests include fellow music makers The Who, 'Mama' Cass Elliot, and The Lovin' Spoonful's John Sebastian.

Friday 5th
The Birds, The Bees & The Monkees album is released in the U.K. It was originally scheduled for June 21st but production difficulties at the RCA pressing plant have caused a delay.

Saturday 6th
● After four weeks on the chart 'D.W. Washburn' stalls on the *Billboard* Hot 100. Peaking at #19, the single is seen as the group's first flop and a mis-step in their career. This month The Coasters issue a single of their version of 'D.W. Washburn,' which has been sitting in the can since late last year. The competition, though minor, does little to help The Monkees' chart performance. 'It's Nice To Be With You,' The Monkees' flipside to 'Washburn,' also peaks this week at a respectable #51. Meanwhile *The Birds, The Bees & The Monkees* holds at #7 for a second week on *Billboard's* Top LPs chart as *Pisces* slips to #115. Internationally, 'Valleri' is a Top 10 placing in Japan, Malaysia, and The Philippines.

Monday 8th
TV NBC reruns episode 50 of the *Monkees* series, *Monstrous Monkee Mash*, at 7:30pm.

● Tuesday 9th

● Eight of Davy's productions – 'You And I,' 'That's What It's Like Loving You,' 'Smile,' 'A Man Without A Dream' version 3, 'Party,' 'I'm Gonna Try,' 'Changes,' and 'War Games' version 2 – are assembled on a single reel today, probably in preparation for Davy to add his lead vocals. Nevertheless, Davy will never add vocal overdubs to 'That's What It's Like Loving You' and 'A Man Without A Dream' version 3, and with the exception of 'You And I' none of these tracks will be given a contemporary release.

● Friday 12th

● Micky marries Samantha Juste at 4:30pm at his home in Laurel Canyon in the Hollywood Hills. Michael, Peter, Davy, and Ward Sylvester are among those in attendance. A post-wedding jam session is held in Micky's home studio with the groom on drums and Peter on lead guitar. Davy recalls: "There were flowers everywhere and I expected to see a little vicar come walking out like at an English garden party. It was a lovely setting, very quiet and very chic! Samantha's long blonde hair was streaming down her back, and she looked more like a princess than a bride."

● Monday 15th

TV At 7:30pm the NBC network reruns episode 55 of the *Monkees* series, *The Monkees Mind Their Manor*.

● Thursday 18th

● Charlie Smalls records a demo of his song 'Opening Night' for Davy at I.D. Sound in Hollywood, and it is possible that this is the recording that will appear on Davy's 1995 *Just For The Record – Volume Two* collection. Davy will cut his own more 'produced' version during 1969.

● Thursday 25th

RECORDING RCA *Hollywood, CA*. Bert Schneider, Jack Nicholson *prod*; Richie Schmitt *eng*; half-inch 4-track; tracking.
1. **'Ditty Diego'** version 1 takes 1-15
   Head master # UZB3-0581
2. **'Ditty Diego'** version 2 takes 1-9
   unissued master # UZB3-0581
Personnel Micky Dolenz, David Jones, Michael Nesmith, Peter Tork (all spoken word).
● Under the direction of Bert Schneider and Jack Nicholson, The Monkees tape a variation on their TV series theme song, as revamped by Nicholson for the upcoming film. The original Boyce & Hart lyrics – "Hey, hey we're The Monkees / People say we monkey around / But we're too busy singing / To put anybody down" – are cast aside as Nicholson comes up with a caustic replacement – "Hey hey we are The Monkees / You know we love to please / A manufactured image / With no philosophies." Titled 'Ditty Diego,' this piece is custom-made for a sequence in which the entire film is previewed in short bursts on 20 small television-shaped screens.

The session marks the first time that the four Monkees have been together in a single recording studio since 1967 – and will be the last such occasion in the 1960s. Standing in front of four separate microphones, which are fed to four individual tracks of a 4-track tape, the group are coached and cajoled by Schneider from the control room and more directly by Nicholson who stands before them in the studio.

As with every other occasion when Micky, Davy, Peter, and Michael are together in a studio, they quickly take control of the session, fighting out their own ideas amongst themselves to establish a group direction. After several acceptable takes, Schneider comments: "Jack, if you can get Mike, Peter, and Davy to pick up

their tempo a little bit, then they will be more in timing with Micky, who's right on with what you're looking for."

Nicholson tells the group: "In other words, if we can get that doggerel kind of …" Peter quickly interjects: "Oh, yeah? Not so much romantic reading, OK?" "Sillier," says Schneider. "As though it's one guy reading it," explains Nicholson, "like Gilbert and Sullivan." The rest of today's takes of version 1 are taped in this manner, with the final pass, take 15, marked as master. It will be mixed at a session tomorrow.

Once Nicholson is sure that take 15 is satisfactory, he has the group attempt a second version of 'Ditty Diego.' "We're going to do one in unison, top to bottom," he says, "and then we're gonna do one jumpin' around." The Monkees do their best to stay in synch with each other as they read the lines in unison, and after take 1 an impressed Nicholson exclaims: "Huh! What about that?"

"Why don't you do one more like that," advises Schneider. "We'll do one more," says Nicholson giddily, "then we'll mess around a little bit. You know what I mean? Fool around."

"My version of fooling around is to get in a car and go home," says Peter bluntly. "OK," replies an amiable Nicholson, "either way." When Davy blows the next take, Peter attempts to slink away. "The longer you stay over there," says Davy to Peter, "the longer it'll be before you get in your car."

This exchange makes Michael laugh. "I like that, Davy!" he giggles. "That's as good as, 'What about the workers?' That was the last one that really cracked me up." After this, Michael quickly counts in the next take, which rapidly falls apart.

"Jack, you're losing control," observes Schneider. The next several passes end in giggles and ad libs as The Monkees crack themselves up. "I'm losing control," admits Nicholson. "You've lost control, Jack," says Schneider.

Although take 7 is labeled as a master, Nicholson is still not satisfied. "I want a new version," he says, discouraged, and asks the group: "You don't want to do a new version, with people Gilbert and Sullivan-ing around, making noise?"

The tape is stopped, and when recording resumes two more attempts are made at 'Ditty Diego.' Neither is complete (or useable). Then Michael suggests that the group say the lines as fast as they can. They do this, breaking in to a bit of 'Zilch' as the take concludes.

Nicholson insists he will direct the band through one more brief attempt but then gives up on the date, saying: "OK, that's all the versions I want today." As The Monkees tear up their lyric sheets, Nicholson exclaims: "Hey! Terrific." Version 2 of 'Ditty Diego' will never be used or released in any form whatsoever.

● Friday 26th

RECORDING RCA *Hollywood, CA*. 'GH' *eng*; quarter-inch mono; mixdown.
1. **'Ditty Diego'** version 1 mixdown of take 15
   unissued master # UZB3-0581
● Five mixes of yesterday's best take are made. Although they offer some interesting variations – like one ending with the sound of a gunshot and another two missing verse six of the dialogue – none is ever publicly heard. The master for 'Ditty Diego' will be revised at a session on August 3rd.

● Monday 29th

TV At 7:30pm the NBC network reruns episode 52 of the *Monkees* series, *The Devil And Peter Tork*. In the studio, the flipside of the next Monkees' single is reduced in preparation for future overdubs.
RECORDING United Recorders *Hollywood, CA*. 'SW' *eng*; half-inch 4-track; reductions.

Micky marries Samantha Juste in the backyard of their Laurel Canyon home. Best man (facing camera) is Micky's friend and one-time TV series stand-in Ric Klein; maid of honor (back to camera) is Micky's sister, Coco.

1. **'As We Go Along'** reductions of take 9
   Head master # WZB5-5342
● Mixes of both the backing track and Micky's lead vocal track are made today using a 4-track machine. These are likely intended for use in the actual movie since the original film tracks all have vocals and instruments separated for later mixing and printing to film as a composite. However, it is not clear if today's reductions are used, since the master for 'As We Go Along' will be further embellished at a session on Wednesday.

AUGUST

● *Monkees Monthly* reports that the group are still in dispute with Screen Gems over contracts, halting any live appearances. Davy is quoted as saying: "We only want what is due to us. Our last tour grossed two million, but we only made a tiny percentage of that. Something has got to be changed. For us the next 12 months will be hard. We want to do a world tour and hope we'll be allowed to do it."
● In a signal that The Monkees' popularity is on the wane, *Tiger Beat* publishes the last ever issue of *Monkee Spectacular*.

● Thursday 1st
RECORDING Original Sound Recording Studio *7120 Sunset Boulevard, Hollywood, CA* 3:00-6:00pm. Carole King *prod*; one-inch 8-track; overdubs.
1. **'As We Go Along'** overdubs onto take 9
   Head master # WZB5-5342
Personnel Ken Bloom (guitar), Danny 'Kootch' Kortchmar (guitar), Tony McCashen (guitar), John Raines (probably percussion).
● With final augmentation today of additional guitar – and possibly percussion, though none is audible in the final production – the master for this recording is now complete and will be mixed later today. An hour after this session wraps, another Monkees session begins several blocks east on Sunset at RCA.
RECORDING RCA *Hollywood, CA* 7:00-10:00, 11:00pm-3:00am. Micky Dolenz *prod*; tracking.
1. **'Mommy And Daddy'**
   The Monkees Present master # WZB5-5310
Personnel Pat Coghlan (instrument unknown), Dom DeMieri (guitar), Micky Dolenz (vocal, piano, possibly drums), unknown (bass).
● This brand new Micky song, taped today under the working title 'Tell Your Mommy,' is written in the style of 'Randy Scouse Git.' With biting lyrics about drug use, the JFK assassination, and the plight of Native Americans, this is a true protest number.
    The first half of the session is dedicated to capturing a backing track, accomplished in 18 takes, while the lengthier second half is given over to adding overdubs to the master. Unfortunately, no session tapes will survive so most other details on the production process of 'Mommy And Daddy' are a mystery. An early mix will be committed to tape on August 8th.
    Micky: "I was going through a period of social revelation. I have a lot of Indian heritage, so that had something to do with it. That was a period when everybody was writing protest songs. I remember sitting there writing it in my little house up in Laurel Canyon on my mom's old piano. Making my little statement."
    Also today, masters are mixed and assembled for The Monkees' movie.
RECORDING RCA *Hollywood, CA*. Richie Schmitt *eng*; quarter-inch mono and stereo; mixdown.

1. **'Can You Dig It'**
   Head master # WZB3-0123
2. **'Long Title: Do I Have To Do This All Over Again'** version 4
   Head master # WZB3-0117
3. **'Porpoise Song'**
   Head master # WZB4-3513
4. **'Circle Sky'**
   Head master # UZB3-9792
5. **'As We Go Along'**
   Head master # WZB5-5342
6. **'Daddy's Song'**
   Head master # WZB3-0110
7. **'Ditty Diego'** version 1
   Head master # UZB3-0581
● All of The Monkees' songs to be featured in their film are mixed and/or assembled in both mono and stereo today. The stereo mixes will be included on the soundtrack album – which will be compiled next month – while the mono mixdowns will be featured in the film. (Many of the mono mixes differ from their stereo counterparts; see the Songography at the rear of the book for specific details.) The one exception is 'Circle Sky,' which in the film will be heard in the live version recorded in May while the soundtrack album will feature the studio rendition from earlier this year. Today's mono mix of 'Porpoise Song' will also be used as a single master when the song is released as a seven-inch in November. 'As We Go Along' will be remixed for single release on August 19th. 'Ditty Diego' will also be mixed again after the master is revised at a session on August 3rd.

● Saturday 3rd
● The album *Mike Nesmith Presents The Wichita Train Whistle Sings* debuts today on the *Billboard* Top LPs chart at #161. The recording will remain a chart item for the next seven weeks, peaking at #144. In the studio, further audio elements are assembled for the group's film.
RECORDING RCA *Hollywood, CA* 3:00-6:30pm. Pat Ieraci and others unknown *eng*; one-inch 8-track; tracking, overdubs.
1. **'Ditty Diego'** version 1 overdub takes 1-17 onto take 15
   Head master # UZB3-0581
2. **'Happy Birthday'** overdub takes 1-9
   Head master # WZB5-5353
Personnel Michel Rubini (piano 1, organ 2).
● Further editing is done on the master of 'Ditty Diego,' including some varispeed work on The Monkees' voices to make them sound more cartoon-like. Then session musician Michel Rubini adds some zany silent-movie styled piano to the track. Some of today's takes are made without The Monkees' voice track, to encourage Rubini to go completely off the deep end with his improvised playing. However, he must still conform to the length of the piece, and so Peter counts out the 32 bars to signal the end of the piece for the pianist.
    Today's final pass, take 17, will be used as the master for the film. It will be further edited to cut out Micky's lines: "To mix it all together / Pictures, sounds and songs / And time and place and weather / And even rights and wrongs." For the soundtrack album these edited results are sped up and slowed down throughout the mix and then tagged with crowd noise from the May 17th Salt Lake City 'concert' and The Monkees' give-me-an-M 'War Chant.' This conglomeration is titled 'Ditty Diego – War Chant' on the album.
    Another task for Rubini is to add some organ to a previously recorded tape of Micky, Davy, and Peter singing the standard 'Happy Birthday' to Michael from a scene in the movie. The final overdub master is an edit of takes 6 and 9. In the final print of the film Rubini's organ track will only be faintly heard – and on the

Peter at RCA studios, Hollywood, fooling around on piano between takes of 'Ditty Diego,' a spoken piece for Head. His recording days for The Monkees are now over.

soundtrack it won't be heard at all since 'Happy Birthday' is excluded from the release. The piece will later turn up as a bonus track on the 1994 CD reissue of *Head*.

● Tuesday 5th

RECORDING Amigo Recording Studios *11114 Cumpston, North Hollywood, CA.* Michael Nesmith *prod*; one-inch 8-track; reductions, overdubs.

1. 'St. Matthew' version 3
Instant Replay master # WZA4-3076
Personnel Michael Nesmith (vocal).
● Michael, unhappy with the master of 'St. Matthew' from June 12th, works to revise the track. First he bounces the Nashville backing track to a new 8-track tape and then adds a fresh vocal performance to the resulting master. This updated master will be mixed on August 21st.

● Wednesday 7th

● Michael becomes a father for the third time as his son Jason is born today. Jason's mother is photographer Nurit Wilde. From 4:00 to 7:00pm Michael is at H.R. Recording Studio (on Melrose Avenue in Hollywood) working with keyboardist Michael Cohen, guitarist Al Casey, bassist Max Bennett, and possibly David Cohen, a.k.a. folk-singer David Blue, on a song called 'Heavy On The Dark.' Michael produces the track for his American Wichita Company, but no further details are known.

● Thursday 8th

RECORDING RCA *Hollywood, CA.* Micky Dolenz *prod*; quarter-inch mono; mixdown.

1. 'Mommy And Daddy'
Anthology master # WZB5-5310
● Micky makes at least two rough mono mixes of his 'Mommy And Daddy' some time today. At this early stage the production is fairly complete, though lacking the brass arrangement that will be added on December 9th. It does however feature an intro that is later trimmed from the master. In 1996 this mono intro-piece will be grafted onto a stereo version for release on Rhino's *The Monkees Anthology*. Aside from this brief, 12-second piece, the rest of today's mixes will remain unissued.

● Saturday 10th

● Peter flies from L.A. to Connecticut for a weekend with his family.

● Monday 12th

TV NBC reruns episode 54 of the *Monkees* series, *The Monkees In Paris*, at 7:30pm.
● Peter returns to Los Angeles from Connecticut.

● Monday 19th

TV At 7:30pm the NBC network reruns episode 56 of the *Monkees* series, *Some Like It Lukewarm*. Meanwhile in the studio 'As We Go Along' is mixed for single release.

RECORDING Wally Heider Recording (3) *Hollywood, CA*. Chris ? *eng*; quarter-inch mono; mixdown.

1. **'As We Go Along'**
    single-only mix master # WZB5-5342

● The unique mono mix of 'As We Go Along' produced at this session will be featured on the final Monkees single of 1968. The release, with 'Porpoise Song' as its A-side, will also be the final Monkees single issued commercially in mono. All future 'stock' singles will be released in stereo – though a mono version of their first 1969 single, 'Tear Drop City,' will be pressed exclusively for radio stations. (At the time of writing, today's mono mix of 'As We Go Along' has yet to find a CD release.)

● Wednesday 21st

● Peter holds a session at the T.T.G. studio in Hollywood from 2:00 to 5:00pm for his own Breakthrough Influence Company (or BRINCO for short).

Today's date is for 'Dream Goin' By' written by his friend Judy Mayhan. In addition to Peter and Mayhan, the session features guitarist Lowell George and Robert McPherson (instrument unknown). A further session for this track will occur on August 26th. Meanwhile, a Monkees mixing session is held at RCA.

RECORDING RCA *Hollywood, CA*. Michael Nesmith *prod*; 'GH' *eng*; quarter-inch stereo; mixdown.

1. **'Some Of Shelly's Blues'**
    Missing Links 2 master # WZA4-3073
2. **'Hollywood'** version 2
    Missing Links 3 master # WZA4-3074
3. **'Don't Wait For Me'**
    Instant Replay master # WZA4-3072
4. **'Propinquity (I've Just Begun To Care)'** version 1
    Missing Links 3 master # WZA4-3070
5. **'Nine Times Blue'** version 4 take 17
    Missing Links 1 master # WZB3-0125
6. **'Carlisle Wheeling'** version 3 take 4
    Instant Replay master # UZB3-9782
7. **'Good Clean Fun'**
    The Monkees Present master # WZA4-3077
8. **'The Crippled Lion'** version 1
    Missing Links 2 master # WZA4-3071
9. **'St. Matthew'** version 3
    Instant Replay master # WZA4-3076

● Michael mixes and compiles a stereo reel featuring almost all of his Nashville tracks plus a few of his other recent productions. Given the *Billboard* report from June 22nd, he may be compiling his side of the proposed Monkees double album – but none of today's mixes will be given a contemporary release.

'Don't Wait For Me,' 'Nine Times Blue,' 'Carlisle Wheeling,' and 'The Crippled Lion' will all be remixed on October 29th and 'Some Of Shelly's Blues' on June 27th 1969. 'St. Matthew' will also be revisited twice at the end of October but it is not clear if any mixes result from those sessions. In 1969 'Good Clean Fun' will be remixed after it is selected for single release, and the following year Michael will record new versions of both 'Hollywood' and 'Propinquity (I've Just Begun To Care).'

RECORDING RCA *Hollywood, CA*. Quarter-inch mono; mixdown.

1. **'I'm A Man'** take 11
    unissued master # UZB3-9781

● For some unknown reason Chip Douglas's backing track of 'I'm A Man' from November 4th 1967 is given a rough mono mix today. Perhaps the song is once again under consideration for completion. Douglas certainly hasn't given up on it, and next year he will make a fresh attempt at getting the band to record the tune.

● Saturday 24th

● The *NME* reports that The Monkees' movie "is running well behind schedule." Although shooting is completed, "there remains the complicated process of editing and overdubbing, during which the group has to hold itself available for studio requirements." The band's British agent Vic Lewis will travel to Hollywood on September 20th to set up a UK tour for The Monkees, says the paper. The group's film will most likely be shifted from Christmas release in Britain to February, when it is hoped that they will be on tour and able to attend the premiere.

● Sunday 25th

● Peter produces two three-hour sessions (3:00-6:00, 7:00-10:00pm) at Wally Heider's studio in Hollywood this evening for his Breakthrough Influence Company. Once again it features his friends Judy Mayhan and Lowell George, and this time the team tackle a second Mayhan composition, 'Everlovin' Ways.' A further session for this will occur on September 11th.

● Monday 26th

● Returning to T.T.G. studio in Hollywood, Peter holds an overdub session for Judy Mayhan's 'Dream Goin' By.' From 3:00 to 6:00pm he employs bassist Mickey Nadel, cellist Frederick Seykora, violinists Bobby Notkoff and Slim Weston, and Joe Relich on viola. A further session will be held for this track on August 28th.

● Wednesday 28th

● Lowell George adds some musical embellishments to Peter's production of 'Dream Goin' By' at T.T.G. studio from 8:00 to 11:00pm. The Peter-produced version of this song will never see the light of day. In 1970 Judy Mayhan will release a new version of the song, produced by Ahmet Ertegun, on her Atco album *Moments*.

● Thursday 29th

● From 8:00 to 11:00pm Peter holds another BRINCO session at T.T.G. studio with Lowell George and Judy Mayhan for unknown work.

● Friday 30th

● *Daily Variety* announces that The Monkees will undertake their first overseas tour next month. On September 18th they will set out on a 12-day jaunt through Australia followed by six days in Japan. Dates are also expected in The Philippines pending the clearance of the start date on their first television special.

SEPTEMBER

● *Monkees Monthly* reports that the band's movie will be called *Head*. With their new Screen Gems contracts finalized, the group set out on a Far East tour that is originally slated to take in Australia, Japan, New Zealand, Hawaii, and The Philippines. Upon their return, the magazine reports, The Monkees may themselves direct their upcoming television specials.

Micky gets in the mood at RCA for work on *Head*'s spoken piece 'Ditty Diego.'

● Early this month Davy returns to Phoenix, Arizona, to visit accident victim Rhonda Cook (see May 11th).
● Michael and Phyllis Nesmith are temporarily separated. Phyllis moves to Northridge, California, where she hopes to resume her college education at CSUN. At the start of The Monkees' Far East tour Michael asks Phyllis to move back to their Bel Air home and to join him in Australia.

● Tuesday 3rd
● *The Hollywood Reporter* notes that The Monkees' movie "*Untitled* is now titled. The Raybert Production for Columbia Pictures will be called *Head*."

● Wednesday 4th
● Another BRINCO session is held with Judy Mayhan and Lowell George from 4:00 to 8:00pm, at I.D. Sound studio in Hollywood, recording the Bob Dylan song 'I Shall Be Released.' They will be assisted by percussionist Tony Cohan. It is likely that Peter is absent from this session; in his place is his BRINCO partner Bob Hammer. A further session for this track will be held next Monday.
● It is possible that some additional mixing for the *Head* soundtrack album takes place today at Western Recorders with engineer Henry Lewy. Masters for the release will be prepared tomorrow.

● Thursday 5th
● Under the guidance of Jack Nicholson, stereo masters for the *Head* soundtrack album are prepared. Nicholson takes particular interest in interweaving dialogue and sound effects from the movie with The Monkees' musical performances.

Peter: "That was something special, you know? Nicholson coordinated that record, made it up from the soundtrack. He made it different from the movie. There's a line in the movie where Zappa says, 'That was pretty white.' Then there's another line in the movie that was not juxtaposed in the movie, but Nicholson put them together in the [soundtrack album], when Mike says: 'And the same thing goes for Christmas.' I mean, that's funny, and that's very different from the movie. It was a different trip from the movie. I thought that was very important and wonderful that he assembled the record differently from the movie. It wasn't just a pale ghost of a copy. It was a different artistic experience."

Mono masters for The Monkees' next single, 'Porpoise Song' coupled with 'As We Go Along,' are also prepped today. The single will be released next month but the *Head* album will be delayed until November.

● Friday 6th
● Micky attends a Janis Joplin concert at the Hollywood Bowl.

● Saturday 7th
● Davy acts as best man at DJ Ken Douglas's wedding in New Albany, Indiana. After the services Davy flies to Detroit for some promotional appearances.
● Ann Moses writes in today's *NME* that The Monkees' film is undergoing some last-minute retooling. "Screen Gems, after several screenings of the film and getting a mixed audience reaction of total confusion, are busy re-editing it. Neither the teenyboppers nor the adults could figure out what's going on! As a result, release date for the movie is likely to be set back somewhat."

● Monday 9th
● Bob Hammer holds a session for Peter Tork's BRINCO from 2:00 to 5:00pm, again at I.D. Sound in Hollywood. Drummer Buddy

Miles and Electric Flag's Herbie Rich add overdubs to Judy Mayhan's September 4th recording of 'I Shall Be Released.' An overdub session for strings scheduled for the same time is cancelled and will be rescheduled for September 11th. A further recording date for this track will be held tomorrow.
TV Just days short of the second anniversary of the debut of *The Monkees*, NBC screens a rerun of episode 49, *Monkees Watch Their Feet*, at 7:30pm. This will turn out to be the final primetime network broadcast of the *Monkees* series.

● Tuesday 10th
● Peter's partner Bob Hammer holds a further BRINCO session at I.D. Sound from 2:00 to 3:00pm, using musician Herbie Rich to add overdubs to 'I Shall Be Released.' Judy Mayhan will later cut a new version of the song at Muscle Shoals studio for her 1970 album *Moments*. Presumably no part of today's recording will be used in that version. Also in the studio today, Davy returns to his production of 'You And I.'
RECORDING RCA *Hollywood, CA* 10:00am-1:30pm. David Jones *prod*; one-inch 8-track; overdubs.
1. **'You And I'** take 2
   Instant Replay master # WZB3-5307
Personnel Bill Chadwick (guitar), Louie Shelton (guitar).
● With help from Bill Chadwick and session veteran Louie Shelton, Davy adds some final six-string sweetening to the already guitar-laden 'You And I.' By the end of this date the production is complete and ready for tomorrow's mix session.

● Wednesday 11th
● Bob Hammer holds a BRINCO session at I.D. Sound from 2:00 to 5:00pm to add overdubs to Judy Mayhan's August 25th recording of 'Everlovin' Ways.' The four musicians employed are bassist Mickey Nadel, violinist Slim Weston, cellist Ray Kelley, and viola-player Harry Hyams. Judy Mayhan will later cut a new version of the song at Muscle Shoals studio for her 1970 album *Moments*. Presumably no part of today's recording will be used in that version. Also in the studio today, Davy mixes 'You And I.'
RECORDING RCA *Hollywood, CA*. David Jones *prod*; quarter-inch mono; mixdown.
1. **'You And I'** take 2
   Anthology master # WZB3-5307
● With a fresh set of guitar overdubs, 'You And I' is given a mono mix. However, when the track is released on next year's *Instant Replay* album it will appear in a later stereo mix. Today's unique mixdown eventually turns up as a rarity on Rhino's 1998 release *The Monkees Anthology*.

● Saturday 14th
● At 6:05pm The Monkees fly to San Francisco from Los Angeles and then to Fiji and Sydney, Australia (via Qantas Airways) to start their Far East tour.
● Today's issue of *Billboard* publishes a picture of Davy finally accepting the group's gold record awards for *The Birds, Bees & The Monkees* album from Ernie Altschuler of Colgems. The caption notes that certification occurred three months ago but The Monkees were too busy to collect their plaques until now.
● Today sees the animated debut on TV of Don Kirshner's series *The Archies*. The first single from this 'group,' 'Bang-Shang-A-Lang,' will creep into the *Billboard* charts next week.

● Sunday 15th
● The group stop over in Fiji on their way to Sydney, Australia.

● Monday 16th

● The Monkees arrive in Sydney, Australia just before 8:00am and are greeted by some 500 fans with fireworks and sparklers. Shortly after their arrival, the group conduct a television interview in the press room at Sydney airport. They are then driven to Miller's Brighton Hotel at Botany Bay where an hour-long press conference is scheduled. (Some of this will survive on film, and an audio portion is later released on the *Monkees Talk Downunder* album.)

After the press conference Peter speaks to DJ Baby John Burgess. He explains that The Monkees have no say in what records are released by them, but they can record whatever they like. He says the person responsible for selecting their single and album releases is Lester Sill. Meanwhile, Michael tells radio station 2UW's Ward Austin that he plans to publish a book in three months. (A portion of both conversations will be featured on *The Monkees Talk Downunder*.)

The Monkees fly to Melbourne at 11:00am where another press conference is slated and the first concert appearance of their tour is due to take place on Wednesday. They stay at the President's Motor Inn. The group's entourage for this tour includes Samantha Dolenz, *Monkees* series executive producer Ward Sylvester, Raybert employee Marilyn Schlossberg, the group's assistant Brendan Cahill, group insiders Bill Chadwick, David Pearl, and Ric Klein, Screen Gems publicist Floyd Ackerman, Peter's girlfriend Reine Stewart, and sound and projections man Winton Teel.

● Tuesday 17th

● The group hold a press conference at the President Motor Inn in Melbourne, Australia at 12midday. (A portion will be released later on the *Monkees Talk Downunder* album.) The event is telecast live on station HSV7 and repeated again at 6:00pm.

After the conference, Davy is interviewed by the *NME's* David Lillicot, who asks him what *Head* is all about. "It's about life," explains Davy, "society, and the way four people – namely Mike, Micky, Peter, and myself – try to get out of the clutches of the establishment. My way is to fight my way out, because I'm a fighter. Peter loves his way out, because he's for love and peace – as we all are, but Peter is a little more extreme. Mike cons his way out, and Micky goes along with anything.

"Oh, it's so very hard to explain. It's just about four ordinary people and we play ourselves for the first time ever. Our true personalities come over. After you've seen it, you'll understand why I can't really tell you about the film. It's a very involved, very complicated thing."

As for music, Davy says that Broadway Rock will be a trend. "I think it's going to be the next thing," he claims. "Broadway Rock is coming in all the time in America with Jose Feliciano and also Harry Nilsson and a lot of others doing it. It's the type of music your mum and dad can listen to and not be offended. I think pop music has to go this way to be accepted by adults who won't listen to 'Hey, hey, we're the Monkees.' You've got to have roots to a song and I think Broadway music has a lot of roots. If only we can get it into our rock'n'roll music. I think the industry is dying for some kind of trend. It's my feeling that it will have to move to Broadway."

● Wednesday 18th

● The Monkees spend the afternoon rehearsing for the opening show of their tour in Australia. After the rehearsal Davy is interviewed by Phil Hunter. He discusses his concept for Broadway Rock with Hunter (and a portion of this conversation will be released later on *The Monkees Talk Downunder*).

PERFORMANCE Festival Hall *Melbourne, Victoria, Australia* 6:00pm & 8:30pm, with The Cherokees, Marcie Jones & The Cookies

● This evening the group perform two concerts at the 6,700-seat Festival Hall in Melbourne. They are backed by veteran Australian combo The Cherokees during their four solo spots. Around this time The Cherokees release a single for Australia's Festival Records consisting of two Monkees rejects, Linzer and Randell's 'I Didn't Know You Had It In You Sally, You're A Real Ball Of Fire' (which they simply call 'Sally') and Boyce & Hart's 'Grey Monday Morning.' The Cherokees also perform the concert's warm-up set along with a group of four Australian girls, Marcie Jones & The Cookies.

● Thursday 19th

PERFORMANCE Festival Hall *Melbourne, Victoria, Australia* 6:00pm & 8:30pm, with The Cherokees, Marcie Jones & The Cookies

● The Monkees perform two further concerts at the Festival Hall.

● Friday 20th

● At 12midday the group return to Sydney, Australia where the touring party stay at the Sheraton Motor Hotel. While at the hotel Peter gives another interview to DJ Baby John Burgess (a portion of which is later released on the *Monkees Talk Downunder* album).

● Saturday 21st

PERFORMANCE Sydney Stadium *Sydney, New South Wales, Australia* 6:00pm & 8:30pm

● The Monkees spend the day shopping for clothing, incense, and candles. This evening they perform two concerts at the 11,000-seat Sydney Stadium. Showers of paper streamers flung by Monkees fans gum up the works of the venue's revolving stage, which has to be rotated manually.

● Sunday 22nd

● The group leave Sydney on a 4:35pm hour-long flight to Brisbane where they and the entourage stay at Lennons Hotel. At the airport the group are greeted by a reported 3,000 fans but are soon herded into a press conference at Lennons, where Channel 9 television reporter Keith Sharpe immediately hits the group with the question: "When do you think you might break up and try something like music?" The group are largely unruffled by such negativity, but Davy decides to pour a glass of water on Sharpe, who retaliates by hurling another glass back at Davy's face. The reporter is then hauled off by two security guards.

● Monday 23rd

PERFORMANCE Festival Hall *Brisbane, Queensland, Australia* 6:00pm & 8:30pm, with The Cherokees, Marcie Jones & The Cookies

● This evening The Monkees perform two sold-out concerts at the 4,500-seat Festival Hall in Brisbane. One reporter describes support act Marcie Jones & The Cookies as "four girls in purple sequined micro skirts."

● Tuesday 24th – Wednesday 25th

● The group enjoy a couple of days off in Brisbane. On Tuesday, Phyllis Nesmith arrives in Australia to join the touring party for the rest of the trip. Davy visits Surfers' Paradise as well as an animal reserve, a bird sanctuary, and some botanical gardens. Peter and his girlfriend Reine Stewart rent a car and drive to Sydney to see the Australian countryside. Marcie Jones & The Cookies throw a party that some of The Monkees attend.

● Thursday 26th

● The Monkees travel to Adelaide where they stay at the South Australian hotel.

Friday 27th
● Michael and Phyllis Nesmith and Micky and Samantha Dolenz visit a game reserve.
PERFORMANCE Centennial Hall *Adelaide, South Australia, Australia* 6:00pm & 8:30pm
● This evening The Monkees play two concerts at this 3,000-seat venue.

Saturday 28th
● The group leave Adelaide on a 1:00pm flight to make another trip back to Sydney for two more concerts at the Sydney Stadium.
PERFORMANCE Sydney Stadium *Sydney, New South Wales, Australia* 6:00pm & 8:30pm
● Today's issue of *Billboard* shows that the group have scored another #1 in The Philippines with the Davy ballad 'It's Nice To Be With You.' The group initially planned to perform some dates there on the current tour but these never happen. Back in their homeland, the *Pisces* album nears the end of its chart run, now at #166, and *The Birds, The Bees & The Monkees* clings to #67.

Sunday 29th
PERFORMANCE Sydney Stadium *Sydney, New South Wales, Australia*
● The Monkees make their last-ever appearances in Australia as a foursome at two more concerts in the 11,000-seat Sydney Stadium. During the second show a 13-year-old fan dies due to heart failure. Unaware of the situation, The Monkees enjoy a post-performance taste of Sydney nightlife at the Here Disco and the Whisky nightclub.

Monday 30th
● The Monkees travel to Tokyo, Japan. When their flight runs directly into a typhoon it is rerouted to Hong Kong. The group are given the option of stopping over in Manila, but despite their current #1 status with 'It's Nice To Be With You' they decide not to suffer the series of painful cholera injections that would be necessary.

OCTOBER

'Porpoise Song' / 'As We Go Along' single is released in the U.S.A. Two selections from The Monkees' forthcoming movie *Head* are issued as the group's eighth single. Originally, Harry Nilsson's 'Daddy's Song' was considered as a single, but Screen Gems objected after realizing that Nilsson had already issued his own version of the song as part of his RCA album *Aerial Ballet*.
● Music coordinator Lester Sill makes a deal with independent record producer Bones Howe for him to become The Monkees' latest

'new' recording manager. Howe has produced hits for bands such as The Turtles, The Association, and The Fifth Dimension and engineered hits for dozens of artists including The Mamas & The Papas, Johnny Rivers, and Jan & Dean.

Tuesday 1st
● The Monkees arrive in Tokyo, Japan where they are greeted by a reported 10,000 fans gathered at the city's airport. The group's movement in the country is limited because of some death threats. They are playing sacred venues such as the Budokan, which upsets some people. But they are able to have some fun, such as touring the Nikon camera factory and testing out motorbikes at the Honda plant.

Wednesday 2nd
● Davy's first child, Talia Elizabeth Jones, is born at Wimbledon Hospital in London, England. The mother is Davy's current girlfriend, Linda Haines.
● In Los Angeles composer Ken Thorne works with a 40-piece ensemble at Goldwyn Studios to record his final orchestral score for *Head*. Elements of these recordings will now be integrated into the *Head* soundtrack album.

Thursday 3rd
PERFORMANCE Budokan Hall *Tokyo, Japan* 4:30pm & 7:30pm
● The Monkees perform two shows at the 10,000-seat Budokan Hall in Tokyo. The group are backed during their solo spots by five-piece group The Floral.

Friday 4th
PERFORMANCE Budokan Hall *Tokyo, Japan*
● The Monkees perform again at the Budokan.
● At RCA studios in Los Angeles tapes for the *Head* soundtrack are revised to incorporate elements from Ken Thorne's score as well as some other fine-tuning.

Saturday 5th
PERFORMANCE Kokusai Hall *Kyoto, Japan* 7:30pm
● The group make their only appearance in Kyoto, in the 2,300-seat Kokusai Hall.
● In Britain the *NME* reports: "The Monkees are now almost certain to tour Britain next spring, this time taking in major cities throughout the country."

LEFT En route to Japan for concerts, the group are diverted to Hong Kong by bad weather – and excite local media interest just as they're leaving. ABOVE Michael faces a barrage of press photographers in Japan during the tour.

The Monkees play Tokyo's Budokan: pictured are the entire arena (MAIN PICTURE) and the group in action (LEFT).

● Sunday 6th
● A concert scheduled in Nagoya, Japan is canceled. Instead the group take the 150-miles-per-hour bullet train to Osaka.

● Monday 7th
PERFORMANCE Festival Hall *Osaka, Japan*
● The group perform in concert at the 2,800-seat Festival Hall in Osaka. One of the concerts during this period is filmed for broadcast on the TBS network, which airs the *Monkees* series in Japan. The band's set during the film is a good example of their varied repertoire for this tour. Songs include: 'Last Train To Clarksville,' 'I Wanna Be Free,' 'D.W. Washburn,' 'Daydream Believer,' 'Cuddly Toy,' 'Salesman,' 'It's Nice To Be With You,' 'Mary, Mary,' the folk traditional 'Cindy' (performed by Peter solo on banjo), 'Peter Percival Patterson's Pet Pig Porky' (spoken word by Peter solo), Chuck Berry's 'Johnny B. Goode' (performed by Michael with backing from The Floral), 'Gonna Build A Mountain' (Davy solo with The Floral), 'I Got A Woman' (Micky solo with The Floral), 'I'm A Believer,' and '(I'm Not Your) Steppin' Stone.'

● Tuesday 8th
PERFORMANCE Festival Hall *Osaka, Japan* 3:30pm
● The Monkees perform the final concert of their Far East tour. They will not perform again in concert as a foursome for another 18 years.

● Wednesday 9th
● Davy travels from Osaka to Tokyo and then on to London to see his newborn daughter and to visit his ailing father.

● Thursday 10th
● Mike, Micky, and Peter depart from Tokyo, Japan at 8:30pm. They will arrive back in Los Angeles at 7:30am the same day.

● Saturday 12th
● The group's new single, 'Porpoise Song,' enters the *Billboard* Hot 100 at #89. The *Pisces* album clocks in at #192 to enjoy its last week as a chart item (but will miraculously reappear on the chart in August 1986 as a reissue on Rhino Records). *The Birds, The Bees & The Monkees*, which registers this week at #80, will remain on the charts for the rest of 1968. 'It's Nice To Be With You' places at #3 in The Philippines.
● *Daily Variety* announces that *Head* will have its world premiere in New York City on November 6th and will open the same day in two theatres, the Greenwich (at 7th Avenue and West 12th Street) and the Cinema Studio (at Broadway and 66th Street).

● Friday 18th
● Jack Nicholson has experimented with various cross-faded endings for the *Head* soundtrack album, and now settles on a final composite of dialogue plus Ken Thorne's end-title score and the 'Porpoise Song.' The result is a five-minute track he calls 'Swami – Plus Strings (Ken Thorne), etc.'

Final album masters are now ready for pressing and the record will be available to the public next month, though not before a further hitch occurs in the printing of the LP jackets. Since these feature a slick of silver mylar, which acts as a mirror for the purchaser to see their own head, the covers are slightly heavier than the normal RCA efforts and many get jammed in the presses until the proper adjustments are made at the factory.

● Saturday 19th
● 'Porpoise Song' climbs to #62 in *Billboard's* Hot 100, but this four-minute single will remain stuck in that position for the rest of its five-week chart run – despite the release to radio stations of an edited version and the looming premiere of *Head* in some major markets. This week also sees the chart debut of the record's beautiful flipside, 'As We Go Along,' at #106. Next week it will slip to #109 and then disappear forever. *The Birds, The Bees & The Monkees* is the band's only charting album, at #80. The only international market in which they still register is The Philippines, where 'It's Nice To Be With You' slips to #4.

● Thursday 24th
RECORDING Michael probably revisits his production of 'St. Matthew' today with engineer Eddie Brackett, possibly at Wally Heider's studio in Hollywood, but it is not known if any further work or mixing is done on the track.

● Friday 25th
● Davy's father, Harry Jones, dies. Sadly, Davy has only just returned to Los Angeles from his U.K. visit. He immediately flies back to Britain to attend the funeral.

● Saturday 26th
● *Billboard* reports that Bones Howe has been signed to handle the group's upcoming recording sessions. Howe is quoted as saying: "I want to get The Monkees out of their TV image musically and into a more contemporary-R&B-C&W vein." Earlier this year Howe was involved in Elvis Presley's 'comeback special' and some Petula Clark programs. His first session for The Monkees is scheduled for November 7th.
● Also in this issue of *Billboard*, NEMS managing director Vic Lewis reports that his recent trip to the U.S. included a meeting with The Monkees. He hopes to bring them to Europe in 1969 for a tour "embracing major cities."
● In the charts *The Birds, The Bees & The Monkees* slips to #88 and 'It's Nice To Be With You' spends its last week in The Philippines' Top 10.

● Tuesday 29th
RECORDING Wally Heider Recording (3) *Hollywood, CA*. Michael Nesmith *prod*; Eddie Brackett *eng*; quarter-inch stereo; mixdown.
1. **'Don't Wait For Me'**
   Instant Replay master # WZA4-3072
2. **'The Crippled Lion'** version 1
   Missing Links 2 master # WZA4-3071
3. **'Carlisle Wheeling'** version 3 take 4
   Instant Replay master # UZB3-9782
4. **'Nine Times Blue'** version 4 take 17
   Missing Links 1 master # WZB3-0125
5. **'Listen To The Band'** version 1
   The Monkees Present master # WZA4-3086
● Working with engineer Eddie Brackett, Michael makes new stereo mixes of some of his productions. Mixes of both 'Don't Wait For Me' and 'Carlisle Wheeling' from today's session will be considered for The Monkees' next album, *Instant Replay*, but only the former makes it to the final line-up. 'Carlisle Wheeling' will be included as a bonus track on the album when it is reissued on CD in 1995.

Both 'The Crippled Lion' and 'Nine Times Blue' will end up on Rhino's *Missing Links* series while today's unique mix of 'Listen To The Band,' with prominent pedal-steel guitar, will be featured as a bonus track on 1994's CD reissue of *The Monkees Present*. The song will be mixed again for release after horns are added to the track on December 9th.

● Thursday 31st

● Michael and Phyllis Nesmith host a Halloween party for some 100 guests including singer-songwriter Donovan and Michael's fellow Monkees, who all appear in costume. Michael dresses as a cowboy, his wife Phyllis as a ballerina, Peter as a pioneer, Davy as a prince, and Micky and his wife Samantha as a priest and a nun. Around this time Davy and his girlfriend Linda Haines elope to Mexico to get married.

RECORDING It is possible that earlier in the day Michael works with engineer Eddie Brackett on 'St. Matthew' but it is not known what work is done or indeed if there any results. There will be no further production dates for this song, which will remain unreleased until Rhino's 1990 compilation *Missing Links Volume Two*.

NOVEMBER

Head album is released in the U.S.A. This soundtrack record is the group's sixth album. The feature film *Head* itself is also finally released this month.

• *Monkees Monthly* reports that the group, upon returning from the Far East, read the script for their TV special and are disappointed. They find it "sloppy" and too like a "fairytale." They insist on a full rewrite but will not direct it themselves, as was once planned.

Head soundtrack album

A1 'Opening Ceremony'
A2 'Porpoise Song (Theme From "Head")' (G. GOFFIN / C. KING)
A3 'Ditty Diego – War Chant'
A4 'Circle Sky' (M. NESMITH)
A5 'Supplicio'
A6 'Can You Dig It' (P. TORK)
A7 'Gravy'
B1 'Superstitious'
B2 'As We Go Along' (C. KING / T. STERN)
B3 'Dandruff'
B4 'Daddy's Song' (H. NILSSON)
B5 'Poll'
B6 'Long Title: Do I Have To Do This All Over Again' version 4 (P. TORK)
B7 'Swami – Plus Strings (Ken Thorne), Etc.'

U.S. release November 1968 (Colgems COSO-5008)
U.K. release late 1969 (RCA 8050).
Chart high U.S. number 45; U.K. none.

● Saturday 2nd

● The *NME* reports that Michael was arrested recently for defacing an American flag. He was in fact wearing the flag in the form of a shirt and thought nothing of it. He had worn the costume as part of the group's recent Far East tour and had drawn some heat from people who thought that he was supporting America's involvement in Vietnam. One of the few topics the entire group agrees on now is their opposition to the war.

● Tuesday 5th

● *The New York Times* runs an ad for *Head*. A fuzzy black-and-white image of advertising guru John Brockman is pictured with the word "HEAD" emblazoned on the top right hand corner. Below is the information: "A COLUMBIA PICTURE – WORLD PREMIERE ENGAGEMENT STARTS TOMORROW – GREENWICH AND CINEMA STUDIO THEATRES." No mention is made of The Monkees or any of the other people associated with the movie. This is part of Raybert's strategy – as recommended to them by Brockman – to attract non-Monkees fans to their film.

Micky: "This guy John Brockman came up with the ad campaign. He was a New York avant-garde promotion and publicity guy. I don't know what he was. Anyway, that was what it was all about: very avant-garde. Bob [Rafelson] was into the New York scene.

"By that time it had all gone very sour because Davy and Mike and I had gone on strike the first day of the filming of the movie to get a better deal. We had discovered finally after so many years that we were getting ripped off pretty bad. So we decided to strike. Peter didn't – he was the scab. I don't think Bob and Bert [Schneider] ever forgave us for that.

"At the time it didn't occur to us; we thought that everything would go on as normal. 'Cos the mechanism was in hand. I was only 22 years old. I remember seeing Bob and Bert in New York and they were a little distant in talking about their other projects. I remember getting the feeling that the bloom had left the flower. At the time, of course, nothing really had changed much. Practically speaking, we were still selling out and playing and recording. It wasn't until years later that I look back and realize what was going on.

"I would have liked to do the television show for another year – but at the time I didn't want to do it at all. It was boring. It was the same old thing every week. We were getting tired of it and it was very difficult to maintain that kind of level of spontaneity and improvisation. It wasn't like going in and reading scripts every week. We were coming up with it all ourselves. Not necessarily every word or line, but having to come up with the spirit of it. Having to improvise and come up with shtick week after week after week. All fresh and spontaneous. The spontaneity was getting old!"

Peter: "We were all in on it together. We were trying to shake off the old Monkee image, but I think that Bert and Bob had given up on The Monkees at that point. They collapsed and that's why *Head* didn't do anything. The publicity decision to have John Brockman's face on the poster and two-minute commercials for *Head* that were so avant-garde as to be positively repulsive. … I think those things were very conscious decisions to [bury] the movie and the entire project. Bert said to me the point was to destroy The Monkees. Charitably, you could say that his point was to break the bubblegum Monkees image. Less charitably, he wanted to be done with the project."

● Wednesday 6th

● The Monkees travel to New York City to attend the premiere of their movie *Head*, which is held not in a cinema but rather at the Columbia Pictures studio on West 54th Street. A party is thrown afterwards for guests including Janis Ian, Andy Warhol, Boyce & Hart, Carole Bayer, Lester Sill, Bert Schneider, Bob Rafelson, Peter Fonda, Peter's brother Nick Thorkelson and his grandma. A discothèque is set up and a room that includes small television sets playing portions of the movie. (The group stay at the Hilton hotel.) Bob Rafelson: "The night *Head* opened they arrested [Jack Nicholson and myself]. Our opening – and there we were slapping stickers all over New York about the movie. The producer and director on 57th and 5th Avenue. I see a guy about to get arrested for selling chestnuts on the street without a license. So I went over

G ⊜ A COLUMBIA PICTURE · WORLD PREMIERE ENGAGEMENT STARTS TODAY

12:00, 2:00, 4:00, 6:00, 8:00, 10:00 THE CINEMA *Studio* **GREENWICH** 1:55, 3:55, 5:55, 7:55, 9:55
Broadway at 66th St. opposite Lincoln Center · TR 4-8445 12th St. & Seventh Ave. · WA 9-3350

and said, 'How much for the chestnuts?' and the cop said, 'He can't sell you the chestnuts.' And I said, 'I'll just give you the money and you give me the nuts and then no one breaks the law.'

"Now, while I'm having this dialectic with the cop, who has a white helmet on, Jack is standing behind the cop trying to slap a *Head* sticker on the helmet. And like a Laurel & Hardy comedy, man, this cop turns around just at the right moment and Jack nails him on the side of his face. Bam! We're handcuffed and up against the walls. A squad car takes us away. We've got a flick opening in an hour. I just wanted to call everybody and tell them we're in jail. And to get on the radio and sell tickets – because Jack and I had this feeling that no one was going to see *Head*."

● A larger ad than yesterday's appears in *The New York Times*, still without cast information but now giving show times and stating "WORLD PREMIERE ENGAGEMENT STARTS TODAY."

● John Maloney of *The Hollywood Reporter* has already seen the film and his rather lengthy analysis hits newsstands just as the film's first audiences get to see it. "The faults of the Raybert production of *Head* are rather neatly symbolized in the title," writes Maloney, "an insistence on playing it both ways, purposely seeking to evolve some detached commentary from seemingly confused material while at the same time playing to the inner circles to be with it, hip now, making small jokes of and for small set attitudes … . Individually, The Monkees are a very talented assemblage. Little effort is made to explore or develop their screen characters or styles. … Box office will depend on the residue of goodwill for The Monkees, not here in their finest hour. The film's psychedelic boutique was more commercial when production began."

● *Daily Variety* is even less impressed than *The Hollywood Reporter*, if that's possible. "*Head* is an extension of the ridiculous nonsense served up on the Screen Gems vidseries that manufactured The Monkees and lasted two full seasons following the same format and, ostensibly, appealing to the same kind of audience. … Writers Bob Rafelson and Jack Nicholson were wise not to attempt a firm storyline as The Monkees have established themselves in the art of the non sequitur and outrageous action. Giving them material they can handle is good thinking; asking them to achieve something more might have been a disaster."

● **Thursday 7th**

● Today's *New York Times* finally runs an ad for *Head* that has the cast listed. The paper also publishes a scathing review of the film. Renata Adler writes: "*Head*, which opened yesterday, might be a film to see if you have been smoking grass, or if you like to scream at The Monkees, or if you are interested in what interests drifting heads and hysteric high-school girls. Dreadfully written by Jack Nicholson (who wrote *The Trip*) and directed by Bob Rafelson who, with Bert Schneider, created The Monkees (on the basis of interviews) as a singing group, the movie is, nonetheless, of a certain fascination in its joining of two styles: pot and advertising. The special effects – playing with perspective, focus, dimension, interstices, symmetry, color, logic, pace – are most accessible to marijuana; the use of pre-packaged stars gives the movie a kind of brandname respectability – like putting Jim Dooley (of the "come on down" commercial) on display in the hashish crowd.

"The Monkees, who are among the least-talented contemporary music groups and know it, are most interesting for their lack of similarity to The Beatles. Going through ersatz Beatle songs, and jokes and motions, their complete lack of distinction of any kind – the fact that fame was stamped on them by hucksters as it might have been on any nice four random, utterly undistinguished boys – makes their performance modest and almost brave. They work very hard and they aren't any good. This keeps them less distant from their own special fans than The Beatles or, say, Bob Dylan and The Beach Boys are. They do not have to bridge the distance of talent or style.

"It will be interesting to see if the underlying fusion works, if taking essentially subversive styles (as in other pot films, such as *Revolution* and *You Are What You Eat*) and covering them with famous mediocrities assures their success. The aesthetic marijuana world is bound to come out importantly in films one way or another. This sort of movie might be the testing ground."

This unreserved putdown of the movie and everyone associated with it will elicit at least one response from a reader, one Richard D. Horwich, whose letter is later published in the paper. "I want to protest at Renata Adler's too-easy dismissal of *Head*," writes Horwich. "Her assumption seems to be that anything without a strong narrative is by definition formless and inchoate, and that anything formless and inchoate must be, as she puts it, 'accessible to marijuana' – that is, I take it, in the mod-transcendentalist-freakout bag.

"I share her weariness with slapdash trivia like *You Are What You Eat*; but I think she's a bit hasty in tossing *Head* onto that particular compost heap. Granted that the title suggests a movie about drugs, and that the presence of The Monkees indicates an alliance with all the adolescent psychedelia we yawned at in *Privilege*, *Wild In The Streets*, *Help!*, and a dozen others. Still *Head* is certainly more than a joining of the styles of 'pot and advertising.' With her sometimes too-literary sensibilities, Miss Adler should know that there are many other ways of achieving coherence in a book or a film than by employing the realistic convention. *Head* is a fantasy, all right, but it's

An enigmatic *New York Times* ad for the group's *Head* movie, featuring the head of advertising guru John Brockman.

not a child's, or a nut's, or a junkie's fantasy; it may be a trip, but not on acid. It owes more to *Finnegans Wake* than to *You Are What You Eat*; it struck me, at least, as more mythic than psyche-delic.

"Miss Adler wants more movies like *Bullitt* (which she praises for its succinctness of plot, though I defy her or anyone else to give a synopsis of it), movies that show 'how things work,' movies that are accretions of realistic detail. Well, *Head* is certainly not that kind of movie; she's right in calling attention to its 'playing with perspective, focus, dimension, interstices, symmetry, color, logic, pace.' But she doesn't think it worthwhile to inquire how interesting the games it plays are. Instead of simply rejecting *Head* because she's tired of other movies like it, let her recognize that this is superior fantasy, and that fantasies about incredible journeys have always had a right to serious consideration, as any reader of Homer, Dante, Strindberg or Joyce should know."

● In Los Angeles, where *Head* has yet to be seen by the general public, The Monkees' newly-appointed record producer, Bones Howe, holds his first session for the group – though no Monkees attend.

RECORDING Wally Heider Recording (3) *Hollywood, CA* 2:00-5:30pm. Bones Howe *prod*; Bones Howe *eng*; one-inch 8-track; tracking.

1. **'A Man Without A Dream'** version 4 takes 1-14
   Instant Replay master # XZB5-0123
2. **'Someday Man'** takes 1-38, + insert piece 1 take
   Instant Replay master # WZB5-5399

Personnel Hal Blaine (drums), Mike Deasy (acoustic guitar 1, electric guitar 2), Larry Knechtel (piano), Joe Osborn (bass), Jimmy Rowles (piano), Tommy Tedesco (acoustic guitar 1, electric guitar 2).

● This is the fifth recording of Goffin & King's 'A Man Without A Dream' counting Peter's demo from 1967, but today's production of the song by Bones Howe will be the first to reach public ears. The early takes taped today are fairly fast in tempo. Howe dedicates take 3 "to the Beach Boys" for no obvious reason other than to keep up with the wisecracks of drummer Hal Blaine. The band then settle into a more gentle groove for take 4 until the song is satisfactorily captured on take 14. There are a few exceptions. Take 8 is stopped abruptly by Howe, who feels it is too fast, and the pass that follows, take 9, is incredibly slow. Howe offers to play Blaine a demo of the song before take 10, but the drummer falls quickly into line without the need of any extra help. The take 14 master will be subject to substantial sweetening during January 1969.

'Someday Man' by Paul Williams and Roger Nichols is the first song not copyrighted by Screen Gems to be recorded by or for the group since 'All Of Your Toys' and will be the only non-Gems-owned song ever released by the original group.

The road to capturing a satisfactory take of 'Someday Man' is a long one. Guitarist Mike Deasy switches from acoustic to an electric instrument. After the early passes, Howe says things sound "sluggish." In general, the band have trouble locking into a groove. On this song the assembled musicians have a habit of cluttering up the arrangement with too many accents, particularly the bass and electric guitar.

Lucky take 13 is the first that the producer considers a saver, but the studio group still have some way to go before they reach perfection. After take 16 Howe suggests that drummer Blaine and guitarist Tommy Tedesco start the song together – which they do on every take that follows. A portion of take 27 will be used in the final master, which also includes pieces of takes 31, 32, and 37, plus part of an insert piece taped at the end of the session. Like today's other song, 'Someday Man' will be sweetened and completed during January 1969.

Bones Howe: "All the [Monkees] were making records on their own and [Screen Gems] were looking for somebody to produce Davy. So I did those two tracks with him, 'Man Without A Dream' and 'Someday Man.' I can't remember how I was approached in the first place. I had a lot of records on the charts, so I guess that probably had something to do with it.

"'Someday Man' by Paul Williams was the first time that they'd ever recorded an 'outside' song. They had always recorded songs either [copyrighted by] Screen Gems or their own material. I was a song 'saver' – if I found a great song I would hang on to the demo, even though the possibility was that someone else might cut it in the meantime. Paul Williams and I were friends going back a long time. When this thing happened with Davy, I played it for [Davy] and he liked it. We were able to convince Colgems that we could do an outside song. Somehow or other they were willing to do this. I guess it was because we looked around and I kept saying to them, 'Find me another song that'll knock this one out of the box.' And no one could find a song that everybody liked better."

Davy recalls later: "On 'A Man Without A Dream' I sang 'With the music of life my soul is out of tune' down in the range that I was supposed to be singing in, not where they had me singing all the time. I'm a baritone and I always have been. I mean, I can hit the notes better now and sing those songs a lot better than I ever did. I don't understand why we were given so little thought and consideration along the line."

● **Saturday 9th**
● *Billboard* reports that *Head* will open in Hollywood, Washington, San Francisco, and Boston by mid-November.
● Bob Rafelson: "[*Head*] was a total disaster on every level. Judging by other people's reaction to me, it was a full-out gas. Nobody saw it; everybody hated The Monkees so much. I went through a very bad trip as a result of *Head*. My vanity was hurt and I doubted my sanity for a while. I couldn't understand how people couldn't see past The Monkees. That was what the movie was about. I admit it was a bit abstract. It was about my relation to The Monkees and the whole perpetration that had taken place. But when the film was reviewed it was looked on as another shuck. Nobody saw it."

● **Monday 11th**
● Today's *New York Times* carries a special ad for *Head*. It reads: "*HEAD* wishes to thank *CUE* Magazine for permission to print this review in advance of its publication in the issue that will appear on newsstands Thursday." What follows is one of the few positive reviews of the film. Reviewer William Wolf concisely and lucidly details this otherwise indescribable work. "After having argued for more creative musicals," writes Wolf, "I was delighted at seeing the extent of inventive musicality inherent in *Head*, a wacky first film for The Monkees.

"In terms of sheer cinema, there is a mountain of creativity adding up to mod impressionism. Using sight and sound to the hilt with great freedom of form, director Bob Rafelson manages to convey the frenzied existence of The Monkees – sudden fame, hilarious escapades, their unreal world in the midst of misery elsewhere in the real one, and sometimes the feeling of everything closing in. There is madcap fun, although not enough to match the exuberance. But the film is refreshingly up-to-date, as if *8?* had been made by a flower child."

Wolf says later: "I don't remember whether I saw a first screening or one of several to which critics were invited. What I do recall is my appreciation of the cinematic inventiveness that *Head* displayed. It was refreshing to watch, and in addition to the amusement provided

by the performances there was the pleasure of seeing a lively piece of film work back in 1968."
● Meanwhile in the studio, sessions commence for the soundtrack to the band's upcoming television special.
RECORDING United Recorders [possibly Western Recorders] ("1") *Hollywood, CA* 2:00-5:30pm. Bones Howe *prod*; Bones Howe *eng*; one-inch 8-track; tracking.
1. **'I Go Ape'** takes 1-12, + intro piece 5 takes
   The Monkees Season 2 DVD master # WZB5-5393
2. **'Wind Up Man'** takes 1-5
   The Monkees Season 2 DVD master # WZB5-5391
3. **'String For My Kite'** version 1 takes 1-5
   unissued master # WZB5-5397
Personnel Hal Blaine (drums 1,3, percussion 2), Mike Deasy (electric guitar), Larry Knechtel (piano 1 [takes 10-12 only], keyboard 2,3), Jimmy Rowles (piano 1 [takes 10-12 only], keyboard 2,3), Joe Osborn (bass 1 [takes 10-12 only], 2,3).
● Now that Bones Howe has the backing tracks for the next potential Monkees single under his belt, he sets about recording the music for the group's upcoming television special.

The first song taped today is an old Screen Gems copyright, 'I Go Ape.' It was Neil Sedaka's second hit record in 1959, composed by Sedaka with his regular collaborator Howard Greenfield. Since The Monkees' TV special is written and produced by Jack Good, this selection should come as no surprise. Old time rock'n'roll is Good's stock-in-trade. After creating such groundbreaking British music television shows as *Oh Boy!* and *6.5 Special*, Good came to America in the mid 1960s and produced *Shindig!* using essentially the same format just a few years later. The show featured all the top recording artists of the British Invasion and the folk-rock era, but it was the regular cast members such as Bobby Sherman and Donna Loren who, prompted by Good, dominated the program with old rock'n'roll medleys. The Monkees' quasi-psychedelic special will be no exception to Good's formula. Guest stars Julie Driscoll, Brian Auger & The Trinity will dominate the program and The Monkees will sing a stack of old rock numbers.

At the start of today's recording session, producer Howe asks the session musicians: "Are you ready to rock'n'roll?" But the taping gets off to a rough start. Due to a technical error, takes 1 to 7 feature only an electric guitar and drums. Starting with take 10 – takes 8 and 9 seemingly go unrecorded – the bass and two pianos are successfully tracked live with the guitar and drums. Take 12 is marked as the master and will receive overdubs of guitar, organ, sax, tambourine, backing vocals, more drums, and a lead vocal from Micky.

To further refine this master, Howe tapes five takes of an intro piece (which will be crudely cut off in the special). The final edited master will be pulled to another reel and is used in the soundtrack to the special. It will subsequently be lost and the song will never receive an official record release. Fans will have to wait until 2003 for Rhino's DVD box set of the *Monkees* second season for the best quality version. (An acetate circulating among collectors features an incomplete version – albeit with the otherwise unused intro piece.)

The syncopated 'Wind Up Man' – the first of several short musical pieces written for the special by Bill Dorsey – is quickly recorded in five takes. It features Hal Blaine on some mechanical-sounding percussion and keyboardists Larry Knechtel and Jimmy Rowles playing a combination of piano and harpsichord, and is flavored with some 'sliding' string noises from guitarist Mike Deasy. Take 5 is marked as the master and will eventually receive the addition of vocals from all four Monkees, probably taped on another date. Like all the tracks featured in the TV special, this final take will later be lost and can only be heard in the special (later included on

2003's *The Monkees Season 2* DVD boxed set).
Another Bill Dorsey composition is taped today, the first version of 'String For My Kite,' intended as a showcase for Davy. The arrangement recorded at this session is lovely, featuring some fine harpsichord playing from Knechtel or Rowles, but it will remain unused and unissued. No further overdubs will be committed to today's track. A second version of the song will be cut on November 18th.

● **Tuesday 12th**
RECORDING Western Recorders (3) *Hollywood, CA* 8:00pm-12midnight, 12:30-3:30am. Bones Howe *prod*; Bones Howe *eng*; one-inch 8-track; tracking.
1. **'Naked Persimmon'** takes 1-12, + ending piece 18 takes, + insert piece 5 takes
   The Monkees Season 2 DVD master # WZB5-5395
2. **'(I Prithee) Do Not Ask For Love'** version 4 takes 1-12, + intro piece 6 takes
   The Monkees Season 2 DVD master # WZB5-5394
Personnel Hal Blaine (drums 1, percussion 2), Dennis Budimir (guitar 1, acoustic guitar 2), Mike Deasy (guitar 1, acoustic guitar 2), Larry Knechtel (keyboard 1,2), Joe Osborn (bass 1,2), Jimmy Rowles (keyboard 1,2), unknown (steel guitar 1, sitar 2 [intro only]).
● Michael's showcase in the upcoming TV special is his exotically-titled 'Naked Persimmon.' The song explores the dichotomy he feels between being a rock musician – 'Monkee Mike' – and the sincere country crooner that he is deep down inside – 'Michael Nesmith.'

Personnel for the track is similar to yesterday's session but includes an uncredited steel player, who may be Michael himself (though he is not heard speaking at all on the session tape, so it is not clear if he attends). Keyboardists Larry Knechtel and Jimmy Rowles play tack piano and electric harpsichord, and Dennis Budimir joins Mike Deasy on guitar. The final pass taped today, take 12, is marked as the master. After the addition of an ending and an insert piece, 'Naked Persimmon' will receive a lead vocal from Michael at another session this month. The master take will be pulled to another reel on November 21st but later this will be lost.

The Monkees' fourth and final version of Michael Murphey's 'Do Not Ask For Love' is taped today. Arranged in a slow raga style, the track makes interesting use of the same session personnel as 'Naked Persimmon.' Hal Blaine switches to a large hand drum, Knechtel and Rowles play piano and electric harpsichord, and the guitarists switch to acoustics. A brief intro piece, slightly faster than the body of the song, is also taped and features a sitar probably played by Deasy or Budimir. Take 12 will be marked as the master and is subject to two vocal overdubs from Peter this month. The final master will subsequently become lost.

● **Wednesday 13th**
● The Monkees are expected among the guests at the gala premiere of The Beatles' animated feature *Yellow Submarine* at Westwood Village's Fox Village theatre (filmed by local television station KHJ Channel 9), but Micky may be the only one to attend as the others are on a promotional tour for *Head*.
● *Weekly Variety* features a full-page ad declaring "HEADs UP! WAY UP!" Selectively quoting from reviews for the *Head* movie – even the bad ones – it announces that the film's "first five days breaks all records at N.Y.'s Greenwich and Cinema Studio Theatres! Combined Gross $16,111." This figure seems like nothing to advertise. Still, the film is set to open on November 20th at Los Angeles's Vogue Theatre, Philadelphia's Trans Lux Theatre, San Francisco's Metro 2 Theatre, Washington's Rosslyn Plaza, and Boston's West End Cinema.

Bob Rafelson: "*Head* was never thought of by me or my partner as a picture that would make money. What I felt was that, since we had made an enormous amount of money for Columbia in their record division and in TV sales, we were entitled to make a picture that would in a sense expose the process."

● Thursday 14th

● Today's *Los Angeles Times* carries an ad for *Head* boasting "INVITATIONAL PREMIERE TUESDAY! The Monkees in Person! Vogue Theatre Hollywood."

● The Monkees (sans Micky) are currently in Washington on a promotional tour to hype *Head*. Today Davy and Peter speak with Mary Ann Seawell of *The Washington Post* who puts together an article titled "The Monkees Aren't Manufactured." Seawall writes: "The Monkees, a rock singing group formed three years ego by two producers who placed an ad announcing auditions for 'four insane boys 17-21,' insist they are not a manufactured product. 'We're not just any four guys off the street. We're the cream of 400 guys off the street,' said Monkee Peter Tork.

"Actually, 650 young men were interviewed before the four were chosen for a Beatle-type television series which ran two years. Three of the quartet were in Washington to promote their new movie *Head* which will open here Nov. 20 at the Rosslyn Theater. Micky Dolenz remained behind in Hollywood. Although critics have attacked them as 'The Beatles run through a Xerox machine' and 'as calculatingly manufactured as a TV dinner,' The Monkees do not seem carbon copies of anyone.

"Peter Tork, the son of a University of Connecticut economics professor, is the 'political' one, He performed solo at a rally for Sen. Eugene McCarthy during the presidential campaign and is considering a career in politics. Tork labels himself a 'conservative radical' and says he might run for sheriff of Los Angeles County in 1970.

"Michael Nesmith, who was a roving folk singer before joining the group, worries about The Monkees' musical image. Once quoted as saying, 'Don't buy us if you want good music,' Nesmith insists that the only decent Monkee album is the 'third one, when they gave us a free hand. On the first two they wouldn't let us make any suggestions and they even threw me out of the studio.' Sighing, he added, 'They're all convinced we're crazy lunatics and don't know who we are.'

"Their rise to fame apparently hasn't overwhelmed The Monkees. Jones says, however, their fame has brought frequent requests for loans from former friends and total strangers. 'A hairdresser who cut our hair asked Mike and me for a few grand to start a business selling Monkee hair. He was going to sell which he had just cut. We gave him the money – I'm sure we'll never see him again.' 'There will come a time,' Peter Tork says, 'when The Monkees are referred to in the past tense.'"

● Saturday 16th

● KHJ-TV (Channel 9) in Los Angeles televises at 5:30pm highlights from Wednesday's premiere of *Yellow Submarine*. Footage of Micky may be included in this broadcast.

● *NME* reports that British group Julie Driscoll, Brian Auger & The Trinity are due to fly to Los Angeles this weekend to spend ten days filming their appearance in The Monkees' television special. "Format of the show has been decided as a satire on the manufactured Monkees, although it is expected that Julie and The Trinity will make a straight appearance. The special will be networked in the U.S. in January, but as yet there are no plans for British transmission."

● *NME* correspondent June Harris reporting on *Head*'s New York opening says the film is "fairly good fun and quite entertaining – even if it has been released a little late in The Monkees' career."

● Sunday 17th

● *The Los Angeles Times*, which has featured ads for *Head* every day since Thursday, runs a blurb for the film exclaiming "INVITATIONAL PREMIERE TUESDAY! Stars! Lights! Glamour! Excitement! The Monkees in Person! Vogue Theatre Hollywood."

● Monday 18th

● The Monkees appear on two local Philadelphia teen-dance television shows to promote the opening of their movie *Head* at the Trans Lux theatre later this week. (The spots were probably taped earlier this month.) In one of these appearances former *Monkees* series guest star and popular DJ Jerry Blavat hosts the group for an interview on his WFIL-TV show *Jerry's Place*. The audience comes up with the questions for this dialogue.

Michael is asked when he will release another album like *Wichita Train Whistle*, to which he replies, "January." He is then asked if he will be in town for the premiere of *Head*. "There's a special screening this evening for the people in the trade," he explains. "The movie opens at the Trans Lux theatre on the 20th. We won't be here. We're doing a TV special, and we have to get back."

Blavat explains to the crowd that The Monkees cannot perform on his show because they are under obligation to NBC and Screen Gems – and presumably still under the "no outside television in the U.S." rule, though they could certainly use the exposure. Blavat goes on to say that fans who see *Head* "will find a whole different thing with The Monkees." Michael jokes: "It's a dirty picture." Presumably also joking is the audience member who asks if The Monkees really play the music for the TV cartoon 'group' The Archies.

"There's a place in the movie where we do something that no other rock'n'roll group has ever done," says Michael. "They film us live in a concert, and the music that we play live in a concert is the music they use for the soundtrack. [It's] the second number in the movie – the song after the 'Porpoise Song' – a song called 'Circle Sky.' And that's the only time you see us play, because the movie is kind of about different stuff. We're not into the same old thing." Michael says the soundtrack album should be out Monday.

"What we did … was drop out for about eight months," says Michael of the film's prolonged production. "Did some real thinking and got our heads together. Everybody out there knows kind of what it's all about. We felt a certain responsibility and obligation to continue. Everybody's growing up – we are, they are."

● Around this time The Monkees are accompanied by another DJ, Long John Wade, to tape an even more serious interview for *The Hy Lit Show* (starring DJ Hy Lit), which is televised on WKBS-TV. Lit asks, "Will somebody fill me in on the movie?" Micky responds: "It's kinda like a collage, I think. It's not quite like our TV show. It's a little more serious in places, and a lot funnier in places." Lit then asks, "Do you play serious parts in this at all?" Micky again: "We kind of play ourselves mostly, more than we have before. … We had a chance to get into a little dramatics at times, and to portray ourselves a little bit, rather than just running around."

"There's cutting up and stuff on it," explains Michael, "but it's not in the same way that we do it on the television show. We do that really … in person, but we do it differently than the way you saw us do it on the television show – because that was like a year ago. The movie is now. I think maybe we're putting some people on, but it's different."

Davy chimes in: "We have Victor Mature in the movie and

Annette Funicello, Ray Nitschke, Carol Doda. We have a lot of losers in the movie! You know what I mean? We take little bits out of different movies. Like we have a little war sequence, and we have a Western sequence, and we have a fight sequence, and a 'sequence' sequence. Different people are going to get different things out of the movie. I think the kids are going to get maybe Monkee TV time out of the movie, but the adults will see it differently. I think young adults will see it much differently than the adults, or the little ones." "The most fun was the character assassination," says Michael. "What's that all about?" wonders Lit. "Well, you have to see the movie for that to make any sense, but just keep that in mind," says Michael. "We had a lot of fun at The Monkees' expense." Lit asks about The Monkees' music. "We're going back to the roots," says Michael. Micky adds: "Each of us has an individual road or path that we're traveling, and we're expounding on those as much as we can individually. There's no group sound. There hardly ever was, really." "There never was," says Davy. "There never was," repeats Micky. "There was a group sound," counters Michael, "but you could only hear it at concerts. Except maybe *Headquarters*, which was the album that we all just sat down and played on. Concerts were mostly what we really sound like. 'Cos in the studio, and *Headquarters*, worrying about a transition at that time and everything, we maybe pulled a few of the punches that we would [have made]. I think, to a man, all of us are kind of up to here with screaming loud psychedelic stuff, you know? I mean, not that it doesn't have its place. Because I sit and do that number too. Jimi Hendrix is the greatest living rock'n'roll guitarist that I know. I mean that's not what we do, you know? I think what we're going to do [on] our next album, after the soundtrack album, is to be a little more representative of the four of us."

"It's going to be a double album," explains Micky, "where we'll each have a side where we produce our own particular sounds, whatever. I'm kind of into electronic music, I have a Moog synthesizer." Michael adds: "Microtonal fantasies." "I'm Broadway Rock," says Davy, "I like Broadway, Feliciano." Micky says: "Mike's country western." And so ends what is perhaps the group's last interview as a foursome.

● Today's *Los Angeles Times* reveals a bizarre list of 'stars' expected at tomorrow night's *Head* premiere: "Hoyt Axton, Leon Bing, Tommy Boyce, Les Crane, Severn Darden, Carol Doda, Peter Fonda, Annette Funicello, Bobby Hart, Bobby Hatfield, Dennis Hopper, John Phillip Law, Peter Lawford, Sonny Liston, Tina Louise, Don Mitchell, Millie Perkins, Carl Reiner, Vito Scotti, Tiny Tim – and many more!" Several other guests will be detailed in tomorrow's ad. The paper also carries a teaser ad with a picture of a phone and the line "DIAL GO-GO-FUN FOR HEAD." Presumably this is some form of hotline set up to stimulate interest in the film.

● Meanwhile in the studio Michael takes over as producer from an inexplicably absent Bones Howe.

RECORDING Wally Heider Recording (3) *Hollywood, CA* 2:00-5:30, 7:00-10:00pm. Michael Nesmith *prod*; one-inch 8-track; tracking.

1. **'Goldie Locks Sometime'** takes 1-7, + intro piece 3 takes
   The Monkees Season 2 DVD master # WZB5-5396
2. **'String For My Kite'** version 2 takes 1-5
   The Monkees Season 2 DVD master # WZB5-5397
3. **'Darwin'** takes 1-3
   The Monkees Season 2 DVD master # WZB5-5392

Personnel Hal Blaine (drums, percussion 1), Dennis Budimir (guitar), Mike Deasy (guitar), Gene Estes (percussion 1, tambourine 2), Jackie Kelso (flute 1), Larry Knechtel (keyboard 1,3, piano 2), Joe Osborn (bass), Jimmy Rowles (keyboard 1,3, piano 2), Louie Shelton (guitar).

● Michael is joined by a slightly expanded studio band for the final

tracking session to produce songs for The Monkees' upcoming TV special. It is not known why he takes over for Bones Howe this evening, though Howe will certainly return to complete his productions of 'A Man Without A Dream' and 'Someday Man' in January 1969.

The date begins with a brief intro piece for 'Goldie Locks Sometime' and then seven takes of the body of the song. The light instrumentation includes triangle, mallets, celeste, flute, tack piano, organ, various percussion, and some electric guitar. It is possible that Shorty Rogers arranged the charts. Take 7 is spliced together with take 3 of the intro piece to create the master backing track. Davy will add a vocal in the next few days and the finished recording will provide the soundtrack for his major dance routine in the production.

A new version of Bill Dorsey's 'String For My Kite' is taped to replace the arrangement from last week, with tonight's rendition is given some gospel overtones by the session keyboard players, Larry Knechtel and Jimmy Rowles. Davy will add a vocal to this track very soon, the lyrics of which he finds rather poignant. He says: "I'm ready to go. I'm ready to work. I'm ready to do anything. But in the end [of the song] I say, '… if I'm going anywhere.' You know, nobody really knows where they're going. Nobody knows if they're going to be dropped overnight. We had a phenomenon for two years. I mean total pandemonium. Everybody wanted to know us. Then it died off a little. Because we were so big, dying off a little looks like oh, wow, they really died off."

The session wraps with three full passes of 'Darwin,' a song intended as a show segue (a brief musical piece that leads into another scene). Keyboards for this one are tack piano and organ. Group vocals are likely added later this week.

● Tuesday 19th
● The Monkees attend the Hollywood invitation-only premiere of *Head* at 8:30pm at the Vogue Theatre on Hollywood Boulevard. The event is covered on local Metromedia Radio stations KLAC and KMET by DJ Elliot Mintz, who is on hand to interview the group. Other attendees include 'Mama' Cass Elliott, Boyce & Hart, Dennis Hopper, Denny Doherty (of The Mamas & The Papas), Frank Zappa, Sonny Liston, actors Sonny Tufts, Tina Louise, and Annette Funicello, and comedy troupe The Committee.

Today's *Los Angeles Times*, in a slight variation on yesterday's report, says the guest list also includes: "Hoyt Axton, Leon Bing, Ruth Buzzi, The Byrds, Timothy Carey, Les Crane, Severn Darden, Carol Doda, Peter Fonda, Bobby Hatfield, Dennis Hopper, Will Hutchins, T.C. Jones, John Phillip Law, Peter Lawford, Don Mitchell, Sal Mineo, Millie Perkins, Robert Redford, Carl Reiner, Vito Scotti, Tiny Tim – and many more!"

The Citizen News reports that the premiere is quite a scene, "with thousands of screaming fans and scores of personalities showing up for the exciting affair. Fans who waited many hours got to see their favorite stars, the highlight moment coming when The Monkees themselves … arrived on the scene and greeted the crowd. It was a delightful evening for everyone, especially the stars themselves, as *Head* turns out to be one of the most unusual movies of the year [and] a highly entertaining film that will intrigue the 'squares,' not bore grown-ups and be an instant success with the teenybopper for whom it was made."

Ann Moses will later file a rather cruel report in the *NME* saying the film "received a mixed reaction from the opening-night audience. You could hear The Monkees in the audience laughing hysterically at certain 'in jokes' in the film, while the remainder sat idly by. The biggest positive reaction was heard for Davy's black-on-white dance number, which was followed by heavy applause." Moses says the film's message was lost on her – and she knew what to expect, having visited the film set. The queen of the teen magazine *Tiger Beat* has now fully shifted her affections from The Monkees to Elvis Presley, currently on the comeback trail.

● Wednesday 20th

● The *Motion Picture Herald* publishes a very sympathetic review of *Head*. Like William Wolf's *Cue* piece, it tends to show more clarity than the film itself. "Professionally known as The Monkees, these four young men have been the victims of abuse, due to the process by which they reached the heights of the musical recording industry. Having been selected from hundreds of applicants, the four were put together, processed, and marketed like a business commodity, smartly packaged and cleverly advertised.

"*Head* is … important because it is a well-made marijuana movie, representing the sense-transference, time lapse, illusionary realm of pot that lends itself to and belongs in film. In some respects, this makes it a bit intramural, but curious adults will surely find much in it pleasing. They will most decidedly have their attention held.

"All six songs have been performed and presented well, with the initial 'Porpoise Song' registering most positively for improvement of the group's image."

● Kevin Thomas of *The Los Angeles Times* is similarly effusive. "Along with *Yellow Submarine*, *Head* is one of the year's most imaginative movies. With even less plot than in the animated Beatles feature, director Bob Rafelson (and his collaborator on the script, Jack Nicholson) takes The Monkees on a freewheeling series of adventures. Since it is as richly colorful as a kaleidoscope, it is tempting to describe it as still another psychedelic trip studded with frequently hilarious non sequiturs. Indeed it can be fully enjoyed as just that, but the way in which Rafelson bombards the screen with what is often no more than the briefest of blackouts reveals his essential seriousness. He begins the picture with The Monkees jumping off a bridge, plunging them into his own fantasy world.

"As intensely personal as this fast-moving picture is, it remains accessible because Rafelson defines his own sense of reality in the way so many of us do – with images of movies that we grew up on. When he places The Monkees in snatches of Westerns, war pictures, or even Maria Montez-type harem epics he is not spoofing these genres but is instead using them to make us aware of what pop culture tells us about ourselves.

"For example, at one point he cuts from a TV screen showing a mindless [children's] cartoon figure exuberantly shooting a rifle to a newsreel of wounded Vietnamese. Rafelson regards The Monkees, so obviously patterned after The Beatles, as losers, and he counterpoints their escapades and songs with a gallery of his own favorite losers – Victor Mature, Timothy Carey, Annette Funicello, Sonny Liston, Carol Doda, T.C. Jones, and Ray Nitschke.

"Key scenes with The Monkees are extensions of their own personalities and interests – e.g., Peter Tork's involvement in Eastern mysticism inspired a funny sequence with a guru (Abraham Soafer). That The Monkees are not The Beatles, indeed, allows Rafelson to comment implicitly on the place the Liverpudlians actually do occupy in our imaginations – just as he so deftly turns back our old movie fantasies upon reality.

"The structure of *Head* is like one of those Chinese boxes within boxes within boxes within boxes, stretching into infinity. This is highly appropriate since the box is Rafelson's central metaphor. For much of the movie The Monkees are literally as well as figuratively 'boxed in' and trying to free themselves from their manufactured images."

Davy recalls: "I was proud to be involved with such good people as Bob Rafelson and Jack Nicholson. If I were making a movie, that wouldn't be the movie I would make, but there's only a certain amount of things you can do with a group of four. One review I read was really funny. It said, 'Two Beatle movies opened in town, one starring The Monkees.' Then the *Los Angeles Times* gave it rave reviews and said it was a masterpiece. It just shows you two different viewpoints."

● Thursday 21st

Unlike *The Los Angeles Times*, the other major newspaper from the group's hometown, the *Herald Examiner*, files a highly negative review of *Head*. While the paper has the usual harsh words for The Monkees, the most cutting remark is saved for producers Raybert. "It is perhaps unseemly to spend so much effort mocking the four youngsters whom they exploited to get rich."

Peter recalls later: "Basically the movie is not the story of The Monkees' release; it is Rafelson's idea of who The Monkees are. Nobody comes off too good in this movie. If you look carefully, Davy gets called a Manchester midget greenie. Micky is a blithering space case. I am some Indian wiseman's mouthpiece who doesn't know what he's doing. Mike is a con man. Nobody looks too good. Bob Rafelson … has a low view of life and he doesn't mind spewing it into your face. He thinks life sucks and he wants you to know that it sucks. If you don't think it sucks, then you're a fool. That's his viewpoint and one he will insist on making part of your life if he possibly can. I think it's pretty low myself.

"It was great to break loose. There's some awfully funny stuff in it, some brilliant scenes. The movie is not pure bad by any stretch. It's just that finally the point of it is pretty grim. 'Nobody gets out of here alive' is the point of the movie. I think it's basically Rafelson's low-life view of life. I think the movie reflects that."

● Friday 22nd

● *NME* publishes a story of Jimi Hendrix's rise to fame as told by Chas Chandler. Hendrix's former manager now claims (see also July 16th 1967) that the guitarist's appearance on The Monkees' tour last summer was nothing short of a publicity stunt. "One of the first encroaches into the American market was when Jimi rather incongruously appeared on The Monkees' tour – rather like putting Count Dracula on with Snow White! An awful lot of people were against that move. I was against it in principle but we knew that putting Jimi on with The Monkees would get him a blaze of publicity across America. And we had an agreement with Dick Clark that Jimi could be pulled off after a few days. When it was decided to take him off we concocted that story about the American Daughters of [the] Revolution objecting to his act and saying he was obscene. That did the trick and we hit every newspaper in the country, with Jimi coming up with little gems about how he had been replaced by Mickey Mouse!"

● Saturday 23rd – Wednesday 27th

● This weekend, production commences on The Monkees' television special, to be titled *33 ⅓ Revolutions Per Monkee*. The plan was to stage the project at NBC's television studios, but a union strike forces a change. Instead of postponing the taping, The Monkees and their crew move operations about an hour away to MGM Studios in Culver City, where they will avoid any union interference. Unfortunately, the MGM facility is better suited to the production of feature films rather than the extensive video chroma key work, or patching of images, that producer Jack Good has in mind. According to Micky, many of the special's larger sets have to be left behind at NBC, and what remains looks rather cheap and makeshift.

Micky: "It was weird and difficult. Just as we were ready to go into production with Jack Good producing, the musicians at NBC went on strike. We weren't allowed to tape at NBC, which is where we wanted to tape in the big studios, so everything had to be done remote at MGM. Nobody had ever tried to tape this kind of complicated thing remote, where they put tape machines and consoles into moving-vans and wire them up with Scotch tape. So it was very laborious out there at MGM. It was a lot of work, a lot of trouble, a lot of waiting – a pain in the ass. Mainly because Jack Good was doing a lot of special effects, which again hadn't been done at the time."

The roots of The Monkees' special are to be found in another project that Jack Good mounted earlier this year in association with Screen Gems, *Innocence, Anarchy And Soul*. Described as "a one-hour show divided into three phases – nostalgic; a satirical sketch on the present pop scene; and a wild guess at the future," the program featured Jerry Lee Lewis and Julie Driscoll, Brian Auger & The Trinity. For *33⅓*, Good reuses this scenario and guests, merely plugging The Monkees into his script, where he creates another "satirical sketch on the present pop scene" by cynically portraying The Monkees as rock's first test tube babies.

Brian Auger: "The premise of the program was that we would grab four guys in off the street – didn't matter who they were – and we would brainwash them into becoming rock stars. Now, Jack explained this to me and I said, 'Well, this is a bit harsh, isn't it, to say we'll grab anybody off the street, we're gonna make them rock stars? Aren't The Monkees gonna go, 'Wait a minute, this is a little bit rough on us?' He said, 'Absolutely not, man. They love the idea.' They turned out to be great guys."

Art Fisher, who co-wrote the show's script with Jack Good, directs *33 ⅓*. The two recently worked together on a James Brown special for Metromedia, but *33 ⅓* is Fisher's network directorial debut – and it will show. The program is meant to be a Darwinian tale of rock music's evolution, hyped by the two as "a new-to-television format – a definitive storyline for a musical variety show." Although there will be obvious moments of innovation and creativity throughout the production, the show's script is really a less sophisticated variation on *Head*.

LEFT **The Monkees perform a rock'n'roll medley for Jack Good's *33 ⅓ Revolutions Per Monkee* TV special.** ABOVE **Working with Little Richard on the set of *33 ⅓*.**

Michael says that Good "was, I think, in some way trying to grind the same ax that *Head* did so beautifully. He did [it] clumsily. Sort of the television version of *Head* in a way."

Peter: "Interesting thing about *33 ⅓* is it's the same as *Head*. I think it's the story that wanted to be told. I think that *33 ⅓* is more human in that sense. It's not as powerful an artistic achievement by any stretch of the imagination. When you look at *Head* now there is an awful lot of stuff in there that beguiles you away from the basic point-of-view of the movie. It's like a time capsule. It's really interesting from that point of view. Styles and behaviors and characters and people."

The *33 ⅓* special will be something of a social time capsule. It combines the old-time rock'n'roll rave-ups of Jack Good's *Shindig!* with featured guests Julie Driscoll, Brian Auger & The Trinity and their progressive neo-jazz workouts (a wild guess at the future?), yet this chaotic blend will be fascinating to watch if only for its incongruous nature.

The failure of the program will be in its use – or non-use – of The Monkees. Whether they be considered a group of musicians, actors, or just four very lucky guys, their television series did change the face and pace of presenting music on television. There is no evidence of another such great leap with *33 ⅓*'s pacing or visuals. Indeed, Raybert's Bob Rafelson and Bert Schneider, creators of the TV series, are absent from this production, with only Ward Sylvester acting on Raybert's behalf. Saddled with the hackneyed format of a musical variety show, most of *33 ⅓* only serves to set up the presence of Jack Good's guest performers.

Davy: "On *33 ⅓* they didn't use us to our full capacity. Everybody knew about the manufactured image and about us being made in a test tube. They should have used our talents and let us perform." Micky: "In a way we were like our own special guests on our own television special. Kinda weird."

The highlights of *33 ⅓* will be in some of the musical segments. The four Monkees are each given solo fantasy sequences, all of which are effective in showing their individual musical points of view. Michael fights it out with his alter ego Monkee Mike in a split-screen rendition of 'Naked Persimmon,' which contains the biting lines: "Tell me Mr. TV man / Just where you make your moral stand. / Which way each day do you take your pay? / Do you walk straight up / Or do you face the other way?"

Peter sits cross-legged for the meditative '(I Prithee) Do Not Ask For Love.' Davy runs through the choreographed 'Goldie Locks Sometime,' which echoes his show-stopping dance work in *Head*, and Micky performs a soulful live duet with Julie Driscoll on 'I'm A Believer.'

Another major sequence taped for the special is Good's inevitable rock'n'roll medley, a feature of nearly all of his programs. The twist here is that the backing is provided by The Buddy Miles Express, including Herbie Rich on keyboards, Billy Rich on bass, Jim McCarty on guitar, and a brass section of James Tatum, Virgil Gonsalves, Tom Hall, and Robert Pittman. The sequence is supposedly set at the Paramount Theater on December 7th 1956, interspersed with black-and-white images of DJ Alan Freed and other early rock iconography.

The Monkees run through 'At The Hop' (with Micky on lead vocals) followed by guest Fats Domino on 'I'm Ready' and Jerry Lee Lewis's quick rendition of 'Whole Lotta Shakin' Goin' On.' Little Richard takes over for 'Tutti Frutti,' then back to Fats for more of 'I'm Ready.' Next it's on to The Monkees and 'Shake A Tail Feather' (with added vocals by The We Three Trio), Fats Domino, who performs 'Blue Monday,' and The Monkees mugging it up for a comical take on The Diamonds' hit 'Little Darlin'.' Then there's a burst of Little

Richard on 'Long Tall Sally,' Jerry Lee Lewis pounds out 'Down The Line,' and *Shindig!* regulars The Clara Ward Singers wrap things up with a quasi-gospel revival of the traditional 'Dry Bones.' The Monkees are seen for little more than three minutes during the 11-minute sequence.

Micky: "I don't remember a lot about that. I remember Jerry Lee Lewis, Fats Domino, and Little Richard all stacked up on pianos – that was unbelievable. That's when we were splitting up even more. Going further and further away from anything."

The special closes with what the show's outline calls "the wild 'Freak-Out' finale," which is meant to be "a pure bit of social commentary on the part of the writers." This frenzied send-off is supposed to show "how society is constantly brainwashed into sameness. In the finale [the writers once again] show how, when people are tired of conformity, they branch off into extreme paths of individualism. With the aid of hundreds of props resurrected from literally scores of old movies, The Monkees, Julie Driscoll, Brian Auger & The Trinity, Buddy Miles Express, Paul Arnold & The Moon Express, zitarist Maryvonne [Pointer] and her Indian musicians, the We Three Trio, and the Jamie Rogers Dancers, augmented by 120 hippies recruited from the Hollywood streets, do their individual things simultaneously. The result is an explosion of sight and sound which ends – literally – with an explosion."

More accurately, the finale begins as a live performance of Michael's 'Listen To The Band' by just the four Monkees and eventually spirals out of control as each of Good's guests are added to the mix.

It will be the last time the four Monkees perform together in the 1960s. During the taping, Peter tells the other Monkees that he is interested in leaving the band. Peter: "The last official get-together I had with The Monkees was when they gave me a $6 watch upon my retirement from the group. They all chipped in and even had it engraved: 'To Peter from the guys at work.'"

Peter will later claim that the seeds of his departure lay in the musical battles of '66. He says: "I'd always had deep doubts ever since 'Clarksville.' I walked in [the studio] and Tommy Boyce and Bobby Hart looked at me with scorn and derision, like: 'What are you doing here, you stupid jerk? Guitar in your hand, you fool.' That was the end of it for me right there. Right there I was done with The Monkees in large measure. I struggled against it with some success at one point. *Headquarters* was great for me, but after *Headquarters* nobody wanted to be a recording group any more. I did what I could, but I didn't feel like there was any reason for me to be there any more. It wasn't what I wanted. I wanted to be in a group and nobody else did."

Peter is the only one who believes in this group ethic. Some will say that no one is more pleased with Peter's departure than Michael, who may have viewed him as an obstacle in the way of his total musical dominance of the group.

Michael: "Well, I was ambivalent. I could understand why he wanted to go, 'cos I did too. But I felt like we hadn't quite finished up and that there were a few things that we should try to do. I was also keen on just not leaving it a loose end. I felt like there was some things that The Monkees were and represented that had not been said or done. I felt if we could have been able to work together, we might have been able to do that. But it was also clear to me that we weren't able to work together. That we weren't really an organic band, so we didn't have the way to do it. So I realized it was best for him to move on and that it would just be a matter of time before I would find my next stage."

The TV special will be broadcast on April 14th 1969 and is later included on the 2003 DVD boxed set *The Monkees Season 2*.

DECEMBER

● Raybert Productions end their association with The Monkees amid some bitterness over the commercial outcome of *Head*. Their final managerial act is to book the group on the television game show *Hollywood Squares*.

Bob Rafelson: "I grooved on those four in very special ways while at the same time thinking they had absolutely no talent."

● Wednesday 4th

● *Head* opens 'wide' at movie houses around Southern California while continuing its special engagement at the Vogue. *Duffy* with James Coburn and James Mason is added as a second feature to help boost ticket sales.

● Wasting no time in getting back to business, the remaining Monkees have some new post-Peter photos shot by their friend Henry Diltz.

● This evening a private party is held at the Whisky A Go Go for Brian Auger and Julie Driscoll. Peter and Micky attend. Buddy Miles performs at the club later in the evening.

● Saturday 7th

● The new three-piece Monkees – Michael, Micky, and Davy – travel to Las Vegas for a photoshoot and a promotional appearance at the Gavin Awards.

● Ann Moses files a report in *NME* about the band's recently

completed TV special. Though she is miffed to have been thrown off the set of Elvis Presley's upcoming *Charro!*, also filming on the MGM lot, she speaks with Davy who outlines the plot. Moses says the completed program is "as yet unsold."

● Stanley Kauffman files a somewhat sympathetic review of *Head* for *The New Republic*. "I've been hearing that in order to enjoy *Head*, you have to be high on pot. I enjoyed it while smoking a cigar. ... [Bob] Rafelson, who organized The Monkees as a young singing group, directed the film, with a well-stocked memory and a pretty fair imagination. Not all of *Head* is funny, or funny enough, but at least it understands that its job is to supply lots of choices, not to be carefully selective."

● Monday 9th

RECORDING RCA *Hollywood, CA*. Shorty Rogers *prod*; one-inch 8-track; overdubs.

1. **'Listen To The Band'** version 1
   The Monkees Present master # WZA4-3086
2. **'Mommy And Daddy'**
   The Monkees Present master # WZB5-5310

Personnel Bud Brisbois (trumpet), Buddy Childers (trumpet), John Kitzmiller (tuba), Don McGinnis (brass), Dick Nash (trombone), Michel Rubini (keyboard), Mike Saluzzi (guitar), Ray Triscari (trumpet).

● Shorty Rogers adds brass (and possibly other instruments) to the productions of 'Listen To The Band' and 'Mommy And Daddy.' Guitar and keyboard are also credited on today's musicians' union contract but seem speculative at best. Both of today's songs will be worked on again at sessions on December 28th.

● Tuesday 10th

● After only a week *Head* ends its city-wide run in the Los Angeles area.

● Wednesday 11th

● *Variety* reports that Don Kirshner has finally settled out-of-court his Monkees dispute with Screen Gems/Columbia. The terms of the settlement are not disclosed, though Kirshner will later claim "it was the biggest settlement in the history of Columbia Pictures."

● Thursday 12th

● The remaining three Monkees shoot a promotional Christmas card at the offices of Screen Gems with photographer Henry Diltz.

● Friday 13th

● *Head* opens 'wide' in theatres across New York. Another Columbia Pictures film, *The Love-Ins*, is added as a second feature to boost ticket sales.

● Sunday 15th

● Davy and Linda Haines's marriage has been deemed 'illegal' by the draft board and so today they once again tie the knot. This time the ceremony takes place at Gretna Green Weddings in Winterhaven, California, with David Pearl acting as best man.

● Tuesday 17th

● After barely more than a weekend showing at theatres throughout the New York City area, *Head* today ends its run as a cinema attraction there. Meanwhile in the studio, Peter officially ends his run as a Monkee.

RECORDING Wally Heider (3) *Hollywood, CA* 7:30-10:30pm. Brendan Cahill *prod*; Rik (Pekkonen?) *eng*; one-inch 8-track; set-up, tracking.

1. **'California, Here It Comes'** takes 1-2
   The Monkees Season 2 DVD no master #

Personnel Mike Barone (trombone), Jack Good (additional vocal), Bob Morin (drums), Peter Tork (vocal, banjo).

● Peter's final duty as a Monkee is to record a vocal for this piece, an off-kilter rendition of the standard 'California Here I Come.' The song is rewritten and geared towards a predicted California earthquake and, fittingly, will be the very last thing heard in the completed TV special. It will also be the very last thing heard from Peter for a very long time. His next vocal performance released to the general public will be in 1976. Unlike the other recordings made for *33 ⅓ Revolutions Per Monkee*, the final master for 'California Here

It Comes' will remain in the vaults, though at the time of writing it has never been released officially on record.

● Friday 20th
RECORDING United Recorders *Hollywood, CA* 4:30-7:30, 8:00-11:00pm. Tommy Boyce & Bobby Hart *prod*; Henry Lewy *eng*; one-inch 8-track; overdubs.
1. **'Me Without You'** overdubs onto take 1
   Instant Replay master # WZB3-3511
2. **'Don't Listen To Linda'** version 2 overdubs onto take 2
   Instant Replay master # WZB3-0187
3. **'Through The Looking Glass'** version 2 overdubs onto take 20
   Instant Replay master # WZB3-3512

Personnel Louie Shelton (guitar).

● Tommy Boyce and Bobby Hart are anxious to get some of their still-unreleased productions from late '67 onto The Monkees' next album and so return to the studio to freshen up these tracks with some added guitar from Louie Shelton. All three songs will be mixed for release on December 28th.

● Saturday 21st
● *NME* officially reports that Peter Tork has left The Monkees and that the group will make their first television appearance without him next week on *Hollywood Squares*. The paper also reports that

Davy will soon tape a solo appearance on the television program *Rowan and Martin's Laugh-In*.

● Monday 23rd – Friday 27th
● The Monkees – now just Micky, Davy, and Michael – make their public debut as a trio on the television game show *Hollywood Squares*. This program is shown each day this week in most major areas.

● Saturday 28th
● In *Billboard*'s last Top LPs chart of the year, the soundtrack to The Monkees' film *Head* debuts at #158. In its 33rd week on the same chart *The Birds, The Bees & The Monkees* slips to #132, still outselling the group's new album. Meanwhile in the studio, masters for the next Monkees album are mixed.

RECORDING RCA *Hollywood, CA*. Dennis ? *eng*; quarter-inch stereo; mixdown.
1. **'Don't Listen To Linda'** version 2 take 2
   Instant Replay master # WZB3-0187
2. **'Me Without You'** take 1
   unissued master # WZB3-3511
3. **'Mommy And Daddy'**
   unissued master # WZB5-5310
4. **'Just A Game'** version 2 take 3
   Instant Replay master # WZB5-5311

5. 'Rose Marie'
   unissued master # WZB3-0140
6. 'Through The Looking Glass' version 2 take 20
   Instant Replay master # WZB3-3512

● Today's stereo mixes of 'Don't Listen To Linda' and 'Through The Looking Glass' are destined for inclusion on The Monkees' next long-player, *Instant Replay*. 'Me Without You' will also appear on that album but not in today's mix, which features a prominent solo played on a calliope (a sort of steam-whistle keyboard). After some minor fine-tuning a new mix of 'Me Without You' featuring more guitar will be prepared some time in the next few days.

Micky's 'Mommy And Daddy,' now sporting Shorty Rogers's horn arrangement, is given its first stereo mixdown today. The results are somewhat rough and the song will be mixed for a third time on January 10th next year.

Two more of Micky's numbers also receive attention during today's date, with 'Just A Game' and 'Rose Marie' both mixed into stereo. Only 'Just A Game' will make it to The Monkees' next album, *Instant Replay*. While 'Rose Marie' is seriously considered for the LP, Micky probably feels the production is still incomplete. Sessions for the track will continue through 1969.

● Michael holds another session for his 'Listen To The Band,' at Gold Star Recording Studios in Hollywood, but precise details are not known.

● Monday 30th

● In a recap of the past year in music, Joe Cappo of *The Chicago Daily News* writes: "If nothing else, the whole country finally got The Monkees off its back. The public wised up to the antics of this synthetic group of musicians who were manufactured in a television test tube."

● Tuesday 31st

● *Variety* reports that The Monkees have been signed by producer Roger Gimbel to appear on *The Glen Campbell Goodtime Hour* television show. Their formal contract will be executed next month (see January 20th 1969).

● Journalist Ann Moses of *Tiger Beat* and *NME* visits Peter at home to get the dirt on his split from The Monkees. "Actually, I wanted to leave the group over two years ago when the first season ended," he admits, "but the guys convinced me not to. I didn't care about all the things that were happening, all the acclaim. I hated the work! It was tough, and I didn't like it. I just wanted to record for all my life.

"Also, the pressure was awful. We were working in an incredibly new environment. Half the crew on the show was young and had very little experience at that level of work. Many of them were getting their first big break. Actually, after the TV show was cancelled it was easier for me to leave. Doing the TV show was the worst. Then came the movie, and I couldn't forego the movie, so I did it.

"You know, there were moments here and there – lots of good, funny stuff happening throughout – but the only time it was really happy was when we were recording the *Headquarters* album. The concerts were fun, but during the concert tours you are removed from your friends except for the guys. And even when we did take a few friends along, it was only a mild relief. The last tour of Australia and Japan wasn't fun because I felt hideously under-rehearsed. I was constantly pushing for rehearsals, and they were constantly saying, 'Well, like, later.' We couldn't get together. Also, we didn't play any new music the last concert tour. It was all old tunes, nothing from our newer albums, and it was a bore."

Peter tells Moses that the other Monkees saw the split coming. "I think they suspected I was leaving anyway. For me, a lot of pressure

was off. When I felt a part of the group, every time someone said something that jarred against my sensibilities I'd raise a huge ruckus and everybody thought I was out of my mind. While we were making the television special, knowing I was not going to be there any longer, I just thought to myself: I don't have to worry about this thing. And I just let everything slide right off my back. They must have thought something was screwy.

"Then I finally told them, 'Gentlemen, I'm in negotiations to resign from the group.' And they said, 'OK, well, there's not much time, we'd better get to work on the special.' So we taped the thing and that's the last I saw of them. The last day of taping, they gave me this little testimonial, memorial watch."

Peter says he is currently pursuing a recording contract for his friend Judy Mayhan (who will eventually sign to Atlantic Records)

but that his own musical plans to form a group with his brother Nick have faltered. As for acting, he says: "I don't like acting, but I may do it some day. I mean, the thing about film work is that it is on-again, off-again. They say, 'Turn on, act up, keep happy, charge, generate.' Then just as quickly, 'Turn off, shut up, keep quiet while everybody else does their work.'"

Now Peter calls the shots for himself. "I usually wake up about nine or eleven," he says of his current routine. "Get up, eat breakfast, read the newspapers, drink coffee, go out, come back in the evening, watch the news, eat dinner, and go to bed.

"Going out means whatever is handy. Sometimes I go over to the Raybert office and hang out with Bert Schneider for a while. Sometimes I go … anywhere, no telling. Right now I'm working with my friend Bob Hammer on a film. I'm going to deliver a lecture on the generation gap in Aspen, Colorado, and I'm going to show a film just to keep them interested.

"I'm free. I don't know what I'll be doing. I'm actually a little apprehensive, because there's no doubt that there are three other incredibly talented fellows out there.

"They're very talented guys. Mike is one of the funniest people I've ever known. Micky is even funnier, and Davy is just as cute as a button. Who could ask for anything more?"

Peter closes the interview with a final remark about his split from the group. "I'm both really relieved and really, really apprehensive. I'm terribly glad and also terribly sad."

LEFT **Stepping out as a trio: Davy, Michael, and Micky.** ABOVE **Michael, Davy, and Micky take over a tree-house belonging to Michael's son for a photoshoot later used on *Instant Replay*, The Monkees' first album as a trio.**

1969

Monkees now a trio: Davy, Michael, and Micky ... Davy makes solo TV appearances ... producer Bones Howe continues Monkees recording sessions ... *Instant Replay* seventh LP, makes #32 ... 'Tear Drop City' ninth single, makes #56 ... concerts as trio, backed by Sam & The Goodtimers ... TV ads for Kool Aid soft drink mix ... TV special *33 ⅓ Revolutions Per Monkee* shown on NBC ... 'Someday Man' tenth single, makes #81 ... Davy, Michael, and Micky resume separate recording sessions ... concerts continue ... *Greatest Hits* compilation LP, makes #89 ... Boyce & Hart return to Monkees production ... 'Good Clean Fun' 11th single, makes #82 ... Saturday TV reruns of *The Monkees* on CBS, some with new music ... *The Monkees Present* eighth LP, makes #100 ... more concerts ... Michael begins a gradual departure from the group.

Jumping for joy? The three-piece Monkees launch themselves into a difficult year.

JANUARY

● *16* magazine reports that The Monkees' television special will be about "a man who manages singing groups – but the groups always desert him when they get successful, so he makes four puppets and teaches them how to sing. The story is supposed to take place in England about a hundred years ago."

● *Monkees Monthly* notes that the group's next single may be Michael's 'Listen To The Band' and that it could be issued as soon as February. They also list an early line-up for ex-Monkee Peter Tork's new band featuring on guitar *The Monkees* series assistant director Jon Anderson, Lowell George also on guitar, Tork on bass, and his girlfriend Reine Stewart on drums.

● Davy begins a series of solo TV appearances and this month tapes an episode of the popular series *Laugh-In*, acting as the show's guest host but not performing musically.

As for the current state of Monkeemania, Davy tells Ann Moses: "Fans will remember that we gave them two years of looking at something other than their mother or father or their schoolbooks. We gave them something. They thought about us. It's something that takes you away from the normal everyday routine. I think we filled a gap.

"You see, two-and-a-half years ago there were lots of groups breaking into the big time, but the scene was like an apple. Half of it was gone on things that had been done before; half of it was still fresh. Nobody had even had a taste of the fresh half – the five-to-ten-year-olds. Nobody was playing to them. Nobody was performing for those people. But we went to them and we filled a little void.

"That's why I get so angry when musicians say, 'Oh, your music is so bad,' because it's not bad to the kids. Those people who talk about 'doing their own thing' are groups that go and play in the clubs that hold 50 people, while we're playing to 10,000 kids. You know it hurts me to think that anybody thinks we're phoney, because we're not. We're only doing what we think is our own thing."

● Saturday 4th

RECORDING Wally Heider Recording (3) *6373 Selma Avenue, Hollywood, CA.* Bones Howe *prod*; Bones Howe *eng*; one-inch 8-track; reductions, overdubs.

1. **'A Man Without A Dream'** version 4 overdubs onto take 14
   Instant Replay master # XZB5-0123
2. **'Someday Man'** overdubs onto composite take
   Instant Replay master # WZB5-5399
Personnel David Jones (vocal).

● Bones Howe, having wrapped his music production work on The Monkees' television special, sets about completing the two potential single tracks he taped for the group in November. This session focuses on adding Davy's lead vocal to the masters. Davy tapes four full passes of his voice on Goffin & King's 'A Man Without A Dream.' Howe then sorts through the performances, simultaneously dubbing down the results to a second 8-track machine – during which procedure the two pianos and two guitars from the previous session are combined to a single track, leaving just the bass and drums on individual tracks. After this is completed Howe edits together the best elements of these four performances (and reductions) into one composite master. The composite master is subjected to further refinement from Davy, who touches up his final lead vocals. Once satisfied, Howe makes a second composite master featuring the best of today's augmentation. It is this second composite master that will be subject to further sweetening at sessions on Friday and Saturday.

As with 'A Man Without A Dream,' Davy tapes four full passes of

the lead vocal for 'Someday Man.' The pianos and guitars are bounced to a single track in the process, but the original bass and drum tracks are kept discrete. After the four vocal takes, Howe runs over the song six more times to arrive at the perfect combination of performances, during which process Davy fine-tunes his vocals. Two further sessions will be held this month to complete the production of 'Someday Man.'

● Thursday 9th

● Micky's wife Samantha gives birth to a baby daughter, Ami Bluebell, at St. Joseph's Hospital in Burbank, California.

● Friday 10th

RECORDING Western Recorders *6000 Sunset Boulevard, Hollywood, CA* 11:00am-2:00pm. Bones Howe *prod*; Bones Howe *eng*; one-inch 8-track; overdubs.

1. **'A Man Without A Dream'** version 4 overdubs onto take 14
   Instant Replay master # XZB5-0123
2. **'Someday Man'** overdubs onto composite take
   Instant Replay master # WZB5-5399
Personnel Don Addrisi (backing vocal), Hal Blaine (tambourine), Joe Osborn (bass), unknown (guitar, backing vocal).

● With Davy's performances on these songs now in the bag, producer Howe adds group backing vocals to the tracks, as performed by Don Addrisi of The Addrisi Brothers along with other uncredited singers (none of The Monkees are audible).

Other overdubs probably taped this evening include a tambourine and two guitar parts (one acoustic 12-string and a baritone guitar put through an amp with heavy tremolo) for 'A Man Without A Dream.' Then 'Someday Man' is sweetened with an electric fuzz guitar, handclaps, and tambourine. It is also possible that bassist Joe Osborn replaces his part on 'A Man Without A Dream' during this session. Brass overdubs for both songs will be added tomorrow afternoon.

RECORDING RCA *6363 Sunset Boulevard, Hollywood, CA.* Quarter-inch mono and stereo; assembly.

1. **'Just A Game'** version 2 take 3
   unissued master # WZB5-5311
2. **'Rose Marie'**
   unissued master # WZB3-0140
3. **'Carlisle Wheeling'** version 3 take 4
   unissued master # UZB3-9782
4. **'Mommy And Daddy'**
   The Monkees Present master # WZB5-5310

● At RCA studios preparations are made for The Monkees' upcoming *Instant Replay* album. During today's master assembly process mixes of these four songs are reviewed but rejected. 'Just A Game' will appear on the forthcoming album, but in stereo and not the mono mixes featured on today's reel. Unique mono mixes of 'Rose Marie' and 'Carlisle Wheeling' are also left on the studio floor, and neither song will appear on the final album. 'Mommy And Daddy' is given a second stereo mix today, but music coordinator Lester Sill will deem the song's lyrics – including lines such as "Ask your mommy and daddy / Who really killed J.F.K.?" – too controversial for release on the LP. The song will remain in the vault until its words are softened by Micky later this year. In 1994 the unadulterated version will appear as a bonus track on the CD reissue of *The Monkees Present*.

● Saturday 11th

● *NME* reports that Davy will soon fly to London to tape an appearance on Welsh vocalist Tom Jones's television series, *This Is*

The trio rehearsing a medley for their appearance on TV's Glen Campbell Goodtime Hour.

Tom Jones. "The *NME* understands it was originally hoped to book The Monkees as a group for the February 16th show – and the possibility that Micky Dolenz and Mike Nesmith will join Davy Jones in the programme still cannot be ruled out. In any event, Davy will be appearing as a singer and not simply in an interview spot." Meanwhile in Hollywood, Bones Howe adds the final production touch of an eight-piece brass section to 'A Man Without A Dream' and 'Someday Man.'

RECORDING Western Recorders *Hollywood, CA* 2:00-6:00pm. Bones Howe *prod*; Bones Howe *eng*; one-inch 8-track; overdubs.

1. **'A Man Without A Dream'** version 4 overdubs onto take 14
   Instant Replay master # XZB5-0123
2. **'Someday Man'** overdubs onto composite take
   Instant Replay master # WZB5-5399

Personnel Conte Candoli (trumpet), Buddy Childers (trumpet), Jim Decker (French horn), Vincent DeRosa (French horn), Bob Edmondson (trombone), Bill Hinshaw (French horn), Lew McCreary (trombone), Dick Perissi (French horn).

● Bill Holman arranges today's brass charts. All eight players are recorded onto a single track of the now brimming 8-track masters for 'A Man Without A Dream' and 'Someday Man.' With the productions now complete, these songs will be mixed on Monday.

● Sunday 12th

● Davy travels to London, England to tape his TV appearance for *This Is Tom Jones*. The taping takes place at Elstree Studios, just north-west of London, where Davy solo performs 'Consider Yourself' from *Oliver!* with accompaniment from the house band.

He later comments to the *NME*: "Doing the Tom Jones show was really weird. When I did *Laugh-In* it was all very off-the-top-of-my-head comedy and gagging. The *Jones* show was a very planned thing and I haven't worked under those conditions for a long time. It was so fantastic to hear people like Nancy Wilson and Rich Little, who were also guests on the show, come up to me and say, 'We

admired what The Monkees have done for the industry.' It was a very good feeling."

● Monday 13th

RECORDING Wally Heider Recording (3) *Hollywood, CA*. Bones Howe *prod*; Bones Howe *eng*; quarter-inch stereo; mixdown.

1. **'A Man Without A Dream'** version 4 take 14
   Instant Replay master # XZB5-0123
2. **'Someday Man'** composite master
   Instant Replay master # WZB5-5399

● Bones Howe mixes down his completed productions for the group. 'A Man Without A Dream' will be included on the group's next album, *Instant Replay*, and on the flipside of their next single, 'Tear Drop City,' rush-released only days from now. 'Someday Man' will follow as a single release in April. It is never featured originally on an album but will eventually be collected as a bonus track on the 1995 CD reissue of *Instant Replay*. The A-side of The Monkees' next single is also mixed today, at a separate session at RCA.

RECORDING RCA *Hollywood, CA*. Quarter-inch mono and stereo; mixdown.

1. **'Tear Drop City'**
   Instant Replay master # TZB3-4731

● Music coordinators Lester Sill and Brendan Cahill hope to shore up The Monkees' sagging commercial fortunes by reviving the sound (and nearly the same song) that started it all: 'Last Train To Clarksville.' Today, someone digs into the vault and resurrects Boyce & Hart's old master of 'Tear Drop City,' originally completed on November 6th 1966. But there is a new twist.

During the mixing process, this once bluesy-sounding rocker, played at the tempo of the Sir Douglas Quintet hit 'She's About A Mover,' will be speeded up almost beyond recognition, resulting in a master that plays a whole nine percent faster than its original recording. This will change the feel of the song totally, giving it a sprightly pace similar to 'Last Train To Clarksville.'

The revised master is mixed into mono and stereo, both in speeded-up mode, though only the stereo will be released to the general public. A promotional single of today's mono mix will be made available to U.S. AM radio stations, which still broadcast in monaural sound. (Overseas mono singles are probably just reductions of today's stereo mix.)

● Saturday 18th

● *NME* publishes an article entitled "Year Of The Monkee Crash." It is essentially a survey of U.K. chart performances and points out that the group went from the second biggest selling act in 1967 to the 25th in 1968. The biggest-selling act of '67, Engelbert Humperdinck, was relegated to fourth place in 1968 – not quite the dramatic fall of The Monkees.

● Monday 20th

● Hank Grant writes in *The Hollywood Reporter*: "The Monkees will be splitting up whether they want to or not (we had it that they wanted to). Not only has Peter Tork quit ... but Micky Dolenz just got his draft notice and Davy Jones is expecting his any day now."
● Despite rumors of their demise, the trio (including Davy, who returns from Britain today) sign a contract with Smo-Bro Productions to appear on television's *The Glen Campbell Goodtime Hour*, a new variety series starring the former Monkees session musician, now a hit-maker in his own right. In addition to a payment for their services, the trio are also due to receive a collective $7,500 "for furnishing special material for use in said program." In return for this one-time payment the group waives all future rights to this "special material."

● Wednesday 22nd

RECORDING RCA *Hollywood, CA* 7:00-10:00pm. Michael Nesmith *prod*; 'HM' *eng*; one-inch 8-track; tracking.
1. **'My Share Of The Sidewalk'** version 2 takes 1-8
    unissued master # WZB3-0109
Personnel Arnold Belnick (violin), Max Bennett (bass), Jules Chaikin (trumpet), Douglas Davis (cello), Bonnie Douglas (violin), John Guerin (drums), James Hughart (bass), Wilbert Nuttycombe (violin), Gene Pello (mallets), Jerome Reisler (violin), Michel Rubini (piano), Paul Shure (violin), Gerald Vinci (violin), unknown (guitar, steel guitar).
● A full year after he first taped this song, Michael attempts an all-new version. Today's arrangement by Don McGinnis is far lighter in feel to the 1968 rendition, and Gene Pello's mallet work and the uncredited steel guitarist give it an almost tropical sound that one can easily imagine Michael singing over in the manner of his 1970s hit 'Rio.' Take 8 from today's session is marked as the master and will be further augmented on Friday.

● Wednesday 22nd – Sunday 26th

● The Monkees are scheduled to rehearse and perform their TV appearance on *The Glen Campbell Goodtime Hour*, taped on Sunday 26th.
● Saturday's *NME* reports that the group's next UK single may be 'Porpoise Song.' The release has been held back to coincide with the as-yet unscheduled premiere of the group's *Head* movie in Britain, mainly because Columbia Pictures has reported very low attendance for the film Stateside. Meanwhile, The Monkees' television special, *33 ⅓ Revolutions Per Monkee*, is now scheduled for a February airing.

● Thursday 30th

● Final masters for The Monkees' *Instant Replay* album are assembled. The long-player will be released next month.

● Friday 31st

RECORDING RCA (C) *6363 Sunset Boulevard, Hollywood, CA* 2:00-5:00pm. Don McGinnis *prod*; Richie Schmitt *eng*; one-inch 8-track; overdubs, mixdown.
1. **'My Share Of The Sidewalk'** version 2 overdubs onto take 8
    unissued master # WZB3-0109
2. **'All The Grey Haired Men'** overdubs onto take 5
    unissued master # WZB3-0179
3. **'If I Ever Get To Saginaw Again'** overdubs onto take 2
    Missing Links 2 master # WZB3-0178
Personnel Douglas Davis (cello), Jack Gootkin (violin), Bob Jung (violin), Del Kacher (possibly guitar), Garry Nuttycombe (viola), George Poole (violin), Heimann Weinstine (violin), William Weiss (violin).
● Further string embellishments are added to these productions under the direction of arranger Don McGinnis. Rough mono mixes of all three tunes are made at the end of today's session but only 'If I Ever Get To Saginaw' will be taken beyond this point (see March 6th).

Work on version 2 of Michael's 'Sidewalk' will stall after this session, leaving this rendition unheard publicly. However, the song will be resurrected by another Colgems group, The New Establishment, later this year (see July 23rd). Likewise, Jack Keller's 'All The Grey Haired Men' will be shelved and, since it has no vocal tracks, is never released.

FEBRUARY

Instant Replay album is released in the U.S.A.
'Tear Drop City' / 'A Man Without A Dream' single is released in the U.S.A.
The Monkees' seventh album and ninth single are both issued in America this month.

Instant Replay album

A1 **'Through The Looking Glass'** version 2 (T. BOYCE / B. HART / R. BALDWIN)
A2 **'Don't Listen To Linda'** version 2 (T. BOYCE / B. HART)
A3 **'I Won't Be The Same Without Her'** (G. GOFFIN / C. KING)
A4 **'Just A Game'** version 2 (M. DOLENZ)
A5 **'Me Without You'** (T. BOYCE / B. HART)
A6 **'Don't Wait For Me'** (M. NESMITH)
B1 **'You And I'** (D. JONES / B. CHADWICK)
B2 **'While I Cry'** version 2 (M. NESMITH)
B3 **'Tear Drop City'** (T. BOYCE / B. HART)
B4 **'The Girl I Left Behind Me'** version 1 (C. BAYER / N. SEDAKA)
B5 **'A Man Without A Dream'** version 4 (G. GOFFIN / C. KING)
B6 **'Shorty Blackwell'** (M. DOLENZ)

U.S. release February 1969 (Colgems COS-115).
U.K. release June 6th 1969 (RCA 8016).
Chart high U.S. number 32; U.K. none.

Tear Drop City single

A 'Tear Drop City' (T. BOYCE / B. HART)
B 'A Man Without A Dream' (G. GOFFIN / C. KING)

U.S. release February 1969 (Colgems 5000).
U.K. release February 28th 1969 (RCA 1802).
Chart high U.S. number 34; U.K. number 46.

● *Monkees Monthly* reports that the trio plan to perform a try-out concert in Hawaii – as they did in 1966 – before hitting the road this year. The magazine further notes that Davy has recently made some solo personal appearances, probably referring to two recent concerts in Alabama (possibly in late 1968), where he may have sung live to pre-recorded Monkees tracks.

During one weekend Davy appeared at the Alabama State Coliseum in Montgomery, where he introduced Andy Kim, Billy Joe Royal, and Boyce & Hart in an event sponsored by radio station WBAM.

The following day he traveled to Birmingham's Municipal Auditorium for a show with Gary Puckett & The Union Gap, Four Jacks And A Jill, and Boyce & Hart again. This event, which drew an audience of 12,000, was presented by radio station WVOK.

● Saturday 1st
● *NME* reports that The Monkees hope to tour Britain in the spring.

● Wednesday 5th
TV The group's appearance on *The Glen Campbell Goodtime Hour* is aired at 7:30pm across the CBS television network. The trio is seen performing a brief live medley – 'Last Train To Clarksville,' 'Salesman,' 'I'm A Believer' – and a comedy sketch concerning their long history together that includes several pre-recorded numbers satirizing historical events from the last 60 years. At the end of this lengthy segment the group lip-synchs (mimes) to their new single, 'Tear Drop City.'

Later in the program the trio appears in a series of skits, loosely about touch-tone telephones, including the performance of a touch-tone 'symphony' and acting as spies. (Both segments will be featured on 2003's *The Monkees Season 2* DVD boxed set.) Their voices are also heard as callers during a skit about provocative hosts of radio talk shows.
● Also airing tonight at 8:00pm on the ABC television network is a new series called *Turn-On* created by the executive producer of *Laugh-In*, George Schlatter. The Monkees have already taped an appearance for this show (see March 12th) but today's premiere installment of *Turn-On* generates so many complaints for its off-color comedy that the show is instantly cancelled. *Turn-On* is one of very few U.S. television series to be pulled after a single broadcast.

● Saturday 8th
● *Billboard* says that the group are planning to promote their latest single heavily. "The Monkees are preparing a concert tour of the U.S. for early spring. The tour will follow a cross-country promotional junket which The Monkees are lining up on behalf of their new single." Also in *Billboard*, the *Head* soundtrack album reaches its peak position of #45.

● *NME* reports that Don Kirshner is finally ready to launch his joint venture with James Bond producer Harry Saltzman, a group (and film) called Toomorrow. This venture will not meet with the kind of success Kirshner has recently tasted with cartoon group The Archies, though it does spawn future star Olivia Newton-John.

● Monday 10th
TV Davy's appearance on television's *Rowan & Martin's Laugh-In*, taped last month, is aired at 8:00pm on the NBC network. This Valentine's Day episode features a series of romantically themed vignettes with Davy acting as guest star.

● Friday 14th
TV Davy's appearance on *This Is Tom Jones*, taped last month, is aired at 7:30pm on the ABC network. Davy performs 'Consider Yourself.' The show also features Herman's Hermits and Nancy Wilson.

● Saturday 15th
● *NME* announces that the group will kick off a coast-to-coast concert tour of America in the spring. The Monkees' British representative, Vic Lewis, will visit them this month to discuss a UK tour for the late spring. The paper also mentions that Michael recently signed a band called The Corvettes to his production company and that his wife Phyllis is recovering from a serious auto accident. The group's TV special has yet to find an airdate, says *NME*, but Davy may soon make a second appearance on *This Is Tom Jones*.

● Sunday 16th
TV Davy's appearance on *This Is Tom Jones* is aired in Britain.

● Saturday 22nd
● The group's new single, 'Tear Drop City,' debuts in *Billboard's* Hot 100 at #87.
● *TV Guide* reports that The Monkees' NBC special now has an April airdate.

● Friday 28th
'Tear Drop City' / 'A Man Without A Dream' single is released in the U.K.

MARCH

● Brendan Cahill and David Pearl take over as the group's personal managers, although they are still financially tied to Raybert. Jerry Perenchio of Chartwell Artists is employed as The Monkees' agent.
● The group are currently preparing for their first concert performances as a trio. They have spotted an all-black R&B band called Sam & The Goodtimers (also called The Goodtimers Band Ltd. in some early press releases) performing at the Red Velvet club in Los Angeles, and decide to recruit them to back the trio musically on the upcoming dates.

The plan is for an all-new stage presentation similar in style to a revue. Not only will the set be musically rearranged to reflect a more soulful direction, but the group's usual rear-projection displays will be revamped to feature completely new film footage, which is mostly shot this month. Michael is at work in his home studio to prepare a tape of sound effects for use in the concerts.

Michael: "It was a very interesting time. Somebody said get a band together. So we put this black R&B band together – and it was just totally weird. But it wasn't any weirder than Jimi Hendrix opening for us. There's a lot of stuff about the whole Monkees experience that I'd classify as at least weird."
● *Tiger Beat* publishes more of the interview that Ann Moses held with Peter Tork on the last day of last year. He said then that he hadn't seen the other members of The Monkees since the taping of the TV special in November. "I caught them on *Hollywood Squares* [in December '68] and I thought they were all right."
● Also in this month's *Tiger Beat* an interview with Davy is published under the heading "Monkeemania is dying, but…" In the piece, Davy proffers an incendiary theory behind the group's sudden drop in popularity, at least on radio. "The record industry is tied up by one guy whose name I can't mention," he intimates. "Most of the radio stations who play our records are run on his format. But he doesn't play our records any more because he's mad [that] we gave our record to somebody else first, about 15 records ago. Then when things started to cool off for The Monkees he helped it cool off by not playing one Monkee record."

Davy admits he has been disappointed by the band's recent singles but is looking forward to future releases. "Micky has written [one] that says, 'Ask your mommy and daddy what happened to the Indians and ask your mommy and daddy who really killed JFK.' Now that's the kind of things that we're into, but we haven't been able to put them out, it's all been 'D.W. Washburn.'"
● *Monkees Monthly* reports that Michael is at work on a solo follow-up to *Wichita Train Whistle Sings*. He plans to tape more tracks in Nashville and possibly cover one of Micky's songs.

● Saturday 1st

● *Instant Replay*, The Monkees' first album as a trio, breaks into *Billboard's* Top LPs chart at #111. It is barely outsold by *Head*, which rates at #104 in its tenth chart week. Meanwhile 'Tear Drop City' climbs to #68 on the Hot 100 singles.
● *NME* publishes an interview with Michael and Davy who discuss their current activities. "We're really getting down to the nitty-gritty," boasts Michael. "It's coming alive! In the spring, we're really going to spring something big on people. And as for TV – we're basically comedians, and we're working on an idea for a series with comedy and no music. Man, I've never been more happy.

"It's not a question of us shaking off the old Monkees' image. We've nothing to escape from. What we did then was valid and honest. I'm not ashamed of it. The reason our next single is 'Tear Drop City,' which was recorded around the time of 'Clarksville,' is that it's almost a concession on our part to certain people. It's one from the archives of Monkee music, one with Peter. You can call it a corporate swan song. And I'm sure it'll be commercially very profitable.

"It was no surprise when Peter left. There were no arguments. About eight or nine months ago we discussed it, and I agreed that the time was right. There were probably other things he would rather do than be a Monkee. So it was no shock. It is a fact that Peter's leaving has had the reverse effect, in that it has brought us together more: we lean on each other more, and now we believe we can develop each of our talents within the context of The Monkees. In the future, we really want to exploit comedy rather than rock'n'roll. Our stock in trade is that we are, simply, comedians. This is what we must concentrate on for television and probably abandon the music."

Davy adds: "The Monkees are more together than ever before. It's not a question of us now being in control of our destinies and [that we weren't] before. It wasn't our destinies we had to worry about in the past, man. It was our souls. … A lot of people have used us in the last three years. There have been many who bettered their own personalities than us personally. There have been a lot of people who have taken credit for our success. We've known where we've been at since the beginning, and the fact that we're now one less only makes us much tighter. Hey, we've been in the studio this week with Donovan, man. He's written a number which he's given to us before recording – 'Valentine's Angel' – and it's really nice. I tell you, The Monkees are getting tighter and it's great."

● Tuesday 4th

● Vic Lewis tells *Variety* that the group will mount their first ever European concert tour in May. The trio are booked for two weeks of shows in London and other provincial cities in Britain. After that they are scheduled to spend a further two weeks performing in continental Europe. Dates and places have yet to be arranged.

● Wednesday 5th

● Over the next two days Michael produces tracks with a group called The Corvettes. The group consists of former members of The Nitty Gritty Dirt Band and Linda Ronstadt's Stone Poneys (who scored a hit with Michael's 'Different Drum' in November 1967). They include future Eagle Bernie Leadon, Chris Darrow, and Jeff Hanna, all on guitars, Nesmith sidekick John London on bass, and John Ware on drums. Ware recalls: "For less than a year, maybe, it was a good, rough, loose country rock machine, and then The Eagles and the Dirt Band tore the thing up. The tracks that Mike did for ABC were disappointing. Mike's production skills had nothing to do with that disappointment – we were fine as a back-up band, but without a songwriter at the helm it was a mess." The recordings, made for Michael's American Wichita production company, include The Corvettes' self-penned 'Back Home Girl' and 'The Lion In Your Heart.' The songs will be mixed at a further session on March 19th.

● Thursday 6th

RECORDING United Recorders *6050 Sunset Boulevard, Hollywood, CA* 2:30-5:30pm. One-inch 8-track; overdubs.

1. **'If I Ever Get To Saginaw Again'** overdubs onto take 2
   Missing Links 2 master # WZB3-0178
Personnel Louie Shelton (electric guitar).
● This production is further embellished with the addition of a country-styled electric guitar part from Monkees session veteran Louie Shelton. Michael may still be in another studio working

with The Corvettes and will probably add his lead vocal to this track tomorrow.

● **Friday 7th**
RECORDING United Recorders (E) *6050 Sunset Boulevard, Hollywood, CA.* Eddie Brackett *eng*; quarter-inch stereo, one-inch 8-track; overdubs, mixdown.
1. 'If I Ever Get To Saginaw Again' overdubs onto take 2
   Missing Links 2 master # WZB3-0178
Personnel Michael Nesmith (vocal).
● In a surprising move, Michael adds his vocal to a song that he did not produce or compose – something he hasn't done since Chip Douglas's reign as producer. It is not known who convinced him to sing this number, but its country flavor suits him. Despite the fact that the final results are also mixed today, 'Saginaw' will never be given a contemporary release. During the 1970s its co-writer Jack Keller will cut another version, with Davy on lead vocals, but this too will remain in the can. In 1990, today's mix of 'Saginaw' will appear on Rhino's *Missing Links Volume Two*.

● **Wednesday 12th**
● This evening should have seen the telecast of the group's appearance on the ABC network show *Turn-On* but the plug was pulled on the show last month (see February 5th) and their spot is never aired nor publicly screened.

● **Saturday 15th**
● The 'Tear Drop City' single peaks at a middling #56 on this week's *Billboard* Hot 100. It will remain on the charts through April 1969 but is the group's second release in a row to miss the Top 20.
● *NME* notes that the group's TV special is now scheduled to air on April 14th.

● **Tuesday 18th**
RECORDING Location unknown. Quarter-inch mono; mixdown.
1. 'Circle Sky' take 6
   single? master # UZB3-9792
● A new mono mix of the studio version of 'Circle Sky' is made today. It is possible that this is intended for a single release overseas. In Greece the song will be featured on a single alongside 'Porpoise Song' but it is not known if today's mono remix is used for that pressing.

● **Wednesday 19th**
● In the studio Michael mixes his two recent productions for The Corvettes, 'Back Home Girl' and 'The Lion In Your Heart.' They will be released together later this year as a single on the Dot label (#45-17244) that does not chart.

● **Friday 21st**
● *Amusement Business* announces that the group are booked for two days in August as headliners at the Colorado State Fair. Their 1969 tour, which kicks off later this month, now has about a dozen dates scheduled.

● **Saturday 22nd**
TV The trio appear as guest stars on Dick Clark's daytime television show *Happening* in an episode titled *Monkee Day*, broadcast on the ABC network. Davy, Micky, and Michael interview and generally clown around with the program's resident hosts Paul Revere and Mark Lindsay of The Raiders. They also disrupt a Raiders musical performance and mock a *Happening* fashion presentation. The

Monkees do not perform any music, although both sides of their new single, 'Tear Drop City' and 'A Man Without A Dream,' are briefly heard as a backdrop to their zany antics.
● Today's issue of British music paper *NME* features a full-page ad for the 'Tear Drop City' single with the added note: "Hope to see you all in May!"

● **Wednesday 26th**
● 'Tear Drop City' enters the British charts today at #46, but will last just one week in this once loyal haven of Monkeedom.

● **Friday 28th**
● The group and an entourage of five others board United Airlines 8:00am flight 382 at LAX bound for Seattle, where they will spend the day. At 8:10pm the entourage board a second flight (United 167) bound for Vancouver where they will perform their first concert as a trio tomorrow night.

● **Saturday 29th**
PERFORMANCE Pacific Coliseum *Vancouver, BC, Canada* 8:30pm, with The 1910 Fruitgum Company, Sam & The Goodtimers; tickets $2-$5; promoted by Northwest Releasing Corporation
● The Monkees' 1969 tour opens to an audience of 5,200 in Canada. At this concert and the rest of the tour the trio are backed musically by Sam & The Goodtimers, which consists of Sam Rhodes (leader, backing vocal), Tony Burrell (bass), Mack Johnson (trumpet), Ernest Lane (keyboards), Thomas Norwood (drums), Clifford Solomon (saxophone), and Willie Webb (guitar), though it is possible at different points during the year's various dates that the line-up fluctuates. Tonight's event opens with sets from The Goodtimers, who perform just three numbers, and bubblegum supremos The 1910 Fruitgum Company.
    Bob Smith of the *Vancouver Sun* writes of this evening's show: "There was a mild lightshow made up of Monkees film clips which gained shouts of joy from the girls but my notes read, 'Was it necessary?' The sound system, lost in the vastness of the Coliseum, was not kind to Micky Dolenz on his rhythm songs, but he strutted ably to compensate. Nor to Davy on his contemporary, serious ballads, which he obviously felt: 'I Wanna Be Free' and [Stevie Wonder's] 'For Once In My Life.' For me, the musical high point came from Mike Nesmith's guitar composition and voice on 'Don't Wait For Me.' With superb restraint, Mike asked for and got silence and then did his own thing. But after the prolonged, high-decibel applause, he shrugged and said, 'OK, come on back, Davy and Micky, let's return to pandemonium.'" Tonight's set also reportedly includes 'Last Train To Clarksville.'
● *NME* says that the group's British dates have now been postponed. "Obviously the boys want to do a lot of work with their new backing band before they undertake such important overseas engagements," says Monkee manager Brendan Cahill. "The European tour has been put back until much later in the year," says U.K. agent Vic Lewis. "I doubt if we shall have them before the autumn. When they do come, the majority of their act will consist of entirely new songs."

● **Sunday 30th**
PERFORMANCE Seattle Center Coliseum *Seattle, WA* 1:30pm, with The 1910 Fruitgum Company, Sam & The Goodtimers, compère KJR DJ B'Wana Johnny; tickets $2.75-$5; promoted by Northwest Releasing Corporation
● For the first show of the tour in the United States, The Monkees draw a crowd of 5,500 fans. The touring party stays at the Seattle

Center Travelodge. Rolf Stromberg of the *Seattle Post* reviews the concert. "It may be presumptuous to say so," he writes, "but on the evidence at the Coliseum, The Monkees are no longer attracting the crowds they once knew when they were big on television.

"The Coliseum was barely a third full for the single appearance of the trio yesterday. Most of the crowd seemed junior-high-school age and under. What they lacked in numbers they made up for in volume. Once more the public address system was turned up to window-shattering heights. And one thing you can say for The Monkees, they come on to put on a show. That they did here. The show was emceed by bulky B'Wana John, complete with white suit and pith helmet."

Janine Gressel writes in *The Seattle Times*: "The Monkees have changed. Since their series ended last spring, Micky, Mike, and Davy have progressed from a single product labeled 'Monkees' to a trio of individualistic artists who perform together as an act. They presented few of their former teen oriented songs at their concert. To establish a point of identification with the audience, they opened their show with one of their biggest hits, 'Last Train To Clarksville.' But the music they are doing now is not in that style.

"Rather than having one type of music, their revue consists of three types built around the individual taste and talent of each performer. Micky concentrates on rhythm and blues, backed by one of the best bands in that field, Sam & The Goodtimers, formerly with Ike & Tina Turner. Davy presents a nightclub style. He sings lyrical love songs such as 'For Once In My Life' and his image is more sophisticated than when he did teen rock. Mike is basically oriented towards country music. He performs alone on acoustic guitar and sings in a sort of Hank Williams style.

"The overall effect of the change is that the group as a whole is more satisfying to listen to, and their concert is far more interesting to attend. Their show is done in a revue manner, with far more solos than group performances. There are several costume changes effected by two-at-a-time while the third is performing. They accompany themselves on few numbers, allowing The Goodtimers to provide most of the instrumental work. The program is far more a stage production than a typical rock concert.

"The Monkees are in the process of succeeding. The changes were made recently and they are still in the process of development. Their performance is not without minor flaws. But on the whole, their show is immensely interesting. It is exciting to see three performers, who could have rested on their laurels, have the nerve and artistic integrity to change a successful style. The new Monkees have risen to the challenge and are succeeding beautifully."

● After tonight's gig the group return to Los Angeles on a Western Airlines flight. The tour is off to a rocky start with attendance less than expected. Gerald Lonn of promoters Northwest Releasing later tells *Amusement Business*: "We lost our shirts. No quarrel with their show – a revue, which is really tremendous. But somehow they didn't draw."

Davy later tells *16*: "I guess that was one of the darkest hours of my life. We got out there and gave everything we have – that's something we always do – but afterwards I couldn't help but wonder if it was all over for us as Monkees."

Michael recalls: "It was surreal. Sam & The Goodtimers were a hard-core, black, lounge, R&B band – and there they were backing us up. We all had a good time, but Davy singing 'For Once In My Life' on stage – these were surreal moments. I just sort of played along with the band and went ahead and fulfilled the obligations that I had. By that time we were a pariah. Not only had people been gunning for us, starting in '67, but now that they were dancing on the graves the vitriol flowed like wine. So it was tough out there."

APRIL

● *Flip* reports that the delay in screening the group's television special is because it has been difficult to find a sponsor.
● *Monkees Monthly* writes that Peter Tork has opened a soup kitchen in New York City's Greenwich Village. The magazine also notes that Davy has given away his interest in the Zilch boutique to chum Jeff Neal and his parents, who run the shop.
● The group begin filming a series of commercials for Kool-Aid soft drink mix. Kool-Aid will be the sponsors of the *Monkees* TV series when it returns for Saturday-morning reruns on September 13th. This first set of commercials, featuring The Monkees dressed in tuxedos will debut during those broadcasts.

● Saturday 5th
● *NME* reports that Peter Tork's new group is called Release. "Three is a quorum for our group," he says of the outfit. "We sometimes have four. We're thinking of having a rotating fourth. Right now the fourth is that girl I'm promoting named Judy Mayhan." The other group members are Tork's girlfriend Reine Stewart on drums and buddy Riley 'Wildflower' Cummings on bass. "We're like Peter's back-up band," says Stewart, "except we happen to be a group instead of a back-up band." Tork says: "If I was having a back-up band I could go into the musicians' union and hire bass, drums, and organ. But I'd rather work with friends because that makes much better music." He hopes to have a record out with Release in a couple of months. The band's repertoire currently includes 'Take A Giant Step,' Slim Harpo's 'Mailbox Blues,' two Peter Tork originals as well as two by his brother Nick, and one each by Mayhan and Wildflower.

● Tuesday 8th
● The Monkees sign a new contract with Screen Gems/Columbia Pictures that revises their original seven-year 1966 deal. The agreement is amended to give the trio "a measure of artistic control." Steve Blauner of Screen Gems tells *Weekly Variety* that the group are now under firm contract until 1973. From this point Screen Gems will receive 15 percent of The Monkees' earnings from concert and personal appearance and an even split from any television or film features. Notably, the group's record royalties – usually their biggest source of income – will remain at the 1966 rate. Blauner claims record sales to date have reached the 35 million mark.

Weekly Variety also notes that the band hope to extend the duration of their concerts from the current 90-minute program to a whopping two-and-a-half-hours, but it is unlikely that they ever perform any show in this extended format. Twenty-four concert dates are now scheduled for the group and they are guaranteed $1m for their efforts. The first record issued under this new pact is the single 'Listen To The Band' coupled with 'Someday Man,' available a week from today.

Micky: "At the time Mike and Davy and I thought that we could just go on forever doing what we did. When you're right in the midst of that – right in the eye of the hurricane – you don't have any idea of what's going on around you. We tried to get management and agents. [We'd] buy our way out of this deal and buy our way out of that deal."

● Thursday 10th
● Michael and Micky appear at a youth rally in the Alabama State Fairgrounds organized by radio station WSGN. Davy arrives late. *The Birmingham News* reports that the group will "bring a new approach

in musical stage presentation" to their concert in Alabama tomorrow night. "The show, designed to appeal to both adults and teenagers, will represent the beginning of a new effort on the part of the band to produce a more sophisticated sound."

● Friday 11th

PERFORMANCE Municipal Auditorium *Birmingham, AL* 8:30pm, with The Wild Vy-Bra-Shuns, Sam & The Goodtimers; tickets $3-$5; promoted by Concerts West
● The group appear on air as guest disc jockeys at radio station WSGN in Birmingham, Alabama, while this evening's concert is reported by *16* magazine as "sold-out, standing room only."

● Saturday 12th

PERFORMANCE Civic Center Arena *Charleston WV* 8:30pm, with Sam & The Goodtimers; tickets $3-$5; promoted by National Shows Inc.
● *Billboard's* Ray Brack reviews this show, performed before a 6,000 capacity audience. "The Monkees are carefully bridging two images," writes Brack. "They performed enough of their hits ('Daydream Believer,' 'Last Train To Clarksville,' etc.) to avoid alienating the vast teenybopper market while adding enough new material to stake out a claim on a more mature market. Representative of the 'new' Monkees was material like [Joe Tex's] 'Show Me,' a blues sung by Micky Dolenz; 'For Once In My Life' and 'I Wanna Be Free,' with David Jones handling the vocals in his best Broadway style; and 'Don't Wait For Me' and 'Listen To The Band,' both pure Nashville, performed by Nesmith."
● *Billboard* reports that the soundtracks of the *Monkees* series will be revised for their upcoming Saturday-morning reruns. "The TV show switch from bubblegum to contemporary music enables The Monkees to pursue a new course in recordings, said Mike Nesmith, a member of the Colgems recording group. The reruns, which CBS will debut on Saturdays in September, will be redubbed to give The Monkees an opportunity to sing compositions written by The Beatles, Donovan, and Jimmy Webb, among others.

"Nesmith said two redubbed songs will be introduced in each episode. The Monkees will follow up their new musical image by producing singles and LPs in a contemporary style, beginning with their new single. The image turnabout from pre-teen music to teen/young-adult sounds followed a contract understanding with RCA and Screen Gems to allow the group creative freedom, including repertoire selection, Nesmith said.

"The next Monkees LP is *Golden Hits* to be released in April, with all product following that album to be under full creative control of the group. The group will pursue individual careers outside of recording and music publishing. A contract forces the trio to record together, not individually, said Nesmith.

"Nesmith, however, has signed an exclusive five-year production contract with Dot Records to produce a minimum of 18 masters each year under the American Wichita Co. logo. He also formed National Mod Records and Runner Music (BMI). Artists to be produced by Nesmith are singer Bill Chadwick, a country-rock group called The Corvettes, and a female vocalist not yet signed."
● *Billboard* shows the band's *Instant Replay* at its Top LPs chart peak of #32. This is a slight improvement over their last album, *Head*, which had a similar chart run of 15 weeks but only reached #45.

● Sunday 13th

PERFORMANCE Bell Auditorium *Augusta, GA* with Sam & The Goodtimers
After tonight's show in Augusta, Micky and Michael attend a private party, but Davy falls ill and returns to the group's motel. The Monkees leave Augusta tomorrow.

● Monday 14th

TV The group's long awaited television special, *33 ⅓ Revolutions Per Monkee*, is finally aired on NBC at 8:30pm. (For full details see November 23rd-27th 1968.) The show replaces an episode of *Laugh-In*, which is regularly seen in this time slot. In certain areas, mainly the West Coast, The Monkees' show runs simultaneously with the 41st annual Academy Awards Oscar presentation, ensuring limited viewing in Hollywood. As a result of low ratings two further Monkees specials that were planned will never be produced. Davy tells *16*: "I think one day that TV special will have more meaning than it does at the moment. I think that we were a little bit ahead of our time in doing it." (The special will later be included on 2003's *The Monkees Season 2* DVD boxed set.)

● Tuesday 15th

'Someday Man' / 'Listen To The Band' single is released in the U.S.A. It is The Monkees' tenth single. Davy: "That was great. 'Some people complain that their life is too short so they hurry it along.' I went to [Screen Gems] many, many times with Paul Williams tunes. Not because Three Dog Night were doing them and not because anybody else was doing them. They were just great tunes. But [Screen Gems] felt they were too sophisticated.

"This one was all right. They accepted that. It *was* a bit complicated for The Monkees at the time. Unfortunately, it never even got a showing. I thought Bones Howe was a bit busy. I felt they were all a bit busy. Carole King telling us how to sing it. Bones Howe busy throwing too much in there. 'My budgets are usually this much, so I must keep them up there.' The Monkees were a garage band and we needed the basic instruments – the rest was personality."

Someday Man single

A 'Someday Man' (R. NICHOLS / P. WILLIAMS)
B 'Listen To The Band' (M. NESMITH)

U.S. release April 15th 1969 (Colgems 5004).
U.K. release June 6th 1969 (RCA 1824).
Chart high U.S. number 81; U.K. number 47.

● Friday 18th

● The group fly United Airlines to Hawaii where they have scheduled a return to the site of their live concert debut in December 1966. The *Honolulu Advertiser's* Wayne Harada, who reviewed their premiere concert in '66, conducts a lengthy interview with the trio today at the Moana Hotel for publication in tomorrow's paper.

Harada describes Davy as more "mature and perceptive, full of hope and energy," while Micky is "skinny as ever, with wild fried hair," and notes that Michael is "still the least demonstrative Monkee: quiet, brooding, sensitive." As for the missing fourth Monkee, Micky says: "I don't get sick of telling people why Peter Tork quit The Monkees. Peter quit because he was tired. He couldn't keep up with the pressures. [We] wanted to do a little more comedy. So he bugged out."

During the talk Michael delivers his usual state-of-the-union address. "The Monkees are really dead. No question about that. When we were out of the TV show, that was it. What Davy, Micky, and Mike are now – today – aren't even remotely connected with the TV show. It's just a name we use – The Monkees – because, obviously, everybody knows The Monkees.

"We're expanding. Specifically, we've just finished the 20th episode of a radio show – a series of mini-dramas. We're looking for the right deal now. I've been producing records. My activities outside of The Monkees have been just the everyday bitches of living. We're still feeling for the right script for another movie. Davy's got a friend working on a Broadway thing for us. And we've been offered another TV series. Whether we'll do it, I don't know.

"I don't like living my life regimented, and that's what a TV series does to your life. Yet I like a series. We have visions of another special, but the next one will have to be extra special.

"I've been writing songs lately. We have one album in the can which was cut one and a half years ago, and would you know it – it's a country kind of thing which sounds like Bob Dylan's latest, *Nashville Skyline*. So they'll say we're copying when it finally comes out. That's strange about composers, though. The public is exposed to their songs at least a year or so after the thoughts emerge in the minds of the composers. Truly."

Asked about The Monkees' slip in popularity, Michael says: "When you start at the top, it's not easy staying there. Me? I'm content as a guitar player. That'll always be my gig. I'll stand there on stage, smile, and wave hello once in a while. It's not a bad life."

Davy, on the other hand, is not ready to let go of success, at least not without a fight. "I've been working hard," he tells Harada. "Constantly moving. As a group, we've been working hard, too, coming together to do such concerts as we're giving here.

"I have entertaining inside me, and that's what really counts. I'd die if I couldn't entertain. I'd be like a horse with a broken leg if I couldn't get in front of an audience. … When I work, I really try to give all I've got, whether there are ten people or 20,000 people in the audience. Maybe as a performer I will be abused – I may not be in demand – but that won't change my feelings."

Micky sums up the group's current status with a proclamation. "I'd just like to tell you we're an entertainment troupe which can do a heck of a lot of things. We give a revue that'll surprise you. Really. Davy and I don't play instruments any more. Back in the old days I was told to be a drummer. I like drums, but I'm not crazy about them. I believe in individuality, and I like to choose. I'm starting to feel out some acting jobs. Meanwhile I'm part of The Monkees. That's just a name for a collective career … [like] The Rat Pack."

● Saturday 19th

PERFORMANCE Honolulu International Center Arena *Honolulu, HI* 8:00pm, with Sam & The Goodtimers, The Ventures, Mickey & Kurt; tickets $3-$5; promoted by Community Concerts
● During the day Micky visits radio station KKUA's Mike Hamlin for a 45-minute interview. At this evening's concert the group perform to 3,500 fans – about 5,000 fewer than their debut show here in '66. The Ventures feature former Monkees session guitarist Gerry McGee, while the Mickey & Kurt duo use pre-recorded tapes and a drum machine to perform cover songs.

Wayne Harada is again on hand to chronicle the group's return to HIC. "To be sure they still do the round of what they call 'Monkee hits.' The screechers [in the audience] greeted such oldies but goldies as 'Last Train To Clarksville,' 'I'm A Believer,' 'Pleasant Valley Sunday,' but the performances were rather tongue-in-cheek, as if they were embarrassed even to do these tunes. Yet it was quite

obvious in interpretation that The Monkees have been attempting to polish what has been proven. A tune like 'Daydream Believer' by pint-sized Jones was revived with soulful nuances combining dance, with wailing vocal. The technique of aural-visual experience first premiered by The Monkees back in 1966 at the HIC was also revived, with variation. When Nesmith rendered 'Salesman' solo, a series of movies of the home variety was flashed onto an overhead screen.

"There were some new tunes for the new Monkees. Two in particular were intriguing specimens – 'Man Without A Dream' by Jones and 'Listen To The Band' by Nesmith. Dolenz continued to shimmy and shake in a furious display of soulmanship, notably on 'Goin' Down,' a swift, unrelenting tongue twister that is so breathtakingly potent. The Monkees' use of a support band of six musicians, augmented occasionally by Nesmith's fine pickings on guitar, and Jones's guitar and Dolenz's drums, was another example of forward strides being taken by the group. Sam, leader of The Goodtimers Ltd. band, chimed in on one tune with The Monkees but also dispensed his palatable blues brand of tunes in a pre-Monkees warm-up sequence.

"The de-emphasis of the group image and the boosting of solo careers seemed indicative of The Monkees' current fling. I'm sure Nesmith would have liked to do more things on unamplified guitar, as he did of 'Don't Wait For Me,' a plaintive country tune. Jones's 'For Once In My Life' belter was that kind of a performance that one might find on a Broadway stage. And again, Micky's preoccupation with soul was in the limelight time and time again."

● Sunday 20th

TV In the wake of the group's Hawaiian visit their *33 ⅓ Revolutions Per Monkee* special is aired on Honolulu's KHON-TV station.

● Thursday 24th

TV The group appear on television's *The Joey Bishop Show*, a late-night talk show broadcast at 11:30pm by the ABC network. The trio backed by Sam & The Goodtimers perform a medley that segues a soulful arrangement of 'I'm A Believer,' sung by Micky with Davy joining in on the choruses, into their latest single 'Someday Man.' Later in the same program the group perform Michael's 'Listen To The Band.'
● Song selection is finalized today for the group's first compilation album, *The Monkees Greatest Hits*, which will be issued in June.

On TV's *Joey Bishop Show* at the end of April with their regular live backing band, Sam & The Goodtimers.

● Saturday 26th

PERFORMANCE Auditorium Theatre *Chicago, IL* 7:30pm, with Sam & The Goodtimers; tickets $3.50-$6.50; promoted by Fred Fried's Triangle Productions
● Among the songs performed by the group tonight at this 4,008-seat venue are 'I'm A Believer,' 'Pleasant Valley Sunday,' 'Tapioca Tundra,' 'I Wanna Be Free,' Joe Tex's 'Show Me' (sung by Micky), 'Daydream Believer,' 'A Man Without A Dream,' 'Goin' Down,' 'Someday Man,' 'Listen To The Band,' 'Don't Wait For Me,' The Esquires' 'Get On Up' (sung by Micky), Stevie Wonder's 'For Once In My Life' (Davy), Chuck Berry's 'Johnny B. Goode' (Michael), and a finale of 'I'm A Believer' with Micky and Davy trading off verses.
● *NME* reports that the BBC has acquired the rights to air *33 ⅓ Revolutions Per Monkee* in Britain. There is also the possibility that the group's TV series will be rerun there, probably to coincide with the opening of BBC-1's color service in November. This would mark the first time that U.K. viewers could see *The Monkees* in color as all previous British broadcasts have been in monochrome.

MAY

RECORDING RCA *Hollywood, CA.* David Jones *prod*; Pete Abbott, 'SF' *eng*; one-inch 8-track; tracking.
1. **'Opening Night'**
   unissued master # XZR3-0360
2. **'Penny Music'** takes 1-9
   Missing Links 3 master # XZR3-0361
Personnel unknown (harpsichord 2, guitar, piano, bass, drums, brass).
● During this month all three Monkees will return – individually – to the studio to record new material. This renewed effort is no doubt hastened by their renegotiated deal with Screen Gems (see April 8th) and today's session marks the first 'Monkees' tracking date since January. Many of the new recordings produced by the group will highlight their fascination with horn-laden arrangements, a style they have playfully dubbed 'Rhythm & Bubblegum,' and today's session possibly features members of their touring band The Goodtimers.
Davy, in his first session as producer since September 1968, starts today's proceedings with 'Opening Night,' which was first demoed in July last year. Molded on the work of Anthony Newley by Davy's pal Charlie Smalls, the song is intended as an aural evocation of the pre-show buzz of a Broadway show. Sadly, no session tapes or personnel information will survive for this ambitious ballad. However, the final master does endure. It runs close to four minutes, highlighted by an extended brass fade-out. Despite its elaborate production, 'Opening Night' will never be mixed or considered for release.
The second song taped is a Broadway-meets-bubblegum tune, 'Penny Music.' Davy monitors the proceedings from behind the mixing desk, joking and cajoling the uncredited musicians through nine takes. The final pass, take 9, is marked as the master, and Davy will overdub vocals sometime before the song is mixed on July 11th, while Bill Chadwick will assist him in adding several layers of background vocals. Also during this period, Chadwick and Jones collaborate on recordings of 'Something To Show For It All' and 'Talking To The Wall.'

● Friday 2nd

● A Monkees concert scheduled for Kiel Auditorium in St. Louis, Missouri, is cancelled for unknown reasons.

● Saturday 3rd

PERFORMANCE Jackson Coliseum *Jackson, MS* 7:30pm, with Sam & The Goodtimers; promoted by Robert Berman
● *Amusement Business* runs an article highlighting the group's recent activities. Davy says: "The remaining three of us will always be together. We might do something on our own, but we'll always come back." Michael says the group is "a comedy group that does music, not vice versa. We might have been four times as big if we never picked up a guitar." Micky concludes: "We started off sticking to the group image, but today we're individuals."
● Britain's *NME* reports May 24th as the air date there for the *33 ⅓ Revolutions Per Monkee* TV special.
● *Billboard's* Hot 100 Bound chart registers the group's latest single, 'Someday Man,' at #133. But the song's chart progress will be blighted when programmers flip the single over, choosing to play Michael's 'Listen To The Band' instead.

● Sunday 4th

PERFORMANCE Civic Auditorium *Houston, TX* with Sam & The Goodtimers; tickets $3-$6; sponsored by radio station KILT, promoted by Concerts West
● This show was originally scheduled for Houston Music Hall and later Sam Houston Coliseum but moved to this smaller venue probably due to slow ticket sales.

● Monday 5th

● Davy makes a brief taped appearance on the NBC network's 8:00pm Grammy awards show, *The Best On Record*. The program is not the awards presentation itself but rather a pre-taped selection of performances by winners. During the broadcast Davy tells a joke about John Lennon and Yoko Ono's nude appearance on their *Two Virgins* album cover and then somehow manages to segue into an introduction of Bobby Goldsboro performing 'Honey.'

● Tuesday 6th

● The group, down south following their recent concert date in Texas, travel to Nashville and the Ryman Auditorium, site of the Grand Ole Opry, to tape an appearance on *The Johnny Cash Show*. This new variety series stars the famed country singer and will debut in June on the ABC network. *NME* reports that Cash invites the trio to his home to go fishing and enjoy a home-cooked meal. Allegedly, Cash tells the group he has never enjoyed working with anyone as much as The Monkees. Later this week they will travel from Nashville to New Mexico.

● Friday 9th

PERFORMANCE Civic Auditorium *Albuquerque, NM* 7:30pm, with Sam & The Goodtimers; promoted by Swanson Attractions

● Saturday 10th

PERFORMANCE Century II Convention Center *Wichita, KS* 7:30pm, with Sam & The Goodtimers; tickets $3-$5; sponsored by radio station KLEO
● Just prior to tonight's show the trio go on the air at KLEO to try to coax a few more fans to attend. "We have a seven-piece band with us now," says Davy, describing their new format. "Rhythm and blues – Micky says it's 'Rhythm & Bubblegum.' It's an all-black band and they're really outasite. Michael's found them and he's working with them and we have a great sound: a big-band sound. Something we've been wanting to do for goodness knows how long."
Their set this evening includes a medley of 'I'm A Believer,' 'Pleasant Valley Sunday,' and 'Tapioca Tundra,' 'I Wanna Be Free,'

In Nashville for a TV appearance on *The Johnny Cash Show* with the revered country artist.

'Show Me,' 'A Man Without A Dream,' 'Daydream Believer,' 'Goin' Down,' 'Someday Man,' 'Listen To The Band,' 'Don't Wait For Me,' 'Get On Up,' 'For Once In My Life,' 'Johnny B. Goode,' and a second, extended version of 'I'm A Believer' with Davy and Micky trading off verses.

● *NME* reports that the group "with an addition of an all Negro band" will kick off the summer season at Forest Hills in New York on June 21st.

● Monday 12th

RECORDING Western Recorders (1) *6000 Sunset Boulevard, Hollywood, CA* 4:30-8:00pm. Chip Douglas *prod*; Eddie Brackett *eng*; one-inch 8-track; tracking.

1. **'Today'** takes 1-8
   unissued master # XZR5-0510
2. **'Steam Engine'** takes 1–8
   Missing Links 3 master # XZR5-0509
3. **'Windy Day At Kitty Hawk'**
   unissued master # XZB5-0575
4. **'I'm A Man'** take 11
   unissued master # UZB3-9781

Personnel Israel Baker (violin 1), Ray Brown (bass 1), Gary Coleman (tympani 1), Vincent DeRosa (French horn 1), Harold Dicterow (violin 1), Henry Diltz (vocal 1), Chip Douglas (vocal 4), Jesse Ehrlich (cello 1), Jim Gordon (drums 1,2), Bill Green (woodwind 1,2), Bob Hardaway (woodwind 1,2), Jan Hlinka (cello 1), Eddie Hoh (tambourine 1,2), Harry Hyams (cello 1), Larry Knechtel (piano 1), Bobby Knight (trombone 1,2), Bill Kurasch (violin 1), Leonard Malarsky (violin 1), Bill Martin (organ 1,2), Lew McCreary (trombone 1,2), Sid Miller (bassoon 1), Bill Peterson (trumpet 1,2), Red Rhodes (steel guitar 1,2), Lyle Ritz (bass 1,2), Ralph Schaeffer (violin 1), Leonard Selic (cello 1), Sidney Sharp (violin 1), Sanford Skinner (trumpet 1,2), Tony Terran (trumpet 1,2), Clarence White (guitar 1*,2) Jerry Yester (guitar 1*), unknown (3). * White or Yester on guitar.

● Chip Douglas, only months after achieving tremendous success with his record productions for The Turtles, finds himself mired in the same group politics that led to his parting with The Monkees in late '67. The Turtles, coasting on their two Douglas-produced Top 10 singles, now wish to produce themselves – without any interference from Douglas.

So, at a loose end, he comes up with a scheme to resume his production duties for The Monkees. Today, he tapes some tracks on which he hopes the group can later add their vocals. The unique twist to his plan is that he is financing this elaborate session himself and plans to sell the finished tracks to Screen Gems.

Adding to the precarious nature of Douglas's scheme is his use, unprecedented for a Monkees session, of nearly 30 musicians, most of whom would in normal circumstances be saved for a less expensive overdub session.

The first track they cut is a soaring ballad intended for Davy, 'Today,' and notable for the involvement of two of Douglas's bandmates from his Modern Folk Quartet (MFQ). The song is arranged by Jerry Yester, who may provide some guitar, and sung by Henry Diltz, whose vocals will be used as a rough guide to help steer the musicians through the piece.

After eight passes with this brimming ensemble, Douglas assembles a three-and-a-half minute composite of what he considers their best performances.

This final edited master starts with the beginning of take 8 cut into the body of take 6 and concludes with the tail of take 5. After this composite master is assembled, Douglas, with some doubling from Yester, will dub his own guide vocal over Henry Diltz's.

But despite Douglas's impressive production work he will be unable to coax Davy into adding his vocals to the track. He will, however, have slightly better luck with the second track that is cut at this session.

Douglas implores the studio musicians to "think of Wilson Pickett" as they tape the next number, 'Steam Engine.' Despite the soul flavor of this driving composition, it in fact features some rather

unusual non-R&B musical elements in the form of Byrds guitarist Clarence White's patented string-bender electric guitar and Red Rhodes's masterful pedal-steel playing, incorporating a fuzz effect on the breaks and solo section.

Takes 1 and 2 are performed at a particularly brisk pace. After some untaped rehearsals, Douglas slows the engine down to achieve a more in-the-pocket groove. The assignment of recording tracks shifts slightly from take 1 to the start of take 3, with White's guitar given its own track for the later takes, where on takes 1 and 2 it shared a track with the steel and organ. The final master for 'Steam Engine' will be an edit of take 7 with a bit of take 8 spliced in. On July 8th Douglas will take the track to RCA to record some vocals with Micky.

Session records indicate that Douglas also made a pass at recording Bill Martin's reflective 'Windy Day At Kitty Hawk' during this session. Tapes for this track will not survive in The Monkees' archive so few other details are available. Regardless of the song's hopeful title, which refers to the Wright Brothers' triumphant first flight, a 'Monkees' version of the track will never get off the ground.

Also at this session Douglas revisits his November 1967 production of Mann & Weil's 'I'm A Man,' dubbing a guide vocal onto the old track. But this minor embellishment does little to entice The Monkees into participating in Douglas's prolonged production.

● Tuesday 13th

RECORDING RCA *Hollywood, CA.* Micky Dolenz *prod;* 'HM' *eng;* quarter-inch stereo; mixdown.
1. **'Mommy And Daddy'** mixdown takes 1-9
   The Monkees Present master # WZB3-5310
● Micky must put to rest his 1968 opus, 'Mommy And Daddy,' before he can create any new material. Working at RCA he creates nine new stereo mixes. At this point the song still features his original biting lyrics, and the resulting mixes differ only slightly from those of the four previous sessions. Screen Gems will remain resolute in their refusal to issue this song because of such lines as "ask your Mommy if she really gets off on all her pills," and so today's work will go unused. Before the next mixdown session on July 1st Micky will relent and rewrite his lyrics, dubbing on a totally new lead vocal some time during the next month.

● Saturday 24th

TV The group's *33 ⅓ Revolutions Per Monkee* is aired in Britain on BBC-2.
● The 'Someday Man' single charts for a final week in *Billboard* at #111 (it peaked on May 10th at #85). This week's *Billboard* Hot 100 Bound chart reflects radio programmers' preference for the single's flipside, with Michael's 'Listen To The Band' debuting at #101.

● Tuesday 27th

RECORDING RCA *Hollywood, CA* 10:00am-1:00, 2:00-5:00pm. Michael Nesmith *prod;* Pete Abbott *eng;* one-inch 8-track; tracking.
1. **'Oklahoma Backroom Dancer'** takes 1-14
   The Monkees Present master # XZB3-0362
2. **'You're So Good'** takes 1-9
   Missing Links 3 master # XZB3-0363
Personnel Max Bennett (bass 1), James Burton (guitar 2), Mike Deasy (guitar 1), Eddie Hoh (drums 1), Earl Palmer (drums 2), Michel Rubini (piano), Louie Shelton (guitar), Bob West (bass 2).
● This session marks the start of a remarkably creative spurt for Michael, who will tape a whopping 15 new backing tracks over the next several days. Today begins with 'Oklahoma Backroom Dancer,' penned by his former Survivors bandmate Michael Martin Murphey.

Six Monkees studio regulars boogie their way through some 14 takes of this Southern-rock number, but Michael, who presides over the session from the control room, chooses their least mannered performance, take 1, as the best and therefore master take.

Using that as his basic track, Michael will eventually add overdubs of his own lead vocal plus an acoustic guitar track as well as tambourine and shaker parts (both on one tape track). It is unclear who plays the latter instruments, but Michael is probably involved. The completed master will be mixed in the next few months and included on the group's October long-player, *The Monkees Present*.

Michael retains the same basic instrumentation but slightly reshuffles the musicians to produce 'You're So Good.' Little is known about the origins of this funky soul rocker, but Michael is obviously tailoring it to showcase Micky's R&B leanings. The final pass from this date, take 9, will be used as a basic track for future overdubs, including brass, on June 26th.

● Wednesday 28th

RECORDING RCA *Hollywood, CA* 10:00am-1:00, 2:00-5:00pm. Michael Nesmith *prod;* Pete Abbott *eng;* one-inch 8-track; tracking.
1. **'Little Red Rider'** version 1 takes 1-11
   Missing Links 3 master # XZB3-0364
2. **'Thirteen's Not Our Lucky Number'** version 2 **'Part 1'** takes 1-3; **'Part 1a'** takes 1-2; **'Part 1b'** take 1; **'Part 2a'** takes 1-2; **'Part 2b'** take 1; **'Intro'** take 1
   unissued master # XZB3-0365
Personnel Max Bennett (bass 1), Hal Blaine (drums), Al Casey (guitar), Larry Knechtel (piano 1, organ 2), Joe Osborn (bass 2), Louie Shelton (guitar).
● In what will become something of a pattern, Michael holds two three-hour sessions today to produce two new songs with the basic instrumentation of two guitars, piano, bass, and drums. The first, 'Little Red Rider,' was originally conceived by Michael as a song called 'Then Starting With Arthur,' and may have been previously recorded in a rough state at Original Sound in Hollywood.

Today's fully realized rendition features a funky arrangement that the session crew are able to breeze through on their first pass but seemingly cannot duplicate again. Takes 2 through 11 are all false starts, leading Michael to tell the musicians: "I'm gonna take the first one. Yeah. We're getting away from it. I'd rather take the first one. Come listen to that."

Using take 1 as the basis, Michael initially experiments with overdubs of tack piano, acoustic guitar, and a lead electric guitar solo. He obviously has some doubts about these since they are all later erased and replaced. A further session for 'Little Red Rider' will occur in New York City on June 17th.

The second half of today's date is devoted to recording a song from Michael's pre-Monkees past, 'Thirteen's Not Our Lucky Number.' First taped in October 1965 for Colpix but never released, the song juxtaposes a Texas stomp like 'She's About A Mover' with some flowing, fuzz-guitar-dominated cowbell rock. These different moods are recorded in short sections intended to be edited together later.

Tracking begins with three takes of what Michael calls 'Part 1.' After the first pass he instructs guitarist Louie Shelton not to play any 'fills' because, as he puts it, he has something up his sleeve for the production. A short false start (take 2) is followed by what Michael will mark as the master take for this section, take 3.

He calls the next segment 'Part 1a.' It is almost identical in structure to 'Part 1' with the exception of a segue point to cut into 'Part 2.' Michael feels Hal Blaine's drumming in take 1 of 'Part 1a' speeds up a little, so a second pass is required. Take 2 is marked as the master. Next comes 'Part 1b,' captured in a single take, and then 'Part 2a,' with take 2 marked as master. 'Part 2b' is knocked off in a single take as is 'Intro.' The whole shebang is edited together immediately to create a composite master lasting less than three minutes, and this will be used for future overdubs. A further session for the track's 'Intro' section will take place next Monday.

● Thursday 29th
RECORDING RCA *Hollywood, CA* 10:00am-1:00, 2:00-5:00pm. Michael Nesmith *prod*; Pete Abbott *eng*; one-inch 8-track; tracking.
1. **'Thank You My Friend'** takes 1-4
   unissued master # XZB3-0366
2. **'Calico Girlfriend'** version 1 takes 1-12
   The Monkees Present master # XZB3-0367
3. **'Lynn Harper'** takes 1-8
   unissued master # XZB3-0368

Personnel Hal Blaine (drums 1,2), Al Casey (guitar 1,2), Carol Kaye (bass 3), Gerry McGee (guitar 3), Joe Osborn (bass 1,2), Earl Palmer (drums 3), Michel Rubini (piano), Louie Shelton (guitar).
● This particularly productive six-hour date produces three brand new Michael originals. The first is a country-tinged jazz waltz, 'Thank You My Friend.' Captured easily in four takes and with the final pass, take 4, marked as the master, this simple but promising tune will be left unadorned and is abandoned after this session.

The studio crew next limbo through 12 playful takes of Michael's samba, 'Calico Girlfriend.' Although the excellent take 7 is listed on the session reel as a "driving mother," the final pass, take 12, is selected as the master and eventually subjected to overdubs of a lead vocal (from Michael), shaker, cowbell, and bongos (and possibly even more shaker and cowbell from some uncredited participants). A note on another tape box hints that someone may have intended that Davy try to sing this number, but alas he will never be involved in the production. Despite the fun-and-frolics feel of today's track, this version of 'Calico Girlfriend' will initially be passed over for release. (It will eventually appear on Rhino's expanded 1994 reissue of *The Monkees Present* where it is titled 'Calico Girlfriend Samba.') Michael will, however, record a second version of the song on February 19th 1970.

After a one-hour break, the session resumes this afternoon with a slightly different crew of musicians but with identical instrumentation to the earlier work. Earl Palmer lays down a funky drum pattern for a song labeled 'Lynn Harper,' though it is stressed on the tape box that this is a working title only. Eight takes are taped, with the final pass marked as the master backing track. Musically, the composition bears a passing resemblance to the new, soulful rendition of 'I'm A Believer' that The Monkees are currently performing on tour, and indeed some of the live backing band, The Goodtimers, will participate in a brass overdub for this recording on June 27th.

● Friday 30th
RECORDING The Sound Factory *6357 Selma Avenue, Hollywood, CA* 2:00-5:00, 6:00-9:00pm. Tommy Boyce & Bobby Hart *prod*; Dave Hassinger *eng*; one-inch 8-track; tracking, overdubs.
1. **'My Storybook Of You'** takes 1-16
   Missing Links 1 master # XZB3-0479
2. **'Suzzana Sometime'** a.k.a. **'Love Bandit'** takes 1-8
   unissued master # XZB3-0593

Personnel Hal Blaine (drums), Larry Knechtel (piano), Joe Osborn (bass), Louie Shelton (guitar).
● As the nation observes Memorial Day, Boyce & Hart hold what will be their final tracking session as producers for The Monkees. Their main focus today is to tape an expansive ballad, 'My Storybook Of You,' which they have composed especially for Davy.

The set-up has Tommy Boyce guiding the four session musicians from the studio floor while Bobby Hart offers his suggestions from the control room of The Sound Factory. A great deal of time is lavished on perfecting this song's improvised tack-piano intro, played by Larry Knechtel. (A tack piano is one with specially hardened hammers for a percussive, jangling sound.) Along the way, Boyce and Hart both chip in their ideas as Knechtel rambles through several unnumbered takes of his part.

Few if any take numbers are called during the session by engineer Dave Hassinger and those that are seem arbitrary. After what may be take 13, Hart suggests that Knechtel adds an extended tack-piano coda to the tail of the song, similar in form to his improvised intro. Knechtel admits that he is "totally confused" as Boyce & Hart converse over the structure of this part, but, regardless, the crew proceeds.

To keep the musicians on course through the countless false starts and unnumbered takes, Boyce occasionally sings an off-mike guide vocal. Eventually, Hassinger announces the day's final pass, take 16 – which accurately would be numbered 28 – and it will be this performance that Boyce & Hart use as their master. A variety of other overdubs will be added to the piece tomorrow.

The second song taped today, 'Suzzana Sometime,' is a funky R&B number, an uncharacteristic style for Boyce & Hart. The session men shift gears accordingly, with Louie Shelton moving from acoustic to electric guitar and Knechtel swapping the more stylized tack piano for a normal piano. After seven passes, of which only the first is complete, the musicians achieve a totally acceptable take 8 that will be used as the basis for all future overdubs. The first embellishment is a second bass part from Joe Osborn that serves to augment his live part from the tracking session. It is also possible that Boyce & Hart add their own rough guide vocals to 'Suzzana' during this session.

The song's lyrics will later be rewritten to form another song, 'Love Bandit,' which will become the officially copyrighted title. But for the time being the master is logged as 'Suzzana Sometime' and will be subjected to some horn overdubs tomorrow.

● Saturday 31st
RECORDING The Sound Factory *Hollywood, CA* 4:00-7:00pm. Tommy Boyce & Bobby Hart *prod*; one-inch 8-track; overdubs.
1. **'My Storybook Of You'** overdubs onto take 16
   Missing Links 1 master # XZB3-0479
2. **'Suzzana Sometime'** a.k.a. **'Love Bandit'** overdub onto take 8
   unissued master # XZB3-0593

Personnel Jules Chaikin (trumpet), Jesse Ehrlich (cello 1), John Gallie (piano 1), Bill Kursach (violin 1), Billy Lewis (drums 1), Jay Migliori (saxophone), Ollie Mitchell (trumpet), Dick Nash (trombone), William Pening (instrument unknown 1), Jerome Reisler (violin 1), Ralph Schaeffer (violin 1), Sidney Sharp (violin 1), Shari Zippert (violin 1),
● Boyce & Hart tinker with what was called 'take 16' of 'My Storybook Of You' from yesterday's session, adding a number of flourishes. In addition to a ten-piece string and horn ensemble arranged by Jimmie Haskell, the duo augment some of yesterday's basic instrumentation: Billy Lewis doubles Hal Blaine's drum track in spots to add some sonic weight, while his fellow Boyce & Hart band member John Gallie plays some standard piano through the song's ending section, reinforcing Larry Knechtel's grandiloquent tack piano.

An addition is also made to the song's last verse of electric guitar, played by an uncredited musician. By the end of the session, 'Storybook' will be ready for vocals, which Davy adds probably some time over the summer. The production will meander through the rest of the year with the possibility of inclusion on *The Monkees Present* (see August 29th) but the song will not be included on that collection or any other original Monkees album. It will later turn up on the 1987 collection *Missing Links* with the shortened title 'Storybook Of You.'

The same horn crew that worked on 'Storybook' also add to yesterday's take 8 of 'Suzzana Sometime.' At some point after this work is completed, Bobby Hart adds an all-new guide vocal to the track with lyrics that change the title to 'Love Bandit.' But production will stall, and neither 'Suzzana Sometime' nor 'Love Bandit' will be issued in any form.

JUNE

The Monkees Greatest Hits compilation album is released in the U.S.A. This is a collection of old album and single tracks.
● The group shoot another set of commercials for Kool-Aid soft drink mix that will be shown when their series returns to television in September.
● *16* reports that Peter Tork recently had a speaking engagement at the annual seminar of the Young Presidents Organization in Aspen, Colorado. He presented a film and gave a speech to help young corporation presidents bridge the generation gap. As an extension of this, Tork hopes to tour a one-man multimedia road-show. The magazine also mentions his group, Release, has yet to select a label for their recordings – but he did recently stop by Micky's house for a four-hour jam session.

Tork: "After I left The Monkees I went through an identity crisis right away. I called up Dick Clark and said: 'Put me on the road.' He said: 'Get a hit record; nobody will recognize you.' I went, 'What?' That was so staggering to me that it completely stopped me cold. I thought 37 promoters would be dying to have me perform."

● **Monday 2nd**
RECORDING RCA *Hollywood, CA* 10:00am-1:00, 2:00-5:00pm. Michael Nesmith *prod*; Pete Abbott *eng*; quarter-inch stereo, one-inch 8-track; tracking, overdubs.
1. **'Never Tell A Woman Yes'** takes 1-5
   The Monkees Present master # XZB3-0369
2. **'Omega'**
   The Monkees Present master # XZB3-0481
3. **'Thirteen's Not Our Lucky Number'** version 2 drum intro takes 1-2
   unissued master # XZB3-0365
Personnel Hal Blaine (drums), Al Casey (banjo 1, electric guitar 2), Larry Knechtel (piano 1*,2*), Michael Nesmith (acoustic guitar 1,2), Joe Osborn (bass 1,2), Michel Rubini (piano 1*,2*). * Knechtel or Rubini on piano.
● Michael, back at work after the Memorial Day holiday weekend, records two more of his songs. The first is a playful ditty that features him on acoustic guitar, tracking live with the other musicians. Captured in a mere five takes, of which only the second and fifth run-throughs are full passes, the production will be completed later with the simple addition of a single lead vocal track from Michael onto take 2. The song will be mixed this summer and included on the trio's October album, *The Monkees Present*.

The second song that Michael starts (and ends) today is his mysterious 'Omega.' Labeled on the tape box as a demo, it is no less produced than any of his other tracks from this time, so the designation seems erroneous. Furthermore, no 'master' version is known to exist of this song. So although 'Omega' has a clearly defined structure, perhaps the 'demo' label just means that in Michael's mind this is a work in progress.

Takes 1–7 of the mid-tempo rock number are lively but halting, with only the first and last takes full passes. From take 8 on, the pace of 'Omega' is slowed to a more laidback groove. Two full takes follow at this new tempo. Hal Blaine comments that he hopes "Lalo Schifrin doesn't get mad" since one section of the song reminds him of Schifrin's theme from *Mission Impossible*, although the similarities are very slight.

Before take 10 Michael instructs the musicians to use the bridge section as an intro. From this point the crew try to implement the change and, although Michael is pleased with the results, they are unable to complete a take. After take 17 it is necessary to change a tape reel – and the remainder of the 'Omega' session will not survive in The Monkees' tape archive. Michael will never complete or revisit 'Omega' after today.

At some point during the session Michael returns to his elaborate production for 'Thirteen's Not Our Lucky Number.' Working with Blaine, he adds two takes of what sounds like a totally improvised solo drum intro. A stereo mix will be made of each pass as a test edit with the beginning of the song, but work on 'Thirteen' will stall after this session and the song will remain unissued. Michael will tape a third version of this song on October 20th 1970.

● **Thursday 5th**
RECORDING RCA *Hollywood, CA* 10:00am-1:00, 2:00-5:00pm. Michael Nesmith *prod*; Pete Abbott *eng*; one-inch 8-track; tracking.
1. **'Good Afternoon'** takes 1-14
   unissued master # XZB3-0370
2. **'Down The Highway' issued as 'Michigan Blackhawk'** takes 1-6
   Missing Links 2 master # XZB3-0371
Personnel Max Bennett (bass), Hal Blaine (drums), Al Casey (guitar), Larry Knechtel (piano), Louie Shelton (guitar).
● For Michael's second session of the week he assembles most of his basic studio crew to tape a breezy soft-rock tune appropriately titled 'Good Afternoon.' In all, 14 takes will be made of this gentle song of unknown source, with only subtle variations in performance. Michael selects take 14 as his potential master. However, no further overdubs will ever be added to the song, which will remain unissued.

After an hour-long break, the session resumes for the taping of Carole King and Toni Stern's 'Down The Highway.' It has a cool, country-rock flavor, perfectly suited to Michael, and is easily captured in just six takes. Michael chooses the final pass, take 6, as his master, eventually adding a set of double-tracked lead vocals to the production. At first it will be passed over for release, but Rhino will later include 'Down The Highway' on the 1990 *Missing Links Volume Two* compilation under the incorrect title of 'Michigan Blackhawk.' Adding to the confusion, a totally different song with the title 'Michigan Blackhawk' will be recorded by Michael on June 10th.

● **Friday 6th**
Instant Replay album released in the U.K.
'Someday Man' / **'Listen To The Band'** single released in the U.K.
● Meanwhile in Hollywood, Michael continues his run of recording sessions with a further date at RCA.

RECORDING RCA *Hollywood, CA* 10:00am-1:00, 2:00-5:00pm. Michael Nesmith *prod*; Pete Abbott *eng*; one-inch 8-track; tracking.
1. **'A Bus That Never Comes'** takes 1-9
   unissued master # XZB3-0447
2. **'London Bridge'**
   unissued master # XZB3-0448
Personnel Max Bennett (bass), Hal Blaine (drums), Al Casey (guitar), Michael Cohen (keyboard 2), Alan Estes (percussion including mallets), Larry Knechtel (piano 1, keyboard 2), Louie Shelton (guitar).
● 'A Bus That Never Comes' is a smooth soft-rock number, like yesterday's 'Good Afternoon,' and features some beautiful marimba work from percussionist Alan Estes. It was written by Jack Keller and Bob Russell, the authors of 'If I Ever Get To Saginaw Again,' and is taped in nine takes. Michael later has Estes overdub congas and bell tree to take 9, but the production never progresses beyond that and is never released.

Session tapes for today's second song, Michael's 'London Bridge,' will not survive, which is a great pity since this intriguing composition is like nothing else in the Nesmith canon. However, the take marked as the master today, take 4, will survive, and it reveals a foreboding, complex production of great majesty.

Instrumentation ranges from strummed acoustic 12-string guitar to a fuzzed-out electric six-string. The spooky organ track, played by one of today's two credited keyboardists, is highlighted by the eerie sound of the instrument being turned off and on. Two sets of drum tracks, some vibes, and bass guitar fill out the sonic picture. The recorded elements are spread fully across all eight tracks of the multi-track recorder, indicating that perhaps the moody 'London Bridge' is intended purely as an instrumental piece. If that is so, then the production of this song is complete – but it will never cross the bridge of commercial availability.

Davy in costume during one of the group's filmed ads for Kool Aid soft drink mix.

● **Saturday 7th**
● In Britain the *Daily Mirror*'s Don Short publicly breaks the news that Davy is married to Linda Haines and is the father of her daughter Thalia. Remarkably, Davy has managed to keep this union a secret from the general public since late last year. The news will shock some of his fans, who consider him as the last 'available' Monkee, and does little to aid the group's floundering career.
● *NME* reports that The Monkees plan to tape an appearance for television's *Andy Williams Show* in August. In fact this never happens, although Davy will make a brief cameo on the program later in the year.

● **Monday 9th**
RECORDING RCA *Hollywood, CA* 10:00am-1:00, 2:00-5:00pm. Michael Nesmith *prod*; Pete Abbott *eng*; one-inch 8-track; tracking.
1. **'Till Then'** takes 1-2
   unissued master # XZB3-0449
2. **'Angel Band'** takes 1-3
   Missing Links 3 master # XZB3-0450
Personnel Max Bennett (upright bass), Hal Blaine (drums), Al Casey (guitar 1, acoustic guitar 2), Michel Rubini (piano 1, harmonium 2), Louie Shelton (guitar 1, acoustic guitar 2).
● After a weekend off, Michael resumes his recording activities with two nostalgic numbers. 'Till Then' sounds like an old standard – and may be, since it carries no writers' credit. To add to the aura of yesteryear all the instrumentation is recorded on a single track of the 8-track master and, as if that were not frugal enough, only two takes are made – with the first merely a long false start. In keeping with the sparse production, take 2 is subjected to just one track of overdubs, consisting of atmospheric chatter and laughter from Michael and an uncredited batch of male and female friends. This bizarre piece will never be released.

Staying with the old-timey vibe, Michael next cuts a traditional gospel song, 'Angel Band,' composed in 1864 by William Bradbury and the Reverend J. Hascall and in the intervening years covered by many artists including The Stanley Brothers.

It's captured in just three takes, of which the first and last are full passes. Michael uses take 3 as his master, later adding a single lead vocal and two tracks of a multi-layered backing vocal choir including male and female voices. The results are excellent but, like most of Nesmith's recent productions, 'Angel Band' will not find contemporary release. In 1996 it will be dusted off for Rhino's *Missing Links Volume Three* (though it is mistakenly credited there as a Nesmith original).

● **Tuesday 10th**
RECORDING RCA *Hollywood, CA* 9:00am-1:30pm. Michael Nesmith *prod*; Pete Abbott *eng*; one-inch 8-track; tracking.
1. **'Little Tommy Blue'** takes 1-5
   unissued master # XZB3-0451
2. **'Michigan Blackhawk'** takes 1-9
   unissued master # XZB3-0452
Personnel Max Bennett (upright bass), Hal Blaine (drums), Al Casey (guitar), Michel Rubini (piano), Louie Shelton (guitar).
● Michael ends his slew of studio work with today's four-and-a-half-hour session. Although he will hold several more overdub and mixdown sessions in the months to come, this will be his final tracking date of the year – and his last ever for The Monkees.

As the title might imply, 'Little Tommy Blue' is an out-and-out slow blues number. The studio musicians are encouraged to really get into this one, and they shout compliments at each other and otherwise whoop it up on mike as they perform live. Only takes 3 and

5 of the five passes committed to tape are complete performances. Michael selects take 5 as his master – and on June 26th will transfer it to a new recording format for The Monkees: two-inch 16-track tape.

Today's session concludes with nine takes of a straight-ahead Chuck Berry-styled rock number, 'Michigan Blackhawk.' (This should not to be confused with the earlier recorded 'Down The Highway' that will issued later under the erroneous title 'Michigan Blackhawk.') There are a number of acceptable and complete takes among today's recordings of the song, and Michael picks take 4 from them as his master. On June 26th 'Michigan Blackhawk' too will be transferred to a new two-inch 16-track tape for further overdubs.

● Thursday 12th

PERFORMANCE City Stadium *Richmond, VA* 9:10pm, with Gary Lewis & The Playboys (co-headliners), B.J. Thomas, The Smash Machine; tickets $1.75-$4.75

● The Monkees perform to a crowd of 5,600 tonight, and the concert is the largest drawing paid activity at the Stadium in a decade (excepting football events). The bill was set to include The Classics IV, but the program runs over causing them to cancel their spot.

Carole Kass of the *Richmond Times Dispatch* writes: "The Monkees are backed by an eight-man group called Sam & The Goodtimers. With three claret-coated stars singing, dancing, and clowning in some of their top hits, the saxophone, trumpet, guitar, drum, and organ gave a strong, solid background mostly of rhythm and blues, some sensitive soft rock and, in the reprise of 'I'm A Believer,' the pronounced swing of the old-new boogie.

"The Monkees drove onto the field in a powder-blue sedan ... greeted by a battering-ram of shrieks. However, more anxious for applause than screams, they waited until the kids quieted down, and then proceeded to perform for one whole, uninterrupted hour. ... There are only three Monkees left since Peter Tork left the group. Mike Nesmith is the only musician left then, and he plays guitar well, establishes the beat, and cues the background band, while curly-haired Micky and little perpetual-motion Davy take turns singing and dancing, keeping the rhythm with maracas and claves, sitting in on the drums, and variously displaying the efforts which keep all three bone thin.

"Although the group was originally conceived as a bunch of clowns for young people, they started appearing as musicians during 'the Monkee Syndrome' as young Nesmith calls it. Now they seem to combine everything: the clowning, the music, and more. Unfortunately, since the show last night was out of doors, the audience missed the slides, lights, movies, and costume changes which usually go with it."

Bill Wasson of the *Richmond News Leader* also attends this show. He writes: "When The Monkees appeared, the police dog protecting the singers from the teenyboppers and five-year-olds woke up and wagged his tail. He had fallen asleep during white soul singer B.J. Thomas's 'Ballad Of Billy And Sue.'

"The Monkees played a medley of their hits to their eager fans, most of whom remained standing throughout the hour-long performance. 'I want to hold your hand,' sang The Monkees, and every 13-year-old in the stadium reached out her hand. Michael Nesmith, the only musician in the group, deserves praise for his sensitive guitar solo 'Don't Wait For Me.' The Monkees were followed by Gary Lewis, son of Jerry Lewis, and The Playboys. Gary and his band are a West Coast group who are rather staid, with none of the acid rock or originality of such groups as The Grateful Dead. It was The Monkees, however, that turned out the crowd, the enthusiasm, and the joy."

● Friday 13th

PERFORMANCE Dome *Virginia Beach, VA* tickets $3.50– $4.50; sponsored by radio station WGH

● The Monkees were scheduled to perform two shows this evening at 7:30pm and 9:30pm, but it is likely that they only give a single evening performance, to a reported audience of just 2,000 fans. The concert is advertised as "The Biggest Sight and Sound Show Ever Presented."

● Saturday 14th

● A Monkees concert originally scheduled for today in Rochester, New York, is cancelled because, just prior to show time, the promoter fails to come up with the group's 'guarantee' cash. *Amusement Business* reports that Greyhound Bus Lines are running a special trip to New York's Forest Hills Music Festival for the group's concert set for the Tennis Stadium on June 21st. In the same issue an announcement is made that the Dane County Junior Fair in Madison, Wisconsin, has secured The Monkees, Eddy Arnold, and television's Gentle Ben as the top attractions for the fair later this year.

● *Billboard* notes that Don Kirshner has another Monkees-style television music group in the works. Kirshner's latest aggregation, which he is forming with the help of animator Ernie Pintoff, will be called The Kowboys and are to perform country-rock music. Ironically, this is the same style pioneered but not popularized by Kirshner's foe, Michael Nesmith. A pilot program called *The Kowboys* will be filmed for 20th Century Fox.

● The group travel to New York City where they stay at Loew's Midtown Motor Inn. Davy spends the day shopping in Greenwich Village at Zilch, which he no longer owns, and Village Oldies, a record shop where the legendary Bleecker Bob sells him some jazz discs.

● Sunday 15th

● The Monkees' June 21st concert appearance set for Forest Hills in New York is officially cancelled. The cancellation is initially reported as due to "contractual rhubarb" but Colgems promotions man Danny Davis later reveals: "We honestly didn't think we could fill the place. So we talked it over with the promoter and decided to postpone the date till a later time." *Amusement Business* later reports

Michael saddles up for another Kool Aid ad.

that all box seats and field chairs for the performance are sold out five weeks before and that cancellation is not due to poor ticket sales.
● This evening Davy escapes the disappointment by taking in a performance of the Broadway musical *Promises, Promises*.

● Monday 16th
TV Still in New York City, The Monkees tape an appearance for *The Tonight Show*, an NBC network program hosted by Johnny Carson. They perform two songs live, 'Daydream Believer' and 'Goin' Down,' and between the songs take part in a painfully long panel discussion that is dominated by Micky's offbeat patter. After discussing Michael's custom-made cowboy outfit, Carson turns to Micky and asks, "Is your tongue black? Look at that!"

"Robitussin," explains Micky, referring to the popular cough syrup. "I thought maybe it just went with the outfit or something," jokes Carson. "There's a cough in my throat, so I have to drink it every day," says Micky, "but I can't show the label, can I?"

"No, I don't think you better show the label," deadpans Carson. "Is there a label?" After the audience erupts with laughter, Carson takes a more serious tack, asking the group if they would rather be known as singers or comedians. "We're a comedy group," asserts Micky. "We were always a comedy group – that's what we were hired for on the television show."

"None of you were professional musicians at all before you got together, were you?" wonders Carson. "I know Mike was and Peter," replies Micky. "Davy had sung on-stage in *Oliver!* and I had played a little guitar, but primarily I think they wanted us to be a comedy group, and the music kind of happened after that. I was told to be the drummer. About two weeks later I had to do my first concert and have somebody else set up the drums."

"You didn't even know how to set up the drums?" muses Carson. "Is this microphone working? Maybe that's our problem: it is working." Davy interjects: "We sit every night and watch you." Micky shrieks: "I'm so excited, I just love you!" much to the audience's amusement. "You wanna give me a swig of that bottle?" quips Carson.

"I have a picture of my wife and child in my case, that I was going to show you," rambles Micky, "but they won't give me my case. I also have a present for you. Real quick, because Mike says they don't have a lot of time to do this. I'm going to give you a present."

"Smart luggage," remarks Carson upon spying Micky's paper bag. "That's the only way to travel." Micky gushes: "Here's my wife and kid." Michael jokes: "The older one's your wife?"

"Here's my *TV Guide* thing on how to hog the camera without seeming pushy on the talk shows," says Micky, referring to an article in last week's *TV Guide*. "I'm supposed to sit in the left chair on the left hand of God, but you don't have a left chair over there." Carson says: "I don't have a God either." Quoting directly from the article, Micky recites: "Best of all, mention that you've tried some of the new food products that they've put on the market. It's delicious – Carson's Crullers."

"We were up in the commissary," offers Davy, "and you're right what you say about it every night. [Michael] had a gross burger." Michael adds: "And a side of ptomaine." Carson concurs: "It's not really very good, is it, to tell you the truth." Then he asks Micky: "What is the gift?" Micky says: "This gift for Ed [McMahon, Johnny's co-host] is *The Great International Paper Airplane Book* by the *Scientific American*." Carson laughs, saying: "I got him that last week."

"This for you is a hologram," continues Micky. "You don't believe me. He thinks I'm out of my mind. It says in my *TV Guide* you gotta be a kook. … Now listen, this is very important, and you won't know how important this is until maybe 20 years from now. This is a three-

dimensional hologram produced by laser. The infraction beams of two laser lights coming together. It's recorded on Kodak Spectrographic 649-F film."

When the audience starts laughing, Micky pleads: "Oh come on! Please listen, 'cos this is incredible. It's the first time that anybody on nationwide television has ever heard this. This is a monochromatic filter – you put this in front of your slide projector, or a high intensity light. Inside, through here, appears a three-dimensional image – on this particular one it happens to be a cannon. You can turn it around and see it on all sides – the front and the back."

After arguing with Michael and Carson that they won't see it on television, Micky explains: "This I got out of a catalog, but in 20 years this will be in your living room. Then at 11:15 will come Johnny Carson. You'll be able to walk around him. Did you see *Forbidden Planet*? Anyone see *Forbidden Planet*? Staff? Can I give you one other thing? This is an article on Clive Baxter, who lives here in New York. … He was one of the four polygraph experts asked to testify before the House Foreign Operations and Government Information subcommittee."

But before Micky can complete his address about Baxter – who proved scientifically that plants can think and respond via polygraph testing – Carson gracefully cuts him off in order to go to a commercial. Micky's enthusiasm to interact with the vastly popular Carson is no doubt genuine and without malice to his bandmates, but the other Monkees are allegedly miffed by his antics. A post-show argument will place further cracks in their already rickety relationship.

● Tuesday 17th
● During the late evening, the group's appearance on *The Tonight Show* is aired by the NBC network. Earlier today, Michael spends some time recording overdubs at New York's legendary Webster Hall.
RECORDING Webster Hall *125 East 11th Street, New York, NY* 4:00-7:00pm. Michael Nesmith *prod*; one-inch 8-track; overdubs.
1. **'Little Red Rider'** version 1 overdubs onto take 1
   Missing Links 3 master # XZB3-0364
Personnel Mack Johnson (trumpet), Lester Robertson (trombone), Clifford Solomon (tenor saxophone).
● Webster Hall was built in 1886 by architect Charles Rentz and first employed as a studio in the 1950s by RCA who were impressed by its extraordinary acoustical properties. It has been used for sessions by Elvis Presley, Tony Bennett, and Frank Sinatra, and today plays host to Michael, two of The Goodtimers, Mack Johnson and Clifford Solomon, plus trombonist Lester Robertson. During the three-hour session Michael supervises overdubs of two tracks of horns onto his master of 'Little Red Rider' from May 28th. Eventually, Michael will add a lead vocal to the song; production will continue on June 26th.

● Thursday 19th
● While his former Monkee mates wait to perform some further dates on the East Coast, Peter Tork is only a few miles away giving a free multi-media extravaganza at the Fond du Lac Fairgrounds County Pavillion in Wisconsin. Billed as *For What It's Worth*, the 8:00pm event (promoted by Spirit Movement 1969) "will have music, slides, lights, and a rap session with the star" in a series of "expressions on worth." Too much! *For What It's Worth* attracts around 1,000 and Tork performs 'Can You Dig It,' 'Take A Giant Step,' and a song called 'Bartender' among others during his set.

● Friday 20th
PERFORMANCE Sorrowtown Theatre *West Springfield, MA* promoted by Ann Corio and Mike Iannucci of TWB and Concert Guild Productions

● The Monkees perform in concert at this theatre at the Coliseum on the Eastern States Exposition Grounds. Top ticket price is $5.00. Also today, the group throw a surprise birthday party for Goodtimers drummer James Norwood. (A concert at one time scheduled for today at the Bushnell Auditorium in Hartford, Connecticut, does not happen.)

Saturday 21st
● The group were scheduled to open the Forest Hills Music Festival tonight but the gig was cancelled on June 15th. Advance tickets were sold at 91 Singer Sewing Centers and through mail-order ads in Metropolitan New York papers, with the remainder placed on sale at the box office on June 2nd. Festival promoters had hoped to net $25,000.

Sunday 22nd
PERFORMANCE **Milwaukee Pop Festival, County Stadium** *Milwaukee WI* with Freddie & The Freeloaders, The Classics IV, Eddie Floyd & The Bar-Kays, The Bob Seger System, Gary Lewis & The Playboys, The Cryan Shames, Tommy James & The Shondells, The New Colony Six, Andy Kim, The Buckinghams, The Royal Guardsmen, The Guess Who; tickets $1.50–$3.50; sponsored by radio station WOKY, promoted by Gerald Purcell Associates
● The Monkees rebound quickly from the cancellation at Forest Hills to perform to the single biggest audience of their careers at this charity show, also known as *M'Woky Fest*. The Monkees perform to

29,041, one of the day's largest audiences, and their set includes 'I'm A Believer' and 'I Wanna Be Free.' According to one report, after the group finish their set a portion of the audience leave for the day, despite the fact that there are many more acts to follow. A revolving stage with a canopy does little to keep out today's icy rain, but the spirits of the audience and performers will not be dampened. The event raises $68,192 for the Children's Outing Association, which provides camping for handicapped and under-privileged kids and senior citizens.

Wednesday 25th
● 'Someday Man' registers for a single week at #47 in the British charts. This will be the group's last U.K. chart entry until March 1980.

Thursday 26th
RECORDING RCA *Hollywood, CA* 2:00-5:00pm. Michael Nesmith *prod*; Pete Abbott *eng*; two-inch 16-track; overdubs.
1. **'Little Red Rider'** version 1 take 1A
   Missing Links 3 master # XZB3-0364
2. **'You're So Good'** take 1A
   Missing Links 3 master # XZB3-0363
3. **'Lynn Harper'** take 1A
   unissued master # XZB3-0368
4. **'Little Tommy Blue'** take 1A
   unissued master # XZB3-0451

Relaxing during a shoot for a Kool Aid ad.

5. **'Michigan Blackhawk'** take 1A
   unissued master # XZB-0452
Personnel Micky Dolenz (vocal 2), Mack Johnson (trumpet 2,3), Michael Nesmith (backing vocal 1), Lester Robertson (trombone 2,3), Clifford Solomon (tenor saxophone 2,3), John Williams (instrument unknown 2,3).
● Back from the East Coast, Michael dabbles with a new recording format: two-inch 16-track tape. Now that he has twice the number of tracks to play with, Michael can add even more overdubs to his recent productions.

Today he transfers his 'Little Red Rider' to the new medium and gives it a new designation, take 1A, although the only additions are a few tracks of harmony backing vocals that pop up just once in the song's bridge. Subsequently this master will be passed over for release, and is not mixed until 1996 when it is released on Rhino's *Missing Links Volume Three*. Michael will record a second version of 'Little Red Rider' on February 20th 1970.

He next returns to his production of 'You're So Good' from May 29th, adding further embellishments to take 9 (now renamed take 1A), including tracks of horns and a lead vocal from Micky. Once again members of The Goodtimers are involved, as well as someone named John Williams, probably another horn player. After this session, 'You're So Good' will be passed over for inclusion on *The Monkees Present*. In February 1970 an incomplete master of the track, lacking today's overdubs, will be sent to producer Jeff Barry to consider for the band's next album. But it will not find a contemporary release and only much later will it appear, on Rhino's *Missing Links Volume Three*.

Take 8 of the tentatively titled 'Lynn Harper' is also given some horn overdubs today, after which it is redesignated as take 1A. Despite this addition the song will remain incomplete and unissued. Two further songs are transferred to 16-track today in the hope of adding more overdubs, but 'Little Tommy Blue' and 'Michigan Blackhawk' will also remain incomplete and unissued.

● Friday 27th
RECORDING RCA *Hollywood, CA* 2:00-5:00pm. Michael Nesmith *prod*; Pete Abbott *eng*; quarter-inch stereo; mixdown.
1. **'Some Of Shelly's Blues'**
   Missing Links 2 master # WZB4-3073
2. **'Carlisle Wheeling'** version 3 take 4
   Instant Replay master # UZB3-9782
● Michael works with engineer Pete Abbott to mix two of his 1968 productions for potential inclusion on *The Monkees Present*. Ultimately both will be passed over. After Michael departs the studio, Davy enters to tape two new numbers.
RECORDING RCA *Hollywood, CA* 8:00pm-12:30am. David Jones, Bill Chadwick *prod*; 'HM' *eng*; one-inch 8-track; tracking.
1. **'French Song'** takes 1-12
   The Monkees Present master # XZB3-0236
2. **'How Can I Tell You'** takes 1-12
   unissued master # XZB3-0237
Personnel Max Bennett (bass), Hal Blaine (drums), Frank Bugbee (acoustic guitar), David Jones (vocal), Michel Rubini (organ 1, piano 2), Louie Shelton (acoustic guitar).
● Davy and Bill Chadwick partner up to produce two new tracks today. The first is 'French Song,' a slow, atmospheric tale of a little boy and girl who go out walking in the rain. Davy provides live guide vocals with every take – a very unusual practice at a Monkees session, and the first time since 'So Goes Love' on July 7th 1966. In fact 'French Song' is very similar in mood to that Goffin & King composition.

Before take 1, Hal Blaine says, "This is the 'French Song,'" and proceeds to count the number off – en françÁais. The arrangement is fully rehearsed and developed from the first pass, but Davy and Chadwick (who supervises the date from the control room) will record multiple takes to achieve a suitably subtle performance. After 12 takes everyone is satisfied and the final pass, take 12, is chosen as the master for further overdubs done on July 1st.

Davy recalls: "I think 'French Song' is one of my better productions. We were thinking a little bit more sophisticated at that particular time. I thought as a record it was absolutely super. That was like our first try at going in and being a producer. It's a really specialized thing, producing. It's not just sort of: go in and turn it on."

The slightly slower 'How Can I Tell You' is a smoky ballad that would be suitable for Sinatra. After a brief, faltering take 1 in which session guitarist Louie Shelton flubs the intro, Davy suggests that Shelton use a pick. Blaine is in a particularly jokey mood and instructs Shelton: "Do it like it was your album, Louie," which at least makes Davy laugh.

After six takes and a few more unnumbered false starts, the musicians have yet to lay down a full pass of 'How Can I Tell You,' leaving Blaine to quip about the loungey material at hand. "You gotta remember," he says, "we haven't worked in motels in a long time." Bill Chadwick shoots back: "Sounds like you've been working in Greyhound bus stations – restrooms." After this playful exchange the crew at last achieve a complete performance and Chadwick says the resulting take 7 is "worth a listen."

Chadwick and Jones decide to try a few more passes and prepare for take 8, though not before Blaine announces that they "ought to do a guest shot on the Lawrence Welk Show next Saturday night." Welk is the king of easy-listening music. Chadwick fires back: "It's already booked," but a less-than-amused Davy says: "Good. I'll make it."

The next few renditions are all complete and useable, but Chadwick asks for just one more. Davy says before take 10: "I love this stuff," referring to the material at hand and perhaps asserting the fact that it should not be a joking matter to the musicians. Blaine doesn't quite get the hint, and after Chadwick instructs Davy to sing "just a little easier in the beginning on this one for me," Blaine is merciless in his comments. "More like Frank [Sinatra] would do it," ribs Blaine. "You know, quarter to two, no one in the place."

Thankfully, the session is just about over. Take 12 is the final recorded take and Davy will eventually attempt to redo his vocals, taping over part of the live track. But he is unhappy with the results and will leave the track incomplete. It will remain unfinished and unissued.

● Saturday 28th
● The group's latest album, the *Monkees Greatest Hits* compilation, debuts on *Billboard*'s Top LPs chart at #163. Despite its retail potential, it will be The Monkees' worst-selling album to date.
● Micky's wife Samantha appears on the daytime music television program *Happening* as a judge in one of the show's weekly band contests.

JULY

● *Tiger Beat* spotlights Peter Tork's new group, Release. The article notes that the band rehearse every day at his North Hollywood pad. Tork says he "plans to let his hair grow and grow."

● *Monkees Monthly* reports that promoter Vic Lewis is hoping to bring the trio over to Britain in September for some live appearances.

● Tuesday 1st

RECORDING RCA *Hollywood, CA*. Micky Dolenz *prod*; Pete Abbott *eng*; quarter-inch stereo; mixdown.

1. **'Mommy And Daddy'** mixdown takes 1-3
   The Monkees Present master # WZB3-5310

● Micky has revised his lyrics and re-recorded his vocals for this song, which is now slated for release on The Monkees' next single. Today is the first of several attempts to mix a master suitable for public consumption. The third mix made today is temporarily considered the master for release, but it will be superseded by a new mix made tomorrow. Micky also tapes a new song at another studio.

RECORDING Sunset Sound Recorders (2) *6650 Sunset Boulevard, Hollywood, CA*. Micky Dolenz *prod*; Bill Lazerus *eng*; one-inch 8-track; tracking, overdubs.

1. **'Music Bridge' a.k.a. 'We'll Be Back In A Minute'** takes 1-29
   Missing Links 3 no master #

Personnel Henry Diltz (banjo), Micky Dolenz (vocal, acoustic guitar), Chip Douglas (bass), unknown (kazoo, claps, slaps).

● Moving to Sunset Sound, Micky records his first all-new track since last year's 'Mommy And Daddy.' His fresh offering lasts less than a minute and is labeled 'Music Bridge.' Its purpose is to give viewers of the upcoming Saturday reruns of the *Monkees* TV series a little musical transition between commercials to let them know that the show will be "back in a minute."

Micky is flanked by friends Chip Douglas on bass and Henry Diltz on banjo, and leads this date playing acoustic guitar (and singing some off-mike guide vocals).

Brendan Cahill, official music supervisor for the reruns, is on hand to time each take in an attempt to record them to a precise length. The goal seems to be a mere 20 seconds. Using the same basic chord structure, Micky, Douglas and Diltz tape a number of variations that are loosely termed during the session as 'fast,' 'slow,' 'slow rock,' and 'fast rock.'

In all, three different versions will be 'completed' today, one slow and two fast. All will receive overdubs of lead and backing vocals from Micky, plus some uncredited knee slaps, handclaps, and kazoo work. At least one of today's versions probably surfaces when the reruns debut in September. One slow and one fast version will later be incorporated into 1996's *Missing Links Volume Three* where they are issued under the presumptive title 'We'll Be Back In A Minute.'

RECORDING Sunset Sound Recorders (2) *Hollywood, CA* 9:00pm-12midnight. David Jones, Bill Chadwick *prod*; Bill Lazerus *eng*; one-inch 8-track; tracking, overdubs.

1. **'If I Knew'** takes 1-21
   The Monkees Present master # XZB3-0591
2. **'French Song'** overdubs onto take 12
   The Monkees Present master # XZB3-0236

Personnel Max Bennett (bass 1), Hal Blaine (drums), David Cohen [a.k.a. David Blue] (acoustic guitar 1), David Jones (vocal), Emil Richards (vibes 2, chimes 2, shaker 2, other percussion 2), Michel Rubini (piano 1, organ 2), Tim Weisberg (flute 2).

● After Micky leaves Sunset Sound, Davy and Bill Chadwick enter to record their new song, 'If I Knew,' and to add some overdubs to their 'French Song'. They use the same set-up as their last session, with Chadwick directing from the control room as Davy sings live with the musicians. The gentle soft-rock 'If I Knew' is well suited to Davy, and the session runs smoothly through 21 takes, despite a few non-

musical, technical glitches. The final pass is selected as the master and Davy later adds further vocal overdubs with some harmonies from Chadwick. A mono mix session will be held for the recording on the 11th.

Bill Chadwick: "I wrote it, but it was easier to get things recorded if you split the credit. So that's what I did. It was actually written about a girl that I had been living with for several years. A girl named Christine. Things were starting to break up and I couldn't figure out why. So I wrote the song.

"It was always easy to work with Davy. He always gave me complete creative freedom. He said whatever you need, whatever you want, you do it. He would oversee it and want to make sure that I wasn't going too far afield. He knew that I was the kind of person who could do that: I could get nuts and have 80 tabla players in there."

Work is also done today on take 12 of 'French Song' from June 27th, adding overdubs of flute, vibes, and percussion, as well as some more organ and drums to augment the basic track. The song will be given a mix on July 9th.

● Wednesday 2nd

RECORDING RCA *Hollywood, CA*. Micky Dolenz *prod*; Pete Abbott *eng*; quarter-inch stereo; mixdown.

1. **'Mommy And Daddy'**
   The Monkees Present master # WZB3-5310

● Micky now feels that yesterday's mix wasn't 'the one' and returns to RCA to mix a revised version of 'Mommy And Daddy.' The differences between yesterday's and today's mixes are sonically subtle. Today's has a less covered, overall brighter tone with somewhat louder background vocals (from Micky and his sister Coco) and has a slightly shorter fade-out section. Otherwise the placement and level of the recorded elements are absolutely identical. Striving to achieve a different sound, Micky will return to RCA to make another mix of the recording on July 10th.

Peter Tork: "I thought 'Mommy And Daddy' was a real interesting song. I'm not sure that I think it goes in quite the right direction musically, but [there are] some really interesting bits on it."

● Saturday 5th

● Peter Tork makes a rare television appearance on the Dick Clark show *Happening*, where he participates as a judge in a band contest. Other guests include Three Dog Night, Stephen Young, and Kathy Garver. Tork will appear in two further segments of the show in the coming weeks.

● A Monkees concert tentatively scheduled for today at the Anaheim Convention Center in Anaheim, California, does not happen.

● Tuesday 8th

RECORDING RCA *Hollywood, CA* 3:00-6:00pm. Chip Douglas *prod*; one-inch 8-track; overdubs.

1. **'Steam Engine'** overdubs onto composite master
   Missing Links 3 master # XZB5-0509

Personnel Micky Dolenz (vocal), Red Rhodes (pedal steel guitar).

● Chip Douglas, who participated in Micky's 'Music Bridge' session a few days earlier, manages to corral Micky into singing on his 'Steam Engine,' one of the items from the producer's speculative self-financed tracking session on May 12th. Not only does Micky officially sponsor this session, by persuading Screen Gems to foot the bill, but acts as union 'leader' for the date and goes so far as to personally sign the union contract. It's a very rare occurrence for a Monkee to sign the paperwork – usually it's one of the session musicians – and this underlines Micky's endorsement of Douglas's session.

Micky is in a good mood throughout the proceedings – at one point extolling on-mike the virtues of Drambuie whisky liqueur – and adds three tracks of lead and some background vocals to the track. Red Rhodes also attends the date to clean up his pedal-steel parts from May. Douglas will eventually add a final production touch of soulful female backing vocals before the song is given a mix on August 28th.

● Wednesday 9th
RECORDING RCA *Hollywood, CA.* David Jones, Bill Chadwick *prod*; quarter-inch stereo; mixdown.
1. **'French Song'** take 12
   The Monkees Present master # XZB3-0236
● At this point, Davy and Bill Chadwick's production features a sound effect of rain that will later be excised from the final master issued on *The Monkees Present*. A mono mix will be prepared on July 11th.

● Thursday 10th
RECORDING RCA *Hollywood, CA.* Micky Dolenz *prod*; Pete Abbott *eng*; quarter-inch stereo; mixdown.
1. **'Mommy And Daddy'** mixdown takes 1-7
   The Monkees Present master # WZB3-5310
● Micky makes yet another attempt at mixing his single master for 'Mommy And Daddy.' Today's features heavy reverb on the lead vocals and some panning moves that at various points have the backing vocals shifting from side to side in the stereo mix. The fade is also longer, and there are significant differences in the placement of instruments in the stereo picture. But as with his previous attempts to finalize this production, Micky obviously feels the mix requires some further tweaking.

Probably some time this month, he arrives at a final mix master that, unlike the previous attempts, features most of the top-end EQ rolled off (a technical term meaning that the treble is turned down) during the entire tape, to give a lo-fi effect. A mono mix of the track will be prepared on July 22nd.

● Friday 11th
RECORDING RCA *Hollywood, CA.* David Jones *prod*; Pete Abbott *eng*; quarter-inch mono; mixdown.
1. **'If I Knew'** take 21
   The Monkees Present master # XZB3-0591
2. **'French Song'** take 12
   The Monkees Present master # XZB3-0236
3. **'Penny Music'** take 9
   Missing Links 3 master # XZR3-0361
● Three of Davy's recent productions are mixed into mono for potential use on the Saturday-morning reruns of the *Monkees* series. 'French Song' will appear on the program on November 29th while today's mix of 'If I Knew' probably pops up on January 24th next year (though it is possible that it may be superseded by a later mono mix prepared on August 4th). In contrast to the first two tunes, today's mix of 'Penny Music' will never be aired and the song will never be originally released. Furthermore, today's tape of the song will later be damaged and 'Penny Music' will have to be remixed for its eventual inclusion on 1996's *Missing Links Volume Three*.

● Saturday 12th
● A further segment from Peter Tork's pre-taped appearance as a judge in Dick Clark's *Happening* band contest is televised by the ABC network. Other guests on this installment include Linda Ronstadt, Chuck Barris, Stephen Young, and Kathy Garver.

● Monday 14th
● Raybert's first post-Monkees production, a film called *Easy Rider*, opens in New York City. It has previously been shown at Cannes, in May. It will achieve the almost instant success that eluded their first feature-length film, *Head*, and will ultimately rake in some $30m.

Bob Rafelson: "We took all the money we made on [The Monkees] and financed *Easy Rider* ourselves. There was no Columbia money there. It was a little frightening. I totally believed in [*Easy Rider* co-star Dennis Hopper], but there are a lot of things that can go wrong while shooting a picture, especially with crazy Dennis. Then of course following the success of *Easy Rider* we were able to make *Five Easy Pieces* [with Jack Nicholson]."

● Wednesday 16th
RECORDING RCA *Hollywood, CA* 7:00-10:00pm. Micky Dolenz *prod*; Pete Abbott *eng*; one-inch 8-track; tracking.
1. **'Bye Bye Baby Bye Bye'** takes 1-11 + ending piece 2 takes
   The Monkees Present master # XZB3-0524
2. **'Midnight Train'** takes 1-5 + ending piece 5 takes
   Changes master # XZB3-0523
Personnel Hal Blaine (drums), James Burton (banjo), Tommy Morgan (harmonica), Joe Osborn (bass), Louie Shelton (electric guitar).
● Now that his production of 'Mommy And Daddy' has been put to bed, Micky has a clear path to record some new material. 'Bye Bye Baby Bye Bye' is a collaboration with his long-time friend Ric Klein and is recorded under the working title 'Second Song.' Shorty Rogers, credited as arranger of the tune, leads the musicians from the floor while Micky and Brendan Cahill look on from the control room.

Take 2 of 'Bye Bye' features Louie Shelton's unique fuzz/wah-wah electric guitar, not repeated on any other performance. After this pass, drummer Hal Blaine starts ribbing Shelton for looking at his watch between takes. "You going to ten?" asks Blaine, referring to the date's finish time. "How many fingers do you use when you play? Take two eggs out of a dozen, how many do you have?" continues Blaine, reinforcing the fact that they are all employed at this evening's session until 10:00pm.

The studio crew meander through another seven passes, eventually reaching take 10 (tonight's magic number). Sensing that they have a potential master, Cahill asks the musicians to tape two takes of an ending piece to edit onto the song's tail.

Despite this added effort, someone obviously feels they can do better, and the musicians perform one final pass, take 11. This will be used as the master and, sometime prior to mixing on July 22nd, Micky will add a lead vocal. Other overdubs on the final production will include some backing vocals from Davy and a track of acoustic guitar from an uncredited player. Notably, 'Bye Bye' will be the only new recording on *The Monkees Present* to feature more than one group member – although Micky and Davy will appear together vocally on a couple of warmed-over Boyce & Hart productions from 1966 that appear on the album.

The second song taped tonight is Micky's 'Midnight Train,' which was demoed more than two years earlier for *Headquarters*. The crew use the same instrumentation as 'Bye Bye' and easily nail the song in just five passes, of which only takes 1 and 5 are complete. After the final pass, five takes of a solo-guitar tag section are performed by Louie Shelton under the direction of Micky. Of these, Shelton's final attempt is edited onto take 5 and the master is now virtually complete. Prior to mixing on July 22nd, Micky will add a lead vocal to the track and (with the help of his sister Coco) some background harmonies.

● Friday 18th

PERFORMANCE Dane County Fair *Madison, WI* tickets $3-$4.50; promoted by Belkin Productions Inc.

Following their performance today The Monkees will travel tomorrow to Lake Geneva, Wisconsin.

● Saturday 19th

PERFORMANCE Majestic Bandstand *Majestic Hills, WI* promoted by Bill Grunow

This evening the group perform at Majestic Hills, between Fontana and Lake Geneva. This show is booked by local impresario Bill Grunow, who runs a series of summer teen dances in the Lake Geneva area.

● Also tonight, at 9:30pm, the group can be seen on the ABC network's *The Johnny Cash Show* in an appearance taped in early May. Cash performs a short burst of 'Last Train To Clarksville' and then introduces The Monkees who continue the song with backing from the house band. But when they get to the second round of "oh no no no's" Micky complains that the song is old and suggests that they sing something "off our new album." Then, accompanied just by Michael's Gibson acoustic guitar, the trio perform a stunning version of Michael's still unissued 'Nine Times Blue.' When they are done, Cash returns proclaiming that the song is "beautiful! Take a bow gentlemen." After this, the trio take part in some scripted patter with Cash about being called weirdos. This is the set-up for a rather embarrassing romp with Cash through Cowboy Jack Clement's 'Everybody Loves A Nut,' the title track of an album of novelty songs that Cash issued in 1966.

● Earlier today viewers could also watch Peter Tork make his third and final pre-taped appearance as a judge in Dick Clark's *Happening* band contest. It marks Tork's final 'new' television appearance of the 1960s. But his fans can take heart since today's issue of *Amusement Business* notes that Screen Gems have sold the *Monkees* TV series into reruns for at least two years.

● In *Billboard* 'Listen To The Band' reaches its peak of #63 on the Hot 100 while the magazine's Top LPs chart registers *The Monkees Greatest Hits* at #95. The album will peak in next week's chart at a disappointing #89.

● *Billboard* also reports that Columbia Pictures have signed Boyce & Hart to a new multi-million-dollar pact. The agreement includes provisions for a Boyce & Hart television series, as well as their own record label, B&H Aquarian. In the five years that Tommy Boyce and Bobby Hart have been associated with Columbia's Screen Gems they have written more than 260 songs that have sold nearly 50 million records. Regardless of these impressive figures, their series will be stillborn and their new label only issues a single 45. The contract does however provide a fresh incentive to include Boyce & Hart's material on The Monkees' upcoming releases.

● Monday 21st

RECORDING RCA *Hollywood, CA.* David Jones *prod*; Pete Abbott *eng*; one-inch 8-track; tracking.

1. 'The Good Earth' takes 1-17
   The Monkees Present master # XZB3-0594
Personnel David Jones (spoken word).

● Back from Wisconsin, Davy tapes a recitation of a poem, 'The Good Earth,' supervised by Brendan Cahill. As the tape starts to roll, Davy announces: "OK, this is 'The Good Earth.' Take 1 – the only take." Nevertheless, he will tape 17 nearly identical passes of this philosophical piece of unknown authorship. It is never issued on an original release, but one take will later be included as a bonus track on the 1994 CD reissue of *The Monkees Present.*

● Tuesday 22nd

RECORDING RCA *Hollywood, CA.* Pete Abbott *eng*; quarter-inch mono; mixdown.

1. 'Bye Bye Baby Bye Bye' take 11
   The Monkees Present master # XZB3-0524
2. 'Midnight Train' take 5
   Changes master # XZB3-0523
3. 'Mommy And Daddy'
   The Monkees Present master # WZB3-5310
4. 'Of You' take 10
   Missing Links 1 master # TZB4-4626

● Since The Monkees' records are no longer issued in true monaural sound, it is quite possible that today's mono mix session is held to generate tapes suitable for inclusion on the Saturday-morning reruns of *The Monkees*, which like all television at this time is broadcast in mono. Now that the group once again have records and television as outlets for their music, many unique mixes will be generated for both mediums.

However, it is not clear if today's mix of 'Bye Bye' – which lacks the acoustic guitar overdub heard on the final stereo master included on *The Monkees Present* – is used when the song is added to the show on November 14th 1970. On the other hand, 'Midnight Train' sounds very close to the released version and it may very well be today's mix that is used for its first television airing on February 21st 1970. Of the other two songs mixed, neither 'Mommy And Daddy' nor the 1966 outtake 'Of You' will ever turn up on the Saturday-morning reruns.

● Wednesday 23rd

● Colgems recording artists The New Establishment tape a version of Michael's previously unissued 'My Share Of The Sidewalk.' The recording is scheduled for release in April 1970, but the band's album will be withdrawn for unknown reasons.

● Thursday 24th – Tuesday 29th

PERFORMANCE The Forum *Mexico City, Mexico* promoted by Javier Castro

● Sunday 27th

PERFORMANCE Plaza Monumental *Jalisco, Mexico* 3:30pm

● The Monkees travel to Mexico City on the invitation of promoter Javier Castro for a long stint at his nightclub, The Forum. *Billboard* reports that the group play to a full house. During their stay in Mexico, they participate in a press conference, probably at their hotel, the Stella Maris. On Sunday the group perform an additional concert at Jalisco's Plaza Monumental. Pictures of this event will feature on the rear sleeve of the band's upcoming album, *The Monkees Present*. These lucrative south-of-the-border cash dates negate other bookings in Reading, Pennsylvania (24th), and two shows scheduled for this weekend in Florida.

● Thursday 24th

In the group's absence, some mixes are prepared in Hollywood for possible use on their upcoming records and TV reruns.

RECORDING RCA *Hollywood, CA.* Tommy Boyce & Bobby Hart *prod*; Pete Abbott *eng*; quarter-inch mono and stereo; mixdown.

1. 'Looking For The Good Times'
   The Monkees Present master # TZB3-4732
2. 'Apples, Peaches, Bananas And Pears'
   Missing Links 1 master # TZB3-4734
3. 'Ladies Aid Society' take 17
   The Monkees Present master # TZB3-4725

Michael and Davy perform in Mexico in July at Jalisco's Plaza Monumental stadium.

4. **'Kicking Stones' a.k.a. 'Teeny Tiny Gnome'** take 11
Missing Links 1 master # TZB3-4726
5. **'I Never Thought It Peculiar'**
Changes master # TZB3-4736
● Following Boyce & Hart's substantial deal with Screen Gems (see July 19th) there is a renewed push from the company to include some of the duo's overlooked productions from 1966 on The Monkees' upcoming releases. Today, five of Boyce & Hart's songs are mixed in both mono and stereo with engineer Pete Abbott.

'Looking For The Good Times,' completed in November 1966, and 'Ladies Aid Society,' completed in September 1966, will both turn up in stereo on the October 1969 album *The Monkees Present*. A mono mix of 'Good Times' will also pop up on two 1970 repeats of *The Monkees*, while today's mono mix of 'Ladies Aid Society' goes unused.

The unique mono mix of 'I Never Thought It Peculiar' will appear on a November 8th *Monkees* but not again since it lacks the backing vocals, strings, and horns added in September. New mono and stereo mixes will be prepared after it is sufficiently sweetened.

Today's mono mix of 'Apples, Peaches, Bananas And Pears' will first turn up on a repeat of *The Monkees* on February 13th 1971. The companion stereo mix will go unused, and when the song is finally included on an album (1987's *Missing Links*) the song will be remixed (in stereo) from the 4-track master. Last but not least, neither of today's mixes of 'Kicking Stones' will ever be used. The song will not appear on the TV series or any of the group's original albums. When the track is issued under the title of 'Teeny Tiny Gnome' on *Missing Links* it will be remixed in stereo from the 4-track master.

AUGUST

● *Tiger Beat* announces that Samantha Dolenz has entered the retail world with her own clothing boutique, One Of A Kind, which is now open at 8003 Santa Monica Boulevard in Hollywood.

● **Friday 1st**
PERFORMANCE Curtis Hixon Hall *Tampa, FL*

● **Saturday 2nd**
PERFORMANCE Trumbull County Fair, Mollenkopf Stadium *Warren, OH* 3:00 & 8:00pm
● The group perform as the "entertainment finale" on the closing day of the county fair. The *Warren Tribune Chronicle* reports that The Monkees "pack 'em in" for these two performances, though overall attendance for the fair is a little reduced as this is the first year that admission is charged for what is usually a free event.

● **Monday 4th**
RECORDING RCA *Hollywood, CA.* David Jones, Bill Chadwick *prod*; 'GH' *eng*; quarter-inch mono; mixdown.
1. **'If I Knew'** take 21
The Monkees Present master # XZB3-0591
● Back from Ohio, Davy supervises a second mono mix of his 'If I Knew.' It is possible that it supersedes the mono mix from July 11th and may be the one later used on the soundtrack of the rerun of the TV-series episode *One Man Shy* on January 24th 1970.

● **Tuesday 5th**
RECORDING RCA *Hollywood, CA.* Brendan Cahill *prod*; 'GH' *eng*; half-inch 4-track; overdubs.
1. **'Love To Love'** take 1A, formerly take 6
Missing Links 3 master # UZB1-4403
2. **'You Can't Tie A Mustang Down'** take 1A, formerly take 3
Daydream Believer And Other Hits master # UZB1-4401
● Just as the original run of *The Monkees* series fueled the need for recorded material, the show's Saturday-morning reruns are generating a similar demand. Under the direction of Brendan Cahill, now officially the group's music coordinator, some of The Monkees' unfinished recordings from their heyday will be considered for use on the program. Today, Cahill works with Davy to complete two of Jeff Barry's leftover productions from early 1967.

Davy adds three tracks of vocals to a 4-track tape of 'Love To Love' that consists simply of a mono mixdown of take 6 of the old backing track from January 21st 1967. For 'Mustang' Davy tapes two attempts at a lead vocal to accompany a mono mix of the backing track, which leaves one empty track on the 4-track tape.

After these additions both masters are given the new take number 1A. Nevertheless, they are never aired on the series or on any original record release.

A rough mix of today's work will be widely bootlegged and 'Love To Love' will later surface semi-officially on the 1979 Australian-only compilation *Monkeemania*, after which it will appear in much better quality on a number of Rhino releases.

As for 'You Can't Tie A Mustang Down,' this middling track will in fact slip out on the 1998 budget collection *Daydream Believer And Other Hits*.

● Wednesday 6th

RECORDING RCA *Hollywood, CA* 9:00am-12:30pm. David Jones, Bill Chadwick *prod*; 'HM' *eng*; one-inch 8-track; tracking.

1. **'If You Have The Time'** takes 1-10
   Missing Links 1 master # XZB3-0576
2. **'Time And Time Again'** takes 1-9
   Missing Links 1 master # XZB3-0592
3. **'French Song'** take 12
   The Monkees Present master # XZB3-0236

Personnel John Guerin (drums 1,2), David Jones (vocal 1,2), Joe Osborn (bass 1,2), Michel Rubini (keyboard 1,2), Louie Shelton (electric guitar 1,2). (It is possible that this list is incomplete and that more musicians participate today.)

● Prior to leaving for a working vacation in Britain, Davy enters RCA for his final tracking session of 1969. Alongside collaborator Bill Chadwick he cuts two new tracks: 'If You Have The Time' and 'Time And Time Again.' As with their recent tracking dates, Davy provides guide vocals throughout the session while Chadwick directs the musicians from the control room. Brendan Cahill is also on hand today to offer advice.

'If You Have The Time' is a bouncy music-hall styled number in the mold of the Beatles song 'Your Mother Should Know.' It is efficiently taped in ten takes, with little variation from performance to performance, and the final take is marked as today's master. Sometime later Davy will replace his live vocal track with a new double-tracked lead. Davy, Chadwick, and some (uncredited) others will also add a track of background vocals to the production. A further instrumental overdub session will take place on November 11th. (Chadwick will record his own version of 'If You Have The Time' under the production direction of Michael Nesmith later this year – see November 13th.)

The session's second song, 'Time And Time Again,' is somewhat more musically inspired. This moody number, with its heavily tremelo'd guitar and haunting calliope (a sort of steam-whistle keyboard, which is played today by session leader Michel Rubini), has real potential.

After Take 2, Chadwick asks Rubini to improvise a new calliope part for the song's intro. Rubini immediately says: "I don't know what to do. Help!" Chadwick replies: "Well, do something." Failing to find anything immediately of musical interest, Rubini reverts to his part as written.

Today's final pass, take 9, is marked as the master and will receive a newly recorded double-tracked lead vocal from Davy, as well as some vocal backgrounds from both Davy and Chadwick. Further instrumental overdubs will be added to the production on November 11th.

According to musicians' union documents, some final production work may be attempted today on Davy and Chadwick's 'French Song.' Although it was mixed in both mono and stereo last month, there is still plenty of time for the pair to update their master for release on *The Monkees Present*.

● Thursday 7th

● Davy flies to London, with wife Linda and baby Thalia in tow, to tape an appearance for an upcoming Tennessee Ernie Ford special. He is scheduled to stay in Britain through August 23rd. The *NME* says Davy will "undertake other TV dates during his visit."

● Saturday 9th

● *Billboard* reports that tickets for The Monkees' August 25th concert at the Central Canada Exhibition are priced at just $1.

● Thursday 14th

RECORDING RCA *Hollywood, CA* 9:30pm-1:00am. Micky Dolenz *prod*; 'Hank M' *eng*; one-inch 8-track; tracking.

1. **'Pillow Time'** version 2 takes 1-21
   The Monkees Present master # XZB3-0577
2. **'Little Girl'** takes 1-13
   The Monkees Present master # XZB3-0578

Personnel Micky Dolenz (vocal, acoustic guitar), Earl Palmer (drums), Ray Pohlman (bass), Louie Shelton (electric guitar).

● On this summer night, Micky holds what will be the final Monkees tracking session of the 1960s. The first song is mistakenly announced by Brendan Cahill as "'Pillow Talk' take 1," but he is quickly corrected by Micky and Shorty Rogers, who say simultaneously: "It's 'Pillow Time.'" This is the Janelle Scott/Matt Willis lullaby that Micky first taped on March 14th 1967 during the *Headquarters* sessions. Whereas the echo-laden '67 rendition was spacey and almost spooky, tonight's performances will be smooth and jazzy, skillfully arranged by Rogers.

Micky adopts Davy's routine of providing live vocals during the tracking, singing and playing acoustic guitar through every sublime take. Despite a few interruptions and flubs, he sounds perfectly at ease throughout the evening, playfully shifting his vocal phrasing to suit the mood of each performance.

Tonight's final pass, take 21 (with the ending from take 20 tacked on), is marked as the master; before mixing, Micky will add four more lead-vocal tracks to the 8-track master in addition to his live take. This offers him a variety of options for mixing, though ultimately he will select just a single vocal performance from these. Completed in the next few days, 'Pillow Time' will be used as the closer for *The Monkees Present*.

The opening track of that album, Micky's 'Little Girl,' is taped next. Using the same recording set-up, Micky sings live and plays acoustic guitar for all 13 takes. The final pass, take 13, is edited together with the ending from take 8 to create a composite master. Micky and his sister Coco will record overdubs of background vocals onto this tape as well as a new lead vocal to replace Micky's live track. 'Little Girl' will be mixed sometime during the next few days.

(A tape box indicates that an otherwise unknown song called 'Pockets Of Life' may be attempted at this session, but it is possibly erased by take 1 of 'Little Girl.')

● Monday 18th

● The Monkees may be scheduled to perform at the Kentucky State Fair in Louisville today, but it is unlikely that this gig takes place since Davy is still in Britain. Michael and Micky will undertake one booking without Davy, on August 24th.

On stage in Mexico: The Monkees perform with the support of their regular backing band, Sam & The Goodtimers.

our popularity is falling off? People come up and say we aren't as big in Britain these days.

"I turn around and say they only think that because the music papers aren't writing about us like they used to. If [the papers] can't get hold of what they want, they give up and use something they can get easily.

"We can still play almost anywhere in the world and pack a theatre. In the States, we have a new series on peak-hour television which will run for two years. But you mustn't think of The Monkees in terms of a group. We were four people, now we are three. We joined Screen Gems as actors who could play a bit of music, not a group who could fool around a bit.

"The Beatles comparison? What a joke. Of course it was. They are a group, a music group, the best that ever happened. How could anyone compare us with them? But I loved it. To be put in the same bracket as The Beatles! But let's be honest, what a joke. If you put a bass guitar in my hands, it becomes an actor's prop. Oh, I can play a couple of notes, but it's a prop, that's all. While I'm here doing the Ernie Ford [television special *The Peapicker In Piccadilly*] the others are hosting shows, compère things. Not guesting, but actually running a whole show. That's how separate we are."

● **Sunday 24th**

● As described by Davy in yesterday's *NME*, Michael and Micky act as emcees this afternoon in *Experience No. 1*, a multi-act music program at the Central Canada Exhibition in Ottawa. With an admission price of 50 cents and a bill of unknown acts – the most noteworthy may be Aretha Franklin's sister, Carolyn – this is yet another bizarre booking for the beleaguered band members. *The Ottawa Citizen* later reviews the event under the heading "Ho hum, we're The Monkees."

"Finding it unnecessary to do more than bask witlessly in their past glories," writes *Citizen* staffer Tracy Morey, "the big visitors, ex-Monkees Mike Nesmith and Micky Dolenz, were delivering emcee jobs without a hint of involvement or style. The line of performing visitors had included a routine Ian & Sylvia-type duo, a folksy sort of Johnny Cash called Eric Erickson, and a pleasant but unexciting quintet called Nora's Truckstop. An amplified sound system somewhat off-kilter, musicians and technicians wandering on and off stage, and 2,500 people feeling a little lonely and neglected in the 12,000 capacity stadium.

"The audience began to dwindle at 4:30pm and the early leavers lost out on a very classy full-scale rock orchestra, including electric cellos and violins, a xylophone, and trumpet. … The program was too long and they tried to draw the kids in with two big names that were unhappily disappointing. Behind the scenes during the concert, Micky claimed he and Nesmith were really very happy doing a non-performing emcee kid of job. Nesmith couldn't really say, since he was tired and sickly after a bad flight from Toronto."

"'It's more difficult than performing, this off-the-cuff routine,' remarks Dolenz, before adding, 'and it's not as rewarding. … The Monkees brought long hair into living rooms. We were just harmless little ding-a-lings and the parents found nothing they could object to, despite the long hair. You have no choice these days but to peak around 19 or 20.'" As for being an adult, Micky tells Morey that it just means "you're someone able to deal with corruption and get along in our corrupt world."

● **Monday 25th**

PERFORMANCE Grandstand, Canadian National Exhibition *Toronto, ON, Canada* 5:30 & 8:30pm, with Sam & The Goodtimers
● Reunited with Davy, The Monkees reportedly appear before 5,000

● **Saturday 23rd**

● Davy tells *NME's* Gordon Coxhill that he is broke. He says to the reporter: "You've got more money than I've got. I owe the taxman quite a bit. I owe money to almost everybody I know, and I've got a pile of unpaid bills at home." Coxhill has difficulty believing this, especially since the interview takes place in Davy's plush Savoy Hotel suite in London. Davy insists that his problem is with Screen Gems, who he claims takes half of every dollar he earns.

"That's why I have to carry on working," he explains. "I've got another two and a half years to go on my contract at Screen Gems, and then they won't see me for dust. Then I'll be the big guy behind the desk, hiring and firing." Davy confesses: "I'm not a singer or a musician. I never have been – The Monkees never were. … Who says

Davy in Britain shooting a scene for a forthcoming Tennessee Ernie Ford TV special.

fans at the first performance, which takes place in sweltering 90-degree heat. DuBarry Campu of Toronto's *The Telegram* provides some detail. "Almost everyone is under 16 – except for sets of parents who have brought along even younger children, many of them two to six. (Was there some misunderstanding here – could they have thought they were bringing the tots to see something even more simian than they ultimately saw?) So – bing, bang, and buzz! Onto the stage come Sam & The Goodtimers Ltd. They're hooked up to enough electric power to blow every fuse in town and they play and shout and stamp about a bit and yell things like, 'Sock it to me.' Despite all the noise, they're just warming us up for The Monkees.

"After a brief break, during which we all had another round of tepid food and drink, The Monkees, all three of them, bound onto the stage. Everyone screams – but this is interesting. These screams sound faintly imitative. These very young teenagers know that's what you do when you're hearing a group like this live – their older sisters have probably told them how it's done. But the Beatles fans had the original patent on sobbing and moaning; swooning was a thousand years ago in the Sinatra era.

"The trio backed by Sam & The Goodtimers are frenetically noisy and active. … The Monkees encourage a lot of rhythmic clapping – which swells the decibel count and gives an illusion of audience participation. When their hands aren't busy clapping, most of the girls use them to wave limply at the stage. … There is a final burst of raucous amplified sound, accompanied by dutiful screaming from the customers, and the show is over. … It's 7:14. The temperature has gone down: it's only 87 degrees."

The cooler temperatures must have drawn a far larger crowd for the second show since *Billboard* reports later that The Monkees pulled in almost 19,000 fans (combined) for today's gigs. *Billboard* also notes that Davy took time out during his visit to Toronto to visit the Hospital for Sick Children.

● **Thursday 28th – Friday 29th**
PERFORMANCE Colorado State Fair *Pueblo, CO* 5:30 & 8:30pm, with Sam & The Goodtimers
● The group appear for two days at the fair, promoted as headliners by fair manager Don Svedman. There has been a report that the appearances were cancelled due to the illness of Davy Jones, but the shows go on as planned. According to the State Fair sales director: "The crowd was not as large as expected but they put on a great show … . Those who attended made enough noise, responding to the entertainment, to make up for those who did not attend." Rainfall at the fairgrounds dampened the visiting crowds. Meanwhile back in Hollywood, final mix and assembly sessions are held for *The Monkees Present*.
RECORDING RCA *Hollywood, CA.* Chip Douglas *prod*; quarter-inch stereo; mixdown.
1. **'Steam Engine'**
   Missing Links 3 master # XZB5-0509
● On Thursday 28th Chip Douglas makes a mix of his 'Steam Engine' for possible inclusion on *The Monkees Present*, but it is obvious from the roughly hewn results that the master is not quite ready for release. The following day, the final masters for the album are compiled and sequenced. Among the songs specifically considered but passed over are Boyce & Hart's 'Apples, Peaches, Bananas And Pears' and 'My Storybook Of You,' Michael's 'Hollywood,' and Jack Keller's 'If I Ever Get To Saginaw Again.'

● **Saturday 30th**
TV The Monkees' *33 ⅓* special is repeated in Britain on BBC-1, replacing the regular *Dee Time* program.

SEPTEMBER

'Good Clean Fun' / **'Mommy And Daddy'** single released in the U.S.A. This is the group's 11th single.
● Britain's *Monkees Monthly* publishes its farewell issue, the result of declining sales.
● *16* magazine features a unique draft of the lyrics for Boyce & Hart's as yet unissued 'My Storybook Of You.' Under the heading "Sing-along with DAVY," *16* writes: "Recently Davy fell head over heels in love – with a song! When Davy heard two of his best friends, songwriters Tommy Boyce and Bobby Hart, working on 'My Storybook Of You,' he told them it was one of the most beautiful tunes he had ever heard and he made them promise that, when they finished it, they would let him record it. Bobby and Tommy are still working on 'My Storybook Of You' for Davy, but at press time they had finished the first draft. Take a look and remember it well – for it's the kind of song that reminds Davy of you." Regardless of this hype, the song will remain unissued (until 1987's *Missing Links*).
● *16* also notes that Peter Tork is now producing Judy Mayhan solo, but their joint group, Release, are still "deciding" on a recording contract.

Good Clean Fun single

A **'Good Clean Fun'** (M. NESMITH)
B **'Mommy And Daddy'** (M. DOLENZ)

U.S. release September 1969 (Colgems 5005).
U.K. release late 1969 or early 1970 (RCA 1887).
Chart high U.S. number 82; U.K. none.

● **Thursday 4th**
PERFORMANCE California State Fair *Sacramento, CA* 8:30pm, with Queen Lily Soap, Sam & The Goodtimers; tickets $3–$5; sponsored by radio station KROY
● The group's set tonight reportedly consists of 'Last Train To Clarksville,' 'I'm A Believer,' 'Pleasant Valley Sunday,' 'Tapioca Tundra,' 'I Wanna Be Free,' 'Show Me,' 'A Man Without A Dream,' 'Daydream Believer,' 'Goin' Down,' 'Someday Man,' 'Listen To The Band,' 'Don't Wait For Me,' 'Summertime' performed by Micky, 'For Once In My Life,' 'Johnny B. Goode,' and 'I'm A Believer.'

John Hurst of the *Sacramento Bee* reviews the performance. "One thing about The Monkees: as musicians they may just be middling to good, but they sure are cheerful. The audience gave them the Star Spangled Banner treatment last night when they appeared in front of the State Fair grandstand – [meaning they] stood through the entire first half of [the group's] show. … When Micky Dolenz dangled his legs over the edge [of the stage] as he sat to sing a song, there was a stampede to touch him. He quickly retrieved his feet and the girls went back to flinging their crumpled wads of paper onto the stage. … The concert opened with a group called Queen Lily Soap, playing a kind of Hebraic-psychedelic rock with occasional lapses into the dance tempo of the hora. Then Sam & The Goodtimers, the six-man group that backs up The Monkees, took over to warm up the audience. … [The Monkees] gave the huge crowd a good show.

Collectively or singly, they performed a baker's dozen of their songs, including two versions of their hit, 'I'm A Believer,' both sung by Jones. One pretty much followed the outline of the original record. The other put it to an effective, medium gospel-rock tempo, then merged into a Dolenz-dominated scat thing that ended the show."

● Friday 5th

RECORDING The Sound Factory *Hollywood, CA* 12midday-3:00pm. Tommy Boyce & Bobby Hart *prod*; overdubs.

1. 'I Never Thought It Peculiar'
  Changes master # TZB3-4736
Personnel Tommy Boyce, Bobby Hart, Ron Hicklin (all backing vocal).
● Boyce & Hart reunite with session vocalist Ron Hicklin, a veteran of their '66 sessions, to overdub some vocal backgrounds for their production of 'Peculiar.' Strings and horns will be added on September 12th.

● Saturday 6th

PERFORMANCE Duluth Auditorium *Duluth, MN* promoted by Variety Theatre International
● After two postponements The Monkees finally perform two concerts here, drawing an audience of 1,376 to the afternoon set and 1,742 to the evening show. The *Duluth News Tribune* reports that, despite the meager turnout, "superior police" have to disperse a crowd of about 200 young girls who converge on the group's motel. "They were disappointed. The Monkees had already left for their afternoon show."

● Friday 12th

RECORDING The Sound Factory *Hollywood, CA* 1:00-5:30pm. Tommy Boyce & Bobby Hart *prod*; Dave Hassinger *eng*; overdubs, mixdown.

1. 'I Never Thought It Peculiar'
  Changes master # TZB3-4736
Personnel Michael Anthony (instrument unknown), Harold Ayres (violin), Tommy Boyce (backing vocal), John DeVoogdt (violin), Chuck Findley (trumpet), Jimmy Getzoff (violin), Bobby Hart (backing vocal), Ron Hicklin (backing vocal), Dick Hyde (trombone), William Hymanson (viola), Joy Lule (violin), Jay Migliori (saxophone), Gary Nuttycombe (viola), Alan Robinson (French horn), Norman Serkin (violin), Frederick Seykora (cello).
● Boyce & Hart work with arranger Jimmie Haskell to add horns and strings to their master of 'I Never Thought It Peculiar,' as well as putting on some further backing vocal overdubs. After the additions are completed they make a mono mixdown of the song for use on the TV series. 'Peculiar' will also be mixed in stereo for The Monkees' next album, *Changes*.

Symbolically, today's date will turn out to be Boyce & Hart's final Monkees recording session – and 'I Never Thought It Peculiar' will be the last song on wht will become the group's swansong as recording artists.

● Saturday 13th

TV At 12midday *The Monkees* returns in a series of Saturday-morning reruns on the CBS network. Today, episode 18 – *I Was A Teenage Monster* – is aired with an updated soundtrack. The original episode's 'Your Auntie Grizelda' is replaced by The Monkees' latest single, 'Good Clean Fun,' which coincidentally enters *Billboard's* Hot 100 Bound chart at #113 today. Today also marks the last chart placement for *The Monkees Greatest Hits* which exits at #162 after a 12-week run.

● Monday 15th

RECORDING Location unknown; half-inch 4-track; overdubs.
1. 'I Didn't Know You Had It In You Sally, You're A Real Ball Of Fire'
  unissued master # UZB1-4414
Personnel Micky Dolenz (lead vocal, backing vocal).
● Micky attempts to make something of the group's stockpile of unfinished masters, adding a lead vocal track to Denny Randell's February 1967 production 'I Didn't Know You Had It In You Sally, You're A Real Ball Of Fire.' The song is way out of date, having echoes of The New Vaudeville Band's 'Winchester Cathedral' which itself was anachronistic in 1966. Nevertheless, the revised master will be transferred to 8-track tape for more potential work on October 3rd.

● Wednesday 17th

TV Davy's solo appearance on *Laugh-In* from February is finally aired in Britain on BBC-2.

● Saturday 20th

TV CBS reruns *The Monkees* episode 23, *Captain Crocodile*, at 12midday.
● In *Billboard*, Micky's 'Mommy And Daddy' makes a brief showing at #110 while 'Good Clean Fun' clings to #100.

● Tuesday 23rd

● Micky and Samantha Dolenz take advantage of the absence of performing or recording obligations for the rest of the month and travel to Hawaii for a vacation where they will spend time with friends Henry Diltz and Chip Douglas.

● Saturday 27th

TV At noon today the CBS network reruns episode 37 of the *Monkees* series, *Art For Monkees Sake*.

● Sunday 28th

● Micky and Samantha return to Los Angeles from Hawaii.

OCTOBER

The Monkees Present album is released in the U.S.A. Michael says later of the group's eighth LP: "That had the black-and-white cover done with Marks-A-Lot [marking pens] and was supposed to be in color. Apparently they wouldn't do a color [printing], because by that time we were, you know, as cold as yesterday's soup. Nobody would spend any money. Besides that, Peter had spent all the royalties on 'Lady's Baby,' bless his heart."

● Friday 3rd

RECORDING RCA *Hollywood, CA*. 'GH' *eng*; one-inch 8-track; transfers.
1. 'I Didn't Know You Had It In You Sally You're A Real Ball Of Fire'
  unissued master # UZB1-4414
2. 'Love Is On The Way'
  unissued master # UZB1-4413
3. 'Sugar Man'
  unissued master # UZB1-4416
● Someone at Screen Gems has managed to coax Micky into singing on Denny Randell's 'Sally,' and so that song and two others are today

The Monkees Present album

A1 'Little Girl' (M. DOLENZ)
A2 'Good Clean Fun' (M. NESMITH)
A3 'If I Knew' (D. JONES / B. CHADWICK)
A4 'Bye Bye Baby Bye Bye' (M .DOLENZ / R. KLEIN)
A5 'Never Tell A Woman Yes' (M. NESMITH)
A6 'Looking For The Good Times' (T. BOYCE / B. HART)
B1 'Ladies Aid Society' (T. BOYCE / B. HART)
B2 'Listen To The Band' version 1 (M. NESMITH)
B3 'French Song' (B. CHADWICK)
B4 'Mommy And Daddy' (M. DOLENZ)
B5 'Oklahoma Backroom Dancer' (M. MURPHEY)
B6 'Pillow Time' version 2 (J. SCOTT / M. WILLIS)

U.S. release October 1969 (Colgems COS-117).
Chart high U.S. number 100.

bounced from 4- to 8-track in the hope of completing them. Although The Monkees' base for record production will make a surprising shift back to New York City next year, producer Jeff Barry will not include any old recordings on the group's next album (except one of his own).

● Saturday 4th

TV The CBS network reruns episode 3 of the *Monkees* series, *Monkees Vs. Machine*, at 12midday. The show's soundtrack is revised to include 'Listen To The Band' in place of 'Saturday's Child.'
● *Amusement Business* magazine runs a potentially damaging article titled "Monkees: Hard Work Ahead On Road Back To The Top." Colgems promotions man Danny Davis is quoted as saying: "I've watched their rise and their demise. The wheel has turned full cycle. Let's face it, the group was a phenomenon in 1967; now they'll have to rebuild." Since *Amusement Business* is published almost exclusively for show bookers and promoters, these words could have a negative effect on future bookings. Additionally it is revealed that CBS asked The Monkees to film some extra segments for their Saturday-morning TV reruns, but for personal reasons they declined. On a brighter note, the promoter of their canceled Forest Hills show says that they might appear at the 1970 festival.

● Monday 6th

TV The Monkees appear as special guest stars on *Laugh-In* at 8:00pm. During the hour-long program they take part in numerous sketches and vignettes, but do not perform musically.

● Thursday 9th

Tickets priced at $2.50 and $3.50 go on sale for a Monkees concert at the Civic Coliseum in Knoxville, Tennessee.

● Saturday 11th

TV At 12midday the CBS network reruns episode 35 of the *Monkees* series, *Everywhere A Sheik, Sheik.*

● Thursday 16th

● Michael and Davy travel to North Carolina on an Eastern Airlines flight. They are greeted by 500 screaming fans upon their arrival at the Raleigh-Durham Airport. A press conference originally set for the Eastern Airlines VIP room is moved when, according to one reporter, the terminal becomes "overrun with teenagers on the roof, banging on windows, breaking through a loading area, and traipsing along the runway. Mike and Davy were rushed into a station wagon that was chased down the roadway."

Later, while eating dinner at their hotel, Mike and Davy are informed that another press conference has been hastily arranged. After sending their meals back to be kept warm, they spend a half-hour with the local press. During this intercourse, Michael explains that Micky is busy recording and will arrive before their first show in North Carolina tomorrow afternoon. He also admits that he is a country & western music purist and has "always dreamed of being a big cowboy star."

Davy tells the press that Michael's songs are "beautiful" but just don't fit into the Monkees mold. He says that Peter Tork has gone back to "his own kind of music" but that he still meets with Tork each week. Michael adds that each band member has been approached about making a film, but they haven't found "the right vehicle" for a group film.

● Friday 17th

PERFORMANCE Dorton Arena, North Carolina State Fair *Raleigh, NC* 3:30 & 7:30pm; tickets $2.50
● The group headline the opening day of the 102nd North Carolina State Fair. Despite the fan fervor that greeted them yesterday, the attendance for their two 50-minute performances is only half of this venue's normal occupancy. Reviewer Bill Morrison writes: "The Monkees opened their act by giving solo turns to each member. The high marks were attained by Davy Jones, who croons in Anthony Newley fashion and shows some sense of lyrics. Micky Dolenz, the rather smart alecky kid with the bride of Frankenstein coiffure, created the act's most embarrassing moments, which reached their nadir in a tortured 'Summertime.' Mike Nesmith, the Texan with the deadpan delivery, blends into the band, a no more than adequate guitarist. Finally, The Monkees' appeal seems limited to a youth group that asks, as one child behind me asked, 'What are personal problems?' Personal problems, honey, are the fate of anyone who pans The Monkees. But I figure: who'll remember in 10 years?" Today's performances gross a total of $23,000.

● Saturday 18th

PERFORMANCE Greenville Memorial Auditorium *Greenville, SC* 3:00 & 8:00pm; tickets $2.50 & $3
Micky and Davy make the cover of the *Greenville News* when they present a copy of *The Monkees Present* to a seven-year-old aphasic fan, Pamela Bowers. Using the group's music and TV series as therapy, she has learned to say her first two words: 'Davy,' and 'Monkees.'
TV At 12midday the CBS network reruns for a second time episode 3 of the *Monkees* series, *Monkees Vs. Machine*. The show's soundtrack is again revised to include 'Listen To The Band' in place of 'Saturday's Child.'
● In *Billboard* the band's current single, 'Good Clean Fun,' peaks at #82 after just five weeks in the chart. It is a difficult song to sell, considering it does not feature the title anywhere in the lyrics and is a hardcore country & western number, and it will disappear from the Hot 100 next week.

● Sunday 19th

PERFORMANCE Civic Coliseum *Knoxville, TN* 2:00pm; promoted by Jim Crockett Promotions
● The group perform a one-hour concert to a near full house of

6,000 at the Coliseum that grosses a total of $16,000. The *Knoxville News-Sentinel* says: "Hundreds of excited girls ran from the Coliseum after the show, around to the rear doors, hoping to get an autograph, but the popular three already had been whisked away in a security movement almost as tight as when Richard Nixon visited the Coliseum as a presidential candidate. The throng pounded on the rear doors, yelling for Davy Jones, Micky Dolenz, and Michael Nesmith. The girls wouldn't believe The Monkees were gone.

"But have hope girls, The Monkees may return in April. John Ringley, vice president of Jim Crockett Promotions which staged [the] show, said he's hopeful of a return engagement. Micky, in a brief interview backstage before the show, said they perform 'mostly on the weekends while the kids are out of school.' A concert on a Sunday afternoon is not rare for them, he said. The group returned last night to Los Angeles, home base. As for the future and a possible TV series or movie, Davy said, 'We're considering a couple of proposals now,' but until a decision the group is grinding out hit recordings."

● Saturday 25th

TV Episode 2 of the *Monkees* series, *Monkee See, Monkee Die*, is shown again today at 12midday. *Amusement Business* reports that the group have soared in the ratings with these CBS reruns. The first three weeks of the run saw top share ratings of 48, 50 and 51 – which translated into over eight million viewers of their Saturday-morning repeats. The magazine also announces a concert date for The Monkees at the Arizona State Fair in Phoenix.

TV Davy makes an oh-so-brief cameo appearance on *The Andy Williams Show*, a variety television program broadcast at 7:30pm by the NBC network. Earlier in the year The Monkees were slated to appear as a group on Williams's program, but this split-second walk-on from Davy is all that will materialize.

● Friday 31st

● Michael participates in the Mexican 1000 buggy race, on a motorcycle. Other famous contestants at this Ensanada event include actors Steve McQueen and James Garner. However, most who participate in the race are not celebrities. Two contestants are fatally injured during the competition.

NOVEMBER

● Michael begins to develop his exit strategy from The Monkees. After watching the group's last two singles flop – both of which featured his songs – he sees very little commercial or creative reason to tie himself to his bandmates. However, his parting from the group will be a gradual process that will take place over the next several months. Although he will continue to perform in concert with The Monkees and film some commercials, Michael makes no secret of his intentions to form a new group. By the end of this month these plans will be made public.

● Saturday 1st

TV At 12midday the CBS network reruns episode 28 of the *Monkees* series, *Monkees On The Line*. The show's soundtrack is revised to include Micky's 'Little Girl' from the group's latest album in place of 'Look Out (Here Comes Tomorrow).' That album, *The Monkees Present*, breaks into the *Billboard* chart today at #187. Although it will have a longer run in the Top LPs section than their last release, *The Monkees Greatest Hits*, it will still only peak at #100.

● Sunday 2nd

TV Davy appears on *Dick Clark's Music Bag* at 7:00pm singing 'Someday Man.' The show is syndicated and so Davy's appearance airs later in some areas.

● Monday 3rd

PERFORMANCE **Memorial Coliseum, Arizona State Fair** *Phoenix, AZ* 6:30 & 8:30pm, with Sam & The Goodtimers; fair admission $1.50 adults, 50¢ children 12 and under

● A reviewer writes: "The Monkees, the original American bubblegum rock group, performed for 6,700 screaming, frenzied enthusiasts [at the early show]. The second performance drew about 7,000. Opening the show and backing The Monkees were Sam & The Goodtimers, a polished soul-and-jazz-oriented band which used to tour with Ike & Tina Turner. Their renditions of 'Come See About Me,' 'Soulful Strut,' and 'The Horse' were well received, but the restless crowd made it obvious whom they all really came to see.

"Those who imagined, wishfully perhaps, that the group's popularity had waned since the days of 'Last Train To Clarksville' and the old Monkees TV show were mistaken; thunderous applause and screaming greeted Mike Nesmith, Davy Jones, and Micky Dolenz as they bounced on-stage. After a bit of clowning around which has come to be expected from performers, the show started with the biggest Monkee hit, 'I'm A Believer,' followed by 'Pleasant Valley Sunday,' 'Tapioca Tundra,' and 'I Wanna Be Free.' While Nesmith, the musically talented member of the trio, contributed a few bits of relatively undistinguished guitar work here and there, Jones and Dolenz amused themselves with the modest demands of the tambourine, the maracas, and the cowbell. The crowd, composed mainly of 11-year-old micro-boppers accompanied by their mommies and daddies, loved every second of it."

TV Michael and Davy possibly appear on the local Phoenix children's television program *Wallace And Company*.

● Tuesday 4th

● Davy pays a visit to Rhonda Cook, the auto-pedestrian accident victim he befriended last year (see May 11th 1968). Davy tells a local paper that Cook is doing fine and made it to The Monkees' concert last night.

● Saturday 8th

TV At 12midday the CBS network reruns episode 58 of the *Monkees* series, *Mijacogeo (The Frodis Caper)*. The show's soundtrack is revised to include a unique mix of 'I Never Thought It Peculiar' in place of 'Zor And Zam.'

● Monday 10th

A full year after the failure of their *Head* movie, Bob Rafelson and Bert Schneider begin a new film project together called *Five Easy Pieces*. Jack Nicholson and Toni Basil, both featured in *Head* and *Easy Rider*, rejoin Rafelson for his second feature-length turn as director, and Monkee staff alumnus Marilyn Schlossberg is on hand as production coordinator. Shooting begins today and runs through January 3rd 1970.

Bob Rafelson: "Because of *Five Easy Pieces*, all these people were requesting to see *Head*. But [at the time *Head*] came out, nobody exhibited it, nobody saw it. My feelings were hurt. I felt rejected, you know? I went through a very sad thing and then I realized that's not why I make pictures. That was never why I wanted to make pictures. It never had anything to do with that. It was always the experience of making the film, the exhilaration. Nothing that happens after the film-shoot can diminish that. So I went out and made another picture. It took me a while to get it together, to find out if I had anything to say."

● Tuesday 11th

RECORDING RCA *Hollywood, CA* 2:00-5:00pm. David Jones, Bill Chadwick *prod*; one-inch 8-track; overdubs.

1. **'If You Have The Time'** take 10
   Missing Links 1 master # XZB3-0576
2. **'Time And Time Again'** take 9
   Missing Links 1 master # XZB3-0592

Personnel Paul Beaver (Moog synthesizer), Michel Rubini (keyboard).
● Keyboardists Paul Beaver and Michel Rubini work today on sweetening two of Davy and Bill Chadwick's productions from August. Synthesizer pro Beaver, last heard on 1967's 'Star Collector,' overdubs two tracks of Moog on both songs. Meanwhile Rubini probably just touches up his own tracks of piano and calliope from August. Both songs are now complete and will be mixed in stereo at the end of the session.

'Time And Time Again' is slated to appear on the group's next album, *Changes*, but (for reasons unknown) will be replaced by 'I Never Thought It Peculiar.' The track will eventually surface on the 1988 CD version of *Missing Links*. 'If You Have The Time' will first appear on a rerun of the *Monkees* series on March 21st 1970. It does not make it to any of the group's original albums and is later collected on the 1987 LP *Missing Links*. (Bill Chadwick has cut his own version of the song, which will find a release much sooner.)

● Thursday 13th

RECORDING Michael works in the studio to mix down Bill Chadwick's own version of 'If You Have The Time.' Michael produced Chadwick's recording of this track recently as a part of his continuing production deal with the Dot label. It will be issued very soon as a single on Dot under the name Bill Chadwick, coupled with a recording of Chadwick's 'Talking To The Wall,' which Michael also produced.

● Saturday 15th

TV CBS reruns *Monkees* episode 34, *The Picture Frame*, at 12midday.

● Friday 21st

RECORDING RCA *Hollywood, CA*. Chip Douglas *prod*; 'GH' *eng*; quarter-inch mono; mixdown.

1. **'Steam Engine'**
   Missing Links 3 master # XZB5-0509
● Production of Chip Douglas's song is now complete and today it is mixed into mono for use on *The Monkees*. 'Steam Engine' will make the first of several television appearances on February 7th 1970, but this excellent track will never appear on any of The Monkees' original albums. In 1979 it will make its quasi-legitimate record debut on the Australian compilation *Monkeemania* – in rather poor fidelity – and then appears on a number of Monkees compilations in a variety of mixes (see Songography at the rear of this book for further details).

● Saturday 22nd

TV The CBS network reruns episode 33 of the *Monkees* series, *It's A Nice Place To Visit*, at 12midday.
● Micky appears at the Valley Teen Center dance in Van Nuys, California. In his youth, Micky was the Center's original disc jockey.

● Monday 24th

TV Davy appears on Tennessee Ernie Ford's television special *The Peapicker In Piccadilly* broadcast on NBC. Other guests include Terry Thomas, Harry Secombe, The Brothers And Sisters vocal group, and The Ambrosian Choir (as heard in the movie *Goodbye Mr. Chips*). The program includes a mini-version of Gilbert & Sullivan's *H.M.S. Pinafore* as well as abundant location filming in London (St. Paul's Cathedral, Regent's Park, Westminster Abbey). Davy and Harry Secombe sing 'Consider Yourself' on an open-topped double-decker bus. Davy sings 'Scarborough Fair' solo on location and also appears in the *H.M.S. Pinafore* production number. All these items were pre-taped in August.

● Saturday 29th

TV CBS reruns episode 6 of the *Monkees* series, *Success Story*, at 12midday. The show's soundtrack is revised to include Davy's 'French Song' in place of 'I Wanna Be Free.'

● Sunday 30th

PERFORMANCE Oakland-Alameda County Coliseum *Oakland, CA* 2:00pm; tickets $3-$5; promoted by Y.B.M.C. (Your Basic Music Company), sponsored by radio station KYA
● A press release preceding today's show says the promoters are expecting a capacity audience in the group's first concert in the San Francisco area since their Cow Palace triumph of 1967. "In addition to giant projections of The Monkees viewed on a special overhead screen, strobe lights, and other special effects, concertgoers will see a full line-up of supporting acts and will witness a live recording session for The Monkees' next album."

A review by Ed Ward in *Rolling Stone* paints a less rosy picture. "Oakland Coliseum is a big place; it holds 24,000 or 30,000 people plus ushers and program hawkers. Unlike a week earlier when the Stones had played, there were only 1,500 (my guess) or 2,000 (the guard's guess) people lost in the dim recesses of this huge plastic hall. Most of them seemed to be between ten and 16, although there were a goodly percentage of over-twenties with slicked-back hair and Woolworth's bell-bottoms, and, as might be guessed, the parents.

"They sat through some of the worst bands I've ever heard, some of whom played only two numbers, and they applauded them. These two Bossjox from KYA appeared on stage in between and tried to get the audience to applaud more, but they knew what they wanted, and from time to time various sections erupted with cries of 'MONKEES!' One of the Bossjox said, 'The Monkees asked me if I thought San Francisco would still go for them,' and I just said, 'Ho-ho-ho, just wait and see.'

"Finally, it happened. Some cardboard music stands, just like the sax section had used in the high-school dance band I'd played in, were set up. The word MONKEES was apparent on the front of them. And out walked these six black guys, five of them in black tuxes, one in a purple tux – Tony and the Goodtimes [sic], formerly backup band for Ike & Tina Turner. They played a tight, slick, professional, derivative rhythm-and-blues set. Tony did some lovable imitations of Otis Redding, some lovable soul routines – 'Lemme hear you say YEAH!' – and some lovable introducing of the band, and then they left the stage, the lights went up, the tension mounted, the audience pleaded, the Bossjox wasted time, the audience keened, the Bossjox wasted time, the audience shrieked, and suddenly there they were: Micky, Davy, and Mike.

"It was strange. Micky and Davy up there trying to do exactly what the band had just gotten through doing with infinitely more finesse (well, professionalism anyway), and getting ten times the response. And Mike, up against the amp, trying to hide behind the band, back to the audience, tuning his guitar, which was inaudible during the entire concert. They ran through 'Daydream Believer,' 'Pleasant Valley Sunday,' 'I Wanna Be Free' – all their hits (except, I

noticed, 'Last Train to Clarksville'). In between were sandwiched little bits of comedy-imitation Smothers Brothers routines, Micky getting sent backstage for messing up a song and coming back wringing out a handkerchief and putting on a crybaby act. The audience was eating it up!

"Mike Nesmith introduced 'Listen To The Band' by saying, 'I'm gonna sing this song 'cos that's what I'm getting paid to do.' Davy Jones sang 'For Once In My Life' and Micky Dolenz sang 'Summertime' with considerable histrionic effort. By the time Nesmith did 'Johnny B. Goode' I was thoroughly confused. They really did think they were doing an R&B show. And girls were SCREEEEAMING and rushing up to take pictures and being held back by security men and throwing beads and candy and notes and SCREEEAMING. Somebody threw up a brightly colored sign, which Dolenz picked up and showed to the audience. It said WE STILL LOVE YOU.

"Back at the hotel Micky Dolenz was being very candid and honest about the whole thing. 'Look,' he said, *The Monkees* is the name of a TV show. I was hired to play the part of a rock'n'roll drummer, but what I am is an entertainer trying to reach an audience of eight-year-old girls. I'm no more a Monkee than Lorne Greene is a Cartwright. There'll be Monkee records in the future, done by Davy and me' – apparently Nesmith is going to start a C&W band – 'but I'm into producing my own films and acting. That's where my roots are.'

"On the bus home. Kathy, 16, from San Francisco, said they were 'out of sight' and proffered no further comment. Bill Marks, 15, from Richmond, was wearing Davy's scarf, which Davy had given him. He was not smoking the cigarette Davy had given him. Celia was 16 and also from San Francisco. She was angry at the guards and the Bossjox who'd promised her a backstage pass and then reneged. But the one who seemed totally out of place was Laura, who was fully 20 years old, and just as starry-eyed as Celia was about Davy Jones, the little English Monkee. She kept on casting glances at the scarf Bill was wearing.

"Dolenz had said, back at the hotel, that Davy intends to go into Broadway shows and nightclub singing, and if Laura is any indication, he's got his audience already. She and Celia talked a little of the last San Francisco Monkees concert. They weren't as good then, she said. In her handbag was a paperback entitled *The Uses Of The Past*."

DECEMBER

● *16* magazine says that Davy has been offered his own network show and may star in a movie called *Scrooge*. (The film will appear at the end of 1970 without him.) Davy is also planning some solo recordings. Micky has purchased a restaurant on the Sunset Strip called The Marquis. Peter Tork's group Release are reported to have gigged, but are yet to secure a recording deal.

Saturday 6th

TV At 12midday the CBS network reruns *Don't Look A Gift Horse In The Mouth*, episode 8 of *The Monkees*. The show's soundtrack is revised to include 'I Never Thought It Peculiar' in place of 'All The King's Horses.'

PERFORMANCE Salt Palace *Salt Lake City, UT* 7:00pm, with Original Caste, Sam & The Goodtimers
● The Monkees perform their final concert of the 1960s. Canada's Original Caste, who have just scored a hit with 'One Tin Soldier,' open the show. Reportedly, The Goodtimers back the Monkees trio on songs such as 'I'm A Believer,' 'Last Train To Clarksville,' 'Listen To The Band,' and 'Mommy And Daddy.' Tonight's audience of 8,223 are also treated to Micky's juggling act as well as lots of rear-projected films of The Monkees in action. This is very likely Michael's last concert appearance with The Monkees until September 1986.

Monday 8th – Friday 12th

TV Davy appears on NBC's daytime show *Letters To Laugh-In* with Judy Carne, Zsa Zsa Gabor, and Jeremy Lloyd.

Friday 12th

● Henry Diltz photographs Davy and Michael at their respective homes. It is not clear if the photos are for group-related purposes.

Thursday 18th

● Davy tapes his appearance for the TV show *Music Scene* at ABC Studios in Los Angeles. He will receive the sum of $5,000 for his services; his appearance will be aired on Monday.

Saturday 20th

TV At 12midday the CBS network reruns episode 47 of the *Monkees* series, *The Christmas Show*.

Monday 22nd

TV Davy's appearance as guest host on *Music Scene* is aired on the ABC network at 7:30pm.
During the program he is seen performing Harry Nilsson's 'Together' live with backing from Sam & The Goodtimers, as well as assisting host David Steinberg in introducing the program's other musical guests. (This episode of *Music Scene* will later be made available on DVD.)

Thursday 25th

● Micky and Samantha Dolenz are probably in Los Angeles, where they are reportedly spotted at a special Christmas gig given by Poco at the Troubadour club.

Saturday 27th

TV At 12midday the CBS network reruns episode 27 of the *Monkees* series, *Monkee Mother*.
● *NME* reports that on Monday Davy will fly to London where he is to discuss with agent Vic Lewis the prospect of British appearances. "One project which may be confirmed during Davy's visit," says the paper, "is a starring role in a West End musical."

Monday 29th

● Davy travels to the U.K. to spend the Christmas holidays there with his wife Linda and daughter Thalia, and he will stay in Britain through February 1970.

Wednesday 31st

TV Britain's ITV network airs Davy's appearance on the Tennessee Ernie Ford special *The Peapicker In Piccadilly*.

ABOVE Ad for the group's first (and last) concert in the San Francisco area since January 1967.

1970

Michael effectively leaves The Monkees, except to make more ads ... Michael secures deal for his new group ... Davy tells press he plans solo career ... reruns of *The Monkees* continue on CBS TV ... Michael's First National Band start recordings ... Micky and Davy record as Monkees with producer Jeff Barry ... 'Oh My My' 12th and last single, makes #98 ... Michael's group release first single, 'Little Red Rider,' and LP, *Magnetic South* ... Changes ninth and last LP, fails to chart ... Micky makes stage-acting debut ... Davy opens his shopping mall in Los Angeles ... Michael's First National Band release second single, 'Joanne,' and play European dates ... Davy and Micky make final Monkees recording session ... second album and third single by First National Band, *Loose Salute* and 'Silver Moon.'

Davy and his daughter Thalia consider the future.

JANUARY

As the year opens, the future of The Monkees is uncertain. The group have completed all their concert bookings as a trio – Michael, Davy, and Micky – but there is increasing public demand for their services following the re-emergence of their TV series on Saturday mornings. They will fulfill this need – and the basic terms of their Screen Gems contract – by taking part in advertisements for their show's various sponsors.

Michael will be a part of all The Monkees' print and filmed advertising this year, but will no longer appear with them in person or on record. Over the next month he begins negotiating a release from the various contracts that tie him to The Monkees. He also secures a deal with RCA for his post-Monkees group, Michael Nesmith & The First National Band.

As he will explain in the liner notes to the group's debut album: "When Johnny Ware, now the drummer of The First National Band, first suggested I start a band, my reaction was distant and a little negative. But he continued to talk and, through the conversation, I sensed some of the same spirit of the same men who have so profoundly influenced me [at this point Hank Williams, Jerry Lee Lewis, and Jimmie Rodgers]. So, two days later, Red Rhodes, John London, Johnny, and myself got together for a trial run and it all seemed to fall into place. Effortlessly and freely the music poured forth. And it was fun. Great fun. We played and sang and laughed for

two weeks. Then I trekked off looking for a way to get all this out of my little rehearsal room."

● Davy is in Britain and is restless to work either as a Monkee or as a solo artist. The Screen Gems contract that he has complained so bitterly about recently keeps him on call for Monkees projects throughout the year but leaves him idle most of the time.

● Micky is no doubt enjoying the time off that The Monkees' reduced schedule affords him. Now that he has a family, he will spend most of his time with his wife, Samantha, and child, Ami, as well as helping with Samantha's boutique and his own real-estate investments in Hollywood, including a restaurant.

● Peter Tork's band Release have released nothing. Their much-talked-about record deal never materialized and Atlantic Records' head honcho Ahmet Ertegun has passed on recording Peter as a solo act for his label. However, Tork does manage to talk Ertegun into signing Release member Judy Mayhan to Atco. Unlike his involvement in Mayhan's earlier demos, Tork will not take part in the production of her album. He will undertake solo live bookings throughout the year.

● Saturday 3rd

● Britain's *NME* carries the dramatic headline "Davy Jones confesses that – 'MONKEES ARE FINISHED.'" Davy says: "So far as I'm concerned, The Monkees are dead. I am planning a new career on my own." The *NME* reports that he does not intend to appear with the group again in public, but will record with them. The group's recording contract has another 18 months to run, but Davy admits that "we are simply not making records now." The planned British reruns in color of the *Monkees* TV series never appeared and the group's movie *Head* has yet to be screened overseas.

Proof of Davy's solo career comes on U.S. television screens today as he hosts *Get It Together*. His guests include Creedence Clearwater Revival and Three Dog Night.

TV Also on the box, the CBS television network reruns for a second time episode 35 of the *Monkees* series, *Everywhere A Sheik, Sheik*, at 12midday.

● Saturday 10th

TV At 12midday the CBS network reruns for a third time episode 3 of the *Monkees* series, *Monkee Vs. Machine*. The show's soundtrack is again revised to include 'Listen To The Band' in place of 'Saturday's Child.'

● Saturday 17th

● *NME* reports that Davy has accepted an offer to appear in a screen version of the Broadway stage show *Baker Street*. He is due to sing four songs in his role as a Baker Street boy. The offer comes from Leslie Bricusse, who wrote the musical and plans to begin production later this year. Davy is also in talks to appear in an unnamed London West End musical.

TV The CBS network reruns episode 42 of the *Monkees* series, *The Wild Monkees*, at 12midday. The show's soundtrack is revised to include 'Looking For The Good Times' from the *Monkees Present* album in place of 'Star Collector.'

● Friday 23rd

● Henry Diltz takes a series of photos of Micky, one of which probably graces the picture sleeve of the next Monkees single.

● Saturday 24th

TV At 12midday CBS reruns *One Man Shy*, episode 13 of *The Monkees*. The show's soundtrack is revised to include Davy's 'If I Knew' in place of the original program's 'I'm A Believer.'

Sunday 25th
● Peter Tork becomes a father when his daughter Hallie Thorkelson is born. Hallie's mother is Peter's longtime girlfriend, Reine Stewart.

Saturday 31st
TV CBS reruns episode 16 of the *Monkees* series, *Son Of A Gypsy*.
● *The Monkees Present* spends its final week (of 14) in *Billboard*'s Top LPs chart, at #160. This will be the group's final album-chart entry of the year.

FEBRUARY

● Michael has successfully extricated himself from his contractual obligations with Screen Gems, except for filming further commercials with The Monkees. He has made a recording deal for his new group with RCA and will return to the studio this month to tape *Magnetic South*, the first in a series of albums for the label.

Michael: "Buying my way out of the contract was pretty simple, 'cos basically what I did was just sign off and leave the royalties there. I knew that I had to get rid of my obligations there so I could move on to my next thing. So it was just an orderly end to a business deal that had finally come to a close. I was ready to move.

"I was a hired writer and a hired actor, and while I had put all of my good-faith creative energies into it, it was not something that grew up around me organically, so I didn't really feel like it was the end of anything."
● The Monkees – Micky and Davy – also return to the studio this month. Screen Gems hope to capitalize on the group's successful Saturday-morning TV reruns and have paired them with producer Jeff Barry – who created their biggest hit, 'I'm A Believer.'

Sunday 1st
● Davy returns home from his British sojourn. He is due in New York for a few days recording this month. The *NME* notes that these sessions will mark "the return of producer Jeff Barry, who was responsible for the production of the group's early hit singles. As reported, Davy now plans to work independently from The Monkees, although he is still committed to recording with them for another 18 months."

Thursday 5th
RECORDING RCA *1133 6th Avenue, New York, NY*. Jeff Barry *prod*; Mike Moran *eng*; tracking.
1. **'I Love You Better'**
   Changes master # ZZB1-4842
2. **'Oh My My'**
   Changes master # ZZB1-4843
3. **'Tell Me Love'**
   Changes master # ZZB1-4844
Personnel unknown.

● Exactly three years after Jeff Barry was last employed as The Monkees' producer, he is reenlisted to concoct some new material for the group. It will be a smoother ride this time for Barry, since Michael is no longer a part of the recording unit, and no one in the group will question Barry's direction or musical decisions. Selecting tunes from his own catalog, Barry tapes these new tracks with a crew of (uncredited) New York session players. Once the tracks are taped, Barry will call in Micky or Davy to add their vocal parts.

The most surprising aspect of Barry's latest work is the heavy soul influence. One could easily imagine that the man who enjoyed one of 1969's biggest hits with 'Sugar Sugar' might conjure up more Archies-like cartoon-styled pop for The Monkees. This is not the case. At least for this first session, Barry takes the group in an R&B direction. Although The Monkees have dabbled in this genre,

LEFT Davy during a shoot for the picture cover of The Monkees' final single, 'Oh My My.' ABOVE The group continue to make ads for Kool Aid soft drink mix, here at an amusement park in San Diego, California.

especially on their recent tour with Sam & The Goodtimers, it is not exactly a good match for their talents.

'Tell Me Love' is a slow R&B ballad by Barry. No session tapes or personnel documents will survive for this or any of his other productions for the resulting *Changes* album. But today is probably just a tracking date, with Micky's vocals added to 'Tell Me Love' at a later date.

The other two songs taped, both by Barry and Andy Kim, will appear on The Monkees' next single. 'Oh My My' features a catchy acoustic guitar riff in E that quickly develops into a churning soul number. It sounds like a Temptations cast-off and is the most off-beat choice for a Monkees A-side since 'D.W. Washburn.' The lyrically inept and similarly soul-flavored 'I Love You Better' will appear on the flipside, both topped off with lead vocals from Micky. Davy probably contributes at least a backing vocal to 'I Love You Better,' but otherwise vocally he takes a back seat to Micky on this project.

Davy is not particularly thrilled by these new recording sessions. He says: "That was Andy Kim and Jeff Barry doing an Andy Kim album. Andy Kim couldn't get it sold so they took his voice off it and they put us on it. That's how that came about. So don't ask me about that album. Please don't ask me. That was a way of keeping Micky Dolenz and me out of the studio so they could sell Partridge Family albums. I have very bad memories about that trip to New York."

Micky: "I was quite happy to do it and quite happy to record as long as somebody wanted to record me. It was as simple as that. At that time we were all thinking we could go on and have our own careers and be solo artists. When the [TV] show went off the air and then Peter quit the group that was basically the end of it. Mike and

Davy and I stayed together for a very brief period of time. Then Mike decided to quit."

● Saturday 7th

● The *NME* gives fans very early warning that Davy will appear in pantomime next Christmas. Details will apparently be firmed up in March when Davy is due to return to the UK. The paper also says that Davy is likely to star in his own TV special.

TV The CBS network reruns *Monkees Get Out More Dirt*, episode 29 of *The Monkees*. The show's soundtrack is revised to include the previously unissued 'Steam Engine' in place of 'The Girl I Knew Somewhere.'

● Monday 9th

● Michael, Micky, and Davy regroup, probably for the first time since December '69, to film a new commercial for their TV-show sponsors, Kool-Aid soft drink mix. They travel two hours south of Los Angeles to an amusement park in San Diego where they spend their day together dressed in white racing outfits and driving bumper cars. Another shoot requires them to pour out Kool-Aid for a group of waiting children, during which Micky holds a large racing trophy. This scene will be used as the tag to the commercial. Photos of Micky and Davy driving bumper cars will appear in a few months on the rear sleeve of the group's *Changes* album.

● Tomorrow, Michael will begin recording a new album of his own. Meanwhile, faithful Monkees recording engineer Pete Abbott makes copies of nine unfinished Monkees multi-track tapes to send to Jeff Barry for review and possible completion. Included are 'Shake 'Em

Up And Let 'Em Roll,' 'Look Down' version 2, 'That's What It's Like Loving You,' 'Smile,' 'I'm Gonna Try,' a completed production of Micky's 'Rose Marie,' 'You're So Good,' 'War Games' version 1, and 'The Ceiling In My Room.' Coupled with the three tracks that Barry has in the can from last Thursday's session, this material could make a standard 12-song Monkees album. However, Barry will pass on working with any of these group outtakes and all nine will be left on the cutting room floor – at least for the time being.

● Tuesday 10th
RECORDING RCA *Hollywood, CA*. Felton Jarvis *prod*; one-inch 8-track; tracking.
1. **'Little Red Rider'** version 2
   Magnetic South master # ZPA3-8135
2. **'Nine Times Blue'** version 5
   Magnetic South master # ZPA3-8150
3. **'Magnolia Simms'** version 2
   unissued no master #

Personnel John London (bass), Michael Nesmith (vocal, acoustic guitar), Red Rhodes (pedal steel guitar), John Ware (drums).
● This session represents the true beginning of Michael's new group, The First National Band. The unit consists of Michael on guitar and vocals, his longtime sidekick John London on bass, pedal steel virtuoso Orville 'Red' Rhodes, and drummer John Ware, formerly of The Corvettes, the country-rock band that Michael produced last year. The First National Band will artfully meld the genres of country and rock and act as an outlet for Michael's prodigious portfolio of songs.

Michael will record three albums filled with his stockpile of songs that never found a place on Monkees records – in a similar way to Beatle George Harrison, whose watershed set, *All Things Must Pass*, will be issued later this year. The main difference is that Harrison releases all his recordings on that one jumbo three-record set, whereas Michael will cautiously issue his discs separately, spaced just a few months apart. Nevertheless, Michael's three albums will carry thematically linked cover art and are conceived as a trilogy.

Speaking of trilogies, this first recording date features three songs from Michael's Monkees past. 'Little Red Rider,' taped last year but passed over for inclusion on *The Monkees Present*, is remade today with less of the soul flavor apparent in Michael's horn-laden 'Monkees' rendition. Now it features some mind-bending steel work from Rhodes, whose sound is processed through a Leslie rotating-speaker cabinet, and will be issued as Michael Nesmith & The First National Band's debut single in May. A further session for this song will occur on the 20th.

In contrast, today's recording of 'Nine Times Blue' is nearly identical to most of Michael's Monkees-era recordings of the song (including the group's performance on *The Johnny Cash Show*). Today's basic 8-track master will be transferred to two-inch 16-track tape on the 20th for further overdubs. When it appears on the *Magnetic South* album it will be skillfully segued with 'Little Red Rider' to form a medley.

Also recorded at this session is a version of 'Magnolia Simms,' a song by Michael and Charlie Rockett previously released on *The Birds, The Bees & The Monkees*. It is not known if today's rendition is ever completed or how it differs from the released 'Monkees' version. It will remain unissued.

Although Felton Jarvis is the credited producer for this and several other recording dates for The First National Band during the first half of the year, he will not in fact attend many sessions. Since Jarvis is the man who signed Michael to RCA, the credit remains as something of a courtesy.

Michael: "Felton came out to LA once during the sessions, on his way to Las Vegas with Elvis [Presley, another artist Jarvis handles for RCA]. He stayed for about an hour and did not provide any production work. I saw him as more of a liaison with [RCA] – I talked to him about money and such. I liked him quite a bit, but he didn't 'produce' *Magnetic South*."

● Saturday 14th
TV At 12midday the CBS network reruns *The Devil & Peter Tork*, episode 52 of *The Monkees*. The show's soundtrack is revised to include 'I Never Thought It Peculiar' in place of the once offensive 'Salesman.'

● Tuesday 17th
● Michael, Micky, and Davy rendezvous at Columbia's 'ranch' lot where they once shot many episodes of their TV series. Today the trio is scheduled to film yet another Kool-Aid commercial. During a break, Micky visits the set of the Sally Field series *The Flying Nun*, the current episode of which is being directed by Jon Anderson, who worked on *The Monkees* and *Head*.

● Thursday 19th
RECORDING RCA *Hollywood, CA* 10:00am-2:30, 3:30-8:00, 9:00pm-12midnight. Felton Jarvis *prod*; Pete Abbott *eng*; tracking.
1. **'Calico Girlfriend'** version 2
   Magnetic South master # ZPA3-8130
2. **'The Keys To The Car'**
   Magnetic South master # ZPA3-8132
3. **'Hollywood'** version 3
   Magnetic South master # ZPA3-8133

Personnel John London (bass), Michael Nesmith (vocal, acoustic guitar), Red Rhodes (pedal steel guitar), John Ware (drums).
● Another session for The First National Band's *Magnetic South* album features two more Monkees rejects. 'Calico Girlfriend' was first taped in May of last year for *The Monkees Present* and today's version is similar, though the old recording's heavy Latin influence has been toned down considerably and replaced with more of a country sensibility. When completed, 'Calico Girlfriend' will kick off *Magnetic South*.

Michael recorded 'Hollywood' twice during 1968 in Nashville (and it was even heard briefly during 1967's *Headquarters* sessions) but a Monkees version was not to be. Today, the song is rearranged with a soft intro and a series of dynamic builds capped off by an extended, free-form fade (including some overdubbed electric piano from an uncredited participant). The finished production will land on side two of *Magnetic South*. Also destined for the second side of the album is an apparently new number, 'The Keys To The Car.' A tale of boundaries, real and imagined, this straightforward, mid-tempo country song includes some superb vocals from Michael.

● Friday 20th
RECORDING RCA *Hollywood*, CA 10:00am-2:30, 3:30-8:00, 9:00pm-12midnight. Felton Jarvis *prod*; Pete Abbott *eng*; one-inch 8-track, two-inch 16-track; tracking, overdubs, transfers.
1. **'Little Red Rider'** version 2
   Magnetic South master # ZPA3-8135
2. **'Mama Nantucket'**
   Magnetic South master # ZPA3-8136
3. **'Joanne'**
   Magnetic South master # ZPA3-8137
4. **'Nine Times Blue'** version 5
   Magnetic South master # ZPA3-8150

Personnel Earl P. Ball (piano 2), John London (bass), Michael Nesmith (vocal, acoustic guitar), Red Rhodes (pedal steel guitar), John Ware (drums 1,2,4).
● In an extension of the February 10th First National Band session, today's date sees the original 8-track masters of 'Little Red Rider' and 'Nine Times Blue' transferred to 16-track tape for overdubbing and completion. Additionally, two newer Nesmith songs are taped today. 'Mama Nantucket' is highlighted by some inspired yodeling from Michael, a great steel break from Rhodes – whom Michael implores to "play your magic steel, El Rojo" – as well as the piano playing of guest musician Earl Ball. (Ball recently appeared on the groundbreaking country-rock albums *Sweetheart Of The Rodeo* by The Byrds and the International Submarine Band's *Safe At Home*.)

The gentle ballad 'Joanne' will become a surprise hit in August, achieving far greater chart success than any of Michael's compositions for The Monkees. In the liner notes to *Magnetic South* he will dedicate 'Joanne' to Jack Nicholson and the actor's girlfriend Mimi Jefferson, who appeared as Lady Pleasure in the 'kissing contest' sequence of *Head*.

● Saturday 21st
TV CBS reruns episode 9 of the *Monkees* series, *The Chaperone*, at 12midday. The soundtrack is revised to include the previously unissued 'Midnight Train' in place of 'This Just Doesn't Seem To Be My Day.' Meanwhile in the studio, Michael's First National Band cut two more tracks.
RECORDING RCA *Hollywood*, CA 10:00am-2:30, 3:30-8:00, 9:00pm-12midnight. Felton Jarvis *prod*; Pete Abbott *eng*; tracking.
1. **'The Crippled Lion'** version 2
   Magnetic South master # ZPA3-8138
2. **'Rose City Chimes'**
   Nevada Fighter & Tantamount To Treason **CD** master # ZPA3-8139

Personnel Earl P. Ball (piano), John London (bass), Michael Nesmith (vocal 1, acoustic guitar), Red Rhodes (pedal steel guitar), John Ware (drums).
● This session produces a new version of 'The Crippled Lion,' Michael's song that he first recorded in Nashville during mid '68, as well as a cover of Bobby Garrett's 'Rose City Chimes.' Garrett is a pedal-steel player who performed with the likes of Ernest Tubb and Hank Thompson, and The First National Band's Red Rhodes obviously feels an affinity for his work. The instrumental will be

included on the flipside of the group's May 1970 debut single but will not feature on *Magnetic South*. Later it will become more commonly available as a bonus track on the 2001 British BMG/Camden-label CD reissue of *Nevada Fighter & Tantamount To Treason*.

● Sunday 22nd
RECORDING RCA *Hollywood*, CA 10:00am-2:30, 3:30-8:00, 9:00pm-12midnight. Felton Jarvis *prod*; Pete Abbott *eng*; tracking.
1. **'Smoke, Smoke, Smoke'**
   Nevada Fighter & Tantamount To Treason **CD** master # ZPA3-8140
2. **'One Rose'**
   Magnetic South master # ZPA3-8141

Personnel Earl P. Ball (piano 1), Billy Dale (instrument unknown), John London (bass), Michael Nesmith (vocal, acoustic guitar), Red Rhodes (pedal steel guitar), John Ware (drums).
● This Sunday session results in two cover tunes, only one of which will wind up on *Magnetic South*. Merle Travis and Tex Williams's ode to cigarettes, 'Smoke, Smoke, Smoke,' will become a live staple of The First National Band's set this year but will not make any of their albums. In 2001 it will be featured as a bonus track on the British CD reissue of *Nevada Fighter & Tantamount To Treason*. Today's other tune, Del Lyon and Loni McIntire's 'One Rose,' is no doubt inspired by the Jimmie Rodgers recording of yesteryear and will land firmly on side two of *Magnetic South*. (Although a musician named Billy Dale is logged on this and several other First National Band session sheets this year, later neither Michael nor John Ware will be able to recall his involvement.)

● Monday 23rd
RECORDING RCA *Hollywood*, CA 10:00am-2:30, 3:30-8:00, 9:00pm-12midnight. Felton Jarvis *prod*; Pete Abbott *eng*; tracking.
1. **'First National Rag'**
   Magnetic South master # ZPA3-8149
2. **'Beyond The Blue Horizon'**
   Magnetic South master # ZPA3-8148
3. **'Born To Love You'**
   unissued master # ZPA3-8131

Personnel Earl P. Ball (piano), Billy Dale (instrument unknown), John London (bass), Michael Nesmith (vocal, acoustic guitar), Red Rhodes (pedal steel guitar), John Ware (drums).
● The *Magnetic South* sessions come to a close today with the taping of some conceptual pieces. Red Rhodes's 'First National Rag' will act as a humorous side break for the album with Michael's announcement "We'll be back right after you turn the record over," while 'Beyond The Blue Horizon,' first heard in the 1930 film *Monte Carlo*, will serve as the album's closing message. It is produced with an array of sound effects and a slow building arrangement to create a beautiful send-off to a hopeful tomorrow.

Michael will dedicate 'Blue Horizon' in the album's liner notes "to the 'Tomorrow' man," leading some to speculate that he means Don Kirshner, whose failed group with Olivia Newton-John was called Toomorrow. However, Michael will later admit that the 'Tomorrow' man is himself. With his departure from The Monkees he has, in the words of this song, said "goodbye to things that bore me." As for his comrades of the last five years, Michael will dedicate *Magnetic South* as follows: "The making of the album to Lester Sill, Bert Schneider, and David, Micky, & Peter."

A version of Cindy Walker's 'Born To Love You' also figures in today's sessions but will not make *Magnetic South*. It will remain unissued, and exact personnel is unknown. Michael will later rerecord the song during his last session for RCA, on March 16th 1973, and the result will be included on that year's *Pretty Much Your Standard Ranch Stash* album.

● Tuesday 24th – Thursday 26th
RECORDING RCA *Hollywood, CA*. Felton Jarvis *prod*; overdubs, mixdown.
● Over these three days *Magnetic South* is completed and mixed. On Thursday 26th The First National Band start their day with a Henry Diltz photo session at Michael's house, and then Michael returns to RCA to complete mixing *Magnetic South*. Diltz had attempted to shoot the band at an RCA session on Wednesday but insufficient light hampered his chances to get useable pictures.

● Saturday 28th
TV At 12midday the CBS network reruns episode 19 of the *Monkees* series, *Find The Monkees*.

MARCH

● *Tiger Beat* reports that The Monkees are now a duo. "There'll be Monkee records and shows done by Davy and me," Micky tells a reporter. "But I'm into producing my own films and acting. That's where my roots are. Mike Nesmith is starting his own country/western group." The magazine notes that Micky has been reading scripts in a search for roles, while Michael has written a script with former *Monkees* series screenwriter Dave Evans. The story involves "a guy who welcomes different people to a little country town and then the action follows the new people around the town." *Tiger Beat* also mentions that Samantha Dolenz's boutique, One Of A Kind, has moved from 8003 Santa Monica Boulevard in Hollywood to 12609 Ventura Place in Studio City – closer to the Dolenz's home.

● Sunday 1st
● Rex Reed of *The New York Times* talks with Jack Nicholson, currently enjoying great acclaim for his part in Raybert's *Easy Rider*. "[Peter Fonda and Dennis Hopper] came in while I was writing and co-producing *Head* with The Monkees," recalls Nicholson of the genesis of the hit *Easy Rider*. "Nobody ever saw [*Head*], man, but I saw it 158 million times. I loved it. Filmically, it's the best rock'n'roll movie ever made. I mean, it's anti rock'n'roll. Has no form. Unique in structure, which is very hard to do in movies."

● Saturday 7th
TV CBS reruns *I've Got A Little Song Here*, episode 12 of *The Monkees*, at 12midday. The show's soundtrack is revised to include 'Steam Engine' in place of Michael's 'Mary, Mary.'

● Sunday 8th
● Micky celebrates his 25th birthday with a party at his home.

● Saturday 14th
TV At 12midday the CBS network reruns episode 20 of the *Monkees* series, *Monkees In The Ring*. The show's soundtrack is revised to include 'Looking For The Good Times' from *The Monkees Present*.

● Saturday 21st
● The *NME* reports that Michael has officially left The Monkees. "Last week he signed a solo recording contract with RCA Victor,

including $20,000 cash up-front. Mike's first album will be released in a couple months. Called *Magnetic South*, the album will be nothing like Mike's first solo album, *The Wichita Train Whistle Sings*, but will be Mike singing some of his own compositions and performing a few standards in new arrangements. Mike recently made a weekend solo appearance at a new club in the San Fernando Valley called Creation, managed by his former chauffeur Alfie Weaver."
TV CBS reruns *Dance, Monkee, Dance*, episode 14 of *The Monkees*. The show's soundtrack is revised to include the previously unissued 'If You Have The Time.'

● Sunday 22nd
● It's possible that Michael Nesmith & The First National Band perform this evening at the Troubadour in West Hollywood, California.

● Wednesday 25th
RECORDING RCA *New York, NY*. Jeff Barry *prod*; Mike Moran *eng*; tracking.
1. **'Ticket On A Ferry Ride'**
   Changes master # ZZB1-5705
2. **'Which Way Do You Want It?'**
   unissued master # ZZB1-5706
3. **'You're So Good To Me'**
   Changes master # ZZB1-5708
Personnel unknown.
● Jeff Barry has decided against using any of The Monkees' outtakes (see February 9th) for his projected album with the group, and so holds another three sessions in the coming days to complete a projected long-player titled *Changes*.
Today's date to record three songs by Barry and Bobby Bloom produces the rather generic pop balladry of 'Ticket On A Ferry Ride' (which will feature a vocal from Micky) and the R&B-flavored 'You're So Good To Me' (which will include one of Davy's rare lead vocals on *Changes*).
The third song, 'Which Way Do You Want It?,' is slated as the penultimate track on side two of *Changes* but for reasons unknown Micky's 'Midnight Train,' recorded in July of last year, will be substituted. 'Which Way Do You Want It?' will remain a mystery as all tapes for the song will be lost.

● Thursday 26th
RECORDING RCA *New York, NY*. Jeff Barry *prod*; Mike Moran *eng*; tracking.
1. **'All Alone In The Dark'**
   Changes master # ZZB1-5707
2. **'Do You Feel It Too?'**
   Changes master # ZZB1-5709
3. **'Ride Baby Ride'**
   unissued no master #
Personnel unknown.
● This further *Changes* session results in three more prospective tracks for the album. 'All Alone In The Dark' started life as a demo for songwriters Steve Soles and Ned Albright, but Jeff Barry is allegedly so taken with the sprightly feel of their rough original that he decides merely to add Micky's vocal on top of their makeshift production. The Davy-sung 'Do You Feel It Too?' is one of the album's better songs, though it makes one lament the lack of quality material on offer during these sessions. The third track taped today, 'Ride Baby Ride,' is a complete mystery. No tapes, credits, or further information will survive of the song, which will not appear in any of the album's provisional track line-ups.

● **Saturday 28th**

TV At 12midday the CBS network reruns episode 19 of the *Monkees* series, *Find The Monkees*.

● In today's *NME* Roy Carr speaks with Don Kirshner, who is still coasting on the #1 success of The Archies' 'Sugar Sugar.' "The most gratifying thing is that it is a cartoon group," says Kirshner, "and to get an award for the best record of 1969 when you have artists like The Beatles, Rolling Stones, and Tom Jones around is for me a great accomplishment. 'Sugar Sugar' is even more important to me because I had previously supervised some of The Monkees' records. But I only want to take credit for the ones I did with The Monkees. That is 'Last Train To Clarksville,' 'I'm A Believer,' and 'A Little But Me, A Little Bit You.' Also I did their first two albums, which sold over four million each, a fact which I think is quite staggering when you think of it.

"Then The Monkees went on to do their own thing. I thought, 'No more Monkees, they've been taken away from me.' But how do I top this? The first group I formed was The Archies, which didn't have four live faces and this helped. Actually, 'Sugar Sugar' was never exposed on television until it became a hit. ... My next project for NBC and 20th Century Fox [is] called The Kowboys – it features four young kids who ride horses and sing like [key Western singing/instrumental group] The Sons Of The Pioneers."

APRIL

'Oh My My' / 'I Love You Better' single is released this month in the U.S.A. This will be Micky and Davy's last single as The Monkees.

● Micky and Davy travel to New York City to overdub vocals onto Jeff Barry's recent productions. Davy visits his old store, Zilch, which is still operating under the auspices of Jeff Neal and his parents. Davy has in fact started a new company called the Zilch Corporation with his pals David Pearl, Bill Chadwick, and Ricky Cooper. Their first venture together rekindles Davy's dream of owning a retail establishment. This month they rent a large space in Beverly Hills for an ambitious project called The Street, an early attempt at an indoor shopping mall.

● Michael and Phyllis Nesmith's spectacular home recently played host to former *Monkees* TV director Jim Frawley and a camera crew. Frawley is in the midst of shooting a motion picture called *The Christian Licorice Store* and uses the Nesmiths' Antello Place abode for the feature's opening sequence. The film will find release next year and includes an appearance by another *Monkees* series alumnus, singer-songwriter Tim Buckley.

● *16* magazine notes that Davy is considering cutting a record on his

own and possibly co-starring in the movie *Fortune And Men's Eyes*. The film deals with homosexuality and the dangers of prison life and will be released next year – without Davy's involvement. *16* also mentions that Micky and Davy are working up a new concert act as a duo.

● **Thursday 2nd**

RECORDING RCA *New York, NY.* Jeff Barry *prod*; Mike Moran *eng*; tracking.

1. **'Acapulco Sun'**
   Changes master # ZZB1-5711
2. **'It's Got To Be Love'**
   Changes master # ZZB1-5709

Personnel unknown.

● Two tracks are taped today to complete the *Changes* album. Both are passable and poppy, though the master for 'Acapulco Sun' features a nasty-sounding tape squeal about two and half minutes into the song, making one wonder if there was any quality control during the making of this album. Micky and Davy probably add their voices to these and the album's other tracks before the final master is prepared next Tuesday.

● **Saturday 4th**

TV At 12midday the CBS network reruns episode 36 of the *Monkees* series, *Monkee Mayor*.

● Today's *NME* carries the headline "After the Monkees and Archies – HERE COME THE BUGALOOS!" Apparently another group modeled on The Monkees' success are to be formed, this one by producer Marty Krofft. "The group – to be named The Bugaloos – will be recruited from auditions in the same way The Monkees were born. And it is to become the starring attraction of a new pop-comedy series, to be screened in America for a minimum of two years by NBC-TV – the company that launched The Monkees! Also confirmed for The Bugaloos is a five-year Capitol disc deal. Krofft – who is being hailed in America as 'the new Walt Disney' – recently produced the *H.R. Pufnstuf* series. ... His project with The Bugaloos is envisaged as a part-live/part-animated series, and production is due to begin in Hollywood in May, with transmission starting in September. The Bugaloos must be an all-British unit, including one colored member and one girl, insists Krofft. ... As with The Monkees, personality is likely to be the deciding factor in their acceptance." The Bugaloos will indeed appear and are – briefly – very popular.

● **Tuesday 7th**

● A master for the now completed *Changes* album is compiled today. At this point it features the following line-up (which will be changed on the 29th). Side One: 'Oh My My' / 'Ticket On A Ferry Ride' / 'You're So Good To Me' / 'It's Got To Be Love' / 'Acapulco Sun' / '99 Pounds.' Side Two: 'Tell Me Love' / 'Do You Feel It Too?' / 'I Love You Better' / 'All Alone In The Dark' / 'Which Way Do You Want It?' / 'Time And Time Again.'

● **Thursday 9th**

RECORDING RCA *Hollywood, CA* 9:30am-2:00, 2:30-7:00, 7:30pm-12midnight. Felton Jarvis, Michael Nesmith *prod*; Kent Tunks, Pete Abbott *eng*; two-inch 16-track; tracking.

1. **'Bye, Bye, Bye'** version 1
   unissued master # ZWA3-1387
2. **'Bye, Bye, Bye'** version 2
   Loose Salute master # ZWA3-1387
3. **'Thanx For The Ride'** version 1
   unissued master # ZWA3-1388

Oh My My single

A 'Oh My My' (J. BARRY / A. KIM)
B 'I Love You Better' (J. BARRY / A. KIM)

U.S. release probably May 1970 (Colgems 5011).
U.K. release probably 1970 (RCA 1958).
Chart high U.S. number 98; U.K. none.

This shot, from April 1970, is one of the last taken of The Monkees as a trio – for a further Kool Aid ad – shortly before Michael's permanent departure.

4. **'Dedicated Friend'** version 1
   unissued master # ZWA3-1389
5. **'Dedicated Friend'** version 2
   Loose Salute master # ZWA3-1389
6. **'American Airman'**
   unissued master # ZWA3-138?

Personnel Earl P. Ball (piano 1,3,4), Glen D. Hardin (piano 2,5), John London (bass 1,2,3,4,5), Michael Nesmith (vocal 1,2,3,4,5, guitar 1,2,3,4,5), Red Rhodes (pedal steel guitar 1,2,3,4,5), John Ware (drums 1,2,3,4,5).

● The First National Band, scarcely a month after completing their yet-to-be-released first album, start to make a second long-player. Today's session focuses on three new numbers, all of which will be recorded twice. Session records suggest that version 1 of 'Bye, Bye, Bye' is a short 2:20 rendition featuring Earl Ball on piano. A second version, also taped today, lasts more than three minutes and has Glen D. Hardin taking Ball's place behind the keys.

Version 1 of 'Dedicated Friend' is probably a long recording of the song, again with Ball on piano, lasting nearly four minutes. By comparison, version 2, also taped today, is a mere two-and-a-half minutes, with Hardin on piano. A first attempt at 'Thanx For The Ride' is also taped, but it is not clear how it differs from the second version recorded next Wednesday. Another mystery from today is 'American Airman.' It will not be issued and there is precious little other information about it.

● Saturday 11th

TV At 12midday the CBS network reruns episode 24 of the *Monkees* series, *Monkees A La Mode*. The soundtrack is updated to include The Monkees' new single 'Oh My My' in the place of the original episode's 'Laugh.'

● Tuesday 14th

● Michael, Micky, and Davy unite for perhaps the last time as The Monkees to film another commercial for Kool-Aid in Palm Springs, California. Photographer Henry Diltz is on hand to shoot some stills of this final get-together. Tomorrow, Michael will return to recording with The First National Band – and is now probably completely free of any Monkee obligations. A tracklisting and June release date for his *Magnetic South* album has now been finalized.

● Wednesday 15th

RECORDING RCA *Hollywood, CA* 7:00-10:00pm, 12:30-1:30am. Felton Jarvis, Michael Nesmith *prod*; Mickey Crawford, Pete Abbott *eng*; two-inch 16-track; tracking, overdubs.

1. **'Thanx For The Ride'** version 2
   Loose Salute master # ZWA3-1390
2. **'Bye, Bye, Bye'** version 2
   Loose Salute master # ZWA3-1387
3. **'Dedicated Friend'** version 2
   Loose Salute master # ZWA3-1389

Personnel Glen D. Hardin (piano), John London (bass), Michael Nesmith (vocal, guitar), Red Rhodes (pedal steel guitar), John Ware (drums).

● The First National Band resume sessions for their second album, *Loose Salute*. 'Thanx For The Ride,' first taped last Thursday with Earl Ball on piano, is remade today with keyboardist Glen D. Hardin. The second versions of 'Bye, Bye, Bye' and 'Dedicated Friend' from Thursday are both overdubbed today, though the recording of these songs will meander through the next several months. During these sessions, production credit will shift from Felton Jarvis to Michael Nesmith, and in June, Jarvis will leave RCA to work exclusively for Elvis Presley.

Friday 17th
● Peter Tork begins a three-night stint performing solo at West Hollywood's Troubadour club. The opening act for these dates is a band called The Earth Disciples.

Saturday 18th
TV CBS reruns *Hitting The High Seas*, episode 44 of *The Monkees*, at 12 midday. The soundtrack is updated to include 'Oh My My' in place of 'Daydream Believer.'

Sunday 19th
● Peter Tork ends his residency at West Hollywood's Troubadour club. Tork will reappear as a solo act next month at McCabe's in Santa Monica, California.

Saturday 25th
TV At 12midday the CBS network reruns episode 48 of the *Monkees* series, *Fairy Tale*.

Wednesday 29th
● The final master for The Monkees' *Changes* album is compiled for a June release. Among the last-minute changes, 'Time And Time Again' and 'Which Way Do You Want It?' are dropped in favor of 'Midnight Train' and 'I Never Thought It Peculiar.'

MAY

'Little Red Rider' / 'Rose City Chimes' single by Michael Nesmith & The First National Band is released in the U.S.A. This is the debut record from Michael's new group.
● *16* reports that Micky has recently been recording a radio serial for eventual syndication. It's a comedy drama with regular characters, and Micky provides the majority of the voices. He has also written a script for a new television series in which he is due to star with Davy. The duo also hope to host a 30-minute special for television.

Friday 1st
RECORDING RCA *Hollywood, CA* 9:30am-1:00, 2:00-5:00, 6:00-9:00, 10:00pm-1:00am. Felton Jarvis, Michael Nesmith *prod*; Pete Abbott *eng*; two-inch 16-track; tracking, overdubs.
1. **'Bye, Bye, Bye'** version 2
   Loose Salute master # ZWA3-1387
2. **'I Fall To Pieces'** version 1
   unissued master # ZWA3-?
3. **'Listen To The Band'** version 2
   unissued master # ZWA3-?
4. **'Conversations'** version 1
   unissued master # ZWA3-?
Personnel Glen D. Hardin (piano), John London (bass), Michael Nesmith (vocal, guitar), Red Rhodes (pedal steel guitar), John Ware (drums).
● Sessions for The First National Band's first album were wrapped in a matter of days, but production of their second, *Loose Salute*, will be a prolonged process. All three new songs taped today will be rejected for release (though they will soon be rerecorded). 'I Fall To Pieces,' popularized by Patsy Cline, will be remade on May 14th; Michael's own 'Listen To The Band' (a single last year for The Monkees) will be recorded for a second time on May 27th; and 'Conversations' – simply a new title for his oft-recorded 'Carlisle

Wheeling' – will be remade on July 16th. Also today, some overdubs are added to the April 9th recording of 'Bye, Bye, Bye' version 2, and production on it will continue on May 26th.

Saturday 2nd
TV The CBS network reruns for a second time *Hitting The High Seas*, episode 44 of *The Monkees*, at 12 midday. The soundtrack includes the new Monkees single 'Oh My My' in place of the original show's 'Daydream Believer.'

Thursday 7th
RECORDING RCA *Hollywood, CA* 7:00-10:00, 11:00pm-2:00am. Michael Nesmith *prod*; Pete Abbott *eng*; two-inch 16-track; tracking.
1. **'First National Dance'**
   Magnetic South & Loose Salute CD master # ZWA3-8279
Personnel John London (bass), Michael Nesmith (vocal, electric guitar), Red Rhodes (pedal steel guitar), John Ware (drums).
● This evening session produces the nearly instrumental 'First National Dance,' which is planned for inclusion on *Loose Salute* but pulled before release (see August 11th). Credited to Ware, London, and Rhodes, it is conceived as the closing track for side one, in the tradition of *Magnetic South*'s 'First National Rag.' It will be unearthed as a bonus track for the 1999 British Camden-label reissue CD *Magnetic South & Loose Salute*. According to musicians' union records, Earl Ball is involved in this session (though he is inaudible on the released mix) and the group possibly try a second (untitled) number, probably untaped.

Saturday 9th
TV At 12midday the CBS network reruns episode 11 of the *Monkees* series, *Monkees A La Carte*.

Tuesday 12th
● Michael produces a demo session for Bill Chadwick at RCA Studios, including the songs 'Tomorrow' and 'Alistair Rascher.' Neither is originally released, though they will later be included on Chadwick's 1992 private cassette-only release *Friendships*.

Wednesday 13th
RECORDING RCA *Hollywood, CA* 7:00-10:00, 11:00am-2:00, 3:00-7:00pm. Michael Nesmith *prod*; Pete Abbott *eng*; two-inch 16-track; tracking.
1. **'Tengo Amore'**
   Loose Salute master # ZWA3-8280
2. **'Lady Of The Valley'**
   Loose Salute master # ZWA3-8282
Personnel John London (bass), Michael Nesmith (vocal, electric guitar), Red Rhodes (pedal steel guitar), John Ware (drums).
● Two Latin-influenced songs by Michael are taped for release on *Loose Salute*. Sung entirely *en españÒol*, the entertaining 'Tengo Amore' is like nothing else in the Nesmith catalog and is highlighted by some exemplary steel work from Red Rhodes. 'Lady Of The Valley' is more conventional – but only slightly. The percussion work and steel tracks add an almost tropical feel and the whole production is topped off by some multi-layered vocals from Michael. Further overdubs will be added to both songs tomorrow.

Thursday 14th
RECORDING RCA *Hollywood, CA* 1:00-4:00, 5:00-9:00, 10:00pm-1:00am. Michael Nesmith *prod*; Pete Abbott *eng*; two-inch 16-track; tracking, overdubs.
1. **'Tengo Amore'**
   Loose Salute master # ZWA3-8280

2. 'Lady Of The Valley'
Loose Salute master # ZWA3-8282
3. 'I Fall To Pieces' version 2
Loose Salute master # ZWA3-8276
Personnel John London (bass), Michael Nesmith (vocal, guitar), Red Rhodes (pedal steel guitar), John Ware (drums).
• A second version of 'I Fall To Pieces' is taped, destined for release on *Loose Salute*. Today's recording will be subject to further augmentation at a session on May 27th.
   Some additional work is also done on yesterday's recordings of 'Tengo Amore' and 'Lady Of The Valley,' but both these tracks are still incomplete and additional production touches will be added later in May.

● Saturday 16th
TV At 12midday CBS reruns *Too Many Girls*, episode 15 of *The Monkees*.

● Tuesday 19th – Sunday 24th
PERFORMANCE Michael Nesmith & The First National Band appear live at the Ice House in Pasadena, California.

● Saturday 23rd
● Ann Moses reports in today's *NME* that Peter Tork recently gave a solo performance at the Troubadour "as a last-minute replacement for Dion. He performed such standards as 'Kansas City,' 'Blue Monday,' 'Get Back,' and three forgettable originals."
TV The CBS network reruns episode 30 of the *Monkees* series, *Monkees In Manhattan*. The soundtrack is revised to include 'Acapulco Sun' from the forthcoming *Changes* album, replacing 'Look Out (Here Comes Tomorrow).'
● The new Monkees single, 'Oh My My,' debuts on *Billboard*'s Hot 100 Bound chart at #116.

● Tuesday 26th
RECORDING RCA *Hollywood, CA* 10:00am-1:00, 2:00-5:00, 6:00-9:00, 10:00pm-1:00am. Michael Nesmith *prod*; Pete Abbott *eng*; two-inch 16-track; overdubs.
1. 'Tengo Amore'
Loose Salute master # ZWA3-8280
2. 'Thanx For The Ride' version 2
Loose Salute master # ZWA3-1390
3. 'I Fall To Pieces' version 2
Loose Salute master # ZWA3-8276
4. 'Bye, Bye, Bye' version 2
Loose Salute master # ZWA3-1387
Personnel Billy Dale (instrument unknown), Glen D. Hardin (keyboard), John London (bass), Michael Nesmith (vocal, guitar), Red Rhodes (pedal steel guitar), John Ware (drums).
● A very full day of overdubs for four songs destined for *Loose Salute*. Despite the industriousness, none of the productions are completed today. 'I Fall To Pieces' will be worked on again tomorrow, while 'Tengo Amore' and 'Bye, Bye, Bye' will be revisited on Thursday, and 'Thanx For The Ride' will be threaded onto the tape machine for the zillionth time on July 13th.

● Wednesday 27th
RECORDING RCA *Hollywood, CA* 10:00am-1:00, 2:00-5:00, 6:00-10:30pm. Michael Nesmith *prod*; Pete Abbott *eng*; two-inch 16-track; tracking, overdubs.
1. 'I Fall To Pieces' version 2
Loose Salute master # ZWA3-8276

2. 'Listen To The Band' version 3
Loose Salute master # ZWA3-8277
3. 'Dedicated Friend' version 2
Loose Salute master # ZWA3-1389
Personnel John London (bass), Michael Nesmith (vocal, guitar), Red Rhodes (pedal steel guitar), John Ware (drums).
● The First National Band record a new version of Michael's 'Listen To The Band' and add overdubs to existing recordings of 'I Fall To Pieces' and 'Dedicated Friend.' Henry Diltz will attend this session to shoot some photos and later goes with Michael and the group for more pictures at Hugo's, the Palomino club, and the Pickwick Riding Stables, all in the San Fernando Valley suburb of Los Angeles.

● Thursday 28th
RECORDING RCA *Hollywood, CA* 10:00am-1:00, 2:00-5:00, 6:00-9:00, 10:00pm-1:00am. Michael Nesmith *prod*; Pete Abbott *eng*; two-inch 16-track; overdubs.
1. 'Tengo Amore'
Loose Salute master # ZWA3-8280
2. 'Lady Of The Valley'
Loose Salute master # ZWA3-8282
3. 'Bye, Bye, Bye' version 2
Loose Salute master # ZWA3-1387
Personnel John London (bass), Michael Nesmith (vocal, guitar), Red Rhodes (pedal steel guitar), John Ware (drums).
● Further unspecified overdubs are added to these three previously recorded tracks. This will be the final *Loose Salute* session for several weeks as The First National Band take on some live bookings and promote their first album, *Magnetic South* (released next month). Recording for *Loose Salute* will resume on July 13th.

● Friday 29th
● This evening and tomorrow Peter Tork performs solo at McCabe's guitar shop in Santa Monica, California. Each performance is scheduled for 8:30pm and Harold Oblong is the support act.

● Saturday 30th
TV CBS reruns *Your Friendly Neighborhood Kidnappers*, episode 4 of *The Monkees*, at 12midday. The soundtrack is updated to include 'Do You Feel It Too?' from The Monkees' next album, *Changes*.

JUNE

Changes album is released in the U.S.A. Although *Teen World* reports that Davy and Micky as a group have another two years to run on their contracts, this will be their final waxing under the Monkees name. It is possible that Micky and Davy undertake a performance as The Monkees during this period in Philadelphia at an event for radio station WFIL.
   Micky: "By that time it was pretty obvious that The Monkees was over. Davy and I were still getting along. Really, we were mainly fulfilling an obligation to the record company to finish the contract. That's what [*Changes*] was all about."
Magnetic South album by Michael Nesmith & the First National Band is released in the U.S.A. Although Michael's new group's first single 'Little Red Rider' failed to chart, this debut LP will be a 'grower' that reaches *Billboard*'s Top LPs listings in October.
● *Tiger Beat* reports that Davy recently hosted a television special called *Presenting*. He will spend most of this month preparing for the

Changes album

A1 'Oh My My' (J. BARRY / A. KIM)
A2 'Ticket On A Ferry Ride' (J. BARRY / B. BLOOM)
A3 'You're So Good to Me' (J. BARRY / B. BLOOM)
A4 'It's Got To Be Love' (N. GOLDBERG)
A5 'Acapulco Sun' (S. SOLES / N. ALBRIGHT)
A6 '99 Pounds' (J. BARRY)
B1 'Tell Me Love' (J. BARRY)
B2 'Do You Feel It Too?' (J. BARRY / A. KIM)
B3 'I Love You Better' (J. BARRY / A. KIM)
B4 'All Alone In The Dark' (S. SOLES / N. ALBRIGHT)
B5 'Midnight Train' (M. DOLENZ)
B6 'I Never Thought It Peculiar' (T. BOYCE / B. HART)

U.S. release June 1970 (Colgems COS-119).
Chart high U.S. none.

opening of The Street, where he serves as hopeful landlord to a marketplace of stalls. Micky has accepted a role in a stage play that opens on June 2nd in Illinois, and won't be around when The Street opens its doors.

● Tuesday 2nd – Sunday 28th
● Micky makes his professional stage-acting debut at the Pheasant Run Dinner Playhouse in St. Charles, Illinois. For three weeks he will appear as a jazz drummer in Howard Lindsay and Russel Crouse's *Remains To Be Seen*. (Weeknight shows start at 8:30pm, plus a Wednesday matinee at 2:30pm. The two Saturday performances are at 6:30 and 10:50pm, and there is a single Sunday show at 7:30pm.)

● Friday 5th – Sunday 7th
PERFORMANCE On these three evenings Michael Nesmith & The First National Band perform at West Hollywood's Troubadour club.

● Saturday 6th
TV CBS reruns for the second time episode 28 of the *Monkees* series, *Monkees On The Line*, at 12midday. The soundtrack again includes 'Little Girl' in place of the original's 'Look Out (Here Comes Tomorrow).'
● The Monkees' latest single, 'Oh My My,' slips into *Billboard*'s Hot 100 today at #99.

● Saturday 13th
TV At 12midday the CBS network reruns *Success Story*, episode 6 of *The Monkees*, for a third time. The soundtrack again includes 'French Song' in place of 'I Wanna Be Free.'
TV The Monkees – Micky and Davy – make an appearance on the music program *Upbeat* to promote their new single, 'Oh My My,' which peaks today at a sorrowful #98 after only four weeks in the charts. (It is possible that *Upbeat* merely shows a tape of a promotional clip that Micky has directed for the single featuring Micky and Davy riding horses and motorcycles.)

● Wednesday 17th
● The Los Angeles *Herald-Examiner* reports that Davy's shopping mall, The Street, is now open for business. "Three years ago, Monkee David Jones thought it high time young Los Angeles

artisans had a 'place' to display their talents and wares, a 'street' of stall-like shops, such as is found in Europe, where space could be rented at a nominal fee without leases and customers could wander around in a casual, soft-sell atmosphere. The idea began as a dream and, up until 24 hours before opening, it looked as if it might stay that way. But it's amazing what no sleep, determination, and a minimum of 20 pairs of hands, all untrained in any form of carpentry, paper hanging, painting (house) or building, can accomplish.

"Jones, along with his Zilch Corporation partners Rick Cooper, Bill Chadwick, and his personal manager, David Pearl, two months ago rented the ground floor of Beverly Hills discotheque, The Factory. When they took it over, it was feet deep in debris, all left by the former interior decorating studio predecessors, and a block long of nothing but unbroken space. A bomb site factory during the second World War, the building is what might be called 'functional,' but that's all. With the help of 10 friends – joined by others as time went on – Jones, Pearl, Chadwick, and Cooper built 21 shops, a market place area where stalls will be located, painted, papered, hung lights, doors, and generally pulled off an impossibility. Everything, including interior walls, had to be built, and since Beverly Hills fire laws do not permit the use of wood, Masonite [hardboard] cast from patterns into molds became a new talent to be learned.

"The Street, its inhabitants, and their friends roamed through in happy bemusement at the opening. Babies and dogs, popcorn and champagne mingled with tie dyes, denim flares, funky laces, and long skirts, wandering in and out of 'Hansel and Gretel,' 'Leather Goods,' 'Daffodil,' 'Pin Mony,' 'Nemo's Fantasy Factory' (antique toys), and 'Geppetto's' (puppets). Some shop interiors weren't finished but the kids didn't mind – they went right on hanging their raw leather hides, arranging their flowers and handmade pottery, hammering and all. It was 'family night' at a medieval fair. In Beverly Hills."

Tiger Beat reports that the opening of The Street was an underwhelming event with few celebrities (just Peter Tork) and even fewer open stalls. The intention is to have a total of 32 shops, plus a public square and sparkling fountain. The businesses are to include a barber shop, juice bar, jewelry, antiques, pottery, and clothes.

● Saturday 20th
TV At 12midday CBS reruns episode 28 of the *Monkees* series, *Everywhere A Sheik, Sheik*, for a third time.

● Saturday 27th
TV At 12midday CBS reruns episode 48 of *The Monkees*, titled *Fairy Tale*, for a second time.

JULY

● *Tiger Beat* reports that Davy is scheduled to appear in a pantomime version of Cinderella in his hometown of Manchester, England.
'Joanne' / **'One Rose'** single by Michael Nesmith & The First National Band released in the U.S.A. The group's second single will break into the charts next month.

● Saturday 4th
TV At 12midday the CBS network reruns for a second time episode 23 of the *Monkees* series, *Captain Crocodile*.

● Saturday 11th

TV At 12midday CBS reruns for a second time *Don't Look A Gift Horse In The Mouth*, episode 8 of *The Monkees*. The show's soundtrack is again revised to include 'I Never Thought It Peculiar' in place of 'All The King's Horses.'

● Monday 13th

● Tonight, Don Kirshner's latest television venture, *The Kowboys*, hits the box. The country-rock soundtrack for this pilot was created by Jeff Barry and Kirshner, showing perhaps that the two have momentarily embraced Michael's years-old musical vision. Not coincidentally, the show stars Michael Murphey and 'Boomer' Castleman – former members of Colgems group The Lewis & Clarke Expedition and the writers of 'What Am I Doing Hangin' 'Round,' 'Oklahoma Backroom Dancer' and a song that Michael will record in a few months, 'Texas Morning.' Unfortunately *The Kowboys* never progresses beyond this single airing.
RECORDING RCA *Hollywood, CA* 10:00am-1:00, 2:00-5:00, 6:00-10:00pm. Michael Nesmith *prod*; two-inch 16-track; overdubs.

1. **'Tengo Amore'**
   Loose Salute master # ZWA3-8280
2. **'Thanx For The Ride'** version 2
   Loose Salute master # ZWA3-1390
3. **'Bye, Bye, Bye'** version 2
   Loose Salute master # ZWA3-1387

Personnel Glen D. Hardin (keyboard), John London (bass), Michael Nesmith (vocal, guitar), Red Rhodes (pedal steel guitar), John Ware (drums).
● Sessions resume for *Loose Salute* with a series of unspecified overdubs. Despite the numerous recording hours already put into perfecting these masters, the process will continue apace for all three songs through the end of July.

● Tuesday 14th

RECORDING RCA *Hollywood, CA* 10:00am-1:00, 2:00-5:00, 6:00-10:30pm. Michael Nesmith *prod*; two-inch 16-track; tracking, overdubs.

1. **'Bye, Bye, Bye'** version 2
   Loose Salute master # ZWA3-1387
2. **'Nadine (Is It You)?'**
   unissued master # ZPA3-8024
3. **'Whole Lotta Shakin' Goin' On'**
   unissued master # ZPA3-8025
4. **'Different Drum'**
   unissued master # ZPA3-8026

Personnel Glen D. Hardin (keyboard), John London (bass), Michael Nesmith (vocal, guitar), Red Rhodes (pedal steel guitar), John Ware (drums).
● Alongside yet more overdubs for 'Bye, Bye, Bye,' The First National Band tape three songs destined for the cutting room floor. Today sees Michael's first serious recording of 'Different Drum,' a hit for The Stone Poneys in late '67 and his most successful composition as a songwriter. He will eventually record a second version that appears on his 1972 album *And The Hits Just Keep On Comin'*.

Jerry Lee Lewis was part of the "musical triumvirate" of influences that Michael namechecked on the back of *Magnetic South*. Today, The First National Band tackles one of Lewis's trademark tracks, 'Whole Lotta Shakin' Goin' On.'

A similarly inspirational figure in Michael's life is Chuck Berry, whose 'Johnny B. Goode' was his showcase number in The Monkees' concerts of 1968 and '69. Berry's 'Nadine' is also taped today and will be subjected to overdubs on July 16th. (According to musicians'

union documents for this session a fifth unnamed track may be taped but no further details are available.)

● Wednesday 15th

RECORDING RCA *Hollywood, CA* 11:00am-1:00, 2:00-5:00, 6:00-9:00, 10:00pm-1:00am. Michael Nesmith *prod*; two-inch 16-track; tracking, overdubs.

1. **'I Fall To Pieces'** version 2
   Loose Salute master # ZWA3-8276
2. **'Tengo Amore'**
   Loose Salute master # ZWA3-8280
3. **'Bye, Bye, Bye'** version 2
   Loose Salute master # ZWA3-1387
4. **'Thanx For The Ride'** version 2
   Loose Salute master # ZWA3-1390
5. **'Lady Of The Valley'**
   Loose Salute master # ZWA3-8282
6. **'Guitar Man'**
   unissued no master #

Personnel John London (bass), Michael Nesmith (vocal, guitar), Red Rhodes (pedal steel guitar), John Ware (drums).
● As the *Loose Salute* sessions continue, The First National Band cut a version of Jerry Reed's 'Guitar Man,' a song popularized by Elvis Presley. This track will never be released. The productions of 'I Fall To Pieces,' 'Tengo Amore,' and 'Thanx For The Ride' are completed today.

● Thursday 16th

RECORDING RCA *Hollywood, CA* 12midday-3:00, 4:00-7:00, 8:00-11:00pm, 12midnight-3:00am. Michael Nesmith *prod*; Pete Abbott *eng*; two-inch 16-track; tracking, overdubs.

1. **'Conversations'** version 2
   unissued master # ZPA3-8278
2. **'Bye, Bye, Bye'** version 2
   Loose Salute master # ZWA3-1387
3. **'Nadine (Is It You)?'**
   unissued master # ZPA3-8024
4. **'Lady Of The Valley'**
   Loose Salute master # ZWA3-8282
5. **'Listen To The Band'** version 3
   Loose Salute master # ZWA3-8277

Personnel John London (bass), Michael Nesmith (vocal, guitar), Red Rhodes (pedal steel guitar 2,3,4,5), John Ware (drums).
● Michael returns to 'Conversations,' a retitled 'Carlisle Wheeling,' which he last taped in May. Finally he achieves a recording of this song that he feels is worthy of release.

Other tracks completed today are 'Lady Of The Valley,' 'Listen To The Band' version 3, and 'Nadine.' Although a studio version of 'Nadine' never finds release, Michael will later perform it in concert, and an Australian concert take will be heard on his 1978 album *Live At The Palais*.

● Saturday 18th

TV CBS reruns for the second time *Monkees A La Mode*, episode 24 of *The Monkees*, at 12midday. The soundtrack is revised to include 'Oh My My' in place of 'Laugh.' Meanwhile in the studio, Michael holds the penultimate session for his *Loose Salute* album.
RECORDING RCA *Hollywood, CA* 12midday-3:00, 4:00-7:00pm. Michael Nesmith *prod*; Pete Abbott *eng*; two-inch 16-track; tracking, overdubs.

1. **'Hello Lady'**
   Loose Salute master # ZPA3-8281

2. 'Dedicated Friend' version 2
Loose Salute master # ZWA3-1389
Personnel Glen D. Hardin (piano), John London (bass), Michael Nesmith (vocal, guitar), Red Rhodes (pedal steel guitar), John Ware (drums).
● The final new song destined for *Loose Salute* is taped this afternoon, Michael's 'Hello Lady.' The angular track will close out the long player after completion during a further session on July 29th. 'Dedicated Friend' is also reviewed and completed during today's date.

● Saturday 25th
TV The CBS network reruns episode 3 of the *Monkees* series, *Monkee Vs. Machine*, for a fourth time, at 12midday. The show's soundtrack is revised to include The Monkees' recording of Michael's 'Listen To The Band' in place of the original show's 'Saturday's Child.'
• The *NME* reports that Michael will soon tour Britain with The First National Band. They are scheduled to arrive in London on September 17th for a ten-day stay before flying to continental Europe for a series of concert appearances. The band will return on October 5th for dates in England and Ireland. *Magnetic South* is due to be released in Britain during September to coincide with these dates.

● Wednesday 29th
RECORDING RCA *Hollywood, CA* 7:00-10:00, 11:00pm-1:00am. Michael Nesmith *prod*; two-inch 16-track; overdubs.
1. 'Hello Lady'
Loose Salute master # ZPA3-8281
2. 'Bye, Bye, Bye' version 2
Loose Salute master # ZWA3-1387
Personnel Bud Brisbois (trumpet 1), Chuck Findley (trumpet 1), Glen D. Hardin (piano 2), Dick Hyde (trombone 1), John London (bass 2), Lew McCreary (trombone 1), Ollie Mitchell (trumpet 1), Michael Nesmith (vocal 2, guitar 2), John Raines (drums 2), Red Rhodes (pedal steel guitar 2).
● This evening seems to wrap the recording sessions for *Loose Salute* – although the album will go through a major change prior to release. An extended brass fade is added to 'Hello Lady,' while 'Bye, Bye, Bye' appears complete after a whopping ten sessions (a number that might make even Peter Tork blush). Nevertheless, an eleventh (!) session for this rollicking track will be held on October 26th. Michael Nesmith & The First National Band will begin recording a new (third) album next month.

AUGUST

● *Tiger Beat* notes that Davy is planning this summer to join a touring company of the musical comedy stage show *The Fantasticks*. He also hopes to perform in South America and Las Vegas.

● Saturday 1st
● *NME* reports that Davy's Christmas pantomime booking has fallen through. "It had been proposed to showcase Davy at one of the Howard & Wyndham chain of theatres," writes *NME*'s reporter, "but, now this company has been taken over, the projected venue is no longer available for panto purposes."
    U.K. agent Vic Lewis says: "As of this moment, there are no plans for Davy to undertake any British engagements."

TV At 12 midday CBS reruns for a second time *The Chaperone*, episode 9 of *The Monkees*. The show's soundtrack is again revised to include 'Midnight Train' in place of 'This Just Doesn't Seem To Be My Day.'

● Saturday 8th
TV The CBS network reruns for a second time episode 16 of the *Monkees* series, *Son Of A Gypsy*, at 12 midday.
● 'Joanne,' Michael Nesmith & The First National Band's second single, enters the *Billboard* Hot 100. It will peak at #21, Michael's highest placing since The Monkees' 1968 single 'D.W. Washburn' (which made #19). The success is made even sweeter by the fact that 'Joanne' is Michael's own song, by his own group, and his own production. What is more, he has succeeded with a track that is uncompromisingly country.

● Tuesday 11th
● Preparations are made today for an October release of The First National Band's second album, *Loose Salute*.
    Sometime in the next month a decision is made to revise the album's track-listing and drop 'First National Dance' in favor of a yet-to-be-recorded tune that can serve as a follow-up single to their current hit 'Joanne.'

● Wednesday 12th
RECORDING RCA *Hollywood, CA* 1:00-4:00, 5:00-8:00, 9:00pm-12midnight. Michael Nesmith *prod*; Pete Abbott *eng*; two-inch 16-track; tracking.
1. 'Nevada Fighter'
Nevada Fighter master # ZPA3-8489
2. 'Tumbling Tumbleweeds'
Loose Salute master # ZPA3-8490
Personnel Michael Cohen (keyboard), Billy Dale (instrument unknown), John London (bass), Michael Nesmith (vocal, guitar), Red Rhodes (pedal steel guitar), John Ware (drums), James Zitro (percussion).
● With their second single having just entered the charts, The First National Band start their third album this afternoon. Sessions kick off with a track titled 'Apology,' but this will later be reworked as 'Nevada Fighter' – which becomes the title of this third album. Next comes a cover of Bob Nolan's 'Tumbling Tumbleweeds,' popularized by The Sons Of The Pioneers and cut by such Western stars as Gene Autry and Roy Rogers. Michael recasts it as a cosmic cowboy anthem. Both of today's recordings will be subject to further overdubs tomorrow.

● Thursday 13th
RECORDING RCA *Hollywood, CA* 11:30am–2:30, 3:30–6:30, 7:30–10:30, 11:30pm-1:30am. Michael Nesmith *prod*; Pete Abbott *eng*; two-inch 16-track; tracking, overdubs.
1. 'Propinquity (I've Just Begun To Care)' version 2
Nevada Fighter master # ZPA3-8488
2. 'Nevada Fighter'
Nevada Fighter master # ZPA3-8489
3. 'Tumbling Tumbleweeds'
Loose Salute master # ZPA3-8490
Personnel Michael Cohen (keyboard), Billy Dale (instrument unknown), John London (bass), Michael Nesmith (vocal, guitar), Red Rhodes (pedal steel guitar), John Ware (drums), James Zitro (percussion).
● The First National Band record unspecified overdubs onto yesterday's tracks and tape 'Propinquity (I've Just Begun To Care).'

Michael originally recorded this in Nashville during 1968, but today the song is performed in a slightly slower arrangement.

All three of the recordings worked on during today's session will be refined tomorrow.

● Friday 14th
RECORDING RCA *Hollywood, CA* 11:30am–2:30, 3:30–5:30pm. Michael Nesmith *prod*; Pete Abbott *eng*; two-inch 16-track; overdubs.
1. **'Propinquity (I've Just Begun To Care)'** version 2
   Nevada Fighter master # ZPA3-8488
2. **'Nevada Fighter'**
   Nevada Fighter master # ZPA3-8489
3. **'Tumbling Tumbleweeds'**
   Loose Salute master # ZPA3-8490

Personnel Michael Cohen (keyboard), Billy Dale (instrument unknown), John London (bass), Michael Nesmith (vocal, guitar), Red Rhodes (pedal steel guitar), John Ware (drums), James Zitro (percussion).
● This third day of sessions for the *Nevada Fighter* album is given over to unspecified overdubs on the three songs tracked thus far. 'Tumbling Tumbleweeds' will be further refined at a session on October 26th.

● Saturday 15th
TV At 12midday the CBS network reruns for a second time *Monkees Get Out More Dirt*, episode 29 of *The Monkees*. The show's soundtrack has been modified to feature 'Steam Engine' in place of 'The Girl I Knew Somewhere.'

● Tuesday 18th
RECORDING RCA *Hollywood, CA* 6:00-9:00, 10:00pm-12midnight. Michael Nesmith *prod*; Pete Abbott *eng*; two-inch 16-track; tracking.
1. **'Rene'**
   Nevada Fighter master # ZPA3-8491

Personnel Michael Cohen (keyboard), John London (bass), Michael Nesmith (vocal, guitar), Red Rhodes (pedal steel guitar), John Ware (drums), James Zitro (percussion).
● After a weekend rest, sessions resume for *Nevada Fighter* with the taping of a short and lovely Red Rhodes instrumental. After completion, 'Rene' will be used to close the album. Work on the piece continues tomorrow.

● Wednesday 19th
RECORDING RCA *Hollywood, CA* 6:00-9:00, 10:00pm-12midnight. Michael Nesmith *prod*; Pete Abbott *eng*; two-inch 16-track; overdubs.
1. **'Rene'**
   Nevada Fighter master # ZPA3-8491

Personnel Michael Cohen (keyboard), John London (bass), Michael Nesmith (vocal, guitar), Red Rhodes (pedal steel guitar), John Ware (drums), James Zitro (percussion).
● Recording on Red Rhodes's 'Rene' wraps today – and the *Nevada Fighter* sessions will not resume until October. In the meantime, the band will tour and slot in the recording of a projected single, 'Silver Moon.'

● Saturday 22nd
TV At 12midday CBS reruns for a third time episode 19 of the *Monkees* series, *Find The Monkees*.

● Saturday 29th
TV CBS reruns for a second time *Monkee Mother*, episode 27 of *The Monkees*, at 12midday.

● Sunday 30th
● *The Los Angeles Times* announces that the writing team of Paul Mazursky and Larry Tucker is splitting up. Since crafting the pilot for *The Monkees* in 1965 the duo has created such movie successes as *I Love You Alice B. Toklas* and *Bob & Carol & Ted & Alice*. The duo's final feature together, *Alex In Wonderland*, premieres in December.

SEPTEMBER

● *Fave* mentions that Michael and his family have moved to Palm Springs, California. Michael and Phyllis are expecting a new addition to their family any day now. *Fave* also notes that an unannounced performance at the Troubadour by Peter Tork and Micky and Coco Dolenz was "experimental" and "unique." The magazine's Johnny Jason says that Tork "is currently releasing a single on which he plays banjo and guitar. It is his own composition and is rather good, as is his musicianship; it's just his voice that doesn't quite make it." (No such release is known to exist.)
● Michael Nesmith & The First National Band travel to London to begin a European tour. In an interview with Britain's *Disc* music paper, he tells Mike Ledgerwood of his Monkees experience. "They couldn't pay me enough money for the abuse I had to take about the group not playing on the records," says Michael. "That's why I had no compunction about accepting the royalty checks. No sir! None at all. Imagine yourself a craftsman pharmacist – and being forced to make shoes. That's what it was like for me."

● Wednesday 2nd
● Peter Tork takes part in a demo session at Sound Center in New York City for two songs by his friend Wendy Erdman. Peter plays bass on 'Help Me Sing the Sun Down' and 'Keep in Touch,' later featured on Wendy's album, *ERDMAN*. Also in the studio, Michael Nesmith & The First National Band hold a one-off session for their next single.
RECORDING RCA *Hollywood, CA* 6:00-10:00, 11:00pm-1:00am. Michael Nesmith *prod*; Dennis Smith *eng*; two-inch 16-track; tracking, overdubs.
1. **'Silver Moon'**
   Loose Salute master # ZPA3-8494

Personnel Michael Cohen (piano), John London (bass), Michael Nesmith (vocal, guitar), Red Rhodes (pedal steel guitar), John Ware (drums).
● Michael has come up with a winning upbeat follow-up to 'Joanne' in 'Silver Moon,' perfectly combining the group's country direction with the happy energy of their live performances. One further session for the song will be held on October 19th. Shortly after its completion the decision is made to add it to the group's imminent second album, *Loose Salute*. This will delay the LP by a month, but 'Silver Moon' is undoubtedly superior to the track it will replace on the LP, 'First National Dance.'

● Friday 4th - Saturday 5th
PERFORMANCE The First National Band play at The Warehouse in Anaheim, California, with Coven and Fresh Air in support.

● Saturday 5th
TV At 12midday the CBS network reruns for a second time *The Wild Monkees*, episode 42 of the *Monkees* series. The show's revised soundtrack includes 'Looking For The Good Times' in place of 'Star Collector.'

Tuesday 8th

TV Michael Nesmith & The First National Band appear on the syndicated evening program *The Allen Show* hosted by Steve Allen. Other guests include 'Mama' Cass Elliot.

Thursday 10th

● Michael's wife Phyllis gives birth to their daughter Jessica Buffler Nesmith.

Friday 11th

● Bob Rafelson's second feature film, *Five Easy Pieces*, is released to great acclaim. Rafelson is elevated instantly to the level of auteur by critics – whom he looks upon with great mistrust. Rafelson tells a reporter: "I can't depend on critical support. From a guy who was considered a complete ass – that's the word people used – with *Head*, I was suddenly brilliant with *Five Easy Pieces*. But I was the same man. You go through that once in a lifetime, never again. Since Jack [Nicholson] and I wrote and produced *Head* together, along with my partner Bert Schneider, we're now telling people we made *Five Easy Pieces* so people would go back to see *Head*. Several critics have asked to do just that."

Rafelson's observations are spot-on, as usual, since *The New York Times* will say exactly that in a piece they run about his new film tomorrow. "Bob Rafelson [is] a young director whose name will probably not be remembered in connection with his first film, *Head*. *Head* suffered from its cast, The Monkees, and from an ad campaign that perhaps did more for the publicist than for the client (you may recall a month when New York was inundated with a mysterious poster – photographs of John Brockman's head), but it was a better movie than most critics allowed. … *Head* was a movie that had nowhere to go except down, but in retrospect doesn't seem all that bad."

Saturday 12th

● *NME* reports that Michael begins his European tour today, starting with four dates in Ireland, almost a week in advance of the previously reported start date of the 17th. The paper publishes an interview with Michael by Alan McDougall under the headline: "Mike – who paid a quarter-million to quit Monkees."

"The Monkees were designed," reminisces Michael, "and well designed too, and did everything they were supposed to. I didn't like them except for the TV show. That won two Emmy awards, so it must have been good. I really needed a job when I joined The Monkees and I made a lot of money with them, Lord have mercy, I made more money than I thought there was in the whole world. And for a while, I spent some time believing I was a superstar. Specially the time we came to London. John Lennon extended every courtesy to me and he was real nice.

"But at the time I was going through a real stubborn time. Our producers were always saying to me, 'Act madcap, act crazy,' and all that. But that isn't my nature, so I preferred to just sit quietly. I guess a lot of people got the impression that I am moody.

"So anyway, I came back to America and bought all the superstar things. You know: a limousine with black windows and a mansion with guards and dogs, and furs and jewels. But after a year, I found it was rusting, it was going bad, and I would have to buy new things. And I realized I had to let my own music come through. I had four years to run on my contract, at $160,000 a year (which adds up to more than a quarter million [neither Michael nor the *NME* can add up]), so I just gave it back to buy my freedom.

"After all, I was the first one to blow the whistle on the studio musicians story. You see, we were two months into [making the TV]

show when I found out, to my withering disappointment, that there was no intention for us to make music. So after we'd had a few hits, I called a press conference without telling any of the Monkee people and just told the reporters the honest truth: that we hadn't played or nothing on any of the first records. I didn't want people to stop buying Monkees records if they enjoyed them – and I got a penny from every record they bought – but I just had to be honest."

As for Nesmith's recent recorded output, he admits: "It's not all that new. I've been sitting on it for about five years. Coming from urban Texas, my roots are more rhythm & blues, but somehow I feel more comfortable in country & western. My music is kinda doped-up L.B.J., kinda acid country.

"My group, The First National Band, are really fine musicians. Our steel guitarist, Red Rhodes, has won the CMA award for best musician for six of the last eight years. The piano player on *Magnetic South* is Glen Hardin, who's now playing over in Vegas with Elvis. Our next album we're using a jazz piano player called Michael Cohen from the Charles Lloyd band. Now he's used to playing complicated stuff. But at first he got real intimidated with us, because our music is so rigidly disciplined. But when you really get going, oh! Sometimes on stage I laugh out loud in the middle of singing a song, because the music is so beautiful. It makes me real happy."

Asked about his former bandmates, Nesmith says: "Well, I see David and Micky socially, but I don't really know what they're up to. And I haven't seen Peter Tork for about two years."

TV Back in the States, at 12midday the CBS network reruns episode 49 of the *Monkees* series, *Monkees Watch Their Feet*.

Wednesday 16th

PERFORMANCE Michael Nesmith & The First National Band play a show at London's Nashville Rooms. It is Michael's first stage appearance in London since July 1967.

Friday 18th

● Jimi Hendrix dies in London. Hendrix had recently attended a gig by Michael in London – either the Nashville Rooms on Wednesday or a private show held for an invited audience during this period. Michael later tells *Guitar World*: "I was surprised to see [Hendrix] in somewhat of a funk. He was not happy with the way his music had developed. He felt stultified somehow. He felt that what he was doing didn't have the substance it once had. I'm not sure he even realized how much substance it ever had. We were standing outside alone in a lobby and I felt a great deal of compassion for him. As he stood there, his eyes kind of drifted off, and I could see him trying to come to terms with some sort of devil or something in his head.

"And he said, 'You know, I think I'm gonna start an R&B band. I gotta do something. I think I'm gonna work with some horns and put together something like Otis does, 'cos that's really where it's at.' I put my arm around him, and I said: 'Jimi, don't you understand, man, you invented psychedelic music. You invented it. Nobody had ever played this before you came along. Why are you going through this crisis of self-confidence right now?' And he didn't say anything, he didn't respond at all, but it was an extraordinary moment in my life, and I think in his as well. He nodded kind of in agreement to that, but in a very humble way. And I went off to Amsterdam, and got the call two days later that he was dead."

Saturday 19th

TV At 12midday the CBS network reruns *Monkees Marooned*, episode 40 of *The Monkees*. The show's revised soundtrack includes the *Changes* track 'Do You Feel It Too?'.

BELL- 88054
STEREO
bell
45 RPM

素敵な女の子
DO IT IN THE NAME OF LOVE
モンキーズ

¥ 400

● Tuesday 22nd

Today marks the end of an era: the final recording session by The Monkees in their original incarnation.

RECORDING Studio unknown *New York, NY*. Jeff Barry *prod*; one-inch 8-track; tracking, overdubs.

1. 'Do It In The Name Of Love'
   Changes master #9918
2. 'Lady Jane' takes 1-9
   Changes master #9919

● Despite the success of the TV reruns of *The Monkees*, the kids who watch are simply not buying the group's new releases in any great quantity. The last single, 'Oh My My,' barely registered on the charts, and *Changes* didn't even get a showing. Although The Monkees – Davy and Micky – are under contract for several more years, Screen Gems will be unwilling to spend any more money on them after this session.

And it's not much of a session.

Jeff Barry turns out two unremarkable pop-soul blends for the duo, who at least are to be heard singing together on these final sides. The tracking session reveals producer Barry directing a crew of unidentified New York session musicians, with the master for 'Do It In The Name Of Love' captured in 16 takes and 'Lady Jane' in just nine.

The results will not be mixed until February 19th 1971, and although the tapes are labeled "Monkees" the songs will be released under the name "Mickey Dolenz & Davy Jones." The misspelling of Micky's name says a lot about this release: the company no longer cares and neither does Micky.

The Monkees are finished in both name and spirit. Micky: "It kind of wound down. There wasn't any great last moment."

Colgems, the label started in 1966 to promote and sell Monkees records, will fold next year, and this final single will be released on another Columbia Pictures venture, Bell.

(The two recordings – 'Do It In The Name Of Love' and 'Lady Jane' – will later be released as a couple of bonus tracks on the 1994 CD reissue of *Changes*.)

● Friday 25th

● Davy tells reporter Penny Pence: "I'm working on a new act and hope to open in Las Vegas in December," though Pence notes that "no official booking has taken place." Davy says that Peter Tork is "growing squash on his mother's farm in Connecticut."

● Saturday 26th

TV CBS reruns *The Spy Who Came In From The Cool*, episode 5 of *The Monkees*, at 12midday. The show's revised soundtrack includes 'All Alone In The Dark.'

● Monday 28th

PERFORMANCE Michael Nesmith & The First National Band begin a week-long cabaret booking in Sheffield, England at the Cavendish and Monk Bretton clubs.

OCTOBER

● *Tiger Beat* reports that Peter Tork "is the most broke ex-Monkee," that Samantha Dolenz's boutique is still going strong, and that Micky is "testing" for some movie roles, including a biopic of comedian Lenny Bruce. Tork: "I gave away a lot of money to friends, on the theory that it would come back to me in the long run." The magazine also notes that Davy has now filled out the stalls at The Street market and can be seen working there regularly. Meanwhile, Screen Gems has shifted its promotional focus from *The Monkees* to another television music program, *The Partridge Family*.

● The First National Band are presently in Europe. Their second album, *Loose Salute*, was originally scheduled for release this month but has been pushed back to accommodate the inclusion of 'Silver Moon,' which will be completed at a session on the 19th.

● Saturday 3rd

TV At 12midday CBS reruns episode 21 of the *Monkees* series, *The Prince And The Pauper*. The show's revised soundtrack includes '99 Pounds' from *Changes*.

● *NME* features a photo of Michael with Ringo Starr, who attended a recent private concert that Michael gave in London for an invited audience. Last month, Starr released his own country album, *Beaucoups Of Blues*.

● Monday 5th

PERFORMANCE Michael Nesmith & The First National Band begin a week-long cabaret booking in Birmingham, England at the Cavendish and Dolce Vita clubs.

● Saturday 10th

● *NME* reviews one of Michael's recent British cabaret gigs, at Sheffield's Baily Club. Ray Nortrop writes: "Mike Nesmith never even made a reference to his former role as a Monkee. For me and the predominately under-25 audience, the 35-minute act was far too short. Everyone appeared to be spellbound by Mike's creative country sound with The First National Band. ... Mike opened with 'Listen To The Band' followed by 'Little Red Rider' and then Red Rhodes performed his first solo, 'Rose City Chimes.' Next Mike, in a very Jim Reeves type of manner, worked his way through 'One Rose.' He continued with his recent U.S. chart success, 'Joanne,' and this was followed by another instrumental spot featuring Red Rhodes – 'Steel Guitar Rag.' Then to conclude the act the pace dramatically

Davy and Micky's final session as The Monkees is for the 'Do It In The Name Of Love' single – issued next year as by 'Davy & Micky.' The designer of this Japanese issue couldn't even find a picture of them together – a telling sign that each of The Monkees is now a solo artist.

increased for the only rock number included in the set, Chuck Berry's 'Nadine.'"

TV CBS reruns for a second time *I Was A Teenage Monster*, episode 18 of *The Monkees*, at 12midday. 'Your Auntie Grizelda' from the original show is again replaced by Michael's 'Good Clean Fun.'

● Friday 16th
PERFORMANCE Michael Nesmith & The First National Band and Davy Jones "and his band" are scheduled to appear at 7:30pm on the same bill at the Las Vegas Ice Palace in Nevada. Also appearing are Sugarloaf (the headliners) and Brothers Reborn. The show is a Mike Tell production with advance tickets priced at $3.50.
● The *Los Angeles Free Press* runs an interview with Bob Rafelson. He tells Jacoba Atlas that there is a thread linking his first two films, *Head* and *Five Easy Pieces*. "I can see a relation between those two films that others can't," says Rafelson. "I mean, I'm not a lizard: I don't change completely every two years."

● Saturday 17th
TV At 12midday CBS reruns episode 26 of the *Monkees* series, *Monkees Chow Mein*.
● Michael Nesmith & The First National Band's *Magnetic South* album enters the *Billboard* Top LPs chart. Despite its musical quality and the presence of a hit in 'Joanne' it will register for a mere three weeks, peaking at #143. Nonetheless it will turn out to be Michael's highest-charting solo album.

● Monday 19th
RECORDING RCA *Hollywood, CA* 10:00am-1:00, 2:00-5:00, 6:00-9:00, 10:00pm-1:00am. Michael Nesmith *prod*; two-inch 16-track; overdubs.
1. **'Silver Moon'**
   Loose Salute master # ZPA3-8494
Personnel Michael Cohen (piano), John London (bass), Michael Nesmith (vocal, guitar), Red Rhodes (pedal steel guitar), John Ware (drums).
● Returned from their travels, The First National Band put in a very full day at RCA to complete their next single, 'Silver Moon.'

● Tuesday 20th
● Master tapes are prepared for a new two-disc compilation of Monkees oldies, *Barrel Full Of Monkees*. Fittingly, it will be issued in January 1971 as the last ever Colgems-label release. Meanwhile, across the hall at RCA, Michael is recording an oldie of his own.
RECORDING RCA *Hollywood, CA* 11:00am-1:00, 2:00-5:00, 6:00-9:00, 10:00pm-12midnight. Michael Nesmith *prod*; two-inch 16-track; tracking.
1. **'Thirteen's Not Our Lucky Number'** version 3
   unissued master # ZPA3-8495
Personnel Michael Cohen (piano), Billy Dale (instrument unknown), John London (bass), Michael Nesmith (vocal, guitar), Red Rhodes (pedal steel guitar), John Ware (drums).
● Michael makes his third attempt to record this unusual song, five years in the making. The tune's co-writer, Michael Cohen, is on hand for the session – but like the previous versions, this 'Thirteen's Not Our Lucky Number' will also remain unissued.

● Wednesday 21st
RECORDING RCA *Hollywood, CA* 12midday-3:00, 4:00-7:00, 8:00pm-12midnight. Michael Nesmith *prod*; two-inch 16-track; tracking.
1. **'Grand Ennui'**
   Nevada Fighter master # ZPA3-8496

Personnel Michael Cohen (piano), John London (bass), Michael Nesmith (vocal, guitar), Red Rhodes (pedal steel guitar), John Ware (drums).
● Sessions for The First National Band's third album resume today with the taping of this very impressive new Nesmith song. When completed it will kick off the stunning *Nevada Fighter*. A further session for 'Grand Ennui' will be held on October 26th.

● Friday 23rd
● Davy appears on the television program *Love American Style* in an installment entitled *Love And The Elopement*.

● Saturday 24th
TV At 12midday CBS reruns for a second time episode 37 of the *Monkees* series, *Art For Monkees Sake*.

● Monday 26th
RECORDING RCA *Hollywood, CA* 10:00am-1:00, 2:00-5:00, 6:00-9:00, 10:00pm-12midnight. Michael Nesmith *prod*; two-inch 16-track; overdubs.
1. **'Grand Ennui'**
   Nevada Fighter master # ZPA3-8496
2. **'Bye, Bye, Bye'** version 2
   Loose Salute master # ZWA3-1387
3. **'Tumbling Tumbleweeds'**
   Loose Salute master # ZPA3-8490
Personnel Michael Cohen (keyboard), John London (bass), Michael Nesmith (vocal, guitar), Red Rhodes (pedal steel guitar), John Ware (drums).
● A day of clean-up work as 'Grand Ennui' and 'Tumbling Tumbleweeds' are overdubbed and the months-old 'Bye, Bye, Bye' is given a final tweak. It will be available in a few days on the group's revamped *Loose Salute* album.

● Friday 30th
● Davy appears on the television program *Danny Thomas In Make Room For Granddaddy*.

● Saturday 31st
TV CBS reruns episode 31 of the *Monkees* series, *Monkees At The Movies*, at 12midday.

NOVEMBER

Loose Salute album by Michael Nesmith & The First National Band is released in the U.S.A.
'Silver Moon' / 'Lady Of The Valley' single by Michael Nesmith & The First National Band is released in the U.S.A. Michael and his group release their second LP and third 45.
● Peter Tork's performance on Wendy Erman's album is released towards the end of this month.

● Saturday 7th
TV At 12midday the CBS network reruns *Hillbilly Honeymoon*, episode 39 of *The Monkees*.

● Saturday 14th
TV CBS reruns episode 50 of the *Monkees* series, *Monstrous Monkee Mash*, at 12midday. For this airing, the soundtrack is modified, with

the original song 'Goin' Down' replaced now with 'Bye Bye Baby Bye Bye' from last year's album *The Monkees Present*.

● Friday 20th
PERFORMANCE Michael Nesmith & The First National Band appear in concert at the KRNT theater in Des Moines, Iowa, at 8:00pm.

● Saturday 21st
PERFORMANCE At 9:00pm Micky, Davy and Peter are scheduled to perform together for half an hour at the Valley REC Center in Van Nuys, California, in a show billed as a 'Freaky, Foxy, Funky Revival.' This will be the last time that these members of The Monkees share a stage until 1976.
TV CBS reruns episode 41 of the *Monkees* series, *Card-Carrying Red Shoes*, at 12midday.
● Michael Nesmith & The First National Band's new single, 'Silver Moon,' creeps into *Billboard*'s Hot 100 Bound chart at #102.

● Monday 23rd
● Davy tapes a TV appearance on *The Merv Griffin Show* which will be aired at a later date.

● Saturday 28th
TV At 12midday the CBS network reruns *Monkees Blow Their Minds*, episode 57 of *The Monkees*.
● Michael's 'Silver Moon' single enters the regular *Billboard* Hot 100. It will peak at #42 early in 1971.

DECEMBER

● Saturday 5th
TV CBS reruns episode 52 of the *Monkees* series, *The Devil And Peter Tork*, at 12midday. For this airing 'Salesman' is again replaced with 'I Never Thought It Peculiar.'

● Saturday 12th
TV At 12midday CBS reruns *The Monkees Paw*, episode 51 of *The Monkees*.

● Saturday 19th
TV CBS airs a seasonal repeat of episode 47 of *The Monkees*, titled *The Christmas Show*.

● Monday 21st
RECORDING RCA *Hollywood, CA*. Michael Nesmith *prod*; Pete Abbott *eng*; two-inch 16-track; tracking.
1. **'Texas Morning'**
   Nevada Fighter master # ZPA3-8497
2. **'Ain't Never Found A Good Woman'**
   unissued master # ZPA3-9228
3. **'Grand Ennui'**
   Nevada Fighter master # ZPA3-8496
Personnel Michael Nesmith (vocal, guitar), Red Rhodes (pedal steel guitar), unknown (other instruments).
● Tensions within The First National Band have caused a split, despite their relative success. Drummer John Ware will recall later that the break-up may have occurred after their Iowa gig on November 20th. Regardless of the details, Michael will finish *Nevada*

Fighter with the help of Red Rhodes and some session players including guitarists James Burton and Al Casey, drummer Ron Tutt, and bassists Joe Osborn and Max Bennett. Exact personnel credits for the remainder of the sessions are unavailable.

Today, Michael and a modified First National Band tape two new songs – 'Texas Morning' and 'Ain't Never Found A Good Woman' – as well as completing what will be the album's opener, 'Grand Ennui.' 'Ain't Never Found A Good Woman' (or possibly 'Never Found A Good Woman' and perhaps by Jack Hardy) will remain unreleased.

● Tuesday 22nd
RECORDING RCA *Hollywood, CA*. Michael Nesmith *prod*; Pete Abbott *eng*; two-inch 16-track; tracking.
1. **'I Looked Away'**
   Nevada Fighter master # ZPA3-8499
2. **'Some Of Shelly's Blues'** version 2
   unissued master # ZPA3-8498
Personnel Michael Nesmith (vocal, guitar), unknown (other instruments).
● Two more songs are taped for *Nevada Fighter* today. One is a cover of Eric Clapton and Bobby Whitlock's 'I Looked Away,' the opening track from their recently released Derek & The Dominos album *Layla And Other Assorted Love Songs*. The second is a new recording of Michael's own 'Some Of Shelly's Blues.' Today's take on the song will not be issued, but Michael and Red Rhodes will cut another version for the 1973 album *Pretty Much Your Standard Ranch Stash*.

● Wednesday 23rd
RECORDING RCA *Hollywood, CA*. Michael Nesmith *prod*; Pete Abbott *eng*; two-inch 16-track; tracking.
1. **'Only Bound'**
   Nevada Fighter master # ZPA3-8493
2. **'Cucurrucucú Paloma'**
   unissued master # ZPA3-9229
Personnel Michael Nesmith (vocal, guitar), Red Rhodes (pedal steel guitar), unknown (other instruments).
● Following yesterday's pattern, another cover and a Nesmith original are taped for *Nevada Fighter*, though this time Michael's wistful 'Only Bound' makes it to the album while his cover of the popular Latin song 'Cucurrucucú Paloma' does not.

This is Michael's final recording session of the year.

Production on *Nevada Fighter* will be completed in January 1971 with the recording of 'Here I Am' (January 4th) and Harry Nilsson and Bill Martin's 'Rainmaker' (January 5th and 20th).

Two other songs recorded at those sessions, 'Roses Are Blooming' (January 4th) and a new version of 'Tapioca Tundra' (January 20th), will be left off the final album. *Nevada Fighter* will be released in May 1971. It completes Michael's musical trilogy, but does not sell as well as the first two volumes, *Magnetic South* and *Loose Salute*.

● Saturday 26th
TV The CBS network reruns *Some Like It Lukewarm*, episode 56 of *The Monkees*, at 12midday.

● Thursday 31st
PERFORMANCE Michael rings in the new year with a performance at Disneyland in Anaheim, California. According to a press release he is accompanied by The First National Band, but the group's line-up is not known. Support acts include The Poppy Family, Ann Peebles, Sound Castle Ltd., and The Rhythm Rebellion.

afterword

Michael Nesmith: "The whole thing was like being in a continuous movie. You keep watching all the things going on around you, but you aren't really part of it. You lose your sense of reality. It always seemed a little wrong. I was never really comfortable in it. I was back at zero, financially, just the way I had been before joining the group. I learned a real lesson with The Monkees. The experience sort of anchored me to the concept of art. I won't let myself get fooled again by the machine."

Peter Tork: "I did think for a long time that it was a mistake to be involved and I didn't want to have anything to do with [The Monkees]. Hey, it really was my life and I really did learn a lot. Any mistakes I made were because I didn't know better."

Micky Dolenz: "There was never a leader of us four. As long as we were under the umbrella, under the wing of a musical entity – a conductor, as it were, in terms of the music – and under the wing of a director, as on the television show, it was great, it was wonderful. The proof is in the pudding. It was phenomenal. But without that, then we're just four kind of loose cannons running around."

Davy Jones: "First of all Peter Tork wasn't with us when we toured and then all of a sudden Mike Nesmith wasn't with us, and Micky and I were together. Then, 'Hey, hey I'm a Monkee,' you know? That's the way it's been ever since – Davy Jones formerly of The Monkees. Davy Jones from The Monkees. I sign autographs now and I say 'Davy Jones' and I put 'The Monkees' under that and most of the fans say, 'You don't have to put that. We know who you are.'"

To say that Michael, Micky, Davy, and Peter would never fully recover from their five years as The Monkees would be something of an understatement. All four did their best to establish individual careers in the arts, but whatever they accomplished would be dwarfed by their Monkee past. As they were to learn, The Monkees as a pop culture phenomenon never really faded away. It just took breaks every so often.

1971

In September 1971, one year after Davy and Micky's last recording session together, *Look* caught up with the dynamic duo. Micky told the magazine: "After the series stopped, I couldn't get work. It wasn't funny. 'Who needs a rock'n'roll drummer?' agents said. It was very tough."

Micky issued a number of impressive solo singles throughout the 1970s but was never able to turn his incredible talent as a singer (or songwriter) into any hits. Despite operating his own home studio, there would be no Micky Dolenz solo album of original material. He had the songs, but without his Monkee mates he lacked the self-confidence to go all the way. Savvy investments kept him afloat and every so often he would appear in television (*My Three Sons*; *Mannix Adam-12*; *Cannon*) or in low-budget movies (*Keep Off My Grass!*; *Linda Lovelace For President*; *Night Of The Strangler*). In Micky's words he "just partied, bought a laser, and went hang gliding."

Davy told *Look* that in the last year he and Micky "were passed from RCA to Screen Gems to a subsidiary company that didn't pay us very much. The only thing that can save us now is our talent. … The residual money is keeping us alive. We're in our third year of reruns."

Davy, as the most popular member of the group, had perhaps the best chance of post-Monkees success. In the summer of 1971 he enjoyed a mild solo hit called 'Rainy Jane,' but a follow-up eluded him. He disliked his label, Bell (the latest subsidiary of Columbia Pictures to inherit The Monkees), as well as the producer they picked for him, Jackie Mills.

Despite telling *Look* that his dream was "to be a Yorkshire farmer and tap dance only on weekends," Davy kept on working, with a steady stream of personal appearances and guest spots on television (*The Brady Bunch*; *Love American Style*; and in animated form on *The New Scooby Doo Movies*).

Peter was the first of the group to break away – and with pals like Crosby Stills & Nash, Peter would surely have been expected to pull off some sort of musical second act. Unbelievably, he would not issue a solo record until 1981 – and that would be just a single of two cover tunes. It was a true disappointment that a man with so much musical promise didn't achieve more.

Michael's solo career started with a bang. Three critically acclaimed solo albums – *Magnetic South*, *Loose Salute*, and *Nevada Fighter* – and two reasonably successful chart singles, 'Joanne,' and 'Silver Moon,' were released in little more than a year. But after that, mainstream acceptance was hard to come by. Michael continued, unfazed, with a slew of quality releases, including an album jokingly titled *And The Hits Just Keep On Comin'*.

1972-73

Saturday morning TV reruns of *The Monkees* moved from CBS to ABC in 1972. By August '73 these airings had run their course. Over the next several years the series would be picked up in syndication across the United States and was probably being seen in more places than the original prime-time airings.

1975-76

The syndicated broadcasts set off a revival of sorts, and two 1976 greatest-hits albums met with as much success as some of the group's original releases. Arista's *The Monkees Greatest Hits* charted for 16 weeks in 1976, reaching #58. This renewed interest coincided with Michael, Micky, Davy, and Peter meeting for the first time since 1968 to discuss a full reunion.

"We met up at my house, up in the Hollywood Hills," Micky told me in the 1990s. "I think it was William Morris [agency] or something expressed an interest in putting the act back together. Everybody was very enthusiastic about it on the surface. You know: 'Oh great; great idea,' but when it got down to the nitty gritty there were too many conflicting feelings and attitudes. Typically, we didn't agree on anything, because you've got to remember that The Monkees was not a group.

"We did have a meeting, but there was still an awful lot of bad blood, you know? I don't mean bad blood, that's not the right term, but there was still an awful lot of competition and stuff. We were all solo personalities and solo artists. We only had the one meeting and I don't think anything else happened after that. There wasn't any animosity: there wasn't a fight or anything. Actually, I remember it being really exciting. We all got together for the first time in quite a few years in the same room and there was a hell of a buzz."

Davy told reporter Ivor Davis during this period: "We did try to get together again. We could have picked up £100,000 to reunite for just one hamburger commercial. Peter and Mike said no. Peter is teaching music and French and playing in local coffee houses. Mike makes country & western discs and is deep into a meditation type of religion."

Soon afterwards Davy and Micky were approached with another offer, from songwriters Tommy Boyce and Bobby Hart. Micky remembers that the duo's approach was: "'Let's get together and do some gigs.' That's when we came up with the idea of the 'Guys that wrote 'em and the Guys that sang 'em.' It sounded like a good idea."

Dolenz, Jones, Boyce & Hart, as they would be known on record, mounted a number of extremely successful tours through 1975 and 1976 playing predominately at amusement parks. Their album on Capitol, *Dolenz, Jones, Boyce & Hart*, was not a success, and soon after its release Micky and Davy struck out on their own.

"Davy and I got a job doing a play, *Tom Sawyer*," recalls Micky. "Then an agent came to us and said, 'Do you and Davy want to go out with a show?' We had to make a decision whether to go out with Tommy and Bobby, or just go out by ourselves, and I think it was just an economic decision. We put together a show. My sister Coco was on it, she sang backups, and another girl. We went out and did, I think, one or two years. A couple of summers just as Dolenz & Jones, doing a lot of the Monkee hits, but a lot of new material too. After that we went to England to do *The Point*. That's when Davy and I split up and I stayed in England."

The Point was a musical based on Nilsson's album of the same name, and towards the end of the run Micky and Davy had a falling out that lasted for years after. Micky found work as a television director in Britain and Davy became something of a journeyman entertainer, taking the stage anywhere there was a spotlight.

1977

Michael, meanwhile, had also spent quite a bit of time in Britain during the mid 1970s. Since the Monkee days he had enjoyed a strong cult following in Britain, which granted him a fluke hit in 1977, 'Rio.' The success of the record meant little in comparison to the journey on which it would take Michael. Asked to create a promotional clip for the song, he went to town and created a conceptual rock video that drew accolades throughout the industry.

Somehow inspired by the success of the primitive home-video game *Pong*, Michael felt that the future of music and videos were inextricably linked. As proof of this, he created a pilot program, *Popclips*, filled with music videos and later sold the idea to Warner Communications as the basis for a 24-hour-a-day music station called MTV. He also opened a video label, Pacific Arts – itself an offshoot of Michael's own record company – and produced the Grammy-award-winning long-form video album *Elephant Parts* (1981).

1980

The Monkees enjoyed renewed success in Japan thanks to a Kodak television commercial that used 'Daydream Believer' for its soundtrack. In the years that followed, Micky, Davy, and Peter all toured Japan individually and were greeted with much fan fervor.

1985

Peter was approached by promoter David Fishof about regrouping The Monkees for a 20th anniversary tour. Micky, Davy, and Peter all climbed on board, and during 1986 and '87 they performed a series of record-breaking concerts. Incredibly, by November 1986 seven Monkees albums were on the *Billboard* charts and a new single from Micky and Peter, 'That Was Then, This Is Now,' had gone Top 40.

This success was due in large part to the re-airing of *The Monkees* series by MTV, in a deal worked out by the show's co-creator Bert Schneider. Just a few days short of the 20th anniversary of the original debut of the series, Michael joined his former bandmates on stage at Greek Theater in Los Angeles for performances of 'Listen To The Band' and 'Pleasant Valley Sunday.' After this, the foursome taped a Christmas video for MTV. But Michael had no intention of any permanent reunion.

1987

Micky, Davy, and Peter recorded a new album together, *Pool It!*, for the Rhino label. It did not reach the artistic heights of their 1960s recordings but did manage a reasonable chart placement of #72.

1989

The four Monkees reunite once more to receive a star on the Hollywood Walk Of Fame and to perform their first full-length concert together since 1968. Micky, Davy, and Peter continued touring without Michael, but not for much longer. Without exposure from MTV, which by now had moved on to other programming, their appeal had waned, as in years past.

1994

Bob Rafelson, Bert Schneider, and Steve Blauner had formed BBS in 1970, a company that absorbed Raybert Productions. In the early 1990s they became interested in releasing a special edition of their movie, *Easy Rider*. Approaching Columbia Pictures, who had distributed the film, they found that all outtake footage and other important elements had been destroyed without their consent.

Because Raybert/BBS were the true owners of the film and not Columbia, they lodged a lawsuit against the entertainment giant and, as a settlement, won back the rights to all of The Monkees' films and recordings. In 1994, Raybert/BBS sold these assets to Rhino Records and thereafter this mighty reissue label became the keepers of The Monkees' archived legacy of tapes and films.

1996

Micky, Davy, and Peter marked their 30th anniversary as The Monkees with another concert tour. However, this time there would be a twist. In each show they would perform a Michael Nesmith song, apologizing for his absence but promising fans that he was back at home working on their new album. Indeed he was, and later that year the group unleashed *Justus*, which was, as the title implied, their first group-only recording since *Headquarters*.

1997

This year was like 1967 in so many ways for The Monkees. Fans loved them; critics did not. When the foursome hit the stage of Wembley Arena in north London in March 1997 it was a jaw-dropping sight. There stood the original band clad in matching red velvet suits, just like those they wore onstage during the 1960s, without any backup musicians, pounding out numbers like 'Sunny Girlfriend' with genuine garage rock fervor. They sounded absolutely like the raw band of 30 years before – and were even road managed by old hand Ward Sylvester. However, by the end of March, Michael had grown weary of working with his bandmates and begged off any future projects with them.

An ABC network television special, *Hey Hey We're The Monkees*, directed by Michael before the split, had its moments of charm, but the magic of their original series was not in evidence.

Since this reunion, Micky, Davy, and Peter have toured, split, and toured again. Despite their differences, these three Monkees have learned to never say never. Although Michael remains the creative missing-link in their group, The Monkees are truly a band of brothers bound together forever on celluloid and magnetic tape.

Micky: "We have an incredible chemistry between the four of us. We always did and we always will. That's what Bob and Bert hired us for: they detected that. That's what the screen tests were all about. So when we get together in a room it's pretty exciting – but it needs an enormous amount of editing and control and direction and containing. It's a bit like a fission reaction, The Monkees. Put the four of us together in a room and things start exploding. If you're lucky, you contain it and you can generate a lot of heat. But if you don't, it very quickly goes critical mass and starts burning a hole through the center of the floor. That's what it was always like."

musicians index

This list of the musicians who played on Monkees records is based on a review of American Federation of Musicians (musicians' union) records, RCA session sheets, original recording-session tapes, and other data.

Contrary to popular belief, The Monkees themselves *did* appear on many of their own recordings, both vocally *and* musically. However, their appearances are *not* listed here. This is a guide to non-Monkee musicians. Vocalists and backing musicians on live recordings have also been omitted from this listing.

Often musicians were paid to play on tracks but on occasion did not perform or their performance was not used in the song's final released production. In such cases where the player's absence can be determined, they are omitted from this listing.

The information here should be seen as an overview of possible appearances and should not be construed as the final word on what actually occurred during these hectic recording sessions.

Dates are rendered in U.S. style: month/date/year.

We apologize for any omissions and will gratefully accept any corrections (see back of book for contact details).

Willie Ackerman drums
Some Of Shelly's Blues/Hollywood version 1 [5/29/68];
Keith Allison guitar
No Time version 1/Blues/Banjo Jam [3/17/67]; Through The Looking Glass version 2/Nashville [12/30/67]; Circle Sky/Auntie's Municipal Court [1/6/68]; Zor And Zam [1/7/68]; Auntie's Municipal Court/While I Cry version 2 [1/15/68]; Auntie's Municipal Court/Daddy's Song [1/16/68]; "No Title" version 1/War Games version 1 [1/23/68]; Nine Times Blue version 2 [2/2/68]; St. Matthew version 2/Nine Times Blue version 3 [2/8/68]; "Untitled" [2/9/68]; D.W. Washburn [2/17/68]; "Untitled?" [2/18/68]; Shake 'Em Up And Let 'Em Roll/Don't

Say Nothin' Bad (About My Baby) [2/24/68];
Chester Anderson instrument unknown
Can You Dig It [2/3/68]
Michael Anthony instrument unknown
I Never Thought It Peculiar [9/12/69]
Victor Arno violin
Theme For A New Love/My Dad/Face Up To It [7/26/65]; P.O. Box 9847 [2/10/68]
Leonard Atkins violin
Hard To Believe/A Man Without A Dream version 2 [9/15/67]
John Audino trumpet
Wichita Train Whistle Sings sessions [11/18-19/67]
Maggie Aue cello
Mr. Webster version 1 [9/24/66]
Harold Ayres violin
I Never Thought It Peculiar [9/12/69]
Israel Baker violin
Until It's Time For You To Go version 1/Thirteen's Not Our Lucky Number version 1 [10/15/65]; *Wichita Train Whistle Sings* sessions [11/18-19/67]; Medley: The Girl I Left Behind Me version 2/Girl Named Love [11/21/67]; Today [5/12/69]
Earl Ball piano
Mama Nantucket [2/20/70]; The Crippled Lion version 2/Rose City Chimes [2/21/70]; Smoke, Smoke, Smoke [2/22/70]; First National Rag/Beyond The Blue Horizon [2/23/70]; Bye, Bye, Bye version 1/Dedicated Friend version 1/Thanx For The Ride version 1 [4/9/70]
Seymour Barab cello
The Day We Fall In Love [11/23/66]
Robert Barene violin
Wichita Train Whistle Sings sessions [11/18-19/67]; Medley: The Girl I Left Behind Me version 2/Girl Named Love [11/21/67]
Mike Barone trombone
California Here It Comes [12/17/68]
Paul Beaver Moog synthesizer
Star Collector [10/4/67]; If You Have The Time/Time And Time Again [11/11/69]
Arnold Belnick violin
Theme For A New Love/My Dad/Face Up To It [7/26/65]; Until It's Time For You To Go version 1/Thirteen's Not Our Lucky Number version 1 [10/15/65]; Hard To Believe/A Man Without A Dream version 2 [9/15/67]; *Wichita Train Whistle Sings* sessions [11/18-19/67]; My Share Of The Sidewalk version 2 [1/22/69]

Gregory Bemko cello
Porpoise Song [2/28/68]
Max Bennett bass (electric and acoustic)
Magnolia Simms [12/2/67]; War Games version 2/Changes/Dream World/The Girl I Left Behind Me version 3/We Were Made For Each Other version 2/It's Nice To Be With You [2/6/68]; Impack [2/17/68]; Zor And Zam [2/17/68]; Porpoise Song [2/28/68]; Wasn't Born To Follow/I'll Be Back Up On My Feet version 3/The Shadow Of A Man/A Man Without A Dream version 3/If I Ever Get To Saginaw Again/All The Grey Haired Men [3/9/68]; Just A Game version 2/Shorty Blackwell [4/9/68]; My Share Of The Sidewalk version 2 [1/22/69]; Oklahoma Backroom Dancer [5/27/69]; Little Red Rider version 1 [5/28/69]; Good Afternoon/Down The Highway [6/5/69]; A Bus That Never Comes/London Bridge [6/6/69]; Till Then/Angel Band [6/9/69]; Little Tommy Blue/Michigan Blackhawk [6/10/69]; French Song/How Can I Tell You [6/27/69]; If I Knew [7/1/69]
Norman Benno oboe
Mr. Webster version 1/Hold On Girl version 1 [9/10/66]
Chuck Berghofer bass
Wichita Train Whistle Sings sessions [11/18-19/67]
Milt Bernhart trombone
Wichita Train Whistle Sings sessions [11/18-19/67]; Impack [2/17/68]; Zor And Zam/The Party/The Poster/I'm Gonna Try [2/17/68]
George Berres violin
Just A Game version 2/Shorty Blackwell [4/9/68]
Maurice Bialkin cello
The Girl I Left Behind Me version 1 [11/23/66]
Hal Blaine drums, percussion
I'll Be Here/The Girl From Chelsea/Show Me Girl [9/25/65]; Take A Giant Step version 1/Let's Dance On version 1 [6/10/66]; All The King's Horses/I Don't Think You Know Me version 1/The Kind Of Girl I Could Love [6/25/66]; Gonna Buy Me A Dog version 1/So Goes Love/Papa Gene's Blues [7/7/66]; I Won't Be The Same Without Her/Sweet Young Thing/You Just May Be The One version 1 [7/18/66]; Mary, Mary/Of You/Do Not Ask For Love version 1 [7/25/66]; Laugh/I'll Be Back Up On My Feet version 1/The Day We Fall In Love [10/28/66]; *Wichita Train Whistle Sings* sessions [11/18-19/67]; The Poster/The Party/I'm Gonna Try [2/15/68]; Impack [2/17/68]; Zor And Zam [2/17/68]; Look Down version 2 [4/6/68]; You And

I/That's What It's Like Loving You/Smile [5/10/68]; A Man Without A Dream version 4/Someday Man [11/7/68]; I Go Ape/Wind Up Man/String For My Kite version 1 [11/11/68]; Naked Persimmon/Do Not Ask For Love version 4 [11/12/68]; Goldie Locks Sometime/String For My Kite version 2/Darwin [11/18/68]; A Man Without A Dream version 4/Someday Man [1/10/69]; Little Red Rider version 1/Thirteen's Not Our Lucky Number version 2 [5/28/69]; Thank You My Friend/Calico Girlfriend version 1 [5/29/69]; My Storybook Of You [5/30/69]; Never Tell A Woman Yes/Omega/Thirteen's Not Our Lucky Number version 2 [6/2/69]; Good Afternoon/Down The Highway [6/5/69]; A Bus That Never Comes/London Bridge [6/6/69]; Till Then/Angel Band [6/9/69]; Little Tommy Blue/Michigan Blackhawk [6/10/69]; French Song/How Can I Tell You [6/27/69]; If I Knew/French Song [7/1/69]; Bye Bye Baby Bye Bye/Midnight Train [7/16/69]
Lou Blackburn trombone
Goin' Down [9/15/67]; *Wichita Train Whistle Sings* sessions [11/18-19/67]; D.W. Washburn/Rose Marie [3/1/68]; I'll Be Back Up On My Feet version 3/It's Nice To Be With You/Rose Marie [3/14/68]
Ken Bloom guitar
Dear Marm [2/16/68]; Porpoise Song [2/26/68]; Look Down version 1 [3/15/68]; Carlisle Wheeling version 4 [5/3/68]; As We Go Along [8/1/68]
Tommy Boyce guitar
Whatever's Right/Tomorrow's Gonna Be Another Day [7/26/66]; Through The Looking Glass [9/10/66]; Looking For The Good Times/I'll Spend My Life With You version 1 [10/26/66]; Don't Listen To Linda version 1/I Never Thought It Peculiar [10/28/66]; Nashville [12/30/67]; Don't Listen To Linda version 2 [12/31/67]
Harold Bradley guitar
The Crippled Lion version 1/Don't Wait For Me [5/29/68]; How Insensitive/Hollywood version 2 [5/31/68]; Good Clean Fun/Listen To The Band version 1 [6/1/68]; St. Matthew version 3 [6/2/68]
David Briggs keyboard
Propinquity (I've Just Begin To Care) version 1 [5/28/68]; The Crippled Lion version 1/Don't Wait For Me [5/29/68]; How Insensitive/Hollywood version 2 [5/31/68]; Good Clean Fun/Listen To The Band version 1 [6/1/68]; St. Matthew version 3 [6/2/68]

And Zam [1/13/68]; D.W. Washburn [2/17/68]; "Untitled?" [2/18/68]; Rose Marie [2/19/68]; Shake 'Em Up And Let 'Em Roll/Don't Say Nothin' Bad (About My Baby) [2/24/68]; Carlisle Wheeling version 3/Nine Times Blue version 4 [4/5/68]; Music Bridge [7/1/69]

David Duke French horn
War Games version 2/Dream World/Changes [2/8/68]; The Girl I Left Behind Me version 3/We Were Made For Each Other version 2/It's Nice To Be With You [2/9/68]; Just A Game version 2/Shorty Blackwell [4/9/68]

Bobby Dyson bass
The Crippled Lion version 1/Don't Wait For Me/Some Of Shelly's Blues/Hollywood version 1 [5/29/68]

Bob Edmondson trombone
Someday Man/A Man Without A Dream version 4 [1/11/68]

Jesse Ehrlich cello
Until It's Time For You To Go version 1/Thirteen's Not Our Lucky Number version 1 [10/15/65]; *Wichita Train Whistle Sings* sessions [11/18-19/67]; Today [5/12/69]; My Storybook Of You [5/31/69]

Wayne Erwin guitar
(Theme From) The Monkees version 1/Let's Dance On version 2/This Just Doesn't Seem To Be My Day [7/5/66]; Take A Giant Step version 2/I'll Be True To You/Saturday's Child [7/9/66]; I Wanna Be Free version 1/I Wanna Be Free version 2/I Wanna Be Free version 3 [7/19/66]; Jokes/Tomorrow's Gonna Be Another Day/Gonna Buy Me A Dog version 2 [7/23/66]; Last Train To Clarksville/I Can't Get Her Off Of My Mind version 1 [7/25/66]; (I'm Not Your) Steppin' Stone/Whatever's Right [7/26/66]; Valleri version 1/(Theme From) The Monkees version 2 [8/6/66]; Words version 1/She [8/15/66]; Ladies Aid Society/Kicking Stones [8/23/66]; Mr. Webster version 1/Hold On Girl version 1/Through The Looking Glass [9/10/66]; Tear Drop City/Looking For The Good Times/I'll Spend My Life With You version 1 [10/26/66]; Apples, Peaches, Bananas And Pears/Don't Listen To Linda version 1/I Never Thought It Peculiar [10/28/66]; Through The Looking Glass version 2/Nashville [12/30/67]

Alan Estes percussion (various including tympani & mallets)
Mr. Webster version 1/Hold On Girl version 1/Through The Looking Glass [9/10/66]; A Bus That Never Comes/London Bridge [6/6/69]

Gene Estes percussion (various including mallets)
Until It's Time For You To Go version 1/Thirteen's Not Our Lucky Number version 1 [10/15/65]; (Theme From) The Monkees version 1/Let's Dance On version 2/This Just Doesn't Seem To Be My Day [7/5/66]; Take A Giant Step version 2/I'll Be True To You/Saturday's Child [7/9/66]; I Wanna Be Free version 2/I Wanna Be Free version 3 [7/19/66]; Last Train To Clarksville/I Can't Get Her Off Of My Mind version 1 [7/25/66]; Valleri version 1/(Theme From) The Monkees version 2 [8/6/66]; Tear Drop City/Looking For The Good Times/I'll Spend My Life With You version 1 [10/26/66]; Apples, Peaches, Bananas And Pears/Don't Listen To Linda version 1/I Never Thought It Peculiar [10/28/66]; The Poster/The Party/I'm Gonna Try [2/15/68]; Goldie Locks Sometime/String For My Kite version 2 [11/18/68]

John Ethridge bass
Nine Times Blue version 2 [2/2/68]; St. Matthew version 2/Nine Times Blue version 3 [2/8/68]; "Untitled" [2/9/68]

Virgil Evans trumpet
Goin' Down [9/15/67]

Gilbert Falco trombone
Ladies Aid Society/Kicking Stones [8/23/66]

Victor Feldman percussion (including mallets)
Wichita Train Whistle Sings sessions [11/18-19/67]; Shorty Blackwell [4/30/68]

Marie Fera cello
War Games version 2/Dream World/Changes [2/8/68]; The Girl I Left Behind Me version 3/We Were Made For Each Other version 2/It's Nice To Be With You [2/9/68]

David Filerman cello
Porpoise Song [2/28/68]

Chuck Findley trumpet
I Never Thought It Peculiar [9/12/69]; Hello Lady [7/29/70]

Elliott Fisher violin
Theme For A New Love/My Dad/Face Up To It [7/26/65]; Medley: The Girl I Left Behind Me version 2/Girl Named Love [11/21/67]

Stan Free keyboard, percussion
99 Pounds/Love To Love/She Hangs Out version 1/A Little Bit Me, A Little Bit You [1/21/67]; I Wanna Be Your Puppy Dog/Love Is On The Way/I Didn't Know You Had It In You Sally, You're A Real Ball Of Fire/Sugar Man [1/22/67]; Poor Little Me/If I Learned To Play The Violin/Black And Blue/Eve Of My Sorrow/The Love You Got Inside [1/26/67]; I Wanna Be Your Puppy Dog/Love Is On The Way/Sugar Man [1/27/67]

Sam Freed violin
Seasons [2/2/68]; War Games version 2/Dream World/Changes [2/8/68]; The Girl I Left Behind Me version 3/We Were Made For Each Other version 2/It's Nice To Be With You [2/9/68]

Al Gafa guitar
The Girl I Left Behind Me version 1/When Love Comes Knockin' (At Your Door) [11/23/66]

John Gallie piano
My Storybook Of You [5/31/69]

Gene Garf organ
A Little You/Baby It's Me/This Bouquet/What Are We Going To Do? [6/15/64]; Theme For A New Love/My Dad/Face Up To It/Maybe It's Because I'm A Londoner/Put Me Amongst The Girls/Any Old Iron/It Ain't Me Babe [7/26/65]

Lowell George guitar
Dear Marm [4/2/68]

Jimmy Getzoff violin
Theme For A New Love/My Dad/Face Up To It [7/26/65]; Until It's Time For You To Go version 1/Thirteen's Not Our Lucky Number version 1 [10/15/65]; *Wichita Train Whistle Sings* sessions [11/18-19/67]; I Never Thought It Peculiar [9/12/69]

Bobby Gibbons guitar
A Little You/Baby It's Me/This Bouquet/What Are We Going To Do? [6/15/64]

Michael Glass instrument unknown
Can You Dig It [1/28/68]; Can You Dig It [1/29/68]

Philip Goldberg viola
P.O. Box 9847 [2/10/68]

Jack Gootkin violin
My Share Of The Sidewalk version 2/All The Grey Haired Men/If I Ever Get To Saginaw Again [1/31/69]

Jim Gordon drums, percussion
All The King's Horses/I Don't Think You Know Me version 1/The Kind Of Girl I Could Love [6/25/66]; Gonna Buy Me A Dog version 1/So Goes Love/Papa Gene's Blues [7/7/66]; Mary, Mary/Of You/Do Not Ask For Love [7/25/66]; D.W. Washburn [2/17/68]; "Untitled?" [2/18/68]; Rose Marie [2/19/68]; Just A Game version 2/Shorty Blackwell [4/9/68]; Today/Steam Engine [5/12/69]

Justin Gordon woodwind
Wichita Train Whistle Sings sessions [11/18-19/67]

Al Gorgoni guitar
You Can't Tie A Mustang Down/99 Pounds/Love To Love/She Hangs Out version 1/Gotta Give It Time/A Little Bit Me, A Little Bit You [1/21/67]; I Wanna Be Your Puppy Dog/Love Is On The Way/Sugar Man [1/22/67]; I Wanna Be Your Puppy Dog/Love Is On The Way/Sugar Man [1/27/67]

Lloyd Green steel
Propinquity (I've Just Begin To Care) version 1 [5/28/68]; The Crippled Lion version 1/Don't Wait For Me/Some Of Shelly's Blues/Hollywood version 1 [5/29/68]; How Insensitive/Hollywood version 2 [5/31/68]; St. Matthew version 3 [6/2/68]

Bill Green woodwind
Today/Steam Engine [5/12/69]

Joseph Grimaldi saxophone
I Didn't Know You Had It In You Sally, You're A Real Ball Of Fire [1/22/67]

John S. Gross bass
Medley: The Girl I Left Behind Me version 2/Girl Named Love [11/21/67]; Circle Sky [12/9/67]

John Guerin drums
My Share Of The Sidewalk version 2 [1/22/69]; If You Have The Time/Time And Time Again [8/6/69]

Louis Haber violin
The Day We Fall In Love [11/23/66]

Bob Hardaway reeds
Today/Steam Engine [5/12/69]

Glen D. Hardin keyboard
Bye, Bye, Bye version 2/Dedicated Friend version 2 [4/9/70]; Thanx For The Ride version 2 [4/15/70]; Bye, Bye, Bye version 2 [5/1/70]; Tengo Amore/Thanx For The Ride version 2/I Fall To Pieces version 2/Bye, Bye, Bye version 2 [5/26/70]; Tengo Amore/Thanx For The Ride version 2/Bye, Bye, Bye version 2 [5/28/70]; Bye, Bye, Bye version 2/Nadine (Is It You)?/Whole Lotta Shakin' Goin' On/Different Drum [7/14/70]; Hello Lady/Dedicated Friend version 2 [7/18/70]

Herbie Harper trombone
D.W. Washburn/Rose Marie [3/1/68]

Bobby Hart keyboard, autoharp
Gonna Buy Me A Dog version 2 [7/23/66]; I Can't Get Her Off Of My Mind version 1 [7/25/66];(I'm Not Your) Steppin' Stone/Whatever's Right [7/26/66]; She [8/15/66]; Ladies Aid Society/Kicking Stones [8/23/66]; Looking For The Good Times [10/26/66]; P.O. Box 9847/Me Without You [12/26/67]; Through The Looking Glass version 2/Nashville [12/30/67]

Jim Helms guitar
Gonna Buy Me A Dog version 1/So Goes Love/Papa Gene's Blues [7/7/66]

Al Hendrickson guitar
New Girl In School/I Love You Really (Versions One – Two) [8/22/66]; War Games version 2/Changes/Dream World/The Girl I Left Behind Me version 3/We Were Made For Each Other version 2/It's Nice To Be With You [2/6/68]; Impack [2/17/68]

Bill Hinshaw French Horn
Wichita Train Whistle Sings sessions [11/18-19/67]; Porpoise Song [2/26/68]; Porpoise Song [2/28/68]; Carlisle Wheeling version 4 [5/6/68]; Someday Man/A Man Without A Dream version 4 [1/11/68]

Jan Hlinka viola
Today [5/12/69]

Whitey Hoggan upright bass
Porpoise Song [2/28/68]

Eddie Hoh drums, percussion
Pleasant Valley Sunday [6/10/67]; Pleasant Valley Sunday [6/11/67]; Pleasant Valley Sunday [6/13/67]; Words version 2/Daydream Believer/Salesman [6/14/67]; Daily Nightly/Love Is Only Sleeping [6/19/67]; What Am I Doing Hangin' 'Round?/Don't Call On Me [6/20/67]; She Hangs Out version 2/Goin' Down [6/21/67]; Yours Until Tomorrow/The Door Into Summer version 2/"I've Got Rhythm"/"Sixty-nine"/Star Collector [6/22/67]; Daydream Believer [8/9/67]; We Were Made For Each Other (Demo) [10/23/67]; I'm A Man/We Were Made For Each Other version 1/Carlisle Wheeling version 1 [11/4/67]; The Girl I Left Behind Me version 2 [11/4/67]; Tapioca Tundra version 1 [11/11/67]; St. Matthew version 1 [12/2/67]; Writing Wrongs [12/3/67]; Circle Sky [12/9/67]; Circle Sky [12/17/67]; Circle Sky/Auntie's Municipal Court [1/6/68]; Zor And Zam [1/7/68]; My Share Of The Sidewalk version 1 [1/9/68]; Daddy's Song/Good Times/The Story Of Rock And Roll version 4 [1/10/68]; Mr. Richland's Favorite Song [1/11/68]; War Games version 1 [1/23/68]; Tears Of Joy (Demo) [1/24/68]; Nine Times Blue version 2 [2/2/68]; St. Matthew version 2/Nine Times Blue version 3 [2/8/68]; "Untitled" [2/9/68]; Shake 'Em Up And Let 'Em Roll/Don't Say Nothin' Bad (About My Baby) [2/24/68]; Can You Dig It [3/8/68]; Today/Steam Engine [5/12/69]; Oklahoma Backroom Dancer [5/27/69]

Milt Holland percussion, mallets
I'm A Man/We Were Made For Each Other version 1 [11/4/67]; Medley: The Girl I Left Behind Me version 2/Girl Named Love [11/21/67]; Changes/Dream World/The Girl I Left Behind Me version 3/We Were Made For Each Other version 2/It's Nice To Be With You [2/6/68]; Impack [2/17/68]; Zor And Zam [2/17/68]; Wasn't Born To Follow/I'll Be Back Up On My Feet version 3/The Shadow Of A Man/A Man Without A Dream version 3/If I Ever Get To Saginaw Again/All The Grey Haired Men [3/9/68]

Bill Hood saxophone
Goin' Down [9/15/67]; D.W. Washburn/Rose Marie [3/1/68]; I'll Be Back Up On My Feet version 3/It's Nice To Be With You/Rose Marie [3/14/68]

Jim Horn baritone saxophone, woodwind
Hard To Believe/A Man Without A Dream version 2 [9/15/67]; *Wichita Train Whistle Sings* sessions [11/18-19/67]; Magnolia Simms [12/2/67]; Valleri version 2 [12/28/67]; Impack [2/17/68]; Look Down version 2 [4/6/68]

Joe Howard trombone
Wichita Train Whistle Sings sessions [11/18-19/67]

Steve Huffsteter trumpet
Ladies Aid Society/Kicking Stones [8/23/66]

Jim Hughart upright bass
Porpoise Song [2/28/68]; My Share Of The Sidewalk version 2 [1/22/69]

Harry Hyams viola
Wichita Train Whistle Sings sessions [11/18-19/67]; Today [5/12/69]

Dick Hyde trombone
Ladies Aid Society/Kicking Stones [8/23/66]; *Wichita Train Whistle Sings* sessions [11/18-19/67]; I Never Thought It Peculiar [9/12/69]; Hello Lady [7/29/70]

William Hymanson viola
I Never Thought It Peculiar [9/12/69]

Jules Jacob woodwind
Wichita Train Whistle Sings sessions [11/18-19/67]; Impack [2/17/68]; Porpoise Song [2/26/68]; Porpoise Song [2/28/68]

Norm Jeffries percussion
Words version 1/She [8/15/66]

Max Johnson trumpet
Little Red Rider version 1 [6/17/69]; You're So Good/"Lynn Harper" [6/26/69]

Plas Johnson saxophone
Goin' Down [9/15/67]

Bob Jung brass, strings
Ladies Aid Society/Kicking Stones [8/23/66]; My Share Of The Sidewalk version 2/All The Grey Haired Men/If I Ever Get To Saginaw Again [1/31/69]

Del Kacher guitar
My Share Of The Sidewalk version 2/All The Grey Haired Men/If I Ever Get To Saginaw Again [1/31/69]

Leo Kahn violin
The Girl I Left Behind Me version 1 [11/23/66]

Anatol Kaminsky violin
Just A Game version 2/Shorty Blackwell [4/9/68]

Artie Kaplan soprano saxophone
I Didn't Know You Had It In You Sally, You're A Real Ball Of Fire [1/22/67]

Armand Kaproff cello
Just A Game version 2/Shorty Blackwell [4/9/68]

Nathan Kaproff violin
Daydream Believer [8/9/67]; Hard To Believe/A Man Without A Dream version 2 [9/15/67]; Seasons [2/2/68]; War Games version 2/Dream World/Changes [2/8/68]; The Girl I Left Behind Me version 3/We Were Made For Each Other version 2/It's Nice To Be With You [2/9/68]; Zor And Zam/The Party/The Poster/I'm Gonna Try [2/17/68]

George Kast violin
Daydream Believer [8/9/67]; War Games version 2/Dream World/Changes [2/8/68]; The Girl I Left Behind Me version 3/We Were Made For Each Other version 2/It's Nice To Be With You [2/9/68]; Zor And Zam/The Party/The Poster/I'm Gonna Try [2/17/68]

Pearl Kaufman harpsichord
Seasons [2/2/68]

Carol Kaye guitar, bass
Theme For A New Love/My Dad/Face Up To It/Maybe It's Because I'm A Londoner/Put Me Amongst The Girls/Any Old Iron/It Ain't Me Babe [7/26/65]; New Girl In School/I Love You Really (Versions One – Two) [8/22/66]; Laugh/I'll Be Back Up On My Feet version 1/The Day We Fall In Love [10/28/66]; "Lynn Harper" [5/29/69]

Jan Kelley cello
Porpoise Song [2/28/68]

Ray Kelley cello

P.O. Box 9847 [2/10/68]; Carlisle Wheeling version 4 [5/6/68]

Jackie Kelso flute
Goldie Locks Sometime [11/18/68]

Myra Kestenbaum viola
I Wanna Be Free version 1/I Wanna Be Free version 2 [7/19/66]

Carole King guitar
As We Go Along [5/30/68]

John Kitzmiller tuba
Wichita Train Whistle Sings sessions [11/18-19/67]; Listen To The Band version 1/Mommy And Daddy [12/9/68]

Manny Klein trumpet
Wichita Train Whistle Sings sessions [11/18-19/67]

Larry Knechtel keyboard, bass
I'll Be Here/The Girl From Chelsea/Show Me Girl [9/25/65]; Take A Giant Step version 1/Let's Dance On version 1 [6/10/66]; All The King's Horses/I Don't Think You Know Me version 1/The Kind Of Girl I Could Love [6/25/66]; I Won't Be The Same Without Her/Sweet Young Thing/You Just May Be The One version 1 [7/18/66]; Mary, Mary/Of You/Do Not Ask For Love [7/25/66]; I'm A Man/We Were Made For Each Other version 1 [11/4/67]; *Wichita Train Whistle Sings* sessions [11/18-19/67]; Look Down version 2 [4/6/68]; You And I/That's What It's Like Loving You/Smile [5/10/68]; A Man Without A Dream version 4/Someday Man [11/7/68]; I Go Ape/Wind Up Man/String For My Kite version 1 [11/11/68]; Naked Persimmon/Do Not Ask For Love version 4 [11/12/68]; Goldie Locks Sometime/String For My Kite version 2/Darwin [11/18/68]; Today [5/12/69]; Little Red Rider version 1/Thirteen's Not Our Lucky Number version 2 [5/28/69]; My Storybook Of You [5/30/69]; Never Tell A Woman Yes/Omega [6/2/69]; Good Afternoon/Down The Highway [6/5/69]; A Bus That Never Comes/London Bridge [6/6/69]

Bobby Knight bass trombone
Hard To Believe/A Man Without A Dream version 2 [9/15/67]; Today/Steam Engine [5/12/69]

Danny 'Kootch' Kortchmar guitar
Dear Marm [2/16/68]; Porpoise Song [2/26/68]; Look Down version 1 [3/14/68]; As We Go Along [5/30/68]; As We Go Along [8/1/68]

Ray Kramer cello
Wichita Train Whistle Sings sessions [11/18-19/67]; My Share Of The Sidewalk version 1/Daddy's Song [1/19/68]

Bernard Kundell violin
Just A Game version 2/Shorty Blackwell [4/9/68]

Bill Kursach violin
Until It's Time For You To Go version 1/Thirteen's Not Our Lucky Number version 1 [10/15/65]; Today [5/12/69]; My Storybook Of You [5/31/69]

Ronnie Lang flute, other wind instruments
Just A Game version 2/Shorty Blackwell [4/9/68]

Charles Larkey bass
Carlisle Wheeling version 4 [5/3/68]

Dick Leith trombone
She Hangs Out version 2/Daydream Believer [8/9/67]; Goin' Down [9/15/67]; My Share Of The Sidewalk version 1/Daddy's Song [1/19/68]; Impack [2/17/68]; Zor And Zam/The Party/The Poster/I'm Gonna Try [2/17/68]

Neil Levang guitar
I'm A Man/We Were Made For Each Other version 1 [11/4/67]

Stan Levey percussion
Impack [2/17/68]; Zor And Zam [2/17/68]; Wasn't Born To Follow/I'll Be Back Up On My Feet version 3/The Shadow Of A Man/A Man Without A Dream version 3/If I Ever Get To Saginaw Again/All The Grey Haired Men [3/9/68]

Billy Lewis drums
(Theme From) The Monkees version 1/Let's Dance On version 2/This Just Doesn't Seem To Be My Day [7/5/66]; Take A Giant Step version 2/I'll Be True To You/Saturday's Child [7/9/66]; I Wanna Be Free version 2/I Wanna Be Free version 3 [7/19/66]; Jokes/Tomorrow's Gonna Be Another Day/Gonna Buy Me A Dog version 2 [7/23/66]; Last Train To Clarksville/I Can't Get Her Off Of My Mind version 1 [7/25/66]; (I'm Not Your) Steppin' Stone/Whatever's Right [7/26/66]; Valleri version 1/(Theme From) The Monkees version 2 [8/6/66]; Words version 1/She [8/15/66]; Ladies Aid Society/Kicking Stones [8/23/66]; Hold On Girl version 1 [9/10/66]/Through The Looking Glass [9/10/66]; Tear Drop City/Looking For The Good Times/I'll Spend My Life With You version 1 [10/26/66]; Apples, Peaches, Bananas And Pears/Don't Listen To Linda version 1/I Never Thought It Peculiar [10/28/66]; P.O. Box 9847/Valleri version 2/Me Without You [12/26/67]; Valleri version 2 [12/28/67]; Through The Looking Glass version 2/Nashville [12/30/67]; Don't Listen To Linda version 2 [12/31/67]; My Storybook Of You [5/31/69]

Cappy a.k.a. Carroll Lewis trumpet
D.W. Washburn/Rose Marie/Daddy's Song [3/1/68]

Marvin Limonick violin
War Games version 2/Dream World/Changes [2/8/68]; The Girl I Left Behind Me version 3/We Were Made For Each Other version 2/It's Nice To Be With You [2/9/68]; Zor And Zam/The Party/The Poster/I'm Gonna Try [2/17/68]

John London bass
Just A Little Love/How Can You Kiss Me [circa '65]; The Girl I Knew Somewhere version 1/All Of Your Toys [1/16/67]; The Girl I Knew Somewhere version 1/All Of Your Toys [1/23/67]; The Girl I Knew Somewhere version 2/Sunny Girlfriend [2/23/67]; Mr. Webster [2/24/67]; Where Has It All Gone version 1/Twelve-String Improvisation/Memphis Tennessee/Where Has It All Gone version 2 [3/7/67]; Calico Girlfriend version 2/The Keys To The Car/Hollywood version 3 [2/19/70]; Little Red Rider version 2/Mama Nantucket/Joanne/Nine Times Blue version 5 [2/20/70]; The Crippled Lion version 2/Rose City Chimes [2/21/70]; Smoke, Smoke, Smoke/One Rose [2/22/70]; First National Rag/Beyond The Blue Horizon [2/23/70]; Bye, Bye, Bye version 2/Dedicated Friend version 2 [4/9/70]; Thanx For The Ride version 2 [4/15/70]; Bye, Bye, Bye version 2 [5/1/70]; First National Dance [5/7/70]; Tengo Amore/Lady Of The Valley [5/13/70]; Tengo Amore/Lady Of The Valley/I Fall To Pieces version 2 [5/14/70]; Tengo Amore/Thanx For The Ride version 2/I Fall To Pieces version 2/Bye, Bye, Bye version 2 [5/26/70]; I Fall To Pieces version 2/Dedicated Friend version 2/Listen To The Band version 3 [5/27/70]; Tengo Amore/Lady Of The Valley/Bye, Bye, Bye version 2 [5/28/70]; Tengo Amore/Thanx For The Ride version 2/Bye, Bye, Bye version 2 [5/28/70]; Bye, Bye, Bye version 2/Nadine (Is It You)?/Whole Lotta Shakin' Goin' On/Different Drum [7/14/70]; I Fall To Pieces version 2/Guitar Man/Tengo Amore/Bye, Bye, Bye version 2/Thanks For The Ride version 2/Lady Of The Valley [7/15/70]; Bye, Bye, Bye version 2/Nadine (Is It You)?/Lady Of The Valley/Listen To The Band version 3/Conversations version 2 [7/16/70]; Hello Lady/Dedicated Friend version 2 [7/18/70]; Hello Lady/Bye, Bye, Bye version 2 [7/29/70]; Nevada Fighter/Tumbling Tumbleweeds [8/12/70]; Nevada Fighter/Tumbling Tumbleweeds/Propinquity (I've Just Begun To Care) version 2 [8/13/70]; Nevada Fighter/Tumbling Tumbleweeds/Propinquity (I've Just Begun To Care) version 2 [8/14/70]; Rene [8/18/70]; Rene [8/19/70]; Silver Moon [9/2/70]; Silver Moon [10/19/70]; Thirteen's Not Our Lucky Number version 3 [10/20/70]; Grand Ennui [10/21/70]; Grand Ennui/Tumbling Tumbleweeds/Bye, Bye, Bye version 2 [10/26/70]

Herb Lovelle drums
The Girl I Left Behind Me version 1/When Love Comes Knockin' (At Your Door) [11/23/66]; You Can't Tie A Mustang Down/99 Pounds/Love To Love/She Hangs Out version 1/Gotta Give It Time/A Little Bit Me, A Little Bit You [1/21/67]; Poor Little Me/If I Learned To Play The Violin/Black And Blue/Eve Of My Sorrow/The Love You Got Inside [1/26/67]

John Lowe bass saxophone, bass clarinet, woodwind
Goin' Down [9/15/67]; *Wichita Train Whistle Sings* sessions [11/18-19/67]; Impack [2/17/68]; Zor And Zam/The Party/The Poster/I'm Gonna Try [2/17/68]

Doug Lubahn bass
Dear Marm [2/16/68]; Porpoise Song [2/26/68]; Look Down version 1 [3/14/68]

Joy Lule violin
I Never Thought It Peculiar [9/12/69]

Edgar Lustgarten cello
Cuddly Toy [4/26/67]; *Wichita Train Whistle Sings* sessions [11/18-19/67]; Seasons [2/2/68]; War Games version 2/Dream World/Changes [2/8/68]; Just A Game version 2/Shorty Blackwell [4/9/68]

Jacqueline Lustgarten cello
Seasons [2/2/68]; The Girl I Left Behind Me version 3/We Were Made For Each Other version 2/It's Nice To Be With You [2/9/68]; Porpoise Song [2/28/68]; Carlisle Wheeling version 4 [5/6/68]

Joe Macho guitar
I Wanna Be Your Puppy Dog/Love Is On The Way/I Didn't Know You Had It In You Sally, You're A Real Ball Of Fire/Sugar Man [1/22/67]

Charlie Macy guitar, banjo
I Wanna Be Your Puppy Dog/Love Is On The Way/I Didn't Know You Had It In You Sally, You're A Real Ball Of Fire/Sugar Man [1/22/67]

Arthur Maebe French horn
War Games version 2/Dream World/Changes [2/8/68]

Leonard Malarsky violin
Wichita Train Whistle Sings sessions [11/18-19/67]; Today [5/12/69]

Bill Martin various including percussion, keyboard
Daydream Believer [8/9/67]; The Door Into Summer (Version Three?)/Love Is Only Sleeping [9/7/67]; We Were Made For Each Other (Demo) [10/23/67]; Today/Steam Engine [5/12/69]

Dewey Martin drums
Lady's Baby version 5 [1/24/68]; Long Title: Do I Have To Do This All Over Again version 4 [1/25/68]; Can You Dig It [1/28/68]; Can You Dig It [1/29/68]; Tear The Top Right Off My Head [2/5/68]; Tear The Top Right Off My Head [2/6/68]; Come On In version 3 [2/8/68]

Lou Mauro bass
You Can't Tie A Mustang Down/99 Pounds/Love To Love/She Hangs Out version 1/Gotta Give It Time/A Little Bit Me, A Little Bit You [1/21/67]

Lincoln Mayorga keyboard
I'll Be Here/The Girl From Chelsea/Show Me Girl [9/25/65]; Until It's Time For You To Go version 1/Thirteen's Not Our Lucky Number version 1 [10/15/65]

Tony McCashen guitar
As We Go Along [8/1/68]

Charlie McCoy harmonica
Listen To The Band version 1/Hollywood version 2/Some Of Shelly's Blues [6/2/68]

Hugh McCracken guitar
You Can't Tie A Mustang Down/99 Pounds/Love To Love/She Hangs Out version 1/Gotta Give It Time/A Little Bit Me, A Little Bit You [1/21/67]; Poor Little Me/If I Learned To Play The Violin/Black And Blue/Eve Of My Sorrow/The Love You Got Inside [1/26/67]

Lew McCreary trombone
Wichita Train Whistle Sings sessions [11/18-19/67]; Magnolia Simms [12/2/67]; Valleri version 2 [12/28/67]; My Share Of The Sidewalk version 1/Daddy's Song [1/19/68]; The Girl I Left Behind Me version 3/We Were Made For Each Other version 2/It's Nice To Be With You [2/9/68]; Impack [2/17/68]; Zor And Zam/The Party/The Poster/I'm Gonna Try [2/17/68]; I'll Be Back Up On My Feet version 3/It's Nice To Be With You/Rose Marie [3/14/68]; Look Down version 1 [3/15/68]; Look Down version 2 [4/6/68]; Someday Man/A Man Without A Dream version 4 [1/11/68]; Today/Steam Engine [5/12/69]; Hello Lady [7/29/70]

Gerry McGee guitar, harmonica
(Theme From) The Monkees version 1/Let's Dance On version 2/This Just Doesn't Seem To Be My Day [7/5/66]; Take A Giant Step version 2/I'll Be True To You/Saturday's Child [7/9/66]; I Wanna Be Free version 1/I Wanna Be Free version 2/I Wanna Be Free version 3 [7/19/66]; Jokes/Tomorrow's Gonna Be Another Day/Gonna Buy Me A Dog version 2 [7/23/66]; Last Train To Clarksville/I Can't Get Her Off Of My Mind version 1 [7/25/66]; (I'm Not Your) Steppin' Stone/Whatever's Right/Tomorrow's Gonna Be Another Day [7/26/66]; Valleri version 1/(Theme From) The Monkees version 2 [8/6/66]; Words version 1/She [8/15/66]; Ladies Aid Society/Kicking Stones [8/23/66]; Mr. Webster version 1/Hold On Girl version 1 [9/10/66]/Through The Looking Glass [9/10/66]; Tear Drop City/Looking For The Good Times/I'll Spend My Life With You version 1 [10/26/66]; Apples, Peaches, Bananas And Pears/Don't Listen To Linda version 1/I Never Thought It Peculiar [10/28/66]; No Time version 1/Blues/Banjo Jam [3/17/67]; P.O. Box 9847/Valleri version 2/Me Without You [12/26/67]; Through The Looking Glass version 2/Nashville [12/30/67]; Don't Listen To Linda version 2 [12/31/67]; Me Without You [2/3/68]; War Games version 2/Changes/Dream World/The Girl I Left Behind Me version 3/We Were Made For Each Other version 2/It's Nice To Be With You [2/6/68]; We Were Made For Each Other version 2/It's Nice To Be With You [2/7/68]; You And I/That's What It's Like Loving You/Smile [5/10/68]; "Lynn Harper" [5/29/69]

Don McGinnis horns, arranger
Ladies Aid Society/Kicking Stones [8/23/66]; Listen To The Band version 1/Mommy And Daddy [12/9/68]

Michael Melvoin keyboard
I'm A Man/We Were Made For Each Other version 1 [11/4/67]; The Girl I Left Behind Me version 3/We Were Made For Each Other version 2/It's Nice To Be With You [2/6/68]; Impack [2/17/68]; Zor And Zam [2/17/68]; Wasn't Born To Follow/I'll Be Back Up On My Feet version 3/The Shadow Of A Man/A Man Without A Dream version 3/If I Ever Get To Saginaw Again/All The Grey Haired Men [3/9/68]

Jay Migliori saxophone
Valleri version 2 [12/28/67]; Look Down version 2 [4/6/68]; My Storybook Of You/Suzzana Sometime a.k.a. "Love Bandit" [5/31/69]; I Never Thought It Peculiar [9/12/69]

Buddy Miles drums
Lady's Baby version 4/Long Title: Do I Have To Do This All Over Again version 1/Seeger's Theme version 2/"?" [1/14/68]; Can You Dig It [1/28/68]; Seeger's Theme version 4 [2/12/68]

Sid Miller bassoon
Today [5/12/69]

Ollie Mitchell trumpet
Hard To Believe/A Man Without A Dream version 2 [9/15/67]; *Wichita Train Whistle Sings* sessions [11/18-19/67]; Magnolia Simms [12/2/67]; Valleri version 2 [12/28/67]; I'll Be Back Up On My Feet version 3/It's Nice To Be With You/Rose Marie [3/14/68]; Look Down version 1 [3/15/68]; Just A Game version 2/Shorty Blackwell [4/9/68]; My Storybook Of You/Suzzana Sometime a.k.a. "Love Bandit" [5/31/69]; Hello Lady [7/29/70]

Red Mitchell bass
Medley: The Girl I Left Behind Me version 2/Girl Named Love [11/21/67]

Joe Mondragon bass
Seasons [2/2/68]

Lou Morell guitar
New Girl In School/I Love You Really (Versions One & Two) [8/22/66]

Tommy Morgan harmonica
Bye Bye Baby Bye Bye/Midnight Train [7/16/69]

Bob Morin drums
California Here It Comes [12/17/68]

Wayne Moss guitar
Propinquity (I've Just Begin To Care) version 1 [5/28/68]; Good Clean Fun/Listen To The Band version 1 [6/1/68]; St. Matthew version 3 [6/2/68]

Alex Murray violin
Daydream Believer [8/9/67]; War Games version 2/Dream World/Changes [2/8/68]; The Girl I Left Behind Me version 3/We Were Made For Each Other version 2/It's Nice To Be With You [2/9/68]; Zor And Zam/The Party/The Poster/I'm Gonna Try [2/17/68]

Dick Nash trombone
Goin' Down [9/15/67]; Listen To The Band version 1/Mommy And Daddy [12/9/68]; My Storybook Of You/Suzzana Sometime a.k.a. "Love Bandit" [5/31/69]

Ted Nash brass, wind
Cuddly Toy [4/26/67]; Just A Game version

2/Shorty Blackwell [4/9/68]
Alex Neiman viola
Wichita Train Whistle Sings sessions [11/18-19/67]
Erno Neufeld violin
Daydream Believer [8/9/67]; Seasons [2/2/68]; War Games version 2/Dream World/Changes [2/8/68]; The Girl I Left Behind Me version 3/We Were Made For Each Other version 2/It's Nice To Be With You [2/9/68]; Zor And Zam/The Party/The Poster/I'm Gonna Try [2/17/68]; Just A Game version 2/Shorty Blackwell [4/9/68]
Harvey Newmark bass
As We Go Along [5/30/68]
Michael Ney drums
Dear Marm [2/16/68]; Porpoise Song [2/26/68]; Look Down version 1 [3/14/68]
Harry Nilsson piano
The Story Of Rock And Roll version 3 [4/21/67]; The Door Into Summer (Version Three?)/Love Is Only Sleeping [9/7/67]; Daddy's Song/Good Times/The Story Of Rock And Roll version 4 [1/10/68]; Mr. Richland's Favorite Song [1/11/68]; Auntie's Municipal Court/While I Cry version 2 [1/15/68]
Jack Nimitz woodwinds
Wichita Train Whistle Sings sessions [11/18-19/67]; Magnolia Simms [12/2/67]
Dick Noel trombone
She Hangs Out version 2/Daydream Believer [8/9/67]; Medley: The Girl I Left Behind Me version 2/Girl Named Love [11/21/67]
Garry Nuttycombe viola
My Share Of The Sidewalk version 2/All The Grey Haired Men/If I Ever Get To Saginaw Again [1/31/69]; I Never Thought It Peculiar [9/12/69]
Wilbert Nuttycombe violin
Hard To Believe/A Man Without A Dream version 2 [9/15/67]; My Share Of The Sidewalk version 2 [1/22/69]
Barrett O'Hara trombone
Wichita Train Whistle Sings sessions [11/18-19/67]
Joe Osborn bass
P.O. Box 9847/Valleri version 2/Me Without You [12/26/67]; Through The Looking Glass version 2/Nashville [12/30/67]; Don't Listen To Linda version 2 [12/31/67]; "No Title" version 1/War Games version 1? [1/23/68]; You And I/That's What It's Like Loving You/Smile [5/10/68]; A Man Without A Dream version 4/Someday Man [11/7/68]; I Go Ape/Wind Up Man/String For My Kite version 1 [11/11/68]; Naked Persimmon/Do Not Ask For Love version 4 [11/12/68]; Goldie Locks Sometime/String For My Kite version 2/Darwin [11/18/68]; A Man Without A Dream version 4/Someday Man [1/10/69]; Thirteen's Not Our Lucky Number version 2 [5/28/69]; Thank You My Friend/Calico Girlfriend version 1 [5/29/69]; My Storybook Of You [5/30/69]; Never Tell A Woman Yes/Omega [6/2/69]; Bye Bye Baby Bye Bye/Midnight Train [7/16/69]; If You Have The Time/Time And Time Again [8/6/69]
Sonny Osborne banjo
Propinquity (I've Just Begin To Care) version 1 [5/28/68]; The Crippled Lion version 1/Don't Wait For Me/Some Of Shelly's Blues/Hollywood version 1 [5/29/68]
Gene Page piano
A Little You/Baby It's Me/This Bouquet/What Are We Going To Do? [6/15/64]
Earl Palmer drums, percussion
A Little You/Baby It's Me/This Bouquet/What Are We Going To Do? [6/15/64]; Theme For A New Love/My Dad/Face Up To It/Maybe It's Because I'm A Londoner/Put Me Amongst The Girls/Any Old Iron/It Ain't Me Babe [7/26/65]; *Wichita Train Whistle Sings* sessions [11/18-19/67]; Magnolia Simms [12/2/67]; Empire/"No Title" version 2 [1/25/68]; War Games version 2/Changes/Dream World/The Girl I Left Behind Me version 3/We Were Made For Each Other version 2/It's Nice To Be With You [2/6/68]; Wasn't Born To Follow/I'll Be Back Up On My Feet version 3/The Shadow Of A Man/A Man Without A Dream version 3/If I Ever Get To Saginaw Again/All The Grey Haired Men [3/9/68]; As We Go Along [5/30/68]; You're So Good [5/27/69]; "Lynn Harper" [5/29/69]; Pillow Time version 2/Little Girl [8/14/69]
Don Peake guitar, arranger (some sessions)
A Little You/Baby It's Me/This Bouquet/What Are We Going To Do? [6/15/64]; Until It's Time For You To Go version 1/Thirteen's Not Our Lucky Number version 1 [10/15/65]
Gene Pello percussion
The Girl I Knew Somewhere version 2 [2/23/67]; My Share Of The Sidewalk version 2 [1/22/69]
William Pening instrument unknown
My Storybook Of You [5/31/69]
Jack Pepper violin
P.O. Box 9847 [2/10/68]
Dick Perissi French horn
Wichita Train Whistle Sings sessions [11/18-19/67]; The Girl I Left Behind Me version 3/We Were Made For Each Other version 2/It's Nice To Be With You [2/9/68]; Just A Game version 2/Shorty Blackwell [4/9/68]; Someday Man/A Man Without A Dream version 4 [1/11/68]
Bill Peterson trumpet
Today/Steam Engine [5/12/69]
Bill Pitman guitar, possibly bass
Theme For A New Love/My Dad/Face Up To It/Maybe It's Because I'm A Londoner/Put Me Amongst The Girls/Any Old Iron/It Ain't Me Babe [7/26/65]; Gonna Buy Me A Dog version 1/So Goes Love/Papa Gene's Blues [7/7/66]; I'm A Man/We Were Made For Each Other version 1 [11/4/67]
Eddie Placidi guitars
The Ceiling In My Room [11/14/67]
Ray Pohlman bass
I'll Be Here/The Girl From Chelsea/Show Me Girl [9/25/65]; Take A Giant Step version 1/Let's Dance On version 1 [6/10/66]; Laugh/I'll Be Back Up On My Feet version 1/The Day We Fall In Love [10/28/66]; I'm A Man/We Were Made For Each Other version 1 [11/4/67]; Pillow Time version 2/Little Girl [8/14/69]
George Poole violin
My Share Of The Sidewalk version 2/All The Grey Haired Men/If I Ever Get To Saginaw Again [1/31/69]
Joe Porcaro percussion (including tympani & mallets)
Just A Game version 2/Shorty Blackwell [4/9/68]
Al Porcino trumpet
She Hangs Out version 2/Daydream Believer [8/9/67]
Seldon Powell saxophone
I Didn't Know You Had It In You Sally, You're A Real Ball Of Fire [1/22/67]
Billy Preston keyboard
Gonna Buy Me A Dog version 1/So Goes Love [7/7/66]
George Price French horn
Theme For A New Love/My Dad/Face Up To It [7/26/65]
Norbert Putnam bass
Propinquity (I've Just Begin To Care) version 1 [5/28/68]; How Insensitive/Hollywood version 2 [5/31/68]; Good Clean Fun/Listen To The Band version 1 [6/1/68]; St. Matthew version 3 [6/2/68]
Lou Raderman violin
Theme For A New Love/My Dad/Face Up To It [7/26/65]
John Raines drums, percussion
Dear Marm [2/16/68]; Porpoise Song [2/26/68]; Carlisle Wheeling version 4 [5/3/68]; As We Go Along [8/1/68]; Hello Lady/Bye, Bye, Bye version 2 [7/29/70]
Bob Rand guitar
I Wanna Be Your Puppy Dog/Love Is On The Way/Sugar Man [1/22/67]
Don Randi keyboard
Laugh/I'll Be Back Up On My Feet version 1/The Day We Fall In Love [10/28/66]; *Wichita Train Whistle Sings* sessions [11/18-19/67]; War Games version 2/Changes/Dream World [2/6/68]; The Poster/The Party/I'm Gonna Try [2/15/68]
Uan Rasey trumpet
Goin' Down [9/15/67]
Bob Ray bass
War Games version 1? [1/23/68]; Tears Of Joy (Demo) [1/24/68]
Clyde Reasinger trumpet
Impack [2/17/68]; Zor And Zam/The Party/The Poster/I'm Gonna Try [2/17/68]
Mac Rebennack a.k.a. Dr. John keyboard
Impack [2/17/68]
Kurt Reher cello
Theme For A New Love/My Dad/Face Up To It [7/26/65]; The Girl I Left Behind Me version 3/We Were Made For Each Other version 2/It's Nice To Be With You [2/9/68]
Jerome Reisler violin
Hard To Believe/A Man Without A Dream version 2 [9/15/67]; My Share Of The Sidewalk version 2 [1/22/69]; My Storybook Of You [5/31/69]
Red Rhodes steel guitar
Wichita Train Whistle Sings sessions [11/18-19/67]; Carlisle Wheeling version 3/Nine Times Blue version 4 [4/5/68]; Today/Steam Engine [5/12/69]; Steam Engine [7/8/69]; Calico Girlfriend version 2/The Keys To The Car/Hollywood version 3 [2/19/70]; Little Red Rider version 2/Mama Nantucket/Joanne/Nine Times Blue version 5 [2/20/70]; The Crippled Lion version 2/Rose City Chimes [2/21/70]; Smoke, Smoke, Smoke/One Rose [2/22/70]; First National Rag/Beyond The Blue Horizon/Born To Love You [2/23/70]; Bye, Bye, Bye version 2/Dedicated Friend version 2 [4/9/70]; Thanx For The Ride version 2 [4/15/70]; Bye, Bye, Bye version 2 [5/1/70]; First National Dance [5/7/70]; Tengo Amore/Lady Of The Valley [5/13/70]; Tengo Amore/Lady Of The Valley/I Fall To Pieces version 2 [5/14/70]; Tengo Amore/Thanx For The Ride version 2/I Fall To Pieces version 2/Bye, Bye, Bye version 2 [5/26/70]; I Fall To Pieces version 2/Dedicated Friend version 2/Listen To The Band version 3 [5/27/70]; Tengo Amore/Lady Of The Valley/Bye, Bye, Bye version 2 [5/28/70]; Tengo Amore/Thanx For The Ride version 2/Bye, Bye, Bye version 2 [5/28/70]; Bye, Bye, Bye version 2/Nadine (Is It You)?/Whole Lotta Shakin' Goin' On/Different Drum [7/14/70]; I Fall To Pieces version 2/Guitar Man/Tengo Amore/Bye, Bye, Bye version 2/Thanks For The Ride version 2/Lady Of The Valley [7/15/70]; Bye, Bye, Bye version 2/Nadine (Is It You)?/Lady Of The Valley/Listen To The Band version 3 [7/16/70]; Hello Lady/Dedicated Friend version 2 [7/18/70]; Hello Lady/Bye, Bye, Bye version 2 [7/29/70]; Nevada Fighter/Tumbling Tumbleweeds [8/12/70]; Nevada Fighter/Tumbling Tumbleweeds/Propinquity (I've Just Begun To Care) version 2 [8/13/70]; Nevada Fighter/Tumbling Tumbleweeds/Propinquity (I've Just Begun To Care) version 2 [8/14/70]; Rene [8/18/70]; Rene [8/19/70]; Silver Moon [9/2/70]; Silver Moon [10/19/70]; Thirteen's Not Our Lucky Number version 3 [10/20/70]; Grand Ennui [10/21/70]; Grand Ennui/Tumbling Tumbleweeds/Bye, Bye, Bye version 2 [10/26/70]; Texas Morning/Ain't Never Found A Good Woman/Grand Ennui [12/21/70]; I Looked Away/Some Of Shelly's Blues version 2 [12/22/70]; Only Bound/Cucurrucucú Paloma [12/23/70]
Sam Rice tuba
Wichita Train Whistle Sings sessions [11/18-19/67]
Emil Richards percussion
A Little You/Baby It's Me/This Bouquet/What Are We Going To Do? [6/15/64]; Theme For A New Love/My Dad/Face Up To It/Maybe It's Because I'm A Londoner/Put Me Amongst The Girls/Any Old Iron/It Ain't Me Babe [7/26/65]; Ladies Aid Society/Kicking Stones [8/23/66]; Shorty Blackwell [4/30/68]; French Song [7/1/69]
Lyle Ritz bass
Until It's Time For You To Go version 1/Thirteen's Not Our Lucky Number version 1 [10/15/65]; The Poster/The Party/I'm Gonna Try [2/15/68]; Today/Steam Engine [5/12/69]
George Roberts trombone
War Games version 2/Dream World/Changes [2/8/68]; Just A Game version 2/Shorty Blackwell [4/9/68]
Howard Roberts guitar
The Poster/The Party/I'm Gonna Try [2/15/68]
Lester Robertson trombone
Little Red Rider version 1 [6/17/69]; You're So Good/"Lynn Harper" [6/26/69]
Alan Robinson French Horn
I Never Thought It Peculiar [9/12/69]
Frank Rosolino trombone
Impack [2/17/68]; Zor And Zam/The Party/The Poster/I'm Gonna Try [2/17/68]
Nathan Ross violin
Just A Game version 2/Shorty Blackwell [4/9/68]
Ethmer Roten flute
Words version 1 [8/15/66]
Henry L. Roth violin
Theme For A New Love/My Dad/Face Up To It [7/26/65]
Jimmy Rowles keyboard
A Man Without A Dream version 4/Someday Man [11/7/68]; I Go Ape/Wind Up Man/String For My Kite version 1 [11/11/68]; Naked Persimmon/Do Not Ask For Love version 4 [11/12/68]; Goldie Locks Sometime/String For My Kite version 2/Darwin [11/18/68]
Michel Rubini keyboard
Take A Giant Step version 2 [7/9/66]; I Wanna Be Free version 1/I Wanna Be Free version 2/I Wanna Be Free version 3 [7/19/66]; Mr. Webster version 1/Hold On Girl version 1/Through The Looking Glass [9/10/66]; Laugh/I'll Be Back Up On My Feet version 1/The Day We Fall In Love [10/28/66]; D.W. Washburn/Rose Marie [3/1/68]; Daddy's Song [4/4/68]; Look Down version 2 [4/6/68]; Just A Game version 2/Shorty Blackwell [4/9/68]; Ditty Diego version 1/Happy Birthday [8/3/68]; Listen To The Band version 1/Mommy And Daddy [12/9/68]; My Share Of The Sidewalk version 2 [1/22/69]; Oklahoma Backroom Dancer/You're So Good [5/27/69]; Thank You My Friend/Calico Girlfriend version 1/"Lynn Harper" [5/29/69]; Never Tell A Woman Yes/Omega [6/2/69]; Till Then/Angel Band [6/9/69]; Little Tommy Blue/Michigan Blackhawk [6/10/69]; French Song/How Can I Tell You [6/27/69]; If I Knew/French Song [7/1/69]; If You Have The Time/Time And Time Again [8/6/69]; If You Have The Time/Time And Time Again [11/11/69]
Ambrose Russo violin
Zor And Zam/The Party/The Poster/I'm Gonna Try [2/17/68]
Leon Russell keyboard
Porpoise Song [2/26/68]
David Sackson viola
The Day We Fall In Love [11/23/66]
Mike Saluzzi guitar
Listen To The Band version 1/Mommy And Daddy [12/9/68]
Buddy Salzman drums
I Wanna Be Your Puppy Dog/Love Is On The Way/I Didn't Know You Had It In You Sally, You're A Real Ball Of Fire/Sugar Man [1/22/67]
Murray Sandry viola
The Day We Fall In Love [11/23/66]
Billy Sanford guitar
Some Of Shelly's Blues/Hollywood version 1 [5/29/68]; Good Clean Fun/Listen To The Band version 1 [6/1/68]
Emmet Sargeant cello
My Share Of The Sidewalk version 1/Daddy's Song [1/19/68]; Seasons [2/2/68]
Russ Savakus bass
The Girl I Left Behind Me version 1/When Love Comes Knockin' (At Your Door) [11/23/66]
Joseph Saxon cello
Until It's Time For You To Go version 1/Thirteen's Not Our Lucky Number version 1 [10/15/65]
Julius Schachter violin
The Girl I Left Behind Me version 1 [11/23/66]
Ralph Schaeffer violin
Until It's Time For You To Go version 1/Thirteen's Not Our Lucky Number version 1 [10/15/65]; *Wichita Train Whistle Sings* sessions [11/18-19/67]; Today [5/12/69]; My Storybook Of You [5/31/69]
Jerry Scheff bass
Porpoise Song [2/28/68]
Harold Schneier violin
Theme For A New Love/My Dad/Face Up To It [7/26/65]
Ralph Schuckett keyboard
Porpoise Song [2/26/68]; Look Down version 1 [3/14/68]
Tom H. Scott trumpet
Goin' Down [9/15/67]
Tom W. Scott brass, wind
Cuddly Toy [4/26/67]

Jim Seals saxophone
Don't Listen To Linda version 1 [10/28/66]
Neil Sedaka keyboard
The Girl I Left Behind Me version 1/When Love Comes Knockin' (At Your Door) [11/23/66]
Leonard Selic viola
Today [5/12/69]
Norman Serkin violin
I Never Thought It Peculiar [9/12/69]
Frederick Seykora cello
I Wanna Be Free version 1/I Wanna Be Free version 2 [7/19/66]; Shades Of Gray [3/22/67]; Shades Of Gray [3/23/67]; Medley: The Girl I Left Behind Me version 2/Girl Named Love [11/21/67]; War Games version 2/Dream World/Changes [2/8/68]; I Never Thought It Peculiar [9/12/69]
Bud Shank flute, other brass, wind
Cuddly Toy [4/26/67]; Seasons [2/2/68]; Just A Game version 2/Shorty Blackwell [4/9/68]
Sidney Sharp violin
Until It's Time For You To Go version 1/Thirteen 's Not Our Lucky Number version 1 [10/15/65]; *Wichita Train Whistle Sings* sessions [11/18-19/67]; Today [5/12/69]; My Storybook Of You [5/31/69]
Jack Sheldon trumpet
War Games version 2/Dream World/Changes [2/8/68]; The Girl I Left Behind Me version 3/We Were Made For Each Other version 2/It's Nice To Be With You [2/9/68]; Impack [2/17/68]; Zor And Zam/The Party/The Poster/I'm Gonna Try [2/17/68]
Louie Shelton guitar
(Theme From) The Monkees version 1/Let's Dance On version 2/This Just Doesn't Seem To Be My Day [7/5/66]; Take A Giant Step version 2/I'll Be True To You/Saturday's Child [7/9/66]; I Wanna Be Free version 1/I Wanna Be Free version 2/I Wanna Be Free version 3 [7/19/66]; Jokes/Tomorrow's Gonna Be Another Day/Gonna Buy Me A Dog version 2 [7/23/66]; Last Train To Clarksville/I Can't Get Her Off Of My Mind version 1 [7/25/66]; (I'm Not Your) Steppin' Stone/Whatever's Right [7/26/66]; Valleri version 1 [8/6/66]; Words version 1/She [8/15/66]; Ladies Aid Society/Kicking Stones [8/23/66]; Mr. Webster version 1/Hold On Girl version 1 [9/10/66]/Through The Looking Glass [9/10/66]; Tear Drop City/Looking For The Good Times/I'll Spend My Life With You version 1 [10/26/66]; Apples, Peaches, Bananas And Pears/Don't Listen To Linda version 1/I Never Thought It Peculiar [10/28/66]; P.O. Box 9847/Valleri version 2/Me Without You [12/26/67]; Valleri version 2 [12/28/67]; Through The Looking Glass version 2/Nashville [12/30/67]; Don't Listen To Linda version 2 [12/31/67]; You And I [9/10/68]; Goldie Locks Sometime/String For My Kite version 2/Darwin [11/18/68]; Me Without You/Don't Listen To Linda version 2/Through The Looking Glass version 2 [12/20/68]; If I Ever Get To Saginaw Again [3/6/69]; Oklahoma Backroom Dancer/You're So Good [5/27/69]; Little Red Rider version 1/Thirteen's Not Our Lucky Number version 2 [5/28/69]; Thank You My Friend/Calico Girlfriend version 1/"Lynn Harper" [5/29/69]; My Storybook Of You [5/30/69]; Good Afternoon/Down The Highway [6/5/69]; A Bus That Never Comes/London Bridge [6/6/69]; Till Then/Angel Band [6/9/69]; Little Tommy Blue/Michigan Blackhawk [6/10/69]; French Song/How Can I Tell You [6/27/69]; Bye Bye Baby Bye Bye/Midnight Train [7/16/69]; If You Have The Time/Time And Time Again [8/6/69]; Pillow Time version 2/Little Girl [8/14/69]
Kenny Shroyer trombone
Wichita Train Whistle Sings sessions [11/18-19/67]; Shorty Blackwell [4/30/68]
Paul Shure violin
Theme For A New Love/My Dad/Face Up To It [7/26/65]; I Wanna Be Free version 1/I Wanna Be Free version 2 [7/19/66]; My Share Of The Sidewalk version 2 [1/22/69]
Sanford Skinner trumpet
Today/Steam Engine [5/12/69]
Eleanor Slatkin cello
My Share Of The Sidewalk version 1/Daddy's Song [1/19/68]; The Girl I Left Behind Me version 3/We Were Made For Each Other version 2/It's Nice To Be With You [2/9/68]
Bill Sleeper drums
Just A Little Love/How Can You Kiss Me [circa '65]
Charlie Smalls piano
The Girl I Left Behind Me version 2 [10/31/67]; The Girl I Left Behind Me version 2 [11/4/67]; The Ceiling In My Room [11/14/67]; Medley: The Girl I Left Behind Me version 2/Girl Named Love [11/21/67]
Paul Smith piano
Magnolia Simms [12/2/67]
Clifford Solomon tenor saxophone
Little Red Rider version 1 [6/17/69]; You're So Good/"Lynn Harper" [6/26/69]
Irving Spice violin
The Day We Fall In Love [11/23/66]
Buddy Spicher fiddle
How Insensitive/Hollywood version 2 [5/31/68]; Good Clean Fun/Listen To The Band version 1 [6/1/68]; St. Matthew version 3 [6/2/68]
Herb Steiner steel guitar
Carlisle Wheeling version 4 [5/6/68]
Joseph Stepansky violin
Just A Game version 2/Shorty Blackwell [4/9/68]
Manny Stevens trumpet
She Hangs Out version 2/Daydream Believer [8/9/67]
Stephen Stills bass, guitar
Come On In version 1/Come On In version 2 [5/1/67]; Lady's Babyversion 3/(I Prithee) Do Not Ask For Love version 3 [12/3/67]; Lady's Baby version 4/Long Title: Do I Have To Do This All Over Again version 1/Seeger's Theme version 2/"?" [1/14/68]; Lady's Baby version 5 [1/24/68]; Long Title: Do I Have To Do This All Over Again version 4 [1/25/68]; Long Title: Do I Have To Do This All Over Again version 4 [1/26/68]; Come On In version 3 [2/68]
Louis Stone violin
The Day We Fall In Love [11/23/66]
Robert Sushel violin
Until It's Time For You To Go version 1/Thirteen's Not Our Lucky Number version 1 [10/15/65]
Paul Suter flute, keyboard
Kicking Stones [9/3/66]
Willard Suyker guitar
The Girl I Left Behind Me version 1/When Love Comes Knockin' (At Your Door) [11/23/66]
Dallas Taylor drums
Look Down version 1 [3/14/68]
Larry Taylor bass
(Theme From) The Monkees version 1/Let's Dance On version 2/This Just Doesn't Seem To Be My Day [7/5/66]; Take A Giant Step version 2/I'll Be True To You/Saturday's Child [7/9/66]; I Wanna Be Free version 3 [7/19/66]; Jokes/Tomorrow's Gonna Be Another Day/Gonna Buy Me A Dog version 2 [7/23/66]; Last Train To Clarksville/I Can't Get Her Off Of My Mind version 1 [7/25/66];(I'm Not Your) Steppin' Stone/Whatever's Right [7/26/66]; Valleri version 1/(Theme From) The Monkees version 2 [8/6/66]; Words version 1/She [8/15/66]; Ladies Aid Society/Kicking Stones [8/23/66]; Mr. Webster version 1/Hold On Girl version 1/Through The Looking Glass version 1 [9/10/66]; Tear Drop City/Looking For The Good Times/I'll Spend My Life With You version 1 [10/26/66]; Apples, Peaches, Bananas And Pears/Don't Listen To Linda version 1/I Never Thought It Peculiar [10/28/66]; The Door Into Summer version 1 [5/29/67]
Tommy Tedesco guitar
A Little You/Baby It's Me/This Bouquet/What Are We Going To Do? [6/15/64]; Theme For A New Love/My Dad/Face Up To It/Maybe It's Because I'm A Londoner/Put Me Amongst The Girls/Any Old Iron/It Ain't Me Babe [7/26/65]; *Wichita Train Whistle Sings* sessions [11/18-19/67]; Look Down version 2 [4/6/68]; Just A Game version 2/Shorty Blackwell [4/9/68]; A Man Without A Dream version 4/Someday Man [11/7/68]
Phil Teele trombone
She Hangs Out version 2/Daydream Believer [8/9/67]; Goin' Down [9/15/67]
Tony Terran trumpet
Hard To Believe/A Man Without A Dream version 2 [9/15/67]; *Wichita Train Whistle Sings* sessions [11/18-19/67]; My Share Of The Sidewalk version 1/Daddy's Song [1/19/68]; Impack [2/17/68]; Zor And Zam/The Party/The Poster/I'm Gonna Try [2/17/68]; Look Down version 2 [4/6/68]; Today/Steam Engine [5/12/69]
Darrel Terwilliger violin
Hard To Believe/A Man Without A Dream version 2 [9/15/67]
Don Thomas guitar
The Girl I Left Behind Me version 1/When Love Comes Knockin' (At Your Door) [11/23/66]; You Can't Tie A Mustang Down/99 Pounds/Love To Love/She Hangs Out version 1/Gotta Give It Time/A Little Bit Me, A Little Bit You [1/21/67]; Poor Little Me/If I Learned To Play The Violin/Black And Blue/Eve Of My Sorrow/The Love You Got Inside [1/26/67]; I Wanna Be Your Puppy Dog/Love Is On The Way/Sugar Man [1/27/67]; Sugar Man [1/28/67]
Bobby Thompson banjo
How Insensitive/Hollywood version 2 [5/31/68]; Good Clean Fun/Listen To The Band version 1 [6/1/68]; St. Matthew version 3 [6/2/68]
Russ Titelman percussion
Porpoise Song [2/29/68]
Ray Triscari trumpet
Just A Game version 2/Shorty Blackwell [4/9/68]; Listen To The Band version 1/Mommy And Daddy [12/9/68]
James Tyrell bass
Poor Little Me/If I Learned To Play The Violin/Black And Blue/Eve Of My Sorrow/The Love You Got Inside [1/26/67]
Gerald Vinci violin
My Share Of The Sidewalk version 2 [1/22/69]
Lance Wakely guitar, possibly bass)
Lady's Baby version 3 [12/17/67]; Lance's/Lady's Baby version 4/Long Title: Do I Have To Do This All Over Again version 1/Seeger's Theme version 2/"?" [1/14/68]; Long Title: Do I Have To Do This All Over Again version 2 [1/22/68]; Lady's Baby version 5 [1/24/68]; Long Title: Do I Have To Do This All Over Again version 4 [1/25/68]; Long Title: Do I Have To Do This All Over Again version 4 [1/26/68]; Long Title: Do I Have To Do This All Over Again version 4 [1/27/68]; Can You Dig It [1/28/68]; Can You Dig It [1/29/68]; Can You Dig It [1/30/68]; Can You Dig It/Merry Go Round version 4 [1/31/68]; Can You Dig It/Long Title: Do I Have To Do This All Over Again version 4 [2/1/68]; Lady's Baby version 5 [2/2/68]; Long Title: Do I Have To Do This All Over Again version 4/Can You Dig It [2/3/68]; Tear The Top Right Off My Head [2/5/68]; Tear The Top Right Off My Head [2/6/68]; Lady's Baby version 5 [2/7/68]; Come On In version 3 [2/8/68]; Tear The Top Right Off My Head [2/8/68]; Come On In version 3 [2/9/68]; Long Title: Do I Have To Do This All Over Again version 4/Seeger's Theme version 3 [2/10/68]; Come On In version 3 [2/11/68]; Seeger's Theme version 4 [2/12/68]; Come On In version 3 [2/13/68]
John Ware drums
Calico Girlfriend version 2/The Keys To The Car/Hollywood version 3 [2/19/70]; Little Red Rider version 2/Mama Nantucket/Nine Times Blue version 5 [2/20/70]; The Crippled Lion version 2/Rose City Chimes [2/21/70]; Smoke, Smoke, Smoke/One Rose [2/22/70]; First National Rag/Beyond The Blue Horizon [2/23/70]; Bye, Bye, Bye version 2/Dedicated Friend version 2 [4/9/70]; Thanx For The Ride version 2 [4/15/70]; Bye, Bye, Bye version 2 [5/1/70]; First National Dance [5/7/70]; Tengo Amore/Lady Of The Valley [5/13/70]; Tengo Amore/Lady Of The Valley/I Fall To Pieces version 2 [5/14/70]; Tengo Amore/Thanx For The Ride version 2/I Fall To Pieces version 2/Bye, Bye, Bye version 2 [5/26/70]; I Fall To Pieces version 2/Dedicated Friend version 2/Listen To The Band version 3 [5/27/70]; Tengo Amore/Lady Of The Valley/Bye, Bye, Bye version 2 [5/28/70]; Tengo Amore/Thanx For The Ride version 2/Bye, Bye, Bye version 2 [5/28/70]; Bye, Bye, Bye version 2/Nadine (Is It You)?/Whole Lotta Shakin' Goin' On/Different Drum [7/14/70]; I Fall To Pieces version 2/Guitar Man/Tengo Amore/Bye, Bye, Bye version 2/Thanks For The Ride version 2/Lady Of The Valley [7/15/70]; Bye, Bye, Bye version 2/Nadine (Is It You)?/Lady Of The Valley/Listen To The Band version 3/Conversations version 2 [7/16/70]; Hello Lady/Dedicated Friend version 2 [7/18/70]; Nevada Fighter/Tumbling Tumbleweeds [8/12/70]; Nevada Fighter/Tumbling Tumbleweeds/Propinquity (I've Just Begun To Care) version 2 [8/13/70]; Nevada Fighter/Tumbling Tumbleweeds/Propinquity (I've Just Begun To Care) version 2 [8/14/70]; Rene [8/18/70]; Rene [8/19/70]; Silver Moon [9/2/70]; Silver Moon [10/19/70]; Thirteen's Not Our Lucky Number version 3 [10/20/70]; Grand Ennui [10/21/70]; Grand Ennui/Tumbling Tumbleweeds/Bye, Bye, Bye version 2 [10/26/70]
Ken Watson percussion
Look Down version 2 [4/6/68]
Julius Wechter percussion
I'll Be Here/The Girl From Chelsea/Show Me Girl [9/25/65]; Laugh/I'll Be Back Up On My Feet version 1/The Day We Fall In Love [10/28/66]
Heimann Weinstine violin
My Share Of The Sidewalk version 2/All The Grey Haired Men/If I Ever Get To Saginaw Again [1/31/69]
Tim Weisberg flute
French Song [7/1/69]
William Weiss violin
My Share Of The Sidewalk version 2/All The Grey Haired Men/If I Ever Get To Saginaw Again [1/31/69]
Bob West bass
All The King's Horses/I Don't Think You Know Me version 1/The Kind Of Girl I Could Love [6/25/66]; I Won't Be The Same Without Her/Sweet Young Thing/You Just May Be The One version 1 [7/18/66]; Mary, Mary/Of You/Do Not Ask For Love [7/25/66]; You're So Good [5/27/69]
Clarence White guitar
Today/Steam Engine [5/12/69]
Jerry Williams percussion
Changes/Dream World/The Girl I Left Behind Me version 3/We Were Made For Each Other version 2/It's Nice To Be With You [2/6/68]
John Williams instrument unknown
You're So Good/"Lynn Harper" [6/26/69]
Stu Williamson trumpet
D.W. Washburn/Rose Marie/Daddy's Song [3/1/68]; Look Down version 1 [3/15/68]
Charles Wright guitar, organ
Empire/"No Title" version 2 [1/25/68]
Jerry Yester bass, guitar
Shades Of Gray/Masking Tape [3/16/67]; I Can't Get Her Off Of My Mind/No Time version 1/Blues/Banjo Jam [3/17/67]; Today [5/12/69]
Neil Young guitar
Carlisle Wheeling version 4 [5/3/68]; You And I/That's What It's Like Loving You/Smile [5/10/68]; As We Go Along [5/30/68]; You And I [6/19/68]; You And I [6/21/68]
Tibor Zelig violin
Wichita Train Whistle Sings sessions [11/18-19/67]
Shari Zippert violin
My Storybook Of You [5/31/69]
Jimmy Zito trumpet
Wichita Train Whistle Sings sessions [11/18-19/67]
James Zitro percussion
Nevada Fighter/Tumbling Tumbleweeds [8/12/70]; Nevada Fighter/Tumbling Tumbleweeds/Propinquity (I've Just Begun To Care) version 2 [8/13/70]; Nevada Fighter/Tumbling Tumbleweeds/Propinquity (I've Just Begun To Care) version 2 [8/14/70]; Rene [8/18/70]; Rene [8/19/70]

songography

This is a listing of the recordings made between 1963 and 1970 by and for the members of The Monkees (unless otherwise noted). The title is followed by the artist if not The Monkees, and then the composer(s) in brackets. The entries feature the most complete personnel listing ever published for each recording, as well as a guide to where each song can be found released on CD. In some cases it also features information about mix variations that exist for individual songs.

'A Bus That Never Comes' (Jack Keller/Bob Russell)
Recorded June 6th 1969
Personnel Al Casey & Louie Shelton (guitars), Larry Knechtel (piano), Max Bennett (bass), Hal Blaine (drums), Alan Estes (percussion including mallets)
unissued

'Acapulco Sun' (Steve Soles/Ned Albright)
Recorded April 2nd 1970
Personnel Micky Dolenz (vocal), all others unknown
Release *Changes* Rhino CD #71798

'A Journey With Michael Blessing' by Michael Blessing (Samuel Ashe/Bob Krasnow/Russell Nields)
Recorded circa 1965
Personnel unknown
Release Colpix single #787

'A Little Bit Me, A Little Bit You' (Neil Diamond)
Recorded January 21st 1967, February 4th 1967, February 6th 1967 & February 8th 1967
Personnel David Jones (lead vocal), Neil Diamond (backing vocal), Al Gorgoni, Don Thomas & Hugh McCracken (guitars), Lou Mauro (bass), Artie Butler (organ), Stan Free (clavinet), Herb Lovelle (drums), Tom Cerone (tambourine), unknown (handclaps, additional backing vocal)
Release *Greatest Hits* Rhino CD #72190. This CD has a mono remix of the final 3-track master. Two different stereo mixes of the incomplete master for this song – missing some overdubs including handclaps – appear on Arista's *Then & Now* CD #A2CD 8432 and Flashback's *I'm A Believer And Other Hits* CD #72883.

'A Little You' by David Jones (unknown)
Recorded June 15th 1964
Personnel David Jones (vocal), Tommy Tedesco, Bobby Gibbons, Al Casey & Don Peake (guitars), Earl Palmer (drums), Red Callender (bass), Gene Page (piano), Gene Garf (organ), Emil Richards (percussion including bells)
unissued

'All Alone In The Dark' Steve Soles/Ned Albright)
Recorded March 26th 1970
Personnel Micky Dolenz (vocal), all others unknown
Release *Changes* Rhino CD#71798

'All Of Your Toys' (Bill Martin)
Recorded January 16th 1967, January 23rd 1967, January 24th 1967, January 30th 1967 & January 31st 1967
Personnel Micky Dolenz (lead & backing vocal, drums), Michael Nesmith (backing vocal, electric 12-string guitar), Peter Tork (backing vocal, harpsichord), David Jones (backing vocal, tambourine), John London (bass)
Release *Headquarters* Rhino CD #71792. This CD features the song's original mono mix from 1967. Additionally, three different remixes have appeared on other Rhino releases. Mix 1 in mono appears on *Missing Links* Rhino CD #70150. Mix 2 in mono appears on the *Listen To The Band* boxed set #70566. Mix 3 appears in true stereo on *Music Box* #76706. The *Headquarters Sessions* CD set #RHM2 7715 features the mono master as well as excerpts from the original session tape for this song and an instrumental-only mix.

'All The Grey Haired Men' (Jack Keller/Bob Russell)
Recorded March 9th 1968 & January 31st 1969
Personnel Mike Deasy, Dennis Budimir & Al Casey (guitars), Max Bennett (bass), Michael Melvoin (harpsichord), Earl Palmer (drums), Stan Levey & Milt Holland (tambourine, vibes), Del Kacher (guitar?), Bob Jung, William Weiss, Jack Gootkin, George Poole & Heimann Weinstine (violins), Garry Nutteycombe (viola), Douglas Davis (cello)
unissued

'All The King's Horses' (Michael Nesmith)
Recorded June 25th 1966 & July 16th 1966
Personnel Micky Dolenz (lead & backing vocal), Michael Nesmith (harmony & backing vocal), Peter Tork & David Jones (backing vocal), Al Casey, Glen Campbell & James Burton (guitars), Hal Blaine (drums), Gary Coleman & Jim Gordon (percussion), Larry Knechtel & Bob West (bass)
Release *Missing Links Volume 2* Rhino CD #70903. This song has appeared in four different mixes. Mix 1, as used on the TV show soundtrack, has never been officially available on CD but was included on the Rhino *Season One* DVD boxed set #976076. Mix 2 is a remix for the *Missing Links Volume 2* CD #70903. Mix 3 is a second remix for the *Listen To The Band* CD boxed set #70566. Mix 4 is a third remix available on the *Music Box* set #76706.

'A Lot Of Livin' To Do' by David Jones (Lee Adams/Charles Strouse)
Recorded circa 1963
Personnel David Jones (vocal), unknown (piano)
Release *Just For The Record* Hercules Promotions CD #Y6120E

'Alternate Title' *see* 'Randy Scouse Git'

'Alvin' (Nick Thorkelson)
Recorded January 20th 1968 & March 13th 1968
Personnel Peter Tork (vocal)
Release *The Birds, The Bees & The Monkees* Rhino CD #71794

'A Man Without A Dream' version 1 (Gerry Goffin/Carole King)
Recorded May 8th 1967
Personnel unknown
unissued

'A Man Without A Dream' demo (Gerry Goffin/Carole King)
Recorded June 22nd 1967
Personnel Peter Tork (acoustic guitar)
unissued

'A Man Without A Dream' version 2 (Gerry Goffin/Carole King)
Recorded August 14th 1967, September 15th 1967 (& possibly other dates)
Personnel Peter Tork (piano), Nathan Kaproff, Wilbert Nuttycombe, Leonard Atkins, Jerome Reisler, Arnold Belnick & Darrel Terwilliger (violins), Vincent DeRosa (French horn), Bobby Knight (bass trombone), Jim Horn (baritone saxophone), Tony Terran & Ollie Mitchell (flugelhorn)
unissued

'A Man Without A Dream' version 3 (Gerry Goffin/Carole King)
Recorded March 9th 1968
Personnel Mike Deasy, Dennis Budimir & Al Casey (guitars), Max Bennett (bass), Michael Melvoin (piano), Earl Palmer (drums), Stan Levey & Milt Holland (tambourine, vibes)
unissued

'A Man Without A Dream' version 4 (Gerry Goffin/Carole King)
Recorded November 7th 1968, January 4th 1969, January 10th 1969, January 11th 1969 & January 13rd 1969
Personnel David Jones (lead & backing vocal), Don Addrisi (& unknown others, additional backing vocal), Tommy Tedesco & Mike Deasy (acoustic guitar), Joe Osborn (bass), Larry Knechtel & Jimmy Rowles (piano), Hal Blaine (drums, tambourine), Conte Candoli & Buddy Childers (trumpet), Lew McCreary & Bob Edmondson (trombone), Vincent DeRosa, Dick Perissi, Jim Decker & Bill Hinshaw (French horn), unknown (additional guitars)
Release *Instant Replay* Rhino CD #71796

'American Airman' by Michael Nesmith & The First National Band (unknown)
Recorded April 9th 1970
Personnel unknown
unissued

'Angel Band' (William Bradbury/Reverend J. Hascall)
Recorded June 9th 1969
Personnel Michael Nesmith (lead & backing vocal), unknown (additional backing vocal), Al Casey & Louie Shelton (acoustic guitar), Michel Rubini (harmonium), Max Bennett (upright bass), Hal Blaine (drums)
Release *Missing Links Volume 3* Rhino CD #72153

'Any Old Iron' by David Jones (Sheppard/Terry)
Recorded July 26th 1965 (and possibly other dates)
Personnel David Jones (vocal), Gene Garf (piano), Red Callender (bass), Al Casey, Carol Kaye, Bill Pitman & Tommy Tedesco (guitar), Emil Richards (percussion), Earl Palmer (drums), unknown (backing vocal)
Release *David Jones* Colpix album #493 (in mono & stereo)

'Apples, Peaches, Bananas And Pears' (Tommy Boyce/Bobby Hart)
Recorded October 28th 1966, October 30th 1966, October 31st 1966 & July 24th 1969
Personnel Micky Dolenz (lead vocal), Ron Hicklin, Tommy Boyce & Bobby Hart (backing vocal), Wayne Erwin, Gerry McGee & Louie Shelton (guitars), Larry Taylor (bass), Billy Lewis (drums), Gene Estes (tambourine, other percussion)
Release *Missing Links* Rhino CD #70150

'As We Go Along' (Carole King/Toni Stern)
Recorded May 30th 1968, July 31st 1968, August 1st 1968 (& possibly other dates)
Personnel Danny 'Kootch' Kortchmar, Ry Cooder, Neil Young, Carole King, Ken Bloom & Tony McCashen (guitars), Harvey Newmark (bass), Earl Palmer (drums), Denny Bruce & John Raines (percussion?), unknown (flute, organ)
Release *Head* Rhino CD #71795. In addition to being available originally in mono on 45 and stereo on LP – the original stereo mix appears on the current CD noted – the song was remixed in stereo for Rhino's *Listen To The Band* CD boxed set #70566. A unique mono mix also appears in the film *Head*, available on Rhino DVD #R2 4460.

'Auntie's Municipal Court' (Michael Nesmith/Keith Allison)
Recorded January 6th 1968, January 15th 1968 & January 16th 1968
Personnel Micky Dolenz (lead vocal), Michael Nesmith (harmony vocal, vocal backgrounds, electric guitar & percussion), Rick Dey (bass), Keith Allison (electric guitar), Eddie Hoh (drums), Bill Chadwick (backing vocal & electric guitar), Harry Nilsson (unknown), unknown (additional vocal backgrounds)
Release *The Birds, The Bees & The Monkees* Rhino CD #71794. The CD contains the song's original stereo mix. A drastically different mono mix is featured on certain pressings – U.S., Canadian, Puerto Rican, Israeli – of the original mono vinyl release. A longer stereo remix is included on the *Listen To The Band* CD boxed set #70566.

'Baby It's Me' by David Jones (Hank Levine/Smokey Roberds/Murray Macleod)
Recorded June 15th 1964 (and possibly other dates)
Personnel David Jones (vocal), Tommy Tedesco, Bobby Gibbons, Al Casey & Don Peake (guitars), Earl Palmer (drums), Red Callender (bass), Gene Page (piano), Gene Garf (organ), Emil Richards (percussion including bells), unknown (backing vocal)
Release *David Jones* Colpix album #493 (in mono & stereo)

'Bandit Of My Dreams' by David Jones] (Anne Orlowski/Aaron Schroeder)
Recorded circa 1963
Personnel David Jones (vocal), unknown (piano)
Release *Just For The Record* Hercules Promotions CD #Y6120E

'Band 6' (Micky Dolenz/Peter Tork/Michael Nesmith/David Jones)
Recorded March 2nd 1967
Personnel Michael Nesmith (steel guitar), Peter Tork (electric guitar), Micky Dolenz (drums)
Release *Headquarters* Rhino CD#71792. The song was originally available in mono and stereo mixes, but the stereo appears on the current Rhino CD noted, while the mono resides on the *Headquarters Sessions* CD set #RHM2 7715. This track was remixed in stereo for the Arista edition of the *Headquarters* CD #ARCD 8602.

"Banjo Jam" (unknown)
Recorded March 17th 1967
Personnel Peter Tork (banjo), Michael Nesmith, Keith Allison & Gerry McGee (guitars), Micky Dolenz (drums), Jerry Yester (bass)
Release *Headquarters Sessions* Rhino CD#RHM2 7715. An unedited version can be downloaded from the Rhino Handmade website at http://www.rhinohandmade.com/rhip/7715/hearthis.mgi2

'The Bells Of Rhymney' demo (Idris Davies/Pete Seeger)
Recorded June 22nd 1967
Personnel Peter Tork (acoustic guitar, vocal)
unissued

'Be My Friend' by David Jones (unknown)
Recorded circa 1965
Personnel David Jones (vocal), all others unknown
Release *Just For The Record* Hercules Promotions CD #Y6120E

'Beyond The Blue Horizon' by Michael Nesmith & The First National Band (Richard A. Whiting/W. Franke Harling/Leo Robin)
Recorded February 23rd 1970
Personnel Michael Nesmith (vocal, acoustic guitar), John London (bass), Red Rhodes (pedal steel guitar), John Ware (drums), Earl P. Ball (piano), unknown (organ, tambourine)
Release *Magnetic South & Loose Salute* BMG/Camden CD #74321 660442

'Black And Blue' (Neil Diamond/Jerry Leiber/Mike Stoller)
Recorded January 26th 1967
Personnel Sal Ditroia, Don Thomas & Hugh McCracken (guitars), James Tyrell (bass), Artie Butler (organ), Stan Free (clavinet), Herb Lovelle (drums)
unissued

"Blues" (unknown)
Recorded March 17th 1967
Personnel Micky Dolenz (vocal, drums), Michael Nesmith (electric 12-string guitar, steel guitar), Peter Tork (piano), Jerry Yester (bass), Keith Allison & Gerry McGee (guitars)
Release *Headquarters Sessions* Rhino CD#RHM2 7715. An unedited version can be downloaded from the Rhino Handmade website at http://www.rhinohandmade.com/rhip/7715/hearthis.mgi2

'Bo Diddley' rehearsal (Ellas McDaniel)
Recorded May 17th 1968
Personnel Micky Dolenz (vocal, drums), Michael Nesmith (electric guitar), Peter Tork (bass), David Jones (maracas (organ & tambourine take 2 only))
unissued

'Born To Love You' by Michael Nesmith & The First National Band (Cindy Walker)
Recorded February 23rd 1970
Personnel unknown
unissued

'Boy Can't Win' by David Jones (unknown)
Recorded circa 1965
Personnel David Jones (vocal), all others unknown
Release *Just For The Record* Hercules Promotions CD #Y6120E

'Bye Bye Baby Bye Bye' (Micky Dolenz/Ric Klein)
Recorded July 16th 1969, July 22nd 1969 (& probably other dates)
Personnel Micky Dolenz (lead & backing vocal), David Jones (backing vocal), Louie Shelton (electric guitar), James Burton (banjo), Tommy Morgan (harmonica), Joe Osborn (bass), Hal Blaine (drums), unknown (additional backing vocal, acoustic guitar)
Release *The Monkees Present* Rhino CD #71797

'Bye, Bye, Bye' version 1 by Michael Nesmith & The First National Band (Michael Nesmith)
Recorded April 9th 1970
Personnel Earl Ball (piano), all others unknown
unissued

'Bye, Bye, Bye' version 2 by Michael Nesmith & The First National Band (Michael Nesmith)
Recorded April 9th 1970, April 15th 1970, May 1st 1970, May 26th 1970, May 28th 1970, July 13th 1970, July 14th 1970, July 15th 1970, July 16th 1970, July 29th 1970 & October 26th 1970
Personnel Michael Nesmith (vocal, electric guitar), John London (bass), Red Rhodes (pedal steel guitar), John Ware (drums), Glen D. Hardin (piano), Billy Dale (instrument unknown), unknown (percussion, organ)
Release *Magnetic South & Loose Salute* BMG/Camden CD #74321 660442

'Calico Girlfriend' version 1 (Michael Nesmith)
Recorded May 29th 1969
Personnel Michael Nesmith (vocal), Al Casey & Louie Shelton (guitars), Michel Rubini (piano), Joe Osborn (bass), Hal Blaine (drums), unknown (shaker, cowbell, bongos)
Release *The Monkees Present* Rhino CD #71797

'Calico Girlfriend' version 2 by Michael Nesmith & The First National Band (Michael Nesmith)
Recorded February 19th 1970
Personnel Michael Nesmith (vocal, acoustic guitar), John London (bass), Red Rhodes (pedal steel guitar), John Ware (drums), unknown (shaker)
Release *Magnetic South/Loose Salute* BMG/Camden CD #74321 660442

'California, Here It Comes' (Buddy DeSylva/Al Jolson/Joseph Meyer)
Recorded December 17th 1968
Personnel Peter Tork (vocal, banjo), Jack Good (additional vocal), Bob Morin (drums), Mike Barone (trombone)
Release *Season Two* DVD boxed set Rhino #970128

'Cantata And Fugue In C&W' (Michael Nesmith)
Recorded March 18th 1967
Personnel Michael Nesmith (electric six-string guitar), Peter Tork (piano), Micky Dolenz (bass), Chip Douglas (bass)
Release *Headquarters Sessions* Rhino CD #RHM2 7715 (mislabeled as "Six-String Improvisation").

'Can You Dig It' demo (Peter Tork)
Recorded June 22nd 1967
Personnel Peter Tork (acoustic guitar)
Release *Headquarters Sessions* Rhino CD #RHM2 7715

'Can You Dig It' (Peter Tork)
Recorded January 28th 1968, January 29th 1968, January 30th 1968, January 31st 1968, February 1st 1968, February 3rd 1968, March 8th 1968 & August 1st 1968
Personnel Micky Dolenz (lead vocal), Peter Tork (guitar & possibly other instrumentation), Lance Wakely (guitar & possibly other instrumentation), Dewey Martin or Buddy Miles (drums), Michael A. Glass & Chester Anderson, Eddie Hoh & Don Demieri (instruments unknown), unknown (bass, percussion including finger cymbals, tambourine, cymbals, bongos)
Release *Head* Rhino CD #71795. In addition to the original stereo mix included on this CD, two alternative mixes have surfaced. Mix 1, an early mono mix from February 1968 featuring Peter on lead vocal in place of Micky, can be heard as a bonus track on the same CD. Mix 2, also in mono, is a shorter edit of the track as featured in the film *Head*, which can now be easily found on the Rhino DVD #4460.

'Carlisle Wheeling' version 1 (Michael Nesmith)
Recorded November 4th 1967 (& possibly other dates)
Personnel Michael Nesmith (vocal, acoustic guitar, organ, percussion), Eddie Hoh (drums; & percussion?), Peter Tork (banjo)
Release *Music Box* Rhino CD #76706. This is the best sounding and most complete mix of the song. Two shorter stereo remixes appear on *Missing Links* #70150 and the *Listen To The Band* CD boxed set #70566.

'Carlisle Wheeling' version 2 by Mike Nesmith/The Wichita Train Whistle Sings (Michael Nesmith)
Recorded circa November 18 or 19th 1967
Personnel Bud Brisbois (trumpet), all others unknown
Release *The Wichita Train Whistle Sings* Dot album #DLP 25861

'Carlisle Wheeling' version 3 (Michael Nesmith)
Recorded April 5th 1968, April 11th 1968, August 21st 1968, October 29th 1968 & January 10th 1969
Personnel Michael Nesmith (vocal, guitar), Chip Douglas (bass), Red Rhodes (pedal steel guitar)
Release *Instant Replay* Rhino CD #71796

'Carlisle Wheeling' version 4 (Michael Nesmith)
Recorded May 3rd 1968
Personnel Neil Young & Ken Bloom (guitars), Charles Larkey (bass), John Raines (drums, percussion), Jacqueline Lustgarten & Ray Kelley (cellos), Herb Steiner (steel guitar), Bill Hinshaw (French horn), Denny Bruce (instrument unknown)
unissued

'The Ceiling In My Room' (David Jones/Dom DeMieri/Bobby Dick)
Recorded November 14th 1967 (and other dates)
Personnel David Jones (lead & backing vocal), Eddie Placidi & Dom DeMieri (guitars), Bobby Dick (bass), Charlie Smalls (piano), Kim Capli (drums), unknown (additional backing vocal)
Release *I'm A Believer and Other Hits* Flashback CD #72883

'Changes' (David Jones/Steve Pitts)
Recorded February 6th 1968, February 8th 1968 (& possibly other dates)
Personnel David Jones (lead vocal), Al Hendrickson, Gerry McGee & Mike Deasy (guitars), Don Randi (piano), Max Bennett (bass), Earl Palmer (drums), Milt Holland & Jerry Williams (percussion), George Kast, Erno Neufeld, Marvin Limonick, Sam Freed, Nathan Kaproff & Alex Murray (violins), Edgar Lustgarten, Frederick Seykora, Marie Fera & Jacqueline Lustgarten (cellos), David Duke, Arthur Maebe & John Cave (French horn), Buddy Childers & Jack Sheldon (trumpets), George Roberts (trombone)
Release *Missing Links Volume 2* Rhino CD #70903

'Circle Sky' (Michael Nesmith)
Recorded December 9th 1967, December 17th 1967, January 6th 1968, January 8th 1968, August 1st 1968 & March 18th 1969
Personnel Michael Nesmith (vocal, guitar, organ, percussion), John S. Gross or Rick Dey (bass), Eddie Hoh (drums, percussion), Keith Allison & Bill Chadwick (additional guitars?)
Release *Head* Rhino CD #71795. This CD features the original released stereo mix with Michael's lead vocal buried. An alternative mix with his vocal more audible can be found on *Missing Links Volume 3* CD #72153.

'Circle Sky' rehearsal (Michael Nesmith)
Recorded May 17th 1968
Personnel Michael Nesmith (electric guitar), Peter Tork (bass), David Jones (organ), Micky Dolenz (drums)
unissued

'Circle Sky' live version (Michael Nesmith)
Recorded May 17th 1968 & May 21st 1968
Personnel Michael Nesmith (vocal, electric guitar), David Jones (organ, percussion), Peter Tork (bass), Micky Dolenz (drums)
Release *Head* Rhino CD #71795

'Come On In' version 1 (Jo Mapes)
Recorded May 1st 1967
Personnel Peter Tork – electric piano & guitars; Steve Stills (bass), Micky Dolenz (drums)
unissued

'Come On In' version 2 (Jo Mapes)
Recorded May 1st 1967
Personnel Peter Tork (electric piano), Michael Nesmith (guitar), Micky Dolenz (drums), Steve Stills (bass)
unissued

'Come On In' version 3 (Jo Mapes)
Recorded February 8th 1968, February 9th 1968, February 11th 1968, February 12nd 1968 & February 13th 1968
Personnel Peter Tork (vocal, bass, tack piano), Lance Wakely (electric guitar), Stephen Stills (electric guitar), Dewey Martin (drums)
Release *Missing Links Volume 2* Rhino CD #70903

'Conversations' version 1 by Michael Nesmith & The First National Band (Michael Nesmith)
Recorded May 1st 1970
Personnel unknown
unissued

'Conversations' version 2 by Michael Nesmith & The First National Band (Michael Nesmith)
Recorded July 16th 1970
Personnel Michael Nesmith (vocal, acoustic guitar), John London (bass), John Ware (drums), unknown (keyboard)
Release *Magnetic South/Loose Salute* BMG/Camden CD #74321 660442

'Cripple Creek' (Traditional)
Recorded March 17th 1967
Personnel Peter Tork (banjo), Keith Allison & Gerry McGee (guitars), Micky Dolenz (drums), Jerry Yester (bass)
Release *Headquarters Sessions* Rhino CD#RHM2 7715

'Cripple Creek' live version 1 (Traditional)
Recorded January 21st 1967
Personnel Peter Tork (vocal, banjo)
Release *Season One* DVD boxed set Rhino #976076. This is only an excerpt of the song as featured in the TV episode *The Monkees On Tour*. The complete live version is thus far unissued.

'Cripple Creek' live version 2 (Traditional)
Recorded August 12nd 1967
Personnel Peter Tork – vocal & banjo
Release *Summer 1967: The Complete U.S. Concert Recordings* Rhino CD #RHM2 7755

'Cripple Creek' live version 3 (Traditional)
Recorded August 25th 1967
Personnel Peter Tork (vocal, banjo)
Release *Summer 1967: The Complete U.S. Concert Recordings* Rhino CD #RHM2 7755

'Cripple Creek' live version 4 (Traditional)
Recorded August 26th 1967
Personnel Peter Tork – vocal & banjo; Kim Capli (drums)
Release *Summer 1967: The Complete U.S. Concert Recordings* Rhino CD #RHM2 7755

'Cripple Creek' live version 5 (Traditional)
Recorded August 27th 1967
Personnel Peter Tork (vocal, banjo), Kim Capli (drums)
Release *Summer 1967: The Complete U.S. Concert Recordings* Rhino CD #RHM2 7755. An alternative mix of this performance appears on Rhino's *Live 1967* CD #70139.

'The Crippled Lion' version 1 (Michael Nesmith)
Recorded May 29th 1968, August 21st 1968, October 29th 1968 (& possibly other dates)
Personnel Michael Nesmith (vocal), Harold Bradley (acoustic guitar), Sonny Osborne (banjo), Lloyd Green (steel guitar), David Briggs (organ), Bobby Dyson (bass), Jerry Carrigan (drums)
Release *Missing Links Volume 2* Rhino CD #70903

'The Crippled Lion' version 2 by Michael Nesmith & The First National Band (Michael Nesmith)
Recorded February 21st 1970
Michael Nesmith (vocal, acoustic guitar), John London (bass), Red Rhodes (pedal steel guitar), John Ware (drums), Earl P. Ball (piano), unknown (percussion)
Release *Magnetic South & Loose Salute* BMG/Camden CD #74321 660442

'Crow On The Cradle' (Sydney Carter)
Recorded November 12nd 1967
Personnel Peter Tork (vocal, acoustic guitar), Karen Harvey Hammer (vocal)
unissued

'Cucurrucucú Paloma' by Michael Nesmith & The First National Band] (Thomas Mendez)
Recorded December 23rd 1970
Personnel unknown
unissued

'Cuddly Toy' (Harry Nilsson)
Recorded April 26th 1967, September 5th 1967 (& probably other dates)
Personnel David Jones (lead & backing vocal, tambourine), Micky Dolenz (harmony & backing vocal, drums), Peter Tork (backing vocal, piano, electric piano), Michael Nesmith (acoustic guitar), Chip Douglas (backing vocal, bass), Bud Shank, Tom Scott & Ted Nash (horns/winds), Edgar Lustgarten (cello)
Release *Pisces, Aquarius, Capricorn & Jones, Ltd.* Rhino CD#71793. In addition to being available originally in mono and stereo mixes – the stereo appears on the current CD noted – the track was remixed twice in stereo: remix 1 appears on the Arista edition of the *Pisces, Aquarius…* CD #ARCD 8603; remix 2 appears on the *Listen To The Band* CD boxed set #70566.

'Cuddly Toy' live version 1 (Harry Nilsson)
Recorded May 17th 1968
Personnel David Jones (lead vocal), Michael Nesmith (electric guitar), Peter Tork (bass), Micky Dolenz (harmony vocal, drums)
unissued

'Daddy's Song' (Harry Nilsson)
Recorded January 10th 1968, January 16th 1968, January 19th 1968, March 1st 1968, March 23rd 1968, April 4th 1968, April 25th 1968 & August 1st 1968
Personnel David Jones (vocal), Michael Nesmith (acoustic & electric guitar), Harry Nilsson (piano), Rick Dey (bass), Eddie Hoh (drums), Tony Terran, Pete Candoli & Buddy Childers (trumpets), Dick Leith & Lew McCreary (trombones), Stu Williamson or Cappy a.k.a. Carroll Lewis (flugelhorn solo), Ray Kramer, Eleanor Slatkin, Emmet Sargeant & Justin DiTullio (cellos), Michel Rubini (additional piano on *Music Box* version only), Keith Allison & Bill Chadwick (instruments unknown)
Release *Head* Rhino CD#71795. In addition to this stereo mix, at least three alternative mixes have been issued. Mix 1, a period mono mix from early '68 featuring Michael on lead vocal, can be heard as a bonus track on the same CD. Mix 2 is the same as the *Head* stereo mix until the final verse when it cuts to a slow, somber vocal from Davy, similar to the version heard in the actual film of *Head*, and an extended remixed fade. This can be found on the *Music Box* CD collection #76706. Mix 3, a mono mix unique to the soundtrack of *Head*, features a slow live final verse from Davy and is similar to the *Music Box* arrangement. It is available on the Rhino *Head* DVD #4460.

'Daily Nightly' (Michael Nesmith)
Recorded June 19th 1967, September 5th 1967, October 4th 1967 (& other unknown dates)
Personnel Micky Dolenz (lead vocal, Moog synthesizer), Michael Nesmith (electric guitar), Peter Tork (organ), Chip Douglas (bass), Eddie Hoh (drums)
Release *Pisces, Aquarius, Capricorn & Jones, Ltd.* Rhino CD#71793. In addition to being available originally in mono and stereo mixes – the stereo appears on the current CD noted – the song appears in an alternative mix, lacking some overdubs, as a bonus track on the same CD.

'Darwin' (Bill Dorsey)
Recorded November 18th 1968
Personnel David Jones, Micky Dolenz, Peter Tork & Michael Nesmith (vocals), Mike Deasy, Louie Shelton & Dennis Budimer (guitars), Joe Osborn (bass), Larry Knechtel & Jimmy Rowles (keyboards), Hal Blaine (drums)
Release *Season Two* DVD boxed set Rhino #970128

'Daydream Believer' (John Stewart)
Recorded June 14th 1967, August 9th 1967, September 5th 1967 (& probably other dates)
Personnel David Jones (lead & backing vocal), Micky Dolenz (backing vocal harmony), Peter Tork (piano), Michael Nesmith (electric guitar), Chip Douglas (bass, percussion, additional keyboard), Eddie Hoh (drums), Bill Martin (bell), Manny Stevens (trumpet, piccolo trumpet), Al Porcino & Pete Candoli (trumpets), Dick Noel (trombone), Phil Teele & Dick Leith (bass trombones), Nathan Kaproff, Erno Neufeld, George Kast & Alex Murray (violins), unknown (handclaps, additional percussion)
Release *The Birds, The Bees & The Monkees* Rhino CD #71794. This CD features the song's original stereo mix. The slightly longer original mono mix can be heard on Flashback's *Daydream Believer And Other Hits* CD #75242. A stereo remix of the song is featured on the Rhino *Listen To The Band* CD boxed set #70566. Also, two instrumental mixes of this song have appeared. Mix 1 is heard on the Japanese-only East-West release *The Monkees Best!!* #AMCY-978. Mix 2, without the song's spoken introduction, is included on Rhino's *The Best Of The Monkees* CD #73875. A 1980s remix with newly recorded drums falls outside the scope of this book.

'The Day We Fall In Love' (Sandy Linzer/Denny Randell)
Recorded Oct 28th 1966 & November 23rd 1966 (and possibly other dates)
Personnel David Jones (vocal), Al Casey & Carole Kaye (guitars), Ray Pohlman (bass), Hal Blaine (drums), Frank Capp & Julius Wechter (percussion), Michel Rubini & Don Randi (keyboards), Irving Spice, Louis Haber & Louis Stone (violins), Murray Sandry & David Sackson (violas), Seymour Barab (cello)
Release *More Of The Monkees* Rhino CD #71791. In addition to being available originally in mono and stereo mixes – the stereo appears on the current CD noted – a stereo remix appears on the Arista edition of the *More Of The Monkees* CD #ARCD 8525.

'Dear Marm' (unknown)
Recorded February 16th 1968 & April 2nd 1968
Personnel Danny Kortchmar, Ken Bloom & Lowell George (guitars), Doug Lubahn (bass), Michael Ney & John Raines (drums, percussion)
unissued

'Dedicated Friend' version 1 by Michael Nesmith & The First National Band (Michael Nesmith)
Recorded April 9th 1970
Personnel Earl Ball (piano), all others unknown
unissued

'Dedicated Friend' version 2 by Michael Nesmith & The First National Band (Michael Nesmith)
Recorded April 9th 1970, April 15th 1970, May 27th 1970 & July 18th 1970
Personnel Michael Nesmith (vocal, guitar), John London (bass), Red Rhodes (pedal steel guitar), John Ware (drums), Glen D. Hardin (piano), unknown (percussion)
Release *Magnetic South & Loose Salute* BMG/Camden CD #74321 660442

'Different Drum' by Michael Nesmith & The First National Band (Michael Nesmith)
Recorded July 14th 1970
Personnel unknown
unissued

'Ditty Diego' version 1 (Jack Nicholson)
Recorded July 25th 1968, July 16th 1968, August 1st 1968 & August 3rd 1968
Personnel Micky Dolenz, Michael Nesmith, David Jones & Peter Tork (spoken word), Michel Rubini (piano)
Release *Head* Rhino CD #71795. The CD also features an excerpt of the July 25th 1968 tracking session for this piece as a bonus track.

'Ditty Diego' version 2 (Jack Nicholson)
Recorded July 25th 1968
Personnel Micky Dolenz, Michael Nesmith, David Jones & Peter Tork (spoken word)
unissued

'Do It In The Name Of Love' (Bobby Bloom/Neil Goldberg)
Recorded September 22nd 1970 (& possibly other dates)
Personnel Micky Dolenz (lead & backing vocal), David Jones (lead & backing vocal), unknown (guitar, piano, keyboard, drums, tambourine, hand claps, additional backing vocal)
Release *Changes* Rhino CD#71798. A remix appears on the Rhino *Listen To The Band* CD boxed set #70566.

'The Dolphins' (Fred Neil)
Recorded November 12nd 1967
Personnel Peter Tork (vocal, acoustic guitar)
unissued

'Donna' by David Jones (Ritchie Valens)
Recorded circa 1965
Personnel David Jones (vocal), all others unknown
Release *Just For The Record* Hercules Promotions CD #Y6120E

'Do Not Ask For Love' *see* '(I Prithee) Do Not Ask For Love)'

'Don't Be Cruel' (Blackwell/Presley)
Recorded March 19th 1967
Personnel Peter Tork (piano), Micky Dolenz (drums)
Release *Headquarters Sessions* Rhino CD #RHM2 7715

'Don't Call On Me' (Michael Nesmith/John London)
Recorded June 20th 1967, July 7th 1967, September 5th 1967, October 9th 1967 (& possibly other dates)
Personnel Michael Nesmith (lead vocal, electric guitar), Peter Tork (organ), Chip Douglas (acoustic guitar, bass), Eddie Hoh (drums, claves), Bob Rafelson (piano on intro only), Micky Dolenz, David Jones, Charlie Rockett, Bill Martin & others (spoken chatter)
Release *Pisces, Aquarius, Capricorn & Jones, Ltd.* Rhino CD #71793. In addition to being available originally in mono and stereo mixes – the stereo appears on the current CD noted – a stereo remix appears on the Arista edition of the *Pisces, Aquarius…* CD #ARCD 8603.

'Don't Call On Me' version 2 by Mike Nesmith/The Wichita Train Whistle Sings (Michael Nesmith/John London)
Recorded circa November 18 or 19th 1967
Personnel Tommy Tedesco (guitar), all others unknown
Release *The Wichita Train Whistle Sings* Dot album #DLP 25861

'Don't Cry Now' by Mike Nesmith/The Wichita Train Whistle Sings (Michael Nesmith)
Recorded circa November 18 or 19th 1967
Personnel Doug Dillard (banjo), all others unknown
Release *The Wichita Train Whistle Sings* Dot album #DLP 25861

'Don't Do It' by Micky Dolenz (Micky Dolenz)
Recording date unknown
Personnel Micky Dolenz (vocal), all others unknown
Release Challenge single #59353. A cash-in 12-inch remix single of this song that appeared in 1986 falls outside the scope of this book.

'Don't Listen To Linda' version 1 (Tommy Boyce/Bobby Hart)
Recorded October 28th 1966 & November 6th 1966
Personnel David Jones (lead vocal), Ron Hicklin & Bobby Hart (backing vocals), Tommy Boyce (acoustic guitar, backing vocal), Wayne Erwin, Gerry McGee & Louie Shelton (guitars), Larry Taylor (bass), Billy Lewis (drums), Gene Estes (percussion), Jim Seals (saxophone)
Release *More Of The Monkees* Rhino CD #71791

'Don't Listen To Linda' version 2 (Tommy Boyce/Bobby Hart)
Recorded December 31st 1967, December 20th 1968, December 28th 1968 (& other dates)
Personnel David Jones (lead vocal), Louis Shelton, Gerry McGee & Tommy Boyce (guitars), Joe Osborn (bass), Billy Lewis (drums), unknown (strings, horns)
Release *Instant Replay* Rhino CD #71796

'Don't Say Nothin' Bad (About My Baby)' (Gerry Goffin/Carole King)
Recorded February 24th 1968
Personnel Micky Dolenz (vocal), Keith Allison (electric guitar), Chip Douglas (bass), Eddie Hoh (drums)
unissued

'Don't Wait For Me' (Michael Nesmith)
Recorded May 29th 1968, August 21st 1968, October 29th 1968 (& probably other dates)
Personnel Michael Nesmith (vocal), Harold Bradley (acoustic guitar), Sonny Osborne (banjo), Lloyd Green (steel guitar), David Briggs (organ), Bobby Dyson (bass), Jerry Carrigan (drums)
Release *Instant Replay* Rhino CD #71796

'The Door Into Summer' version 1 (Bill Martin/Chip Douglas)

Recorded May 29th 1967
Personnel Micky Dolenz (drums), Chip Douglas & Larry Taylor (acoustic guitars), Peter Tork (keyboard)
unissued? (It is possible that elements of this version were used in the final released version)

'The Door Into Summer' version 2 (Bill Martin/Chip Douglas)
Recorded June 22nd 1967
Personnel Chip Douglas – guitars, piano, bass & percussion; Eddie Hoh (drums)
unissued

'The Door Into Summer' version 3? – released version (Bill Martin/Chip Douglas)
Recorded August 23rd 1967, August 24th 1967, September 5th 1967, September 7th 1967, October 3rd 1967, October 4th 1967 (& probably other dates)
Personnel Michael Nesmith (lead vocal, possibly guitar), Micky Dolenz (harmony vocal, possibly drums), Peter Tork (keyboard), Chip Douglas (guitar, bass), Eddie Hoh (drums), unknown (percussion), Bill Martin & Harry Nilsson (instruments unknown)
Release *Pisces, Aquarius, Capricorn & Jones, Ltd.* Rhino CD #71793. In addition to being available originally in mono and stereo mixes – the stereo appears on the current CD noted – an alternative mono mix from October 3rd '67 featuring a different vocal track among other things is also included on that CD.

'Down The Highway' issued under the title 'Michigan Blackhawk' (Carole King/Toni Stern)
Recorded June 5th 1969
Personnel Michael Nesmith (vocal), Al Casey & Louie Shelton (guitars), Larry Knechtel (piano), Max Bennett (bass), Hal Blaine (drums)
Release *Missing Links Volume 2* Rhino CD#70903. This song was issued under the title 'Michigan Blackhawk' in error. The song 'Michigan Blackhawk' remains unissued.

'Do You Feel It Too?' (Jeff Barry/Andy Kim)
Recorded March 26th 1970
Personnel David Jones (vocal), all others unknown
Release *Changes* Rhino CD#71798

'Dream Girl' by David Jones (Van McCoy)
Recorded circa December 1964
Personnel David Jones (vocal), all others unknown
Release Colpix single #764 & *David Jones* album #493 (in mono & stereo)

'Dream World' (David Jones/Steve Pitts)
Recorded February 6th 1968, February 8th 1968, March 13rd 1968 (& possibly other dates)
Personnel David Jones (lead vocal), Al Hendrickson, Gerry McGee & Mike Deasy (guitars), Don Randi (harpsichord), Max Bennett (bass), Earl Palmer (drums), Milt Holland or Jerry Williams (tambourine), George Kast, Erno Neufeld, Marvin Limonick, Sam Freed, Nathan Kaproff & Alex Murray (violins), Edgar Lustgarten, Frederick Seykora, Marie Fera & Jacqueline Lustgarten (cellos), David Duke, Arthur Maebe & John Cave (French horns), Buddy Childers & Jack Sheldon (trumpets), George Roberts (trombone)
Release *The Birds, The Bees & The Monkees* Rhino CD #71794

'D.W. Washburn' (Jerry Leiber/Mike Stoller)
Recorded February 17th 1968, March 1st 1968, April 3rd 1968 & April 23rd 1968
Personnel Micky Dolenz (vocal), Bill Chadwick & Keith Allison (guitars), Henry Diltz (banjo), Chip Douglas (bass), Jim Gordon (drums), Michel Rubini (tack piano), Stu Williamson & Cappy a.k.a. Carroll Lewis (trumpets), Herbie Harper & Lou Blackburn (trombones), Bill Hood (saxophone), Larry Bunker (glockenspiel), unknown (additional backing vocal)
Release *Greatest Hits* Rhino CD #72190. This release features an April 1968 stereo mix. The original mono single mix can be heard on Flashback's *Daydream Believer And Other Hits* CD #75242.

'Early Morning Blues And Greens' (Jack Keller/Diane Hilderbrand)
Recorded March 22nd 1967 (and possibly other dates)
Personnel David Jones (lead vocal, maracas), Michael Nesmith (electric 12-string guitar), Peter Tork (harmony vocal, electric piano, organ), Micky Dolenz (drums), Chip Douglas (bass), unknown (additional percussion)
Release *Headquarters* Rhino CD #71792. In addition to being available originally in mono and stereo mixes – the stereo appears on the current CD noted, while the mono resides on the *Headquarters Sessions* CD set #RHM2 7715 – this track was remixed in stereo for the Arista edition of the *Headquarters* CD #ARCD 8602. Additionally, the *Headquarters Sessions* set features an instrumental mix of the song.

'East Virginia' (Traditional)
Recorded March 11st 1967
Personnel Peter Tork (vocal, banjo), Micky Dolenz (vocal)
Release *Headquarters Sessions* Rhino CD #RHM2 7715

'Empire' (Michael Nesmith)
Recorded January 25th 1968
Personnel Michael Nesmith (electric guitar), Charles Wright (electric guitar, organ), Ron Brown (bass, tambourine), Earl Palmer (drums, percussion)
unissued

'Eve Of My Sorrow' (Jeff Barry/Joey Levine/Jerry Leiber/Mike Stoller)
Recorded January 26th 1967
Personnel Sal Ditroia, Don Thomas & Hugh McCracken (guitars), James Tyrell (bass), Artie Butler (organ), Stan Free (clavinet), Herb Lovelle (drums)
unissued

'Face Up To It' by David Jones (Roger Atkins/Gerry Robinson)
Recorded July 26th 1965 (and possibly other dates)
Personnel David Jones (vocal), Elliott Fisher, James Getzoff, Victor Arno, Henry L. Roth, Paul Shure, Arnold Belnick & Lou Raderman (violins), Kurt Reher & Harold Schneier (cellos), James Decker & George Price (French horns), Gene Garf (piano), Red Callender (bass), Al Casey, Carol Kaye, Bill Pitman & Tommy Tedesco (guitars), Emil Richards (percussion), Earl Palmer (drums)
Release *David Jones* Colpix album #493 (in mono & stereo)

"Fever" (unknown)
Recorded 1967
Personnel Peter Tork (piano), Micky Dolenz (drums), David Jones (tambourine), Chip Douglas (bass)
Release *Headquarters Sessions* Rhino CD #RHM2 7715

'First National Dance' by Michael Nesmith & The First National Band (John Ware/John London/Orville Rhodes)
Recorded May 7th 1970
Personnel Michael Nesmith (vocal, electric guitar), John London (bass), Red Rhodes (pedal steel guitar), John Ware (drums), unknown (percussion)
Release *Magnetic South & Loose Salute* BMG/Camden CD #74321 660442

'First National Rag' by Michael Nesmith & The First National Band (Orville Rhodes)
Recorded February 23rd 1970
Personnel Michael Nesmith (announcement, acoustic guitar), John London (bass), Red Rhodes (pedal steel guitar), John Ware (drums), Earl P. Ball (piano)
Release *Magnetic South & Loose Salute* BMG/Camden CD #74321 660442

'Forget That Girl' (Douglas Farthing Hatlelid)
Recorded March 7th 1967, March 8th 1967, March 10th 1967 & March 11st 1967
Personnel David Jones (lead & backing vocal, maracas), Michael Nesmith (electric 12-string guitar), Peter Tork (backing vocal, electric piano), Micky Dolenz (backing vocal, drums), Chip Douglas (backing vocal, bass), unknown (acoustic guitar)
Release *Headquarters* Rhino CD #71792. In addition to being available originally in mono and stereo mixes - the stereo appears on the current CD noted, while the mono resides on the *Headquarters Sessions* CD set #RHM2 7715 – this track was remixed in stereo for the Arista edition of the *Headquarters* CD #ARCD 8602. Additionally, the *Headquarters Sessions* set features some rehearsals of the song, excerpts from a backing vocal overdub session, and an instrumental mix.

'Forget That Girl' live version 1 (Douglas Farthing Hatlelid)
Recorded August 12nd 1967
Personnel David Jones (lead vocal), Michael Nesmith (electric 12-string guitar), Peter Tork (backing vocal, organ), Micky Dolenz (drums)
Release *Summer 1967: The Complete U.S. Concert Recordings* Rhino CD #RHM2 7755

'Forget That Girl' live version 2 (Douglas Farthing Hatlelid)
Recorded August 25th 1967
Personnel David Jones (lead vocal), Michael Nesmith (electric 12-string guitar), Peter Tork (backing vocal, organ), Micky Dolenz (drums)
Release *Summer 1967: The Complete U.S. Concert Recordings* Rhino CD #RHM2 7755

'Forget That Girl' live version 3 (Douglas Farthing Hatlelid)
Recorded August 26th 1967
Personnel David Jones (lead vocal), Michael Nesmith (electric 12-string guitar), Peter Tork (keyboard), Micky Dolenz (drums)
Release *Summer 1967: The Complete U.S. Concert Recordings* Rhino CD #RHM2 7755

'Forget That Girl' live version 4 (Douglas Farthing Hatlelid)
Recorded August 27th 1967
Personnel David Jones (lead vocal), Michael Nesmith (electric 12-string guitar), Peter Tork (backing vocal, keyboard), Micky Dolenz (drums)
Release *Summer 1967: The Complete U.S. Concert Recordings* Rhino CD #RHM2 7755. An alternative mix of this performance appears on Rhino's *Live 1967* CD #70139.

'Forget That Girl' live version 5 (Douglas Farthing Hatlelid)
Recorded May 17th 1968
Personnel Michael Nesmith (electric guitar), Peter Tork (organ), Micky Dolenz (drums)
unissued

'For Pete's Sake' (Peter Tork/Joey Richards)
Recorded March 25th 1967
Personnel Micky Dolenz (lead & backing vocal, drums), Peter Tork (backing vocal, electric guitar), David Jones (backing vocal, tambourine), Michael Nesmith (electric 12-string guitar), Chip Douglas (bass)
Release *Headquarters* Rhino CD #71792. In addition to being available originally in mono and stereo mixes – the stereo appears on the current CD noted, while the mono resides on the *Headquarters Sessions* CD set #RHM2 7715 – this track was remixed in stereo for the Arista edition of the *Headquarters* CD #ARCD 8602. Additionally, the *Headquarters Sessions* set features an instrumental mix of this song.

'French Song' (Bill Chadwick)
Recorded June 27th 1969, July 1st 1969, July 9th 1969 & July 11st 1969
Personnel David Jones (vocal), Louie Shelton & Frank Bugbee (acoustic guitars), Michel Rubini (organ), Max Bennett (bass), Hal Blaine (drums), Tim Weisberg (flute), Emil Richards (vibes, chimes, shaker, other percussion)
Release *The Monkees Present* Rhino CD #71797

'Games' demo NOT THE MONKEES (David Crosby)
Recorded February 16th 1968
Personnel David Crosby (vocal, guitar)
unissued

'The Girl From Chelsea' by David Jones (Gerry Goffin/Carole King)
Recorded September 25th 1965 (and possibly other dates)
Personnel David Jones (vocal), Glen Campbell & Al Casey (guitars), Ray Pohlman & Larry Knechtel (bass), Lincoln Mayorga (piano), Hal Blaine (drums), Julius Wechter (percussion), unknown (backing vocal)
Release Colpix single #789

'The Girl I Knew Somewhere' version 1 (Michael Nesmith)
Recorded January 16th 1967, January 23rd 1967, January 24th 1967, January 30th 1967 & January 31st 1967
Personnel Michael Nesmith (lead vocal, electric 12–string guitar), Peter Tork (backing vocal, acoustic guitar, harpsichord), Micky Dolenz (backing vocal, drums), David Jones (backing vocal, tambourine) John London (bass)
Release *Headquarters* Rhino CD #71792 features an original mono mix from 1967. This version of the song has never appeared in true stereo. However, the *Headquarters Sessions* set #RHM 7715 does feature stereo excerpts from this song's recording session, as well as an instrumental-only mix.

'The Girl I Knew Somewhere' version 2 (Michael Nesmith)
Recorded February 23rd 1967
Personnel Micky Dolenz (lead & backing vocal, drums), Michael Nesmith (backing vocal, electric & acoustic 12-string guitar), Peter Tork (backing vocal, harpsichord), John London (bass, tambourine)
Release *Greatest Hits* Rhino CD #72190 features a stereo remix. Numerous variations are available of this track. The original mono single mix appears on Flashback's *I'm A Believer And Other Hits* CD #72883. An alternative mono mix from the '60s – missing the backing vocal from the instrumental break – appears on the *Headquarters Sessions* CD set #RHM 7715. The original stereo mix appears on Arista's *Then & Now* CD #A2CD 8432, while a further stereo remix with a longer ending is featured on the *Listen To The Band* CD #70566. The *Headquarters Sessions* set includes excerpts from various sessions for the song as well as an instrumental-only mix.

'The Girl I Knew Somewhere' live version 1 (Michael Nesmith)
Recorded August 12nd 1967
Personnel Micky Dolenz (lead vocal, drums), Michael Nesmith

(harmony vocal, electric 12-string guitar), Peter Tork (backing vocal, organ), Davy Jones (bass)
Release *Summer 1967: The Complete U.S. Concert Recordings* Rhino CD #RHM2 7755

'The Girl I Knew Somewhere' live version 2 (Michael Nesmith)
Recorded August 25th 1967
Personnel Micky Dolenz (lead vocal, drums), Michael Nesmith (harmony vocal, electric 12-string guitar), Peter Tork (backing vocal, organ), Davy Jones (bass)
Release *Summer 1967: The Complete U.S. Concert Recordings* Rhino CD #RHM2 7755

'The Girl I Knew Somewhere' live version 3 (Michael Nesmith)
Recorded August 26th 1967
Personnel Micky Dolenz (lead vocal, drums), Michael Nesmith (harmony vocal, electric 12-string guitar), Peter Tork (backing vocal, bass), Davy Jones (organ on ending only)
Release *Summer 1967: The Complete U.S. Concert Recordings* Rhino CD #RHM2 7755. An alternative mix of this performance appears on Rhino's *Live 1967* CD #70139.

'The Girl I Knew Somewhere' live version 4 (Michael Nesmith)
Recorded August 27th 1967
Personnel Micky Dolenz (lead vocal, drums), Michael Nesmith (electric 12-string guitar), Peter Tork (backing vocal, organ), Davy Jones (instrument unknown)
Release *Summer 1967: The Complete U.S. Concert Recordings* Rhino CD #RHM2 7755

'The Girl I Knew Somewhere' live version 5 (Michael Nesmith)
Recorded May 17th 1968
Personnel Micky Dolenz (lead vocal, drums), Michael Nesmith (electric guitar), Peter Tork (organ)
unissued

'The Girl I Left Behind Me' version 1 (Neil Sedaka/Carole Bayer)
Recorded November 23rd 1966 (and possibly other dates)
Personnel David Jones (vocal), Willard Suyker, Al Gafa & Don Thomas (guitars), Neil Sedaka (keyboard), Russ Savakus (bass), Herb Lovelle (drums), Julius Schachter & Leo Kahn (violin), Maurice Bialkin (cello), unknown (backing vocal)
Release *Instant Replay* Rhino CD #71796. An instrumental mix of this track – sans Davy's vocal track – appears on Davy's self-released *Just For The Record Volume Two* CD.

'The Girl I Left Behind Me' version 2 / 'Girl Named Love' (Neil Sedaka/Carole Bayer)
Recorded October 31st 1967, November 7th 1967 & November 21st 1967
Personnel David Jones (vocal), Charlie Smalls (piano), Eddie Hoh (drums), Red Mitchell, John Gross & Red Callender (basses), Milt Holland (tympani, bell, tambourine, other percussion), Elliott Fisher, Robert Barene & Israel Baker (violins), Frederick Seykora (cello), Vincent DeRosa (French horn), Dick Noel (trombone), unknown (acoustic guitar, additional percussion)
Release *Music Box* Rhino CD #76706 features a remix done exclusively for that collection. An earlier reverb-laden remix – missing the song's intro – was featured as a bonus track on the Rhino reissue of *The Birds, The Bees & The Monkees* CD #71794.

'The Girl I Left Behind Me' version 3 (Neil Sedaka/Carole Bayer)
Recorded February 6th 1968, February 9th 1968 (& possibly other dates)
Personnel David Jones (vocal), James Burton, Al Hendrickson, Gerry McGee & Mike Deasy (guitars), Michael Melvoin (harpsichord), Max Bennett (bass), Earl Palmer (drums), Milt Holland & Jerry Williams (percussion), Erno Neufeld, Sam Freed, George Kast, Alex Murray, Marvin Limonick & Nathan Kaproff (violins), Eleanor Slatkin, Kurt Reher, Marie Fera & Jacqueline Lustgarten (cellos), Buddy Childers & Jack Sheldon (trumpets), David Duke, Vincent DeRosa & Dick Perissi (French horns), Lew McCreary (trombone), unknown (bell, tympani)
unissued

'Girl Named Love' *see* 'The Girl I Left Behind Me' version 2

'Goin' Down' (Diane Hilderbrand/Peter Tork/Michael Nesmith/Micky Dolenz/Davy Jones)
Recorded June 21st 1967, July 5th 1967, September 15th 1967, September 23rd 1967, October 3rd 1967, October 4th 1967 (& possibly other dates)
Personnel Micky Dolenz (lead vocal), Michael Nesmith & Peter Tork (electric guitars), Chip Douglas (bass), Eddie Hoh (drums), John Lowe (bass saxophone, bass clarinet), Plas Johnson, Buddy Collette & Bill Hood (saxophones), Tom Scott, Uan Rasey, Bud Brisbois & Virgil Evans (trumpets), Richard Nash, Lou Blackburn, Dick Leith & Phil Teele (trombones)

Release *Greatest Hits* Rhino CD #72190. In addition to being available originally in mono and stereo mixes – the stereo appears on the CD noted – this song appears as a bonus track in a slightly longer alternative mono mix from September 23rd 1967 on Rhino's expanded reissue of the *Pisces, Aquarius, Capricorn & Jones, Ltd.* album CD#71793. The second season of the TV series includes a version with an alternative vocal track on the episodes *The Wild Monkees* and *Monkees In Texas*. A brief instrumental version of the song, without any vocal, can be heard in the episode *The Monkees Paw*. All three of these oddities can now be found on Rhino's *Season Two* DVD boxed set #970128.

'Goldie Locks Sometime' (Bill Dorsey)
Recorded November 18th 1968 (& probably other dates)
Personnel David Jones (vocal), Mike Deasy, Louie Shelton & Dennis Budimer (guitars), Joe Osborn (bass), Larry Knechtel & Jimmy Rowles (keyboards), Hal Blaine (drums, percussion), Gene Estes (percussion), Jackie Kelso (flute)
Release *Season Two* DVD boxed set Rhino #970128

'Gonna Build A Mountain' live version 1 (Leslie Bricusse/Anthony Newley)
Recorded January 21st 1967
Personnel David Jones (vocal), Bobby Hart (organ), Gerry McGee (guitar), Larry Taylor (bass), Bill Lewis (drums)
unissued

'Gonna Build A Mountain' live version 2 (Leslie Bricusse/Anthony Newley)
Recorded August 12nd 1967
Personnel David Jones (vocal), Dom DeMieri & Eddie Placidi (electric guitars), Bobby Dick (bass), Kim Capli (drums)
Release *Summer 1967: The Complete U.S. Concert Recordings* Rhino CD#RHM2 7755

'Gonna Build A Mountain' live version 3 (Leslie Bricusse/Anthony Newley)
Recorded August 25th 1967
Personnel David Jones (vocal), Dom DeMieri & Eddie Placidi (electric guitars), Bobby Dick (bass), Kim Capli (drums)
Release *Summer 1967: The Complete U.S. Concert Recordings* Rhino CD#RHM2 7755

'Gonna Build A Mountain' live version 4 (Leslie Bricusse/Anthony Newley)
Recorded August 26th 1967
Personnel David Jones (vocal), Dom DeMieri & Eddie Placidi (electric guitars), Bobby Dick (bass), Kim Capli (drums)
Release *Summer 1967: The Complete U.S. Concert Recordings* Rhino CD#RHM2 7755

'Gonna Build A Mountain' live version 5 (Leslie Bricusse/Anthony Newley)
Recorded August 27th 1967
Personnel David Jones (vocal), Dom DeMieri & Eddie Placidi (electric guitars), Bobby Dick (bass), Kim Capli (drums)
Release *Summer 1967: The Complete U.S. Concert Recordings* Rhino CD#RHM2 7755. An alternative mix of this performance appears on Rhino's *Live 1967* CD #70139.

'Gonna Buy Me A Dog' version 1 (Tommy Boyce/Bobby Hart)
Recorded July 7th 1966
Personnel Al Casey, Glen Campbell, James Burton, Jim Helms & Peter Tork (guitars), Hal Blaine (drums), Gary Coleman & Jim Gordon (percussion), Billy Preston (organ), Bill Pitman (bass)
unissued

'Gonna Buy Me A Dog' version 2 (Tommy Boyce/Bobby Hart)
Recorded July 23rd 1966 & July 24th 1966
Personnel Micky Dolenz & Davy Jones (vocal), Gerry McGee, Wayne Erwin & Louie Shelton (guitars), Larry Taylor (bass), Billy Lewis (drums), Bobby Hart (organ)
Release *The Monkees* Rhino CD #71790. In addition to being available originally in mono and stereo mixes – the stereo appears on the CD noted – an instrumental mix was featured on the TV episode *Monkees Blow Their Minds*. This is now available on Rhino's *Season Two* DVD boxed set #970128.

'Good Afternoon' (unknown)
Recorded June 5th 1969
Personnel Al Casey & Louie Shelton (guitar), Larry Knechtel (piano), Max Bennett (bass), Hal Blaine (drums)
unissued

'Good Clean Fun' (Michael Nesmith)
Recorded June 1st 1968, August 21st 1968 (& possibly other dates)
Personnel Michael Nesmith (vocal), Norbert Putnam (bass), Bobby

Thompson (banjo), Jerry Carrigan (drums), David Briggs (piano), Wayne Moss (guitar), Harold Bradley or Billy Sanford (additional guitar), Lloyd Green (steel guitar), Buddy Spicher (fiddle), unknown (percussion)
Release *The Monkees Present* Rhino CD #71797. This release features the song's original stereo mix. A unique stereo remix is included on Rhino's *Listen To The Band* CD boxed set #70566.

"The Good Earth" (unknown)
Recorded July 21st 1969
Personnel David Jones – recitation
Release *The Monkees Present* Rhino CD #71797

'Good Times' (Harry Nilsson)
Recorded January 10th 1968
Personnel Michael Nesmith (electric guitar), Harry Nilsson (piano, vocal; Eddie Hoh (drums), Rick Dey (bass)
unissued

'Gotta Give It Time' (Jeff Barry/Joey Levine)
Recorded January 21st 1967
Personnel Al Gorgoni, Don Thomas & Hugh McCracken (guitars), Lou Mauro (bass), Artie Butler (organ), Herb Lovelle (drums), Tom Cerone (tambourine)
unissued

'Grand Ennui' by Michael Nesmith & The First National Band (Michael Nesmith)
Recorded October 21st 1970, October 26th 1970 & December 21st 1970
Personnel Michael Nesmith (vocal, guitar), John London (bass), Red Rhodes (pedal steel guitar), John Ware (drums), Michael Cohen (piano), unknown (percussion)
Release *Nevada Fighter & Tantamount To Treason* BMG/Camden CD #74321 822352

'Guitar Man' by Michael Nesmith & The First National Band (Jerry Reed)
Recorded July 15th 1970
Personnel unknown
unissued

'Happy Birthday' (Mildred Hill/Patty Smith Hill)
Recorded August 3rd 1968 (& probably other dates)
Personnel Micky Dolenz, David Jones & Peter Tork (vocal), Michel Rubini (organ)
Release *Head* Rhino CD #71795

'Hard To Believe' (David Jones/Kim Capli/Eddie Brick/Charlie Rockett)
Recorded August 23rd 1967, September 5th 1967, September 6th 1967, September 9th 1967, September 15th 1967 & September 23rd 1967
Personnel David Jones (vocal), Kim Capli (guitar, drums, shaker, bass, piano, cowbell, claves, other percussion), Nathan Kaproff, Wilbert Nuttycombe, Leonard Atkins, Jerome Reisler, Arnold Belnick & Darrel Terwilliger (violins), Vincent DeRosa (French horn), Bobby Knight (bass trombone), Jim Horn (baritone saxophone), Tony Terran & Ollie Mitchell (flugelhorns)
Release *Pisces, Aquarius, Capricorn & Jones, Ltd.* Rhino CD #71793. In addition to being available originally in mono and stereo mixes – the stereo appears on the current CD noted – a stereo remix appears on the Arista edition of the *Pisces, Aquarius...* CD #ARCD 8603.

"Hawaiian Song" (Micky Dolenz?)
Recorded September 7th 1967
Personnel Micky Dolenz (vocal, sleigh bells), unknown (drums)
unissued

'Hello Lady' by Michael Nesmith & The First National Band (Michael Nesmith)
Recorded July 18th 1970
Personnel Michael Nesmith (vocal, guitar), John London (bass), John Ware (drums), Red Rhodes (pedal steel guitar), Glen D. Hardin (piano), John Raines (drums, percussion), Chuck Findley, Ollie Mitchell & Bud Brisbois (trumpets), Dick Hyde & Lew McCreary (trombones)
Release *Magnetic South & Loose Salute* BMG/Camden CD #74321 660442

'Hold On Girl' version 1 (Jack Keller/Ben Raleigh/Billy Carr)
Recorded September 10th 1966 & September 24th 1966
Personnel David Jones (lead & backing vocal), Ron Hicklin, Tommy Boyce, Micky Dolenz & Bobby Hart (backing vocals), Wayne Erwin, Gerry McGee & Louie Shelton (guitars), Larry Taylor (bass), Billy Lewis (drums), Alan Estes (tympani), Michel Rubini (harpsichord), Norman Benno (oboe)
Release *Missing Links Volume 2* Rhino CD#70903

'Hold On Girl' version 2 (Jack Keller/Ben Raleigh/Billy Carr)
Recorded October 14th 1966, October 23rd 1966 & October 27th 1966 (and possibly other dates)
Personnel David Jones (lead & backing vocal), Micky Dolenz (backing vocal), all others unknown
Release *More Of The Monkees* Rhino CD #71791. In addition to being available originally in mono and stereo mixes – the stereo appears on the CD noted – this track was remixed for the Arista CD release of *More Of The Monkees* #ARCD-8525.

'Hollywood' version 1 (Michael Nesmith)
Recorded May 29th 1968
Personnel Billy Sanford (acoustic guitar), Larry Butler (organ), Lloyd Green (steel guitar), Bobby Dyson (bass), Sonny Osborne (banjo), Willie Ackerman (drums)
unissued

'Hollywood' version 2 (Michael Nesmith)
Recorded May 31st 1968, June 2nd 1968, August 21st 1968 (& possibly other dates)
Personnel Michael Nesmith (vocal, guitar), Felton Jarvis & Harold Bradley (guitar), Lloyd Green (steel guitar), Bobby Thompson (banjo), David Briggs (piano), Norbert Putnam (bass), Buddy Spicher (fiddle), Kenneth Buttrey (drums), Charlie McCoy (harmonica)
Release *Missing Links Volume 3* Rhino CD #72153

'Hollywood' version 3 by Michael Nesmith & The First National Band (Michael Nesmith)
Recorded February 19th 1970
Personnel Michael Nesmith (vocal, acoustic guitar), John London (bass), Red Rhodes (pedal steel guitar), John Ware (drums), unknown (keyboard)
Release *Magnetic South & Loose Salute* BMG/Camden CD #74321 660442

'How Can I Tell You' (David Jones/Bill Chadwick)
Recorded June 27th 1969
Personnel David Jones (vocal), Louie Shelton & Frank Bugbee (acoustic guitars), Michel Rubini (piano), Max Bennett (bass), Hal Blaine (drums)
unissued

'How Can You Kiss Me' by Mike & John & Bill (Michael Nesmith)
Recorded circa 1965
Personnel Michael Nesmith (vocal, guitar), John London (bass), Bill Sleeper (drums)
Release Omnibus single #239

'How Insensitive' (Antonio Carlos Jobim/Vincius DeMoraes/Norman Gimbel)
Recorded May 31st 1968 (and possibly other dates)
Personnel Michael Nesmith (vocal, guitar), Harold Bradley (guitar), Lloyd Green (steel guitar), David Briggs (piano), Bobby Thompson (banjo), Norbert Putnam (bass), Buddy Spicher (fiddle), Kenny Buttrey (drums)
Release *Missing Links Volume 3* Rhino CD #72153

'Huff Puff' by Micky Dolenz (Gary Pipkin)
Recording date unknown
Personnel Micky Dolenz (vocal), all others unknown
Release Challenge single #59372

'I Can't Get Her Off Of My Mind' version 1 (Tommy Boyce/Bobby Hart)
Recorded July 25th 1966 (and possibly other dates)
Personnel David Jones (lead vocal), Wayne Erwin, Gerry McGee & Louie Shelton (guitars), Larry Taylor (bass), Billy Lewis (drums), Gene Estes (marimba), Bobby Hart (tack piano, autoharp), unknown (additional backing vocal)
Release *The Monkees* Rhino CD #71790

'I Can't Get Her Off Of My Mind' version 2 (Tommy Boyce/Bobby Hart)
Recorded March 17th 1967 & March 19th 1967
Personnel David Jones (lead vocal, percussion), Michael Nesmith (electric 12-string guitar), Peter Tork (tack piano), Micky Dolenz (backing vocal, drums), Jerry Yester (bass)
Release *Headquarters* Rhino CD #71792. In addition to being available originally in mono and stereo mixes – the stereo appears on the current CD noted, while the mono resides on the *Headquarters Sessions* CD set #RHM2 7715 – this track was remixed in stereo for the Arista edition of the *Headquarters* CD #ARCD 8602. Additionally, the *Headquarters Sessions* set features an instrumental mix of the song.

'I Can't Get Her Off Of My Mind' live version (Tommy Boyce/Bobby Hart)

Recorded January 21st 1967
Personnel David Jones (lead vocal), Michael Nesmith (electric 12-string guitar), Peter Tork (backing vocal, bass), Micky Dolenz (backing vocal, drums)
unissued

'I Didn't Know You Had It In You Sally, You're A Real Ball Of Fire' (Denny Randell/Sandy Linzer)
Recorded January 22nd 1967, January 28th 1967, September 15th 1969 & October 3rd 1969
Personnel Micky Dolenz (lead vocal), Charlie Macy (banjo), Joe Macho (bass), Don Butterfield (tuba), Artie Kaplan (soprano saxophone), Joseph Grimaldi & Seldon Powell (saxophone), Stan Free (tack piano), Buddy Salzman (drums), Artie Butler (percussion), unknown (backing vocal, tambourine)
unissued

"I Don't Know Yet" (unknown)
Recorded April 24th 1967
Personnel Micky Dolenz (drums), unknown (electric guitar, bass)
unissued

'I Don't Think You Know Me' version 1 (Gerry Goffin/Carole King)
Recorded June 25th 1966, July 16th 1966 & August 30th 1966
Personnel Michael Nesmith (vocal), Micky Dolenz (vocal), Al Casey, Glen Campbell & James Burton (guitars), Hal Blaine (drums), Gary Coleman & Jim Gordon (percussion), Bob West (bass), Larry Knechtel (organ), unknown (backing vocal)
Release *Missing Links* Rhino CD #70150 has Michael singing lead vocal. A slightly different remix of this song, still with Michael on lead vocal, was made for the *Music Box* release #76706. *The Monkees* Rhino CD #71790 has a mix with Micky on lead vocal, specially prepared as a bonus track for this expanded reissue of the band's first album.

'I Don't Think You Know Me' version 2 (Gerry Goffin/Carole King)
Recorded October 13rd 1966 & October 27th 1966
Personnel Peter Tork (lead & backing vocal), Micky Dolenz & David Jones (backing vocal), all others unknown
Release *More Of The Monkees* Rhino CD #71791. Two mixes – with the same personnel – have appeared of version 2 mix 1: a remix made for the *Listen To The Band* box set; and an original mono mix included as a bonus track on the expanded edition of *More Of The Monkees*.

'I Fall To Pieces' version 1 by Michael Nesmith & The First National Band (Hank Cochran/Harlan Howard)
Recorded May 1st 1970
Personnel unknown
unissued

'I Fall To Pieces' version 2 by Michael Nesmith & The First National Band (Hank Cochran/Harlan Howard)
Recorded May 14th 1970, May 26th 1970, May 27th 1970 & July 15th 1970
Personnel Michael Nesmith (vocal, acoustic guitar), John London (bass), Red Rhodes (pedal steel guitar), John Ware (drums), Glen D. Hardin (piano), Billy Dale (instrument unknown), unknown (percussion)
Release *Magnetic South & Loose Salute* BMG/Camden CD #74321 660442

'If I Ever Get To Saginaw Again' (Jack Keller/Bob Russell)
Recorded March 9th 1968, January 31st 1969, March 6th 1969 & March 7th 1969
Personnel Michael Nesmith (vocal), Louie Shelton (electric guitar), Mike Deasy, Dennis Budimir & Al Casey (acoustic guitars), Max Bennett (bass), Michael Melvoin (harpsichord), Earl Palmer (drums), Stan Levey & Milt Holland (tambourine, vibes), Del Kacher (guitar?), Bob Jung, William Weiss, Jack Gootkin, George Poole & Heimann Weinstine (violins), Garry Nutteycombe (viola), Douglas Davis (cello)
Release *Missing Links Volume 2* Rhino CD #70903

'If I Knew' (David Jones/Bill Chadwick)
Recorded July 1st 1969, July 11st 1969 & August 4th 1969
Personnel David Jones (lead & backing vocal), Bill Chadwick (additional backing vocal), David Cohen (acoustic guitar), Michel Rubini (piano), Max Bennett (bass), Hal Blaine (drums)
Release *The Monkees Present* Rhino CD #71797

'If I Learned To Play The Violin' (Artie Resnick/Joey Levine)
Recorded January 26th 1967 & February 4th 1967
Personnel David Jones (vocal), Sal Ditroia, Don Thomas & Hugh McCracken (guitars), James Tyrell (bass), Artie Butler (organ), Stan Free (clavinet), Herb Lovelle (drums), Tom Cerone (tambourine)
Release *Hey Hey, We're The Monkees* nu.millennia CD-ROM #CD0131

'If You Have The Time' (David Jones/Bill Chadwick)
Recorded August 6th 1969 & November 11st 1969
Personnel David Jones (lead & backing vocal), Bill Chadwick (backing vocal), Louie Shelton (electric guitar), Michel Rubini (piano), Joe Osborn (bass), John Guerin (drums), Paul Beaver (Moog synthesizer), unknown (additional backing vocal, guitar)
Release *Missing Links* Rhino CD #70150

'If You Love Me (Really Love Me)' by David Jones (Marguerite Monnot/Geoff Parsons/Edith Piaf)
Recorded circa 1963
Personnel David Jones (vocal), unknown (piano)
Release *Just For The Record* Hercules Promotions CD #Y6120E

'I Go Ape' (Neil Sedaka/Howard Greenfield)
Recorded November 11st 1968 (& other dates)
Personnel Micky Dolenz (lead vocal), Mike Deasy (electric guitar), Joe Osborn (bass), Larry Knechtel & Jimmy Rowles (keyboards), Hal Blaine (drums), unknown (saxophone, tambourine, backing vocal)
Release *Season Two* DVD boxed set Rhino #970128

'I Got A Woman' live version 1 (Ray Charles)
Recorded January 21st 1967
Personnel Micky Dolenz (vocal), Bobby Hart (organ), Gerry McGee (guitar), Larry Taylor (bass), Bill Lewis (drums)
Release *Season One* DVD boxed set Rhino #976076. This version is only an excerpt of the song with overdubbed vocal, as featured in the TV episode *The Monkees On Tour*. The complete live version is thus far unissued.

'I Got A Woman' live version 2 (Ray Charles)
Recorded August 12nd 1967
Personnel Micky Dolenz (vocal), Dom DeMieri & Eddie Placidi (electric guitars), Bobby Dick (bass), Kim Capli (drums)
Release *Summer 1967: The Complete U.S. Concert Recordings* Rhino CD #RHM2 7755

'I Got A Woman' live version 3 (Ray Charles)
Recorded August 25th 1967
Personnel Micky Dolenz (vocal), Dom DeMieri & Eddie Placidi (electric guitars), Bobby Dick (bass), Kim Capli (drums)
Release *Summer 1967: The Complete U.S. Concert Recordings* Rhino CD #RHM2 7755

'I Got A Woman' live version 4 (Ray Charles)
Recorded August 26th 1967
Personnel Micky Dolenz (vocal), Dom DeMieri & Eddie Placidi (electric guitars), Bobby Dick (bass), Kim Capli (drums)
Release *Summer 1967: The Complete U.S. Concert Recordings* Rhino CD #RHM2 7755

'I Got A Woman' live version 5 (Ray Charles)
Recorded August 27th 1967
Personnel Micky Dolenz (vocal), Dom DeMieri & Eddie Placidi (electric guitars), Bobby Dick (bass), Kim Capli (drums)
Release *Summer 1967: The Complete U.S. Concert Recordings* Rhino CD #RHM2 7755

'I'll Be Back Up On My Feet' version 1 (Sandy Linzer/Denny Randell)
Recorded Oct 28th 1966 (and possibly other dates)
Personnel Micky Dolenz (vocal), Al Casey & Carol Kaye (guitar), Ray Pohlman (bass), Hal Blaine (drums), Frank Capp & Julius Wechter (percussion), Michel Rubini & Don Randi (keyboard), unknown (additional backing vocal)
Release *Missing Links Volume 2* Rhino CD #70903

'I'll Be Back Up On My Feet' version 2 (Sandy Linzer/Denny Randell)
Recorded August 23rd 1967
Personnel Michael Nesmith (electric guitar), unknown (bass, drums)
unissued

'I'll Be Back Up On My Feet' version 3 (Sandy Linzer/Denny Randell)
Recorded March 9th 1968, March 13rd 1968 & March 14th 1968
Personnel Micky Dolenz (lead & backing vocal), unknown (additional backing vocal), Mike Deasy, Dennis Budimir & Al Casey (guitars), Max Bennett (bass), Michael Melvoin (harpsichord), Earl Palmer (drums), Stan Levey & Milt Holland (tambourine, quica), Ollie Mitchell & Buddy Childers (trumpets), Lew McCreary & Lou Blackburn (trombones), Bill Hood (saxophone)
Release *The Birds, The Bees & The Monkees* Rhino CD #71794

'I'll Be Here' by David Jones (unknown)
Recorded September 25th 1965 (and possibly other dates)
Personnel David Jones (vocal), Glen Campbell & Al Casey (guitar),

Ray Pohlman & Larry Knechtel (basses), Lincoln Mayorga (piano), Hal Blaine (drums), Julius Wechter (percussion)
unissued

'I'll Be True To You' (Gerry Goffin/Russ Titelman)
Recorded July 9th 1966, July 13rd 1966 & July 16th 1966
Personnel David Jones (lead vocal), Ron Hicklin, Bobby Hart & Tommy Boyce (backing vocals), Wayne Erwin, Gerry McGee & Louie Shelton (guitars), Larry Taylor (bass), Billy Lewis (drums), Gene Estes (glockenspiel)
Release *The Monkees* Rhino CD #71790 (In addition to originally being available in mono and stereo mixes - the stereo appears on the current Rhino CD noted above - this track was remixed for the Arista CD release of **The Monkees** #ARCD-8524)

'I'll Spend My Life With You' version 1 (Tommy Boyce/Bobby Hart)
Recorded October 26th 1966 & November 12nd 1966
Personnel Micky Dolenz (lead vocal), Ron Hicklin (harmony & backing vocal), Bobby Hart (backing vocal), Wayne Erwin, Gerry McGee & Louie Shelton (guitars), Tommy Boyce (acoustic guitar & backing vocal), Larry Taylor (bass), Billy Lewis (drums), Gene Estes (bells)
Release *More Of The Monkees* Rhino CD#71791

'I'll Spend My Life With You' version 2 (Tommy Boyce/Bobby Hart)
Recorded March 4th 1967, March 9th 1967, March 10th 1967, March 11st 1967 & March 18th 1967
Personnel Micky Dolenz (lead vocal, electric 6-string guitar), Michael Nesmith (steel guitar), Peter Tork (harmony vocal, acoustic 12-string guitar, organ, celeste), David Jones (tambourine), Chip Douglas (bass)
Release *Headquarters* Rhino CD #71792. In addition to being available originally in mono and stereo mixes – the stereo appears on the CD noted, while the mono resides on the *Headquarters Sessions* CD set #RHM2 7715 – this track was remixed in stereo for the Arista edition of the *Headquarters* CD #ARCD 8602. Additionally, the *Headquarters Sessions* set features an instrumental mix of the song.)

'I Looked Away' by Michael Nesmith & The First National Band (Eric Clapton/Bobby Whitlock)
Recorded December 22nd 1970 & January 4th 1971
Personnel Michael Nesmith (vocal, guitar), all others unknown
Release *Nevada Fighter & Tantamount To Treason* BMG/Camden CD #74321 822352

'I Love You Anyway' by David Jones (unknown)
Recorded circa 1965
Personnel David Jones (vocal), all others unknown
Release *Just For The Record* Hercules Promotions CD #Y6120E

'I Love You Better' (Jeff Barry/Andy Kim)
Recorded February 5th 1970 (& probably other dates)
Personnel Micky Dolenz (lead vocal), David Jones (backing vocal), all others unknown
Release *Changes* Rhino CD #71798

'I Love You Really' versions 1-3 (Stu Phillips)
Recorded August 22nd 1966
Personnel David Jones (vocal), Lou Morell, Al Hendrickson & Carol Kaye (guitars & bass), unknown (drums)
Release *Season One* DVD boxed set Rhino #976076

'I'm A Believer' (Neil Diamond)
Recorded October 15th 1966 & October 23rd 1966
Personnel Micky Dolenz (lead & backing vocal), David Jones (backing vocal; & possibly Peter Tork along with unknown others), Neil Diamond (acoustic guitar), Buddy Salzman (drums), all others unknown
Release *More Of The Monkees* Rhino CD #71791. In addition to being available originally in mono and stereo mixes – the stereo appears on the current CD noted – this track has appeared in three other mixes. Mix 1 features an alternative lead vocal from Micky and is available as a bonus track on the same CD noted. Mix Two, a remix of the original backing track with no vocal, is on the Japanese-only East West *The Monkees Best!!* CD #AMCY-978. Mix 3, a third remix, features backing vocals overlaid onto the original backing track and is on Rhino's *The Best Of The Monkees* CD#73875.

'I'm A Believer' live version 1 (Neil Diamond)
Recorded January 21st 1967
Personnel Micky Dolenz (lead vocal, drums), Michael Nesmith (electric 12-string guitar), Peter Tork (backing vocal, organ), David Jones (backing vocal, bass)
unissued

'I'm A Believer' live version 2 (Neil Diamond)
Recorded August 12nd 1967
Personnel Micky Dolenz (lead vocal, drums), Michael Nesmith

(electric 12-string guitar), Peter Tork (backing vocal, organ), David Jones (backing vocal)
Release *Summer 1967: The Complete U.S. Concert Recordings* Rhino CD #RHM2 7755

'I'm A Believer' live version 3 (Neil Diamond)
Recorded August 25th 1967
Personnel Micky Dolenz (lead vocal, drums), Michael Nesmith (electric 12-string guitar), Peter Tork (backing vocal, organ), David Jones (bass, backing vocal)
Release *Summer 1967: The Complete U.S. Concert Recordings* Rhino CD #RHM2 7755

'I'm A Believer' live version 4 (Neil Diamond)
Recorded August 26th 1967
Personnel Micky Dolenz (lead vocal, drums), Michael Nesmith (electric 12-string guitar), Peter Tork (backing vocal, organ), David Jones (bass, backing vocal)
Release *Summer 1967: The Complete U.S. Concert Recordings* Rhino CD #RHM2 7755. An alternative mix of this performance appears on Rhino's *Live 1967* CD #70139.

'I'm A Believer' live version 5 (Neil Diamond)
Recorded August 27th 1967
Personnel Micky Dolenz (lead vocal, drums), Michael Nesmith (electric 12-string guitar), Peter Tork (backing vocal, organ), David Jones (bass, backing vocal)
Release *Summer 1967: The Complete U.S. Concert Recordings* Rhino CD #RHM2 7755

'I'm A Man' demo NOT THE MONKEES (Barry Mann/Cynthia Weil)
Recorded October 10th 1967
Personnel Chip Douglas (vocal), unknown (bass, piano, organ, drums)
unissued

'I'm A Man' (Barry Mann/Cynthia Weil)
Recorded November 4th 1967, August 21st 1968 & May 12nd 1969
Personnel Chip Douglas (vocal), Al Casey, Neil Levang & Bill Pitman (guitars), Ray Pohlman (bass), Larry Knechtel (piano), Michael Melvoin (organ), Eddie Hoh (drums), Milt Holland & Gary Coleman (percussion, tympani)
unissued

'I'm Gonna Try' (David Jones/Steve Pitts)
Recorded February 15th 1968 & February 17th 1968
Personnel Davy Jones (vocal), Al Casey, Michael Deasy, Howard Roberts (guitars), Lyle Ritz (bass), Don Randi (harpsichord), Hal Blaine (drums), Gary Coleman & Gene Estes (tambourine, marimba), Buddy Childers, Tony Terran, Clyde Reasinger & Jack Sheldon (trumpets), Lew McCreary, Milt Bernhart, Frank Rosolino & Dick Leith (trombones), John Lowe (saxophone, woodwinds), Erno Neufeld, George Kast, Nathan Kaproff, Marvin Limonick, Alex Murray & Ambrose Russo (violins)
Release *The Birds, The Bees & The Monkees* Rhino CD #71794

'(I'm Not Your) Steppin' Stone' (Tommy Boyce/Bobby Hart)
Recorded July 26th 1966 (and possibly other dates)
Personnel Micky Dolenz (lead vocal), Tommy Boyce (backing vocal), Wayne Erwin (backing vocal, guitar), Gerry McGee & Louie Shelton (guitars), Larry Taylor (bass), Billy Lewis (drums), Bobby Hart (organ, backing vocal), unknown (foot stomps, handclaps, tambourine)
Release *More Of The Monkees* Rhino CD #71791. In addition to the most common mixes – the stereo appears on the current CD noted, while the mono is included on *Greatest Hits* CD #72190 – this track has appeared in several other mixes. Mix 1 is a remix for the *Listen To The Band* CD boxed set #70566. Mix 2 is a karaoke remix featuring just the song's instrumental track and backing vocal for *The Best Of The Monkees* CD#73875. Mix 3 is available on only *some* original US mono vinyl pressings of the *More Of The Monkees* album. It lasts several seconds longer than any other available version of the song.

'(I'm Not Your) Steppin' Stone' live version 1 (Tommy Boyce/Bobby Hart)
Recorded January 21st 1967
Personnel Micky Dolenz (lead vocal, drums), Michael Nesmith (electric 12-string guitar), Peter Tork (backing vocal, organ), David Jones (backing vocal, tambourine)
Release *Season One* DVD boxed set Rhino #976076. This version is only an excerpt of the song with overdubbed vocals, as featured in the TV episode *The Monkees On Tour*. The complete live version is thus far unissued.)

'(I'm Not Your) Steppin' Stone' live version 2 (Tommy Boyce/Bobby Hart)
Recorded August 12nd 1967
Personnel Micky Dolenz (lead vocal, drums), Michael Nesmith (electric 12-string guitar), Peter Tork (backing vocal, bass, organ),

David Jones (backing vocal, maracas)
Release *Summer 1967: The Complete U.S. Concert Recordings* Rhino CD #RHM2 7755

'(I'm Not Your) Steppin' Stone' live version 3 (Tommy Boyce/Bobby Hart)
Recorded August 25th 1967
Personnel Micky Dolenz (lead vocal, drums), Michael Nesmith (electric 12-string guitar), Peter Tork (backing vocal, bass), David Jones (backing vocal, tambourine)
Release *Summer 1967: The Complete U.S. Concert Recordings* Rhino CD #RHM2 7755. An alternative mix of this performance appears on Rhino's *Live 1967* CD #70139.

'(I'm Not Your) Steppin' Stone' live version 4 (Tommy Boyce/Bobby Hart)
Recorded August 26th 1967
Personnel Micky Dolenz (lead vocal, drums), Michael Nesmith (electric 12-string guitar), Peter Tork (backing vocal, bass), David Jones (backing vocal, maracas)
Release *Summer 1967: The Complete U.S. Concert Recordings* Rhino CD #RHM2 7755. An alternative mix of this performance appears on Rhino's *Listen To The Band* box set #70566.

'(I'm Not Your) Steppin' Stone' live version 5 (Tommy Boyce/Bobby Hart)
Recorded August 27th 1967
Personnel Micky Dolenz (lead vocal, drums), Michael Nesmith (electric 12-string guitar), Peter Tork (backing vocal, bass), David Jones (backing vocal, maracas)
Release *Summer 1967: The Complete U.S. Concert Recordings* Rhino CD #RHM2 7755

'Impack' (Michael Nesmith)
Recorded February 17th 1968
Personnel Al Casey, Mike Deasy & Al Hendrickson (guitar), Max Bennett (bass), Michael Melvoin & Dr. John (Mac Rebennack) (keyboard), Hal Blaine (drums), Milt Holland & Stanley Levey – conga & tambourine; Buddy Childers, Tony Terran, Clyde Reasinger & Jack Sheldon (trumpet), Lew McCreary, Milt Bernhart, Frank Rosolino & Dick Leith (trombone), Jules Jacob, Jim Horn, Gene "Cip" Cipriano & John Lowe – sax & woodwinds
unissued

'I Never Thought It Peculiar' (Tommy Boyce/Bobby Hart)
Recorded October 28th 1966, July 24th 1969, September 5th 1969 & September 12nd 1969
Personnel David Jones (lead vocal), Ron Hicklin & Bobby Hart (backing vocals), Tommy Boyce (backing vocal, acoustic guitar), Wayne Erwin, Gerry McGee & Louie Shelton (guitars), Larry Taylor (bass), Billy Lewis (drums), Gene Estes (bells), Jay Migliori (saxophone), Dick Hyde (trombone), Chuck Findley (trumpet), Alan Robinson (French horn), Harold Ayres, Joy Lule, John DeVoogdt, Norman Serkin & Jimmy Getzoff (violins), Frederick Seykora (cello), William Hymanson & Gary Nuttycombe (viola), Michael Anthony (instrument unknown)
Release *Changes* Rhino CD #71798

"Instrumental #1" (unknown)
Recorded June 1967?
Personnel Michael Nesmith (acoustic guitar), Peter Tork (organ), Chip Douglas (bass), Eddie Hoh (drums), unknown (electric guitar)
unissued

"Instrumental #2" (unknown)
Recorded June 1967?
Personnel Michael Nesmith (acoustic guitar), Peter Tork (organ), Chip Douglas (bass), Eddie Hoh (drums), unknown (electric guitar)
unissued

'(I Prithee) Do Not Ask For Love' version 1 (Michael Martin Murphey)
Recorded July 25th 1966 & October 18th 1966 (and possibly other dates)
Personnel Micky Dolenz (vocal), James Burton, Glen Campbell, Al Casey, Mike Deasy & Peter Tork (guitars), Bob West (bass), Hal Blaine (drums), Jim Gordon & Gary Coleman (percussion), Michael Cohen & Larry Knechtel (keyboards)
Release *Missing Links Volume 2* Rhino CD #70903 features a stereo remix from the 1980s. A more recent stereo remix can be found on *Music Box* #76706.

'(I Prithee) Do Not Ask For Love' version 2 (Michael Martin Murphey)
Recorded December 3rd 1967
Personnel Peter Tork (electric guitar)
unissued

'(I Prithee) Do Not Ask For Love' version 3 (Michael Martin Murphey)
Recorded December 3rd 1967
Personnel Peter Tork (vocal, electric guitar), Stephen Stills (electric guitar)
unissued

'(I Prithee) Do Not Ask For Love' version 4 (Michael Martin Murphey)
Recorded November 12nd 1968 & November 17th 1968
Personnel Peter Tork (vocal), Hal Blaine (percussion), Mike Deasy & Dennis Budimer (acoustic guitars), Joe Osborn (bass), Larry Knechtel & Jimmy Rowles (keyboards), unknown (backing vocal, sitar)
Release *Season Two* DVD boxed set Rhino #970128

'It Ain't Me Babe' by David Jones (Bob Dylan)
Recorded July 26th 1965 (and possibly other dates)
Personnel David Jones (vocal), Gene Garf (piano), Red Callender (bass), Al Casey, Carol Kaye, Bill Pitman & Tommy Tedesco (guitars), Emil Richards (percussion), Earl Palmer (drums), unknown (backing vocal)
Release *David Jones* Colpix album #493 (in mono & stereo)

'It's Got To Be Love' (Neil Goldberg)
Recorded April 2nd 1970
Personnel Micky Dolenz (vocal), all others unknown
Release *Changes* Rhino CD #71798

'It's Nice To Be With You' (Jerry Goldstein)
Recorded February 6th 1968, February 7th 1968, February 8th 1968, March 14th 1968, April 25th 1968 (& possibly other dates)
Personnel David Jones (vocal), James Burton, Al Hendrickson, Gerry McGee & Mike Deasy (guitars), Michael Melvoin (keyboard), Max Bennett (bass), Earl Palmer (drums), Milt Holland or Jerry Williams (tambourine), Erno Neufeld, Sam Freed, George Kast, Alex Murray, Marvin Limonick & Nathan Kaproff (violins), Eleanor Slatkin, Kurt Reher, Marie Fera & Jacqueline Lustgarten (cellos), Buddy Childers, Jack Sheldon & Ollie Mitchell (trumpets), David Duke, Vincent DeRosa & Dick Perissi (French horns), Lew McCreary & Lou Blackburn (trombones), Bill Hood (saxophone)
Release *Greatest Hits* Rhino CD #72190 features an April 1968 stereo mix. The original mono single mix can be heard on Flashback's *Daydream Believer And Other Hits* CD #75242.

'I've Got A Lot Of Livin' To Do' *see* 'A Lot Of Livin' To Do'

'I've Got Rhythm' (Eddie Hoh)
Recorded June 22nd 1967
Personnel Eddie Hoh (drums)
unissued

'I Wanna Be Free' slow demo version by Boyce & Hart] (Tommy Boyce/Bobby Hart)
Recorded circa 1965
Personnel Tommy Boyce & Bobby Hart (vocal), all others unknown
Release *Season One* DVD boxed set Rhino #976076 (as featured in the unaired version of the pilot TV episode).

'I Wanna Be Free' fast demo version by Boyce & Hart (Tommy Boyce/Bobby Hart)
Recorded circa 1965
Personnel Tommy Boyce & Bobby Hart (vocal), all others unknown
Release *Season One* DVD boxed set Rhino #976076 (as featured in the unaired version of the pilot TV episode).

'I Wanna Be Free' version 1: slow (Tommy Boyce/Bobby Hart)
Recorded July 19th 1966 & July 24th 1966
Personnel David Jones (vocal), Wayne Erwin, Gerry McGee & Louie Shelton (acoustic guitars), Michel Rubini (harpsichord), Paul Shure & Bonnie Douglas (violins), Frederick Seykora (cello), Myra Kestenbaum (viola)
Release *The Monkees* Rhino CD #71790. In addition to being available originally in mono and stereo mixes – the stereo appears on the current CD noted – this track has appeared in three other mixes. Mix 1 was a stereo remix for the Arista CD release of *The Monkees* #ARCD-8524. Mix 2 was a second stereo remix, for the *Listen To The Band* CD boxed set #70566. Mix 3 was a remix of the original backing track with no vocal, for the Japanese-only East-West *The Monkees Best!!* CD #AMCY-978.

'I Wanna Be Free' version 2: slow (Tommy Boyce/Bobby Hart)
Recorded July 19th 1966
Personnel Wayne Erwin, Gerry McGee & Louie Shelton (acoustic guitars), Billy Lewis (drums), Gene Estes (bells, chimes), Michel Rubini (harpsichord), Paul Shure & Bonnie Douglas (violins), Frederick Seykora (cello), Myra Kestenbaum (viola)
unissued

'I Wanna Be Free' version 3: fast (Tommy Boyce/Bobby Hart)
Recorded July 19th 1966 & July 24th 1966
Personnel David Jones & Micky Dolenz (vocals), Wayne Erwin, Gerry McGee & Louie Shelton (guitars), Larry Taylor (bass), Billy Lewis (drums), Gene Estes (tambourine), Michel Rubini (organ)
Release *Missing Links Volume 2* Rhino CD #70903. Version 3 has appeared in two different mixes. Mix 1 is a remix for the CD noted; mix 2 is a second remix, for the *Music Box* release #76706.

'I Wanna Be Free' live version 1 (Tommy Boyce/Bobby Hart)
Recorded January 21st 1967
Personnel David Jones (lead vocal), Michael Nesmith (electric 12-string guitar), Peter Tork (bass), Micky Dolenz (drums)
Release *Season One* DVD boxed set Rhino #976076. This version is only an excerpt of the song with overdubbed vocal, as featured in the TV episode *The Monkees On Tour*. The complete live version is thus far unissued.

'I Wanna Be Free' live version 2 (Tommy Boyce/Bobby Hart)
Recorded August 12nd 1967
Personnel David Jones (lead vocal), Michael Nesmith (electric 12-string guitar), Peter Tork (bass), Micky Dolenz (drums)
Release *Summer 1967: The Complete U.S. Concert Recordings* Rhino CD #RHM2 7755

'I Wanna Be Free' live version 3 (Tommy Boyce/Bobby Hart)
Recorded August 25th 1967
Personnel David Jones (lead vocal), Michael Nesmith (electric 12-string guitar), Peter Tork (bass), Micky Dolenz (drums)
Release *Summer 1967: The Complete U.S. Concert Recordings* Rhino CD #RHM2 7755

'I Wanna Be Free' live version 4 (Tommy Boyce/Bobby Hart)
Recorded August 26th 1967
Personnel David Jones (lead vocal), Michael Nesmith (electric 12-string guitar), Peter Tork (bass), Micky Dolenz (drums)
Release *Summer 1967: The Complete U.S. Concert Recordings* Rhino CD #RHM2 7755. An alternative mix of this performance appears on Rhino's *Live 1967* CD #70139.

'I Wanna Be Free' live version 5 (Tommy Boyce/Bobby Hart)
Recorded August 27th 1967
Personnel David Jones (lead vocal), Michael Nesmith (electric 12-string guitar), Peter Tork (bass), Micky Dolenz (drums)
Release *Summer 1967: The Complete U.S. Concert Recordings* Rhino CD #RHM2 7755

'I Wanna Be Free' live version 6 (Tommy Boyce/Bobby Hart)
Recorded May 17th 1968
Personnel David Jones (vocal), Michael Nesmith (electric guitar), Peter Tork (organ, bass), Micky Dolenz (drums)
unissued

'I Wanna Be Your Puppy Dog' (Denny Randell/Sandy Linzer)
Recorded January 22nd 1967 & January 27th 1967
Personnel Charlie Macy, Al Gorgoni, Ralph Casale, Bob Rand & Don Thomas (guitars), Joe Macho (bass), Stan Free (clavinet), Buddy Salzman (drums), Artie Butler (tambourine), unknown (handclaps)
unissued

'I Want To Love You' by David Jones (unknown)
Recorded circa 1965
Personnel David Jones (vocal), all others unknown
Release *Just For The Record* Hercules Promotions CD #Y6120E

'I Was Born In East Virginia' *see* 'East Virginia'

'I Won't Be The Same Without Her' (Gerry Goffin/Carole King)
Recorded July 18th 1966, July 30th 1966 & August 30th 1966
Personnel Michael Nesmith (lead & backing vocal), James Burton, Glen Campbell, Al Casey, Mike Deasy & Peter Tork (guitars, 'dano' bass), Hal Blaine (drums), Gary Coleman & Frank DeVito (percussion), Larry Knechtel (piano), Bob West (bass), unknown (additional backing vocal)
Release *Instant Replay* Rhino CD 71796. The song also appears in remixed form on the *Listen To The Band* CD boxed set #70566.

"Jam #1"
Recorded August 23rd 1967
Personnel Michael Nesmith (electric guitar), unknown (bass, drums)
unissued

"Jam #2"
Recorded August 23rd 1967
Personnel Michael Nesmith (electric guitar), unknown (bass, drums)
unissued

'Jericho' (Traditional)
Recorded March 11st 1967
Personnel Peter Tork & Micky Dolenz (vocals)
Release *Headquarters* Rhino CD #71792. A longer edit of this performance is included on the *Headquarters Sessions* set #RHM2 7715.

'Joanne' by Michael Nesmith & The First National Band (Michael Nesmith)
Recorded February 20th 1970
Personnel Michael Nesmith (vocal, acoustic guitar), John London (bass), Red Rhodes (pedal steel guitar), unknown (keyboard)
Release *Magnetic South & Loose Salute* BMG/Camden CD #74321 660442

"Jokes" not actually intended for The Monkees (Tommy Boyce/Bobby Hart)
Recorded July 23rd 1966
Personnel Wayne Erwin, Gerry McGee & Louie Shelton (guitars), Larry Taylor (bass), Billy Lewis (drums)
unissued

'Just A Game' version 1 (Micky Dolenz)
Recorded March 28th 1967
Personnel Micky Dolenz (vocal, electric six-string guitar), Peter Tork & David Jones (percussion), Chip Douglas (bass)
Release *Headquarters Sessions* Rhino CD #RHM2 7715

'Just A Game' version 2 (Micky Dolenz)
Recorded April 9th 1968, June 7th 1968, June 13rd 1968, December 28th 1968, January 10th 1969 (& possibly other dates)
Personnel Micky Dolenz (vocal, acoustic guitar), Coco Dolenz (backing vocal), Tommy Tedesco (acoustic guitar), Max Bennett (bass), Michel Rubini (harpsichord), Jim Gordon (drums), Joe Porcaro (percussion), Bud Shank, Ted Nash & Ronnie Lang (flutes), Bud Brisbois, Buddy Childers, Ray Triscari & Ollie Mitchell (trumpets), George Roberts (trombone), Vincent DeRosa, Dick Perissi & David Duke (French horns), Erno Neufeld, Anatol Kaminsky, Nathan Ross, George Berres, Joseph Stepansky & Bernard Kundell (violins), Edgar Lustgarten, Armand Kaproff & Justin DiTullio (cellos)
Release *Instant Replay* Rhino CD #71796

'Just A Little Love' by Mike & John & Bill; also credited as Mike Nesmith (Michael Nesmith)
Recorded circa 1965
Personnel Michael Nesmith (vocal, guitar, harmonica), John London (bass), Bill Sleeper (drums)
Release Omnibus single #239 & Edan Single #1001

'Just Another Dream' demo (unknown)
Recorded January 24th 1968
Personnel Peter Tork (vocal, piano)
unissued

'The Keys To The Car' by Michael Nesmith & The First National Band (Michael Nesmith)
Recorded February 19th 1970
Personnel Michael Nesmith (vocal, acoustic guitar), John London (bass), Red Rhodes (pedal steel guitar), John Ware (drums)
Release *Magnetic South & Loose Salute* BMG/Camden CD #74321 660442

'The Kind Of Girl I Could Love' (Michael Nesmith/Roger Atkins)
Recorded June 25th 1966 & July 16th 1966
Personnel Michael Nesmith (lead & backing vocal, steel guitar), Micky Dolenz, David Jones & Peter Tork (backing vocals), Al Casey, Glen Campbell & James Burton (guitars), Hal Blaine (drums), Gary Coleman & Jim Gordon (percussion), Larry Knechtel & Bob West (basses)
Release *More Of The Monkees* Rhino CD #71791. In addition to being available originally in mono and stereo mixes – the stereo appears on the current CD noted – this track has been remixed in stereo for two other releases. Mix 1 appears on the Arista CD release of *More Of The Monkees* #ARCD-8525; mix 2 is a second remix, for the *Music Box* release CD #76706.

'Kiss And Hug' by David Jones (unknown)
Recorded circa 1965
Personnel David Jones (vocal), all others unknown
Release *Just For The Record* Hercules Promotions CD #Y6120E

'Kicking Stones' a.k.a. **'Teeny Tiny Gnome'** (Lynn Castle/Wayne Erwin)
Recorded August 23rd 1966, August 27th 1966, September 3rd 1966 & July 24th 1969
Personnel Micky Dolenz (lead vocal), Ron Hicklin & Tommy Boyce (backing vocals), Wayne Erwin (guitar, backing vocal), Gerry McGee & Louie Shelton (guitars), Larry Taylor (bass), Billy Lewis (drums), Emil

Richards (vibes), Bobby Hart (keyboard, backing vocal), Dick Hyde & Gilbert Falco (trombones), Steve Huffsteter (trumpet), Don McGinnis & Bob Jung (horns), Paul Suter (flute, organ)
Release *Missing Links* Rhino CD #70150

'Kitty Hawk' see 'Windy Day At Kitty Hawk'

'Ladies Aid Society' (Tommy Boyce/Bobby Hart)
Recorded August 23rd 1966, September 3rd 1966 & July 24th 1969
Personnel David Jones (lead vocal), Micky Dolenz, Ron Hicklin & Tommy Boyce (backing vocals), Wayne Erwin (guitar, backing vocal), Gerry McGee & Louie Shelton (guitar), Larry Taylor (bass), Billy Lewis (drums), Emil Richards (percussion), Bobby Hart (piano, backing vocal), Dick Hyde & Gilbert Falco (trombones), Steve Huffsteter (trumpet), Don McGinnis & Bob Jung (horns)
Release *Instant Replay* Rhino CD #71797

'Lady Jane' (Jeff Barry)
Recorded September 22nd 1970 (& possibly other dates)
Personnel David Jones (lead & backing vocal), Micky Dolenz (lead & backing vocal), unknown (acoustic guitars, piano, keyboards, drums, tambourine, finger snaps, handclaps, additional backing vocal)
Release *Changes* Rhino CD #71798

'Lady Of The Valley' by Michael Nesmith & The First National Band (Michael Nesmith)
Recorded May 13rd 1970, May 14th 1970, May 28th 1970, July 15th 1970 & July 16th 1970
Personnel Michael Nesmith (vocal, electric guitar), John London (bass), Red Rhodes (pedal steel guitar), John Ware (drums), unknown (percussion)
Release *Magnetic South & Loose Salute* BMG/Camden CD #74321 660442

'Lady's Baby' version 1 (Peter Tork)
Recorded November 12nd 1967
Personnel Peter Tork (vocal, acoustic guitar), Karen Harvey (backing vocal)
unissued

'Lady's Baby' version 2 (Peter Tork)
Recorded November 12nd 1967 & December 1st 1967
Personnel Peter Tork (lead vocal, acoustic guitar, bass, clavinet), Karen Harvey (harmony & backing vocal)
unissued

'Lady's Baby' version 3 (Peter Tork)
Recorded December 3rd 1967 & December 17th 1967
Personnel Peter Tork – lead vocal, acoustic guitar, bass & harpsichord; Stephen Stills (guitar), Karen Harvey (harmony & backing vocal), Lance Wakely (instrument unknown)
unissued

'Lady's Baby' version 4 (Peter Tork)
Recorded January 14th 1968 & January 19th 1968
Personnel Peter Tork (vocal, bass, acoustic guitar), Lance Wakely & Stephen Stills (electric guitars), Buddy Miles (drums)
unissued

'Lady's Baby' version 5 (Peter Tork)
Recorded January 24th 1968, January 25th 1968, February 2nd 1968, February 7th 1968, March 13rd 1968 & March 17th 1968
Personnel Peter Tork (lead vocal, guitar), Karen Harvey Hammer (backing vocal), Justin Hammer (sound effects), Steve Stills (electric guitar), Lance Wakely (bass (& guitar?), Dewey Martin (drums)
Release *The Birds, The Bees & The Monkees* Rhino CD #71794. An alternative mono mix from March 17th 1968 – without baby effects – is included on Rhino's *Missing Links* CD #70150.

'Lance's' (Lance Wakely)
Recorded January 14th 1968
Personnel Peter Tork (bass), Lance Wakely (acoustic guitar)
unissued

'Last Train To Clarksville' (Tommy Boyce/Bobby Hart)
Recorded July 25th 1966 (and possibly other dates)
Personnel Micky Dolenz (lead vocal), Wayne Erwin, Gerry McGee & Louie Shelton (guitars), Larry Taylor (bass), Billy Lewis (drums), Gene Estes (tambourine), unknown (additional backing vocal)
Release *The Monkees* Rhino CD #71790. This is the original stereo mix. The original mono mix appears on Arista's *Then & Now* CD #A2CD 8432.

'Last Train To Clarksville' live version 1 (Tommy Boyce/Bobby Hart)
Recorded January 21st 1967
Personnel Micky Dolenz (lead vocal, drums), Michael Nesmith

(electric 12-string guitar), Peter Tork (backing vocal, bass), David Jones (backing vocal, tambourine)
Release *Season One* DVD boxed set Rhino #976076 features only an excerpt of the song with overdubbed vocal, as featured in the TV episode *The Monkees On Tour*. The complete live version is thus far unissued.

'Last Train To Clarksville' live version 2 (Tommy Boyce/Bobby Hart)
Recorded August 12nd 1967
Personnel Micky Dolenz (lead vocal, drums), Michael Nesmith (electric 12-string guitar), Peter Tork (backing vocal, bass), David Jones (backing vocal, tambourine)
Release *Summer 1967: The Complete U.S. Concert Recordings* Rhino CD#RHM2 7755

'Last Train To Clarksville' live version 3 (Tommy Boyce/Bobby Hart)
Recorded August 25th 1967
Personnel Micky Dolenz (lead vocal, drums), Michael Nesmith (electric 12-string guitar), Peter Tork (backing vocal, bass), David Jones (backing vocal, tambourine)
Release *Summer 1967: The Complete U.S. Concert Recordings* Rhino CD#RHM2 7755

'Last Train To Clarksville' live version 4 (Tommy Boyce/Bobby Hart)
Recorded August 26th 1967
Personnel Micky Dolenz (lead vocal, drums), Michael Nesmith (electric 12-string guitar), Peter Tork (backing vocal, bass), David Jones (backing vocal, tambourine)
Release *Summer 1967: The Complete U.S. Concert Recordings* Rhino CD#RHM2 7755. An alternative mix of this performance appears on Rhino's *Live 1967* CD #70139.

'Last Train To Clarksville' live version 5 (Tommy Boyce/Bobby Hart)
Recorded August 27th 1967
Personnel Micky Dolenz (lead vocal, drums), Michael Nesmith (electric 12-string guitar), Peter Tork (backing vocal, bass), David Jones (backing vocal, tambourine)
Release *Summer 1967: The Complete U.S. Concert Recordings* Rhino CD#RHM2 7755

'Last Train To Clarksville' rehearsal (Tommy Boyce/Bobby Hart)
Recorded May 17th 1968
Personnel Micky Dolenz (drums), Peter Tork (bass), David Jones (organ)
unissued

'Laugh' (Hank Medress/Phil Margo/Mitch Margo/Jay Siegal)
Recorded Oct 28th 1966 (and possibly other dates)
Personnel David Jones (lead & backing vocal), Jeff Barry (backing vocal), Al Casey & Carole Kaye (guitars), Ray Pohlman (bass), Hal Blaine (drums), Frank Capp & Julius Wechter (percussion), Michel Rubini & Don Randi (keyboards), unknown (additional backing vocal)
Release *More Of The Monkees* Rhino CD #71791. In addition to being available originally in mono and stereo mixes – the stereo appears on the current CD noted – an alternative mix of this track appeared in the TV series one episode *Monkees In The Ring*. This is now available on the Rhino *Season One* DVD boxed set #976076.

'Let It Happen' *see* 'If You Love Me (Really Love Me)'

'Let's Dance On' demo by Boyce & Hart (Tommy Boyce/Bobby Hart)
Recorded circa 1965
Personnel Tommy Boyce & Bobby Hart (vocal), all others unknown
Release *Season One* DVD boxed set Rhino #976076 (as featured in the unaired version of the TV pilot episode).

'Let's Dance On' version 1 (Tommy Boyce/Bobby Hart)
Recorded June 10th 1966
Personnel Sonny Curtis, Glen Campbell & James Burton (guitars), Hal Blaine (drums, Latin percussion), Larry Knechtel (keyboard), Ray Pohlman (bass)
unissued

'Let's Dance On' version 2 (Tommy Boyce/Bobby Hart)
Recorded July 5th 1966, July 9th 1966 & July 16th 1966
Personnel Micky Dolenz (lead & backing vocal), Tommy Boyce, Ron Hicklin & Peter Tork (backing vocals), Wayne Erwin (guitar, backing vocal), Gerry McGee & Louie Shelton (guitars), Larry Taylor (bass), Billy Lewis (drums), Gene Estes (maracas, tambourine), Bobby Hart (organ, backing vocal)
Release *The Monkees* Rhino CD #71790

'Listen To The Band' version 1 (Michael Nesmith)
Recorded June 1st 1968, June 2nd 1968, October 29th 1968,

December 9th 1968, December 28th 1968 (& probably other dates)
Personnel Michael Nesmith (vocal, electric guitar), Wayne Moss (guitar), Harold Bradley or Billy Sanford (additional guitar), David Briggs (piano), Lloyd Green (steel guitar), Norbert Putnam (bass), Jerry Carrigan (drums), Charlie McCoy (harmonica), Mike Saluzzi (guitar), Michael Rubini (keyboard), Dick Nash (trombone), Buddy Childers, Bud Brisbois & Ray Triscari (trumpets), John Kitzmiller (tuba), Don McGinnis (brass), unknown (percussion)
Release *Greatest Hits* Rhino CD #72190. This song has appeared in four distinct mix/edits over the years. Mix 1 was first issued as a single in 1969, features a short organ and drum break, and can be found on Rhino's *Greatest Hits* CD #72190 and *Anthology* CD #75269. Mix 2 originally appeared on the *Monkees Present* album. It is a lengthier edit of the track featuring a longer organ and drum break. It can be found on Rhino's CD of *The Monkees Present* #71797. Mix 3 is a unique stereo remix – all other mixes of this song are mono or fake stereo – featuring the short organ and drum break lifted from the single master. It can be found on Rhino's *Listen To The Band* CD boxed set #70566 and more recently the *Music Box* collection CD #76706. Mix 4 is a rough mix from October 29th 1968 and is missing the brass overdubs added later that year. It can be found as a bonus track on Rhino's CD of *The Monkees Present* #71797. A live performance of this song featuring the four Monkees is included in the *33 1/3 Revolutions Per Monkee* special on Rhino's *Season Two* DVD boxed set #970128.

'Listen To The Band' version 2 by Michael Nesmith & The First National Band (Michael Nesmith)
Recorded May 1st 1970
Personnel unknown
unissued

'Listen To The Band' version 3 by Michael Nesmith & The First National Band (Michael Nesmith)
Recorded May 27th 1970 & July 16th 1970
Personnel Michael Nesmith (vocal, guitar), John London (bass), Red Rhodes (pedal steel guitar), John Ware (drums), unknown (piano, percussion)
Release *Magnetic South & Loose Salute* BMG/Camden CD #74321 660442

'Little Girl' (Micky Dolenz)
Recorded August 14th 1969
Personnel Micky Dolenz (lead & backing vocal, acoustic guitar), Coco Dolenz (backing vocal), Louie Shelton (electric guitar), Ray Pohlman (bass), Earl Palmer (drums)
Release *The Monkees Present* Rhino CD #71797

'Little Red Rider' version 1 (Michael Nesmith)
Recorded May 28th 1969, June 17th 1969 & June 26th 1969
Personnel Michael Nesmith (lead & backing vocal), Louie Shelton & Al Casey (guitars), Larry Knechtel (piano), Max Bennett (bass), Hal Blaine (drums), Mack Johnson (trumpet), Lester Robertson (trombone), Clifford Solomon (tenor saxophone), unknown (cowbell)
Release *Missing Links Volume 3* Rhino CD#72153

'Little Red Rider' version 2 by Michael Nesmith & The First National Band (Michael Nesmith)
Recorded February 10th 1970 & February 20th 1970
Personnel Michael Nesmith (vocal, guitar), John London (bass), Red Rhodes (pedal steel guitar), John Ware (drums), unknown (percussion)
Release *Magnetic South & Loose Salute* BMG/Camden CD #74321 660442

'Little Tommy Blue' (unknown)
Recorded June 10th 1969 & June 26th 1969
Personnel Al Casey & Louie Shelton (guitars), Michel Rubini (piano), Max Bennett (bass), Hal Blaine (drums)
unissued

'London Bridge' (Michael Nesmith)
Recorded June 6th 1969
Personnel Al Casey & Louie Shelton (guitars), Larry Knechtel & Michael Cohen (keyboards), Max Bennett (bass), Hal Blaine (drums), Alan Estes (mallets)
unissued

'Long Title: Do I Have To Do This All Over Again' version 1 (Peter Tork)
Recorded January 14th 1968
Personnel Peter Tork (electric guitar), Buddy Miles (drums), Lance Wakely & Stephen Stills (electric guitar or bass)
unissued

'Long Title: Do I Have To Do This All Over Again' version 2 (Peter Tork)
Recorded January 20th 1968

Personnel Peter Tork (acoustic guitar)
unissued

'Long Title: Do I Have To Do This All Over Again' version 3
Recorded January 22nd 1968 (Peter Tork)
Personnel Peter Tork (electric guitar), Lance Wakely (bass)
unissued

'Long Title: Do I Have To Do This All Over Again' version 4
(Peter Tork)
Recorded January 25th 1968, January 26th 1968, January 27th 1968, January 28th 1968,
February 1st 1968, February 3rd 1968, February 4th 1968, February 10th 1968, February 12nd 1968, February 14th 1968, February 15th 1968 & August 1st 1968
Personnel Peter Tork (lead & backing vocal, guitar), David Jones (backing vocal), Steve Stills (guitar), Lance Wakely (guitar, bass), Dewey Martin (drums), unknown (tambourine, handclaps)
Release *Head* Rhino CD #71795. In addition to this stereo mix, a slightly different mono mix – with a cold ending – can be heard in the film *Head*, available on the Rhino DVD #4460.

'Look Down' version 1 (Carole King/Toni Stern)
Recorded March 14th 1968 & March 15th 1968
Personnel Danny 'Kootch' Kortchmar & Ken Bloom (guitar), Doug Lubahn (bass), Ralph Schuckett (keyboard), Dallas Taylor & Michael Ney (drums, percussion), Ollie Mitchell & Stu Williamson (trumpets), Lew McCreary (trombone)
unissued

'Look Down' version 2 (Carole King/Toni Stern)
Recorded April 6th 1968, April 25th 1968 (& probably other dates)
Personnel David Jones (vocal), Tommy Tedesco, Al Casey & Dennis Budimir (guitars), Larry Knechtel (bass), Michel Rubini (piano), Hal Blaine (drums), Ken Watson (percussion), Jules Chaikin & Tony Terran (trumpets), Lew McCreary (trombone), Jim Horn & Jay Migliori (saxophones)
Release *Missing Links Volume 3* Rhino CD #72153

'Looking For The Good Times' (Tommy Boyce/Bobby Hart)
Recorded October 26th 1966, October 30th 1966, November 6th 1966, November 12nd 1966 & July 24th 1969
Personnel David Jones (lead vocal), Micky Dolenz (harmony vocal), Ron Hicklin (backing vocal), Wayne Erwin, Gerry McGee & Louie Shelton (guitars), Tommy Boyce (acoustic guitar, backing vocal), Bobby Hart (organ, backing vocal), Larry Taylor (bass), Billy Lewis (drums), Gene Estes (tambourine)
Release *The Monkees Present* Rhino CD #71797 features the original mono mix. The song also appears as a stereo remix on the *Listen To The Band* CD boxed set #70566.

'Look Out (Here Comes Tomorrow)' (Neil Diamond)
Recorded October 15th 1966 & October 23rd 1966
Personnel David Jones (lead vocal), Micky Dolenz, David Jones, Peter Tork (backing vocals), Neil Diamond (acoustic guitar), Buddy Salzman (drums), all others unknown
Release *More Of The Monkees* Rhino CD #71791. In addition to being available originally in mono and stereo mixes – the stereo appears on the current CD noted – this track was remixed in stereo for four other releases. Mix 1 appears on the Arista CD release of *More Of The Monkees* #ARCD-8525. Mix 2 is a second stereo remix, for the *Listen To The Band* CD boxed set #70566. Mix 3 features an instrumental break edited out of the song for record release and an unused narration from Peter Tork. This appears as a bonus track on the expanded reissue of *More Of The Monkees*. Mix 4, similar to mix 3 but lacking the narration from Tork, appears on the *Music Box* CD set #76706. Mix 4 also closely resembles a mix of the song heard only in the TV episode *Monkees In Manhattan*, which is now available on Rhino's *Season One* DVD boxed set #976076.

'Love Is Only Sleeping' (Barry Mann/Cynthia Weil)
Recorded June 19th 1967, July 10th 1967, September 5th 1967, September 7th 1967, September 23rd 1967, October 1st 1967 (& probably other dates)
Personnel Michael Nesmith (lead vocal, electric guitar), Micky Dolenz (backing vocal), Peter Tork (organ), David Jones (backing vocal, tambourine), Chip Douglas (backing vocal, bass, acoustic guitar), Eddie Hoh (drums), unknown (handclaps, additional percussion), Bill Martin & Harry Nilsson (instruments unknown)
Release *Pisces, Aquarius, Capricorn & Jones, Ltd.* Rhino CD #71793. In addition to being available originally in mono and stereo mixes – the stereo appears on the current CD noted – this song appears on the same CD as a bonus track in an alternative mix, lacking many overdubs.

'Love Is On The Way' (Denny Randell/Sandy Linzer)
Recorded January 22nd 1967, January 27th 1967, January 28th

1967 & October 3rd 1969
Personnel Charlie Macy, Al Gorgoni, Ralph Casale, Bob Rand & Don Thomas (guitars), Joe Macho (bass), Dom Cortese (accordion), Stan Free (percussion, mallets), Buddy Salzman (drums), Artie Butler (percussion), unknown (vocal, additional drums)
unissued

'Love To Love' (Neil Diamond)
Recorded January 21st 1967, February 4th 1967, February 5th 1967 & August 5th 1969
Personnel David Jones (lead vocal), Al Gorgoni, Don Thomas & Hugh McCracken (guitars), Lou Mauro (bass), Artie Butler (organ), Stan Free (clavinet), Herb Lovelle (drums), Tom Cerone (tambourine)
Release *Missing Links Volume 3* Rhino CD #72153 features a stereo remix. A mono remix appears on the *Listen To The Band* CD boxed set #70566.

'The Love You Got Inside' (Jeff Barry/Andy Kim/Jerry Leiber/Mike Stoller)
Recorded January 26th 1967
Personnel Sal Ditroia, Don Thomas & Hugh McCracken (guitars), James Tyrell (bass), Artie Butler (organ), Stan Free (clavinet), Herb Lovelle (drums)
unissued

'Lynn Harper' (Michael Nesmith)
Recorded May 29th 1969 & June 26th 1969
Personnel Gerry McGee & Louie Shelton (guitars), Michel Rubini (piano), Carol Kaye (bass), Earl Palmer (drums), Mack Johnson (trumpet), Lester Robertson (trombone), Clifford Solomon (tenor saxophone), John Williams (instrument unknown)
unissued

'Magnolia Simms'
version 1 (Michael Nesmith/Charlie Rockett)
Recorded December 2nd 1967
Personnel Michael Nesmith (vocal, guitar), Paul Smith (tack piano), Max Bennett (bass), Earl Palmer (drums), Ollie Mitchell (trumpet), Jim Horn & Jack Nimitz (woodwinds), Lew McCreary (trombone)
Release *The Birds, The Bees & The Monkees* Rhino CD #71794

'Magnolia Simms' version 2 by Michael Nesmith & The First National Band (Michael Nesmith/Charlie Rockett)
Recorded February 10th 1970
Personnel unknown
unissued

'Mama Nantucket' by Michael Nesmith & The First National Band (Michael Nesmith)
Recorded February 20th 1970
Personnel Michael Nesmith (vocal, acoustic guitar), John London (bass), Red Rhodes (pedal steel guitar), John Ware (drums), Earl Ball (piano), unknown (percussion)
Release *Magnetic South & Loose Salute* BMG/Camden CD #74321 660442

'Mary, Mary' (Michael Nesmith)
Recorded July 25th 1966 & July 27th 1966
Personnel Micky Dolenz (lead & backing vocal), James Burton, Glen Campbell, Al Casey, Mike Deasy & Peter Tork (guitar), Bob West (bass), Hal Blaine (drums), Jim Gordon & Gary Coleman (percussion), Michael Cohen & Larry Knechtel (keyboards)
Release *More Of The Monkees* Rhino CD #71791. In addition to being available originally in mono and stereo mixes – the stereo appears on the current CD noted – this track was remixed in stereo for two other releases. Mix 1 appears on the Arista CD release of *More Of The Monkees* #ARCD-8525. Mix 2 appears on the *Listen To The Band* CD boxed set #70566.

'Mary, Mary' live version 1 (Michael Nesmith)
Recorded January 21st 1967
Personnel Micky Dolenz (lead vocal, drums), David Jones (backing vocal, tambourine; drums on ending only), Michael Nesmith (electric 12-string guitar), Peter Tork (backing vocal, bass)
Release *Season One* DVD boxed set Rhino #976076. This is only an excerpt of the song with overdubbed vocal, as featured in the TV episode *The Monkees On Tour*. The complete live version is thus far unissued.

'Mary, Mary' live version 2 (Michael Nesmith)
Recorded August 12nd 1967
Personnel Micky Dolenz (lead vocal, drums), David Jones (backing vocal, maracas; drums on ending only), Michael Nesmith (electric 12-string guitar), Peter Tork (backing vocal, bass)
Release *Summer 1967: The Complete U.S. Concert Recordings* Rhino CD #RHM2 7755

'Mary, Mary' live version 3 (Michael Nesmith)
Recorded August 25th 1967
Personnel Micky Dolenz (lead vocal, drums), David Jones (backing vocal, maracas; drums on ending only), Michael Nesmith (electric 12-string guitar), Peter Tork (backing vocal, bass)
Release *Summer 1967: The Complete U.S. Concert Recordings* Rhino CD #RHM2 7755

'Mary, Mary' live version 4 (Michael Nesmith)
Recorded August 26th 1967
Personnel Micky Dolenz (lead vocal, drums), David Jones – backing vocal, maracas (& drums on ending only); Michael Nesmith (electric 12-string guitar), Peter Tork (backing vocal, bass)
Release *Summer 1967: The Complete U.S. Concert Recordings* Rhino CD #RHM2 7755

'Mary, Mary' live version 5 (Michael Nesmith)
Recorded August 27th 1967
Personnel Micky Dolenz (lead vocal, drums), David Jones (backing vocal, maracas; drums on ending only), Michael Nesmith (electric 12-string guitar), Peter Tork (backing vocal, bass)
Release *Summer 1967: The Complete U.S. Concert Recordings* Rhino CD #RHM2 7755. An alternative mix of this performance appears on Rhino's *Live 1967* CD #70139.

'Mary, Mary' live version 6 (Michael Nesmith)
Recorded May 17th 1968
Personnel Micky Dolenz (vocal, drums), Michael Nesmith (vocal, electric guitar), Peter Tork (bass)
unissued

"Masking Tape" (unknown)
Recorded March 16th 1967
Personnel Michael Nesmith (electric 12-string guitar), Peter Tork (electric six-string guitar), David Jones (tambourine), Micky Dolenz (drums), Jerry Yester (bass)
Release *Headquarters Sessions* Rhino CD #RHM2 7715

'Maybe It's Because I'm A Londoner' by David Jones (Gregg)
Recorded July 26th 1965 (and possibly other dates)
Personnel David Jones (vocal), Gene Garf (piano), Red Callender (bass), Al Casey, Carol Kaye, Bill Pitman & Tommy Tedesco (guitars), Emil Richards (percussion), Earl Palmer (drums)
Release *David Jones* Colpix album #493 (in mono & stereo)

'Memphis Tennessee' (Chuck Berry)
Recorded March 7th 1967
Personnel Michael Nesmith (electric 12-string guitar), Peter Tork (electric six-string guitar), Davy Jones (tambourine), Micky Dolenz (drums), John London (bass)
Release *Headquarters Sessions* Rhino CD #RHM2 7715

'Merry Go Round' version 1 (Peter Tork/Diane Hilderbrand)
Recorded December 17th 1967
Personnel Peter Tork (lead vocal, acoustic guitar)
unissued

'Merry Go Round' version 2 (Peter Tork/Diane Hilderbrand)
Recorded January 20th 1968 (and possibly other dates)
Personnel Peter Tork (vocal, piano, bass)
unissued

'Merry Go Round' version 3 (Peter Tork/Diane Hilderbrand)
Recorded January 22nd 1968
Personnel Peter Tork (vocal, piano, bass)
unissued

'Merry Go Round' version 4 (Peter Tork/Diane Hilderbrand)
Recorded January 31st 1968 (& probably other dates)
Personnel Peter Tork (vocal, piano, organ, bass), Lance Wakely (instrument unknown)
Release *Missing Links Volume 3* Rhino CD #72153

'Me Without You' (Tommy Boyce/Bobby Hart)
Recorded December 26th 1967, February 3rd 1968, December 20th 1968 & December 28th 1968
Personnel David Jones (vocal), Louis Shelton & Gerry McGee (guitars), Joe Osborn (bass), Bobby Hart (keyboard), Billy Lewis (drums), unknown (backing vocal, horns, tambourine, calliope)
Release *Instant Replay* Rhino CD #71796. An alternative mono mix of the song with added fuzz guitar appears as a bonus track on the same CD.

'Michigan Blackhawk' (Michael Nesmith)
Recorded June 10th 1969 & June 29th 1969
Personnel Louie Shelton & Al Casey (electric guitars), Michel Rubini (piano), Max Bennett (bass), Hal Blaine (drums)

unissued (The song 'Down The Highway' was mistakenly issued under this title on Rhino's *Missing Links Volume 2*. 'Michigan Blackhawk' itself remains unissued)

"Micky In Carlsbad Caverns"
Recorded March 14th 1967
Personnel Micky Dolenz (voice)
Release *Headquarters Sessions* Rhino CD #RHM2 7715

'Midnight Train' demo (Micky Dolenz)
Recorded February 1967
Personnel Micky Dolenz (vocal, guitar), Coco Dolenz (harmony vocal)
Release *Missing Links Volume 3* Rhino CD #72153. This recording also appears in a slightly different mix on the *Headquarters Sessions* CD set #RHM2 7715.

'Midnight Train' (Micky Dolenz)
Recorded July 16th 1969 & July 22nd 1969
Personnel Micky Dolenz (lead & backing vocal), Coco Dolenz (additional backing vocal), Louie Shelton (electric guitar), James Burton (banjo), Tommy Morgan (harmonica), Joe Osborn (bass), Hal Blaine (drums)
Release *Changes* Rhino CD#71798

'Mommy And Daddy' (Micky Dolenz)
Recorded August 1st 1968, August 8th 1968, December 9th 1968, December 28th 1968, January 10th 1969, May 13th 1969, July 1st 1969, July 2nd 1969, July 10th 1969, July 22nd 1969 (& probably other dates)
Personnel Micky Dolenz (lead & backing vocal, piano, drums?), Coco Dolenz (backing vocal), Dom DeMieri (guitar), Pat Coghlan (instrument unknown), Mike Saluzzi (guitar), Michael Rubini (keyboard), Dick Nash (trombone), Buddy Childers, Bud Brisbois & Ray Triscari (trumpets), John Kitzmiller (tuba), Don McGinnis (brass), unknown (bass)
Release *The Monkees Present* Rhino CD #71797. This CD also features an early mix as a bonus track, highlighted by an almost entirely different set of lyrics. A further unique mix/edit appears on Rhino's *Anthology* CD #75269.

'Mr. Richland's Favorite Song' (Harry Nilsson)
Recorded January 11th 1968
Personnel Michael Nesmith (electric guitar), Harry Nilsson (vocal, piano), Rick Dey (bass), Eddie Hoh (drums)
unissued

'Mr. Webster' version 1 (Tommy Boyce/Bobby Hart)
Recorded September 10th 1966 & September 24th 1966
Personnel Micky Dolenz (lead & backing vocal), Wayne Erwin, Gerry McGee & Louie Shelton (acoustic guitars), Larry Taylor (bass), Michel Rubini (harpsichord), Alan Estes (tympani), Norman Benno (oboe), Maggie Aue (cello)
Release *Missing Links Volume 2* Rhino CD #70903

'Mr. Webster' version 2 (Tommy Boyce/Bobby Hart)
Recorded February 24th 1967
Personnel Micky Dolenz (lead vocal, guitar), David Jones (backing vocal, tambourine), Michael Nesmith (steel guitar), Peter Tork (piano), John London (bass)
Release *Headquarters* Rhino CD #71792. In addition to being available originally in mono and stereo mixes – the stereo appears on the current CD noted, while the mono resides on the *Headquarters Sessions* CD set #RHM2 7715 – this track was remixed in stereo for the Arista edition of the *Headquarters* CD #ARCD 8602. Additionally, the *Headquarters Sessions* set features an instrumental mix of the song.

'Misty' by David Jones (Johnny Burke/Erroll Garner)
Recorded circa 1963
Personnel David Jones (vocal), unknown (piano)
Release *Just For The Record* Hercules Promotions CD #Y6120E

'More' by David Jones (Marcello Ciorciolini/Norman Newell/Nino Oliviero/Riz Ortolani)
Recorded circa 1963
Personnel David Jones (vocal), unknown (piano)
Release *Just For The Record* Hercules Promotions CD #Y6120E

'Music Bridge' released under the title 'We'll Be Back In A Minute' (Micky Dolenz)
Recorded July 1st 1969
Personnel Micky Dolenz (lead & backing vocal, acoustic guitar, & possibly other recorded elements), Chip Douglas (bass), Henry Diltz (banjo), unknown (kazoos, knee slaps, handclaps)
Release *Missing Links Volume 3* Rhino CD #72153

'Mustang' *see* 'You Can't Tie A Mustang Down'

'My Dad' by David Jones (Barry Mann/Cynthia Weil)
Recorded July 26th 1965 (and possibly other dates)
Personnel David Jones (vocal), Elliott Fisher, James Getzoff, Victor Arno, Henry L. Roth, Paul Shure, Arnold Belnick & Lou Raderman (violins), Kurt Reher & Harold Schneier (cellos), James Decker & George Price (French horns), Gene Garf (piano), Red Callender (bass), Al Casey, Carol Kaye, Bill Pitman & Tommy Tedesco (guitars), Emil Richards (percussion), Earl Palmer (drums)
Release *David Jones* Colpix album #493 (in mono & stereo)

'My Share Of The Sidewalk' version 1 (Michael Nesmith)
Recorded January 9th 1968, January 19th 1968 & March 13th 1968
Personnel David Jones (lead vocal), Michael Nesmith (vocal, piano, guitar), Rick Dey (bass), Eddie Hoh (drums), Tony Terran, Pete Candoli & Buddy Childers (trumpets), Dick Leith & Lew McCreary (trombones), Ray Kramer, Eleanor Slatkin, Emmet Sargeant & Justin DiTullio (cellos)
Release *Missing Links* Rhino CD #70150

'My Share Of The Sidewalk' version 2 (Michael Nesmith)
Recorded January 22nd 1969 & January 31st 1969
Personnel James Hughart & Max Bennett (basses), Michel Rubini (piano), John Guerin (drums), Gene Pello (mallets), Jules Chaikin (trumpet), Paul Shure, Jerome Reisler, Arnold Belnick, Wilbert Nuttycombe, Gerald Vinci & Bonnie Douglas (violins), Douglas Davis (cello), Del Kacher (guitar?), Bob Jung, William Weiss, Jack Gootkin, George Poole & Heimann Weinstine (violins), Garry Nutteycombe (viola), unknown (additional guitars, steel guitar)
unissued

'My Song In #7' (Peter Tork)
Recorded January 24th 1968
Personnel Peter Tork – guitar
unissued

'My Storybook Of You' (Tommy Boyce/Bobby Hart)
Recorded May 30th 1969 & May 31st 1969
Personnel Davy Jones (lead & backing vocal), Tommy Boyce & Bobby Hart (backing vocal), Louie Shelton (acoustic guitar), Larry Knechtel (tack piano), John Gallie (piano on ending only), Joe Osborn (bass), Hal Blaine & Billy Lewis (drums), Sidney Sharp, Jerome Reisler, Shari Zippert, Bill Kursach & Ralph Schaeffer (violins), Jesse Ehrlich (cello), Jules Chaikin & Ollie Mitchell (trumpets), Dick Nash (trombone), Jay Migliori (saxophone), William Pening (instrument unknown), unknown (electric guitar)
Release *Missing Links* Rhino CD #70150

'Nadine (Is It You)?' by Michael Nesmith & The First National Band (Chuck Berry/Alan Freed)
Recorded July 14th 1970 & July 16th 1970
Personnel unknown
unissued

'Naked Persimmon' (Michael Nesmith)
Recorded November 12nd 1968 (& other dates)
Personnel Michael Nesmith (lead & backing vocal), Mike Deasy & Dennis Budimer (guitars), Joe Osborn (bass), Larry Knechtel & Jimmy Rowles (keyboards), Hal Blaine (drums), unknown (steel guitar)
Release *Season Two* DVD boxed set Rhino #970128

'Nashville' NOT THE MONKEES (Tommy Boyce/Bobby Hart)
Recorded December 30th 1967
Personnel Tommy Boyce (vocal, acoustic guitar), Louis Shelton, Gerry McGee, Wayne Erwin & Keith Allison (guitars), Joe Osborn (bass), Bobby Hart (tack piano), Billy Lewis (drums)
unissued

'Nevada Fighter' by Michael Nesmith & The First National Band (Michael Nesmith)
Recorded August 12th 1970, August 13rd 1970, August 14th 1970
Personnel Michael Nesmith (vocal, guitar), John London (bass), Red Rhodes (pedal steel guitar), John Ware (drums), Jim Zitro (percussion), Michael Cohen (keyboard), Billy Dale (instrument unknown), unknown (dobro)
Release *Nevada Fighter & Tantamount To Treason* BMG/Camden CD #74321 822352

'Never Tell A Woman Yes' (Michael Nesmith)
Recorded June 2nd 1969 (& other unknown dates)
Personnel Michael Nesmith (vocal, acoustic guitar), Al Casey (banjo), Michel Rubini or Larry Knechtel (piano), Joe Osborn (bass), Hal Blaine (drums)
Release *The Monkees Present* Rhino CD #71797

'Never Will I Ever' by David Jones (unknown)
Recorded circa 1965
Personnel David Jones (vocal), all others unknown
Release *Just For The Record* Hercules Promotions CD #Y6120E

'The New Recruit' by Michael Blessing (Arranged, Copyrighted & Adapted by Sam Ashe/Bob Krasnow)
Recorded circa 1965
Personnel Michael Nesmith (vocal), all others unknown
Release Colpix single #787. Also available on Rhino's *The Colpix/Dimension Story* #71650.

'Nine Times Blue' demo (Michael Nesmith)
Recorded circa 1967
Personnel Michael Nesmith (vocal, acoustic 12–string guitar)
Release *Missing Links Volume 3* Rhino CD #71792. A slightly different and longer mix of this performance is available on Rhino Handmade's *Headquarters Sessions* set #RHM2 7715.

'Nine Times Blue' version 1 by Mike Nesmith/The Wichita Train Whistle Sings (Michael Nesmith)
Recorded circa November 18 or 19th 1967
Personnel Bud Brisbois (trumpet), Doug Dillard (banjo), Red Rhodes (pedal steel guitar), all others unknown
Release *The Wichita Train Whistle Sings* Dot album #DLP 25861

'Nine Times Blue' version 2 (Michael Nesmith)
Recorded February 2nd 1968
Personnel Michael Nesmith (acoustic guitar), Keith Allison (electric guitar), John Ethridge (bass), Eddie Hoh (drums)
unissued

'Nine Times Blue' version 3 (Michael Nesmith)
Recorded February 8th 1968
Personnel Michael Nesmith (vocal, acoustic guitar), David Jones (vocal), Keith Allison & Bill Chadwick (electric guitars), John Ethridge (bass), Eddie Hoh (drums)
unissued

'Nine Times Blue' version 4 (Michael Nesmith)
Recorded April 5th 1968, August 21st 1968 & October 29th 1968
Personnel Michael Nesmith (vocal, guitar), Chip Douglas (bass), Red Rhodes (pedal steel guitar)
Release *Missing Links* Rhino CD #70150

'Nine Times Blue' version 5 by Michael Nesmith & The First National Band (Michael Nesmith)
Recorded February 10th 1970 & February 20th 1970
Personnel Michael Nesmith (vocal, acoustic guitar), John London (bass), Red Rhodes (pedal steel guitar), John Ware (drums)
Release *Magnetic South & Loose Salute* BMG/Camden CD #74321 660442

'99 Pounds' (Jeff Barry)
Recorded January 21st 1967, February 4th 1967, February 6th 1967, February 8th 1967
Personnel David Jones (lead vocal), Al Gorgoni, Don Thomas & Hugh McCracken (guitars), Lou Mauro (bass), Artie Butler (organ), Stan Free (clavinet), Herb Lovelle (drums), Tom Cerone (tambourine), unknown (backing vocal, handclaps)
Release *Changes* Rhino CD#71798

'No Time' version 1 (Hank Cicalo)
Recorded March 17th 1967 & March 20th 1967
Personnel Michael Nesmith (electric 12-string guitar), Peter Tork (piano), Micky Dolenz (drums), Jerry Yester (bass), Keith Allison & Gerry McGee (guitars)
Release *Headquarters Sessions* Rhino CD#RHM2 7715

'No Time' version 2 (Hank Cicalo)
Recorded March 28th 1967 (and possibly other dates)
Personnel Micky Dolenz (lead vocal, drums), David Jones (backing vocal, tambourine), Michael Nesmith (electric guitar), Peter Tork (piano), Chip Douglas (bass), unknown (additional backing vocal, electric guitar)
Release *Headquarters* Rhino CD#71792. In addition to being available originally in mono and stereo mixes – the stereo appears on the current CD noted, while the mono resides on the *Headquarters Sessions* CD set #RHM2 7715 – this track was remixed in stereo for the Arista edition of the *Headquarters* CD #ARCD 8602. Additionally, the *Headquarters Sessions* set features an instrumental mix and highlights from the tracking session for the song.

'No Title' version 1 (Michael Nesmith)
Recorded January 23rd 1968
Personnel Michael Nesmith (organ), Keith Allison (electric guitar), Joe Osborn (bass), Kim Capli (drums)
unissued

"No Title" version 2 (Michael Nesmith)
Recorded January 25th 1968
Personnel Michael Nesmith (organ), Charles Wright (electric guitar),

Ron Brown (bass), Earl Palmer (drums)
unissued

'Of You' (Bill Chadwick/John Chadwick)
Recorded July 25th 1966, July 27th 1966 & July 22nd 1969
Personnel Michael Nesmith (lead vocal), Micky Dolenz (harmony vocal), James Burton, Glen Campbell, Al Casey, Mike Deasy & Peter Tork (guitars), Bob West (bass), Hal Blaine (drums), Jim Gordon & Gary Coleman (percussion), Michael Cohen & Larry Knechtel (keyboards)
Release *Missing Links* Rhino CD #70150 has a stereo remix from the late 1980s featuring a harmony vocal from Micky. An original mono mix from late '66 with just Michael's vocal appears on *Music Box* Rhino CD #76706.

'Oh My My' (Jeff Barry/Andy Kim)
Recorded February 5th 1970 (& probably other dates)
Personnel Micky Dolenz (lead vocal), all others unknown
Release *Changes* Rhino CD #71798

'Oklahoma Backroom Dancer' (Michael Martin Murphey)
Recorded May 27th 1968
Personnel Michael Nesmith (vocal), Louie Shelton & Mike Deasy (guitars), Michel Rubini (piano), Max Bennett (bass), Eddie Hoh (drums), unknown (acoustic guitar, tambourine, shaker)
Release *The Monkees Present* Rhino CD#71797

'Omega' (Michael Nesmith)
Recorded June 2nd 1969
Personnel Michael Nesmith (acoustic guitar), Al Casey (electric guitar), Michel Rubini or Larry Knechtel (piano), Joe Osborn (bass), Hal Blaine (drums)
unissued

'One Rose' by Michael Nesmith & The First National Band (Del Lyon/Loni McIntire)
Recorded February 22nd 1970
Personnel Michael Nesmith (vocal, guitar), John London (bass), Red Rhodes (pedal steel guitar), John Ware (drums)
Release *Magnetic South & Loose Salute* BMG/Camden CD #74321 660442

'Only Bound' by Michael Nesmith & The First National Band (Michael Nesmith)
Recorded December 23rd 1970
Personnel Michael Nesmith (vocal, guitar), Red Rhodes (pedal steel guitar), all others unknown
Release *Nevada Fighter & Tantamount To Treason* BMG/Camden CD #74321 822352

'Opening Night' (Charlie Smalls)
Recorded May 1st 1969
Personnel David Jones (lead & backing vocal), unknown (guitar, piano, brass, bass, drums)
unissued

'Papa Gene's Blues' version 1 (Michael Nesmith)
Recorded July 7th 1966, July 16th 1966 & July 30th 1966
Personnel Michael Nesmith (lead vocal), Micky Dolenz (harmony vocal), Al Casey, Glen Campbell, James Burton, Jim Helms & Peter Tork (guitars), Hal Blaine (drums), Gary Coleman & Jim Gordon (percussion), Bill Pitman (bass)
Release *The Monkees* Rhino CD #71790. In addition to being available originally in mono and stereo mixes – the stereo appears on the current CD noted – this track was remixed in stereo for two other releases. Mix 1 appears on the Arista CD release of *The Monkees* #ARCD-8524; mix 2 on the *Listen To The Band* CD boxed set #70566.

'Papa Gene's Blues' live version (Michael Nesmith)
Recorded January 21st 1967
Personnel Michael Nesmith (lead vocal, electric 12-string guitar), Peter Tork (backing vocal, bass), David Jones (backing vocal, maracas, tambourine), Micky Dolenz (backing vocal, drums)
unissued

'Papa Gene's Blues' version 2 by Mike Nesmith/The Wichita Train Whistle Sings (Michael Nesmith)
Recorded circa November 18 or 19th 1967
Personnel Bud Brisbois (trumpet), all others unknown
Release *The Wichita Train Whistle Sings* Dot album #DLP 25861

'The Party' (David Jones/Steve Pitts)
Recorded February 15th 1968 & February 17th 1968
Personnel David Jones (lead vocal), Al Casey, Michael Deasy, Howard Roberts (guitars), Don Randi (organ), Lyle Ritz (bass), Hal Blaine (drums), Gary Coleman & Gene Estes (percussion including tambourine & marimba), Buddy Childers, Tony Terran, Clyde Reasinger & Jack Sheldon (trumpets), Lew McCreary, Milt Bernhart, Frank Rosolino & Dick Leith (trombones), John Lowe (saxophone, woodwind), Erno Neufeld, George Kast, Nathan Kaproff, Marvin Limonick, Alex Murray & Ambrose Russo (violins)
Release *Missing Links* Rhino CD #70150

'Penny Music' (Michael Leonard/Bobby Weinstein)
Recorded May 1st 1969 & July 11st 1969
Personnel David Jones (lead & backing vocal), Bill Chadwick (backing vocal), unknown (guitar, piano, harpsichord, bass, drums, brass)
Release *Missing Links Volume 3* Rhino CD #72153

"Peter Gunn's Gun" (Henry Mancini)
Recorded March 1967
Personnel Michael Nesmith (steel guitar), Peter Tork (piano), Micky Dolenz (drums), David Jones (tambourine), Chip Douglas or Jerry Yester (bass)
Release *Headquarters* Rhino CD #71792. The recording also appears in a slightly different mix on the *Headquarters Sessions* CD set #RHM2 7715.

'Peter Percival Patterson's Pet Pig Porky' (Peter Tork)
Recorded June 10th 1967 & October 4th 1967
Personnel Peter Tork (spoken word)
Release *Pisces, Aquarius, Capricorn & Jones, Ltd.* Rhino CD #71793

'Pillow Time' version 1 (Janelle Scott/Matt Willis)
Recorded March 14th 1967
Personnel Micky Dolenz (voice, zither)
Release *Headquarters* Rhino CD #71792. A longer edit of this performance is included on the *Headquarters Sessions* set #RHM2 7715.

'Pillow Time' version 2 (Janelle Scott/Matt Willis)
Recorded August 14th 1969
Personnel Micky Dolenz (vocal, acoustic guitar), Louie Shelton (electric guitar), Ray Pohlman (bass), Earl Palmer (drums)
Release *The Monkees Present* Rhino CD #71797

'Pinball Machine'
Recorded January 24th 1968
Personnel Michael Nesmith (player)
unissued

'Pleasant Valley Sunday' (Gerry Goffin/Carole King)
Recorded June 10th 1967, June 11st 1967, June 13rd 1967 (& possibly other dates in June)
Personnel Micky Dolenz (lead vocal, possibly guitar), Michael Nesmith (backing vocal, electric guitar), Peter Tork (backing vocal, piano), David Jones (backing vocal), Eddie Hoh (drums, percussion), Chip Douglas (bass, possibly backing vocal), Bill Chadwick (acoustic guitar)
Release *Pisces, Aquarius, Capricorn & Jones, Ltd.* Rhino CD #71793 features the original stereo album version. A significantly different and shorter mono mix appeared on the song's original single release, but this can now be heard on such Rhino releases as *Music Box* #76706, *Greatest Hits* #75785, and *Anthology* #75269. A unique stereo remix of the song is featured on the *Listen To The Band* boxed set #70566. Two instrumental mixes have also appeared: mix 1 is on the Japanese-only East-West release *The Monkees Best!!* #AMCY-978; mix 2, slightly shorter and with the stereo channels reversed, appears on Rhino's *The Best Of The Monkees* #73875.

'P.O. Box 9847' (Tommy Boyce/Bobby Hart/Bob Rafelson)
Recorded December 26th 1967, February 10th 1968 (& probably other dates)
Personnel Micky Dolenz (lead vocal), Louis Shelton & Gerry McGee (electric guitars), Joe Osborn (bass), Bobby Hart (tack piano), Billy Lewis (drums, percussion), Victor Arno & Jack Pepper (violins), Philip Goldberg (viola), Ray Kelley (cello), unknown (tabla, backing vocal, marxophone, handclaps)
Release *The Birds, The Bees & The Monkees* Rhino CD #71794. In addition to being available originally in mono and stereo mixes – the stereo appears on the current CD noted – this track was also remixed in stereo for the *Listen To The Band* boxed set #70566. A rough mix from the period – featuring Moog synthesizer and no strings – is included as a bonus track on *The Birds...* CD noted.

'Poor Little Me' (Jeff Barry/Andy Kim)
Recorded January 26th 1967
Personnel Sal Ditroia, Don Thomas & Hugh McCracken (guitars), James Tyrell (bass), Artie Butler (organ), Stan Free (clavinet), Herb Lovelle (drums), Tom Cerone (tambourine)
unissued

'Porpoise Song' (Gerry Goffin/Carole King)
Recorded February 26th 1968, February 28th 1968, February 29th 1968, April 3rd 1968 & August 1st 1968
Personnel Micky Dolenz (lead vocal), Davy Jones (backing vocal), Danny 'Kootch' Kortchmar, Ken Bloom, possibly others (guitars), Doug Lubahn (bass), Leon Russell & Ralph Schuckett (keyboards), John Raines & Michael Ney (drums, percussion), Russ Titelman (cymbals), Bill Hinshaw & Jules Jacob (brass, woodwind), Jacqueline Lustgarten, Jan Kelley, Gregory Bemko & David Filerman (cellos), Clyde 'Whitey' Hoggan, Jim Hughart, Max Bennett & Jerry Scheff (upright basses), unknown (additional backing vocal)
Release Head *Rhino CD #71795* features the original stereo LP mix, lacking the song's coda. The full version can be heard on the Rhino Handmade *Nuggets: Hallucinations* compilation CD #RHM2 7821, which features the mono 45 mix, or *Greatest Hits*, which includes a period stereo mix. A stereo remix appears on the *Listen To The Band* CD boxed set #70566.

'The Poster' (David Jones/Steve Pitts)
Recorded February 15th 1968, February 17th 1968 & March 13rd 1968
Personnel David Jones (lead & backing vocal), unknown (additional backing vocal), Al Casey, Michael Deasy, Howard Roberts (guitars), Don Randi (organ), Lyle Ritz (bass), Hal Blaine (drums), Gary Coleman & Gene Estes (percussion including tambourine & glockenspiel), Buddy Childers, Tony Terran, Clyde Reasinger & Jack Sheldon (trumpets), Lew McCreary, Milt Bernhart, Frank Rosolino & Dick Leith (trombones), John Lowe (saxophone, woodwind), Erno Neufeld, George Kast, Nathan Kaproff, Marvin Limonick, Alex Murray & Ambrose Russo (violins)
Release *The Birds, The Bees & The Monkees* Rhino CD #71794

'Prithee' *see* '(I Prithee) Do Not Ask For Love'

'Propinquity (I've Just Begun To Care)' version 1 (Michael Nesmith)
Recorded May 28th 1968, August 21st 1968 (& other unknown dates)
Personnel Michael Nesmith (vocal), Wayne Moss (acoustic guitar), David Briggs (organ), Lloyd Green (steel guitar), Norbert Putnam (bass), Sonny Osborne (banjo), Kenny Buttrey (drums)
Release *Missing Links Volume 3* Rhino CD #72153

'Propinquity (I've Just Begun To Care)' version 2 by Michael Nesmith & The First National Band (Michael Nesmith)
Recorded August 13rd 1970, August 14th 1970
Personnel Michael Nesmith (vocal, guitar), John London (bass), Red Rhodes (pedal steel guitar), John Ware (drums), Jim Zitro (percussion), Michael Cohen (keyboard), Billy Dale (instrument unknown)
Release *Nevada Fighter & Tantamount To Treason* BMG/Camden CD #74321 822352

'Put Me Amongst The Girls' by David Jones (Hank Levine)
Recorded July 26th 1965 (and possibly other dates)
Personnel David Jones (vocal), Gene Garf (piano), Red Callender (bass), Al Casey, Carol Kaye, Bill Pitman & Tommy Tedesco (guitars), Emil Richards (marimba), Earl Palmer (drums), unknown (backing vocal)
Release *David Jones* Colpix album #493 (in mono & stereo)

"Question Mark" a.k.a "?" (unknown)
Recorded January 14th 1968
Personnel Peter Tork (bass), Stephen Stills & Lance Wakely (electric guitars), Buddy Miles (drums)
unissued

'Randy Scouse Git' (Micky Dolenz)
Recorded March 2nd 1967, March 4th 1967 & March 8th 1967
Personnel Micky Dolenz (lead vocal, drums, tympani), David Jones (backing vocal), Michael Nesmith (electric guitar), Peter Tork (backing vocal, piano, organ), Chip Douglas (bass)
Release *Headquarters* Rhino CD #71792. In addition to being available originally in mono and stereo mixes – the stereo appears on the current CD noted, while the mono resides on the *Headquarters Sessions* CD set #RHM2 7715 – this track was remixed in stereo for the Arista edition of the *Headquarters* CD #ARCD 8602. Additionally, the *Headquarters Sessions* set features an excerpt from the song's recording sessions, an alternative version, an instrumental mix, and an alternative mix with an unused 'tag' piece.

'Randy Scouse Git' live version 1 (Micky Dolenz)
Recorded August 12nd 1967
Personnel Micky Dolenz (lead vocal, tympani), David Jones (backing vocal, drums) Michael Nesmith (electric guitar), Peter Tork (backing vocal, organ)
Release *Summer 1967: The Complete U.S. Concert Recordings* Rhino CD #RHM2 7755

'Randy Scouse Git' live version 2 (Micky Dolenz)
Recorded August 25th 1967

Personnel Micky Dolenz (lead vocal, tympani), David Jones (drums), Michael Nesmith (electric 12-string guitar), Peter Tork (backing vocal, organ)
Release *Summer 1967: The Complete U.S. Concert Recordings* Rhino CD #RHM2 7755

'Randy Scouse Git' live version 3 (Micky Dolenz)
Recorded August 26th 1967
Personnel Micky Dolenz (lead vocal, tympani), David Jones (drums), Michael Nesmith (electric 12-string guitar), Peter Tork (backing vocal, organ)
Release *Summer 1967: The Complete U.S. Concert Recordings* Rhino CD #RHM2 7755. An alternative mix of this performance appears on Rhino's *Live 1967* CD #70139.

'Randy Scouse Git' live version 4 (Micky Dolenz)
Recorded August 27th 1967
Personnel Micky Dolenz (lead vocal, tympani), David Jones (backing vocal, drums) Michael Nesmith (electric 12-string guitar), Peter Tork (backing vocal, organ)
Release *Summer 1967: The Complete U.S. Concert Recordings* Rhino CD #RHM2 7755

"Rehearsal Jam #1" (unknown)
Recorded May 17th 1968
Personnel Michael Nesmith (electric guitar), Peter Tork (bass)
unissued

"Rehearsal Jam #2" (unknown)
Recorded May 17th 1968
Personnel Michael Nesmith (electric guitar), Peter Tork (bass), David Jones (maracas), Micky Dolenz (drums)
unissued

'Rene' by Michael Nesmith & The First National Band (Orville Rhodes)
Recorded August 18th 1970 & August 19th 1970
Personnel Michael Nesmith (guitar), John London (bass), Red Rhodes (pedal steel guitar), John Ware (drums), Jim Zitro (percussion), Michael Cohen (keyboard)
Release *Nevada Fighter & Tantamount To Treason* BMG/Camden CD #74321 822352

'Ride Baby Ride' (unknown)
Recorded March 26th 1970
Personnel unknown
unissued

'Riu Chiu' version 1 (Traditional)
Recorded August 24th 1967 & September 7th 1967
Personnel Micky Dolenz, David Jones, Michael Nesmith & Peter Tork (vocals)
Release *Season Two* DVD boxed set Rhino #R2 970128

'Riu Chiu' version 2 (Traditional)
Recorded October 3rd 1967
Personnel Micky Dolenz, Michael Nesmith, Peter Tork & Chip Douglas (vocals)
Release *Missing Links Volume Two* Rhino CD #70903

'Rose City Chimes' by Michael Nesmith & The First National Band (Bobby Garrett)
Recorded February 21st 1970
Personnel Michael Nesmith (acoustic guitar), John London (bass), Red Rhodes (pedal steel guitar), John Ware (drums), Earl P. Ball (piano), unknown (percussion)
Release *Nevada Fighter & Tantamount To Treason* BMG/Camden CD #74321 822352

'Rose Marie' (Micky Dolenz)
Recorded February 19th 1968?, March 1st 1968, March 13th 1968, March 14th 1968, June 7th 1968, June 13th 1968, December 28th 1968, January 10th 1969 (& possibly other dates)
Personnel Micky Dolenz (vocal, acoustic guitar), Peter Tork (acoustic guitar), Keith Allison (electric guitar), Chip Douglas? (bass), Jim Gordon? (drums), Michel Rubini (piano), Stu Williamson, Cappy a.k.a. Carroll Lewis, Ollie Mitchell & Buddy Childers (trumpets), Herbie Harper, Lou Blackburn & Lew McCreary (trombones), Bill Hood (saxophone), Larry Bunker (tambourine)
Release *Missing Links* Rhino CD #70150 features a stereo remix from the final 8-track master of the song. An original, much faster mix featuring different lyrics is included as a bonus track on the expanded CD reissue of *Instant Replay* #71796. Despite their differences, both are both derived from the same master and are not two separate versions of the song.

'St. Matthew' version 1 (Michael Nesmith)
Recorded December 2nd 1967

Personnel Michael Nesmith (vocal, guitar), Chip Douglas (bass), Eddie Hoh (drums)
unissued

'St. Matthew' version 2 (Michael Nesmith)
Recorded February 8th 1968
Personnel Michael Nesmith (vocal, acoustic guitar), John Ethridge (bass), Keith Allison (electric guitar), Eddie Hoh (drums)
unissued

'St. Matthew' version 3 (Michael Nesmith)
Recorded June 2nd 1968, June 12th 1968, August 5th 1968 & August 21st 1968
Personnel Michael Nesmith (vocal, electric guitar), Wayne Moss & Harold Bradley (guitars), Bobby Thompson (banjo), Lloyd Green (steel guitar), David Briggs (piano), Norbert Putnam (bass), Jerry Carrigan (drums), Buddy Spicher (fiddle), unknown (organ, percussion)
Release *Instant Replay* Rhino CD#71796 features an original stereo mix from the 1960s featuring a heavy Leslie-speaker effect on the entire mix. Two relatively similar stereo remixes of the song have also appeared. Mix 1 was prepared in 1989 for *Missing Links Volume 2* CD#70903. Mix 2, featuring some Leslie effect on Michael's vocal, was prepared in 1991 for the *Listen To The Band* boxed set #70566.

'Salesman' (Craig Smith)
Recorded June 14th 1967, July 15th 1967, September 5th 1967 (& probably other dates)
Personnel Michael Nesmith (lead vocal, electric guitar, shaker), Peter Tork (acoustic guitar?), Micky Dolenz & David Jones (backing vocal), Chip Douglas (nylon-string guitar, bass, possibly backing vocal), Eddie Hoh (drums)
Release *Pisces, Aquarius, Capricorn & Jones, Ltd.* Rhino CD #71793. In addition to being available originally in mono and stereo mixes – the stereo appears on the CD noted – a variety of alternative mixes have appeared. Mix 1 is an original mono mix from September 5th 1967 with a spoken tag from Michael; it was rejected for original release on the *Pisces, Aquarius…* album and is now featured as a bonus track on the Rhino CD noted. Mix 2 is a stereo remix issued on Arista's CD reissue of the *Pisces, Aquarius…* album #ARCD-8603. Mix 3 is a longer stereo remix created for the Rhino *Listen To The Band* boxed set #70566 and featuring the spoken tag from Michael.

'Saturday's Child' (David Gates)
Recorded July 9th 1966 (and possibly other dates)
Personnel Micky Dolenz (lead vocal), Ron Hicklin & Tommy Boyce (backing vocals), Bobby Hart (organ, backing vocal), Wayne Erwin (guitar, backing vocal), Gerry McGee & Louie Shelton (guitars), Larry Taylor (bass), Billy Lewis (drums), Gene Estes (tambourine)
Release *The Monkees* Rhino CD #71790 features the original stereo mix. The original mono mix appears on Arista's *The Monkees* CD #ARCD-8524.

'Seasons' (Michael Nesmith)
Recorded February 2nd 1968
Personnel Michael Nesmith (acoustic guitar), Joe Mondragon (bass), Pearl Kaufman (harpsichord), Bud Shank (flute), Erno Neufeld, Nathan Kaproff & Sam Freed (violins), Edgar Lustgarten, Justin DiTullio, Emmet Sargeant & Jacqueline Lustgarten (cellos)
unissued

'Seeger's Theme' demo (Pete Seeger)
Recorded January 30th 1967
Personnel Peter Tork (acoustic guitar, whistling)
Release *Headquarters Sessions* Rhino CD #RHM2 7715

'Seeger's Theme' version 1 (Pete Seeger)
Recorded November 12nd 1967
Personnel Peter Tork (acoustic guitar, whistling, humming)
unissued

'Seeger's Theme' version 2 (Pete Seeger)
Recorded January 14th 1968
Personnel Peter Tork (electric guitar), Stephen Stills & Lance Wakely (electric guitar, bass), Buddy Miles (drums)
unissued

'Seeger's Theme' version 3 (Pete Seeger)
Recorded January 20th 68, January 22nd 68 & February 10th 1968
Personnel Peter Tork (acoustic guitar, whistling, bass, handclaps), Lance Wakely (instrument unknown)
unissued

'Seeger's Theme' version 4 (Pete Seeger)
Recorded February 12nd 1968 & February 13th 1968
Personnel Peter Tork (whistling, guitar, bass, banjo), Lance Wakely (guitar), Buddy Miles (drums)
Release *Missing Links Volume 2* Rhino CD #70903

'Shades Of Gray' (Barry Mann/Cynthia Weil)
March 16th 1967 & March 22nd 1967
Personnel David Jones (lead & backing vocal, maracas, tambourine), Peter Tork (lead & backing vocal, piano), Micky Dolenz (backing vocal, drums), Michael Nesmith (steel guitar), Jerry Yester (bass), Frederick Seykora (cello), Vincent DeRosa (French horn)
Release *Headquarters* Rhino CD #71792. In addition to being available originally in mono and stereo mixes – the stereo appears on the current CD noted, while the mono resides on the *Headquarters Sessions* CD set #RHM2 7715 – this track was remixed in stereo for the Arista edition of the *Headquarters* CD #ARCD 8602. Additionally, the *Headquarters Sessions* set features an instrumental mix of the song.

'The Shadow Of A Man' (Helen Miller/Howard Greenfield)
Recorded March 9th 1968
Personnel Mike Deasy, Dennis Budimir & Al Casey (guitars), Max Bennett (bass), Michael Melvoin (organ), Earl Palmer (drums), Stan Levey & Milt Holland (tambourine, vibes)
unissued

'Shake 'Em Up And Let 'Em Roll' (Jerry Leiber/Mike Stoller)
Recorded February 24th 1968
Personnel Micky Dolenz (lead & backing vocal), Bill Chadwick (acoustic guitar), Keith Allison (electric guitar), Chip Douglas (bass), Henry Diltz (clarinet), Eddie Hoh (drums), unknown (additional backing vocal)
Release *Missing Links Volume 3* Rhino CD #72153

'She' (Tommy Boyce/Bobby Hart)
Recorded August 15th 1966 & August 27th 1966
Personnel Micky Dolenz (lead & backing vocal), Ron Hicklin, Tommy Boyce, Peter Tork & David Jones (backing vocals), Wayne Erwin (backing vocal, guitar), Gerry McGee & Louie Shelton (guitars), Larry Taylor (bass), Billy Lewis (drums), Norm Jeffries (tambourine), Bobby Hart (organ, backing vocal), unknown (additional tambourine)
Release *More Of The Monkees* Rhino CD #71791. In addition to being available originally in mono and stereo mixes – the stereo appears on the current CD noted – this track was remixed in stereo for two other releases: mix 1 appears on the Arista CD release of *More Of The Monkees* #ARCD-8525; mix 2 on the *Listen To The Band* CD boxed set #70566.

'She Hangs Out' version 1 (Jeff Barry/Ellie Greenwich)
Recorded January 21st 1967, February 4th 1967, February 6th 1967 & February 10th 1967
Personnel David Jones (lead vocal), Al Gorgoni, Don Thomas & Hugh McCracken (guitars), Lou Mauro (bass), Artie Butler (organ), Stan Free (clavinet), Herb Lovelle (drums), Tom Cerone (tambourine), unknown (backing vocal)
Release *Missing Links Volume 3* Rhino CD#72153 features the original mono version intended for single release in 1967. A slightly longer remix from 1991 appears on the *Listen To The Band* CD boxed set #70566.

'She Hangs Out' version 2 (Jeff Barry/Ellie Greenwich)
Recorded June 21st 1967, July 3rd 1967, August 9th 1967, September 5th 1967, September 23rd 1967 (& probably other dates)
Personnel David Jones (lead & backing vocal), Micky Dolenz (backing vocal), Michael Nesmith (electric guitar), Peter Tork (organ), Chip Douglas (backing vocal, bass), Eddie Hoh (drums), Manny Stevens, Al Porcino & Pete Candoli (trumpets), Dick Noel (trombone), Phil Teele & Dick Leith (bass trombones), unknown (additional electric guitar, tambourine, handclaps, other percussion)
Release *Pisces, Aquarius, Capricorn & Jones, Ltd.* Rhino CD#71793. In addition to being available originally in mono and stereo mixes – the stereo appears on the current CD noted – a longer stereo remix appears on the Arista edition of the *Pisces, Aquarius…* CD #ARCD 8603. An early mix – without horns – is featured in the second season TV episode *Card Carrying Red Shoes*, which can now be found on Rhino's *Season One* DVD boxed set #970128.

"She'll Be There" (unknown)
Recorded February 1967
Personnel Micky Dolenz (vocal, guitar), Coco Dolenz (harmony vocal)
Release *Missing Links Volume 3* Rhino CD #72153. This recording also appears in a slightly different mix on the *Headquarters Sessions* CD set #RHM2 7715.

'She Said To Me' NOT THE MONKEES (unknown)
Recorded May 8th 1967
unknown (vocal, guitar), Chip Douglas (harmony vocal)
unissued

'She's So Far Out She's In' (Baker Knight)
Recorded January 16th 1967
Personnel Michael Nesmith (electric 12–string guitar), Peter Tork

(bass), Micky Dolenz (drums), David Jones (maracas)
Release *Headquarters Sessions* Rhino CD#RHM 7715

'She's So Far Out She's In' live version (Baker Knight)
Recorded January 21st 1967
Personnel Michael Nesmith (lead vocal, electric 12-string guitar), Peter Tork (backing vocal, bass), David Jones (backing vocal, tambourine), Micky Dolenz (backing vocal, drums)
unissued

'Shorty Blackwell' (Micky Dolenz)
Recorded January 19th 1968, February 4th 1968, February 15th 1968, April 9th 1968, April 30th 1968, June 7th 1968
Personnel Micky Dolenz (lead & backing vocal, piano), Coco Dolenz (lead harmony & backing vocal), Michel Rubini (piano), Max Bennett (bass), Tommy Tedesco (electric 12-string guitar), Jim Gordon (drums, percussion), Joe Porcaro, Victor Feldman & Emil Richards (percussion including tympani & mallets), Bud Brisbois, Buddy Childers, Ray Triscari & Ollie Mitchell (trumpets), George Roberts & Kenny Shroyer (trombones), Vincent DeRosa, Dick Perissi & David Duke (French horns), Bud Shank, Ted Nash & Ronnie Lang (flutes), Erno Neufeld, Anatol Kaminsky, Nathan Ross, George Berres, Joseph Stepansky & Bernard Kundell (violins), Edgar Lustgarten, Armand Kaproff & Justin DiTullio (cellos), Bill Chadwick (instrument unknown)
Release *Instant Replay* Rhino CD #71796

'Show Me Girl' by David Jones (Gerry Goffin/Carole King)
Recorded September 25th 1965 (and possibly other dates)
Personnel David Jones (vocal), Glen Campbell & Al Casey (guitars), Ray Pohlman & Larry Knechtel (basses), Lincoln Mayorga (piano), Hal Blaine (drums), Julius Wechter (percussion)
unissued

'Silver Moon' by Michael Nesmith & The First National Band (Michael Nesmith)
Recorded September 2nd 1970 & October 19th 1970
Personnel Michael Nesmith (vocal, guitar), John London (bass), Red Rhodes (pedal steel guitar), John Ware (drums), Michael Cohen (piano), unknown (percussion)
Release *Magnetic South & Loose Salute* BMG/Camden CD #74321 660442

'Since I Fell In Love With You' by David Jones (unknown)
Recorded circa 1965
Personnel David Jones (vocal), all others unknown
Release *Just For The Record* Hercules Promotions CD #Y6120E

'Six-String Improvisation' see 'Cantata And Fugue In C&W'

"Sixty-nine" (Eddie Hoh)
Recorded June 22nd 1967
Personnel Eddie Hoh (drums)
unissued

'Smile' (David Jones)
Recorded May 10th 1968
Personnel David Jones (lead & backing vocal), unknown (additional backing vocal), Neil Young (electric guitar), Gerry McGee (acoustic guitar), Joe Osborn (bass), Larry Knechtel (electric piano), Hal Blaine (drums)
Release *Instant Replay* Rhino CD #71796

'Smoke, Smoke, Smoke' by Michael Nesmith & The First National Band (Merle Travis/Tex Williams)
Recorded February 22nd 1970
Personnel Michael Nesmith (vocal, acoustic guitar), John London (bass), Red Rhodes (pedal steel guitar), John Ware (drums), Earl P. Ball (piano), Bill Dale (dobro), unknown (percussion)
Release *Nevada Fighter & Tantamount To Treason* BMG/Camden CD #74321 822352

'So Goes Love' (Gerry Goffin/Carole King)
Recorded July 7th 1966 & July 16th 1966
Personnel David Jones (lead & backing vocal), Al Casey, Glen Campbell, James Burton, Jim Helms & Peter Tork (guitars), Hal Blaine (drums), Gary Coleman & Jim Gordon (percussion), Billy Preston (electric piano), Bill Pitman (bass)
Release *Missing Links* Rhino CD #70150

'Someday Man' (Roger Nichols/Paul Williams)
Recorded November 7th 1968, January 4th 1969, January 10th 1969 & January 13rd 1969
Personnel David Jones (vocal), Don Addrisi & unknown others (backing vocals), Tommy Tedesco & Michael Deasy (guitar), Joe Osborn & Larry Knechtel & Jimmy Rowles (pianos), Hal Blaine (drums, percussion), Conte Candoli & Buddy Childers (trumpets), Lew McCreary & Bob Edmondson (trombones), Vincent DeRosa, Dick

Perissi, Jim Decker & Bill Hinshaw (French horns), unknown (additional electric guitar)
Release *Instant Replay* Rhino CD #71796

'Some Of Shelly's Blues' version 1 (Michael Nesmith)
Recorded May 29th 1968, June 2nd 1968, August 21st 1968, June 27th 1969 (& probably other dates)
Personnel Michael Nesmith (vocal), Charlie McCoy (harmonica), Billy Sanford (acoustic guitar), Larry Butler (organ), Lloyd Green (steel guitar), Bobby Dyson (bass), Sonny Osborne (banjo), Willie Ackerman (drums)
Release *Missing Links Volume 2* Rhino CD #70903 features a stereo remix of the song. An original stereo mix from the '60s is included on Rhino's *Music Box* CD collection #76706.

'Some Of Shelly's Blues' version 2 (Michael Nesmith)
Recorded December 22nd 1970
Personnel unknown
unissued

'Sometime In The Morning' (Gerry Goffin/Carole King)
Recorded October 13th 1966 & October 27th 1966
Personnel Micky Dolenz (lead & backing vocal), David Jones, Peter Tork, possibly unknown others (backing vocals), all others unknown
Release *More Of The Monkees* Rhino CD #71791. In addition to being available originally in mono and stereo mixes – the stereo appears on the current CD noted – this track was remixed twice in stereo, featuring a more prominent double-tracked vocal from Micky and similar to the original mono mix. Mix 1 appears on the Arista CD release of *More Of The Monkees* #ARCD-8525 while mix 2 appears on the *Listen To The Band* CD boxed set #70566.)

"Song #2" demo (unknown)
Recorded January 24th 1968
Personnel Peter Tork (instrument unknown)
unissued

"Special Announcement"
Recorded October 9th 1967
Personnel Peter Tork (spoken word, dog barks), Bob Rafelson & Steve Pitts (dog barks)
Release *Pisces, Aquarius, Capricorn & Jones, Ltd.* Rhino CD #71793

'Star Collector' (Gerry Goffin/Carole King)
Recorded June 22nd 1967, July 6th 1967, October 4th 1967, October 16th 1967 (& probably other dates)
Personnel David Jones (lead & backing vocal), Micky Dolenz (harmony & backing vocal), Michael Nesmith (electric guitar), Peter Tork (organ), Chip Douglas (backing vocal, bass, possibly electric guitar); Eddie Hoh (drums), Paul Beaver (Moog synthesizer), unknown (additional backing vocal)
Release *Pisces, Aquarius, Capricorn & Jones, Ltd.* Rhino CD #71793. In addition to being available originally in mono and stereo mixes – the stereo appears on the current CD noted – this track is also featured in a longer alternative mix on the same CD. Another alternative mix is included in the second season TV episode *The Wild Monkees*. This is now available on Rhino's *Season Two* DVD boxed set #970128.

'Steam Engine' (Chip Douglas)
Recorded May 12th 1969, July 8th 1969, August 28th 1969 & November 21st 1969
Personnel Micky Dolenz (lead & backing vocal), Clydie King, Chip Douglas, Jerry Yester, unknown others (backing vocals), Clarence White (guitar), Red Rhodes (steel guitar), Lyle Ritz (bass), Bill Martin (organ), Jim Gordon (drums), Eddie Hoh (tambourine), Bill Green & Bob Hardaway (reeds), Tony Terran, Sanford Skinner & Bill Peterson (trumpets), Bobby Knight & Lew McCreary (trombones)
Release *Missing Links Volume 3* Rhino CD #72153 features an original mix from 1969. The song was also remixed for the Rhino *Listen To The Band* CD boxed set #70566. Two unique vinyl-only mixes appear on Rhino's *Monkee Business* picture disc and a fan-club single on the Monkees Relived label.

'Storybook Of You' see 'My Storybook Of You'

'The Story Of Rock And Roll' version 1 (Harry Nilsson)
Recorded March 18th 1967
Personnel Michael Nesmith (electric six-string guitar), Peter Tork (piano), Micky Dolenz (drums), Chip Douglas (bass)
Release *Headquarters Sessions* Rhino CD #RHM2 7715

'The Story Of Rock And Roll' version 2 (Harry Nilsson)
Recorded March 19th 1967
Personnel Michael Nesmith (electric six-string guitar), Peter Tork (piano), Micky Dolenz (drums), Chip Douglas (bass)
Release *Headquarters Sessions* Rhino CD #RHM2 7715

'The Story Of Rock And Roll' version 3 (Harry Nilsson)
Recorded April 21st 1967
Personnel Micky Dolenz (drums), David Jones (percussion), Harry Nilsson (piano), Chip Douglas (bass)
unissued

'The Story Of Rock And Roll' version 4 (Harry Nilsson)
Recorded January 10th 1968
Personnel Michael Nesmith (electric guitar), Harry Nilsson (piano), Eddie Hoh (drums), Rick Dey (bass)
unissued

'String For My Kite' version 1 (Bill Dorsey)
Recorded November 11st 1968
Personnel Mike Deasy (electric guitar), Joe Osborn (bass), Larry Knechtel & Jimmy Rowles (keyboards), Hal Blaine (drums)
unissued

'String For My Kite' version 2 (Bill Dorsey)
Recorded November 18th 1968
Personnel David Jones (vocal), Mike Deasy, Louie Shelton & Dennis Budimer (guitars), Joe Osborn (bass), Larry Knechtel & Jimmy Rowles (pianos), Hal Blaine (drums), Gene Estes (tambourine)
Release *Season Two* DVD boxed set Rhino #970128

'Sugar Man' (Denny Randell/Sandy Linzer)
Recorded January 22nd 1967, January 27th 1967, January 28th 1967 & October 3rd 1969
Personnel Al Gorgoni, Ralph Casale, Bob Rand, Charlie Macy & Don Thomas (guitars), Joe Macho (bass), Stan Free (percussion, mallets), Buddy Salzman (drums), Artie Butler (drums, percussion), unknown (vocal, organ, additional percussion)
unissued

'Summertime Is Fun Time' by David Jones (unknown)
Recorded circa 1965
Personnel David Jones (vocal), all others unknown
Release *Just For The Record* Hercules Promotions CD #Y6120E

'Sunny Girlfriend' (Michael Nesmith)
Recorded February 23rd 1967
Personnel Michael Nesmith (lead vocal, electric 12-string guitar, acoustic guitar), Peter Tork (electric six-string guitar), Micky Dolenz (harmony vocal, drums), David Jones (backing vocal, maracas), John London (bass)
Release *Headquarters* Rhino CD #71792. In addition to being available originally in mono and stereo mixes – the stereo appears on the current CD noted, while the mono resides on the *Headquarters Sessions* CD set #RHM2 7715 – this track was remixed in stereo for the Arista edition of the *Headquarters* CD #ARCD 8602. Additionally, the *Headquarters Sessions* set features three alternative mixes of the master: mix 1 is a remix featuring just acoustic guitar, maracas, and vocal; mix 2 features a rough vocal from Nesmith; mix 3 is an instrumental mix of the song.

'Sunny Girlfriend' live version 1 (Michael Nesmith)
Recorded August 12nd 1967
Personnel Michael Nesmith (lead vocal, electric 12-string guitar), Peter Tork (backing vocal, bass), Micky Dolenz (harmony vocal, drums), David Jones (backing vocal, tambourine)
Release *Summer 1967: The Complete U.S. Concert Recordings* Rhino CD #RHM2 7755

'Sunny Girlfriend' live version 2 (Michael Nesmith)
Recorded August 25th 1967
Personnel Michael Nesmith (lead vocal, electric 12-string guitar), Peter Tork (backing vocal, bass), Micky Dolenz (harmony vocal, drums), David Jones (backing vocal, tambourine)
Release *Summer 1967: The Complete U.S. Concert Recordings* Rhino CD #RHM2 7755

'Sunny Girlfriend' live version 3 (Michael Nesmith)
Recorded August 26th 1967
Personnel Michael Nesmith (lead vocal, electric 12-string guitar), Peter Tork (backing vocal, bass), Micky Dolenz (harmony vocal, drums), David Jones (backing vocal, tambourine)
Release *Summer 1967: The Complete U.S. Concert Recordings* Rhino CD #RHM2 7755. An alternative mix of this performance appears on Rhino's *Live 1967* CD #70139.

'Sunny Girlfriend' live version 4 (Michael Nesmith)
Recorded August 27th 1967
Personnel Michael Nesmith (lead vocal, electric 12-string guitar), Peter Tork (backing vocal, bass), Micky Dolenz (harmony vocal, drums), David Jones (backing vocal, tambourine)
Release *Summer 1967: The Complete U.S. Concert Recordings* Rhino CD #RHM2 7755

'Sunny Girlfriend' rehearsal (Michael Nesmith)
Recorded May 17th 1968
Personnel Michael Nesmith (electric guitar), David Jones (organ), Micky Dolenz (drums)
unissued

'Sunny Girlfriend' live version 5 (Michael Nesmith)
Recorded May 17th 1968
Personnel Michael Nesmith (lead vocal, electric guitar), Peter Tork (bass), David Jones (backing vocal, tambourine), Micky Dolenz (harmony vocal, drums)
unissued

'Suzzana Sometime' a.k.a. 'Love Bandit' (Tommy Boyce/Bobby Hart)
Recorded May 30th 1969 & May 31st 1969
Personnel Tommy Boyce & Bobby Hart (vocals), Louie Shelton (electric guitar), Larry Knechtel (piano), Joe Osborn (bass), Hal Blaine (drums), Jules Chaikin & Ollie Mitchell (trumpets), Dick Nash (trombone), Jay Migliori (saxophone)
unissued

'Sweet Young Thing' version 1 (Michael Nesmith/Gerry Goffin/Carole King)
Recorded July 18th 1966 & July 27th 1966
Personnel Michael Nesmith (lead vocal), Micky Dolenz & Peter Tork (backing vocals), Jimmy Bryant (fiddle), James Burton, Glen Campbell, Al Casey, Mike Deasy & Peter Tork (guitars, 'dano' bass), Hal Blaine (drums), Gary Coleman & Frank DeVito (percussion), Larry Knechtel (piano), Bob West (bass), unknown (additional backing vocal)
Release *The Monkees* Rhino CD #71790. In addition to being available originally in mono and stereo mixes – the stereo appears on the current CD noted – this track was remixed in stereo for two other releases. Mix 1 appears on the Arista CD release of *The Monkees* #ARCD-8524; mix 2 on the *Listen To The Band* CD boxed set #70566.

'Sweet Young Thing' live version 1 (Michael Nesmith/Gerry Goffin/Carole King)
Recorded January 21st 1967
Personnel Michael Nesmith (lead vocal, electric 12-string guitar; Peter Tork (backing vocal, bass), David Jones (backing vocal, tambourine), Micky Dolenz (backing vocal, drums)
Release *Season One* DVD boxed set Rhino #976076. This is only an excerpt of the song with overdubbed vocal, as featured in the TV episode *The Monkees On Tour*. The complete live version is thus far unissued.

'Sweet Young Thing' live version 2 (Michael Nesmith/Gerry Goffin/Carole King)
Recorded August 12nd 1967
Personnel Michael Nesmith (lead vocal, electric 12-string guitar), Peter Tork (backing vocal, bass), David Jones (backing vocal, maracas), Micky Dolenz (backing vocal, drums)
Release *Summer 1967: The Complete U.S. Concert Recordings* Rhino CD #RHM2 7755

'Sweet Young Thing' live version 3 (Michael Nesmith/Gerry Goffin/Carole King)
Recorded August 25th 1967
Personnel Michael Nesmith (lead vocal, electric 12-string guitar), Peter Tork (backing vocal, bass), David Jones (backing vocal, tambourine), Micky Dolenz (backing vocal, drums)
Release *Summer 1967: The Complete U.S. Concert Recordings* Rhino CD #RHM2 7755

'Sweet Young Thing' live version 4 (Michael Nesmith/Gerry Goffin/Carole King)
Recorded August 26th 1967
Personnel Michael Nesmith (lead vocal, electric 12-string guitar), Peter Tork (backing vocal, bass), David Jones (tambourine), Micky Dolenz (drums)
Release *Summer 1967: The Complete U.S. Concert Recordings* Rhino CD #RHM2 7755

'Sweet Young Thing' live version 5 (Michael Nesmith/Gerry Goffin/Carole King)
Recorded August 27th 1967
Personnel Michael Nesmith (lead vocal, electric 12-string guitar), Peter Tork (backing vocal, bass), David Jones (backing vocal, tambourine), Micky Dolenz (drums)
Release *Summer 1967: The Complete U.S. Concert Recordings* Rhino CD #RHM2 7755. An alternative mix of this performance appears on Rhino's *Live 1967* CD #70139.

'Sweet Young Thing' version 2 by Mike Nesmith/The Wichita Train Whistle Sings (Michael Nesmith/Gerry Goffin/Carole King)

Recorded circa November 18 or 19th 1967
Personnel Doug Dillard (banjo), Bud Brisbois (trumpet), all others unknown
Release *The Wichita Train Whistle Sings* Dot album #DLP 25861

'Symphony Is Over' NOT THE MONKEES (unknown)
Recorded May 8th 1967
unknown (vocal, guitar)
unissued

'Take A Giant Step' version 1 (Gerry Goffin/Carole King)
Recorded June 10th 1966
Personnel Sonny Curtis, Glen Campbell & James Burton (guitars), Hal Blaine (drums, Latin percussion), Larry Knechtel (keyboard), Ray Pohlman (bass)
unissued

'Take A Giant Step' version 2 (Gerry Goffin/Carole King)
Recorded July 9th 1966 (and possibly other dates)
Personnel Micky Dolenz (lead & backing vocal), Wayne Erwin, Gerry McGee & Louie Shelton (guitars), Larry Taylor (bass), Billy Lewis (drums), Gene Estes (percussion including bells), Michel Rubini (harpsichord), Bob Cooper (oboe), unknown (additional backing vocal)
Release *The Monkees* Rhino CD #71790 features the original stereo mix. The original mono mix appears on Arista's *The Monkees* CD #ARCD-8524. An alternative, early mono mix – distinguished by a single vocal from Micky and fewer backing vocal – appears in the TV series episode *The Chaperone*, which is now available on Rhino's DVD boxed set #976076 of the first season of *The Monkees*.

'Take A Giant Step' live version (Gerry Goffin/Carole King)
Recorded January 21st 1967
Personnel Micky Dolenz (lead vocal, drums), Michael Nesmith (electric 12-string guitar), Peter Tork (backing vocal, bass), David Jones (backing vocal, tambourine)
unissued

'Take Me To Paradise' by David Jones (Steve Venet/Toni Wine)
Recorded December 1964
Personnel David Jones (vocal), all others unknown
Release Colpix single #764

'Tapioca Tundra' version 1 (Michael Nesmith)
Recorded November 11st 1967 & March 13rd 1968
Personnel Michael Nesmith (vocal, whistling, percussion, electric guitar, acoustic guitar), Eddie Hoh (drums), unknown (bass, additional percussion)
Release *The Birds, The Bees & The Monkees* Rhino CD #71794. In addition to being available originally in mono and stereo mixes – the original stereo mix appears on the current CD noted – this track has also appeared in an alternative, originally unused stereo mix from the 1960s. This oddity turns up on the *Music Box* CD set #76706, the Flashback release *Daydream Believer And Other Hits* CD #75242, and the *Listen To The Band* boxed set #70566.

'Tapioca Tundra' version 2 by Mike Nesmith/The Wichita Train Whistle Sings (Michael Nesmith)
Recorded circa November 18 or 19th 1967
Personnel James Burton (guitar), all others unknown
Release *The Wichita Train Whistle Sings* Dot album #DLP 25861

'Tear Drop City' (Tommy Boyce/Bobby Hart)
Recorded October 26th 1966, October 30th 1966, October 31st 1966, November 6th 1966 & January 13rd 1969
Personnel Micky Dolenz (lead vocal), Ron Hicklin, Tommy Boyce & Bobby Hart (backing vocals), Wayne Erwin, Gerry McGee & Louie Shelton (guitars), Larry Taylor (bass), Billy Lewis (drums), Gene Estes (tambourine)
Release Instant Replay Rhino CD #71796 features the original stereo mix. The song also appears in remixed form on the Rhino *Listen To The Band* CD boxed set #70566. Additionally, a mono mix was briefly issued as a promotional-only single in 1969.

'Tears Of Joy' demo (unknown)
Recorded January 24th 1968
Personnel Michael Nesmith (electric 12-string guitar), Bob Ray (bass), Eddie Hoh (drums)
unissued

'Tear The Top Off My Head' demo (Peter Tork)
Recorded June 22nd 1967
Personnel Peter Tork (acoustic guitar, vocal)
unissued

'Tear The Top Right Off My Head' (Peter Tork)
Recorded February 5th 1968, February 6th 1968, February 8th

1968, February 12nd 1968
Personnel Peter Tork (vocal, guitar, possibly bass), Lance Wakely (guitar, harmonica, possibly bass), Dewey Martin (drums), Ron Brown (possibly bass)
Release *Missing Links Volume 3* Rhino CD #72153

'Teeny Tiny Gnome' *see* 'Kicking Stones'

'Tell Me Love' (Jeff Barry)
Recorded February 5th 1970 (& probably other dates)
Personnel Micky Dolenz (lead vocal), all others unknown
Release *Changes* Rhino CD #71798

'Tema Dei Monkees' (Tommy Boyce/Bobby Hart/Nistri)
Recorded July or August 1966 and March 1967
Personnel Micky Dolenz (lead & backing vocal), Wayne Erwin, Gerry McGee & Louie Shelton (guitars), Larry Taylor (bass), Billy Lewis (drums), Gene Estes (tambourine)
Release *Missing Links Volume 3* Rhino CD #72153. An instrumental mix of this version appears as a karaoke track on the Japanese-only release *The Monkees Best!!* East-West CD #AMCY-978. A different, longer mix of the vocal version can be found on the rare Italian-only album *I Monkees In TV* #FIPS 34056.

'Tengo Amore' by Michael Nesmith & The First National Band (Michael Nesmith)
Recorded May 13rd 1970, May 14th 1970, May 26th 1970, May 28th 1970, July 13rd 1970 & July 15th 1970
Personnel Michael Nesmith (vocal, guitar), John London (bass), Red Rhodes (pedal steel guitar), John Ware (drums), Glen D. Hardin & Billy Dale (instruments unknown), unknown (harpsichord, percussion)
Release *Magnetic South & Loose Salute* BMG/Camden CD #74321 660442

'Texas Morning' by Michael Nesmith & The First National Band (Michael Murphey/Boomer Castleman)
Recorded December 21st 1970 & January 6th 1971
Personnel Michael Nesmith (vocal, guitar), Red Rhodes (pedal steel guitar), all others unknown
Release *Nevada Fighter & Tantamount To Treason* BMG/Camden CD #74321 822352

'Thank You My Friend' (Michael Nesmith)
Recorded May 29th 1969
Personnel Al Casey & Louie Shelton (guitars), Michel Rubini (piano), Joe Osborn (bass), Hal Blaine (drums)
unissued

'Thanx For The Ride' version 1 by Michael Nesmith & The First National Band (Michael Nesmith)
Recorded April 9th 1970
Personnel Earl Ball (piano), all others unknown
unissued

'Thanx For The Ride' version 2 by Michael Nesmith & The First National Band (Michael Nesmith)
Recorded April 15th 1970, May 26th 1970, July 13rd 1970 & July 15th 1970
Personnel Michael Nesmith (vocal, acoustic guitar), John London (bass), Red Rhodes (pedal steel guitar), John Ware (drums), Glen D. Hardin (piano), unknown (organ, percussion)
Release *Magnetic South & Loose Salute* BMG/Camden CD #74321 660442

'That's What It's Like Loving You' (David Jones/Steve Pitts)
Recorded May 10th 1968
Personnel Neil Young (electric guitars), Gerry McGee (acoustic guitar), Joe Osborn (bass), Larry Knechtel (organ), Hal Blaine (drums)
unissued

'Theme For A New Love (I Saw You Only Once)' by David Jones (Hank Levine/Berdie Abrams)
Recorded July 26th 1965 (and possibly other dates)
Personnel David Jones (vocal), Elliott Fisher, James Getzoff, Victor Arno, Henry L. Roth, Paul Shure, Arnold Belnick & Lou Raderman (violins), Kurt Reher & Harold Schneier (cellos), James Decker & George Price (French horns), Gene Garf (piano), Red Callender (bass), Al Casey, Carol Kaye, Bill Pitman & Tommy Tedesco (guitars), Emil Richards (percussion), Earl Palmer (drums)
Release Colpix single #789 & *David Jones* album #493 (in mono & stereo)

'(Theme From) The Monkees' demo by Boyce & Hart (Tommy Boyce/Bobby Hart)
Recorded circa 1965
Personnel Tommy Boyce & Bobby Hart (vocals), all others unknown
Release *Season One* DVD boxed set Rhino #976076

'(Theme From) The Monkees' early version (Tommy Boyce/Bobby Hart)
Recorded circa 1966
Personnel Micky Dolenz, Tommy Boyce & Bobby Hart (vocals), all others unknown
Release *The Monkees* Rhino CD #71790

'(Theme From) The Monkees' version 1 (Tommy Boyce/Bobby Hart)
Recorded July 5th 1966, July 9th 1966 (and possibly other dates)
Personnel Micky Dolenz (lead vocal), Ron Hicklin & Tommy Boyce (backing vocals), Wayne Erwin (guitar, backing vocal), Gerry McGee & Louie Shelton (guitars), Larry Taylor (bass), Billy Lewis (drums), Gene Estes (tambourine), Bobby Hart (organ, backing vocal), unknown (finger snaps)
Release *The Monkees* Rhino CD #71790

'(Theme From) The Monkees' version 2 (Tommy Boyce/Bobby Hart)
Recorded August 6th 1966 (and possibly other dates)
Personnel Micky Dolenz (lead & backing vocal), Wayne Erwin & Gerry McGee (guitars), Larry Taylor (bass), Billy Lewis (drums), Gene Estes (tambourine), unknown (additional backing vocal)
Release *Missing Links Volume 3* Rhino CD #72153. A karaoke remix of this version – featuring just the song's instrumental track – is available on *The Best Of The Monkees* CD#73875. *See also* 'Tema Dei Monkees.'

'Thirteen Is Not Our Lucky Number' version 1 by Michael Nesmith (Michael Nesmith/Michael Cohen)
Recorded October 15th 1965 (and possibly other dates)
Personnel Michael Nesmith (vocal), Israel Baker, Arnold Belnick, James Getzoff, Bill Kursach, Ralph Schaeffer, Sidney Sharp & Robert Sushel (violins), Dennis Budimir & Don Peake (guitars), Frank Capp & Gene Estes (percussion), Jesse Ehrlich & Joseph Saxon (cellos), Lincoln Mayorga (harpsichord), Lyle Ritz (bass)
unissued

'Thirteen Is Not Our Lucky Number' version 2 (Michael Nesmith/Michael Cohen)
Recorded May 28th 1969 & June 2nd 1969
Personnel Al Casey & Louie Shelton (guitars), Larry Knechtel (organ), Joe Osborn (bass), Hal Blaine (drums), unknown (cowbell, piano, additional electric guitar)
unissued

'Thirteen Is Not Our Lucky Number' version 3 by Michael Nesmith & The First National Band (Michael Nesmith/Michael Cohen)
Recorded October 20th 1970
Personnel unknown
unissued

'This Bouquet' by David Jones (Hank Levine/Smokey Roberds/Murray Macleod)
Recorded June 15th 1964 (and possibly other dates)
Personnel David Jones (vocal), Tommy Tedesco, Bobby Gibbons, Al Casey & Tommy Tedesco (guitars), Earl Palmer (drums), Red Callender (bass), Gene Page (piano), Gene Garf (organ), Emil Richards (percussion including bells), unknown (strings, backing vocal)
Release Colpix single #784 & *David Jones* album #493 (in mono & stereo)

'This Just Doesn't Seem To Be My Day' (Tommy Boyce/Bobby Hart)
Recorded July 5th 1966, July 9th 1966 (and possibly other dates)
Personnel Davy Jones (lead & backing vocal), Wayne Erwin (guitar, additional backing vocal), Gerry McGee & Louie Shelton (guitars), Larry Taylor (bass), Billy Lewis (drums), Gene Estes (percussion including bells), Joseph DiTullio (cello), Ron Hicklin, Tommy Boyce & Bobby Hart (additional backing vocals)
Release *The Monkees* Rhino CD #71790. In addition to being available originally in mono and stereo mixes – the stereo appears on the current CD noted – this track was remixed for the Arista CD release of *The Monkees* #ARCD-8524.

'Through The Looking Glass' version 1 (Tommy Boyce/Bobby Hart/Red Baldwin)
Recorded September 10th 1966 & September 24th 1966
Personnel Micky Dolenz (lead & backing vocal), Ron Hicklin, Davy Jones & Bobby Hart (backing vocals), Wayne Erwin, Gerry McGee & Louie Shelton (guitars), Tommy Boyce (acoustic guitar, backing vocal), Larry Taylor (bass), Billy Lewis (drums), Alan Estes (tympani, tambourine), Michel Rubini (tack piano)
Release *Missing Links Volume 3* Rhino CD #72153

'Through The Looking Glass' version 2 (Tommy Boyce/Bobby Hart/Red Baldwin)

Recorded December 30th 1967, December 20th 1968, December 28th 1968 (& other dates)
Personnel Micky Dolenz (vocal), Louis Shelton, Gerry McGee, Wayne Erwin & Keith Allison (guitars), Joe Osborn (bass), Wayne Erwin & Keith Allison (guitars), Joe Osborn (bass), Bobby Hart (tack piano), Billy Lewis (drums), unknown (strings, horns)
Release *Instant Replay* Rhino CD #71796. An alternative mix with more horns and different vocals appears as a bonus track on the same CD.

'Ticket On A Ferry Ride' (Jeff Barry/Bobby Bloom)
Recorded March 25th 1970 (& probably other dates)
Personnel Micky Dolenz (vocal), all others unknown
Release *Changes* Rhino CD#71798

'Till Then' (unknown)
Recorded June 9th 1969
Personnel Michael Nesmith, unknown others (laughter), Al Casey & Louie Shelton (guitars), Max Bennett (upright bass), Michel Rubini (piano), Hal Blaine (drums)
unissued

'Time And Time Again' (David Jones/Bill Chadwick)
Recorded August 6th 1969 & November 11st 1969
Personnel David Jones (lead & backing vocal), Bill Chadwick (backing vocal), Louie Shelton (electric guitar), Michel Rubini (calliope), Joe Osborn (bass), John Guerin (drums), Paul Beaver (Moog synthesizer), unknown (additional electric guitar)
Release *Missing Links* Rhino CD #70150. A 1994 stereo remix appears on the expanded CD reissue of *Changes*, Rhino CD #71798.

'Title' (unknown)
Recorded January 18th 1968
Personnel Micky Dolenz (conga), unknown (Moog synthesizer, tack piano, tympani)
unissued

'Today' (Chip Douglas)
Recorded May 12nd 1969
Personnel Clarence White or Jerry Yester (guitar), Red Rhodes (steel guitar), Lyle Ritz & Ray Brown (basses), Bill Martin (organ), Larry Knechtel (piano), Jim Gordon (drums), Gary Coleman (tympany), Eddie Hoh (tambourine), Bill Kurasch, Leonard Malarsky, Ralph Schaefer, Israel Baker, Harold Dicterow & Sidney Sharp (violins), Harry Hyams, Jan Hlinka & Leonard Selic (violas), Jesse Ehrlich (cello), Bill Green & Bob Hardaway (reeds), Sid Miller (bassoon), Tony Terran, Sanford Skinner & Bill Peterson (trumpets), Bobby Knight & Lew McCreary (trombones), Vincent DeRosa (French horn)
unissued

'Tomorrow's Gonna Be Another Day' (Tommy Boyce/Steve Venet)
Recorded July 23rd 1966 & July 26th 1966 (+ possibly other dates)
Personnel Micky Dolenz (vocal), Gerry McGee (electric guitar, harmonica), Wayne Erwin & Louie Shelton (electric guitars), Larry Taylor (bass), Billy Lewis (drums), Tommy Boyce (acoustic guitar), unknown (tambourine, handclaps)
Release *The Monkees* Rhino CD #71790 features the original stereo mix. The original mono mix appears on Arista's *The Monkees* CD #ARCD-8524.

'Tumbling Tumbleweeds' by Michael Nesmith & The First National Band (Michael Nesmith)
Recorded August 12nd 1970, August 13rd 1970, August 14th 1970 & October 26th 1970
Personnel Michael Nesmith (vocal, guitar), John London (bass), Red Rhodes (pedal steel guitar), John Ware (drums), Jim Zitro (percussion), Michael Cohen (keyboard), Billy Dale (instrument unknown)
Release *Nevada Fighter & Tantamount To Treason* BMG/Camden CD #74321 822352

"Twelve-String Improvisation" (unknown)
Recorded March 7th 1967
Personnel Michael Nesmith (electric 12-string guitar), Peter Tork (electric six-string guitar), Davy Jones (tambourine), Micky Dolenz (drums), John London (bass)
Release *Headquarters Sessions* Rhino CD #RHM2 7715

'Two-Part Invention In F Major' version 1 (Johann Sebastian Bach)
Recorded March 1967
Personnel Peter Tork (piano)
Release *Headquarters Sessions* Rhino CD #RHM2 7715

'Two-Part Invention In F Major' rehearsal (Johann Sebastian Bach)
Recorded May 17th 1968
Personnel Peter Tork (organ)
unissued

"unknown #1" (unknown)
Recorded November 12nd 1967
Personnel Peter Tork (acoustic guitar, humming)
unissued

'Until It's Time For You To Go' version 1 by Michael Nesmith (Buffy Sainte Marie)
Recorded October 15th 1965 (and possibly other dates)
Personnel Michael Nesmith (vocal), Israel Baker, Arnold Belnick, James Getzoff, Bill Kursach, Ralph Schaeffer, Sidney Sharp & Robert Sushel (violins), Dennis Budimir & Don Peake (guitars), Frank Capp & Gene Estes (percussion), Jesse Ehrlich & Joseph Saxon (cellos), Lincoln Mayorga (harpsichord), Lyle Ritz (bass)
Release Colpix single #792

'Until It's Time For You To Go' version 2 (Buffy Sainte Marie)
Recorded circa 1967
Personnel Michael Nesmith (vocal, acoustic guitar)
Release *Headquarters Sessions* Rhino CD #RHM2 7715

'Until It's Time For You To Go' version 3 (Buffy Sainte Marie)
Recorded circa 1967
Personnel David Jones (vocal), Michael Nesmith (acoustic guitar)
unissued

'Untitled' demo (Peter Tork)
Recorded June 22nd 1967
Personnel Peter Tork (acoustic guitar)
unissued

"Untitled" (unknown)
Recorded February 9th 1968
Personnel Eddie Hoh, John Ethridge, Bill Chadwick, Bobby Donaho & Keith Allison (instruments unknown)
unissued

"Untitled ?" (unknown)
Recorded February 18th 1968
Personnel Bill Chadwick, Keith Allison, Henry Diltz, Chip Douglas & Jim Gordon (instruments unknown)
unissued

'Valleri' version 1 (Tommy Boyce/Bobby Hart)
Recorded August 6th 1966 & August 27th 1966
Personnel David Jones (lead vocal), Ron Hicklin, Bobby Hart, Tommy Boyce & Micky Dolenz (backing vocals), Wayne Erwin (guitar, backing vocal), Gerry McGee & Louie Shelton (guitars), Larry Taylor (bass), Billy Lewis (drums), Gene Estes (tambourine)
Release *Missing Links Volume 2* Rhino CD #70903. This version has appeared in two different mixes. Mix 1 is a stereo remix for the CD noted. Mix 2 is a second stereo remix, for the *Music Box* set #76706. The original mono mix appears in two first-season episodes of the TV series, *Captain Crocodile* and *Monkees At The Movies* and can be found on Rhino's *Season One* DVD boxed set #976076.
***

'Valleri' version 2 (Tommy Boyce/Bobby Hart)
Recorded December 26th 1967
Personnel David Jones (lead vocal), Louis Shelton & Gerry McGee (electric guitars), Joe Osborn (bass), Billy Lewis (drums, tambourine), Jay Migliori & Jim Horn (saxophones), Ollie Mitchell & Roy Caton (trumpets), Lew McCreary (trombone), unknown (backing vocal)
Release *The Birds, The Bees & The Monkees* Rhino CD #71794. In addition to being available originally in mono and stereo mixes – the stereo appears on the current CD noted – this track was remixed in stereo for the *Listen To The Band* box set #70566. Some later releases feature a 'cold' ending rather than the fade of the original stereo and mono issues. These are the same stereo mix simply without the fade.

'Wanderin' by Mike Nesmith (Michael Nesmith)
Recorded circa 1963
Personnel Michael Nesmith (vocal, guitar)
Release Highness single #HN-13

'War Games' version 1 (David Jones/Steve Pitts)
Recorded January 23rd 1968
Personnel David Jones (lead vocal), Michael Nesmith (acoustic guitar), Keith Allison (electric guitar), Joe Osborn or Bob Ray (bass), Eddie Hoh (drums), unknown (organ)
unissued

'War Games' version 2 (David Jones/Steve Pitts)
Recorded February 6th 1968, February 8th 1968 (& possibly other dates)
Personnel David Jones (lead vocal), Al Hendrickson, Gerry McGee & Mike Deasy (guitars), Don Randi (harpsichord), Max Bennett (bass), Earl Palmer (drums), George Kast, Erno Neufeld, Marvin Limonick,

Sam Freed, Nathan Kaproff & Alex Murray (violins), Edgar Lustgarten, Frederick Seykora, Marie Fera & Jacqueline Lustgarten (cellos), David Duke, Arthur Maebe & John Cave (French horns), Buddy Childers & Jack Sheldon (trumpets), George Roberts (trombone), unknown (additional drums, tambourine)
Release *Missing Links* Rhino CD #70150

'Wasn't Born To Follow' (Gerry Goffin/Carole King)
Recorded March 9th 1968
Personnel Mike Deasy, Dennis Budimir & Al Casey (guitars), Max Bennett (bass), Michael Melvoin (harpsichord), Earl Palmer (drums), Stan Levey & Milt Holland (percussion including mallets)
unissued

'The Water Is Wide' (Traditional)
Recorded November 12nd 1967
Personnel Peter Tork (vocal, acoustic guitar)
unissued

'We'll Be Back In A Minute' *see* 'Music Bridge'

'Well, Well' by Mike Nesmith (Michael Nesmith)
Recorded circa 1963
Personnel Michael Nesmith (vocal, guitar), unknown (percussion, backing vocal)
Release Highness single #HN-13

'We Were Made For Each Other' demo (Carole Bayer/George Fischoff)
Recorded October 23rd 1967
Personnel Chip Douglas, Eddie Hoh, Rodney Dillard, Doug Dillard & Bill Martin (instruments unknown)
unissued

'We Were Made For Each Other' version 1 (Carole Bayer/George Fischoff)
Recorded November 4th 1967
Personnel Al Casey, Neil Levang & Bill Pitman (guitars), Henry Diltz (banjo), Larry Knechtel & Ray Pohlman (basses), Michael Melvoin (organ), Eddie Hoh (drums), Milt Holland & Gary Coleman (percussion, vibes)
unissued

'We Were Made For Each Other' version 2 (Carole Bayer/George Fischoff)
Recorded February 6th 1968, February 7th 1968, February 8th 1968, March 13th 1968 (& possibly other dates)
Personnel David Jones (vocal), James Burton, Al Hendrickson, Gerry McGee & Mike Deasy (guitars), Michael Melvoin (harpsichord), Max Bennett (bass), Earl Palmer (drums), Milt Holland & Jerry Williams (percussion including mallets), Erno Neufeld, Sam Freed, George Kast, Alex Murray, Marvin Limonick & Nathan Kaproff (violins), Eleanor Slatkin, Kurt Reher, Marie Fera & Jacqueline Lustgarten (cellos), Buddy Childers & Jack Sheldon (trumpets), David Duke, Vincent DeRosa & Dick Perissi (French horns), Lew McCreary (trombone)
Release *The Birds, The Bees & The Monkees* Rhino CD #71794

'What Am I Doing Hangin' 'Round?' (Travis Lewis/Boomer Clarke)
Recorded June 20th 1967, September 5th 1967 (& probably other dates)
Personnel Michael Nesmith (lead vocal, electric guitar), Micky Dolenz & David Jones (backing vocal), Doug Dillard (electric banjo), Chip Douglas (backing vocal, bass), Eddie Hoh (drums)
Release *Pisces, Aquarius, Capricorn & Jones, Ltd.* Rhino CD 71793. In addition to being available originally in mono and stereo mixes – the original stereo mix appears on the current CD noted – this track was remixed twice for CD release: mix 1 appears on the Arista CD release of *Pisces, Aquarius...* #ARCD-8603; mix 2 on Rhino's *Listen To The Band* boxed set #70566.

'What Are We Going To Do?' by David Jones (Hank Levine/Smokey Roberts/Murray Macleod)
Recorded June 15th 1964 (and possibly other dates)
Personnel David Jones (vocal), Tommy Tedesco, Bobby Gibbons, Al Casey & Don Peake (guitars), Earl Palmer (drums), Red Callender (bass), Gene Page (piano), Gene Garf (organ), Emil Richards (percussion including bells), unknown (backing vocal)
Release Colpix single #784 & *David Jones* album #493 (in mono & stereo). Also available on Rhino's *The Colpix/Dimension Story* R2 71650.

'Whatever's Right' (Tommy Boyce/Bobby Hart)
Recorded July 26th 1966
Personnel Wayne Erwin, Gerry McGee & Louie Shelton (electric guitars), Tommy Boyce (acoustic guitar, partial vocal), Larry Taylor (bass), Billy Lewis (drums), Bobby Hart (autoharp), unknown (percussion)
unissued

'What Seems To Be The Trouble, Officer' by Michael Blessing (Bob Krasnow/Michael Nesmith)
Recorded circa 1965
Personnel Michael Nesmith (vocal, harmonica, guitar)
Release Colpix single #792

'When Love Comes Knockin' (At Your Door)' (Neil Sedaka/Carole Bayer)
Recorded November 23rd 1966 (and possibly other dates)
Personnel David Jones (vocal), Willard Suyker, Al Gafa & Don Thomas (guitars), Neil Sedaka (keyboard), Russ Savakus (bass), Herb Lovelle (drums), unknown (percussion)
Release *More Of The Monkees* Rhino CD 71791

'Where Has It All Gone' version 1 (Michael Nesmith)
Recorded March 7th 1967
Personnel Michael Nesmith (electric 12-string guitar), Peter Tork (electric six-string guitar), Davy Jones (tambourine), Micky Dolenz (drums), John London (bass)
Release *Headquarters Sessions* Rhino CD #RHM2 7715

'Where Has It All Gone' version 2 (Michael Nesmith)
Recorded March 7th 1967
Personnel Michael Nesmith (electric 12-string guitar), Peter Tork (organ), David Jones (tambourine), Micky Dolenz (drums), John London (bass)
Release *Headquarters Sessions* Rhino CD #RHM2 7715

'Which Way Do You Want It?' (Jeff Barry/Bobby Bloom)
Recorded March 25th 1970
Personnel unknown
unissued

'While I Cried' version 1 by Mike Nesmith/The Wichita Train Whistle Sings (Michael Nesmith)
Recorded circa November 18 or 19th 1967
Personnel Jimmy Zito – fugal horn; Other personnel unconfirmed
Release *The Wichita Train Whistle Sings* Dot album #DLP 25861

'While I Cry' version 2 (Michael Nesmith)
Recorded January 14th 1968
Personnel Michael Nesmith (vocal, guitar), Rick Dey (bass), Eddie Hoh (drums), Keith Allison, Bill Chadwick & Harry Nilsson (instruments unknown), unknown (backing vocal)
Release *Instant Replay* Rhino CD #71796

'Who Will Buy' (Lionel Bart)
Recorded December 3rd 1967
Personnel Peter Tork (electric guitar)
unissued

'Whole Lotta Shakin' Goin' On' by Michael Nesmith & The First National Band (Sunny David/Dave Williams)
Recorded July 14th 1970
Personnel unknown
unissued

'Wind Up Man' (Bill Dorsey)
Recorded November 11st 1968
Personnel Michael Nesmith, Peter Tork, David Jones & Micky Dolenz (vocals), Mike Deasy (electric guitar), Larry Knechtel & Jimmy Rowles (keyboards), Joe Osborn (bass), Hal Blaine (percussion)
Release *Season Two* DVD boxed set Rhino #970128

'Windy Day At Kitty Hawk' (Bill Martin)
Recorded May 12nd 1969
Personnel unknown
unissued

'Words' version 1 (Tommy Boyce/Bobby Hart)
Recorded August 15th 1966 & August 27th 1966
Personnel Micky Dolenz & Peter Tork (lead & backing vocal), Ron Hicklin, Bobby Hart, Tommy Boyce & David Jones (backing vocals), Wayne Erwin (backing vocal, guitar), Gerry McGee & Louie Shelton (guitars), Larry Taylor (bass), Billy Lewis (drums), Norm Jeffries (tambourine, chimes), Ethmer Roten (flute)
Release *Missing Links Volume 2* Rhino CD #70903. A unique mix of this version – with a drum fill in place of the backwards tape section – appears in the TV episode *Monkees In Manhattan*, which can be found on Rhino's *Season One* DVD boxed set #976076.

'Words' version 2 (Tommy Boyce/Bobby Hart)
Recorded June 14th 1967, June 15th 1967 (& possibly other dates in June)
Personnel Micky Dolenz (lead vocal), Peter Tork (counter vocal, organ), Michael Nesmith (backing vocal, electric guitar, percussion), David Jones (percussion, backing vocal?), Chip Douglas (backing

vocal, bass), Eddie Hoh (drums)
Release *Pisces, Aquarius, Capricorn & Jones, Ltd.* Rhino CD #71793 features the song's original stereo mix. The original mono mix – featuring a great deal more reverb – can be heard on Rhino's *Greatest Hits* CD#72190. Two stereo remixes have also appeared: mix 1 is included on Arista's CD of *Pisces, Aquarius...*; mix 2, a slightly longer remix, is on Rhino's *Listen To The Band* boxed set #70566.

'Writing Wrongs' (Michael Nesmith)
Recorded December 3rd 1967 & March 13th 1968
Personnel Michael Nesmith (vocal, piano, electric guitar, organ), Rick Dey (bass), Eddie Hoh (drums, percussion)
Release *The Birds, The Bees & The Monkees* Rhino CD #71794

'You And I' (David Jones/Bill Chadwick)
Recorded May 10th 1968, June 19th 1968, June 21st 1968, September 10th 1968 & September 11st 1968
Personnel David Jones (lead & backing vocal), Gerry McGee & Neil Young (guitars), Bill Chadwick & Louie Shelton (additional guitars), Joe Osborn (bass), Larry Knechtel (organ), Hal Blaine (drums)
Release *Instant Replay* Rhino CD #71796. An alternative mono mix from September 11st 1968 appears on Rhino's *Anthology* CD #75269.

'You Can't Judge A Book By The Cover' live version 1 (Willie Dixon)
Recorded January 21st 1967
Personnel Michael Nesmith (vocal, maracas), Bobby Hart (organ), Gerry McGee (guitar), Larry Taylor (bass), Bill Lewis (drums)
Release *Season One* DVD boxed set Rhino #976076. This is only an excerpt of the song with overdubbed vocal, as featured in the TV episode *The Monkees On Tour*. The complete live version is thus far unissued.

'You Can't Judge A Book By The Cover' live version 2 (Willie Dixon)
Recorded August 12nd 1967
Personnel Michael Nesmith (vocal, maracas, harmonica), Don DeMieri & Eddie Placidi (electric guitars), Bobby Dick (bass), Kim Capli (drums)
Release *Summer 1967: The Complete U.S. Concert Recordings* Rhino CD #RHM2 7755

'You Can't Judge A Book By The Cover' live version 3 (Willie Dixon)
Recorded August 25th 1967
Personnel Michael Nesmith – vocal & maracas; Don DeMieri & Eddie Placidi (electric guitars), Bobby Dick (bass), Kim Capli (drums)
Release *Summer 1967: The Complete U.S. Concert Recordings* Rhino CD #RHM2 7755

'You Can't Judge A Book By The Cover' live version 4 (Willie Dixon)
Recorded August 26th 1967
Personnel Michael Nesmith (vocal, maracas), Don DeMieri & Eddie Placidi (electric guitars), Bobby Dick (bass), Kim Capli (drums)
Release *Summer 1967: The Complete U.S. Concert Recordings* Rhino CD #RHM2 7755

'You Can't Judge A Book By The Cover' live version 5 (Willie Dixon)
Recorded August 26th 1967
Personnel Michael Nesmith (vocal, harmonica, maracas), Don DeMieri & Eddie Placidi (electric guitars), Bobby Dick (bass), Kim Capli (drums)
Release *Summer 1967: The Complete U.S. Concert Recordings* Rhino CD #RHM2 7755. An alternative mix of this performance appears on Rhino's *Live 1967* CD #70139.

'You Can't Judge A Book By The Cover' (Willie Dixon)
Recorded December 3rd 1967
Personnel Peter Tork (electric guitar)
unissued

You Can't Tie A Mustang Down (Jeff Barry)
Recorded January 21st 1967, February 4th 1967 & August 15th 1969
Personnel David Jones (vocal), Al Gorgoni, Don Thomas & Hugh McCracken (guitars), Lou Mauro (bass), Artie Butler (organ), Herb Lovelle (drums), Tom Cerone (tambourine)
Release *Daydream Believer And Other Hits* Flashback CD #75242

'You Just May Be The One' version 1 (Michael Nesmith)
Recorded July 18th 1966 & July 27th 1966
Personnel Michael Nesmith (lead & backing vocal), James Burton, Glen Campbell, Al Casey, Mike Deasy & Peter Tork (guitars, 'dano' bass), Hal Blaine (drums), Gary Coleman & Frank DeVito (percussion),